BORN OF THE MORNING STAR

DUSTY RHOADES HEER

COVER ART: KAREN CLARK YEAGER

Born To Ride The Morning Star
All Rights Reserved.
Copyright © 2020 Dusty Rhoades Heer
v1.0 r1.0

The opinions expressed in this manuscript are solely the opinions of the author and do not represent the opinions or thoughts of the publisher. The author has represented and warranted full ownership and/or legal right to publish all the materials in this book.

This book may not be reproduced, transmitted, or stored in whole or in part by any means, including graphic, electronic, or mechanical without the express written consent of the publisher except in the case of brief quotations embodied in critical articles and reviews.

Outskirts Press, Inc.
http://www.outskirtspress.com

ISBN: 978-1-9772-1805-6

Cover Photo © 2020 Karen Clark Yeager. All Rights Reserved – Used With Permission.

Outskirts Press and the "OP" logo are trademarks belonging to Outskirts Press, Inc.

PRINTED IN THE UNITED STATES OF AMERICA

Born To Ride The Morning Star

FOR SYLVIA

      There is no greater feeling in this life than when two people deeply and truly care for and love each other. Then they become one. The memories that we shared have created an everlasting bond that will never be broken. Thank you for making me feel that I am the luckiest man on the face of this Earth. You are the only one that I have and will love forever.

Born To Ride The Morning Star

The vital breath, perpetually pulsating

Love blossoms sprout from new earth

Mother Earth

Where we arise and depart

Enduring timeless cycles

Always and never the same

Fleeting glimpses

Of other lives

In other worlds

That we have lived

And will live

Beyond the beyond

On the dawn of creation

At the source of everlasting light

Illuminating from her celestial beacon

This angel of sunrise

Sprinkles her cosmic seeds

While she rides the morning star

SYLVIA

The name Sylvia, derived from the French word Sylvain, means of the forest. From the Latin word for forest, Silva, and its meaning is spirit of the wood. The mythological god of the forest was associated with the figure of Silvanus.

It dates back to the fifth century as used by Rhea Silvia, mother of Remus and Romulus, who founded Rome.

In Shakespeare's 1591 play, "The Two Gentlemen of Verona," Silvia is portrayed as a perfect lady, leading to its widespread use.

The many variations of the name Sylvia: Sylvette, Silvana, Zilvia, Sylvaine, Zilvie, Sylvène, Silvie, Sylviane, Sylva, Silva, Sylwia.

Sylvia is the modern spelling in English, Scandinavian, and German-speaking countries of the Latin name Silvia, the feminine form of Silvius.

People with this name are excellent at analyzing, understanding, and learning. They tend to be mystics, philosophers, scholars, and teachers. Because they live so much in the mind, they tend to be quiet and introspective, and are usually introverts.

After what happened, there are really only two choices for me. One is to wallow in despair, follow the crushing wave of desolation that engulfs me, and allow the unyielding grip of a meaningless existence to entice me to the precipice, that leads to slipping over to the dark side.

The other choice is to carry on. Move forward. Accept the comfort and empathy of my family and close friends. Take walks in the woods. Listen to the birds sing. Appreciate the beauty of nature and wildlife. Be thankful for being alive. Be grateful for having my freedom, my health, a roof over my head, a comfortable bed to sleep in, food to eat, clothes on my back, a nice car to take me where I need to go. I do cherish these things. *I do not take them lightly or for granted.* But the incomprehensible reality can be so overwhelming that it makes it difficult to remember what the right choice should be.

All of us have our own story to tell. That is what makes us unique. No matter how wonderful or how dreadful, happy or sad, magic or tragic; there are billions of individual stories out there. The vast majority goes untold. This is why I feel the urgency to tell our story before it is too late.

My life changed forever in the third week of July, 1983. That is when I first met Sylvia. Beautiful Sylvia. Long blonde hair. Hazel eyes. Sweet smile. She had a special knack for knowing how to dress. She could take any outfit and make it look classy, elegant, or fashionable; especially her attire for all the different seasons and holidays at the school where we taught. She could look sexy wearing sweatpants around the house

I always envisioned Sylvia when she was a little girl being like Heidi, from Johanna Sypri's beloved children's book, published in German in 1881. Heidi is an orphan who is sent away by her aunt to live with her hard-hearted grandfather in the Swiss Alps. She is caring, courageous, and funny; and quickly melts his heart. *This is Sylvia.* Heidi saves up all her soft, white rolls for Grandma, so that she wouldn't have to chew the hard bread. *This is Sylvia.* She rescues the basketful of kittens from the clock tower. *This is Sylvia.* Heidi inspires us to be more open and caring of others. *This is Sylvia.*

Sylvia was a month past her 30th birthday, and I was a month away from my 37th birthday, when we first met. Our birthdays, June 18th & August 20th, always fell on the same day of the week. And they always will. I thought this was really unique. We met under strange circumstances, yet destiny prevailed, or we would have never met at all.

Sylvia had come to Syracuse in the fall of 1979 from Virginia, when her first marriage started to head in the wrong direction; to visit her mother, Ursula, who was going through a similar situation. Sylvia was married to an American Air Force guy at the end of October, 1971, when she was only 18 years and a little over 4 months. She had just graduated from Zweibrücken American High School, a Department of Defense-Overseas Dependents Schools, in Zweibrücken, Germany, on June 3rd, 1971. This was because her stepfather, Art, was an American Army man, from Brooklyn, stationed in Germany.

Gunter, Sylvia's birth father, was a month before his 20th birthday when Sylvia was born. Ursula was just 17 and 6 months. He only knew Sylvia for less than 5 months before leaving for Canada to find work. He was a laborer, installing insulation. He went by boat, landing in Québec City and then headed south by train. Once he found work, he wanted Ursula and Sylvia to come join him. Sylvia's maternal grandmother was totally against this idea. This is when Art, Sylvia's eventual stepfather, entered the picture and both families' lives were changed from this point on.

Sylvia was born on June 18, 1953 in Augsburg, Germany, a city in the region of Swabia, Bavaria. Augsburg is located 57 miles northwest of Munich. It is the third oldest German city, after Neuss and Trier. Augsburg was founded by the Romans in 15 BC. Leopold Mozart, father of Wolfgang Amadeus Mozart, was born here in 1719. He became known as a leading music teacher, taught his son, discovered his talent, and managed his career.

As you can see, I've been known to drift off to many tangents in my storytelling. But I bring it all back eventually, that's just how my mind works. I'm going to quote a paper that Sylvia wrote for her Child Psychology course at Cazenovia College in November, 2003:

"I have chosen a time in my childhood going all the way back to Kindergarten. I remember many times of my growing up, but I will start there, because it is my earliest memory.

As I mentioned before, I was born of German parents in Augsburg, Germany. My first language was German for the first 2-3 years of my life. I was born in 1953 and at that time many young Germans were leaving the country for brighter shores. My father went to Canada to find a new job and living space for my mother and me. When he sent for her, she had already met my stepfather and decided, with the help of her mother, not to leave with a child and travel across the ocean to an uncertain future.

My mother, being as young as she was, with a child, heeded her mother's warning, that it wasn't a great idea. I loved my grandmother very much. She was only doing for her daughter and granddaughter what she thought was the best. She was afraid for us. She was not fond of my birth father, but what parent thinks his or her children have found the perfect mate.

So, with my new stepfather, we moved to Monterey, California, where I started Kindergarten. I was from a country that did a few things differently. Dress, food, customs, even though a lot was similar to the American ones. I immediately felt different. I spoke with an accent; my clothes were different and I loved sauerkraut!!! The other kids picked up on this right away and I felt very self-conscious. I wasn't wearing dirndls, but I did have a pair of tights that were thicker than usual with a wild print on them. The kids would chase me and pretend I was a wild tiger. I was confused, but played into the game and chased them back, even though my heart was not into it. I did not like it at all. I had a dress that had a bowtie on the top and the kids wondered why I was wearing a boy's shirt. I ripped it off the next time I had to wear it. My mother patiently sewed it back on because I told her it came off and I didn't know how. I didn't want to hurt her feelings. I loved the dress before this and didn't want to tell her it was a stupid dress in the States. My mother was learning to speak English at the time and was adjusting to her new life as well. I seem to have understood that even at a young age, so I ended up wearing the dress again and was glad the school year was almost over.

Even my teacher seemed to have an issue. I don't know if I was difficult or she just did not have the patience to repeat the things I did not understand the first time. That has helped me with my foreign students. I find myself getting impatient sometimes and have to remind myself that I was once in the same boat.

My stepfather was not easy to please. He was very critical and was not a confidence booster. He always found something wrong. My mother ended leaving after 23 years. She managed to hold her own and started life over without him.

When I was 18, I found out he was not my real father. I wasn't upset or shocked. I believe that I was almost glad. I was fortunate to have a loving family on my mother's side that thought I was more than I thought I was. My American family loved me too, but did not show it the same way. I traveled all over the United States and Europe for 18 years, which was incredible. My travels introduced me to people that believed I was special and not a failure at the things I did.

This story could go on and on and I don't want to sound as if I have regrets. I have been very fortunate in my life, but I do believe there were protective factors which made me more resilient in the face of stressful times. I always managed to find the brighter side of things. I was always told that 'good comes from bad' and I believe that is true in some cases. I was nurtured in an environment not easy to deal with, but have turned out to be a competent, caring adult."

Because Art became a 30-year Army veteran, completing a tour in Korea and two tours in Vietnam; Ursula was left, with the help of her parents, to raise Sylvia and her other two daughters that she had with him, Debbie and Karen. After his tours, he was stationed at several Army bases across the United States and Germany. Like other military families, they moved around frequently and the girls attended many different schools. Sylvia went to Kindergarten, as mentioned before in her paper, in Monterey, California. It was here when she became a

United States citizen, in February, 1959. She spent many of her elementary school years in Munich, Germany. After that, it was schools in Smithtown, Long Island; Greenwich, Connecticut; and Bayshore, Long Island. Then back to Germany to Würzburg and Zweibrücken to finish high school in Business Curriculum. In the summer of 1971, she worked in a Data Systems Office in Zweibrücken as a summer hire secretary.

Sylvia was 18 years, 4 months, and 11 days young when she got married on October 29, 1971. She worked and lived where he was stationed, as a bookkeeper for the American Express Company at the Zweibrücken Air Force Base, from November, 1972-March, 1973. Then as a bookkeeper at the Bank of America, Travis Air Force Base, Fairfield, California, from August, 1973-March, 1974; cashier/teller for the Beale Air Force Exchange in Marysville, California, from August, 1974-March, 1975; bank teller at the Santa Barbara Savings & Loans, Santa Barbara, California, from April, 1975-November, 1975; secretary at the Air Force Recruiting Office in Fredericksburg, Virginia, from 1976-1979. At some point in 1979, their marriage began to fall apart.

We never talked too much about it. I don't think she wanted to relive it. I'm sure they enjoyed some good times in the early years, but it did not end well. It ended in divorce. They had no children. Looking at some pictures now, I feel almost a sense of jealousy, not knowing her in her late teens and twenties. But that is a little ridiculous. It wasn't meant to be. I was blessed to have been with Sylvia for three-quarters of her adult life. The first 18 years of her life were childhood and all the different elementary, middle and high schools. Then an 8-year period of a young marriage, the last year of it not being a pleasant one. After that, a period of around 3 years and 8 months, where she was trying to deal with a divorce, adjusting to a totally unfamiliar city in Syracuse, and got involved in a relationship for 2 years that was going nowhere, and in hindsight, wished had never happened in the first place. Then a year of breaking away and trying to gain her independence for the first time in her life.

I have several friends who met in high school, over 57 years ago, had children and grandchildren, and are still happily married today. I was never married, although I came very close when I was 20 and 8 months young and she was 18. It was only a 5-month relationship, 2 months of it I was away in Great Lakes, Illinois, going through basic training in the Naval Reserves. It is a long and complex story that I'd rather not delve into. I was so naive and very fortunate that the marriage never happened, allowing me to move forward with my life.

I had a few relationships, most of them temporary, in my travels. The only other one was over a three-year period from March, 1974, when I came back to Syracuse to visit from Austin, Texas, until the summer of 1976. It always seemed star-crossed from the beginning. A hiatus for a few years, then a visit to Austin from her in the spring of 1979, when I was living back in Austin. I left Austin for good in July, 1979 and returned to Syracuse, where I have lived ever since. Trying to see if there was any chance for a new start in this relationship, but there was none. It just wasn't meant to be. Again, I was fortunate that it didn't work out, or I never would have met Sylvia, the one and only love of my life.

So many factors had to have been in place for us to meet. This is true for almost all relationships. First of all, we both had to be alive. A little obvious, but definitely true. If Sylvia had never left Germany, or had stayed married, we never would have met. If I had gotten and stayed married, we never would have met. If Art hadn't been assigned to Syracuse as a recruiter at the end of his Army career, and moved here with Ursula, we never would have met. If they weren't going through a divorce, we probably never would have met.

Ursula was on her own, living in the Carriage House East Apartments in Manlius and working at the Addis Company, a downtown department store, when Sylvia came up to see her in the fall of 1979; not knowing who else to turn to, as her marriage was coming to the end. She didn't know where else to go. Ursula left Syracuse the next year for Charleston, South Carolina, where her sister, Lori, was living. She has been there ever since. If Sylvia had gone with her to Charleston, we never would have met. She had gotten involved in this ill-fated relationship, so she stayed here. From our perspective, that's the only good thing that came out of it. The same could be said about the relationship that I was in that I mentioned before. If either of those relationships had worked out, we never would have met. But they weren't meant to be. *Ours was.*

I was playing on a softball team with a group of guys that I had always played against. The team that I had played on for years had disbanded and these guys asked me to play for them. I was leery, as they had a reputation for partying too much in those days. You never knew what physical or mental state that they would be in at game time. They were the only team in history, that I knew of, that wore jeans to play softball. All different kinds and styles of jeans. We hadn't won a game all season, until the third week of July. It was a really hot and humid night. They invited me to come over to this house, that had one of those above ground pools in the backyard, to celebrate our first victory. We cooled off in the pool, throwing a frisbee around, while drinking a few beers.

They wanted to go down to a bar in downtown Syracuse, Liberty Kelly's, the name of our team, to celebrate some more. Knowing their desires to get high and "party," I was understandably reluctant to go down there. Meanwhile, Sylvia faced a similar situation. Her younger sister, Karen, was visiting from Atlanta. She knew the guys on the team, having gone to high school here, and wanted to go down to the bar and take Sylvia with her. Sylvia had been involved in a weird, and in hindsight for her, embarrassing relationship for about two years, with someone who was friends with these guys. I knew this guy, so I would have to agree with her assessment. It had been over for at least a year now, but he was still not accepting it and continued to bother her, so she was not enthusiastic about going down there and possibly running into him and dealing with that.

We probably never would have met if both of us hadn't reluctantly gone down to that bar, that night in July, 1983. This defined the true meaning of *meant to be.* I had a premonition that I had seen Sylvia before, when I saw her standing there. (Sounds like a familiar song, I believe.) This bar was really not known for or conducive for dancing. It was just a bar and tables, with a jukebox and a small floor area next to it. I didn't hesitate and went over and asked Sylvia to dance. She always remembered what song it was, "Stand Back," by Stevie Nicks. I've always been known to be really good at trivia, especially sports, history, television, music and other sometimes useless information; but I couldn't recall what song it was that we first danced to. I thought it was some Fleetwood Mac song, but Syl remembered. *She always remembered. Nothing ever got past Syl.*

We went over to a friend's house after the bar and I can remember sitting on a couch next to her. It was like we were teenagers again. I remember subtly trying to put my arm around her, holding hands and talking. I asked her out on a date, and a few days later, picked her up at St. Joseph's Hospital, where she was working as a receptionist. We went to a bar in the Syracuse University area and had a couple of beers and nice conversations. Another similar date followed a few days after that, and we spent the night together.

Karen and Sylvia were into the song, "The Safety Dance," by the group, Men Without Hats. They would dance around the house, on Lancaster Avenue, where Syl was renting a room, not far from the Syracuse University campus; singing, "It's safe to dance, S-A-F-E-T-Y dance, it's safe to dance." I never knew, until I researched this recently, that Men Without Hats were from Montréal. Montréal will hold a special significance for us, as you will find out later in our story. I always regretted not going up to Montréal for the Summer Olympics in 1976, being only a 4 hour, 250 miles north, drive from Syracuse. Even not having any tickets for the events, just being around an Olympic atmosphere and seeing all the people from all over the world, would have been an incredible experience.

Another group that was very popular at that time was Men at Work from Australia. Their song, "Down Under," was a number one song on the charts in Australia, New Zealand, Canada, United States, United Kingdom, Denmark, Germany, Ireland, Italy, Switzerland and many other countries. I bought tickets to go and see them at the Saratoga Performance Art Center on Saturday, August 7th, and asked Syl if she would like to go. She was very excited to go with me to see them.

It had now been over two weeks since we first met that night at the bar. I asked her out to go to the movies on Friday night, August 6th. I told her that I would pick her up at 9 for the 9:30 movie. I had a softball game earlier that night at Hopkins Road Park in Liverpool, about a half hour away. My plan was to have a teammate follow me to Goodyear Tire, close to the park, to surprise Sylvia by putting four new tires on my 1978 Buick Regal, for the trip to Saratoga for the concert. Of course, per "Murphy's Law,": "Whatever can go wrong, will go wrong;" the game went to extra innings and I was running behind in my planned time to get back home and shower and get ready to pick up Sylvia for the movie. I got a ride back to Goodyear, but my mistake was not calling her and telling her I might be a few minutes late, but we could still be there on time for the movie. There were no cell phones then, but I still felt that I could be there to pick her up, pretty close to the scheduled time.

In the meantime, Karen wanted to go to this party where she knew a lot of people and convinced Sylvia that I was going to stand her up. First of all, I would never do that, and I was looking forward to going to the movie and to the concert the next day. That's all that was on my mind. I raced home by 8:30 and immediately called her. They had made the decision that I was not going to call and left for this party. Syl was hesitant, but after a failed marriage and divorce, and an ill-fated two-year relationship, and with Karen's encouragement; decided to leave and not wait for my call. I would have understood them leaving if I hadn't called by 9, but I was home in time to call and still pick her up on time for the movie. I kept calling all night long and was so angry and disappointed that she would think that I would stiff her like that. I guess she had people in her ear with preconceptions and stereotypes about me. But she didn't know me that well then, even though we seemed to have hit it off and were moving in a positive direction toward a possible long-term relationship.

Saturday morning came, and I had a makeup softball game due to a previous rainout. I hadn't slept very well thinking about the night before. I went and played the game and then decided to go over to Sylvia's place to get an explanation as to what had happened. It was a good thing that I was persistent, instead of just saying, "She didn't believe in me, so this is not going to work;" or we would have never gotten together. Very fortunate for me as well, to have Sylvia in my life forever.

I drove over to her place around noon and there she was, crying and distraught, her shirt and the screen door were both ripped. The ill-fated relationship guy, who must have heard from some of his friends that Sylvia was now dating me, had come over to confront her. Lucky for him that he wasn't still there when I arrived. This altered my perspective, as she did not need another confrontation. Instead, I asked her what had happened and then said,

"Look, if you trust me, why don't you bring some clothes and come with me and get out of here. We can go over to my place and you can take a shower, change clothes and be safe. I have the Men at Work tickets if you think you still might want to go."

1983

August (7th): Our very first trip together: Saratoga, New York (Men at Work Concert)

August (8th): Montréal, Canada (Auberge Belvedere Inn)

We went to my place and she showered and changed clothes. She trusted me and I think right then and there started to believe in me. This was the true beginning of our lifelong relationship. We drove the 150 miles east to Saratoga and enjoyed a great concert, which ended around midnight. I then asked Syl if she would like to drive up to Montréal to spend the night. (Once more, the special significance of Montréal, to be revealed later.) She was excited about the spontaneity of this. We drove 193 miles north and arrived past two in the morning. We found a place that was open, the Auberge Belvedere Inn. The bar was still open, so we had a drink, then went to our room and just held each other for the rest of the night, actually morning. I had forgotten the name of this place until I was sorting out some things and found this postcard that she had saved. We had breakfast and went clothes shopping, dodging the pouring rain. On the drive home, I asked her what she did on that Friday night. She told me she felt weird about going to that party and staying all night there. I never wanted to find out too many details and I think she appreciated that. To be honest, it was something that always bothered me somewhat, but sometimes you just have to put things behind you and let it go.

Syl began moving her clothes and things over to my place the following week. One day, my friend Steve drove me over to my place. When we pulled in front of the house, there was Syl, sitting on the front steps. Steve looked at her and exclaimed, "Wow, who is that doll?" I told him that was my girlfriend. I took a long look at Syl, wearing a jean skirt and a colorful peasant blouse, and gazed up to the heavens and asked to let her be *the one*. My prayers were answered.

By the middle of August, less than a month after that first meeting and dance in the bar, we were living together. And we have lived together ever since. This first place of ours was the second floor of a house I had been renting. It was in a rough, urban inner-city section. I also remember around this time that I had a City League softball game at Burnet Park, near the Zoo. I had gone to the park earlier to warm up. Sylvia came later with the girlfriend of a teammate. When she was walking over to the field in the distance, one of the other guys saw her and shouted,

"Who the heck is that?"

I responded, "That's my new girlfriend."

He answered back, "Yeah, *right!*"

Then Syl came up to me and kissed me. He had an astonished look on his face.

And I never felt so good in my life.

A Silent Life Within

Beyond melting patterns

Of uninhibited design

Appeared the golden crickets

Glowing like harbor lights

Transparent through endless nights

Beckoning me to follow

Never stopping to look back

I entered quickly with no regrets

Deep into the unknown

Engulfing all I've ever known

I feel the strength of my tears

Held back for so many years

Suddenly all became still

A moment of universal harmony

Silhouetted by a crimson sky

Sailing upon a summer breeze

Over the ebb and flow

Of ageless seas

Gliding soft blue

In her silken hue

Doing her child-like dance

As I float into her velvet trance

Beautiful mysteries begin to unfold

Secrets that can never be bought or sold

    We lived here, at 123 Clyde Avenue, on the south side of Syracuse, for over 6 months. I had lived here for 2 years previously. Sylvia was still working at the hospital and I was working for a landscaping company and doing interior house painting in the winter, as I never considered snow plowing, as most of the other landscapers did. In November, Syl decided that she wanted to get a cat. She had seen an ad in the paper for a place to adopt animals. We drove to a house in a rundown neighborhood. What we found was an elderly woman who had at least 40 dogs and cats, living in a crowded and unsanitary environment. The lady asked for references before Syl could adopt a cat. How ironic was that, an animal hoarder, asking for references? Syl gave her my brother-in-law's name and the woman had heard of him and let her take the cat. Tom is my younger sister, Julie's husband, and a well-known veterinarian. Syl saw a gray tabby cowering in the corner and took her. No wonder she was always kind of a skittish cat. On the way back home, the song, "Roxanne" by The Police came on the radio, and that's what we decided to name her. Soon after, shortened to Roxy.

1984

February: North Syracuse (We moved into our first house that we owned together: 108 Elm Street, at the end of February)

August: Sandy Pond, NY

In February of 1984, my younger brother, Marty, had his job transferred to Binghamton and put his house in North Syracuse up for sale. It seemed like the right opportunity for us to buy our first house. We didn't have many assets or credit history, no bad credit, but doing the transaction between family members and the sale price was low, so it worked out for both sides. Marty and his wife, Marti, took their two young sons, Kenny and Justin, and moved to Binghamton in the middle of February. My dad and Syl went out to the house, 108 Elm Street, and worked for two weeks cleaning and painting. I was laid up with a cast on my leg, with torn ligaments, from an injury that occurred while playing in a City League basketball game. Roxy laid next to me the whole time. Moving day came and some of my softball team friends were helping us move. We loaded everything up and they drove away. Syl went with them to let them into the house. I did a last check around our Clyde Avenue house, and to bring Roxy out with me, so she wouldn't freak out.

I don't know what Roxy's life was like before we adopted her, but I'm sure it was not a pleasant one. Just as I was about to leave, Roxy somehow slipped out the side door and was hiding in the neighbors' open garage. I needed to get out there and help the guys with moving all our things, but I couldn't just leave Roxy behind. Syl would have never forgiven me and I could never have done that. Roxy was being stubborn and finally I coaxed her over to the side door with some food and calmly calling her. I didn't put her in a cage in the car, letting her roam free.

She kept crawling under my legs near the brake and gas pedals. We finally made it out there. The guys gave me grief, as they were just about done, but I had Roxy, and that was a good thing.

The house on Elm Street became a nightmare at times. It was in a lower middle-class neighborhood with the houses close together. The downstairs area was a converted garage. The den had a drop ceiling and just a thin carpet covering a cement floor. The bedroom also had a drop ceiling and neither room, although big, were insulated. We had a wood stove installed in the bedroom so we wouldn't freeze to death. An attached blower sent warm air out to the den and upstairs. But it was so hot in the bedroom when the fire was really going, that we could never wear clothes in there, at the most, just shorts and a tee shirt. It was put on four huge slates of Pennsylvania Blue Stone, where you had to be careful not to whack yourself getting up in the middle of the night, or any time for that matter; to go upstairs to the kitchen or the only bathroom. Looking back at it now, we were very fortunate to not have the house go up in flames, as the extension pipe for the smoke to go out went through that drop ceiling. One time, we heard all this buzzing, and it turned out there was a gigantic bees nest in that drop ceiling. I could reach right up in there. We had to call the bee exterminator. We had to call him another time, as I had noticed a small hole in the basement foundation and sealed it up. It turned out this was an entry and exit for bees, unbeknownst to me. I went into the dark basement and went to turn the lights on, pulling the string attached to the light bulb. I screamed in pain, as there were hundreds of bees on that string and thousands more throughout the basement.

In July of 1984, my brother had moved back to Syracuse when his job hadn't worked out. They lived in an apartment until they eventually bought a house in Brewerton. But they weren't allowed to have any pets in the apartment, so they asked us if we wanted to take their six-month-old cat, Katmandu. Syl was excited to have a companion for Roxy. I don't know if the same could be said for Roxy. She wandered away one day through the woods past the backyard. We had to go on an all-out search for her and finally found her over by an elementary school. It took a while for Roxy to warm up to the situation, but eventually she did.

Syl stopped working at the hospital when we moved. During our 6 years and 2 months on Elm Street, Syl worked several different jobs. She worked for Tom as a veterinarian's aide at Liverpool Animal Hospital and also for another vet, Dr. Raile, in Liverpool. A few years later, she worked as a receptionist for two different supply companies, one in Manlius and one in downtown Syracuse. She had to drive long distances from our house, which was difficult in the winter. We had no garage, so our cars were buried in snow most of the time for five months. Somehow, we managed to survive these long, cold winters. It seemed like I was always out shoveling snow. She also worked for a friend's framing shop in Liverpool and framed all our Mayan prints from Mexico, the big John Lennon poster from the "Imagine" album, as well as many other prints, with beautiful frames. Syl was so talented in most everything she did.

That first full summer together, I introduced Syl to the sand dunes and sandy beaches of Lake Ontario, 50 miles north of Syracuse. Lake Ontario is the major influence on the weather for Syracuse and all of Central New York, helping to fuel the lake effect that creates the frequent winter blizzards. But in the summer, it is really beautiful and feels like you are at the ocean.

Some of my closest friends, that I have known since high school for over 57 years, and remain close friends today, used to go to a camp annually from 1963 through 1968. We were 17 to 22-year-old kids during this time period. This camp was located right on Lake Ontario, named Rainbow Shores, a few miles from a popular beach, Sandy Pond. There were several cabins, with a bar and restaurant on the premises.

We would go there at the end of the summer, for a week of drinking beer, playing marathon poker games, shooting pool, midnight tackle football, basketball, swimming, going to local bars for music; before we would head back to college or jobs. Wild and crazy guys, but plenty of fond memories.

Alphabetically, by first name or nickname, the original "Campers" were: "Audie," Brian, "Dust," "Eff," Frank, Jimmy, "Maph," "Mossy," Steve, "Tish," Wardie, "Whale." ("The Dirty Dozen," if you will.) We've lost four along the way: Frank, "Moss," "Whale," "Eff." The rest of us are left to carry on. We still reminisce about those crazy, funny times when we get together, and we greatly miss our friends; who left us way too soon.

1985

(end of) March & April: Tampa, Florida

Rocky Point

Busch Gardens

Sunken Gardens

Sea World

Steinbrenner Field

    This was our first vacation together. We flew to Tampa and went to our hotel, Rocky Point, located on Tampa Bay. I had found it in a brochure at the travel agency when I booked the trip. It fit our budget, but the place was in a transition period of being sold and was in a rundown condition. The beach lived up to its name, but it was a great sight to see dolphins swimming by in the bay in the morning. We would drive over for the day to the beaches at Clearwater and Saint Petersburg.

    We had a wonderful time at Busch Gardens and Sunken Gardens. Also, at SeaWorld, where Syl went with one of the trainers to the side of the pool and got a kiss from Shamu. I don't regret experiencing SeaWorld, but I'm glad that they are closing most of them down now. We were never advocates of the capture and captivity of all these dolphins and whales.

We also went to a Yankees spring training game. It was fun, but those were the days before we started using sunscreen. Got serious sunburns, which was not fun.

One night, Sylvia and I and Steve, who was down here visiting his mother, went to a comedy club called Chuckles to see Jay Leno. This was seven years before he would take over as "The Tonight Show" host from Johnny Carson in 1992, staying until 2009.

We were seated in the front row, so he chose to interact with us. He asked me what I did for a living and I told him that I worked for a landscaping crew. He countered with asking me if I felt like the Indian, with the tear in his eye, in the television commercials when I was out there working. This commercial was first aired on Earth Day in 1971 with a Native American shedding a tear about litter in one of the country's most well-known public service announcements, "Keep America Beautiful." It would be just as poignant and relevant if they aired them again today, and I think they should. The actor went by the name of Iron Eyes Cody, but actually was an Italian-American actor, born Espera Oscar de Corti in 1904. He passed away in 1999.

Next Jay turned his attention to Sylvia. He started talking about cats and asked her if she had any, which she said we had two. (We didn't get Jeopardy until a year and eight months after this.) He asked Syl what brand of cat food the cats were fed and she told him Nine Lives. He equated that to his cats getting fed Fancy Feast. Then if you tried to switch brands, after they were used to and liked a certain brand, they could be starving and not eat the different brand. Syl definitely agreed with him.

Finally, he asked Steve what he did for a living and Steve said he was involved in a business that sold and installed Redwood Hot Tubs. Jay asked him how the business was going, a quick quip about it must be hot, when Steve said, "One step at a time." It was actually a pretty good comeback, but Jay didn't really hear it, as he had moved on from us and to a different part in his standup routine.

It was cool interacting with him, especially what he moved on to become in his career after this. After the show, Jay was just sitting there at the bar by himself, as everyone left the club and told him that they enjoyed the show. We did the same, and always regretted not sitting down and hanging out with him for a while. It was not that late, we were not in any hurry, and he was looking for conversation. He didn't drink or smoke, just sitting there waiting. I guess we were a little shy or something, I don't know why, we had already bantered with him during the show. Definitely an opportunity and an experience that we all let slip away.

1986

April: Antigua

Dian Bay

Long Bay

English Harbour

Nelson's Dockyard

Clarence House

Fig Tree Hill

Shirley Heights

Half Moon Bay

Hawksbill Beach

Darkwood Beach

Dickenson Bay

July: Sonnenberg Gardens

Letchworth State Park

August: Thousand Islands

Seneca Falls

Lakemont & Dundee

Watkins Glen

September: Gananoque, Canada & Thousand Islands

October: Letchworth State Park (cabin)

I had saved my money that I earned from my painting jobs for these vacations. I always looked for the best possible deals that I could find. In those days, the airfares and hotels were much more inexpensive than they are today. We went before my landscaping work began for the season and Syl was able to take a vacation from her work. We survived the long and cold Syracuse winter and made our plans to escape for some warmth. I felt guilty going, as my dad had become sick and faced an uncertain future. But he was not seeking any medical treatment and it became a very frustrating situation. We left in April for two weeks and fortunately had some time to spend with him when we came back. He passed away, far too young, at 69 and almost 5 months, on May 14, 1986.

    We flew into Saint Maarten and then on to Antigua. Antigua is an island in the West Indies, one of the Leeward Islands in the Caribbean Region. Antigua has hundreds of beaches. They boast that they have one for every day of the year. It was cloudy and rainy when we arrived. They don't get that much rain in April, but we found out later that they had been experiencing storms for the past three or four days. This became a prelude to the first of many vacation stories for us.

    During my 21-year teaching career, all the Lower School teachers were assigned lunch room tables. This was for students in Grades 1-5. I don't know why I started telling my stories at lunch, but I guess it's because I'm a storyteller by nature. Once I started, there was no turning back. I became known for this and the kids loved to hear the stories and couldn't wait to sit at my table. Usually there were eight or nine kids at your table, for a three-week period, before the new tables were assigned. Some kids sat at my table numerous times over their years in Lower School. Other kids were never assigned to my table and couldn't believe it. When I would begin to tell a story, some of the older kids from other tables would start mingling around my table, and a small crowd would form.

"Oh, yeah, I remember that one. Great one!"

Syl would feel compelled to come over and shoo them back to their own tables, so I wouldn't get in trouble with the administrators. I could usually finish the stories in this three-week time period, but sometimes, due to vacations or whatever, new table assignments were not completed and the kids were at the table for twice as long, six weeks. I would have to resort to telling some backup stories and animal stories. I told the kids that I could only tell appropriate stories, when the main menu of stories had been told, and I had to move on to the backup and animal stories. I remember one day after stating this, one boy asked,

"Can you please tell us some of your inappropriate stories?"

Holding back a grin, I said I could not. A lot of the kids told their parents about these stories and most of the parents thought they were great. There were probably some who didn't know what to make of these stories and me telling them to their children. You know how stories can get misinterpreted when passed along to second or third hand parties. In fact, there was one boy who was acting rude and dismissive one day, when I was trying to tell a story.

I said to him, "Look, you don't have to like my stories or even listen to them, but you don't need to be rude to me. The other kids like the stories, how come you don't?"

"Because I don't believe that you ever wrestled a bear."

Talk about how stories can get misconstrued! I told him that I never wrestled a bear, never said that I ever wrestled a bear, and whoever you heard that from got it all wrong. I told him that all my stories were true and I would never lie about them. From then on, he started listening to the stories and really liked them.

At one time, I was going to write a book about them with the title of "Dusty's Lunchtime Stories." It would have been a much shorter book than what I'm writing now, but I can now interweave them into this book about our entire history and relationship. In fact, three of these stories occurred on this vacation in Antigua.

We picked up our rental car at the airport. A man named Slane drove us out to our rental place, Dian Bay, situated on a cliff on the far east side of the island. It was a bottom half of a condo, owned by a woman from Toronto. I had found it in a brochure at the travel agency for an inexpensive rate. It probably is three or four times that amount now. That price allowed us to stay an additional week. The woman was not there, so we had the place to ourselves, which was nice. Slane was listening to the cricket match on the radio as we drove through the small town of Willikies as we arrived at Dian Bay. Slane then informed us I had to give him my driver's license and $20, for an Antiguan driver's license, and he would take the rental car with my license and return in an hour. It wasn't clear to me why we couldn't have taken care of this at the airport. I must have been very naive, but at this point there didn't seem to be any other alternatives. I had also paid for daily accident and collision coverage from his rental company, S. & L. Rental, at the airport. It was a smart thing that I did, as you will find out in the second of our Antiguan stories.

As we entered our condo, the intoxicating aromas of the beautiful flowers engulfed us. There were: agave, pink & white bougainvillea, pink & white desert rose, pink & white hibiscus, laceleaf, purple shower, Trinidadian frangipani and try alice. The condo had a large bedroom, living room, kitchen, and wicker furniture. The kitchen had everything you needed: blender, toaster, dishes, cups and glasses. Off the living room was a large sliding glass door. We would leave it open in the morning and little colorful birds would fly in. Leaving out the back of the condo led us down a descending sequence of steps, surrounded by the beautiful flowers, to a lagoon. There was a sailboat that was anchored in the lagoon the entire time of our vacation. We could hear a constant and pleasant tinkling sound at night, as it gently rocked back and forth. This lagoon was surrounded by the Caribbean Sea and the Atlantic Ocean.

Slane did return an hour later with our car, my license, and the Antiguan driver's license. We unpacked our things and the weather started to clear up.

"Moon Jellyfish"

We put on our bathing suits and headed down to the lagoon. I always asked the kids, as I began this story, to tell me what they thought the two people sitting in lounge chairs at the edge of the lagoon, should have said to us as we entered the water. The sun was beginning to set in brilliant colors as a full moon was rising at the same time.

"Isn't this beautiful, honey?" I remarked to Syl.

She agreed and everything seemed so right, until a few minutes later, it wasn't. I started swimming and then felt something wrap around me and then excruciating pain. All of a sudden, I started jumping up and down and screaming. Syl thought maybe I was just acting silly in the water and trying to startle her. Seconds later, she was also jumping up and down and screaming. Either I had flipped what had wrapped around me onto her, or we had swum through a whole school of whatever was causing us so much pain. We both started to make a mad dash to shore. As we were running past the couple, the woman informed us,

"Oh yeah, I got stung yesterday."

So, the question I posed to the kids, "Should they have warned us about the possibility of getting stung?"

Maybe they didn't want to spoil our good time. Maybe they thought it was funny and would be a good show. You don't want to think that way, but it was strange. We found out later that we were stung by Moon Jellyfish. It was like hot burning coals on our bodies, especially our chests. We had these red welts and the ensuing pain for several days. We also learned that during storms, the Moon Jellyfish get swept into the lagoon or go there seeking shelter.

The next day another woman and some kids were stung, while the woman's husband, who was windsurfing, was not. I guess it was just a matter of being in the wrong place at the wrong time.

"Dead Man's Curve"

Because we were dealing with these painful welts on our bodies, we were unable to sit in the sun, so we went cruising around the island. We were driving around the Shekerley Mountains, on the southwest part of the island. We came to a place called "Dead Man's Curve," named for its past history of people dying in driving accidents. There were no guard rails, just the mountains on the right side, and an over 1,300 feet plunge down to protruding boulders in the Atlantic Ocean, on the left side. A road so narrow that there was only space for one vehicle at a time. And you might encounter a cow or two just standing there. The drive had beautiful views, but definitely nerve-racking. We managed to make it safely back to the condo, but we kept hearing this loud noise coming from the car.

The next morning, we were driving around and the noise kept getting louder and louder. I checked for flat tires or the muffler or loose pipes hanging underneath the car, but didn't notice anything. We decided it would be wise to go out to the airport and have Slane check it out and maybe get a different car. As we approached the entrance to the terminal, which was about half a mile away, the right front tire flew off the car! The car was all crumpled on the passenger side, Sylvia's side, as it crashed to the ground. I shut off the car and checked on her. She was shaken up, but unhurt. I jumped out of the car and ran after the tire, which was hurtling toward exiting cars. A couple of cars bounced the tire, as it then started rolling across this field on the left. I finally retrieved it and brought it back to the car. I looked at the tire and noticed it had only two lug nuts. Maybe the other three had come off when it crashed. I then checked the other tires and they all had only one or two lug nuts on them. *Are you kidding me?* You don't think to see if all the tires have all five lug nuts on them when you get your rental car. From then on, I always checked, that's for sure. And what was going on here, is somebody stealing lug nuts?

People must have reported what had happened, as Slane came down from the rental office. At first, he was sort of giving us a hard time to get another car, until I pointed out the lug nut situation. He avoided the issue, offering no explanation, but got another car for us. I immediately checked the tires to make sure they all had five lug nuts securing them. We had our backpacks and some other things in the trunk that we had to transfer to the new car. But behind a small compartment in the trunk, I had put our new binoculars. He was rushing us and we forgot to take the binoculars. I realized the binoculars were missing the next day and called him to have him check the trunk and return them to us. He said nobody had found them, which was a lie. If he is still alive today, he is probably using them to watch his cricket matches.

The bigger issue is, what if that tire had flown off the day before, driving on "Dead Man's Curve?" I don't even want to think about it. The result would not have painted a pretty picture in all probability. Fate and lady luck both were on our side that day. Both of these stories, "Moon Jellyfish" and "Dead Man's Curve," happened on the first three days of our vacation.

We were hoping for better days ahead. We walked down to Long Bay, not far from the condo, and went swimming there in the Atlantic Ocean. We never swam in the lagoon again after being stung by the Moon Jellyfish. We spent many of our days at Darkwood Beach, a favorite spot of the locals.

We drove through Fig Tree Hill, up the ancient volcanic hills of the Parish of Saint Mary, past old sugar mills and little churches, to the steep farmlands of banana, mango and coconut groves. (Figs are what Antiguans call bananas.) And further on through the lush vegetation of the rainforest.

An amazing event happened that we had the privilege of observing on the night of April 11th. We were having a wonderful dinner in our kitchen that Syl had prepared: her usual fantastic big salad, fresh vegetables and fish that we had bought at the market. Seemingly out of nowhere appeared this huge object, illuminating the dark sky with this unmistakable red flashing tail. It was something that we had never ever seen before. We had seen shooting stars, meteor showers, visible planets, lunar and solar eclipses, but nothing ever like this. Maybe our eyes were playing tricks on us after a couple of Piña Coladas. The next day we found out, after talking to other people who had seen what we did, that what we had witnessed was Halley's Comet. It is visible from Earth every 75 or 76 years. The Chinese had the earliest observation in 240 BC. It is named after Edmond Halley, an English astronomer, who in 1705 correctly predicted the 1758 return of a comet that had previously been observed in 1682. The comet returned again in 1835, 1910, and now in 1986.

Samuel Langhorne Clemens, famously known by his pen name, Mark Twain, was born on November 30, 1835 and died of a heart attack on April 21, 1910, just one day after the comet appeared the brightest in its history. Twain was quoted as saying,

"I came in with Halley's Comet in 1835. It is coming again next year, and I expect to go out with it. It will be the greatest disappointment of my life if I don't go out with Halley's Comet. The Almighty has said, no doubt: Now here are these two unaccountable freaks; they came in together, they must go out together."

On April 11, 1986, Halley's Comet passed the closest to the Earth on its outbound journey and the closest it came during its passage. A once in a lifetime experience for us. It will return on July 28, 2061.

Cloud Dancers

Feel the rhythm

Way down in your toes

Abandon the skeleton

And forget all your woes

The hour is late

But the time is right

Let's dare to tempt fate

And dance through the night

Drums pound like a runaway train

Its signals flashing green

Echoes waltz inside my brain

Wildest vision I've ever seen

Now the last tango

As the moon starts to sigh

Recklessly we soar

Click our heels against the sky

Calypso fever vibrates our souls

Passions explode from a magic guitar

We hop aboard a note and begin to float

Reaching out for our own special star

    I wish we could be like Star Trek and just energize ourselves back to all these special places and magical moments in time and hang out there for a while. No limits or constraints, only leaving the adventure we are experiencing when we are ready to transport ourselves to the next one.

"Shorty's Glass Bottom Boat"

    The third "Lunchtime Story" on this Antiguan vacation happened on the next to last day of our trip. We had driven across the island several days before, to purchase our tickets to go on this excursion aboard an old sailing ship, "The Crimson Pirate," which was used in the 1952 movie starring Burt Lancaster. They take you out to Great Bird Island, renowned for its numerous bird population: brown pelicans, West Indian whistling ducks, frigate birds, and red-billed tropicbirds. This island is the only place on Earth where you can see the Antiguan racer, a harmless snake. There's also the endangered Ameiva Griswoldi lizard. The only way to get there is by tour boat. Arriving at the island, they would serve lunch and there would be steel drum music, and later, time for bird-watching.

  We were really looking forward to it, being the last full day of the vacation, as we would be flying home the following day. We got up early, packed up what we needed for the day, and left to be at the ship on time. We wanted to allow for any possible delays on the road, and as we were running a little behind our schedule, skipped breakfast. When we got to the place where we had purchased the tickets, there was a different man there, and he informed us that there was no boat going out today. We asked him why and he just told us there was no boat going out today. No reason given. No alternatives for us, as tomorrow we were going back home. He did give us back $80, $40 per ticket for the boat tour that now no longer existed, and two tee shirts that said, "Holy Shirt" on them. Frustrated and angry, we drove to nearby Dickenson Bay and went into the bar and restaurant to get some breakfast.

  We sat there talking about how we couldn't believe that our trip had been canceled and how disappointed we were that we weren't able to get out on the water. A short local man was sitting next to us and overheard our conversation.

"I can take you out on the water."

"Really? What kind of boat do you have?"

"I have a glass bottom boat."

"How much is it?"

"I will take you out for $10 each."

    I looked at Syl and both of us were skeptical, as he had these huge eyes that looked like they were bugging out of his head. They looked bloodshot, as if he was stoned or had stayed up all night. But we really wanted to go out on a boat on our final day and accepted his offer. He told us that his name was Shorty, (of course), and to follow him to his boat. We hadn't even ordered breakfast yet, but he was ready to go.

    We followed him to the boat. It was a decent-sized boat, with an upper deck and there was a glass bottom, although it was pretty scratched. Shorty loaded up his boat with two metal lockers, one with masks, snorkels, and fins; the other had orange juice, pineapple juice, rum and ice. He brought along a young local man, probably in his early 20's, as his helper, who seemed reluctant to go. He looked like he had been up all night, as he spent most of his time on this trip sleeping. He was a nice-looking young man. Couldn't really say the same about Shorty, and it was hard to determine how old he was.

    Then off we went. Well, sort of. There was no pull cord to start the motor. Shorty took this loose rope, put it between his toes, wrapped it around the motor, then pulled on the rope to start the motor. We would go for a while and the boat would stall out. He would again take the rope, put it between his toes, wrap it around the motor, pull the rope to start the motor. Go for a while and then stall out. You get the picture. We followed this same routine, all the way out to our unannounced destination, somewhere in the Caribbean. Our skepticism of taking this boat trip was growing stronger by the minute, but at this point we knew there was no turning back, and we were in it for the long haul.

I asked Shorty, "Are there any sharks where we are going?"

"Just out at the reef," Shorty replied.

"And where are we going?"

"Out to Cades Reef."

We found out later when we returned home and did some research, that Cades Reef was a coral reef that had spiny lobsters, conch, parrotfish, octopus, barracudas, Hawksbill turtles, moray eels, Eagle rays, and Nurse and Reef sharks. Both of these sharks supposedly pose little threat to divers and snorkelers. Supposedly. Except maybe one feeling a little too curious or threatened. You obviously expect to find a variety and abundance of sea creatures living in and around a coral reef; but if we would have known about the barracudas, eels, rays and sharks, we probably wouldn't have gone diving in the water by the reef. But we had no time for research before going on this boat trip, as it was a spur of the moment decision.

This news wasn't sitting well with Syl. She had me go and tell Shorty that when we got out to the reef, she would not be snorkeling, because she didn't know how to swim. I asked her if she was sure and she said yes, as she didn't know if she really trusted these guys, and her fear of a possible shark encounter. I informed Shorty of what she wanted me to tell him.

We decided to make the best of the situation and went up to the top deck and sat in the sun and had a couple of rum punches. It was really hot in the sun, nearly 90 degrees, and we hadn't eaten anything all day. I told Syl that I was going to dive in and take a swim. I put my mask and fins on, not bothering with the snorkel. I'm a good swimmer, although I wouldn't consider myself a really strong swimmer for any kind of long distances. When it comes to snorkeling, I have a tendency to breathe in, rather than breathe out, which is the obvious technique for snorkeling. But I can hold my breath for a long time underwater, so I just do that. I dove in and had no idea what was happening on the opposite side of the boat.

In the meantime, Syl had the same idea to cool off and decided to dive in. She had completely forgotten that she had told me to tell Shorty earlier that she didn't know how to swim. Shorty saw her dive in and just thought here was a crazy American blonde woman, who had a couple of rum drinks in the hot sun, and had lost her mind. (When I would tell the kids this story, as part of my "Lunchtime Stories," I would never mention that we had a couple of rum drinks.) He panicked and dove in after her, trying to grab her hand and rescue her. Syl was a good swimmer, like me, not a strong long-distance swimmer, but good enough. She was resisting Shorty trying to grab her hand to help her, still not having full trust in these guys, thinking maybe he was trying to hurt her. During this struggle, she raked her thigh across a piece of coral and now had a bleeding gash in the water, not what you want with sharks around in this reef. I don't care if these sharks were not supposed to be aggressive, nobody knows how they will react when they smell blood in the water.

Syl knew she had been cut and finally realized that Shorty was trying to help her. He got her back in the boat and woke up the young guy. I returned to the boat and everyone was freaking out. We ripped up some towels and wrapped them around Syl's thigh as a tourniquet. Shorty immediately started to head back. He put the rope between his toes, then around the motor, started the boat, it went for a while, stalled out. Repeated this routine again and again until we eventually, and I mean eventually, in the most extensive sense of the word; made it back to Dickenson Bay.

I got medical attention for Syl: antiseptic and clean bandages for the gash. It was an uncomfortable last night and plane trip home for her, but she healed nicely, and only had a barely visible scar as a reminder of this ordeal. The craziest thing of all was when we were leaving, we saw at least 20 regular tourists lining up to pay their tickets to go out on Shorty's Glass Bottom Boat. We were thinking they had no idea what kind of trip that they were about to embark upon.

We packed up the next morning and drove to the airport. As we were returning the rental car, guess who was there waiting for us? Slane, asking for a "contribution" toward the damage to the first car, due to the tire incident. My guess was that he had put the car insurance money in his pocket, never expecting anything bad to happen. (I had no credit cards back then, just paid for everything in cash.) I told him we had paid for the insurance to cover this very type of situation. He wasn't too thrilled. That rental company was fortunate that we were very naive in those days and didn't sue them for not having the correct amount of lug nuts on each tire. It could have been a bigger disaster than it was. I also asked him to please send me the binoculars when they found them. That never happened.

Never saw them again. If he is still alive today, he is using them, watching his cricket matches.

I remember bringing back five huge conch shells in a duffel bag, some of them protruding from the sides of the bag. There is no way that you could ever bring them back through the airport today. Still have one of the shells, located alongside the steps of the back deck of our house.

Antigua was still a fantastic vacation, despite experiencing and surviving these three bizarre stories. We saw beautiful island vistas, hiked through a rainforest, observed colorful birds, were surrounded by the aroma of exotic flowers, strolled on sandy beaches, swam in turquoise waters, had wonderful dinners, and witnessed a once in a lifetime event, Halley's Comet.

In July, we drove 70 miles to Sonnenberg Gardens, located at the north end of Canandaigua Lake, one of the Finger Lakes in Upstate New York. It is a beautiful and historic estate with nine formal gardens, an antique greenhouse complex, and a Victorian mansion.

Later in July, we made our first of many trips to Letchworth State Park, renowned as "The Grand Canyon of the East." It is located in Castile, New York, about a two and a half hour, 115 miles west, drive from Syracuse. A 17 mile stretch of the Genesee River roars through the park's scenic gorge, with three major waterfalls, and cliffs as high as 600 feet, surrounded by lush forests. This is where I first saw the statue of Mary Jemison, famously known as "The White Woman of the Genesee." It struck an unexplainable chord in me, one that I knew I needed to explore.

In August, we took trips to the Thousand Islands, Lakemont, Dundee, Watkins Glen, and Taughannock Falls.

The Thousand Islands are a group of 1,864 islands in the Saint Lawrence River, on the border of both the United States and Canada. There are elaborate island mansions, the most famous are: "Millionaires' Row," Boldt Castle on Heart Island, and Singer Castle on Dark Island. It is a unique and beautiful area, 100 miles north of Syracuse.

Lakemont is a hamlet in the town of Starkey. This is where I spent my wonderful childhood, attending Dundee Central School, in Dundee, a small town 3 miles away. Lakemont is 26 miles south of Geneva, where Hobart and William Smith colleges are located. Linda graduated from Dundee Central and then attended and graduated from William Smith. There she met her husband, John, who was from Passaic, New Jersey, and attending Hobart. They were married for over 50 years and had three children, Susan, Stephanie, and Matt, together. It is a scenic drive from Geneva to Lakemont, with Seneca Lake, from the Iroquois meaning "place of stone," the widest and deepest of the Finger lakes, appearing on your left. There are vineyards everywhere and many wineries, which weren't around when we were growing up. Penn Yan, named for "Pennsylvania Yankee," is twelve miles away, on Keuka Lake.

Watkins Glen is 13 miles south of Lakemont, with its State Park renowned for its natural beauty. The two-mile hike through a series of gorges, rare plants, and 19 waterfalls is an amazing experience.

Taughannock Falls is northwest of Ithaca, near the town of Trumansburg, 65 miles south of Syracuse. The falls cascade to a drop of 215 feet, one of the highest east of the Rocky Mountains.

In September, we drove 113 miles to Gananoque, Canada, on the Canadian side of the Thousand Islands for Labor Day weekend.

In October, we returned to Letchworth State Park to stay in a cabin over Columbus Day weekend. This was the first year of four consecutive years that we stayed there over the same long weekend. There was a group of cabins and a communal building in the center with bathrooms and showers. The cabin was rustic, with bunk beds, a small refrigerator and stove, a wooden table and chairs, and a wood burning stove in the middle. I would bring a small television to try and watch the Major League Baseball playoffs from the top bunk bed, but the reception was really poor. Syl would bring a tablecloth, candles, a vase for wildflowers, everything to enhance our experience. We would make breakfast and sit outside on the picnic table and eat it. Then bring what we needed in our backpacks, along with sandwiches that she made, some fruit, and hike all day through the woods; seeing the brilliant colored leaves and sparkling streams and waterfalls. We would return before dark and Syl would make her usual beautiful salad and whatever we were having for dinner. I would make some hot rum and cider drinks and get the wood stove going. I would try to watch the baseball games, as Syl would sit by the wood stove reading her books. Wouldn't mind being there right now.

One morning, Syl made some biscuits and the first batch came out too hard. I threw them out in the woods in the back of the cabin for the birds and animals. Big mistake. The raccoons must have been watching me and discovered the biscuits. This was the year that there were warning signs about a possible rabies scare with the raccoons. Later in the night, I was going to walk out in the total darkness with my flashlight, over to the communal building to go to the bathroom. I opened the back door and there were 40 or 50 raccoons, several right outside the door, a truly scary sight in itself; but made even scarier with this rabies warning. They were standing on their hind legs, with their paws outstretched in full begging position. The rest were advancing toward the cabin like zombies, with their eyes eerily silhouetted against the total blackness. They must have figured out that this was the place where the "biscuit boy" lived. I decided that there was no way I was going out there. We just used a bucket to pee in and dumped it in the morning. I never threw food in those woods ever again.

Later in October, we adopted another cat. We went out to Craig and Leslie's annual Champagne Harvest party, where everyone brought a bottle of champagne, beer, wine, homemade breads and soups, salads, all sorts of delicious food and desserts. Leslie let a new litter of kittens out to run around in the living room for all to see and possibly adopt. Syl loved this orange and white kitten, who had seven toes on each paw, called "dew claws," and wanted to adopt her. Craig called us when they were ready to be taken home. Just before Christmas, we went back out to their house in Lafayette and picked her up.

We named her Jeopardy because she was always seeming to cause trouble. After a while we shortened it to Jeppy. She was small, but feisty. Roxy and Mandu accepted her, but she was really attached to Mandu. We bought Marty and Marti's waterbed when we bought their house, and one night we felt a warm trickle in the bed. She had peed in the waterbed. Then we noticed a little rip where she had scratched it. We had to empty out the waterbed and get rid of it. So now we had three cats.

1987

March: Saint Croix, Virgin Islands
- Frederiksted
- Frederiksted Pier
- Rainbow Beach
- Fort Frederiksted
- Caribbean Museum
- Saint Patrick Church
- Saint George Village Botanical Garden
- Rainforest
- Estate Whim Museum & Great House
- Christiansted
- National Historic Site
- Customs House
- Fort Christiansvaern
- Harbor
- Carambola Beach Resort
- Cramer Park
- Buck Island Reef

Saint John

Trunk Bay

May: Sonnenberg Gardens
　　　Taughannock Falls
　　　Niagara Falls & Marineland

July: Lake Placid
　　　Skaneateles Lake
　　　Seneca Lake

August: Watkins Glen

September: Cape Cod
　　　East Harwich
　　　Provincetown
　　　Hyannisport
　　　Sandwich
　　　Martha's Vineyard

October: Letchworth (cabin)

December: Trinkaus Manor, Oriskany

The following year, in March, 1987, we flew to the island of Saint Croix, one of the Virgin Islands, along with Saint Thomas and Saint John. The Virgin Islands are a western island group of the Leeward Islands, which are the northern part of the Lesser Antilles. They form the border between the Caribbean Sea and the Atlantic Ocean.

I had found this hotel, The Royal Dane, in Frederiksted, in a travel brochure. It was very old and around 1820 had survived a fire and was now renovated. As we entered the front door, a very heavy woman with a chain dog collar around her neck, who was the bartender, took one look at us and said,

"Are you sure that you two are in the right place?"

We said that we were. There was a courtyard around the center area surrounded by exotic flowers and plants. Tables were nicely decorated and set up for dining. On the outer edges of the courtyard were rooms. There were a few rooms and a fitness center on the second level, but we were discouraged from taking a room up there. Syl went to check it out and discovered the fitness room displayed explicit gay sexual magazines. The few rooms on this level were reserved for "close friends." I never went up there. We were assigned a room right off the courtyard next to a jacuzzi.

These were the days when the AIDS epidemic was first becoming known to the public. There was widespread fear, paranoia, and misunderstanding back then. I have never been homophobic, nor will I ever be.

"Not that there's anything wrong with that!" (from a Seinfeld episode). But it was a new and overwhelming experience to be the only straight couple where we were staying.

The owners of the Royal Dane were gay and had invited their friends and friends of friends to come down and stay there. It was a safe haven for them. For me, I didn't have to worry about anyone checking out Sylvia. They were more interested in checking me out. Some of these guys were obviously gay, very feminine and proud of it. Some maybe, possibly, if you were a straight observer. But some you would have never ever guessed were gay.

The first morning we ate out in the courtyard where they had fruit juices in ice buckets, croissants, pastries, and breakfast items. They had a coffee cart that came around the courtyard to the rooms. After the first uncomfortable morning for me, I told Syl from now on to go and get our juice and breakfast and bring it back to the room, while I got the coffee from the cart. They would have a large group in the hot tub, right off our room, at night. We never went in there. But we adjusted to the routine, as nothing was going to stop us from enjoying our vacation. We ate in the courtyard one evening and the food was delicious, but the portions were tiny and way overpriced. It was more about the presentation. This became an inside joke for us through the years, when we were served dinner at an upscale restaurant and the portions were tiny and overpriced. When this happened, I would always comment, "What's this, the Royal Dane?"

Another inside joke for us was one night they had a steel drum band playing in the courtyard, not far from our room. Normally, we would be out there to enjoy the music, but I was trying to watch the first-round game of the 1987 NCAA Basketball Tournament with Syracuse playing Georgia Southern. This was the tournament where Syracuse lost to Indiana on a last second shot by Keith Smart, the most heart-breaking loss in Syracuse's storied basketball history; especially when we had the lead in the final minutes and missed some crucial foul shots that would have ensured the National Championship for us. It still haunts Syracuse fans to this day. Anyway, the band had ended and we were getting ready for bed, when a local man burst into the room. We were in our underwear, but fortunately for all of us, not being intimate. Our door was unlocked, as he mistakenly thought our room was where an after party was going to take place. He said in embarrassment,

"My face may look like I am smiling, but I am not happy."

That became a funny quote for us throughout the years. Syl ran into him in town a week later while she was doing the laundry and he was still telling her how sorry he was.

The first few days we went across the street to Rainbow Beach. Nice name, but kind of a rocky beach, and where the cruise ships came in. We started to explore the town of Frederiksted; the shops, (one was Sylvia's Boutique, Sylvia being a common name on the island), streets, and historic sites: Fort Frederik, the Caribbean Museum, the beautiful Botanical Garden, the Estate Whim Museum & Great House, and the Rainforest. Many of the same flowers and plants that we found in Antigua were here, such as bougainvillea, frangipani, and hibiscus; but there were also aloe vera, bird of paradise, cactus, casha bush, century plant, crown of thorns, cup of gold, flower yellow trumpetbush, ginger thomas, plumbago, and tan tan. We also saw many old abandoned sugar mills. Off Mahogany Road, there is a big barn where they take fallen mahogany trees and cut them up and carve them into all kinds of beautiful furniture.

One day, we took a boat, "The Reef Queen," out to Buck Island. After that, we started exploring the town of Christiansted, on the northeastern coast of Saint Croix. We went down to the waterfront, a National Historic Site with the Customs House and Fort Christiansvaern, which was built in the 18th century to protect the town from pirate attacks. You can see the cannons on its battlements.

We asked some of the locals where they went to the beach and they told us about Cramer Park. It is a remote beach on the north shore of Saint Croix's east end, near Point Udall, surrounded by Knight Bay and Boiler Bay. Palm trees, soft white sand and calm shallow water. We went there almost every day. I wish we were there now.

We were driving around the island and came upon the Renaissance Saint Croix Carambola Beach Resort & Spa. We had heard that Eric Clapton and Elton John had stayed there, as we pulled up to the guard gate. The guard waved to us and we waved back. I'm not sure who he thought we were, but he never asked us anything, so we drove right in. It was a beautiful place, built on a sugar plantation. Carambola is another word for starfruit. The pool was magnificent. We went swimming and posed for a few pictures, wishing we were staying here rather than the Royal Dane. Syl overheard an older man commenting to his wife,

"Those people don't belong here."

Maybe the dead giveaway were these inexpensive souvenir towels that we were using, with palm trees and the words Virgin Islands on them, that we had bought at the airport. I noticed that everyone had these big, fluffy, complementary yellow towels. I wanted them. I grabbed two and went out to the beach, overlooking the Caribbean Sea, behind the pool. Taking a chance of getting into potential trouble, with security guards all around, I stuffed the two towels into my now bulging backpack. We returned a few days later to the Carambola, but it was a different guard and he wanted to know what room we were in. We turned around and headed back to Cramer Park. Years later, we were watching an episode of Robin Leach's "Lifestyles of the Rich and Famous," and the show featured an actor who was walking down the beach at the Carambola, with one of those yellow towels draped around him. We used those towels for many years until they eventually wore out.

Syl and I decided to take a day trip to visit Saint John. We took a seaplane over and returned by ferry. Upon boarding the seaplane, the pilot asked me to sit in the back row, on the right side, to balance the weight. There were only six passengers, four women and us. As we took off, I noticed the door opposite me, where no one was sitting, was not latched tightly. The door was rattling around and water was coming in. I informed the pilot of this, but he just told me to put my feet up against the door to keep it shut. That's how I rode over in the seaplane to Saint John.

It reminded me of the most terrifying ride that I was ever on. I went down to Tampa, Florida in the spring of 1977 to visit a friend. We went to Disney World and went on the Space Mountain Ride, an indoor, dark, high speed, space-themed, steel roller coaster in the Magic Kingdom theme park. It had just opened in January, 1975. My friend and his girlfriend were in one "car" and I was with my friend's sister in another. The smaller person sat in front and the other person in the back and a little higher. I was reading the "star map" before we loaded. Height: 60 feet; Drop: 26 feet; Length: 3,196 feet; Speed: 28 mph;

Duration: 2:30 minutes; G-force: 3.7. Then through the "space tunnel," passing by "space windows" in the walls featuring planets and spaceships. Riders are deposited into the "space station" before loading. As we started down the runway, I noticed that the safety bar, that goes across you and locks into place to keep you from flying out of your seat; the lock was broken and thus not functional. I was trying to get the attendant's attention, waving frantically at him. He just thought I was waving like everyone else to the spectators, as we started the countdown: "10, 9, 8, 7, 6, 5, 4, 3, 2, 1, blastoff!" I was not believing my predicament! I held the bar down with all my might, as I envisioned myself being hurtled into this artificial world of darkness and steel. And instant death. The terror I felt seemed like an eternity. Twists and turns in near complete darkness, including the steepest drop of 39 degrees, before passing through a red swirling wormhole. I was relieved beyond description when the ride finally ended, with me in one piece. I vowed that I would never go on a roller coaster again.

We arrived safely in Saint John and started to explore this beautiful island. One of the first things we saw was the manchineel tree. There was a sign in front of it that read:

"The leaves, bark, and fruits of these trees contain a caustic sap which may be injurious if touched. Columbus described the small green fruits as 'death apples.' The trees are common along Caribbean shores. Avoid contact with any part of this tree."

I'm sure many people learned the hard way. It can cause blistering burns, inflammation in contact with skin and mucous membranes, and your throat can swell up. Doesn't sound like a very pleasant experience. They are also found in Central America, northern part of South America, Gulf of Mexico and South Florida. The fruit is also known as "poison guava" and "manzana de muerte." So, we were very careful to stay away from these trees.

    We made our way down to Trunk Bay, named for the Leatherback Turtle, locally known as "trunks." It is one of the most pristine beaches in the Caribbean and one of the most photographed, rated as one of the finest beaches in the world. Its aqua blue water, beautiful white sand beach, towering coconut palm trees and snorkeling trail make it very popular. We quickly found that out as soon as we put our towels down and got settled, a cruise ship had come in and all these people stormed the beach. A group of girls put their towels down, not just adjacent to ours, but actually overlapping our towels. Sometimes people never cease to amaze me with their cluelessness or rudeness. We relocated to the west end of the beach, where there were fewer people, and enjoyed a relaxing afternoon of sun, swimming and watching Bananaquits, also known as "sugar birds," before catching the last ferry back to Saint Croix.

                Once in a Blue Moon

Long ago

But never forgotten

Etched in my memories

The ways we touched each other

Magic moments we remember by heart

That secret glow

Only true lovers get to know

Maybe for once

In a blue moon

We can share a toast

To all the smiles and tears

To those dreams that did come true

To the destiny and fortune

Of having a friend for life

    In May, day trips to Sonnenberg Gardens and Taughannock Falls. Over Memorial Day weekend, we drove 162 miles west to Niagara Falls and Marineland. We took the "Maid of the Mist" boat tour, where you put on these yellow raincoats, and then they take you to the base of the falls. Starting and ending on the American side, crossing briefly into Ontario; feeling the dense mist of spray inside the curve of Horseshoe Falls, hearing the thunderous roar of the falls and seeing rainbows. Maid of the Mist I was launched on May 27, 1846. Then came II in 1854, III in 1885, IV in 1892. On April 22, 1955, a fire burned two of the boats at the Canadian docks. On July 28, 1955, V was launched, made entirely of steel. This is the one that we took. There was VI in 1990, and VII in 1997: 80 feet long, weighing 145 tons, and capable of carrying 600 passengers.

In July, we took the four hour, 200 miles north drive, our first of many more to come; to Lake Placid, a village in the Adirondack Mountains of New York State. Adirondack was a term given to the Algonquin tribe by their Mohawk neighbors, meaning "barkeaters." We went swimming in Mirror Lake and also took walks around the lake. To go on private Lake Placid, you have to take the pontoon boat tour, unless you are fortunate enough to own one of the stately manors or camps on the lake. This 16-mile tour takes about an hour and we took it every time we went to Lake Placid. There was always something new to see and discover.

We hiked up to the summit of Whiteface Mountain, 4,867 feet, where you have a 360-degree view of the Adirondacks. On a clear day, you can see Vermont and the skyscrapers of Montréal, 80 miles away. The 1980 Winter Olympics held their alpine skiing events here. These same Olympics famously hosted the "Miracle on Ice," where the United States ice hockey team beat the Soviet Union. There is an Olympic Museum in the village, commemorating Lake Placid hosting both the 1932 & 1980 Winter Olympics, the only North American city to do so.

We visited The John Brown Farm Historical Site, the home and final resting place of abolitionist John Brown, where he moved in 1849 to lead freed slaves in farming. His body, along with family members and other followers, was returned here after being hanged in Charlestown, Virginia, in December, 1859. The hanging took place less than two months after the assault on the U.S. Arsenal at Harpers Ferry, in an attempt to start an armed slave revolt, which was one of several events that led to the Civil War in our country.

We loved walking around the village, people watching many international visitors, eating at the many restaurants, and getting some homemade ice cream.

Later in July, day trips to Skaneateles and Seneca Lakes, two of the eleven Finger Lakes. Most people think there are only five, looking like human fingers on a map. The Native Americans said it was the hand of The Creator.

I was trying to figure out an acronym for the Finger Lakes when I taught Geography to the third and fourth grade students. I had taught them HOMES, which somebody had come up with before me; for the Great Lakes, the largest group of freshwater lakes on Earth, on the borders of the United States and Canada. HOMES stands for: Huron, Ontario, Michigan, Erie, Superior. I finally came up with one for the Finger Lakes to teach the students, so this is mine and mine alone. SHOCK stands for: Seneca & Skaneateles, Hemlock & Honeoye, Otisco & Owasco, Canadice & Canandaigua & Cayuga & Conesus, and Keuka.

Skaneateles means "long lake" in the Iroquoian language. It is the cleanest of the Finger Lakes, its pure water used by the city of Syracuse and other municipalities, unfiltered for its drinking supply. It is the second cleanest lake in the United States after Crater Lake in Oregon. We took the scenic drive to Skaneateles several times every year; in the summer, to go out on friends' boats on the lake, walk around the village and look inside all the charming stores, get a fish-fry and an ice cream. In the fall, see the trees with their brilliant colors, do the same routine as the summer, except for the boat rides.

In August, another day trip to Watkins Glen.

In September, we took the six hour, 370 miles east, drive to Cape Cod, one of our favorite all-time places, where we spent many summer vacations. Being on the Cape is definitely a unique experience that can be described, but not truly felt, unless you spend some time there. Cape Cod is a hook-shaped peninsula that juts out into the Atlantic Ocean from mainland Massachusetts. You can drive through all the quaint villages from Woods Hole all the way up to Provincetown. So many things to do and see: ponds, bays, ocean beaches, lighthouses, hiking trails, Whale Watches, seafood shacks.

We stayed with my Aunt Gloria on our first trip to the Cape, at her house in East Harwich, considered the Lower Cape. She had been living here alone for about a year, after the passing of her husband, Bob, my mother's younger brother. Uncle Bob had owned and cooked at a restaurant, the Hickory House, in North Syracuse. I washed dishes there in the summer after my junior year in high school. After selling the restaurant, they moved to Greenwich, Connecticut, where Bob worked as a chef at the Daycroft School. Then they had their dream house built here on the Cape, where they planned to spend their retirement.

Soon after they came to East Harwich, Bob unexpectedly passed away in September, 1986. My dad passed away that same year in the middle of May. A couple of years before, my cousin Peter, the youngest of their four sons, had died in a car accident. We went to that sad funeral. So, Gloria had gone through two monumental losses and was now facing life on the Cape alone.

We had had some fun and good conversations together, along with sharing home-cooked meals and going to some concerts in the park. I helped her move some furniture and washed her skylights. We drove my mom up to visit and stay with Gloria in subsequent years, as Mom had a fear of driving across bridges, and you had to drive across the Bourne or Sagamore bridges to get on the Cape.

Syl and I drove to Provincetown, at the northern tip of the Cape, for the first of our many Whale Watches. We saw fin, humpback, and right whales breaching and swimming in the open ocean. An impressive sight. Then back on land after four hours on the water. This seaside town is on the site of the Mayflower's landing in 1620. Here you can see the towering Pilgrim Monument and the Provincetown Museum. "P-town" is a longtime haven for artists and the gay community. We got an ice cream and sat on a bench, watching all the men and women, some seemingly interchangeable, in a never-ending parade, just doing their thing and glad to be "out there." Then strolling around the houses with their beautiful flower boxes and neatly maintained gardens.

We also took day trips to the Kennedy Compound in Hyannis and the Heritage Museums & Gardens, with their antique cars, in Sandwich. One day, we took the ferry from Hyannis over to Martha's Vineyard, an island just south of Cape Cod, and back. We went on the bus tour up to Gay Head Light, a historic lighthouse on the westernmost point of the island, first built in 1799.

1988

February: Mexico

Cancun (airport)

Merida

Chichen-Itza

Uxmal

Cancun

Tulum

Xel-Ha

July: Old Forge (Palmer Point)

Southwick

Skaneateles Lake

Cooperstown

September: Lake Placid

Ausable Chasm

Fort Ticonderoga

October: Letchworth (cabin)

November: Nature Conservancy Hike (Pennsylvania)

In February, 1988, we flew into Cancun and from there to Merida, the capital of the Yucatan Peninsula. We divided this vacation into two parts, the first half spent in

Merida and visiting two important Mayan Ruins, the second half in Cancun and visiting another important Mayan Ruin.

Merida is not only the capital, but it is also the largest city of the Yucatan Peninsula. The hotel where we were staying had an outside breakfast area, named "Las Sombrillas," meaning umbrellas for the sun. All the tables had huge multi-colored umbrellas. Every morning they would bring you a different freshly squeezed juice: guava, mango, orange, pineapple, watermelon. They were so refreshing I can taste them now. We took long walks around this city, seeing and feeling the influence of both the Mayan and Colonial heritage. The main center is the Plaza de la Indepencia, bordered by the Merida Cathedral and the white limestone Iglesia de la Tercera Orden, both colonial era churches built using materials from ancient Mayan temples. We also visited the Mayan World Museum of Merida, the Museo Casa Montejo, Plaza Grande, and Kabah.

Syl and I took a day trip in a white van with another couple, facing each other the way the seats were situated; for 74 miles south to Chichen-Itza, pronounced "CHEE-chen-EET-za," the name meaning, "At the mouth of the well of the Itza," one of the most famous Mayan Ruins. The main attraction is "El Castillo," The Castle. It is "The Kukulkan Temple of Chichen Itza Mayan Pyramid," Kukulkan being The Feathered Serpent God. This pyramid rises 79 feet above the Main Plaza. It has 4 sides, each with 91 stairs, facing a cardinal direction; then including the top step, combine for a total of 365 steps, the number of days in a solar year. We climbed these steps to the top, no easy feat. Then descended all the way down this dark and dank passageway that was definitely not for the faint of heart.

Other attractions were: the "Temple of the Warriors," the "Cult of the Cenote," where they performed human sacrifices to the Rain God, Chac, and gold and jade ornaments were also thrown in, and the "Wall of the Skulls," which you observed as you entered the Ball Court, "pok-ta-pok" in Mayan and "juego de pelota" in Spanish. This is the largest court known in the Americas, 554 feet long and 231 feet wide. The game was played with a twelve-pound rubber ball, using only your elbows, hips, and knees; to try and put it in stone hoops set high on the court walls. (That had to hurt.) The losers were put to death and the losing captains depicted on the "Wall of the Skulls." Certainly, would not want to be on the losing team, or even worse, captain of the losing team. Talk about intimidation!

Another day trip took us 50 miles south of Merida and 90 miles southwest of Chichen-Itza, to Uxmal, pronounced "Ush-mal," the name meaning, "Thrice Built" or "What is to Come." Uxmal is a very important Mayan Ruin site, maybe not as well known as Chichen-Itza, but equally as impressive. It also feels more peaceful than Chichen-Itza. Even the names of its buildings give you a more peaceful feeling: "Pyramid of the Magician," "Nunnery Quadrangle," "Governor's Palace," (its central doorway is aligned with Venus), "House of Turtles," "House of the Pigeons," "House of the Old Woman," "Cemetery Group," and "Great Pyramid."

We had arranged a taxi, through the hotel, for our trip to Uxmal. We were surprised when our taxi was a late sixties model Chevy Camaro, with a two-tone brown and rust colored paint job. Many crosses and religious beads hung from the rear-view mirror. Our driver was a pleasant local young man named Esubio. As he drove, he would cross himself, first to his forehead, then to his left shoulder, then to his right shoulder, and finally to his lips; where he would make a loud and pronounced smacking noise. He would repeat this same sequence every few minutes, to the point where it was becoming comical. Out of respect for his religious beliefs, we didn't say anything for the first part of the trip. But after a while, our curiosity made us ask him why he did this loud smacking noise every time. It wasn't as if he did his routine upon each new town or village that we passed through, which maybe we could understand, but he did it constantly.

He explained, "That he was blessing all the vehicles on the road to have safe travels and all the people to have long and healthy lives."

He said he wanted to strongly send his message out every time he touched his lips. Hard to argue with his explanation, but needless to say, it was a journey we will never forget. Esubio stopped in a town before we got to Uxmal and walked us over to this tree, the sapodilla tree, and grabbed a couple of leaves for us to chew. It was chicle, a gum from the latex of this tree, used as the main ingredient in chewing gum. Definitely tasted like chewing gum. The Wrigley family, owners of the Chicago Cubs Major League baseball team, (Wrigley Field), made their fortune using this process. They started in 1893 with Juicy Fruit chewing gum and Wrigley's Spearmint.

Syl and I flew back to Cancun for the second half of our vacation. It was very modern and touristy, like a Mexican Fort Lauderdale. But from here it was closer to visit Tulum, an important Mayan Ruin. We decided on taking a tour bus to Tulum and Xel-Ha. In hindsight, a taxi would have been a better choice, a little more expensive, but more intimate and more free time to spend at the beach at Tulum. With our hotel's location, we were the first people to be picked up by the bus, then picking up everyone else from their hotels; then waiting for everyone to be dropped off on the way back, to be the last ones off the bus. Oh well, live and learn. It was still worth it and we had a great day.

Tulum, meaning "Place of the Dawning Sun," is 90 miles south of Cancun, on the Caribbean coastline of the Yucatan Peninsula; the only Mayan Ruin not located in the jungle or rainforest. It was an ancient Mayan port city; whose ruins are well preserved. The main building, "El Castillo," is perched on a rocky cliff above the white sand beach and turquoise sea. There is also "The Temple of the Descending God," carefully aligned with Venus. Formerly a walled city, it was one of the last to be built by the Mayans.

From Tulum the bus took us to Xel-Ha, pronounced "Chel-Ha" or "Shell-uh," about 15 miles away on the Riviera Maya. It is a Natural Aquarium and Tropical Lagoon, where its name means "where the water is born." They gave us fins, masks, and snorkels, and also a box lunch. We were hoping that there would be no weird incidents like we encountered on Shorty's Glass Bottom Boat. We saw an amazing array of colorful fish in our underwater adventure, to complete a wonderful day.

We spent a week over the Fourth of July, in a rustic cabin, on Fourth Lake at Palmer Point, 100 miles north of Syracuse, between Old Forge and Inlet, New York, in the Adirondacks. Also, in July, day trips to Southwick Beach, Skaneateles, Cooperstown, and Beaver Lake.

In September, back to Lake Placid to hike Whiteface Mountain and to Ausable Chasm, a sandstone gorge, called the "Grand Canyon of the Adirondacks." We took the majestic hike through the upper chasm, walking on natural stone walkways, where you see: "Rainbow Falls," "Elephant's Head," "Column Rock," "Hyde's Cave" and "Mystic Gorge." Then through the lower chasm on a guided raft ride through the Ausable River. Then a day trip to Fort Ticonderoga. In October, back to the cabin at Letchworth over Columbus Day weekend. In November, we went on a group hike with a Nature Conservancy group, in the woods of northern Pennsylvania.

1989

February: Mexico

    Merida

    Progreso

    Dzbilchaltún

    Uxmal

June: Cooperstown

July: Old Forge (Palmer Point)

    Southwick

    Thousand Islands (Clayton)

August: Catskills

    Olana Castle

    Mahayana Temple

    Prattsville

    Woodstock (Opus 40)

    Bethel (Festival Site)

September: Skaneateles Lake

Moravia (Fillmore Glen)

October: Letchworth (cabin)

    Naples, NY (Wine Festival)

    Cummings Nature Center

December: Lake Placid

    In February, we flew to Miami and from there to a return trip to Mexico. This time we stayed in Merida the entire vacation. Took a day trip by bus to Progreso, a port city on the Gulf of Mexico, about 30 miles north of Merida. Large cruise ships come in here and it is a center for both the fishing and container industries. You could see by the way the palm trees on the beach were bent, indicating the direction of the hurricanes when they hit land. We spent the day at Malecon Beach, near the over four-mile-long pier, the longest pier in the world; it was beautiful with its pristine white sand, followed by a nice seafood dinner. Somehow, we missed our return bus home and had to wait several hours for another bus with a collection of beggars, hawkers, stray dogs and seemingly unsavory characters. We were so glad when we finally got back to the hotel after midnight.

    The following night we walked down the beautiful Paseo de Montejo, and stopped in a traditional Yucatan restaurant called "Las Yardas," for a pizza and beers. They serve the beers, cervezas, in these tall fishbowl-shaped glasses that taper down to a very narrow stem. It is nearly impossible to sip from these glasses. You pretty much are chugging the cervezas. We each had one of these, (that's all you needed), and shared a pizza with green peppers and black olives. I don't know if I ate a bad olive or pepper, or the combination of that and drinking the cerveza in that manner, but I started to feel really sick on the way back to our hotel. Syl was fine. I bought a couple of Coca-Colas from a street vendor outside the hotel, and I'm so glad I did, especially considering that I rarely drink soda, if anything a Ginger Ale. I got violently sick in the middle of the night, hugging the toilet bowl. And I never throw up. I can honestly say that I can count the times that I have in my life using less than all my fingers. Amazingly, Syl never heard me and she hears everything. *And I mean everything.* When I thought I was finished, I had to do more, where it became the "dry heaves." Lovely topic, isn't it? The only good thing about it is, after you get it all out, you begin to feel better. Drinking the two cokes really saved me, as the carbonation helped to settle my stomach.

"The Long Walk Leaving The Mayan Ruins"

This is another one of "Dusty's Lunchtime Stories." I began by telling the kids that I may have gotten food poisoning from a bad olive or green pepper on a pizza the night before, without going into all the details. I was still feeling lousy the next morning. Obviously, I didn't get a restful sleep and I looked pale and my legs felt weak, a flu-like feeling. My stomach felt empty, yet I didn't feel like eating anything. Drank some bottled water, but not as much as we do today, so I'm sure that I was dehydrated as well. We had planned to visit a small Mayan Ruin, 10 miles north of Merida, and decided to go anyway.

Dzibilchaltún, pronounced "Zeeb-ill-chal-tune," is the "place where there is writing on flat stones." Many memorial stones are found at the site. We inquired at the hotel about tours to Dzibilchaltún and they were charging forty dollars per person. It seemed high to me for this short trip when we could take the bus for twenty pesos each. In hindsight, we probably should have taken the tour, but then we wouldn't have had the experience that we did and be able to include this as one of the "Lunchtime Stories."

So, we got on a bus with all the locals, who were carrying chickens and all kinds of produce and other things, and headed up the Merida/Progreso Highway. Nobody had told us that where the bus dropped you off, there was still at least a three-mile walk, maybe longer, from the main highway to the actual site. We weren't aware of this, as we started walking in the general direction of the ruins. A woman archaeologist, with her van full of children that she had adopted from her travels to many ancient ruin sites in Central and South America and Mexico, stopped to offer us a ride; assuming correctly that we had no idea how far it was from the main highway to the ruins of Dzibilchaltún. We got in the van and gladly accepted the ride, especially considering the way I was feeling.

Syl and I started exploring the ruins and came upon a cenote, derived from a Mayan word for well. This one was not like the human sacrifice ones found at Chichen-Itza. Cenote Xlacah, meaning "old town" in Maya, according to a plaque near the water's edge, is 144 feet deep. I dove in and hundreds of curious silver fish surrounded me. They moved in perfect synchronicity to my every move. I spread my arms out, they spread in both directions. I brought my arms back in, they came back in. I dove down, they dove down. I came back up; they came back up. They didn't bite or get in my face. It was a really cool experience. Syl dove in after me and they moved as she moved. The water was refreshing, as it was a hot and humid day, but I still felt weak and "under the weather."

After spending hours exploring Dzibilchaltún, taking pictures, and watching several little Mayan kids pitching pennies against the walls of the ruins; we noticed the lowering sun was casting shadows on the main building, "The Temple of the Seven Dolls," the only known Mayan temple with windows. Twice a year, on the spring and fall equinoxes, the rising sun shines into the East Window and out the West Window and illuminates the doorway. This illumination during the spring equinox signified the time to plant crop seeds, and the illumination during the fall equinox signified the time to begin harvesting.

It was now time for us to leave and try and find a ride back to the main highway and get a bus back to Merida. We soon realized that everyone had left, even the gift shop was closed. I was feeling worse and there was an impending storm nearby. Just then, a taxi pulled up with two couples in their twenties, that looked like they had just come from a wedding or some formal event. They got out of the taxi and were huddled up, as if they were doing drugs or a drug deal of some sort was going down. (Once again, I never mention any inappropriate aspects when telling these stories to the kids. I feel that it is important to point this out, as the kids looked up to me as a role model and I always tried to act like one.) The taxi driver got out and I went over and asked him if we could get a ride, at least back to the main road, if I gave him $20. I heard later that taxis take you to the highway for 10 pesos each, but since the site closes at 5 o'clock, there were none around anymore. He could have squeezed us in the front seat and made a quick $20 for a ride to the main highway. So, here is what he says to us:

"You know how you get to the highway?"

And he proceeded to lift one leg up, then the other.

"You go a onesie, then a twosie, that is how you do it."

He said this while laughing at our plight. They all got back in the taxi and he waved at us with a devious smile as they drove off. I'll never forget this. I was thinking of his rudeness in comparison to Esubio's religious compassion and showing us where to find the chicle leaves.

We had no choice now, but to start walking back to the main road before this storm came, or darkness set in, or both. Syl and I began this unforgettable journey. The heat was unbearable and I was feeling weaker than ever and we hadn't eaten all day or drank hardly any water. It was humid and sticky, our clothes clung to our bodies, and mosquitoes constantly buzzed us. We had read that there were puma that lived around here. The sky was getting darker by the minute and there were loud claps of thunder and lightning flashes in the distance, but becoming closer and closer. Out of nowhere, workers came out of the fields carrying machetes, heading home after their day's work, startling us to say the least. We passed through a small village with decaying ancient churches, barefoot kids running around, packs of wild dogs barking and attentively looking in our direction. The most disconcerting thing of all were trucks full of men standing in the back and riding around yelling and pointing at us. We weren't sure if they were field workers or just ill-intentioned men, probably drunk and looking for trouble. Let's rephrase that, looking to bring trouble your way. It was not a comfortable situation. We were imagining the worst possible scenario and didn't want to see it happen to us. So, we kept looking straight ahead and just kept moving.

  Finally, we made it almost to the highway, when these two guys pulled up in their jeep, offering us a ride. They looked like Crocodile Dundee characters with their safari outfits and hats. I have no idea where they were when the ruins closed. They said they were archaeologists, so maybe they were out on the site somewhere. They looked a little shady and Syl was wary about accepting a ride from them. But it was almost dark now, the storm was coming, and we had no idea when or if a bus would be coming by. We got in the jeep and headed down the highway toward Merida. We didn't feel that comfortable with these guys, but we had to admit we were glad to be out of the predicament that we had just gone through. They drove us down the highway into Merida and asked us what hotel we were staying at. Maybe we were being paranoid, but it just didn't feel right to let them know. We had them drop us off at San Francisco, a big store that carried everything from clothes to food to alcohol. And me, being "Mr. Practical," had us stock up on bottled water and food supplies, as long as we were here, the store being a few miles from the hotel. So even after this long, and at the end, stressful day, and me still feeling sick and weak; we walked from the store to the hotel, me with four jugs of bottled water, two under my arms and carrying two, and Syl carrying two bags of food supplies. Finally, we arrived back at the hotel, totally exhausted.

It took me a couple of days of rest and food to regain my strength. We took a tour van on a return trip to Uxmal. I can remember climbing up one of the ruins with Syl and then wanting to take some pictures from the very top. Syl didn't want to go to the top. I went ahead and all of a sudden, all these policemen were frantically blowing their whistles for me to come down. I didn't realize they were doing some renovations at the top, (there weren't any workers up there), and I began taking some pictures from the top before I realized the whistles were for me. I came down and apologized and that was the end of it. This time we stayed for the light show at night, which was impressive.

In June, a day trip, 93 miles, to Cooperstown. July, a return trip to Old Forge over the Fourth, in a different cabin, at Palmer Point. Also, in July, Southwick Beach on Lake Ontario and Clayton, in the Thousand Islands, for the Antique Boat Show.

In August, we drove 180 miles southeast down to the Catskill Mountains and discovered two seemingly "out of place" things. One was the Mahayana Temple, a Chinese Buddhist temple located in a forest in South Cairo, New York. The other was Olana Castle, a Persian-inspired mansion on 250 acres in the Hudson River Valley. It was the home of artist Frederic Edwin Church, (1826-1900), and his family. The mansion is filled with original sketches and paintings by Church. It has an art collection of objects from around the world.

We were staying in these Honeymoon Lodge cabins for a couple of nights on our way to Bethel for the 20th anniversary of the Woodstock Music Festival, which I'm happy to say that I was a part of. (I'll get back to this later.) We saw in a brochure that in Prattsville there was Pratt Rock Park, that "Ripley's Believe it or Not" called "New York's Mount Rushmore," by the side of Route 23 on the outskirts of Prattsville. The town was renamed after Zadock Pratt, a congressman who built a tannery larger than any other in the world at the time. His life is depicted through stone carvings at Pratt Rock. The carvings are of: Zadock, his son, a horse, and an arm holding a sledgehammer. We visited the small museum there and went to take a hike and see the stone carvings. We must have gone right by the carvings or were expecting something more spectacular. Either way, we wound up in this open field. It was hot and humid, mosquitoes and black flies were buzzing us, and our feet were getting cut up by the mowed corn stalks through our sandals. We were not happy campers after an hour or so of this, and decided to head back, although still determined to see these carvings; especially after having endured all that we had. On the way out, we noticed the carvings and were thinking, "Is this what they were talking about?" It was my birthday also, just to top it off. We went to a restaurant, splashed some cold water on us in the bathroom, and enjoyed a nice birthday dinner.

We headed to Woodstock the next day for lunch and a walk around town, checking out the many craft, music, and pottery shops and restaurants. We read about this place called Opus 40 and decided to go and experience this. Opus 40 is the amazing project of 37 years by Harvey Fite, who was known for his work in restoring the Mayan civilization at Copan. It is a unique place of bluestone ramps, terraces, and sculptures; built around fountains, pools and trees; out of bedrock half a mile deep. In 1938, Harvey, one of the founders of the Bard College Fine Arts Department, purchased an abandoned quarry in the town of Saugerties. He purchased an additional 76 acres over time, where he built his home, studio, garage, blacksmith shop, and the Quarryman's Museum. He died three years before the original 40-year plan was completed. Opus 40 holds many art exhibits, concerts and lectures. We weren't lucky enough to attend a concert there, but I imagine that it would be incredible.

After this, we drove 70 miles to Bethel Woods, White Lake, the site of the infamous "Woodstock Music & Art Fair," held on Max Yasgur's Farm, August 15th-18th, 1969. Some people have said that if all the people who claimed to be at Woodstock actually were there, then 10 million would have attended. There might be some semblance of truth to that, but all I know is that *I was there*. Actually, even ran into two of my closest friends from Syracuse, Brian and Steve, there. Sylvia was just 16 and 2 months then, and was not allowed to go, unless she came up with a good story and snuck away for at least the weekend. I could see her trying to do it, but she didn't, and always wished that she would have. I was within a few days of turning 23. I almost didn't go to Woodstock. Looking back on it, it was really a fluke that I did.

Before I explain that, I must preface this by talking about what had transpired less than two weeks before. I hitchhiked with two friends from Syracuse down to Atlantic City, New Jersey to attend a music festival, the Atlantic City Pop Festival, August 1st-3rd. It has later, over the years, been called "The Great Lost Rock Festival," attended by over 100,000 people at the Atlantic City Race Track, with the stage created by Buckminster Fuller.

Friday night the performers were: Iron Butterfly, Procol Harum, Crosby, Stills & Nash, Booker T & the MG's, Joni Mitchell, (who I was not familiar with at this time.) In the following years, she became one of my favorites. She was Syl's favorite artist, bar none. *Syl lived and breathed her music.* There was a severe thunderstorm that was approaching as Joni was playing and she walked off the stage. I was thinking, "Wow, who was that?" And then she was gone. The storm passed through and then came: Chicago Transit Authority, Santana, (incorrectly announced as the Santa Ana Blues Band), and Johnny Winter.

The weekend brought steamy conditions, hot and humid, and I can remember workers spraying the crowd with water from huge hoses to cool off.

Saturday: Jefferson Airplane, Creedence Clearwater Revival, Lighthouse, ("Crazy World of") Arthur Brown, B.B. King, Paul Butterfield Blues Band, Tim Buckley, The Byrds, Hugh Masakela, and American Dream.

Sunday: Janis Joplin, Canned Heat, Mothers of Invention, Sir Douglas Quintet, Three Dog Night, Dr. John, ("The Night Tripper"), Joe Cocker, Buddy Rich Big Band, Little Richard, and the Moody Blues. Amazing music. We hitchhiked back to Syracuse feeling like we had just experienced something special. Because of this, I was not overly enthusiastic about the upcoming Woodstock festival.

There was a guy that lived down the street from my parents' house that went to the same private school that I did, two years younger than me. He kept trying to convince me to go to Woodstock with him and his friends. I was resistant to this idea, mainly because of the recent Atlantic City Festival, and I really didn't travel in the same circle of friends as him or his friends. Luckily for me, I finally relented and decided to go. It was a life-changing experience and one of the best decisions I've ever made. I have to give him credit for his persistence. He was now a car salesman and all his friends sold cars or insurance. We met at one of his friend's houses on Friday afternoon, August 15th. These guys were "weekend warriors," working their salesmen jobs during the week, and on the weekends, they transformed into motorcycle guys; changing from their suit coats and ties into motorcycle-looking outfits, some even using their ties as bandanas around their heads. I've been on a motorcycle twice in my life, this being my second and last time. I understand the feeling of freedom on the open road, but the risk of a life-threatening injury in a potential catastrophic accident, far outweighs the thrill. From my perspective, I would much rather take my chances galloping on a horse in the desert.

But riding down to the Woodstock Festival, 193 miles south from Syracuse on a motorcycle, was a great decision, despite getting bugs smashed into our face shields, and getting soaked battling the rain; as we could weave our way through all the thousands and thousands of cars and other vehicles, that were backed up for miles and miles trying to get in. Once we were into the site, there were no real plans, as they went their way and I went mine. (Sounds like a Dylan song.) Somehow, I don't really know how, we met sometime after Jimi Hendrix was finished playing, at the end, near the stage, and rode back home.

What I remember doing during my four days there, was mainly listening to all the incredible music acts; at all hours of the morning, afternoon, evening, and late at night.

Just resting or catching a little sleep here and there. Walking down the road to the small General Store and greeting throngs of people with a smile or waving the peace sign. I remember surviving the storms in tents that people invited me into and meeting new people from all over the country. I remember sliding in the aftermath of mud and then skinny-dipping in the pond with a human chain, everyone in unison singing,

> "Row, row, row your boat
>
> Gently down the stream
>
> Merrily, merrily, merrily, merrily
>
> Life is but a dream."

That to me is what it was all about.

I'm having these flashbacks from 20 years ago, as Syl and I drive up to the festival site and park the car. I'm recounting these experiences to her, as we are taking pictures by the plaque, commemorating where the original stage was; and also, the pond and the open field where everyone gathered to hear the music. And what music it was.

Friday night: Richie Havens, (starting the concert off around 5 in the afternoon), Sweetwater, Bert Sommer, Tim Hardin, Ravi Shankar, (played through the rain), Melanie, Arlo Guthrie, (started around midnight), and Joan Baez (1 a.m.)

Saturday: Quill, (started shortly after noon), Country Joe McDonald, Santana, John Sebastian, (was just attending, not scheduled to play, as they needed someone to fill that time slot), Keef Hartley Band, The Incredible String Band.

Saturday night: Canned Heat, Mountain, Grateful Dead, Creedence Clearwater Revival, (started at 12:30 Sunday morning), Janis Joplin & The Kozmic Blues Band (2 a.m.), Sly and the Family Stone (3:30 a.m.), The Who (5 a.m.), Jefferson Airplane (8 a.m.)

Sunday afternoon: Joe Cocker and The Grease Band, (thunderstorms rolled through and there was an over three-hour delay), Country Joe and the Fish.

Sunday night: Ten Years After, The Band, Johnny Winter (midnight), Blood, Sweat & Tears (1:30 a.m.), Crosby, Stills, Nash & Young (3:30 a.m.), Paul Butterfield Blues Band (6:00 a.m.), Sha Na Na (7:30 a.m.)

Jimi Hendrix/Gypsy Sun & Rainbows, (name of the group at the time), closed Woodstock, playing from 9 until 11 in the morning, even though half of the crowd had gone home. His stirring version of the National Anthem will never be forgotten.

Just as we were taking in these nostalgic moments, a bunch of rednecks started yelling at me. I don't know what else to call them, maybe an even more appropriate term. They were shaggy, tattooed, drunk, and high on who knows what.

"Hey, you, leave your wife."

I wasn't sure they were talking to me, but we were the only ones in the vicinity. Syl wanted us to keep on moving to avoid any confrontation. Sometimes I can be foolish and challenge the situation out of personal pride and self-righteousness. But in this case, discretion was definitely the better part of valor. We kept moving, but they yelled the same thing several more times. Finally, I had enough and shouted back to them,

"This is not what the true spirit of Woodstock was all about."

"Hey, F~~~ you. Leave your wife."

We had the same uncomfortable and fearful feelings as we did with all the guys in the trucks yelling at us on the road out of Dzibilchaltún. We kept on going and avoided what could have been a dangerous incident.

Later we came upon a young guy, probably stoned, roasting an ear of corn over a small fire that he had made, just appreciating his surroundings. He smiled and asked if we wanted to roast some corn. We politely said no, but thanked him for offering. Our spirits felt restored as we walked back to the car. They have a museum there now, that was built in 2008, but unfortunately wasn't there then. We talked about going down there in the summer of 2009, for the 40th anniversary, but we never made it. We planned on going down for the 50th anniversary in August, 2019, but it wasn't meant to be.

One of these days I will take a ride back down there and check out the museum and imagine Syl being there with me.

Whisper of the Wind

Ivory-tipped clouds drift so far away

I closed my eyes tight for awhile

Wishing nobody ever had to be lonely

    cold or hungry

    hated for their beliefs

    or trapped by self-deception

Ageless secrets

Hidden forever

Suspended beyond a silent horizon

Who can see past the edge

What lies there

Hard to reach standing still

    whispers the wind

    with her infinite wisdom

    into once deaf ears

I awoke

Faced the unexplored expanse

Ready to follow tomorrow's light

    Back to the cabin at Letchworth State Park over Columbus Day weekend. This was our fourth consecutive year staying in the cabin and would turn out to be our last.

    In December, after Christmas, we spent several days in Lake Placid, experiencing its beauty, with all the lights and majestic mountains glistening with snow. Walking around the town, looking in the beautifully decorated shops, and eating in the restaurants with the fireplace crackling with a glowing fire. Then we could go back to the hotel, after driving and walking, braving the elements, to relax in the hot tub.

1990

April: Erieville, NY (moved to our new house)

July: Cooperstown

Skaneateles (Ursula visit)

August: Lake Placid (& High Falls Gorge)

On January 10th, 1990, a friend of ours came over to visit us in our house in North Syracuse. She was working for a real estate company, called Help-U-Sell Real Estate, which had a novel idea that they would only earn half the commission, but the tradeoff was that they would only do half the normal work involved in selling a house. In other words, they would get you started, printing up flyers and placing ads. But the physical part of meeting prospective buyers and showing the house and whatever else was your responsibility. Of course, they would be at the closing to get their commission. After a few glasses of wine, it sounded like a good idea. The next day I put a "For Sale" sign in the front yard in the snow. We sold the house in a couple of months and found a house way out in the country, 30 miles from Syracuse. Erieville is a hamlet south of the town of Nelson, south of Tuscarora Lake. We never would have thought about moving this far away; but our real estate friend had this in her private listings, we wouldn't have known about it otherwise. I guess after living in a congested neighborhood, close to a main road with a gas station, laundromat, and other businesses on the corner of our side street and the main road; we were definitely ready, after 6 years and 2 months, to get as far away from this kind of living as possible.

The house was actually a double-wide trailer that had been converted into a house, with a foundation built underneath it and a wood frame around it and a shingled roof. There was a wood stove in the living room that we kept going to stay warm in the winter. There was a shed out back for storing wood and another barn-like structure that was not completely finished inside. It had a large open room upstairs that served as a storage space for us, as we had no attic or basement. Another room that I had designs of remodeling for an office, never materialized, as it had no heat, so it was too cold in the winter and too hot in the summer. The long uphill driveway of stones made it impossible for our Chevy Cavalier to make it to the top in the winter; so, it was parked down below at the entrance to the driveway from the main road, also made of stones.

We were ill-equipped for the weather and living conditions out there. We were like "Mr. and Mrs. Paul Bunyan" maintaining our five acres. I had a small Toro lawn mower that took me three days to mow the entire lawn, and the front lawn was completely and steeply uphill. Then a week later, you had to do it all over again. I mowed extra paths to the woodshed, barn and garden, which we dug out and Syl diligently maintained. I split 12 cords of wood each year, with an ax, as I was afraid of using a chainsaw. (I still am.) The nearest store was Kay's General

Store for basic supplies about 3 miles away. But to get to a supermarket, it was 11 miles away, so 22 miles round trip.

The first year we would park the car at the bottom of the driveway during the long winter and put our groceries in one of those round plastic "flying saucers" type sleds and walk up the hill to the house. It was a romantic moonlit evening as I said to Syl,

"Isn't this beautiful, honey?" She agreed. Syl loved it out here and it definitely was a welcome change from our previous house.

Syl got a job in Hamilton, 12 miles away, as an Emergency Room receptionist at Community General Hospital, across from Colgate University. She worked the late shift from 3 o'clock in the afternoon until midnight. There were students, local workers, and farmers that came in. More often than not, someone would come in right before her shift ended and she rarely got out of there on time. An example was a farmer, that somehow had a pitchfork impaled in his thigh, that came in just before midnight. Why he was working with a pitchfork at that hour is beyond my comprehension. Then Syl would have to drive the 12 miles of pitch-black back country roads with no street lights and hundreds of luminous deer eyes staring at her from the side of the road. Sometimes, if I needed the car, I would take her in and pick her up. These were the days without cell phones, so a lot of waiting around ensued.

I was working my landscaping jobs and some painting jobs in the winter. This also included a massive amount of snow shoveling. I had to get the snow away from the front door to get access to the deck and shovel that off to reach the long driveway, which took hours to do. Then it would snow again. Erieville gets at least twice as much snow as Syracuse, where it is measured at Hancock Airport. That is saying something, as Syracuse is the snowiest city in the United States with populations of 100,000 or more, averaging 125 inches per year, most years closer to 150 inches, and the record at over 190 inches. When I wasn't painting or snow shoveling or doing house chores, like bringing in wood and keeping the wood stove going, I began writing my screenplay.

My screenplay is called, "White Woman of the Genesee," the Mary Jemison story. I became intrigued by her story that first time we went to Letchworth State Park in the summer, before we started staying in the cabin over Columbus Day weekends for four consecutive years. There was a statue of a young woman carrying her papoose on her back near the Glen Iris Inn. I found out that the wealthy industrialist, a partner in a company involved in the malleable iron business, William Letchworth; had learned about Mary's life story and had her remains brought from the reservation near Buffalo, where she had lived her final 10 years, to his estate in western New York. This location was former Seneca Indian territory, who were forced out after the Revolutionary War, as they had been allies of the British. He named it "Glen Iris," after the Greek Goddess of Rainbows. Letchworth was raised a Quaker and noted for his charitable work and was elected as President of the New York State Board of Charities. Also, a well-known philanthropist, he turned over his Glen Iris Estate, over 1,000 acres, to New York State in 1906, four years before his death. It is now called Letchworth State Park.

I went into the gift shop at the Glen Iris Inn and saw this book, "The Life of Mary Jemison," by James Seaver. Seaver was a retired schoolteacher, who on November

29th, 1823, met with Mary Jemison, who was then 80 years old; and wrote down her life story, as she recounted it to him over three days. I started doing more research and had the idea that her story would make a great movie. I learned how to write a screenplay by reading numerous books on the subject: how to set scenes, do dialogue, using the required, for directors and actors alike, placement and spacing. This was not a new subject, as there have been numerous children's books and other narratives written from Seaver's book and translated in different languages around the world. My screenplay is not an original idea, it is based on Seaver's book, thus an adapted screenplay. Nonetheless, written in a different and original format, with my own dialogue. I remember seeing an article from Arch Merrill, a noted author, journalist, and poet, who was known for his historical writings and folklore of Upstate New York, writing about Mary Jemison; "I wonder how Hollywood has always overlooked her story." Seeing that made me more determined and enthusiastic to transform Seaver's book into a screenplay.

 I borrowed a big IBM computer from my friend, Al, who owned his own small insurance company, to type up my screenplay. Hardly anyone had a personal computer in those days. I certainly didn't, as I have always been technologically challenged, although I have adapted and improved over the years. In hindsight, he said he should have loaned me his son's word processor. Better yet, I should have gone out and bought my own. But money was very tight then, and as I wrote everything out by hand, I didn't feel the urgency to buy any devices. That's how I started. I took notes, did more research, and wrote the first draft of my screenplay, 120 pages, by hand. My plan was to take it into a typing service to have it typed professionally. While reading and rereading my draft, I started editing, crossing out this and adding that, making so many revisions that I wound up writing a second draft, again by hand.

I'm writing this present-day story on a Samsung Galaxy tablet, new to me, as I just got it this past winter; as well as a new Samsung smartphone, as my previous smartphone of five years just froze up and faded away. Anyway, I decided to save the money, by not taking it to a typing service and typing it myself, borrowing Al's computer. He assumed it would take a week, maybe two, to type my screenplay. Boy, was he wrong! I can't explain it, and neither could he, about how this computer was set up. It was basically set up to type about one and a half page business letters, and then it would lock up and not let you type anymore; until you kept tapping on the lock key button for around 30 seconds, when it would unlock and let you type another page and a half, before it would lock up again. I was surprised that he didn't know how to rectify this situation, but he didn't. We even called up the home office of IBM in Redmond, Washington and they couldn't offer us a solution. There was also this issue that the margin arrows wouldn't let you know where you were on the page until you were at the bottom of the page. This was not good, as you have to be seven spaces up from the bottom of the page when typing your screenplay, using the proper format.

So, I would start typing and get to the bottom of the page with no warning. Delete those seven lines and go back up seven spaces. Retype those seven lines on the next page. Then halfway down that second page, the computer would lock up. Tap the lock key for 30 seconds until it is released and start typing again. Come to the bottom of the page and type the last seven lines all over again. I got a rhythm going and completed 40 pages, believe it or not. Syl came home late one night and was tired and went to bed. I was on a roll and kept typing until three o'clock in the morning. I didn't want to disturb her to ask questions. I was thrilled with my progress and accomplishment and decided to get some sleep. I unplugged the computer and went to bed. The next day I was telling Syl about all the obstacles that I faced in typing the screenplay and I had finished 40 pages. She said that I hoped you saved it. Nobody had told me to do that, that's how naive I was. Disappointment would definitely be an understated word on how I was feeling. So back to the drawing board, following the same arduous procedures until I restored those 40 pages and saved it this time.

I had another incident one night, when I was making a revision and put the cursor at the period of a sentence, instead of before the first word. Pages started flying back through each other as I panicked and just unplugged the computer. I was ready to tear my hair out. Syl was working, so I couldn't ask her advice if I was making the revision the right way. Another 20 pages had to be restored, again following the same procedures. It took me almost three months to type up the screenplay after these incidents, revisions, editing typos and retyping. Needless to say, Al had to borrow another computer for his business before this one was returned to him.

This was a project that took over two years to complete. It has been "sitting on the shelf" for almost 28 years now, since the end of June, 1992. I sent the screenplay out to a friend of mine's nephew, who was the son of a Hollywood movie executive at Miramax. He thought it had merit, but said, "that he felt that it was uncomfortably similar" to the "Last of the Mohicans." It is from the same time period, but this is a unique story of one woman's life. How many different movies have been from the Civil War period? Or the Old West? Or from World Wars? Ironically, years later, a friend told me about a New York Times article from that era he read that said that

Seaver's "The Life of Mary Jemison" was more popular than James Fenimore Cooper's "The Last of the Mohicans" at that time. I think that the Hollywood guy was more interested in seeing an action movie screenplay.

I also selected nine potential agents and sent out a cover letter and synopsis to them. Never got back one response, not even a rejection. I know that you have to be persistent; so many famous movies, like "Rocky," were rejected multiple times. Even when they accepted it, they didn't want Sylvester Stallone to play Rocky. He held out and it won the Best Picture Oscar in 1976. Can you imagine Stallone not being Rocky?

I can see "White Woman of the Genesee" being on the big screen. I always wanted Julie Christie to play middle-aged and then old and really old Mary. It would have to be the latter now. It needs the right director, actors, cinematographers, crew, to make it all happen, like any movie does. Probably a professional screenwriter to fine tune it. I have no problem with that. If not the big screen, it would make a great two-part mini-series on the Hallmark Channel or HBO or TNT. The blueprint is there. So, to anyone who happens to read this book and has any ideas on how to bring Mary's story to life, I'd love to hear them. I just looked up Mary Jemison on my smartphone and noticed that there have been several documentaries posted on YouTube since 2007. All I know is that I had this screenplay idea since 1990 and copyrighted it in 1992. Maybe my time has passed, but I would still like to see her story in a full-length movie or mini-series.

We enjoyed swimming at Eatonbrook, a manmade reservoir two miles away, and walking up our road to Stoney Pond State Forest. In July, our first summer here in 1990, we took a day trip to Cooperstown. In August, we returned to Lake Placid for four days. One day we drove 8 miles east to Wilmington to hike the High Falls Gorge, with four waterfalls, pristine forests and incredible rock formations.

1991

January: Lake Placid

July: Alexandria Bay (Thousand Islands)

    Wellesley Island

    Kingston, Ontario, Canada

    Wolfe Island

October: Unadilla, NY (Spectacular Bid)

We made it through another tough winter out in the backwoods, shoveling snow and keeping the wood stove going. I was doing some painting jobs and writing my screenplay. Syl was working the late shift at the hospital. We drove up to Lake Placid in January for a few days.

In July, we went up to Alexandria Bay in the Thousand Islands region. A doctor who worked at the hospital in Hamilton, also worked occasionally at a hospital in Alexandria Bay, and had a house there, offered it for a few days stay to some of his staff. Syl took him up on it and we went up there. It was a cute house right in town with exercise equipment and all the furnishings.

We went to Wellesley Island State Park, on the Saint Lawrence River. Another day we drove up to Kingston, Ontario, Canada, and then took the ferry over to Wolfe Island, the largest of the Thousand Islands. The island was once part of the Mohawk hunting lands.

Its original name, Ganounkouesnot, meant "Long Island Standing Up." It was later called Grand Island by the French, and in 1792 renamed Wolfe Island after British General James Wolfe. We had a beautiful day at the beach there.

One evening we were getting ready to go out to dinner and Syl had taken her shower. I started to take mine when I heard Syl frantically yelling from downstairs that water was pouring through the dining room ceiling. What we learned later was that there were actually new copper pipes for the shower plumbing, but whoever did the work had it connected to an old pipe to the shower. I never understood why some workers aren't thorough enough on their jobs. If that final connecting pipe was a new copper one, this catastrophe never would have happened. When the old pipe burst, unbeknownst to us, the water was scalding hot and I screamed in pain. I got out and went downstairs and water was pouring over a mahogany door, streaking it and the dining room chandelier was filled with water. I tried to empty the water out of it, but even though the wall switch was off, the current that was still running through it sent an electric shock that knocked me across the room. I guess I was lucky that there weren't any permanent damages to me. We enlisted the help of a young guy across the street and over the next few days he got the copper piping and fixed the problem. But there was a lot of water damage to mop up. This nice opportunity to stay at this house turned into a major headache.

In October, I saw this news report that Spectacular Bid, a famous thoroughbred racehorse from 1978 through 1980, had been sold from the Claiborne Farm in Kentucky to the Milfer Farm in Unadilla, New York, in 1991. This really caught my attention and Syl and I drove up on a beautiful autumn colorful foliage day to Unadilla, southwest of Oneonta, 50 miles from Erieville, to see him. The farm was filled with fields and horses and paddocks. The owners greeted us and took us to where Spectacular Bid was, treating us like we were potential horse buyers, as they showed us around their farm. We were casually dressed and drove up in our Chevy Cavalier. We didn't pretend to be anything that we were not, but we were extended the royal treatment. Speaking of royalty, there stood Spectacular Bid, looking spectacular. He was a gray, the Champion Two-Year-Old in 1978, the Champion Three-Year-Old in 1979, the Champion Older Male Horse and the Horse of the Year in 1980. He won the Kentucky Derby and the Preakness Stakes, the first two legs of The Triple Crown, in 1979. The story goes that he stepped on a stray safety pin the morning of the Belmont Stakes, probably costing him the Belmont, as well as The Triple Crown. He had won 12 consecutive races before the Belmont. In 1980, he was undefeated in 9 races and became the Horse of the Year. He entered the Racing Hall of Fame in 1992 and was voted 10th on the Top 100 U.S. Racehorses of the 20th Century.

At the end of the 1980 season, he retired to stud at Claiborne Farm. Secretariat was also retired there. They became friendly and would sometimes race each other. Eventually he was sold and moved to Unadilla 11 years later. This is when we saw him. He loved Sylvia. I have a couple of pictures in our photo albums of Syl & Bid. She nuzzled next to him and stroked his head and mane and fed him a carrot. He was truly enjoying it. So was Syl. Now, I love horses and was riding when I was seven years old. (I will tell you the story of my childhood horse and another horse story, when I was in my mid-20's, later on in this book.) I went to pet him and he became very skittish. It almost seemed like a gender thing, as he only had eyes for Syl. He had good taste. It was such a thrill to see him up close and personal. He passed away in June, 2003.

1992

July: Cooperstown

August: Chittenango Falls

October: Manlius ("The Bluffs," Mom's townhouse)

November: Canastota (moved into Pheasant Run Townhouse)

Another winter of relentless snow and work and the appeal of backwoods living was losing its appeal. This was the spring that I was typing up my screenplay through all the obstacles I recounted earlier. Syl was working at the hospital, and my landscaping job was a long round trip ride five days a week, and then driving back country roads to pick up Syl at the hospital. She had worked out a ride to the hospital from a co-worker. I mentioned to Syl that I wanted to sell the house because of the distance, the winters, and all the constant work. We did have some family, from in and out of town, come to visit. Some friends also came out, but they became few and far between. We did enjoy the beautiful country, our gardens, the swimming at Eatonbrook, and the hikes up to Stoney Pond. Syl was resistant to selling the house at this point.

"Let's just test the waters. If we don't get any interest, then we know we are meant to live out here longer."

She reluctantly agreed to that and in the beginning of June, I put a "For Sale by Owner" sign, with some rocks around it, in the ditch near the road, close to the entrance of our driveway. A week or two later, a guy called, interested in buying the house. He was about the same age as me and we had some common friends. He worked in Oneida and had to drive all the way from where he lived, in the Westcott Street area, a bohemian section where I had lived in different houses in the 1970's; and near where Syl was living when I first met her. Ironically, we moved back to this area less than two years later. We agreed on a price, shook hands, had a beer, and that was it. He wanted to move in on September 1st, but we said we needed an extra month. He had sold his house and had to be out at the end of August; but he was house-sitting for a friend who was in India for a month, and could stay there until the end of September. We had until the end of September to move. But in September he started bringing in a sailboat, three motorcycles, (one was a classic Indian), and some other things he stored out by the shed.

Reality was setting in. We were strongly thinking of moving to Arizona. I had lived in Tucson in 1971 and 1972 and my brother Marty and his family had moved out to Phoenix at the end of August in 1989. We had talked about this possibility before, but Syl was never excited about it. Financially, we would have the money that we had put down on the house and also the money we had paid for repairs and improvements. This would give us a start to get a house and live for a while until we found work. Syl could get a job, as she had worked at banks, hospitals, military bases, supply companies, and for veterinarians. I could probably find landscaping work, although they could hire the Mexican workers for the lowest wages. The summers are brutally hot, for house painting jobs also. It is a dry heat, not the humidity like in Florida and Texas, but still unbearable when you are working in 115 to 120-degree temperatures. I had my screenplay and some other writing ideas, but they weren't paying the bills.

Sylvia's sister, Karen, came up from Atlanta for a week. We had tried to discourage her from coming, or at least not staying with us at this time, as our lives were in a total state of flux. Most of our things were packed up in boxes and stored in the front room. But she wanted to come up and be with Bruce, our musician friend. They were having a great time hanging out together, in our house, as we were contemplating our future. I have to admit that I started to get "cold feet" about moving out to Arizona, with no jobs and thinking about the hot summers. This is after Syl was ready to make the move to Arizona, mainly to make me happy. That's the kind of person she was. The fall colors were starting to turn, as we took walks around Green Lakes and drove around looking for houses, just being curious as to what was out there. Most of them we felt were out of our price range at the time. In hindsight, we probably could have worked something out, but we didn't know. Live and learn. We finally decided against moving to Arizona and as it turned out, it was the greatest decision that we ever made in our lives and careers.

We found a townhouse to rent in Canastota, a village 25 miles southeast of Syracuse. "Kniste Stota" was the name used by the Oneida Nation, meaning "cluster of pines near still waters." It is home to the International Boxing Hall of Fame, mainly due to Carmen Basilio, a boxing legend who was from there. They were older townhouses, but nicely modernized inside. The main drawback was that you could hear noises from the adjoining attached townhouses. We put a Security Deposit down and were planning to move in on October 1st; but the woman whose townhouse we were going to move into, was having a house built and encountered some delays, and wasn't going to be out for another month. At this point we could have nullified our lease and gotten our Security Deposit back. We had moved out of Erieville on September 30th and now had to put all our belongings and furniture in a storage unit. We thought about searching for another house, but after looking at prospective houses for a month and packing and moving, we just needed a break.

My mom had moved into a townhouse, "The Bluffs," outside the village of Manlius, two years earlier; after our family had lived on Rugby Road, near Eastwood, for 28 years. She offered her remodeled basement, complete with a bathroom and shower, bedroom and living room, to us for the month of October. She even let us bring our three cats with us. That was an adventure! So, we gladly accepted, and here we were, living in my mom's basement with our three cats, in total limbo with our lives. Syl had given her notice at the hospital, as it would have been too great a distance to continue to work there, and I was still working my landscaping job for another month or two.

Mom was the Head of the Lower School at Manlius Pebble Hill School, a Private School in Dewitt, New York.

One of her teachers, an assistant in Pre-K, needed to have a replacement for a few months, as she would be away on maternity leave. Mom asked Syl if she would be interested in taking that teacher's place. She had worked all those different jobs that I had mentioned before, but never any in education. If Syl had still been working at the hospital, that offer probably would not have taken place. At this moment was when fate stepped in and changed our lives forever.

     We moved into the townhouse on November 1st, had our things moved out of storage, unpacked all our boxes, and got the townhouse in order. Syl started her teaching job a few weeks later and I was finishing up the landscaping season, raking and hauling away all the fallen leaves. We did get our money back that we had put down on the house and also in repairs and improvements. This sustained us when we were between jobs or just working part-time, until eventually it evaporated. After the closing costs, we made a net profit of $4,000. We decided, since we didn't move to Arizona, to use this money and stay in Tucson for a month. Syl worked her teaching job through December, January, and the first half of February, when the Winter Break at school started. I was doing some interior painting jobs. We were enjoying living in the townhouse with our three cats, not being so far away from everything, although Canastota is not exactly around the corner either. Also, not the constant work of house repairs, wood splitting, snow shoveling and mowing five acres. I still did some fine-tune shoveling of the walks and our back patio, but not what I had to do in Erieville for two and a half years.

1993

(mid) February - (mid) March: Tucson, Arizona
- Colossal Caves
- Saguaro Desert Monument

Phoenix
- Glendale (Marty & Marti's house)
- Scottsdale
- Tombstone
- Mission San Xavier Del Bac
- Botanical Gardens
- Sonora Desert Museum
- Old Tucson Studios
- Sabino Canyon

Nogales, Mexico
- Mount Lemmon

Phoenix
- Glendale
- Sabino Canyon
- Kitt's Peak
- Tohono Chul Park

Catalina State Park

May: Sackets Harbor

July: Deruyter Lake

August: Southwick Beach

Cape Cod (East Harwich)

It was twenty below zero when Patty came to our townhouse early in the morning to give us a ride to the airport. Her car was struggling to stay running in these inhumane weather conditions, but it did. When we arrived in Tucson, it was only in the mid-60's, but the sun was shining and it felt wonderful to us, considering the frozen tundra we had just escaped from. I got a monthly discounted rate at a Best Western, which included breakfast and a daily two hour, with free drinks, "Happy Hour." We always tried to make it back from our daily excursions before the 7 p.m. deadline to get our free drinks of beer or wine, sometimes Whiskey Sours, and hang out by the pool or take them back to our room. They had an outdoor hot tub by the pool. At night, we would sit in it, gazing up at the clear night skies with millions of stars, with steam coming off our heads, dive into the heated pool, feeling cool after being in the hot tub, take a swim, and then get back in the hot tub.

The first four days were flying to Tucson and getting settled at the Best Western; experiencing Colossal Cave Mountain Park; Saguaro National Monument, where we hiked the Signal Hill Trail and saw petroglyphs of the ancient Hohokam people; a day trip to Phoenix: exploring downtown Phoenix, visiting Marty & Marti in Glendale, and them taking us to Stonewall Farm Arabian Horses in Scottsdale.

After that, we took a day trip to Tombstone. I was feeling under the weather with flu-like symptoms, similar to how I felt that day in Dzibilchaltún, but fortunately without the high heat and humidity. I must have picked up the virus back in Syracuse and it was now kicking in. It was nothing I ate that I knew of, I was not throwing up, but just had that empty stomach, weak-legged, whitish facial coloring, kind of feeling, with chills, and a headache. *Other than that, I was feeling fine.*

Tombstone was known as "The Town Too Tough to Die." You feel like you have just stepped back in time walking the Old West streets of Wyatt Earp and Doc Holliday in the Historic District. People still live in Tombstone today, and have ever since it became a boomtown with the discovery of a silver mine in 1879. We went into Big Nose Kate's Saloon and Syl got a beer. All I could think of that would appeal to me was a hot chocolate. We saw the reenactment of "The Gunfight at The OK Corral," The Bird Cage Theatre, Silver Mine, Courthouse, and many more attractions. Finally, we went up to Boot Hill Cemetery, where I was feeling so lousy by then, the wind felt cold whipping through me; I laid down among the tombstones and told Syl to just leave me right here, "to bury me with my sneakers on."

It was still a neat experience going to Tombstone, I just wish I would have felt normal. We sat by the pool for a couple of days, as the weather warmed up into the 70's, and I started to feel more like myself again. We took a day trip to see the Mission San Xavier Del Bac, a historic Spanish

Catholic Mission, known as the "White Dove of the Desert." It is a really impressive sight when you first see this Spanish Colonial architecture, its whiteness gleaming in the sun. Other day trips were to the Botanical Gardens, Sonora Desert Museum, and Old Tucson Studios, where many Westerns, such as "Rio Bravo;" "Gunfight at the OK Corral;" "Three Amigos;" "Tombstone," (with Kurt Russell and Val Kilmer); and several John Wayne movies were filmed. Also, television series "High Chaparral," episodes of "Bonanza," and "Little House on the Prairie." In 1995, an arson burned down most of the sets and it took 18 months to restore them.

We hiked in Sabino Canyon, in the Santa Catalina Mountains and the Coronado National Forest north of Tucson.

One day we drove about 40 miles south to the border and crossed into Nogales, Mexico. I was looking for rings, silver with turquoise stones, at a more inexpensive price than you could find in Tucson. A lot of seedy characters walking around in this place. We were in one little shop and this Mexican guy kept staring at us. I said to him,

"Como esta?"

He unfolded a switchblade knife and held it up in the air. Syl grabbed my arm and whisked us out of there, before there was any further escalation of this possible confrontation. It was like flashbacks of Dzibilchaltún, walking back from the ruins; and Bethel, at the Woodstock Festival site. I don't know why we seem to attract these potentially dangerous situations. We later found a store to buy our rings and were glad to cross the border and return to Tucson.

A few days later, we drove 46 miles to Mount Lemmon, up winding and curving roads on the Catalina Highway, in the Coronado National Forest north of Tucson, to an elevation of over 9,000 feet, the highest point in the Santa Catalina Mountains. Here you'll find a totally different atmosphere and environment than in the valley below, with alpine forests and snow! It was like we were back home. I packed and threw a few snowballs in the village of Summerhaven, near the summit.

There were return trips to Phoenix and Sabino Canyon, followed by a drive to Kitt Peak National Observatory, 56 miles southwest from Tucson, in the Quinlan Mountains in the Sonoran Desert. Kitt Peak has the largest collection of astronomical instruments in the northern hemisphere. It became famous for having the first telescope used to search for asteroids that would have the possibility of an impact with Earth.

We went to Tohono Chul Park in Tucson, where the impressive Botanical Gardens are. There were all different types of cacti, but one that caught my eye was the "Teddy Bear Cactus." The sign in front said, "Do not touch the Teddy Bear Cactus." It looked so cute and fuzzy, and of course being the fool that I am sometimes, I proceeded to touch it anyway. Bad move. Instant agony. All these tiny thorns were imbedded in my hand and even tweezers couldn't get them out. It took weeks to finally get them all out. That's *why* they have the warning sign.

It would be the longest vacation that we ever took, well worth using our net gain from the Erieville house; to see some amazing sights and serve as a scouting mission to see if we would want to ever live here. Of course, this was February and not the four-month period of unbearable heat. Also, the scarcity of rivers and lakes. The desert has its own unique beauty, and if you could live here for the winter, that would be really nice.

We flew back to Syracuse, just in time to be a part of "The Great Blizzard of 1993," where we had 43 inches of snow over three days, March 13th-15th. I think we had more in Canastota, and I'm sure there was a whole lot more in Erieville. It took weeks to dig out and melt.

I was working for a landscaping crew and had to drive 32 miles from Canastota to Nedrow, (64 miles roundtrip), on the south side of Syracuse, five days a week. Syl was doing some secretarial work over the summer for a Spanish teacher at MPH. She found out that the administrators and teachers were impressed with her replacement teaching, and she was hired as a full-time assistant teacher in First Grade, for the upcoming school year, starting in September, 1993.

Over Memorial Day weekend, we drove up to Sackets Harbor, 80 miles north in the Thousand Islands region. The Navy built a major shipyard and its headquarters for the Great Lakes here for the War of 1812. The Army built forts and barracks to defend the village and Navy shipyard. Today it is the Sackets Harbor Battlefield State Historic Site and some of these stone buildings have been converted into places you can rent. It was definitely a slice of history, but I remember that it was uncomfortably hot and humid that weekend. We had some nice dinners in the village.

In August, we took Mom with us and drove to Cape Cod, where we all stayed at Aunt Gloria's house, the first time we had returned to the Cape since our initial visit in 1987. Syl and I would go off on our own to the ocean, hiking trails, and driving around, scouting potential future places to stay, and return for dinner. We all went to some antique shops and outdoor lawn concerts together.

Syl started teaching in September. I had to drive her to school early in the morning and then on to my landscaping job. I would pick Syl up at school after 5:30, as they had coerced her into also working the after school Extended Day Program; where she was an assistant to a woman in her 70's, a former Kindergarten teacher at another school, who knew Mom from her church.

There were only 20 kids then, but she was inadequately prepared for this job, having no First Aid or CPR training; plus being very small and frail to handle physical emergencies. She used to gather the kids and have a prayer session before they could eat their snacks, actually blessing the small cartons of milk. She would even tape up the unfinished milk cartons and give them to the parents when they came to pick up their kids.

Syl loved her teaching job, but couldn't stand this situation working with this woman in Extended Day, and was more than happy when I came to pick her up and get her out of there.

We enjoyed our autumn walks and foliage drives and spent our second Thanksgiving and Christmas at the townhouse with our three cats.

1994

February: Charleston, South Carolina

Historic District

      Waterfront & Battery Park

      Magnolia Plantation

      Audubon Swamp

      Edisto Island

      Middleton Place

      Boone Hall Plantation

      Isle of Palms

April: Manlius (Our Wedding at Mom's townhouse)

      Cazenovia (Reception, Brewster Inn)

      Nags Head, North Carolina (Honeymoon)

      Cape Hatteras Lighthouse

      Botanical Gardens

      Kill Devil Hills

      Hatteras

August: Sandy Pond

    In January, after the holidays, we started thinking about moving closer to Syl's teaching job. The prospect of packing up all of our things and moving again was not an appealing thought. We enjoyed the comforts of the townhouse and that they took care of the maintenance; but the distance from our jobs and the fact that you could hear noises from the adjoining townhouses, took precedence in our decision. We started looking around at houses to rent closer to school, not wanting to get involved with any apartments or townhouses.

In the middle of February, we took our first of many trips to Charleston, South Carolina, where Ursula had relocated to; wanting to get as far away from Art and Syracuse as she could. Ursula's sister and Sylvia's aunt, Lori, had met her husband, Chuck, in Germany, and had relocated with him to Charleston. Lori arranged a live-in partner relationship for Ursula with Ben, a South Carolina native and southern gentleman, who had lost his wife and was looking for companionship. Ursula accepted this offer and moved to Charleston. Ben and Ursula became more than just companions and stayed together for over 33 years. They considered themselves married, but were never officially married; as Ursula needed to keep her child support payments, which she felt she had earned and deserved, and her military benefits coming from Art. Sylvia could have moved with her mother to Charleston, but would have had to get a new job and eventually an apartment. Here she had a job and some new friends and decided to stay. Lucky for me. And I'm sure Syl would say lucky for her. We were lucky to have found each other and stay together.

I first met Ursula when she came to visit us in July, 1990, a couple of months after we had moved out to Erieville; but this was our first visit to Charleston to meet Ben, Debbie and her daughters, Lindsey and Erica, Lori and her family, and several of Syl's cousins. Also, there was Syl's grandmother and an uncle visiting from Germany. This was Ursula's mother, who along with

Ursula's father, had helped raise Sylvia before Ursula married Art. Syl hadn't seen her grandparents since 1973 and never got the chance to see her grandfather again. Syl was so happy to see her grandmother and it was fortunate that she did, as her grandmother passed away in Germany not that long after this visit.

Charleston, "The Holy City," is a port city that was founded in 1670, as Charles Town, honoring King Charles II of England. We strolled down the cobblestone streets, looking at houses that peer out behind wrought iron fences and gates and flowers and gardens. Then down to the Battery and Waterfront Park, both overlooking Charleston Harbor. The Battery is a fortified seawall at the southernmost tip of the Charleston Peninsula, where the Ashley and Cooper Rivers meet. It is lined with antebellum homes and wonderful views of Fort Sumter, Castle Pinckney, and Sullivan's Island Lighthouse. There is also White Point Garden, with its large oak trees and oyster shell paths. "Rainbow Row" is the name for a famous row of thirteen colorful historic houses. Walking past restaurants, shops, and historic buildings, you turn off the main street, take a right, and a couple of blocks away is the Atlantic Ocean.

Further down you witness a troublesome time in our past. There you see the seemingly never-ending former slave market. Half of the slaves that came over here came through Charleston. It seems unfathomable to even think it once existed, but it did, and there are still racial divides in the United States, and for that matter, around the world, to this day. These slave market buildings are now utilized for a huge and diverse flea market, selling just about anything you could think of. Chuck and Lori had a space in the market selling old bottles that were hundreds of years old, that Chuck and his son Frankie found under houses, doing their exterminator work.

We visited three of the most prominent plantations: Magnolia Plantation, Middleton Place, and Boone Hall Plantation. With their moss-covered oak trees and beautiful gardens, you immediately find yourself drifting back in time. The entrance to Boone Hall, "Avenue of Oaks," is spectacular and has been used in many movies. Audubon Swamp Garden is a cypress and tupelo swamp on the grounds of Magnolia. At one time, it served as a reservoir for the plantation's rice cultivation. Middleton is an 18th century rice plantation, with America's oldest landscaped gardens. They were all amazing places to visit, seeing the historic houses and smelling the azaleas and all the other colorful flowers, but the reason they existed in the first place is something I just can't justify in my mind.

Syl and I went to the ocean at Edisto Island and Isle of Palms and to a nature park, Palmetto Park, in Mount Pleasant. We all stayed at Ben and Ursula's cute house in North Charleston, where we enjoyed many home-cooked meals.

We flew back to Syracuse after nine days. Our vacations were now determined by the designated vacations at school. The summers, (except for this upcoming summer of 1994, which I'll explain shortly), from the last week of June through the first week in September, were free for us to go and stay longer than nine or ten days.

Syl started back at school and I had some painting jobs until landscaping started again in April. I had decided to switch landscaping jobs to a smaller crew, with a guy that I knew, that was a brother of one of the guys that was in that group of people that Sylvia hung out with, when she first came to Syracuse. I had mixed feelings, as the former job was with a good friend of mine, Ted, who I've known since high school and played on many softball teams with and hundreds of pick-up basketball games. But I didn't want to have to drive so far, the crew was bigger, and minimal pay. Actually, Syl had also done some work for Ted, working with one of our friend's daughters, putting down mulch and planting flowers at some banks and other locations. Syl was under the impression that spreading the mulch and planting the flowers was all they had to do, not having to go get the mulch and flowers in a truck with faulty brakes and then unload the mulch and flowers. Syl didn't need this heavy lifting with chronic back issues. It was hard enough doing the spreading and planting. This was in the summer of 1993. After a few jobs like this, Syl started doing the secretarial work for the Spanish teacher at school that summer, before being offered a full-time position starting in the fall.

  Ted was an incredibly hard worker and had started his business from scratch by himself. I'll always give him credit for hiring me, when I had to learn to mow with those 650-pound Scag mowers, as a total rookie. When I first started practicing, I was using the lowest gear and when I went to turn, the mower was whipping me around. The other guys were zipping around in the highest gear with no problem. The first real time out, we were mowing this big house up on a steep hill, the last week in April, after days of rain. There were four guys, each mowing separate strips. Somehow, I got up on the steepest part of the hill, when the mower started sliding on a muddy part, and I feared the mower would start sliding down the hill and my feet would get caught underneath it. I could let it go flying down the hill and smash into the expensive cars below to save myself. But I held on with all my might and motioned with head bobs that I was in trouble. Ted saw me, shut off his mower, and came over and took the mower out of my hands. He couldn't stop the mower from sliding and wound up flying down the hill, somehow avoiding getting his feet caught up underneath and not smashing the cars in the driveway. It was a close call, even for him, and I don't think I would have been so lucky. I started to get the hang of it and we would drive to all these business complexes and private homes and with just one other guy, we could mow fifteen to twenty lawns a day.

Syl always looked out for me and made me excellent dinners, always with a fantastic big salad. She would pack lunches when we went to the beach, the lake, or the park. She would pack me lunch for work and I became the butt of the crew's jokes, as they referred to my lunch as "Dusty's Gourmet Lunch." I think deep inside they were probably jealous. They would pull up to a fast food place and gobble down their burgers, nuggets, fries, and soda in a few minutes. I would stay in the truck and open up my cooler. Syl had everything neatly sealed: a couple of sandwiches in Ziploc bags, plastic containers with cherry tomatoes, carrots, hard boiled eggs, sliced fruit. I would have to eat it as we drove to the next mowing job.

Some of the safety precautions were not there and started to concern me by the end of the summer. The trucks had faulty brakes and you had to keep pumping them and almost had your foot on the brakes to the floor in order to stop. There were two wooden planks to load the mowers onto the back of the truck, not solid wide metal ones. A slip off the planks with the mower either way, loading on or taking off the truck, would have had serious consequences. Ted had taken off the locking devices when the mowers were running and you put them in the park gear, sort of like taking the catalytic converter off a car, I guess for some kind of better efficiency.

One day in late August, the whole crew was mowing a business complex. While I was mowing, I noticed some Kleenex on the lawn. Nothing looks worse than mowing over Kleenex. The rest of the crew wouldn't have worried about it, but me being "Mr. Meticulous," having my living habits more aligned with Felix Unger than with Oscar Madison; put the mower in park and went to pick up the Kleenex. In hindsight, I should have shut the mower off, so the blades weren't still running, but I didn't, and this is when the locking devices being taken off came into play. I went to go pick up the Kleenex and the mower took off, did a 360 degree turn and ran over my foot, before I realized what had just happened.

This was like something out of a Stephen King novel, my worst nightmare becoming a reality. It seemed similar to victims of a shark attack when they have been bitten, but don't know the extent of their injuries, until they are out of the water. I didn't even know if I had a foot left. I was afraid to look down. Somehow, I grabbed the mower before it could do further damage to buildings, cars, or people, and turned the blades off. I sat down and checked out my sneaker. The other guys kept mowing, thinking I just had a stone in my sneaker or something. My sneaker was cut through and the top part of my right foot had a cut on the bone. The only thing that saved me possibly losing my foot was that the blades were set at a higher level in July and August, when the grass is not as high. If they had been set at a lower level when the grass is higher, like in May and June, the result would have been disastrous. Many years later, I had surgery on that foot. This is when I started thinking about maybe finding a new crew to work for, closer and safer. I think Ted tightened up his equipment over the years after this, but I was looking out for my own best interests. I finished that year out, working through November.

After our vacation over the Winter Break in Charleston, we searched for houses to rent and found one close to the Westcott Street section, at the outer area of Syracuse University, two blocks from Barry Park. We gave our mandatory one month's notice on the townhouse at the end of March.

Sylvia and I had been together for 10 years and 9 months. We had always considered ourselves "married to each other" in every important way: love, trust, affection, caring, best friends, protection, faithful, sexual, financial, intellectual. When I first met Syl, she had just finalized all the divorce documents a year earlier, but they had been separated for three years. Then this three-year period of coming to a strange city, not knowing anyone but her mother, and enduring a weird relationship that I have mentioned several times before. She had just broken away from this, and also now was officially divorced, and started to enjoy her independence for the first time in her life. It was amazing when we met that she wanted to have a full-time relationship again. The only explanation was that it was meant to be, *and this time for both of us, forever.*

We had to work out a few things over the first couple of years, but after that it was smooth sailing. Maybe Syl would have said yes, if I had asked her to marry me, after we had bought and moved into our first house at the end of February, 1984. Maybe she didn't want to get married again and go through another divorce. I didn't want to get rejected or ruin this loving relationship we had now established. Then the years went by with traveling, our jobs, family, moving to different houses and all the work each entailed. I guess that I just got tired of introducing Syl as my girlfriend, or my lady, or my wife. She was my best friend, so she was way beyond being called just my girlfriend. She deserved better than that. Syl was a lady, but to be introduced like that seemed contrived and corny. And to say that this is my wife, when we weren't officially married with the license and the ring, even though we considered ourselves married with all the things that really count; seemed as if this wasn't really true, that we were just making it up.

      I asked Syl to marry me, and without hesitation, she said yes. She was so happy. We were both happy. So, on Saturday, April 16th, 1994, we got married. We just had a family wedding at Mom's townhouse, which was always nicely decorated. Marty and Marti were in Arizona and couldn't really afford to come back. Linda and John lived far away also. Dad had passed away around 8 years earlier. He would have been proud to have been there. At least he got to know Sylvia for almost three years. So, it was Mom, Tom and Julie and their children, Em and Jeff, and a woman who was licensed to perform weddings that Mom knew. It was a beautiful ceremony and Syl looked stunning in her white dress and white pearls. Then we all went out to the elegant Brewster Inn, a Gilded Age mansion built in 1890, on lovely Cazenovia Lake, for the reception. It was a truly wonderful day. *And it has been ever since.*

Wherever Freedom Flies

Magical memories

Naked and free

Like ancient mountains

Rising out of the sea

We go back so long ago

Secrets for only us to know

Lovers of distant pasts

Survivors of the wintry blasts

Haunting echoes in a forgotten land

At the crossroads I blindly stand

Hoping someday you'll burst into view

Together we'll greet the golden dew

But wherever freedom flies

Whether desert or paradise

There's one thing I can see

In my heart you'll always be

    Syl and I went to Nags Head, North Carolina, in the Outer Banks, for our honeymoon, over the Spring Break. We flew into Norfolk, Virginia and then rented a car and drove 80 miles south to Nags Head. We went to the famous Cape Hatteras Lighthouse, Botanical Gardens, Kill Devil Hills, to the Wright Brothers National Museum; Bodie Island Lighthouse, Jockey's Ridge, the largest sand dune on the east coast and a hang glider's paradise; and days at the beach on Hatteras Island, a barrier island dividing the Atlantic Ocean and the Pamlico Sound. We took the ferry one day over to Ocracoke Island, where Blackbeard the Pirate, Edward Teach, was killed here in 1718 and buried here. The historic white lighthouse tower is the second oldest operating lighthouse in the United States. We saw a few wild horses on the island, but only from a distance. Also drove through Salvo, where we saw the second smallest Post Office building in the United States, measuring 8 feet by 12 feet, built in 1910.

    Syl and I returned home and had three days to pack all our things and move once again; this time to a house we were renting, on Jerome Street, a side street off Westcott Street. Syl was doing her teacher's assistant job, as well as being the assistant at Extended Day. I started working for this new landscaping crew; just the guy who ran it, one other guy and me. The guy who ran it had a newer truck and some private lawns and a few clean-ups at apartment complexes, which were really nasty to clean up. But it became a very inconsistent job, to say the least. He would call in the early morning and tell us where to meet him. I think at night he would be getting high, and then in the morning telling us we must repent our sins and accept Jesus into our lives, sometimes even singing hymns. What a hypocrite! I tolerated it, needing the work, and worked through May and into June. At the same time, Syl was tolerating her after school job. She loved teaching, but this additional after school job made for an extra-long day in both hours and stress. Plus, we were unpacking everything and getting the house set up.

    Syl signed up to work some of the summer programs at school, the first one starting in the middle of June for two weeks, after all the graduations. The calls for landscaping were getting more and more inconsistent, sometimes not even a call at all. At least on Ted's crew, you knew where to meet, at his house, and there was always steady work. I told this guy that I couldn't go on like this and he was defensive about it. Just when I was wondering what direction to head in next, fate stepped in and our lives were changed forever.

Syl was to be the Director of Intersession I, a two-week program watching 13 kids from 8 a.m. to 5 p.m., Monday through Friday. A woman who was a friend of Mom's from church, and the assistant Librarian at school, was scheduled to be Syl's assistant for this two-week program. She was supposed to be there on the opening Monday, but at the last minute told Syl that she couldn't make it, as she was getting her car serviced. Obviously, she was not being very responsible, as she could have done her car earlier, or made arrangements to have someone take her place for the first two days. I think she had something to do the next day as well, if I remember correctly. It didn't seem to bother her to leave Syl hanging like that, to not even have the chance to get a replacement for the first two days. I was not getting any calls for work for several days after the first week in June, so I told Syl that I would help her do the program those first two days.

We loaded the kids in the school van and drove up to Sandy Pond, over an hour away. We went swimming in Lake Ontario, threw a frisbee around, played on the playground, ate our lunches, read stories. This seemed to be my true calling, being with kids. They loved me and I loved them. This would later evolve into teaching and being the Director of the Extended Day Program, and a few years later, Syl would join me as Co-Directors of the Extended Day Program; where we became almost legendary, and finished out our careers running the program.

I worked the next day as well and I was enjoying it and Syl was enjoying having me be there as well, not only as a male figure for the boys, but also not real thrilled at the woman either. She called that night, expecting to start work on Wednesday, as if nothing had changed. Syl told my mom that she wanted me to work the program with her and the woman had not treated her fairly. Mom was reluctant, being a friend of hers, but found some secretarial work that she could do for her, as she was counting on the money from the program. She had a lot of nerve, the way she handled it. But it was lucky for me. In the long run, for both of us.

Syl and I worked those two weeks and then I got hired for the summer programs. I was moving on, moving forward, putting all those landscaping jobs in the rear-view mirror. We worked the Kinderplace Program, for that age group, which included children from all over the Central New York area, not just for MPH children, for 6 weeks. The first week, on a Friday, there was an incident that we'll never forget. This program ended at three o'clock in the afternoon and the parents would come and pick up their children. It wasn't Monday, where it was a new experience, especially for the new parents who weren't MPH parents. All of the summer programs that followed the two-week Intersession One program, were open to the entire Central New York Community. The parents had been picking up their children all week by three o'clock in the afternoon, so they knew the routine. On Friday, all the children had been picked up by 3 o'clock, except for this 5-year-old girl, who we didn't know very well yet, as she didn't go to MPH. It became 3:15, then 3:30, 3:45, 4:00. These were the days, not only of no cell phones, but us having no emergency phone numbers for the parents of the children. That would change after incidents like this. We called the parents at home, getting no answer. We asked permission from an administrator to take the girl and drive over, in our car, to the address we had been given for her. It was now 4:30. The little girl trusted us and was actually pretty calm through this. We pulled in the driveway and saw her parents sitting on their deck having cocktails. Incredibly, neither of them looked at each other and said anything that resembled embarrassment or remorse. Maybe the alcohol dictated that. It was so weird. I don't remember any extreme apologies or gratitude. They were back at the program on Monday, as if this incident was long forgotten and never happened. There were times when there was confusion over which parent was supposed to pick up their child or children; sometimes both showed up and sometimes neither, until we kept calling and one of them came. They always felt embarrassment, remorse, and were apologetic, unlike that couple sitting and drinking on their deck.

Syl and I even created our own two-week program in August. The last two weeks of the summer programs, Intersession II, I ran by myself, as Syl wanted a break. One of the Lower School teacher's daughters was my assistant. It was different not having Syl with me, but I gained valuable experience having to do all the planning and almost everything by myself.

Parents, especially faculty with children in our programs, started taking notice of me. Baxter, the Headmaster, offered me a job as the Assistant to that older woman, of the Extended Day Program. This was great news, not only for me, but for Syl; relieving her of that job, to have normal hours and not have that stress. Whenever I would see Baxter in the store or elsewhere, I would throw my "two cents in," that I would love to have a day-time position as well, just to express my willingness to accept any opportunity that might come up.

There was an annual party at Baxter's house, catered, with plenty of beer, wine, and music, that took place on the Friday afternoon after a full week of meetings, speeches, seminars, workshops, and getting the classrooms ready; for the start of classes the day after Labor Day. Toward the end of the party, Baxter looked over at me and said, "I'll give you an extra $5,000 to be the afternoon Pre-K Assistant." I didn't know if it was the wine influencing his decision and whether I should show up at noon the first day of classes or not.

I showed up just before noon and saw him and signed my contract, which consisted of Pre-K Assistant from noon until three, then Extended Day Assistant until 5:30, usually later by the time all the kids got picked up and we cleaned up and locked the doors; and also being the Director, with Sylvia as my Co-Director, of all the Vacation Programs: the two-week Christmas Break Program, the one-week each of the Winter Break Program and the Spring Break Program, and the two-week program in June, after the graduations, and before all the other area public schools were finished for the summer. These were all included in my job description.

We were now married, gone on a honeymoon, moved into a new house, worked all the summer programs, and both of us now had full-time positions at MPH. We enjoyed our foliage drives and hikes in the fall, and we spent our first Thanksgiving and Christmas here on Jerome Street with our three cats. *Life was good.*

1995

April: Green Gate Inn, Camillus, NY

July: Lake Placid

July: Toronto, Canada

    Scarborough Bluffs

August: Cape Cod

    Orleans (Penny Lane)

    Provincetown (Whale Watch)

October: Ithaca

    Another winter was now here. Roxy became sick and we took her in to see Tom at the Liverpool Animal Hospital. He informed us that she had an inoperable tumor and should be put to sleep to end her suffering. On January 10th, Roxy was put to sleep. That was a sad day. Syl took it very hard. She had such an incredible compassion for animals, being so helpless when they become injured or sick.

    We took another trip up to Lake Placid in July. Later in July, we drove 250 miles northwest up to Toronto, to see "The Phantom of the Opera." It was a fantastic show, except for what was offered as part of the V.I.P. package, that I had paid for and surprised Syl with. I assumed that there would be food, so we didn't eat dinner. We entered a special offstage room and they had no food whatsoever. No hors d'oeuvres, not even a variety of cheeses and crackers, just these red gummy candies with the Phantom's face on them. Very disappointing. They gave us free drinks, so we took advantage of that. These guys wearing white gloves seated us in the preferred seating section, so that was nice.

In August, we returned to Cape Cod and stayed in the town of Orleans. We had seen an ad to rent half of a small house, so we called and made the arrangements. It was located on *Penny Lane*, so that sealed it for us. We drove up to Provincetown one day for another Whale Watch. We hadn't seen any whales in our initial 15 miles, so the captain went an additional 10 miles, which is a lot farther than they normally go. Out of nowhere, three humpbacks swam right next to the boat, dove under the boat, then reappeared heading toward another Whale Watching Boat. You could hear all the people from that boat "oohing and aahing" as the whales swam under their boat. Then they headed back our way, seemingly paused for maximum effect, as they waved their tail flukes in unison, silhouetted against the setting sun, then dove down to the depths and disappeared. Easily one of the greatest scenes that we have ever had the privilege to witness.

1996

April: Charleston, South Carolina

    Folly Beach

  Atlanta, Georgia

    Botanical Gardens

Coca-Cola Museum

Stone Mountain

Charleston

July: Sandy Pond

Fair Haven

August: Thousand Islands

Mink Island

Heart Island: Boldt Castle

Lancaster, Pennsylvania

Willow Valley

Amish Village

New Hope, Pennsylvania

August-September: Cape Cod

Orleans (Penny Lane)

Nantucket

October: Tinker Falls

We went back to Charleston two years later, after our initial visit, over the Spring Break at school. I had spent my first two years at MPH in Pre-K and as the Assistant Director, then the Director of the Extended Day Program. I came in at noon my first year, as I mentioned before, and was in Pre-K for over three hours before doing Extended Day for the rest of the afternoon. That first year, after lunch and some classroom activities, I would bring out the dozen cots, (it became 13 after another child enrolled in January), for their nap time. Sometimes I wish I could hop in my own cot for a nap, especially on those cold winter days. They always looked so inviting with their sleeping bags, pillows, fluffy slippers, and favorite stuffed animals. I would read children's books to them before nap time and they wouldn't fall asleep, as they would be so engrossed in the books. I started to read books like "The Education of Little Tree" and Hemingway's "The Old Man and the Sea," leaving out any inappropriate language and parts, of course. This seemed to work, as I had five boys on my lap or hanging on to me, ready to fall asleep. One of the boys, who was one of the speakers for the senior class of 2008, said in his speech at graduation,

"I'd like to thank Dusty, for every time I start to read Hemingway now, I fall asleep."

The administrators liked how I related to the kids and my work ethic and offered me a full-time position as the Pre-K assistant, coming in at 7:30 in the morning, working all day and still retaining my position as the Extended Day Director; in addition to being the Director of the Vacation Breaks' Programs. We did that two-week program in June for 20 years, providing us money for our vacations. It was Intersession I originally, became Playscape for most of our years, then changed to Funscape the last few years. I always liked Playscape for the name, it just sounded better.

Syl was the full-time assistant in first grade for her first six years, before becoming the assistant in Kindergarten for the remainder of her teaching career. After my first couple of years as the Director of Extended Day, working with other people, they installed Syl as the Co-Director of Extended Day. All of a sudden, I went from Director to Co-Director. If this had been anyone other than Syl, I would not have been thrilled. The pay was equal and gave Syl a chance to shine a little more, and now we both went in at the same time, and worked the Extended Day Program together. It was not easy working with your wife, or your husband either. Many parents marveled at how we did it and said that they would find it difficult, if not impossible, to do. This became a blessing in disguise for us, as we became known for being a trusted team that the parents could count on for discipline, learning, safety, and most importantly, fun, for their children.

We were still very much involved in the daily classroom activities as well, Syl in Kindergarten and helping out the teachers with these kids in Art, Foreign Language, (French), and Music. Besides the Music teacher and two Physical Education teachers, I was the only male teacher in the Lower School, Pre-K through fifth, at this time. I was not in Pre-K anymore, being totally involved in the second grade, third & fourth, (a combined grade called "The Blend"), and fifth grade. I also taught Geography in "The Blend" and Physical Education in Kindergarten, first, second, third and fourth grades. Each Lower School teacher also monitored their own lunch room table for students from first grade through fifth, where I began to tell "Dusty's Lunchtime Stories." I never really had any breaks, just a few minutes at the end of the day to check my mailbox;

then go down to the dining hall to gather up all the kids and walk them across campus, after the buses had gone, for Extended Day. In addition, I still did the Vacation Programs with Syl as part of my job. Syl got paid for them and after this year, I started to also. They discontinued the Christmas Vacation Program after this, but we did the Winter Break Program for another 6 years for extra vacation money, but stopped doing the Spring Break Program, so we could go to Charleston and other places. I thought we had done the 1996 Spring Break Program, but our pictures from our photo albums show that we were in Charleston and Atlanta and pictures don't lie.

So down to Charleston in April; then we drove 300 miles northeast to Atlanta with Ursula to visit Syl's sister, Karen, and her partner, Dave, and father of their year-old son, Andrew, for five days. Syl and I went to the Botanical Gardens and with Karen to the Coca-Cola Museum and Stone Mountain. Drove back the 300 miles to Charleston for the rest of the vacation, going to Folly Beach several days, and with Ursula to Charles Towne Landing.

We took day trips to Sandy Pond and Fair Haven, both on Lake Ontario, in July. In August, we went up to Gary and Patty's camp on Mink Island. The only way to get there was by boat, after you parked your car at the Schermerhorn Marina. We went in their boat to Heart Island, where Boldt Castle is.

Later in August, we drove 260 miles south to Lancaster, Pennsylvania with Mom, to visit her friends, Mr. and Mrs. Brooks, who had moved to Willow Valley from Syracuse. They used to live near Drumlins, and we all often went swimming in their pool. Syl and I drove around the beautiful countryside and visited the Amish Village.

We then drove 265 miles north to New Hope, Pennsylvania with Mom, where my dad was born and raised. I remember visiting there with Dad when I was nine years old, going to a Phillies-Pirates game and immediately being intrigued by the right fielder for the Pirates, Roberto Clemente, who was playing in his rookie season in 1955. He became one of my all-time favorite players, along with Willie Mays and Hank Aaron. That would be my dream outfield and I'll stack that up against anyone else's. In this game, I can remember the third basemen for the Phillies, named Willie "Puddin' Head" Jones, hitting a couple of home runs to left field.

My dad grew up living with his mother in a row house right next to the canal. He and his friends would dangerously dive off the bridge into the canal below. My grandmother owned a group of row houses, Mom told us on this trip, which I never knew. When she passed away, Mom and Dad wanted to take care of her affairs as soon as possible and sold them for $20,000. The people who bought them invested around $100,000 into each one, for renovations and upgrades, and wound up selling them for *a million dollars each.* Who knew that New Hope would reinvent itself into a prominent arts and crafts community and this section and these houses would be worth that much? My parents certainly didn't. Mom said that my grandmother also had an antique doll collection that was worth a fortune that they had just gotten rid of. Mom said she could have kicked herself for that, when she became more aware of antiques and their values later on.

Dad grew up without a father. My sisters and brother and I were under the impression that he had left when Dad was two years old and nobody knew what had happened to him. Or that he had passed away. It was always a mysterious situation and it wasn't until the last years of Mom's life that she told us that Dad's father was actually an alcoholic and lived somewhere in New Hope. We never knew that every Christmas, Dad would drive down to New Hope and meet with him and bring him Christmas presents. I don't know any more details than that.

My dad was actually one of those guys that walked through snow drifts to get to school and back. There was a big coal burning furnace in their house that Dad would shovel coal in to keep the house warm in the winter. He put his mother in a nursing home near Syracuse when she got sick in her final years. We never got a chance to know her that well and what her life was really like.

At the end of August and early September, through Labor Day, we went back to Cape Cod and stayed again in Orleans on Penny Lane and took a day trip on the ferry to Nantucket Island. We always loved going to the Cape and swimming in the cool ocean, driving around the different towns with all the quaint houses and shops, visiting the lighthouses, hiking in the marshes and woods, Whale Watches off Provincetown; just soaking up the whole ambience and atmosphere that is unique to the Cape.

1997

April: Charleston

Fort Moultrie

Beaufort, South Carolina

May: Thousand Islands

(June) July: Cape Cod

    Orleans (Penny Lane)

    Provincetown (Whale Watch)

    Harwich (Lavender Farm)

    Truro (Cape View Motel)

August: Thousand Islands

    Mink Island

November: Williamsburg, Virginia

    Gettysburg, Pennsylvania

    Syl and I went back down to Charleston over the school Spring Break in April. We went to Fort Moultrie, on Sullivan's Island, built to protect the city of Charleston. The first fort, formerly named Fort Sullivan, built of palmetto logs, inspired the flag and nickname of South Carolina, as "The Palmetto State." We took a day trip to Beaufort, 70 miles southeast from Charleston, with Ursula and Ben. Beaufort, with its magnolia trees and Antebellum houses, has been the scenic backdrop for many movies. We walked the Beaufort Movie Tour to many of the sites where these films were made: "The Great Santini" (1979), (Antebellum home); "The Big Chill" (1983), (Antebellum home and the scene on the long dock); "The Prince of Tides" (1991); "Daughters of the Dust" (1992); "A Perfect World" (1993); "The Fugitive" (1993); "Forrest Gump" (1994), (the Vietnam War scenes on Hunting Island, and the famous oak where Jenny and Forrest spend time together); "The War" (1994); "The Jungle Book" (1994); "Chasers" (1994); "Something to Talk About" (1995); "White Squall" (1996); "Last Dance" (1996); "Gone Fishin'" (1997); "G.I. Jane" (1997). After we were there came: "Forces of Nature" (1998); "Rules of Engagement" (2000), (Vietnam War scenes on Hunting Island); and "Legend of Bagger Vance" (2000). Really cool and I'm sure more to come.

After the school year and our two-week program in June had ended, we headed to Cape Cod for over a week through the Fourth of July. We again stayed in Orleans on Penny Lane, went to Provincetown for another Whale Watch, and to the Lavender Farm in Harwich. We went up the National Seashore to Truro and our future favorite beach, Head of the Meadow, and spent one night at our future favorite place to stay, the Cape View Motel in Truro.

In August, we drove up to Thousand Islands to spend a few days with Gary and Patty at their camp on Mink Island and going out on their boat on the Saint Lawrence River.

In November, we took Mom and drove 520 miles south, down to see my sister, Julie, and her husband, Tom, and their children, Em and Jeff; to Williamsburg, Virginia for Thanksgiving. Syl and I strolled around the Colonial Williamsburg site, with buildings from the 17th, 18th, and 19th centuries. Costumed workers work and dress as people did in 18th century Colonial America.

On the way back home to Syracuse with Mom, we drove 230 miles north from Williamsburg to Gettysburg, where we spent the night at a motel. It was a rainy day in Gettysburg as we started off at the Gettysburg Museum and Visitor Center; where in the auditorium there, you can see the battle unfold by these lights on this big board, which depicted the number and positioning of each Army, the Union and the Confederate. It is really enlightening, well worth the small price of admission. We went through the extensive museum of uniforms, weapons, all sorts of artifacts and memorabilia. Then on to the Gettysburg National Battlefield, where you can just feel its haunting presence of bloodshed from three days of non-stop fighting and killing, from July 1st-3rd, 1863. The battle involved the largest number of casualties of the Civil War, around 50,000, out of the 160,000 who fought here; and the turning point in the war for the Union forces. I went outside to take pictures of the monuments as we drove around the battlefield. Syl and Mom stayed in the car, as it was raining. There are over 1,200 monuments honoring the veterans of each state, as well as 40 individual monuments, honoring Generals and some unique civilians.

November Nights

The bare trees huddled together

By the frozen lake, dimly lit

Talking about the weather

Wondering if they would make it

Thinking about a time gone by

Nothing seemed near

Shaking their limbs with a sigh

Nothing seemed clear

Cold and distant blows the wind

Stinging with an icy hum

Treated as if they had sinned

Yearning for better times to come

1998

April: Charleston, SC

    Cypress Gardens

    Savannah, Georgia

    Winchester, Virginia

June-July: Ottawa, Canada

    Hull (Museum of Civilization), (Canadian Museum of Nature), (Hull-Wakefield Steam Train)

    July: Fair Haven (Karen and Andrew visit)

Lake Ontario: (Eff and Kathy's camp)

August-September: Cape Cod

Truro

Provincetown (Whale Watch)

Dennis Port ("Coffin Cove")

Dennis (Cape Cod Bay)

October: Taughannock Falls

November: Westfield, Massachusetts

Northampton, Massachusetts

Another trip to Charleston over the Spring Break at school in April. We decided to drive the 900 miles, instead of flying this time. The first day we drove 10 hours, 600 miles south, to Rocky Mount, North Carolina, and spent the night there. The next day, we drove 5 hours, 300 miles further south, to Charleston.

Syl and I took a day trip, driving 30 miles to Cypress Gardens. We went on a boat tour through the 80-acre blackwater bald cypress and tupelo swamp with a guide. It was both beautiful and eerie, as the tannin in the water makes everything appear bigger than they actually are. This property has been used as a set for over 15 movies, including: "Swamp Thing" (1982); "The Patriot" (2000); "Cold Mountain" (2003); "The Notebook" (2004);

and "North and South" (2004). We walked through the Botanical Gardens and the swamp trails, with many gator eyes checking us out from the murky green pond in there. Syl wanted to get out of there as soon as possible, if not sooner.

Another day trip, driving 108 miles south to Savannah, Georgia, a two-hour drive from Charleston, with Ursula and Ben. It was a very hot and humid day, as we went on the River Walk and also the "Midnight in the Garden of Good and Evil" Tour, from the best seller book by John Berendt in 1994.

On our 900 miles north drive back to Syracuse, there was a massive accident on the highway, causing a major traffic delay. They diverted all the cars through this sleepy little South Carolina town, where the people were sitting on their porches, watching all the cars go by, the most exciting event they had seen in a long time. When we returned to the highway, we could see several cars burning in the distance from the accident. As we drove through North Carolina, we could see this ominous funnel cloud heading our way. We decided to keep on driving and found out later that a tornado had indeed touched down. We drove to Winchester, Virginia and spent the night there. In the morning, we strolled around this historic city and then drove back home.

At the end of June, we drove 200 miles north up to Ottawa, Canada, only three hours from Syracuse. Ottawa is the capital of Canada. I mean *all of Canada*. A lot of people don't realize this, that it is the capital of the second largest country in the world by area, almost four million square miles, with its 10 provinces: Alberta, British Columbia, Manitoba, New Brunswick, Newfoundland & Labrador, Nova Scotia, Ontario, Prince Edward Island, Québec, and

Saskatchewan; and 3 territories: Northwest Territories, Nunavut, and Yukon.

We stayed at the Holiday Inn in Hull, the oldest part of the city of Gatineau, Québec, located on the west bank of the Gatineau River and the north shore of the Ottawa River, directly opposite Ottawa. In late 2001, the city changed its name from Hull to Gatineau, although most people still call it Hull. It is home to most of the area's French population. We took the river cruise on the Ottawa River and could see the Parliament Buildings, Canadian Museum of Civilization, (now called the Canadian Museum of History), Rideau Falls, and the Prime Minister's residence. We went to the Museum of Civilization, which was amazing. The first exhibition featured artifacts and majestic totem poles from the Indigenous Peoples of the Pacific Northwest Coast. The second exhibition featured the traveling treasures and tomb of King Tut, as well as statues and artifacts of ancient Egypt. The third exhibition was all about Canadian history, with a special display of its railroads.

We walked along the Rideau Canal, with all the beautiful flowers and the many cyclists. In the winter, people skate on the frozen canal to work, stopping for a coffee or hot chocolate from the vendors along the way.

On July 1st, we walked across the bridge to Parliament Hill, where the Parliament Buildings are located. It was a cloudy day, trying to clear up after raining the night before. This was Canada Day, like our Fourth of July. It is the National Day of Canada, celebrating the anniversary of July 1, 1867 of the Constitution Act, called the British North America Act in 1867; which united the three separate colonies of the Province of Canada, Nova Scotia, and New Brunswick, into a single Dominion within the British Empire, called Canada. Originally called Dominion Day, the holiday was renamed in 1982, the year the Canada Act was passed. Celebrations take place throughout the country, as well as around the world; but Ottawa is the main place to come to, being the capital, on this day.

There were two gigantic screens set up on either side of the lawn at Parliament Hill to see the musical acts, playing one after another, on the stage set up there. The lawn was wet and muddy from the previous night's rain, as we contemplated where we could sit, on the sides or in the back, for the evening shows. Food vendors were all around and there were a lot of people here in the afternoon, but nothing compared to what we would encounter later on. We had our picture taken with a Royal Mountie policeman, who was more than happy to do it. Colorful hot air balloons were floating in the sky, one being a Royal Mountie on his horse. You had to do a double take, as it appeared as an optical illusion, it looked so real.

There was a free admission that we found about at the Canadian Museum of Nature, so we decided to take a walk and find it. We walked for miles down Embassy Row where the international embassies are located. It was farther than we thought. We entered and saw a life size Tyrannosaurus rex, which was impressive, and spent time looking at the galleries: Fossil Gallery, Earth Gallery, Mammal Gallery, Water Gallery, Bird Gallery, Nature Live, Stone Wall Gallery, Landscapes of Canada Gardens, and The Canada Goose Arctic Gallery.

It was now time to head back. Thousands of people were now streaming toward Parliament Hill, draped in Canadian flags and many with their faces painted with maple leaf designs on them. There were dancers with native costumes performing. The restaurants were packed, but we managed to get a table outdoors at one after a long wait. It was dark as we finally got to the vicinity of Parliament Hill. Our afternoon discussion of where we might sit was now a moot point. Hundreds of thousands of people filled the area as far as you could see. Now we realized the importance of the Canada Day celebration in Ottawa. When the crowd started singing "O Canada" in unison, you could hear a pin drop.

  The next day we went back to Parliament Hill to see the impressive "changing of the guards." After that was over, we took a ride on the Hull-Wakefield Steam Train, a 1907 Swedish steam locomotive, using Swedish passenger cars that were built in the 1940's. It was a 20-mile ride through the scenic Gatineau Hills and beside the Gatineau River to the tourist town of Wakefield. Two guys with guitars played and sang, providing entertainment and fun for all the passengers.

  We drove to Cape Cod for the last week in August and the first week in September through Labor Day weekend. Mom told us about a house that she and Dad had rented on the Cape, 25 years or so ago. She couldn't believe that she had forgotten to mention this to us before. We were thinking about a new place to rent anyway, as we had spent one night at the Cape View Motel in Truro the summer before and thought about staying there again. She wasn't sure if the woman who owned the house was still alive. We called her, and sure enough, she was still alive. Mrs. Coffin was in her late 80's now, a widow, and still renting out this house, "Coffin's Cove," in Dennis Port. It was on a small street in a neighborhood with other houses all around. She pulled up in her car, it was amazing that she was still driving. Mrs. Coffin was a native Cape Codder, a very small woman, that if you were following her car, you wouldn't think that anyone was driving. She was very pleasant and we signed the rental agreement. There was a pond bordering the back yard with birds and ducks. The house needed some work and we cleaned up a lot of things and I patched some screens. It was comfortable enough, but a farther drive from the Mid Cape, rather than Orleans on the Lower Cape; to drive up the National Seashore to Truro and Provincetown on the Outer Cape, where we spent most of our time.

We went down to Cape Cod Bay in Dennis to watch the spectacular sunsets and drove to Provincetown for another Whale Watch. We never got tired of seeing these amazing creatures in the wild.

We were watching the weather station about this nor'easter that was making its way from the south up the coast to New England. Usually we check out of our rental place on Monday, Labor Day, and spend a few last hours at the beach; shower and change there, get some sandwiches along the way, and head back to Syracuse. Then dealing with all the people leaving the Cape, and all the other traffic and delays in the seven-hour drive; to finally get home, and go to MPH early in the morning, for four days of teachers' meetings and workshops. This is when reality sets in that your summer vacation is over. Because of this forecast, we decided to just check out and forego the beach and leave earlier. We weren't aware of what had happened at one o'clock in the morning in Syracuse and the surrounding areas. There were no cell phones then. It's a famous event in Syracuse weather history now: "The Labor Day Storm of 1998," like the infamous "Blizzards of 1966 and 1993."

Two fierce thunderstorms, called "derechos," with wind gusts up to 115 miles per hour, had come from the west and struck northern and central New York State; while the other one had started in southeastern Michigan, then moved through northeastern Ohio, Pennsylvania, New Jersey, and Long Island. We pulled into Syracuse as it was getting dark out and it was one of the eeriest sights that we had ever seen. It looked like a war zone: street lights out, trees uprooted, power lines down and wires sparking everywhere. The main road to get to our house was blocked by the police.

We drove to MPH to see the damage there. There were huge trees down across the parking lot, one being a tree that was on the school logo next to the Farmhouse, where the business offices were located. We knew there would be no meetings on Tuesday. It took them days to clear up the damage, as we could hear the whirring of chainsaws during our meetings. We took some side roads to our house, barely making it past fallen limbs and downed power lines. A tree had fallen on our backyard fence and our hanging plants had been blown off the front porch, as you could see that's where the fiercest winds had gone through. But our house and roof had been spared, so we were lucky.

Meanwhile, at Mom's house, my brother Marty was visiting from Arizona and staying with Mom in her guest apartment in the basement. It was very dark down there, with no windows, and close to being soundproof also. Marty went to bed before the storm came and slept right through the night, totally unaware of what was happening to Mom. She had gone to bed, fortunately climbing up her long flight of steep stairs to her bedroom. But when the storm came through, with the sound of a freight train, rattling the windows and shaking the walls; she was too afraid to move and just stayed in bed, hoping for the best.

Luckily, she was okay and no damages to her townhouse, but a harrowing experience that she would never forget.

We drove 220 miles southeast to Westfield, Massachusetts, where Linda and John had now moved to; a 4-hour drive with Mom, for Thanksgiving. They had lived and raised their family in Portland, Oregon for 20 years; then Boise, Idaho for almost 2 years; 3 years in Dallas, Texas; now Westfield, due to John's job transfers.

1999

May: Dorchester, London, Ontario, Canada

    Niagara Falls, Canada

July: Amelia Island, Florida

    Fernandina Beach, Florida

    Saint Augustine, Florida

August: Lakemont, NY (Ursula and Mom)

    Dorchester, London, Ontario, Canada

    Cazenovia Lake (President Clinton)

Syl and I were very interested in bidding on this vacation package to Amelia Island, Florida, one of the items up for bids at an annual MPH auction, held a week before the Spring Break. This was a really pleasant gala event with beautiful artwork donated by teachers, friends, and parents of the school, for the silent auction. There was a cocktail hour, with appetizers and free drinks, a chance to mingle and observe the art work and everyone all dressed up. Then on to separate tables, a very nice dinner, speeches, and an auctioneer, to let anyone bid on vacation packages donated by friends and parents of the school, around 70 different items. We had our eyes on this one-week vacation to Amelia Island. Mir, one of the other teacher assistants, was planning to sit next to me, as Syl was sitting next to me on the other side. She had her purse on the chair, but went over to talk to somebody, and her husband moved it and sat down next to me. I thought it seemed rude, as he was drinking quite a bit and getting more obnoxious. She seemed a little annoyed when she came back, but didn't want to create a scene, and sat down next to him. He had heard us talking about the Amelia Island package and said that when the bidding began on it, he was going to bid on it to raise the bid. I asked him why he wanted to do that and he responded,

"Just trying to keep it interesting."

We were not really thrilled by this. We had overheard him saying to Mir that he thought that the "Fly Fishing in Montana" vacation package seemed like something he might want to bid on. Both of these vacations were way down the list in the program booklets, I think Montana was the 59th item and Amelia was the 64th, something close to that. By the time these packages came up for bidding, a lot of people had left or had already gotten the packages that they had the winning bid on. I had never bid on anything at an auction before, and when the Montana trip came up, I decided to do to him what he had proposed doing to us. The auctioneer announced that "Fly Fishing in Montana" was now open for bidding. Several people were bidding on it, as it got to $550. I raised my auction number, #47, (a cardboard number on a wooden stick), and the auctioneer acknowledged it. The guy who started all this wasn't bidding at all. "Five-fifty going once, five-fifty going twice;" as my face was turning red, the husband had a devilish grin on his face, and Syl was kicking me under the table, not believing that we were going to miss out on a chance to bid on Amelia Island. Finally, somebody bid $600 and I thought I was off the hook. As the auctioneer was finalizing the bid, the bidder apparently had gone to the bathroom when the auctioneer wanted him to come and claim the bid.

"Where is the $600 bid? I know we had one. All right then, I know we had a $550 bid. Number #47, I believe. Where's #47?"

I felt like crawling under the table. This "Fly Fishing in Montana" package did not include airfares and I've never fished a day in my life. I thought I was spared this embarrassment, but now it was back again. Fortunately, the $600 bidder returned and claimed his winning bid. I had let myself get egged on and almost paid for it. We had several people bidding on Amelia Island along with us, but they eventually dropped out, and I thought we had won the bid at $650. I think the auctioneer stretched it out to $700, but we were glad to win it, paid the bid, and signed the rental agreement. I never bid on anything again, except for something at the silent auction, that we never won. It became a funny story at future auctions, but it would not have been funny if the outcome had been different.

One weekend in May, Sylvia and I drove 278 miles west, to Dorchester, 12 miles outside of London, Ontario, Canada. I was going there to play in a Senior Softball tournament for the Syracuse Merchants, the most powerful team in Central New York at the time. Senior Softball started at age 50, (you could turn 50 anytime that year to be eligible.) I was now starting at 52 and 9 months with this tournament, as Senior Softball was introduced to Syracuse only the year before. After the tournament was over, we visited Niagara Falls again, this time on the Canadian side.

We went down to Amelia Island in the middle of July. The vacation package that we had paid for at the auction was a beautiful house owned by MPH parents. We had taught their daughter in Lower School and she had just graduated from fifth grade. There were some unbelievable mansions in this community. This house was not like those, but very nice with a view from the back of the house of the Intracoastal Waterway. Looking past the marshes, you could see the huge barges, boats, and ships. We found out that they used to have a pool in the back, but closed it when alligators started to come up there. They had bicycles there and we rode them all over the island, watching out for all the golf carts that people used, not only for playing golf, but as their transportation around this community. We went to the communal pool area with fountains, food places, and access to the beach by the ocean.

Amelia Island is part of the Sea Islands chain of barrier islands, on Florida's Atlantic Coast. It has a history of Spanish, French, British, and American rule, having had 10 different flag changes. The United States flag has flown continuously over the island since 1862. We visited the Amelia Island Lighthouse, the oldest lighthouse in Florida, Fort Clinch, and historic Centre Street, whose buildings date back to the 19th century. Many pirates came here, including famous ones like Blackbeard and Jean Lafitte, because the port is one of the deepest on the southeast coast, allowing the large pirate ships to enter, even at low tide. We spent a day exploring Fernandina Beach; and a day trip to Saint Augustine, the "Ancient City," founded by Spanish explorers in 1565. It is the oldest city in the continental United States. We visited The Castillo de San Marcos National Monument, a 17th century Spanish stone fortress, with views of the Saint Augustine Inlet. It is the oldest masonry fort in the United States, built with coquina, a soft limestone of broken shells, and served as a fort for over 200 years.

  Then on to Ponce de León's Fountain of Youth Archaeological Park, which has been believed to be the possible landing site of Juan Ponce de León, a Spanish explorer and conquistador and the first Governor of Puerto Rico. In 1513, looking for the island of Bimini, he led the first known expedition to La Florida, ("covered with flowers"), which he named during his first voyage to the area. He was supposedly searching for the Fountain of Youth, but there has been no evidence to support this story. The myth is that when Ponce de León saw the Native American Timucuans, he thought they were so tall, (he was barely 5 feet), and handsome with their high cheekbones, that it must be because of the purity of the water they were drinking. In the Spring House at the Archaeological Park, you can fill a paper cup with water from the Spring of Eternal Hope and each cup will add five years to your life. It did not taste very good, it had a sulfurous smell and taste, but I figured I had nothing to lose and it was free, so I drank five cups. I think Syl could only manage two, maybe three cups.

We also went to hear our friend Bruce, who was from Syracuse, but now living in Saint Augustine, play at a waterfront bar one night.

Ursula came to visit us in August, and one day we drove to Lakemont, for a reunion there. After retiring in June, 1995, my mom had done some substitute public school teaching for a couple of years and had even worked at a nursery school not far from her townhouse. She was now being a tour guide for the Erie Canal Park Boat Tours, a two-mile historic and educational excursion. She overheard a woman talking about a reunion in Lakemont, a place she said that nobody had heard of.

"That's not true. Lakemont was where we spent seven years, raised our family, and were probably the best years of my life."

The woman had a flyer that she gave to Mom and off we went. It was held on the lawn in front of the church where not only did Christians attend, but was also shared with the Mennonite population that had settled here now. Mom reunited with a woman friend who lived up the street from our old house, in the same house she lived in back when we left there in 1960. Ursula had a good time, as she loved meeting and talking with new people, and she also won three raffle prizes. I really didn't know anyone except one guy, who had never left Lakemont, but loved it there. It is a beautiful area. There was another guy who kept talking to me as if I was Marty. I had to keep reminding him that I was Marty's older brother.

Later in August, we went back up to Dorchester, Canada for the Canadian Championships of Senior Softball.

The last week in August we went to the New York State Fair, held annually in Syracuse. We had heard that President Bill Clinton was speaking at a luncheon there. It was a very hot and humid day as the crowd outside this building waited for him to come out. Several elderly women had to be treated for heat exhaustion. Art was with us and also feeling the effects of the heat and humidity, plus being a right-wing conservative, didn't care much for President Clinton anyway. He went and sat on a bench in the shade. Two hours later, people from the luncheon emerged, several of them MPH parents that we knew, but no President Clinton. We found out later that the Secret Service had taken him out the back door. He showed up at the Chicken Coop food stand within The Fair, but unless you were there before the police cordoned it off, you couldn't get in there to see him.

The next day we went out to our favorite park, Lakeside Park on Cazenovia Lake, to sit in the sun, have lunch, read, and swim in the lake. We had heard that President Clinton was going to attend a fundraiser for donors, at a house owned by MPH parents on Cazenovia Lake. This house was in the opposite direction of how we usually leave the park to drive back to our house. As we were leaving the park, I decided to take a chance and drive toward that house. As we approached, you could feel the atmosphere changing, as there were Police and Secret Service cars all around and a crowd had gathered across the street from this house. I parked the car and we got out and started walking toward the crowd. A woman friend of ours, and a MPH parent, waved to us from the front of the crowd. We waved back and proceeded to bypass the crowd and get up by her. No Police or Secret Service personnel stopped us or bothered to inspect the camera held by a strap around my neck, not your best security procedure. We waited for a while and finally President Clinton appeared, looking good with a tan and wearing a light blue long sleeve shirt. He crossed the street and shook hands and greeted everyone, starting from the back and working his way to the front where we were. Hillary was with him, but all the attention was on him. As he shook our hands, he was definitely giving Syl a visual double take. He got in his black limousine as the Secret Service guys closed the doors, but then he got out of the other side and waved to the crowd and some more photo opportunities, much to their dismay. It was still a really cool experience for us.

Syl and I started another school year, another fall, Thanksgiving, and Christmas, as another year had passed.

Y2K was an abbreviation for "year 2000" and as that year approached, many feared that computer programs storing year values as two-digit figures, such as 99, would cause worldwide problems; including the disruption of electricity, water services, food delivery, banking systems, and transportation. People were preparing for the apocalypse. It never happened.

Sylvia became fully aware of my nightmares soon after we started living together in the middle of August, 1983. She knew when to turn the lights on and calm me down, telling me, "Everything is okay, you were just having a nightmare." Sometimes I would relive a basketball or softball game that I had played in. Sometimes I would be laughing, which was a good sign. But more often than not, I would be screaming or running away from something. It seemed that they would occur when I was in a new or unfamiliar place, whether a guest in somebody's house or on vacation. I wouldn't have any for months, then I would have them for several nights in a row. I've startled plenty of people along the way, including family, friends, and obviously Syl.

I believe it all originated from a couple of near tragic childhood experiences that are evidently buried deep within my subconscious. Two of these are "Dusty's Lunchtime Stories," the first and second of these stories.

"Quicksand"

I was around five years old and our family lived in a house on Fairmount Avenue, off Buckley Road, in Liverpool, a northern suburb of Syracuse. There were several houses in the neighborhood, but at our end, there were only a few houses, with more being built. One of these was directly across the street from us. The builders had just poured the cement for the foundation and had ropes around it. There were no "Keep Off" signs, basically the ropes signifying this. A boy, the same age, who lived down the street, came over to play with me. I can visualize him, but I can't recall his name. It was a hot summer's day as we wandered across the street, wanting to see what was inside those ropes.

Curiosity got the best of me, as I stepped inside the ropes and boldly put a foot inside the wet cement. I tried to pull it out, but the cement was hardening around my right leg and I couldn't. I was trying to back out, but gravity forced my left leg forward and it also got stuck. All of a sudden, I started to sink in this wet cement like I was in quicksand. Not that I knew what that felt like, but I knew I now found myself in a very scary predicament. I started sinking down further, both legs covered up to my waist. I yelled for the boy to get some help for me. He didn't go over to my parent's house, as he didn't want me to "get into trouble." (Great logic, right? I guess that's how you think when you are only five years old.) He ran down the street looking for help. I was slowly sinking further into this "quicksand" of wet, but hardening cement, now covering me up to my chest. These are the kinds of accidents that you read about in the paper, where a child was unattended for just a minute and drowned in the pool. Or to read about me with an incident like this. I was panicking, and the more I struggled, the deeper I sank. *The only thing that was not covered now was my head.* Just then a man came with the boy.

My recollection is fuzzy whether he was related to the boy or just a man who lived down the street. But I can vividly see him like it was yesterday. He was a short, stocky man, definitely Italian. The top of his head was bald and glistening in the sun. He had let the hair on the sides and back of his head grow long. He was one of those guys that have hair growing uncontrollably out of their arms, back, chest, and legs. He wore shorts and a white tank top, his pot belly prominently displayed. Not hesitating, he stepped over the rope and reached down with all his strength and pulled me out. I'll never forget him. I think I got scolded by my parents for playing over there when you weren't supposed to. I never told them all the details, so as to not scare them anymore than what all parents worry about, something tragic happening to their children. This was the first of many near-death experiences that I have had, and the beginning of the origin of my nightmares.

"Falling Through The Ice"

The second story of "Dusty's Lunchtime Stories" was the closest near-death experience of my life, and an even more powerful subconscious origin of my nightmares. I was 10 years and 7 months old in late March, 1957, when a group of friends and I went to play ice hockey on a frozen pond, about a mile from our house in Lakemont. The pond was still frozen, but the outer edges were starting to melt, as spring was approaching. We put our skates on and played for a couple of hours. They all left when the sun was beginning to fade, as I decided to stay and practice a few more slap shots. Not a very wise decision. I told the kids to never go out on the ice alone, or for that matter, never swim in the ocean, lake, river, or pool alone; or climb, hike, or be in the woods by yourself.

I started skating around the pond, taking a few shots, when I got too close to the thin ice at the edge and fell in. I began to drift toward the center of the pond, becoming extremely disoriented. I knew that I had to turn my body around toward the direction of the hole that I had created when I fell in, but I kept drifting in the other direction. *I'll always remember looking up and seeing only ice and touching the frozen pond above me with my now waterlogged gloves.* Somehow, I still don't know how, for what seemed like an eternity, I managed to turn my body around and swim toward the opening and get out. Obviously, fate must have been smiling on me that day. My clothes, from head to toe, were totally soaked and frozen. It doesn't take long in these conditions to develop hypothermia, a condition when your core body temperature dips below 95 degrees.

Darkness was imminent as I held my boots in my arms and started running, with my frozen skates still on, across the field toward home. I could not feel my fingers to even attempt to untie the double knot laces of my skates. My legs felt like lead weights as I was literally frozen stiff.

Tears of anguish turned to icicles upon my face. Somehow, someway, I made it home.

My worried parents immediately leaped into action. They removed my wet and frozen clothes and put dry warm clothes: long thermal underwear, turtleneck, sweatpants, sweatshirt, sweater, heavy socks, winter hat, and gloves, on me; then wrapped blankets all around my shivering body and sat me near the fireplace with a blazing fire.
Mom brought me some hot soup and a grilled cheese sandwich. I was feeling a whole lot better than I was a while ago, that's for sure.

My fingers and toes did incur some frostbite, but fortunately not severe enough for any amputations. I still deal with the consequences of this incident, not only that the tips of my fingers become numb and tingly when the temperature dips below 40 degrees, and my feet can suffer these symptoms as well; but the psychological effects of being all alone under the ice, and the fear of drowning, creating the root cause of my nightmares.

Lost At Last

I reached out

Not knowing why

Groping blindly

Choking upon my hollow tongue

The wind howled

At the silent moon

Night shadows stop to watch

Waiting in the naked light

Retracing my steps

Near the cold dawn

Remembering those times

But now they are gone

It's closing hour

Sad, the year gone by

Muffled cries far away

Never to be heard

"Stories About My Brother"

This is the third story in "Dusty's Lunchtime Stories." My brother, Marty, and I had a great environment in our childhoods. We moved to Lakemont when I was a month past my 7th birthday and Marty was 2 years and 4 months old. He grew quickly, and within 3 years was hanging out with me, and pretty much doing all the things that I was doing. I had my own group of friends that I played football, basketball, and baseball with, but Marty and I did so many things together. We would run down through three miles of woods to get to Seneca Lake and go swimming. We would play tackle football in our front yard and whiffle ball home run derby over this hedgerow in our front yard. When the students at Lakemont Academy would go home on holidays and vacation breaks, we would have the whole gymnasium to ourselves. I would have Marty make 100 layups in a row, and if he missed, he would have to start all over again. This is Marty's recollection and reluctantly, but probably accurately, I would have to agree. Even though this was a big brother to little brother scenario, it made Marty into an excellent basketball player; both in high school, and years later, playing with me on many championship teams in local leagues.

  The first story within these stories was when we were playing sock baseball, using a pair of rolled-up socks as the baseball. You had to be creative in those days, as there were no nerf balls then. We would have loved to have had nerf balls. We also used rolled-up socks to play indoor basketball, shooting them into a piece of cardboard with a hole cut out of it and pinned to the wall. It was a rainy day, as we were restless and started to play a game of sock baseball. You used your fist to hit the rolled-up sock and then circled the "bases;" which consisted of touching the bed post on Marty's bed for first base, touching the far wall for second base, touching the bedpost on my bed for third base, and touching the window sill, in front of a window that led out to the roof, for home. There was a huge tree that hung over the roof. Mom had recently waxed the linoleum floor in our room. Marty was up as I pitched the rolled-up sock in. He swung and hit it deep into the hallway. I chased after it as he reached first, then second, and was rounding third and heading for home. I threw it at him as he ducked and slid for home. The window sill was only a foot off the floor and there was no screen in the window. What happened next was still visually one of the funniest things that I have ever seen, as long as he wasn't seriously injured. He slid so fast on the newly waxed floor that he went up and over the window sill and went flying out the window onto the roof. (The kids really laughed when I told them this part.) Dad had to get up on the ladder to get him down. He had scrapes on his chest and some bruises, but was okay. I can still see it today; it was like out of a cartoon.

  The second story within these stories came on a hot summer night in late August. Our team, the Dundee Hawks, had won the local Little League championship. We were having an end of the season picnic and having a game for fun with our younger Minor League team. There were a lot of older and younger brother combinations on both teams and all the parents were there enjoying the evening. Everyone was switching positions on our team and just playing nice and easy, not competitively, against our younger counterparts. It was getting late as I asked someone to come in and take my place as the catcher, the position that I played at this time. Nobody helped me out, as they didn't want to put on the mask, chest protector, and shin guards the catcher wears, on this hot and humid night. It was getting really hard to see as they announced that this would be the final batter.

  As fate would have it, it was Marty, who played for the Minor League team. The batboy, an overweight kid who just wanted to be a part of the team, went in to pitch. He could barely reach the plate. I got as close as I could to the batter, Marty, and leaned forward in order to try and catch his short pitches. He managed to throw one in and Marty, instead of stepping forward with his front foot, the proper way to hit a baseball, instead stepped *backwards* with his back foot, commonly called "stepping in the bucket;" and instead of making contact with the baseball, clocked me in the back of my head and knocked me out cold. When I came to, quite sometime later, (I still had the caught ball firmly entrenched inside my mitt), the concerned parents were all standing around me. There was no concussion protocol back then and I wasn't even taken to the hospital. Marty was really scared as some of my friends were saying to him, "Dusty is going to get you back for this." You know, the big brother to little brother syndrome in those days.

    This is the third and final story within these stories about my brother. I had this big lump on the back of my head for about two weeks after the baseball bat incident. Marty and I went across the little road in front of our house, that led to the school, Lakemont Academy, over to the athletic fields to play one on one baseball, with a real baseball. When Marty pitched to me, I would usually hit it to left field, and it would roll to where there was a wooden shed that stored mowers and tools for maintenance of the athletic fields. There were also bees that had a hive there that Marty wasn't too thrilled about chasing the ball near it.

    After a while, I guess he had enough of this. I don't know if it was deliberate, or his aim was off, but he pitched one in and hit me smack on my ear. As I screamed in pain, and also because of clocking me in the back of the head with the bat two weeks earlier; he was so scared at what I might do to him, he ran across the road and went inside the house to get a Bible. Holding my ear in pain, I made my way to the porch, where he was hiding behind Mom, and he started to read the 23rd Psalm:

"Yea, though I walk through the valley of the shadow of death, I will fear no evil."

The kids always got a kick out of this and laughed really hard.

Another big brother to little brother scenario. We somehow managed to live and play together throughout our childhoods and adulthoods and remain best friends to this day.

"Nightmares"

This is another one of "Dusty's Lunchtime Stories," actually two stories within the main story. I've told you about my two biggest nightmare stories, "Quicksand" and "Falling Through The Ice," and why they still cause me to have nightmares.

Another nightmare story, "Alien Dreams," was when I was a junior at Pebble Hill School. This was the name of the school before they merged with The Manlius School, a military academy, in 1970, to form Manlius Pebble Hill School, where Sylvia and I taught. Our family moved to Syracuse at the end of the summer of 1962, when I had just turned 16.

You know when you are having a dream, not necessarily a nightmare, and everything is so vivid and clear; and then just as you are about to wake up, the dream starts to fade away and you can only remember bits and pieces, fragments, of the dream? The kids, even at their young ages, knew what I was talking about. At least most of them. I always wanted to get up and write down what my dream was about when I was in this clear dream-like state, but it never seemed to happen. One night I was having a very vivid dream and woke up and told myself that I was going to write my dream down before it started to fade away. I went over to my desk, in the middle of the night, still in a dream-like state, and wrote down my dream. I was so proud of myself that I had finally accomplished this and maybe it would offer some clues and insight into my nightmares. I went back to bed and managed to fall asleep. When I woke up, I looked at my desk, now remembering that I had actually done this. There it was: three pages, with paragraphs, sentences with first letters capitalized, spaces between words, punctuation including periods. But not one word was an actual word as we know words.

It was: "Xypt bwsy nmcv qlkj psda rghv."

The kids looked as astonished at me as I did when I first saw what I had written. (I wrote this one sentence down in the back of an address book at this time.) Was this a secret code for something? Did aliens come and abduct me and force me to write this down? Or instruct me to write this down? What did it all mean? I should have kept these three pages somewhere. Maybe they are buried amongst all the things I have saved over the years and still need to sort out. But I doubt it. I was afraid someone would discover it and think I was very weird, especially being a new student in school. I didn't think that it was in my best interest to tell anyone about this. I could fake it now and make it up and just recreate it, but I'm not like that. I know that *this really did happen.*

The second "Lunchtime Story," "Stopping the Train," in "Nightmares;" was one night when Syl and I were sleeping in our bed and I was having a bad dream. I dove across the bed and on top of Mrs. Heer. (I always referred to Sylvia as Mrs. Heer at school or when telling these "Lunchtime Stories.")

Some of the younger kids didn't even know that we were married, as everyone knew me as "Dusty." It was just an easy name to say. They tried to say Mr. Heer sometimes, but got confused and it came out,

"Mr. He, Dus, I mean Mr. Dusty."

I would say, "It's either Mr. Heer or Dusty. 'Mr. Dusty' would be a good name for a vacuum cleaner."

Sometimes when we would say hello at Extended Day and give each other a kiss, some of the kids that didn't know we were married would say,

"I saw Dusty kissing Mrs. Heer."

Sylvia woke up and exclaimed,

"What are you doing?"

"I'm saving you from the train."

As if I could dive across the railroad tracks and stop the train! What, did I think that I was Superman in my dream? But this seemed so clear to me that this was happening in real time.

Sylvia calmed me down and I went back to sleep. She had to appreciate the idea that I would go to any lengths to protect and save her from any type of danger, but these were the kinds of unexpected things that she had to deal with when I drifted off into my dream world.

These were four of my "Lunchtime Stories," plus the three I told earlier on our vacation in Antigua in April, 1986; seven so far, halfway through the total "appropriate" stories.

I went to Morocco in November, 1969, with two college friends, Tomás and "Catman;" who were both local guys from where I went to college, the University of Wisconsin, in Madison, Wisconsin. They were pretty good friends, but I had a group of closer friends that I hung around with. I knew Tomás from playing on a softball team with him. He wasn't Hispanic, he was actually Irish Catholic; he got his name from a Spanish class in high school, and it stuck with him. "Catman's" real name was Pat, he was a hockey player and I guess his cat-like moves on the ice earned him his nickname.

After the Woodstock Festival, I returned to Syracuse in the last week of August, 1969 and worked with a landscaping crew from then until the middle of October. I always knew guys who were looking for extra help mowing and raking leaves, as the summer help had gone back to college. I probably should have gone back as well, but I just had this wanderlust, this free spirit to travel, to explore the world, much to my parents' disappointment. I went out to Madison to visit some friends and see if there were others who felt the same way that I did. This is where Tomás and "Catman" came in, as they were on the same wavelength as I was. Actually, the original trio included another guy on our softball team named Mike, nicknamed "East." He had graduated the year before, and was just hanging out on campus, taking some time off before he knew he would go back to his hometown, St. Louis, and begin a lifelong business career. He was an heir to the Anheuser-Busch empire, so his future was pretty much secured. We all started exchanging ideas and came up with a plan to go to Europe. That is what I had been looking for, a new frontier. "Catman" really wanted to go, but at this time had no money to make it a reality. We agreed to book our own flights and meet at JFK airport in New York City the first week in November.

They really didn't know me that well, just a guy from Syracuse they played softball and had a few beers with, and who had gone to Woodstock. They had no guarantees, except a verbal one and a handshake, that I would show up on time at the airport. Nor did I for that matter. There were no cell phones or Internet. I remember flying down to JFK and not knowing to take the shuttle over to get the international flight. The weather was raw, cold and windy, as I went outside into the elements with only a light jacket and no hat or gloves, carrying my suitcase; walking all the way to a distant terminal, freezing my ears and fingers and everything else off. If memory serves me correctly, we missed our flight, but they were nice enough to wait for me. I'm sure they had their doubts, but they were glad to see me.

We all had bought round trip tickets to London for around $300. I washed dishes at the Hotel Syracuse Country House for two weeks after I got back from Madison; and also sold my record album collection and some old golf clubs, for spending money. Luckily, there was a later flight and we flew to London. We stayed there for three days, sightseeing and walking around. I remember throwing a frisbee around in Hyde Park when a "Bobby," a slang term for a member of London's Metropolitan Police, derived from the name of Sir Robert Peel, who established the force in 1829; came over to us, (I can still see him now), and said,

"No propelling objects in the park, lads."

"East" was handling things better than we were at this point. I couldn't understand the way the Londoners spoke, with their cockney accent, in asking for directions or ordering food. "East" was on top of this and figuring out the restaurant bills, with the pounds and shillings and pence, better than us. We were staying in a cheap rooming house and left a note for "Catman" on the information bulletin board there at the airport and at the rooming house.

On the second night, I overheard "East" talking with Tomás about spending a few more days in London and then flying back home. This probably stemmed from a conversation that they had during the day when "East" asked him about where we might be going after London. We had made no definitive plans before embarking on this journey, basically just "winging it," making it up as we went. Tomás told him that he just wanted to get to where it was warm, head south toward Spain and maybe into Morocco. There was a friend of Tomás' from Madison that had been to Morocco in the summer and said it was amazing. I think the thought of going there and the unknown caused great concern for "East." I pretended I was sleeping as he tried to convince Tomás to return back home with him. I couldn't believe that I was hearing this. There was no way that I was going to go back home after a few days in London; not after landscaping, washing dishes, selling things, to scrape up enough money to get to Europe in the first place. I was at least going to hang around London, maybe even take the ferry to France and back, until my money ran out. I had my plane ticket to get back home.

They weren't too concerned about what my plans might be, but Tomás was not about to go back home after a few days in London either. "East" went to call his father from the pay phone at the rooming house. I think he was looking for some reassurance from his father that he was making the right decision about returning home, but instead his father wanted him to "act like a man" and face the unknown. I guess the prospect of the unknown was too much for him to handle at this time. The next day "East" took a taxi to Heathrow airport and returned home. We couldn't believe it. I never saw him again.

But more astonishing than that, the next day when we were figuring out where to go and how to proceed, "Catman" shows up at the rooming house! Don't ask me how he found us, there were no cell phones or Internet, so I am clueless on how this happened. The only explanation was that when he left Madison, Tomás had told "Catman" to check the information board at the airport. You know how those things usually go, but this time the information led him to the rooming house and to us. I guess he had finally managed to get some loans from several friends and here he was!

The next day, "Catman," Tomás, and I took the train from London to the "White Cliffs of Dover," white chalk cliffs rising 350 feet from the sea, a region of 8 miles of English coastline, facing the Strait of Dover and France. We took the shuttle to the ferry terminal and then rode the ferry to Calais, France, about an hour and a half to cross the 26 miles of the English Channel; the body of water that separates southern England from northern France, and links the southern part of the North Sea to the Atlantic Ocean. It is the busiest shipping area in the world.

We rented a car, a Simca, in Calais and then drove 182 miles south to Paris, arriving at night 3 hours later. We spent the next day walking around, had dinner, and then decided to leave at night and drive 316 miles north to Amsterdam. We drove 126 miles to the border in Brussels, Belgium, and continued on to Amsterdam. We walked around Amsterdam for a few days, but it was getting really cold now. We decided to head south and drive to Algeciras, Spain, 24 hours of driving time to cover over 1,500 miles. We drove all through the night, 11 hours, 675 miles south from Amsterdam to Bordeaux, stopped there for a while; and then drove over 7 more hours, 430 miles south to Madrid. We spent the day there, after sleeping for the night. From Madrid, we drove the final over 6 hours, 410 miles south to Algeciras, a port city and the largest city on the Bay of Gibraltar, where we spent the night.

The next day we boarded the ferry with our car for the two-hour, 40 miles trip across the Strait of Gibraltar, which connects the Atlantic Ocean to the Mediterranean Sea, to Tangier, Morocco. The Rock of Gibraltar is impressive, made of limestone and jutting out of the Strait, 1,400 feet high.

"Hercules Caves"

This is another one of "Dusty's Lunchtime Stories." The Rock of Gibraltar is one of the two Pillars of Hercules, the other Pillar being Jebel Musa in Morocco, on the African side of the Strait. In ancient times, the two points marked the limit of the known world. It was thought that these caves served as a resting place for the Roman God, Hercules, while he was performing his "Twelve Labors."

Legend has it that Hercules stayed here before doing his "Eleventh Labor," which was to get golden apples from the Hesperides Garden. Instead of having to cross the great Atlas Mountain, Hercules used his superhuman strength to smash through it, connecting the Atlantic Ocean to the Mediterranean Sea, and formed the Strait of Gibraltar.

"Catman," Tomás, and I drove one day to Cape Spartel, 9 miles west of Tangier, to the Caves of Hercules. The cave has two openings, one to sea and one to land. The sea opening is known as "The Map of Africa," believed to have been created by the Phoenicians, which is in the shape of Africa when looked at from the sea. When we got there, it was past the closing time of 4 o'clock in the afternoon. There was a big chain blocking the entrance. We decided to step over the chain and climb up to the top. I was wearing cowboy boots, not the smartest footwear for climbing. You wouldn't want to slip and plunge 1,000 feet and crash on the huge boulders protruding from the sea down below. We were nervous, but young and foolish, and kept going. I remember passing along a small camera and taking pictures once we entered the cave. We probably didn't have the flash on, but either way, none of the pictures came out. You could hear the deafening roar of the mighty ocean and see the effects of millions of years of waves pounding in and out of the entrance of the cave to form beds, benches, and chairs made of stone. You could visualize Hercules resting here.

It was getting late and the sun was setting on the beach where the Atlantic Ocean meets the Mediterranean Sea, where the only person that you could see for miles was a man riding his donkey packed with supplies. We now realized there was no way that we could return the same way we came. We kept going until we were just about at the end, when appearing out of nowhere, deep inside the caves, were all these eyes that made us jump a few feet off the ground. They posed no danger to us, they were "holy men," around 30 of them, wearing nothing but white loincloths and turbans; staring out at the sea and preparing to die. They were no longer eating, only meditating, beginning their spiritual journey toward eternity.

We started our return trip, feeling our way among the rocks in darkness, somehow making it back in one piece; although we had many bumps and bruises and cuts on our arms, hands, and shins when we finally got back to the parking lot where the car was. We stayed in Tangier for another month or so before returning home. We rode camels, sipped mint teas in the market in Medina in the afternoons, and walked around the mazes of black cats in the alleys, listening to the sounds of the wailing music at night in this mysterious city.

I went back to Europe in early May, 1970, traveling with one of my closest friends, Steve, who I've known since 1963, and remain close friends today. We left right at the time of the shootings of unarmed college student protesters by the Ohio National Guard at Kent State University. This was a time of great turmoil in our country: with the Vietnam War and all the protests, including the Democratic National Convention in Chicago in 1968; now this; President Nixon and the Watergate break in and scandal, still to come. We flew from New York City to Madrid, with intentions to return to Tangier, Morocco. While waiting in Madrid for a few hours before our flight, we were sitting in this small park with a wrought iron fence around it. I was taking a nap, with my back up against the fence on this hot and sunny day, when I felt the sharp point of a bayonet in my back. It was one of Dictator Franco's policemen telling me,

"You need to have a shirt on to stay in the park."

I was wearing a tank top and said to him that this was a shirt. He told me that this was *not* a shirt and to leave the park. I wasn't about to argue with him and we left the park. This is what we were dealing with in those days.

We flew to Tangier and they would not let us in unless we cut our hair. They were under orders from the United States Government to screen "all hippie types" from entering Morocco. Our hair was not really that long, we've had much longer hair since then. It was curly, not looking like businessmen by any means, but not really ridiculous either. We took the ferry from Ceuta, a Spanish city on the north coast of Africa, 25 miles from Algeciras, and tried to enter Morocco from there; but that didn't work either, unless we cut our hair. Steve would have if I did, but it was the principle of the thing to me at this time and I refused to do it, much to Steve's disappointment. At least he could say he was actually in Africa and crossed the Strait of Gibraltar and saw the Rock of Gibraltar.

"Frisbee Trilogy"

This is another one of "Dusty's Lunchtime Stories." Throwing a frisbee around at the beach, park, or wherever, was a staple activity for us and our friends. We never went anywhere without a "fris." Steve and I took two frisbees with us for our trip, figuring that would be sufficient to carry us through the spring and summer. The frisbee craze started in California in 1964, but it hadn't reached any widespread popularity in Europe; as I mentioned before, with the English "Bobby" coming up to us in Hyde Park and telling us, "No propelling objects in the park, lads," on the previous trip.

We had returned to Algeciras, trying to figure out where we were going next. We started throwing the frisbee around in the streets; over the head tosses, curving it from left to right and right to left tosses, catching it behind the back and between the legs. A crowd began to gather, girls in their balconies checking us out, and their boyfriends not too thrilled about it. We were having fun and loving it. A large group of young boys started following us around and they led us to a soccer field. We were showing them how to throw the frisbee and then told them to run really far and we would throw it to them. When it came time to catch it, they would let it drop and then started to kick it around like a soccer ball. I guess we should have expected it. The only problem was that in kicking it so much, they put a big crack in it, almost splitting it in two. We had some athletic tape and patched it up.

Steve and I stayed in Malaga, Spain for almost a week and then took a train to Rome. We now had a taped up frisbee and the remaining unused one. This is part two of the trilogy. We went to a park one day and started throwing the frisbee around, doing our usual routines. Again, a crowd of people gathered, watching us intently, as this was something that they had never seen before. Out of the corner of my eye, I noticed a young boy, who was crippled and was forced to wear heavy metal leg braces, watching us with total amazement. You could sense that he enjoyed watching us, but would have given anything to do what we were doing, just being able to walk would have obviously been enough. That put everything in perspective and we walked over to him and gave him the frisbee.

The kids always asked, "Did you give him the taped up frisbee?"

"No, we gave him the new frisbee."

The kids liked that. The look on the boy's face was one of astonishment and gratitude and one that I'll always remember to this day. I hope that one day some medical breakthrough happened for him and they found a cure that allowed him to walk. We'll never know, but for that brief moment in the afternoon in the park in Rome, we were able to bring a little ray of sunshine into his life.

We took day trips by train to Florence, Venice, Pisa, and Milan. After spending the day walking around Milan, we got on a late afternoon train to take the three-hour trip back to Rome, to arrive before dark. We showed our tickets and then walked to the back of the train, to the very last car, to see if we could just sleep and wake up in Rome. It was hot outside and not much cooler inside. We fell asleep and when we awoke and looked outside, all we saw were the vast trainyards of Milan! Rubbing our eyes in disbelief and looking out again, it was apparent that this was a reality. This car had been disconnected and we were not part of the train. It almost felt like this was deliberate, considering the hassles we had encountered in Spain and Morocco. We were never given any warning that this would happen or any explanation why it did happen. We had to walk through the trainyards in the heat and wait several hours for the next train back to Rome, not arriving until late at night. We didn't sit in the last car of any train ever again.

We had someone take a picture of us throwing a frisbee in front of the Colosseum. (I still have this picture.) After a few more days in Rome, we decided to take a train to Copenhagen, Denmark, a scenic 24 hours, 950 miles north journey. It remains my favorite city with its Tivoli Gardens, The Little Mermaid Statue, castles, palaces, museums, canals, and lakes. You can go down Hans Christian Andersen Boulevard and be greeted by friendly shopkeepers and buy *real* Danish pastries. The Strøget, "the walking street," is a famous three-quarter mile stretch, pedestrian friendly, with no motorized vehicles allowed; with many shops and a popular hangout for the city's street performers. At Amagertorv Square, you can see performances by acrobats, magicians, and musicians. One day there was a commotion as this guy was walking down the Strøget in July, wearing a lime green jumpsuit, covered in rhinestones, with a high collar, and surrounded by his entourage. It was Liberace, and that was a sight to see!

We went to a park one day and started throwing the taped up frisbee around. This is the third and final part of the "Frisbee Trilogy." Once again, we attracted a group of people watching us do our thing. I can't remember who threw it, but it was a wayward toss that landed in the middle of this pond in the park. I would have dived in the pond, not even caring what was in it, to get the frisbee, if using a long stick to retrieve it had proven to be unsuccessful. Just as we were mulling over our options, this great white egret swooped down on the pond and grabbed the frisbee in its mouth. Realizing that this was not something that it wanted to eat, the egret proceeded to drop the frisbee over the cliff, as we watched in disbelief! These were the days of no Internet, cell phones or Federal Express. By the time we could have written a letter to someone back home to send us additional frisbees, we would have been ready to return to the United States. So now we were relegated to taking rolled up socks, like Marty and I used to do in our childhood bedroom, to throw into trash containers, simulating playing basketball; or to kick around, like an early Western version of the hacky-sack, which wasn't invented until 1972, and didn't gain national popularity until the early 1980's.

Steve was always up early and gone before me, never leaving a message as to his whereabouts. He enjoyed being mysterious and is still like this today. One morning, 5 o'clock in the morning, he had gone down to an all-night coffee shop to bring back some pastries. There he met an Englishman, from Kent, England, named Colin, but he went by "Digby." He had lost his passport, had no money or shoes. Steve befriended him and brought him back to our hotel. We gave him an extra pair of sneakers and he just started hanging out with us. "Digby" was pencil thin and had these big clear green eyes. He was like a chameleon; he could be in the park and just blend in with the trees. He told us that he had names for all the trees in Hyde Park. He also told us that all he wanted to do in his life was to play bass with Jimi Hendrix.

We had met some girls in the park, Lulu and Viva, who had invited us to join them and their friends for a home-cooked meal. Lulu was half Inuit and half Danish. Her Danish father was a fisherman who had fished up in Greenland and met Lulu's Inuit mother there. They took us hiking in the woods and they would know to tell you which flowers and berries that you could eat and which ones you could not. They took us to Dyrehaven, commonly known as "Deer Park," a forest park 8 miles north of Copenhagen, with huge ancient oak trees. It has herds of 2,100 deer: 1,700 Fallow Deer, 300 Red Deer, and 100 Sika Deer. If you are really quiet and still, and out of sight, you can get within 20 yards of them and watch two stags battling it out for dominance of the herd; charging full speed at each other, smashing their heads together with their huge antlers entwined. The sights and sounds were incredible.

When we visited Lulu and Viva and their friends, "Digby" had nothing to bring over, so he went around and washed everyone's feet as his contribution. He was definitely one of a kind. One day, out of the clear blue, some friends of his from England found out where he was staying, just how "Catman" had found us on the previous European trip. They had a van, a new passport, clothes, sneakers, a supply of tea, and were headed to India. "Digby" hugged us, expressed how grateful he was for taking him in, got in the van and was gone. We never saw him again, but think of him often.

We took a 228 miles north bus trip with the girls to Frederikshavn, and then another 25 miles to Skagen, Denmark's northernmost town on the Jutland Peninsula, known as "the top of Denmark," where Viva's parents lived. We were all hanging out in the little guest house behind the main house when Viva's parents summoned her. They decided that they weren't too thrilled with their 18-year-old daughter and her 18-year-old best friend being with two American guys and wanted us to leave. Like *immediately*. We really didn't have any bad intentions, just laughing and talking with them; basically, continuing on to our next destination. It was an uncomfortable situation there and we knew there was no alternative but to leave. *Immediately*. Steve and I walked down this road and somehow found a bus out there, in the middle of nowhere, to Frederikshavn.

We then decided to go to Norway and hopped on a ferry to Oslo; a cold, windy, 12-hour excursion across the rough and choppy North Sea. We took a train to Lillehammer, who eventually hosted the 1994 Winter Olympics, and found a cabin there. It was chilly up there, mid-50's some days, even in the summer. Unbeknownst to us, the sun doesn't set until 11 at night and rises before 3 in the morning. There is a place way up by the Arctic Circle, where the sun sets at midnight and almost immediately rises again, thereby having an equal amount of 12 hours each of sunlight and darkness. I had bought the newly released cassette of the Beatles' "Let it Be" in Oslo. When we were listening to it that night, with no clocks or watches around, we didn't realize it was such a late sunset or such an early sunrise, and couldn't believe we had been listening to it for what we thought was an incredibly long time.

Lulu and Viva later joined us in Lillehammer and then we took a 10-hour boat ride across the North Sea to Hamburg, Germany. There was this large group of tough-looking Norwegian sailors that kept staring at Steve and me. One had a pair of fingernail clippers that he pointed to his head, and then to us, while we were all out on the open front deck. It was a very awkward and nervous predicament, as they were drinking more and more, and singing, more like bellowing, their seafaring songs louder and louder. We avoided their stares and eventually moved away from them to the lower deck when most of them had passed out. We were so glad to get off that boat unscathed and hitchhiked to the Hamburg train station, where we boarded a train going to Amsterdam.

The 6 hours, 230 miles south train ride was going along smoothly, winding its way through the German countryside; when these German police officials, dressed like they were right out of a World War II movie, came aboard at the German-Holland border asking for tickets and passports. We all showed them our tickets and handed them our passports, not worried about anything, as we were legal citizens of our countries and not carrying any illegal drugs or anything. That all changed quickly, as they conferred with each other and then with stern faces and voices, ordered all of us off the train. They separated the girls from us and took us to these small interrogation rooms, making us feel like we were in Nazi Germany. Not like we were there, obviously, but we could imagine what it must have been like. They started interrogating us, pointing to this stamp in our passports.

"Was ist das?"

They were pointing to this MASTURBEE stamp, in red ink, prominently stamped in each of our passports. I remembered that "Digby" had such a stamp and had obviously stamped our passports with this. He was not a mean person, I guess he thought it was funny or something to remember him by. I never knew what it meant then, he never told us anything about it, and I still don't know what it is supposed to mean today. They became even more adamant now,

"Was ist das MASTURBEE stamp? Was country ist das?"

We found out later that the girls were crying and really scared, not knowing what was going on. Finally, I said to a policeman who spoke English,

"Look, we don't know either. We just hand our passports over to the officials as we enter a new country. We have no clue what this stamp is or why it was put there."

Eventually, and reluctantly, they let us go. We boarded another train, as these guys eyeballed us all the way until we arrived in Amsterdam.

We spent several days in Amsterdam, walking around and exploring the city, and then it was time for us to say our good-byes and fly back home.

"Desert Cactus"

This is another one of "Dusty's Lunchtime Stories." I was living in Tucson, Arizona in 1971 and one day went horseback riding with my friend Ray, from Syracuse, who had been living in Tucson for several years. We asked the guys who owned the horse ranch how far we were allowed to take them.

"Just don't take them all the way to Phoenix."

It was a typical late winter Tucson day, sunny with a beautiful blue sky and mild temperatures. We took our shirts off and tied bandanas around our heads and rode off into the desert. Everything was calm and peaceful, until suddenly my horse started bucking violently and threw me off, right into this cactus that had these long spikes sticking out. Out of nowhere, we could see the reason that he became spooked. It was a rattlesnake, coiled and rattling its tail, sounding like castanets, sounding its alarm. We moved away from it and kept our distance, as it retreated back into its hole, that we must have ridden over.

Fortunately, I was wearing jeans, as I had a bunch of these long spikes in my butt. (Kids always get a kick out of the word butt; they can't help it. Just like the Pre-Kers and Kindergarteners can't stop laughing when you say underwear. Eventually they move on from underwear, yet butt remains a constant for laughs.)

I pulled the cactus spikes, one by one, from my butt through the jeans, each one as painful as the next. I had serious puncture wounds and it took me several weeks to heal up. Any type of encounter with cacti is usually not a pleasant one. Ray had been spared, but we soon realized that my horse had 20 or more of these spikes in the soft velvet of his nose. We threw a shirt over his eyes and had to hold the reins, as he was bucking and resisting us trying to pull the spikes from his nose. We took turns between holding the reins and pulling the spikes out. After a while, even as painful as it was for him, he realized that we were trying to help him and calmed down a little, but this was still a long ordeal to pull out all the spikes.

We walked the horses all the way back to the stables, where we explained what had happened. They said that we had done the right thing and were appreciative of how we handled the situation. They put some ointment on the horse's nose and led him to his, we're sure, eagerly awaited stall.

"Stepping On A Sea Porcupine"

Another one of "Dusty's Lunchtime Stories." This story has elements of both the last two "Lunchtime Stories," these being the frisbee and sharp spiked objects from nature. It was the winter of 1973 and I was living with some friends in Coconut Grove, Florida. One warm and picture-perfect day, I went with a friend of mine, "Bush," to Crandon Park, an urban park in Miami, on the northern part of Key Biscayne. We were throwing a frisbee around on the beach when "Bush" threw one way over my head and into the ocean. He was making no effort to go and get it.

I said, "Go get it. You made the bad toss."

He said, "You go get it. It's your frisbee."

I don't know why he was being so difficult about this. It was kind of an unwritten rule that the person who made the bad toss went and got it, especially when it involved landing far away from shore out in the ocean. After bantering for a while, we made the totally stupid decision to both go running in the ocean, at the same time, to retrieve it. I mean, he should have gone after it in the first place; but we could have at least shot fingers, odd or even, or flipped a coin, or something other than the illogical decision that we came up with. It wasn't like this was the last taped up frisbee and we were over in Europe like Steve and I were. And frisbees only cost $3 in those days, so that wasn't it either. I guess the best explanation about getting it and not leaving it out in the ocean, at least from my point of view, was I didn't want to see any ocean creature die from swallowing it or something.

You know how when you look out into the ocean and there's a big area of clear blue-green water, and then beyond that there is this area of dark, murky water? Well, that's where the frisbee was. We both ran full blast into the ocean, at the same time, until we got to the dark and murky area. I grabbed the frisbee and we both started to run back, when I felt this excruciating pain in my right foot, as if I had just stepped on a bed of thorns. Actually, I had. I soon found out that I had the misfortune of stepping on a sea urchin, or "sea porcupine." Nothing happened to "Bush," of course. I made it to shore and people started gathering around, making all sorts of suggestions.
There were at least 20, three-inch spikes, "quills," with barbed hooks on each end, in the bottom of my foot.

The lifeguard came over and was trying to use a fingernail clipper to break the skin and get them out. That wasn't working, as the skin around the quills was forming an impenetrable wall. Others tried tweezers, again to no avail. Someone even tried breaking the skin with their Swiss Army Knife, and that failed also. Finally, I said that I'd had enough of this poking around and just wanted to go home. I figured that if I stayed off of it and soaked my foot in hot water with Epsom salts, the skin would soften enough so I could get the quills out. The area around each of the quills was now purple, apparently from the venom, as the urchin that I had stepped on, "to add insult to injury," was venomous. There are 950 species of sea urchins, inhabiting all oceans and depth zones. Not all of them are venomous, maybe only 10 species. Well, I stepped on one of those 10. I kept soaking my foot for three days, but as each day passed, my foot was getting more and more swollen. It was beginning to look like I had elephantiasis or something. Now I began to get worried, as this venom could cause paralysis or a serious infection that could even lead to death. I was thinking that I should probably go to the hospital, which I was trying to avoid, as I had very limited financial resources and no medical insurance.

    One of my friends knew this guy who was a deep-sea diver and told him about my situation. He came over to see me and told me that he had plenty of experience in getting poisoned by sea urchins. He wore fins while diving, so he didn't step on them. But he has brushed up against them, as they hide in coral reefs. He said vinegar is sometimes helpful, but with the number of quills and the advanced stage I was now in, there was only one solution; and we needed to start this right away or there could be dire consequences. This solution was soaking in *pure ammonia.* (Your normal household cleaning solutions are only 10% ammonia.) So, we had two buckets, one filled with 100% ammonia and the other with cold water. I would soak my foot in the ammonia for a minute, as long as I could stand the burning sensation. Then into the cold water for several minutes. This process was repeated, day and night, for three days, until the skin was starting to peel off my foot. But you could see the purple venom starting to fade and the hard circles around the quills softening. Eventually we were able to get tweezers on the barbs of the quills and pull them out, one by one. My foot was very sore for weeks, as we applied antibiotic ointment on the puncture wounds. But it was a great feeling of relief to have the quills finally out, and the end result could have been much worse.

"The Almost South American Plane Crash"

This is another one of "Dusty's Lunchtime Stories." In November, 1978, I flew down to Santa Cruz, Bolivia to visit some friends and explore the possibility of starting a business of buying and importing woven hats, socks, gloves, and alpaca coats and sweaters. The flight from Miami to La Paz, over 3,000 miles, almost 7 hours, was beautiful on a sunny day flying over the Andes Mountains. People had told me that you get a headache in the middle of your forehead as you get off the plane at the airport in La Paz, because of its elevation: 13,325 feet above sea level; making it the highest international airport in the world. I found this to be true.

I went to board the flight from La Paz to Santa Cruz, when all these people made a mad dash to show their tickets and board. When I got there, they said the plane was full and I had to take the next plane, even though I had my ticket for this flight. I guess they overbooked and it was pretty much a first come, first serve, type of deal. I don't think this would happen today, but it did then. I waited for the next flight, and this time I boxed out people trying to storm passed me, like a basketball player trying to secure a rebound; and made sure I was not going to miss this flight. One hour to cover 340 miles and I was there. Spent a week in Santa Cruz, visiting national parks and botanical gardens, as well as attending this music festival, which was spectacular. Every group was amazing, some even sounded like Santana.

One day I took a bus ride with all the native people, to check out a village at the top of this mountain road, where they sold all kinds of colorful woven hats, socks, alpaca coats and sweaters. There would be three or four buses, directly behind each other, on a narrow road with a gigantic drop off on one side to the valley below, and the mountain on the other side. The bus driver would just be basically in neutral, not using any brakes, as people that were getting off near the small towns where they lived, would just get out and bump up against the mountain wall, which was just a few feet from the bus. The drivers obviously know what they are doing, as they do this every day, but any mishap or rolling back into the other buses would set off a chain reaction that would be catastrophic. It was a "Dead Man's Curve" feeling.

I flew back to La Paz and had to wait there for the next flight that went from there, with a stop in Lima, Peru, and then on to Mexico City. I got on the plane and sat behind a young man in his mid-twenties. We struck up a conversation and he told me that he was a photographer from Chile. We watched in total amazement and disbelief as two groups of passengers boarded the plane. One group was around 50 men in military uniforms, with all sorts of medals on them, and all of them wearing guns. They were all being subservient to this one-man wearing sunglasses and having the most medals. Joaquin told me that this was the military dictator, Padilla, from a recent military coup. Bolivia had a very unstable government throughout the

1960's, 1970's, and into the early 1980's, with many military coups and dictators. The other group was even larger, over 100 Mennonites; men, women, and children relocating from Bolivia to start a new farming community in Mexico. The men wore light blue shirts with black suspenders, black trousers, and straw hats. The women wore white blouses, light blue full-length dresses and light blue bonnets. Two seats to the left and in front of me was a young mother with her young son; they, along with Joaquin and me, being the only four people, beside the pilots and crew, that weren't a member of these two large groups. This would be a long 2 hours, 670 miles flight.

    A Mennonite man sat down next to me in the middle seat, as I was in the window seat, and his wife, holding their baby, next to him in the aisle seat. As we were preparing for takeoff, he leaned next to me and literally started to smell me, putting his nose in my armpit. I gave him a look and he backed away. I had short hair, had showered, and was dressed nicely, with a short-sleeved dress shirt, casual dress pants, and clean socks and casual dress shoes. I don't think they used deodorant, if anything, they smelled a little funky. Maybe they weren't used to someone that used deodorant. Then the baby started crying when we got up in the air, and he took the baby from his wife, and grabbed him and started violently shaking him. It was a very strange scene as Joaquin and I looked on in astonishment. This went on for over a minute, as we were wondering if we should intervene and stop him. Finally, the baby stopped crying and he handed him back to his wife. I wouldn't want to be that child, or any child or young girl or woman for that matter, growing up in that environment; as they are required to walk *behind* the men.

    A storm was brewing as we flew over the Andes heading for the Lima, Peru airport. This was the scariest flight that I have ever been on, and I have been on plenty of planes experiencing serious turbulence caused by fog, rain, snow, and wind gusts. Lightning flashes illuminated the sky and the plane, crackling dangerously close to us. Joaquin and I looked at each other with the same thought, that if we were going to go down, we couldn't believe it was with these two groups of people. I have to admit that I was definitely scared. The only thing that kept my fear away was the young woman two seats in front and to the left of me, shaking with fear and holding on to her son for dear life. I went up to comfort her and kept telling her that everything would be okay, although the way things were going, I wasn't sure that this would be true. The plane was swerving way to the left and then to the right, barely missing the mountains, with lightning constantly flashing all around us. I guess the Bolivian pilots are used to these dangers and are almost like kamikaze pilots. Somehow, they managed, with a harrowing landing, to bring the plane into the Lima airport.

 We had to spend a couple of days and nights in Lima, until these storms were totally out of the area, as the Peruvian pilots are much more cautious than the Bolivian pilots. Eventually we flew the 6 hours, 2,650 miles into Mexico City and it was an incredible scene; as the customs officials had to not only check all the guns from the military guys, but then the nightmare of going through hundreds of burlap bags of farming tools like pitchforks, shovels, and hoes, from the Mennonites. This was like back in those days and for a lot of years when they permitted smoking on planes. Can you believe they ever allowed it, with all that jet fuel on board? Smoking on domestic airliners, based in the United States, was banned on all domestic flights with a duration of 2 hours or less, in 1988. It took 12 more years to ban smoking on all domestic and international flights in 2000. It's incredible, when you really think about it, that there weren't any catastrophic events as a result of this former policy.

    I went back to Austin, Texas where I had a small apartment. I played basketball in Adams Park with a group of regulars, and after playing for hours in the heat and humidity, we would go over to Barton Springs Pool in Zilker Park, where we would cool off in the natural spring fed water. As I mentioned earlier, I returned to Syracuse in July, 1979. I wish I would have met Sylvia then, but it wasn't meant to be until four years later.

2000

April: Charleston, South Carolina

June: Sodus Bay, NY (Chimney Bluffs)

July: Padanaram MA

    Cape Cod (Cape View Motel)

       Truro (Highland Light)

       Provincetown (Whale Watch)

August: Dorchester, London, Ontario, Canada

    It was the year 2000 now, all the 1900's were in the past. Syl and I had been together for 16 years and 9 months now; as we went down to visit Ursula and Ben, her sister

Debbie, and the rest of Syl's family in Charleston, in April over the school Spring Break. This was our fifth visit to Charleston: February in 1994, and each April in 1996, 1997, and 1998. It was always nice to feel the warm air and see the springtime blooms of azaleas, camellias, daffodils, dogwoods, flowering pear, honeysuckle, jasmine, roses, tea olive, and wisteria. We had survived yet another tough winter, but we always knew there would be many more to come.

Where Hell Froze Over

Three-thirty in the afternoon

The sun decides to make a guest appearance

Hangs around for an hour or so

Can't stay too long

Must meet its curfew

Silently slips behind the hills

Punches out for the day

As dusk arrives for the night shift

And the show continues

Ice-packed snow

Coldly crunches

Beneath my aimless steps

A slow, sad murmur

With no place left to go

Whips through the naked trees

Lost inside the depth of winter

I think even Jack Frost

Would be afraid to visit here

    In June, we took a day trip to Chimney Bluffs State Park, on the southern shore of Lake Ontario, east of Sodus Bay, NY. The park is named for the large clay formations at the water's edge that we could see from the hiking trails. We visited the Sodus Point Lighthouse, originally built in 1824 and rebuilt in 1870, and the small museum inside.

    In July, it was back to Cape Cod, stopping in Padanaram, MA, about an hour from the Cape, where Linda and John had now moved to from Westfield. This time we stayed the whole time at the Cape View Motel in Truro, where we had checked it out and spent one night and a day there in July, 1997. We went to the Head of the Meadow Beach in Truro and one day drove up to Provincetown for another great Whale Watch boat tour.

    In August, we drove up to Dorchester, near London, Ontario, Canada, for the Senior Softball Canadian Championships. This time we, the Syracuse Merchants team, won it, as we should have won the year before, in a controversial championship, called the "gold chain game."

This is also the year that we first met Willie, who was in Pre-K and attended our Extended Day after school program at MPH. Debbie, Willie's mother, was the Vice Chancellor at Syracuse University, and Willie's father, Tom, was an Economics Professor, at SU also. They had come from Indiana University to Syracuse in August of 1999, where they enrolled Willie at MPH that fall. We didn't get to know Tom and Debbie that school year, not until the end of Willie's Kindergarten year, but after this would begin a close friendship that is still maintained today.

2001

February: Arizona

    Peoria

    Phoenix

    Carefree

    Montezuma Castle

    Flagstaff

    Sunset Crater Volcano

    Grand Canyon

    Walnut Canyon National Monument

   Sedona

   Peoria

April: Virginia

   Williamsburg (Mom)

   Jamestown

   Norfolk

   Southern Memorial

July: Delaware

   Bethany Beach

   Delmarva Peninsula

   Assateague Island

   Rehoboth Beach

August: Old Forge (Water Safari)

   Lake Placid (Ursula)

   Whiteface Mountain

   Wilmington

   Lake Placid Boat Tour

September: Las Vegas (Dusty)

Skaneateles Lake

Tinker Falls

October: Lakemont and Dundee

November: Padanaram, MA (Mom)

Cape Cod

Race Point

Highland Light

    January 1st brought the official start of the 21st century. We flew out to Phoenix, Arizona over the school Winter Break in the middle of February, to visit Marty and Marti in Peoria, a suburb in the northwest part of Phoenix. The following day we drove to downtown Phoenix, the 5th largest city in the United States, and walked and explored the city. We took a day trip with Marti to Carefree, Arizona for this massive flea market and another day trip to Cave Creek. After three days there, we headed north to go to the Grand Canyon. Syl had never been there, I had gone there at the end of 1971.

    Our first stop was at Montezuma Castle National Monument, one of the best-preserved cliff dwellings in North America. The five-story, 20 room structure, built into soft limestone, is about 100 feet above the trail below. The walls are made of fieldstones, held together with a mortar of mud and clay, constructed by farmers of the Southern Sinaguan culture; having nothing to do with Montezuma, the ruler of the Aztec culture. European settlers mistakenly gave it this name and it remains today. We hiked the trail along Beaver Creek and another trail past Montezuma Well, used by the Sinagua people over 600 years ago.

We then drove 50 miles north to Flagstaff, where it was a totally different environment of pine trees and snow. Then on to Sunset Crater, an ancient volcano that erupted over 900 years ago. The Wupatki National Monument, on the outskirts of Sunset Crater, protects one of five Ancestral Pueblo ruins. They continue to be sacred to the Hopi, Navajo, and Zuni people today. Then we drove another 68 miles to the Grand Canyon.

If you have never been to the Grand Canyon, it is something everyone should experience in their lifetime. You can see all the pictures of it, but there is nothing that compares to witnessing it in person. Its red rock reveals millions of years of geological history, carved by the Colorado River. It is 277 river miles long, 18 miles wide and a mile deep. The sunlight creates a myriad of patterns at different times of the day, just an overwhelming sense of awe of nature's power and beauty. When we got there, a helicopter was flying right next to the canyon wall.

I said to Syl, "Wow, they really bring you close to the walls on these helicopter tours!"

It turned out that this was a police helicopter, searching for a woman who was reported missing from the night before. All that was found from above were her shoes. We read in the news in the following days, after they found her body; was that she was taking pictures alone, had gone over the guardrail to do so, must have slipped and unfortunately plunged to her death. They said that on average, nine people die each year in the Grand Canyon, some by not following the warning signs to stay behind the guardrails. We took pictures of each other and had someone take pictures of us together and we were pretty close to the edge of the boulders ourselves. I've had Syl take plenty of pictures of me standing on a cliff's or mountain's edge, as she would tell me to not get so close to the edge, and she was right.

So now there was police tape put around the area that they were searching for the woman. We noticed an elderly Japanese couple sitting on a huge boulder, watching their grandson jumping from one big boulder to another, with a large crevice in between. We were trying to convey to them that this was dangerous and that police were searching for a woman's body who had fallen nearby. They told the boy not to jump anymore. Then a busload of Japanese tourists got out and were standing perilously close to the edge of the boulders, near the scene where they were searching for the woman. They were laughing and talking and taking pictures. Not much we could do, but a quick misstep or slip could be fatal for someone.

It was a beautiful weather day, sunny with blue skies, around 40 degrees on a late February day in Arizona; the kind of day that you felt comfortable with wearing jeans, a sweatshirt, and a short-sleeved fleece vest or light jacket. I wore my vest and Syl wore her jacket. We hiked all over, awestruck with the Grand Canyon's beauty, ever changing with the way the sunlight created myriad patterns, illuminating the canyon walls.

Just before we were getting ready to leave, there were two young women in their twenties, one taking pictures of the other, as she leaned up against the guardrail.

It was getting very windy and we were concerned, especially after the police search, for the girl getting her picture taken, to not lean against the guardrail. Her friend was trying to tell her the same thing. We were keeping our distance, to not be in the camera's range, so if something bad were to have happened, I don't think I could have gotten there fast enough to save her. We waited to make sure she came away from the guardrail after the picture taking, and told them about the police helicopter. Hopefully they will be more careful after this. These incidents show how, in the blink of an eye, fatal accidents can occur here.

We spent two more days hiking and exploring the Grand Canyon, then started to drive back to Peoria. We stopped at Walnut Canyon National Monument, 10 miles southeast of Flagstaff, where Walnut Creek has carved a 600 feet deep canyon of limestone and sandstone. As it flows east, it eventually joins the Little Colorado River, en route to the Grand Canyon. We hiked the Rim Trail and then the Island Trail, which descends steeply, 185 feet, by going down 200 steps. At an elevation of 7,000 feet, it was definitely a challenge. There are about 20 Sinaguan cliff dwellings, some that are still intact. The valley floor has many walnut trees, from which the canyon and creek were named.

From there we drove 45 miles south to Sedona, a desert town surrounded by red-rock buttes, steep canyon walls, and pine forests. It is a beautiful place, with the sunlight shining on all the incredible rock formations. We hiked the trails and sat in the sun in Oak Creek Canyon, then had lunch in town and checked out some of the New Age shops, which are plentiful here.

We drove 112 miles further south back to Peoria, spending three more days with Marty and Marti, before flying back home.

Over the school Spring Break in April, we drove 520 miles south to Virginia with Mom, to visit Tom and Julie for Easter. Mom had gotten this free place to stay for two nights, with breakfasts and dinners, to listen to a promotion for time shares, and given it to us. We took a day trip to the Colonial National Historical Park site, which includes Jamestown. At the Jamestown Settlement, near the site of the original colony, they reenact life in 17th century Virginia; from the arrival of English colonists on May 14, 1607, the first successful English settlement on the mainland of North America, and the original colonial James Fort, built in 1610. There is a village depicting the culture of the Powhatan Indians. We climbed aboard the replicas of the original settlers' ships: the "Susan Constant," "Godspeed," and "Discovery," that sailed from England to Virginia in 1607.

We took a day trip, 45 miles south, to Norfolk, home to a massive naval base on Chesapeake Bay. My dad was stationed here in the early 1940's when he was in the Navy. He would train men who were preparing to go to the front lines in World War II. Under his command were some well-known professional athletes; among them pro basketball players, Bobby Davies and Dolph Schayes.

In July, Syl and I went on a vacation to Delaware, driving 6 hours, 375 miles south, to Bethany Beach. From our hotel balcony, we could watch the ospreys come and go and tend to their young, in a huge nest that they had built on top of this wooden platform in the marshes. We took a day trip to the Delmarva Peninsula, the 170-mile-long peninsula of land in between the Chesapeake Bay and the

Atlantic Ocean, that contains Delaware and parts of the eastern shores of Maryland and Virginia. We drove 25 miles to Assateague Island, a 37-mile-long barrier island facing the Atlantic Ocean. The northern part of the island is in Maryland, while the southern part is in Virginia. It is famous for its wild horses.

We weren't sure if we would see any wild horses. When we were on Ocracoke Island seven years earlier, we knew there were wild horses there, but we only saw a few specks in the distance. We stopped at the small, but informative museum here and started driving to the beach.

What happened next reminded us of the scene in "Back to the Future III" when Marty McFly is about to go back to the Old West and bring Doc Brown back to the future. Marty is concerned that he will be confronted by Indians as he drives the Delorean toward the drive-in movie screen at 88 miles per hour. Doc tells him that he is not thinking fourth dimensionally and that it will transport him to 1885 and the Indians won't even be there. Then Marty arrives in 1885 to Indians charging right toward him.

We were wondering if we would see any wild horses this time, when just like the scene in the movie, there were all these horses charging full blast right in front of our car. We looked out the windshield in disbelief and yelled, "Horses!" as we swerved at the last minute to avoid hitting them, which obviously would have been a disaster. There were horses everywhere on the beach. We had learned about their history at the museum, that they were brought here in the late 17th century by mainland owners to avoid fencing laws and taxation of livestock. They eventually left, leaving behind the horses. So, these wild horses are descendants of the original domestic horses.

The horses are split into two main herds, one in Virginia and one on the Maryland side of Assateague. They are separated by a fence at the Maryland/Virginia State Line. The National Park Service manages the Maryland herd and the Chincoteague Volunteer Fire Department manages the Virginia herd, known as the "Chincoteague Ponies," keeping the herd at around 150 adults. Marguerite Henry's famous book, "Misty of Chincoteague," takes place during a traditional Chincoteague festival called "Pony Penning." On the last Wednesday of July, a herd of horses is rounded up and they swim from Assateague Island to nearby Chincoteague Island. The next day, most of the young foals are auctioned off, with the proceeds going to the Chincoteague Fire Department.

These horses have learned to live in a tough environment with scorching heat and mosquitoes. Some have been hit and killed by cars when they come to the road and beg for food. People have been bitten, kicked, and knocked down. Once we parked the car and got settled on the beach, we noticed one couple, farther down in front of us, that were eating on their blanket, and a group of horses had forced them off their blanket, up into the dunes. The horses were battling each other for their food, biting and kicking each other. We cautiously began to eat our lunch that Syl had packed. First, there were two horses about 30 feet away; then four about 20 feet away; then six about 10 feet away; then eight staring at you, right next to your blanket. You get the picture, it's actually pretty scary. We decided to eat our lunch up near our car.

We would be lying there, closing our eyes in the sun, when you could hear a rumble of horses, like something out of the Old West; come charging over the dunes heading for the ocean. There were hundreds of horses on the beach, some foals just lying there in the sand, you weren't sure if they were alive or not, but they were. Some horses were swimming in the ocean. Then two groups would come down the beach in opposite directions, and when they met, the leaders of their groups would have a stare down. One of the leaders would bow his head and submit to the other, as the dominant leader would lead his group past the other group. There was horse manure on the beach that you would have to watch where you were walking. We took pictures among the horses. In one picture, I am surrounded by horses, and I included it in my first children's book, "From The Horse's Mouth: The True Story of Zippy Chippy." It is definitely a unique experience to visit here.

    Syl and I went boogie boarding, riding the waves into shore. We took one last ride and I came out okay, but Syl crash-landed near the shore, where there was a huge dip caused by beach erosion that you couldn't see. She had smashed her neck and her hair was all disheveled and she had a cut on her chin. She was lucky that it wasn't even more serious, like being paralyzed. Syl was stunned and I bandaged up her chin and we left. After this incident, she was reluctant to go boogie boarding again. Before this, Syl had loved to ride the waves, and was actually better at it than me. She went a couple of times in later years, but nervously and not too far out, and only where it was flat, like on a sandbar.

    One night we strolled along the boardwalk at Rehoboth Beach. The next day it was time to pack up and head home. While we were leaving Delaware and waiting at a toll booth, I could see this car in my rearview mirror going, and I'm not exaggerating here, 120 miles an hour and closing fast. There were all these young guys in the car, and I don't know if they were out for a crazy joy ride, or being chased by the cops, or what. They almost crashed into some cars at the adjacent toll booth. Hopefully the cops tracked them down before they could do any future damage to themselves or to others. We were glad they weren't behind us. You never know what you might encounter on a road trip.

In August, we took Liam and Willie up to Old Forge, in the Adirondacks, driving 100 miles northeast from Syracuse, to Water Safari. Liam was the son of Joe, the former, and at that time, Assistant Headmaster at MPH. We had first met Tom and Debbie at the end of Willie's Kindergarten year. They had college students to pick him up in the morning and bring him to school and pick him up after Extended Day and bring him home. But there was a two-week period from the middle to the end of August, when Tom and Debbie returned to their positions at Syracuse University, and the students wanted to have some time to themselves; where they needed people to watch Willie. We said we could do it, as it meant extra money for us to pay for our vacations. This arrangement evolved into a long-time friendship that still exists today. We would work the two-week program in June at MPH after the graduations, and then have the last week in June, all of July, and the first two weeks of August to ourselves; to go on a vacation or two and enjoy the summer.

We would play miniature golf with the boys and go for ice cream, play card games, (teaching them how to play "Pitch"); play "Pass the Pigs," (a counting game throwing small rubber pigs, that when they landed in certain positions, had designated points assigned to them); that we made popular at Extended Day, and the kids not only had fun playing, but everyone had their "Pass the Pigs" nicknames, that they retained for years. If they couldn't come up with their own nickname, I would ask them what their favorite color was and then what their favorite animal was. There were some strange or funny combinations, like "Purple Elephant." That's how Syl got her nickname, "Turquoise Dolphin." Even high school kids would remember their "Pass the Pigs" nicknames. Mine was "Magic Dust." The kids also learned math by counting their point totals on each throw. I'd pitch batting practice to Willie and Liam and we'd take them to their Little League games. We played Bocce Ball and Home Run Derby in the backyard; as well as ping-pong, with a floating table in the pool; and P.I.G. basketball, into a small portable backboard with a net, in the pool. All this went on all through their Lower School years and even into Middle School.

  I was with Liam, and Syl with Willie, as we went down the dark tunnel on the water slide. The boys loved it, but it was not much fun for me, getting thrown around inside the tunnel, whacking my butt and back against the walls; and fearing that I would crush Liam, as you get airborne as you exit the tunnel and see daylight again. We floated on the water rafts and enjoyed the wave pool, as it felt good on a hot summer day.

  At the end of August, Ursula came up from Charleston for a visit and we drove up to Lake Placid for a few days. We stayed at a hotel with a view of Whiteface Mountain and drove into Wilmington for breakfast. We also took the Lake Placid Boat Tour. Over Labor Day weekend, we took my mom and Ursula out to Skaneateles.

  I flew out to Las Vegas in September to play in the Senior Softball World Championships with the Syracuse Cyclones. The new manager of the Syracuse Merchants, the team that I was one of its original players and the starting third baseman; had made a political decision, and had put me in a position to accept a backup role or find a new team. I had received this information via a phone call from him the day before we were to leave on our Delaware vacation. I agonized over this in disbelief and Syl had to listen to me talk about this situation, ad nauseam, the whole way driving down to Delaware. What made this more troubling to me, was the fact that I had already purchased my round-trip plane tickets to Las Vegas for the World Championships. This was a big deal for the team, as we previously had only played in local or regional tournaments, or the Canadian Championships in Dorchester, Canada, in 1999 and 2000. I just wanted to finish the season out, experience the World Championships, and see what would happen after that. It seemed so vitally important at the time, now it seems so trivial and irrelevant.

    I had written a long letter to the manager and mailed it out before we left for Delaware for nine days, extolling my virtues and contributions to the team; including never missing a tournament, a local league game, practice, indoor batting practice in the cages during the winter, team functions such as banquets or birthday parties, on and on. I thought when I got back that his response would be to reconsider his position and let me finish out the season. Much to my astonishment, disappointment, and then anger, his response was curt and sarcastic. He even sent a new guy on the team to collect my equipment bag and uniform, much to this guy's embarrassment, almost like a loyalty duty to the Godfather he was forced to perform.

    The one thing that he did for me, probably more for himself, to not have to deal with this problem anymore; was to give my phone number to Jack, the manager of the Cyclones. I had these messages from him on my answering machine when we got back from Delaware. I didn't call him for almost two weeks, still thinking things would work out with the Merchants, and also Jack had said that he was from Cortland, so I was under the impression that he was calling about me playing for a team from Cortland; which was at least 30 miles from Syracuse and I didn't want to drive that far. I really didn't realize that this was for the Cyclones or who they were. They probably thought that I was being a "prima donna." I finally called and they invited me to come out and play in a league game with them. When I arrived on their team side of the field, they all greeted me warmly with hugs and made me feel so welcomed, the opposite of what I had just gone through.

It was a doubleheader and Jack had me sitting out the first game. I was now wondering what was going on and if this was worth it. He had let "Stump," (a guy whose arms, legs, and torso resembled a tree stump, thus the nickname), play the first game. He was the regular third baseman, who was a good hitter with power, also a good fielder with a strong arm; but he had a nagging back injury and his mobility, which was limited before, was even more so now. Jack asked him, out of courtesy and respect, something the manager of the Merchants wouldn't have considered; if it was okay for me to take his place for the second game. "Stump," whose back was really bothering him now, agreed.

I was nervous, as all of us are, when we are trying to make a good impression; whether it be in sports, the classroom, or social circles, for the first time. I have to say I played out of my mind that night, feeling like I was back in my thirties again. I didn't make any errors, in fact I made all sorts of diving stops and leaping line drive catches in the field; as well as hitting doubles, triples, in the gap homers, flying (at least for me), around the bases and helping us easily win the game. A lot of the guys had seen me play before and knew that I was good, or they wouldn't have asked me to join their team, but they had never seen me play like this before. It was a wonderful feeling, unwanted by a team a few weeks before, and now making the Cyclones feel like they had just picked up a prized free agent, giving them new hope for a strong showing at the World Championships. In fact, some of the guys were half-kiddingly talking about calling the manager of the Merchants, playing at another field, and telling him that we had just discovered a new third baseman for him.

The rest of the Cyclones had their plane tickets to Las Vegas, but I now had to scramble to get mine and travel by myself. The manager of the Merchants had made all the guys on their team contribute $20 each to reimburse me for my plane tickets, making them culpable, almost like accomplices; instead of just taking care of it himself out of the team fund, and not making them feel a part of what was his decision about me.

I left on Thursday, September 6th, and Nicky, my friend from Syracuse, picked me up at the airport. I've known Nicky for a long time and gave him his nickname, "Condor," because of his annoying defensive presence when he played basketball with our weekly pick-up games at the MPH gym. He was only average in height, but had a long wingspan, getting in your face while guarding you. Nicky had been working for Speedway Motorsports in Charlotte, North Carolina, before moving out to Las Vegas to manage this same company at the Las Vegas Motor Speedway. People can pay to race exotic cars, like Ferrari, Lamborghini, Aston Martin, Porsche, Corvette, Audi, and Mercedes. The movie, "Driven," starring Sylvester Stallone, who also wrote the screenplay, paid millions to use some of these exotic cars, some involved in crashes, in the film. This movie was just being released at this time.

As I entered the airport, I noticed all these people playing the slot machines as they waited for their planes to depart. I thought to myself how foolish this all seemed. Nicky picked me up and we drove to his house to meet his wife and year-old daughter. We had a nice pasta dinner and he drove me to my hotel in the Fremont Street area, "Old Vegas," the original downtown Las Vegas. This was the Four Queens, which has been in operation since 1966. To get to the elevators and up to your room, you had to walk through the casino with everyone drinking, smoking, playing slots, craps, blackjack, roulette, you name it. They had it all.

My room faced the Fremont Street side, where there was a nightly show of lights, the Visa Vision on a gigantic LED canopy, with loud music. It was a spectacular sight, but hard to get to sleep. They told me at the desk that the show would be over by one o'clock in the morning, but that wasn't true, it went on for hours after that. In the morning, I asked for a room on the opposite side of the hotel, away from the lights and music, where all the rest of the team had their rooms.

It was very hot, over 100 degrees, as we played on Friday and Saturday. We finished with three wins and three losses, just missing advancing out of our group bracket into the playoff round on Sunday. We did beat two teams from California, but our last game was cut short due to time limits. There were no teams waiting to play, and we were so mad that we never got the chance to have our last two at bats, to rally and have a chance to win and advance.

We cruised the Strip on Sunday, but we would have rather been at the field, still playing. Nicky came over and picked me up around seven to go out on the town. He pulled up to the Venetian for valet parking and in front of the hotel, waiting to get in, were hundreds of people standing behind this red velvet rope, guarded by two hotel employees. We walked up and the Maître D' saw Nicky and yelled,

"Nicky!"

The two employees unhooked the rope and led us past all these people, who looked on in disbelief. He gave us a special table and our dinner and drinks were on the house. From there we went to Mandalay Bay, where again hundreds of people were standing behind the red velvet rope waiting to get in. Another Maître D' sees Nicky and yells,

"Nicky!"

Again, the rope was unhooked and we were let in, and the people were in disbelief. This was all very cool, but I was starting to wonder what the deal was. We rode on the glass *outdoor* elevator up to the top floor. Exciting, but scary at the same time. The bartender saw us and yelled, "Nicky!" and gave us free drinks. We went out on the balcony and gazed at the incoming planes, lined up one after the other. Nicky was telling me that there are four or five planes arriving in Vegas at all times. You could see the beam of light from the Luxor Hotel, one of the few things that are visible from space, along with the Great Barrier Reef and The Great Wall of China. We came back inside and went to a place where a band was playing. Same routine, velvet rope behind which all these people were waiting to get in, them seeing Nicky and letting us in past all the other people.

I finally had to ask him, "What's the deal here, Nicky? It's if you're treated like the mayor of Las Vegas."

"Well, they like to come out to the racetrack and race the cars, and I take care of them, and I like to eat and drink."

I was thinking about having a great time here at Mandalay Bay, but in October, 2017, it was the scene of the biggest mass killing in U.S. history.

It was a wonderful whirlwind evening. The only disappointment was that it ended too soon. Nicky's mother was very sick at the time and he needed to drop me off back at the Four Queens around 11:30, so he could get up early and go to church and then visit his mother in the hospital. (She passed away not too long after this.) I had hoped to stay out for a few more hours, as I had to get a taxi at four in the morning, to go to the airport for an early flight.

So now I was back at the Four Queens, with four hours to kill, before going up to my room to pack my things and get the taxi; and I didn't want to lie down and take the chance of falling asleep and missing the taxi. I went into the casino and started playing the slot machines. I made a pact with myself to only spend $10, as I needed the money I had left for the taxi and spending money at the airports. When that $10 was gone, I was done. I was playing 50 cents at a time; I'd go up $5 or so, and then go down $5 or so. This went on for a couple of hours, while they kept supplying me with free drinks. Then I started to lose a little more and was down to the last quarter of my $10 limit. I put it in, three matching things came up, lights were flashing, sirens were going off. I had won! I won $250, enough to reimburse myself for my flights, which was great. But if I had put in 50 cents, which I had been playing the whole time, I would have won $500. Oh well, at least I won. I gathered up my coins, putting them in plastic Four

Queen cups, (which I still have), and took them over to where they converted the quarters into dollars.

While waiting at the airport for my plane to depart, I started using my spare change to play a slot machine, the very same thing I thought was foolish when I had arrived in Las Vegas.

I got back to Syracuse in the early afternoon on Monday, September 10th, and actually went to school and did my Extended Day job, with no sleep. The next morning at school started out like a normal day, until one of the Kindergarten teachers turned on the television in her classroom, as someone had called her to tell her about a plane that had crashed into the Twin Towers. Usually the television was only used for educational videos, but the kids were out of the classroom for one of their "special" classes, like Art, Foreign Language, Library, Music, or PE; so we turned it on and watched in disbelief, and then in horror, as the second plane smashed into the other tower and we started realizing that this was a terrorist attack.

It turned out that the other Syracuse Cyclones team, the 60 and over team, (who are now the 75 and over team), who had arrived on Sunday, the 9th, and would start playing on the 11th; had to rent vans to drive back to Syracuse when their tournament was over, as there were no planes flying for days after the attack. Ironically, the Merchants team, who were scheduled to start their tournament a few days later, could not get any flights past Detroit, as there were potential attacks planned for Las Vegas. They never made it out there for the World Championships that year. Poetic justice. There were two guys on their team that made it out there; one guy was afraid of flying and had taken a train from Syracuse to Las Vegas, and the other guy was at a conference in Palm

Springs and drove from there to Vegas. These two guys, combined with the 60's team guys, who stayed after their tournament was over; played against a 50's team, and came surprisingly close to winning the championship.

There was a Middle School student at MPH whose father was a pilot for American Airlines and was one of the first, if not the first, to see the plane crash into the Twin Towers. Air Traffic Control asked him if he had seen what had just happened. He confirmed it and diverted his landing into New York City and took the bewildered passengers to Canada. He was so freaked out by this that he didn't fly again for several years.

In October, we took a day trip to Lakemont and Dundee. In November, we drove with Mom to visit Linda and John and their son, Matt, who was living with them at this time; to Padanaram, an hour from the Cape, for Thanksgiving. The next day Syl and I drove to the Cape for a couple of days, spending the night in a hotel there. It was a sunny, light jacket day, as we walked on the Head of the Meadow Beach at Truro, and went up to Race Point, where there were kites flying everywhere in a colorful display, silhouetted by the blue sky; and a late afternoon stop at Highland Light. We went back to Padanaram the next day to pick up Mom, had lunch down by the boats, then drove back home.

2002

February: Maui, Hawaii

Lahaina

Wailea Beach Resort

Haleakala Volcano

Kapalua ("Lava Walk")

Napili Bay (The Mauian Hotel)

Iao Valley State Park

Makena Beach ("Big Beach")

Whale Watch (The Carthaginian)

Lahaina Town (Front Street)

June: Glen Burnie, Maryland

    Baltimore (Inner Harbor)

    National Aquarium

July: Cape Cod

    Truro (Cape View Motel)

    Head of the Meadow Beach

    Highland Light

    Salt Pond

August: Old Forge (Water Safari)

    Pratt's Falls

Green Lakes

Cazenovia Lake

Old Forge (Water Safari)

October: BaltimoreWoods

November: Mount Lebanon, NY (Shaker Village)

    Syl and I went to Hawaii over our Winter Break in February. There was heavy security at all the airports after "9/11" as we flew to Chicago, then Los Angeles, and on to Maui, where Tish and Mary had moved to. They had lived in Los Gatos, California for around 8 years before moving back to Syracuse for several years. When they lived in California, they had gone on vacations to Maui with other friends and had always thought about living there. They bought a condo in Lahaina and we decided to visit them. They picked us up at night at the airport and put leis around our necks. Their car was made for only two people with hardly any trunk space. Tish drove our rented car with me and Mary drove their car with Syl. Tish wanted to stop at Walmart on the way, to buy a folding table for their patio, while he had access to a larger vehicle. We stopped and got the table and some gallons of milk, as it was only $6 a gallon there, the cheapest that you could find on the island; because it cost so much to have food and beverage products shipped there. Maui is very expensive, as is the rest of the Hawaiian Islands.

    Their condo was nice, but small, and we slept on a fold out bed in the living room. I remember watching the 2002 Winter Olympics from Salt Lake City, Utah, with them. The first day, we went with them over to visit their

English friends, Brian and Joyce. We had tea with them on their balcony on a beautiful sunny, in the 80's, day. It felt strange, but "when in Rome," or in this case, Maui, just going with the flow.

Then we drove to Wailea Beach Resort to visit Dave, Tish's business partner, and his wife, Mary, and their high school daughter and her friend. We knew them, as they were from Syracuse, and had come here on vacation, and this was their last day at this resort. I had recently seen a show on television ranking the top resorts in the United States and Wailea was at the top of the list. It was an amazing place with five pools, spa, fountains, golf courses, restaurants, right on the Pacific Ocean. I was just going around taking pictures, soaking it all in. It costs $700, up to $1,300 a night to stay here, way out of our league. They had a cabana on the beach, and when they went up to their room to shower and change, Syl and I hung out inside there for a while.

The next day we drove up to Haleakalā, the East Maui Volcano, that forms more than 75 percent of the island. The tallest peak is over 10,000 feet and its name means "House of the Sun." It is much cooler up there, you need your sweatshirt or light jacket, as we walked and took pictures by the Visitor Center at 9,740 feet; and of Haleakalā Crater, with its spectacular vistas, everchanging with fog, shadows, and sunlight. The drive back down was an adventure, descending rapidly around the winding road with scurrying nene, known as the Hawaiian goose, the state bird, and maybe a cow just standing there. This descent, with Tish driving, reminded us of coming back down from Whiteface Mountain in Lake Placid, but even steeper and scarier. There were cyclists flying down the road, probably exhilarating, but as far as I'm concerned, extremely dangerous.

On October 18, 2018, astronomers using the Pan-STARRS 1 telescope on Maui, identified "1I/'Oumuamua," the first known object from interstellar space to visit our solar system. In other words, the first object to visit our solar system *from another solar system.* I find this to be incredibly significant. Not too many people, beyond the scientific community, are aware of this. The "1I" designates it as the first interstellar object, and "Oumuamua" is a Hawaiian word for "messenger," reaching out to us from the past. It is thought to have escaped from an alien star system, millions or perhaps billions of years ago. It is speeding away from us in a different direction, never to return.

Brian, Tish and I played golf one sunny and warm day, on a public course that Tish knew, for only $27 for greens fees and a cart. I was taking pictures of the spectacular views from the course between shots, with the ocean on one side and the mountains on the other side.

Speaking of golf courses, we, (Syl, me, Tish, Mary, Dave and Mary, their daughter and her friend); walked along the road adjacent to the Kapalua Resort, where the Sentry Tournament of Champions is held during the first week in January on the Plantation Course. We took the "Lava Trail" walk, this part of the Northwest Maui coast is both beautiful and rugged, down to millions of years-old lava rocks next to the crashing waves of the ocean.

After spending three days at Tish and Mary's condo in Lahaina, we were ready to start our own adventure. We had booked a room at The Mauian Hotel, right on Napili Beach, on crescent-shaped Napili Bay. This is where Tish and Mary had stayed with their friends when they went to Maui from California on vacations. Tish made a big pancake breakfast for all of us in the morning and then

Syl and I drove over to The Mauian. There was a big chalkboard as you entered the hotel with the names of the new guests on it. It felt great seeing your names on it and they welcomed you with leis, the Hawaiian symbol of affection. We checked in and went down to the beach in the afternoon. In the evening, they had a welcoming party with everyone bringing a dish and a guy playing a ukulele and singing Hawaiian songs, which was nice; and Tish and Mary came over and joined in. Later on, it felt good finally being in our own room.

We spent the following day at the beach, swimming and lying in the sun. From Napili Beach you had a clear view of Molokai, where they have the largest sea cliffs in the world. Later in the afternoon, we drove to Iao Valley State Park, which was designated a National Natural Landmark in 1972. We walked the Iao Lookout Trail, a trail of Hawaiian flora and lush greenery, where a natural rock formation named "Kuka Emoku," commonly known as "The Needle," rises 1,200 feet from the valley floor. Iao, (pronounced "EE-ow"), means "cloud supreme."

One day we went on a Whale Watch with Tish and Mary on the boat, Carthaginian. Appearing literally out of nowhere, directly in front of the boat, was a gigantic humpback whale. It happened so fast that I didn't even get a picture of it. But that image is permanently burned into our minds. It was the singular most spectacular thing we'd ever seen on a Whale Watch, but nothing can compare for us the entire experience of the Whale Watch of August, 1995 in Cape Cod; with the three humpbacks waving their tail flukes in unison, silhouetted against the setting sun. But this humpback, rising out of the ocean depths with an incredible vertical leap, just a couple of feet from the boat, was truly awe-inspiring.

Syl and I started driving to Makena Beach, also known as "Big Beach" or "Oneloa Beach," the furthest south part of Maui, past Wailea and Kihei. It is one of the longest beaches on Maui, with beautiful blue-green water. In Makena State Park there is a 360 feet tall dormant volcanic cinder cone called "Pu'u Olai." George Harrison and Eric Clapton were said to own houses here in the private sector. We walked the soft sandy beach and swam in the ocean. As I'm writing this, I have seen from news reports that there have been several tiger shark attacks off Makena Beach this year, with two fatalities. If we had known that tiger sharks were a danger there, we probably wouldn't have gone swimming.

It seemed like there were clouds that just hovered over Napili Beach, so we needed to drive elsewhere to have the enjoyment of sitting in the sun, although they still had amazing sunsets here. We would drive 15 minutes to Lahaina Beach and it would be sunny there. One day after a quick rain, there was a double rainbow that dominated the sky. Rainbows are a common occurrence; in fact, the University of Hawaii's teams are called the "Rainbow Warriors." We went down to Front Street with its many shops, art galleries, restaurants, and the famous banyan tree, which takes up almost a whole city block.

Syl and I were thinking of driving the "Road to Hana," also called the "Hana Highway," an infamous narrow two-lane highway of 64 miles of hairpin curves; connecting Kahului with the tiny town of Hana in east Maui. It is known for its beautiful scenery of jungle, the famous "Seven Sacred Pools of Oheo," the Twin Falls waterfalls, Honomanu Bay, and much more. Tish even had a guided tour cassette tape of the things to see and the things to avoid along the way. Unfortunately, we had read reports that there were outbreaks in Hana of dengue fever, a tropical disease caused by the bite of a mosquito, causing high fever, rashes, headache, and vomiting. So, we decided not to go, a decision that we always regretted, to not have this experience, but we erred on the side of caution. I wish we had never seen this report and just gone for it. I also read that at the Palapala Ho'omau Church that was built in 1857 and is still standing, is known as the burial ground of the famous aviator, Charles Lindbergh, "Lucky Lindy." This was significant, as our family claim to fame was that my maternal grandmother was a cousin of his and that side of my family are all Lindbergs, (shortened), as this was my mom's maiden name, and they were all of Swedish descent. So that would have been really cool to see, but we missed out on this experience.

    We had a wonderful vacation in Maui, but the major regret, besides not doing the "Highway to Hana" trip, was not asking for a couple of extra personal days off, thus limiting our trip to nine days. We checked out of The Mauian on our last day and went over to Tish and Mary's condo for a few hours, to sit in the sun and swim in the complex's pool, before we had to leave for the airport. But we had to keep looking at the time, so we could shower and change and get to the airport on time. We said good-bye and wished we were staying a few days longer, as we drove out to the airport on a beautiful, sunny, blue sky, Hawaiian afternoon. We flew to San Francisco, arriving there at five in the morning, then on to Chicago, and arrived in Syracuse in the early afternoon, due to the time difference. And believe it or not, we showed up at school and did our Extended Day program, jet lag and all. Perhaps foolishly, but this was true dedication to our jobs.

    Tish and Mary sold their condo a few years later and moved back to the states, near Orlando, Florida. If it wasn't for them living in Maui, chances are we wouldn't have made it there, and we never returned.

In the last week of June, after finishing our two-week program at school, we drove over 5 hours, 335 miles south, down to Glen Burnie, a suburb of Baltimore, Maryland, to play in a tournament with the Syracuse Cyclones 55's team. I was firmly entrenched now as the starting third baseman for the Cyclones and valued for my abilities and liked as a person by my manager and my teammates.

Syl and I drove down to Baltimore's Inner Harbor and had a nice seafood dinner and walked around the harbor. When the tournament was over, we stayed an extra day and went to the National Aquarium in the Inner Harbor, where in addition to all their regular impressive exhibits, they had an incredible Seahorses and Seadragons Exhibit.

In July, we drove to Cape Cod for another vacation, staying at the Cape View Motel in Truro; going to the Head of the Meadow Beach near there, taking walks around the trails at the Salt Pond Visitor Center on the National Seashore, and many other walks around different sites and trails. We also went to the museum and lighthouse at Highland Light in North Truro, the oldest and tallest lighthouse on the Cape, built in 1797, rebuilt in 1853, and replaced in the same location with the current structure in 1857. In 1996, it was moved back 450 feet from the edge of a 125 feet high cliff, due to erosion.

Karen and Andrew came to visit in late July and into the first week of August. We all went up to Old Forge to Water Safari, hiked Pratt's Falls, walked the trails at Green Lakes, and went swimming in Cazenovia Lake.

Later in August, we did some of the same things with Liam and Willie: Pratt's Falls, Cazenovia Lake, Water Safari in Old Forge, and playing many rounds of miniature golf.

In October, we hiked in Baltimore Woods Nature Center in Marcellus, west of Syracuse, and a day trip to Skaneateles with Mom. In November, we took a drive to Mount Lebanon, NY, staying at a winter resort offering a promotional package, for a couple of days, enjoying their hot tub. We took a day trip to the Shaker Village near there, seeing the remnants of The Great Stone Barn.

2003

April: St. Augustine, Florida

Orlando, Florida

Disney World Resort

Disney World & Epcot

Tampa, Florida

Clearwater Beach

St. Augustine, Florida

Jacksonville, Florida

June: Thousand Islands (Mink Island)

July: Cape Cod

    Truro (Cape View Motel)

    Head of the Meadow Beach

    Highland Light & Salt Pond

August: Skaneateles Lake

    Thousand Islands (Mink Island)

    Skaneateles (Ursula visit)

    Pratt's Falls (Liam & Willie)

    Over the Spring Break, Syl and I flew down to Jacksonville, Florida at night, to get our rental car and then drive to Saint Augustine to visit our friend Bruce for a few days, and drive from there to Orlando to the Disney World Resort. I had made the arrangements for the car rental in Syracuse, using my bank debit card, which I had always done in the past, with no problems. Neither of us had credit cards, we just always used our debit cards. We arrived late at night and went to get our car at the rental desk. The woman said we couldn't rent a car using our debit card. I told her that I had always used it in the past with no problems and that they had accepted my reservation in Syracuse with it. She consulted with her manager and they were refusing to give us a car. I can understand their logic with it, but this was not told to us in Syracuse. I told them we weren't leaving this line, with all these other people waiting behind us, until we got our car. I apologized to the people waiting, but I was not going anywhere until I got the car that we had made previous arrangements for.

    This situation reminded me of the Seinfeld episode where Jerry, upon learning that they ran out of cars, is admonishing the rental agent for knowing how to take reservations, just not knowing how to hold reservations, which is the real purpose of the reservation. They finally relented and gave us our car around midnight and we drove 40 miles south to Saint Augustine.

    We spent a few days with Bruce, swimming in the pool, and walking the trails around where his apartment complex was. Then we left and drove 110 miles south to the Walt Disney World Resort near Orlando.

    Our family doctor, Mary, and at that time, an MPH parent of two adopted girls from China, Haley and Taylor, had generously offered us her timeshare in the Disney World Resort. It was a gorgeous place, with an outside balcony overlooking a pond and a gazebo, and beautiful plants and flowers. There were two other women, who were partners, and their adopted Chinese girls, staying in their timeshare below the one we were in. Mary and her partner, Sheila, and their girls, stayed with them. We took the girls to the pool, crowded with many children, and I let them ride on my back like I was a dolphin or a whale.

    Syl and I spent a day at Planet Hollywood in Disney Springs and had dinner at the "House of Blues" restaurant. Another day we went to Epcot, a theme park of 300 acres, twice the size of Disney's Magic Kingdom. We went to see "Honey, I Shrunk the Audience," a 3D film spin off of the 1989 "Honey, I Shrunk the Kids" movie. The audience feels like they have been shrunk to miniature size, having to avoid many human-sized obstacles. We jumped up in our seats when the mouse went running under seats, the tail tickling your chair; and the hungry dog; also when the snake feels like it's coming out of the screen right at you, as you are looking at it; and more special effects, with your 3D glasses.

We went to the "Living Seas" Pavilion, where they take you on a journey to Sea Base Alpha on the ocean floor; and then a seacab tour of the pavilion's almost six million gallon Caribbean Coral Reef Aquarium, where you learn about the wonder and mystery of the world's oceans.

After this, we walked around and visited the international pavilions, sampling food from many countries. Sitting on a tiled bench of multi-colors and designs with Syl in the Moroccan Pavilion, and the tiled multi-colored archways and walls surrounding us; reminded me of my time in Tangier, Morocco, in the autumn of 1969. At night, we saw the spectacular fireworks show, "Illuminations: Reflections of Earth." At the end, the Earth Barge display shows the message, "Peace on Earth, Good Will to Men," in multiple languages. Epcot was an amazing experience.

The following day, Syl and I took a drive to Clearwater Beach, enjoying the sun, feeling the soft sand between our toes, and swimming in the ocean.

On the last night, Syl and I, and Mary and Sheila, and the other two women, and the four little girls, all donned these black tee shirts: with Syracuse University, Men's Basketball NCAA Champions, 2003, inside a diamond ring with orange lettering, that Mary had bought for all of us. We took some group pictures with these shirts. Then Mary treated all of us to a wonderful dinner at Fulton's Crab House in Disney Springs.

Syl and I left the next day and drove back to Saint Augustine to stay with Bruce at his apartment complex for a few days, swimming in the pool and enjoying the nice weather. We went out one evening to hear Bruce play at a club near Jacksonville, stopping to walk on this pier and take some pictures in the late afternoon beforehand. We were eating dinner at this club and listening to Bruce, when this guy in his early twenties came roaring into the club on his motorcycle, stopping just a few feet from our table. We were not at all thrilled by this, one slip-up with his brakes could have resulted in serious injury, especially to us.

There was a big party for him, as he was shipping out to Afghanistan the next day. One of his friends gathered up all the women that were there, including Syl, to be in a group picture with him, so he could show it to all his service buddies. Syl reluctantly did it.

Bruce started playing Marvin Gaye's song,

"What's Going On."

I respected Bruce for his convictions, as he is, as well as us, about as anti-war as you can get. But it could have been a confrontation, except these people were too drunk to pick up on the words that he was singing, like "war is not the answer." It was still a tense situation. We went for a walk on the beach afterwards, and spent another day at the pool, before driving back to Jacksonville to return the rental car and catch our flight back to Syracuse.

We found out at the ticket counter that the flight had been canceled due to mechanical problems and they booked us in a hotel near the airport. We had to call the administrators and tell them that we would be unable to make it back on Monday and most of Tuesday, but would be there to do Extended Day on Tuesday. This hotel had two pools, one on an upper level that nobody came to, so we had a peaceful day on Monday sitting in the sun and swimming in the pool. It was a nice change from all the madness at the Disney Resort pools, but we did have a wonderful experience staying at Mary's timeshare there.

After finishing the school year and our two-week program in June, we went up to the Thousand Islands and spent four days at Gary and Patty's camp on Mink Island. Gary's father had built the family camp, where their family spent their summer childhoods, on their boat cruising the Saint Lawrence River. Gary was an expert boatsman, he knew where all the shoals and dangers were on the river, and could find his way safely around the river at night if he had to. Gary had built his and Patty's camp himself from scratch. He had to transport all the materials from the marina to the campsite in a small boat, including a huge bay window. He also built a big shed, deck, and dock. I remember laying the first pipe in the ground with him. Gary is a plumber, so he knew how to do all of that. It is a beautiful place, with a loft where they sleep. Some family and guests stay in a small room on the first floor, which we did the first time we stayed with them. But after Gary's father passed away and he finished building his own camp, we stayed at the old camp when we went up there.

They kept the old camp, until recently, for family and guests. It had a lot of charm, with many wooden carvings and flower boxes of ducks and mallards and loons that were carved and painted by his father. We had to move a few things around and have Gary turn on the old outside water heater. We had to bring up bins of our bedding and supplies and load them on their boat, cross the river from the marina to the dock in front of the old camp, and then carry them up these long, steep stairs. There was a large piece of plywood behind the bed, where we would have to check for these gigantic wolf spiders, and definitely try to kill them. Obviously, we did not want to get bitten by them. They were in other places as well, so we were always on the lookout for them, sleeping with "one eye open," so to speak.

But it was nice to get up in the morning, make our breakfast, and walk down the stairs and swim in the river. It was a short walk through the woods to their new camp. We would go out on the river in their boat, drive to Boldt Castle on Heart Island, ride around and then anchor somewhere; to take a swim, eat our sandwiches and drink a couple of beers while listening to music, and watch the loons dive. We would return to "our camp" later in the afternoon, after spending a beautiful sunny day on the river, to shower and change; then go to their camp, where Patty and Sylvia made fantastic salads and other dishes, while Gary grilled salmon and whatever else they were having. We ate out on the deck with music playing and then went back out on the boat to watch the sunset. We would return before dark and then sit by the glowing chiminea on the deck, drinking wine, listening to the beavers swimming in the river, and gazing at the star-filled night sky.

In fact, this was the year that Mars and Earth were the closest in nearly 60,000 years, 34.6 million miles. NASA said that won't happen again until 2287. I wonder where we all will be then. *Definitely not here*. The next close approach, according to NASA, will be 38.6 million miles in 2020, so most of us will be around for that. There was a full moon reflecting a long yellow path on the river and adjacent to it was a red path reflecting Mars. It was truly an amazing sight, maybe not quite as amazing as the viewing of Halley's Comet in Antigua in April, 1986; but still worthy of being called amazing and something we will always remember.

In July, we went back up to Cape Cod and again stayed at the Cape View Motel in Truro. We spent most of our sunny days at the Head of the Meadow Beach in Truro. I would go boogie boarding as much as I could, checking the tide charts to see when the big sand bar was exposed. Syl would also go boogie boarding, a little closer to shore, but since her incident at Assateague Island two years earlier, she never rode the waves again like she used to do. I would go way, way out, always searching for that perfect wave. I probably should have invested in a wetsuit, as the ocean water was always chilly at the Cape. Even on a hot and humid sunny day, it took a few minutes to get used to that first initial shock before taking the plunge. Once that was accomplished, it felt so refreshing. I did wear an anti-rash shirt, but after a while, when my fingers and toes were so numb and tingling that I could no longer feel them; I was forced to come out and take a break and warm my body temperature back to normal before I could venture back out again. We would lie in the sun, reading our books and eating the delicious lunch that Syl had made.

We drove through all the towns, looking at the quaint houses, and stopped for an ice cream. We went to the National Seashore Visitor Center and hiked the trails there around Salt Pond and took our usual visit to Highland Light. Our favorite dinner places were: The Hearth 'n Kettle Restaurant and the Jailhouse Tavern in Orleans; The Whitman House Restaurant in Truro, but most of the time we ate in the bar area, the Bass Tavern; and Moby Dick's Cape Cod Seafood Restaurant in Wellfleet. Moby Dick's was always a unique experience. The first time that we ever went there, we saw an incredibly long line waiting to get in, but nobody seemed to mind, as they were all laughing and talking and having a good time. We found out this was because you could bring your own beer or wine, so people were drinking while they were waiting. We drove to the

Package Store down Route 6 and bought a bottle of wine to bring back for dinner. We had a little wine while proceeding in line and then you ordered your dinners. They call out your name when your table is ready and seat you at your table and bring your dinners and an ice bucket for your wine. Smooth jazz music plays in the background as you eat incredibly fresh seafood. We got to know the owner, Todd, as we turned him on to some of the jazz CD's we brought with us, such as Craig Chaquico, and he would play them while we ate our dinner. It has been open since the summer of 1982, and takes the New England clam shack to a whole new level.

In August, we went back up to the Thousand Islands to hang out with Gary and Patty on Mink Island, again staying at the old camp.

Ursula came up for a visit and stayed with us on Jerome Street. We spent time with Tom, Debbie, and Willie at their pool. Willie would call her "Urska" then, she always liked that, and would mention it often. We took a day trip to Skaneateles, walking out on the lake pier and in the little park. We walked around town, checking out all the unique shops, and had lunch at Doug's Fish Fry. Another day we went to Cazenovia, walked around town checking out their unique shops, ate our take out lunch from Angel's Deli, while we sat in the park pavilion by the lake. In the following days, we took Ursula and Mom back out to Cazenovia to visit the historic Lorenzo House, where they were having a giant craft show on the front lawn. We took Ursula to the Brewster Inn, an iconic mansion built in 1890, for a wonderful dinner. We also took Ursula on a tour of the Syracuse University campus.

After Ursula returned to Charleston, we again watched Willie for two weeks before we would return to

MPH for a week of teachers' meetings, workshops, and getting the classrooms ready for the start of another school year, the day after Labor Day. We took Willie and Liam to Pratt's Falls one day, hiking and collecting fossil rocks. The four of us played a lot of miniature golf at Fairmount Glen, in the same location for over 65 years, known as the "Augusta National of Miniature Golf," because of its lush landscape. We also played at Big Don's Wild River, Hickory Hill, and Mini Golf in Cortland; and we always went for ice cream afterwards. We swam and played P.I.G. basketball in the pool, played Bocce in the backyard, and played "Pitch" card games and "Pass the Pigs."

2004

April: Fort Myers, Florida

      Edison & Ford Winter Estates

      Downtown Fort Myers

      Edison House

      Historical Museum

      Sanibel Island

      Bowman Beach

      Ding-Darling Wildlife Preserve

      Captiva

      Fort Myers Beach

July: Thousand Islands

Mink Island

August: Kiawah Island, South Carolina

Kiawah Island Golf Club

Charleston, South Carolina

Fort Sumter

    Syl and I survived another long winter in Syracuse. I had to constantly shovel our driveway so we could get to work. We never called in sick or missed a day of school. On Friday nights, we would rent a couple of videos and Syl would make dinner and I would get the fireplace ready. We would watch the videos with a nice fire going, something to look forward to.

    Over the Spring Break in April, we flew down to Fort Myers, Florida. Fort Myers was built on the banks of the Caloosahatchee River and named after a Civil War general. Long before the United States Army built a fort there in the 1830's, the Seminole Indians had chosen this spot for their villages. And long before the Seminoles, "the ancient ones," the Calusa, had built earth and shell living mounds along the south side of the river. There were plenty of creeks that the Calusa and Seminoles could use as watery escape routes into the Everglades. From there, they could travel east to the Atlantic Ocean, south to the Florida Keys, or to the salt marshes near Cape Sable. Fort Myers, known as the "Gateway to the Tropics," was incorporated in August of 1885.

We visited the Edison-Ford Winter Estates, the historic winter homes of Thomas Edison and Henry Ford. Edison first visited Southwest Florida in 1885 and purchased the property to build a vacation home. Ford purchased the adjacent piece of land in 1916. The main features are: the Edison Botanical Gardens, the Edison Rubber Laboratory, and the Edison Museum. When you first enter the property, you can't miss the gigantic banyan tree, more than an acre in diameter, by Edison's house, with the sign that reads:

"Given to Edison by Firestone in 1925. Circumference of aerial roots 390 ft." We found out that: "The tree was brought from India in a butter tub and was two inches in diameter and four feet high when given by Harvey Firestone and planted by Edison in 1925. It is a member of the rubber family."

We walked through the impressive botanical gardens, seeing some exotic specimens, such as the African Sausage Tree, bearing hot-dog shaped fruit. Then on to the museum which contains hundreds of inventions, artifacts, and exhibits. We never knew that Edison held more than 1,000 United States patents, and that he submitted patent paperwork for a record 65 years. The electric light bulb, the phonograph, and the motion picture were obviously his most famous inventions; but you learn about his lesser known ones: the talking doll, the electric train, alkaline batteries, a fruit preserver, and a stencil pen, which became the tattoo stylus.

The following day we went to downtown Fort Myers, better known as the River District or the "City of

Palms," which is aptly named as you drive down McGregor Boulevard. Cattle drivers used to drive their cattle down what is now McGregor Boulevard to ships docked at Punta Rassa. We walked along the waterfront of the Caloosahatchee River with its brick-lined streets and art galleries, shops, and restaurants, and had lunch there. Then we went to the Historical Museum, located in what was once the Fort Myers Depot of the Atlantic Coastline Railroad. This museum is dedicated to preserving not only the history of Fort Myers, but of Southwest Florida as well. Exhibits date back to prehistoric times, with fossils of giant sea creatures and dinosaurs. Other exhibits include: Spanish explorers, Native Americans, a Calusa Indian Village, an old fort, the old riverfront wharf, the re-creation of 19th century Fort Myers, the Cracker House, and an old Pullman railcar.

Syl and I spent many days on Sanibel Island and Captiva Island. As you drive over the Sanibel Causeway into Sanibel, there were always several low-flying pelicans that were seemingly checking you out or maybe welcoming you, as they flew right at and then over your car. We stopped at the Information Center and found out about a wildlife refuge and this public beach, that we always went to after that.

We drove down Sanibel-Captiva Road until we came to the J.N. "Ding" Darling National Wildlife Refuge. It was established in 1945 and occupies one-third of Sanibel Island's 6,400 acres; and is a prime spot for bird-watching the 245 species that come through the mangrove estuary each year. We found out that the tall pink birds wading in the water aren't flamingos, but rather roseate spoonbills. You drive through the refuge, park the car on the side of the road, getting out to observe alligators, dolphins, and manatees. There are white egrets stalking their prey. We walked along the boardwalk of the Calusa Mound Trail, seeing mounds left behind by the ancient Calusa; seeing snake plants under gumbo-limbo trees, sea grapes, cactus, saw palmettos, giant poincianas, wild coffee, a grove of lime trees, bromeliads, and a mangrove forest with enormous 30 feet tall white mangroves.

Jay Norwood "Ding" Darling was a political cartoonist and by 1917 his cartoons were syndicated across the country and would appear in 130 daily newspapers. He started his 50-year career in 1900 and won two Pulitzer Prizes. One of his favorite bird-watching locations was on Sanibel Island, and this refuge was set aside to honor his lifelong work in wildlife conservation.

Bowman's Beach Park is now recognized as one of the Top 10 Beaches in the world by U.S. News Travel and by Travelocity as one of the Top 25 Beaches in the United States. We didn't know these ratings when we went there, just that it was a nice beach. We had to drive further down Sanibel-Captiva Road and then park the car in the lot and put money in the meter. We walked on the several miles of white sandy beach, swam in the Gulf of Mexico, and collected all sorts of colorful shells. Before we left, we rinsed off in the outdoor showers and changed out of our bathing suits. We drove over to Captiva Island, north of Sanibel, to catch the beautiful sunset. (Less than four months after we left, on August 13th, a Category 4 Hurricane, named Charley, came roaring through, packing winds of 150 miles per hour; splitting the north end of Captiva in two.)

We drove down the road and pulled over into a secluded spot, where we changed in the car into casual dress clothes for dinner. Syl and I had become quite adept at changing out of bathing suits, or shorts and tee shirts, into casual dress clothes; in Cape Cod, the Caribbean, Florida, Mexico, and many other places. We had a nice dinner at the Jacaranda Restaurant on Sanibel Island before we drove back to our hotel in Fort Myers.

One day we went over to Fort Myers Beach to visit some friends, MPH parents Bruce and Lynn, and their three children, B.J., Kelley, and Sawyer. We were invited to come over and have lunch and hang out for the afternoon and early evening with them where they were staying, The Pink Shell Beach Resort, between Estero Bay and the Gulf of Mexico. You can't miss this place, gleaming with its pink color in the sun. After lunch, we threw a frisbee around with the kids on the beach and then went for a swim in the Gulf of Mexico. As we waded in, we noticed all these little creatures with spines that help them move along the ocean floor and bury themselves in the sand. They were sand dollars, relatives of sea urchins and sea stars. If you pick them up gently in the palm of your hand and the spines are moving, then they are alive. There were thousands of them there, so we called it "Sand Dollar Heaven."

When you think of sand dollars, you envision the white, bleached out version of their exoskeletons that you find on the beach or can buy at souvenir shops. Obviously, they are not still alive. "The Sand Dollar Legend" is an Easter and Christmas favorite, which tells a story that includes the five slits representing the wounds on Jesus Christ when he was on the cross; a star in the middle representing the Star of Bethlehem, that led the Wise Men to the manger where Christ was born; the outline of the Easter lily, a sign of the Lord's Resurrection; and on the back is the outline of a Poinsettia, the Christmas flower. If you break open the sand dollar, five "doves" emerge, the "doves" of the peace and joy of Christmas. There are always five doves every time you open one.

The kids and I were so excited to see live sand dollars, that we filled up some plastic buckets and brought them up to show Sylvia. She immediately told us that it was illegal to collect live sand dollars and that there was a hefty fine for that. She asked what we were thinking, and I guess in our excitement, we weren't thinking about what we were doing and the potential consequences. We took them back down to the water and put them back where they belonged.

In July, I started experiencing excruciating pain in one of my teeth. I had gone to my regular dentist for observation and x-rays, but he had found nothing. I was in such discomfort and pain, it was overwhelming. Syl called an endodontist late at night on July 2nd to explain my situation, but he wanted to talk directly to me. I didn't even want to hold the phone next to my face. He told me to meet him at his office at ten in the morning, on Saturday, July 3rd. I couldn't even put that side of my face on the pillow. Syl took me down there and I waited for at least half an hour, as he casually strolled in the office in his warm up outfit; talking on the phone about his golf date, as I writhed in pain. Finally, he saw me and gave me the hot and cold test, as I was thinking to myself, "Just dig a hole and bury me in it," that's how intense the pain was. I kept feeling the pain in my lower right jaw, but the tests indicated to him that it was in the upper right. Sometimes this can happen, commonly known as referred pain, where nerve endings may fool the brain into thinking the pain is coming from a different place than it is actually coming from. He gave me some antibiotics, but forgot to give me any pain pills, and sent me home for the Fourth of July weekend.

Syl and I drove out with Mom to Linda and John's new house in Cazenovia for the Fourth. They had sold their house in Padanaram and had moved here in May. They had all this great food, but I could only manage to eat a small bite of salmon and a couple of raspberries. I sat in a recliner as they all went across the street to watch the fireworks. It was unfortunately the most miserable Fourth of July that I have ever experienced, before or since.

    I went to see another endodontist, who finally diagnosed the pain I was feeling in my lower right jaw. It turned out that I had a golf ball-sized abscess that had spread inside to my neck. He had to lance it and get all the abscess out. He said I was lucky that I saw him when I did, as this is poison going into your bloodstream, and if not eliminated, can even be fatal. He wasn't sure if that tooth could be saved, but he managed to save it. I still had more pain in other areas and he had to drill through some of my crowns and do several root canals. That summer, I wound up going to the dentist *eighteen times,* driving back and forth to downtown Syracuse. I had to go back to my regular dentist and have him seal up the small holes in the crowns, that they had to drill in order to do the root canals. Even after all this, a few weeks later, I was experiencing severe pain again. What did I do to deserve this? I had to go see another endodontist who discovered that I had two impacted wisdom teeth! These were my remaining wisdom teeth. They put me under and extracted them. A few years later, I had to have a titanium implant for a tooth in my lower left jaw; the last major issue I've had.

    One of the physical nemeses in my life has been my left front tooth. When our family moved from Liverpool to Lakemont in October, 1953, when my Dad got the job at Lakemont Academy, I was the new kid in second grade at Dundee Central School. We went out on the playground at recess and the class bully, "Skippy" Evans, pushed me off the monkey bars and chipped my left front tooth. I'm sure, if he's even still alive, that he doesn't remember my name or this incident. But I've always remembered his name. How could I forget, as this was something that impacted me my whole life? I was in a lot of pain as my parents came and took me to the dentist. I can remember him putting this black rubber mask over my face, probably nitrous oxide. I can also remember the smell of cigarette smoke in the office, not too wise when there is flammable gas around, but this was a country dentist's office in the early 1950's. He had to use this file to smooth out my tooth, which was all jagged, for hours.

    I went back to school the next day and "Skippy" offered me half of his peanut butter and jelly sandwich. Instead, I punched him in the face, giving him a bloody nose, and he never bothered me again. But I've had to deal with my front tooth, as I mentioned before, all my life. I now had a chipped front tooth, probably still two-thirds of it, for over eight years. This is how I looked in all my childhood pictures back then.

    Our family had moved from Lakemont at the end of the summer in 1960, when Dad decided to accept a public school teaching position at East Irondequoit Central School, near Rochester, New York. We lived in Webster, just a five-minute walk to Webster Central School, where I went for my freshman and sophomore years. Mom got a job working in the Audio-Visual Department at Webster. I'm assuming the reason was an increase in his salary, but it was a decision he would quickly regret. At Lakemont Academy, he was the Chairman of the History Department, teaching World History, American History, and Problems of Democracy; also, Athletic Director and Head Coach of varsity football, varsity baseball, and varsity track, and even coached the debate team. Plus, the diversity of the students who came from all over the world. When I looked at the old yearbooks, there were students from China, Cuba, South America, and even Persia.

One student's name that intrigued me was Gardner McKay, who went on to star in the television series, "Adventures in Paradise," created by James Michener. It ran on ABC from 1959 until 1962, with McKay as Adam Troy, the captain of the schooner Tiki III, which sailed the South Pacific looking for passengers and adventure. I always liked the concept of the show, I wish they would bring it back in reruns on the TVLand channel. He led a colorful life, abandoning the spotlight to move to the Amazon jungle. Later in his life he became a successful playwright and author. He died at his home in Honolulu at age 69 in November, 2001.

At East Irondequoit, Dad was no longer Chairman of the History Department, just teaching World and American History courses. He no longer was Athletic Director or Head Coach, just an Assistant Coach. Plus, there were at least 30 students in his classes, compared to 10 students per class, what he was used to at Lakemont; and obviously there wasn't the diversity of students that Lakemont provided. Dad was unhappy in his decision to leave Lakemont and gave his notice to not renew his contract at East Irondequoit when the school year was over. I remember him being a carpenter's helper that summer in 1961. He was tanned, muscular, and in great shape at 44 and 6 months old. That fall, he was selling Encyclopedia Britannica's door to door and being a substitute teacher at Webster.

When I was a freshman at Webster, I was 5 feet, 2 inches tall, (short), and weighed 100 pounds. Toward the latter part of my freshman year and into the beginning of my sophomore year, I grew 9 inches and 50 pounds, where

I was now 5 feet, 11 inches and 150 pounds. I was always one of the fastest kids in my class growing up and I was always involved in sports: football, basketball, baseball, and track. As a freshman, I could do a triple flip on the trampoline in gym class and land on my feet. I had a little blond brush cut and played point guard on the junior varsity basketball team.

This all changed my sophomore year. I had a new body now. Some of the kids didn't even recognize me at first when we returned to school. I still was athletic and coordinated, but this new body took some time to get used to and realize there were things that I used to be able to do, but now longer could. The first one happened on Columbus Day, Monday, October 9th, 1961, when the football team had a practice on the school holiday. I had been on the junior varsity team my freshman year, and had passing skills, but was too small to get any meaningful playing time. But now I had a new body and was the starting quarterback on the junior varsity team and third-string varsity quarterback, running the scout team this day. There was a play where I faked a handoff to the halfback on the right side of the line, and with a sleight of hand move, put the ball on my left hip, commonly called "a bootleg," and ran for 40 yards down the left sideline, before being pushed out of bounds. The coaches were impressed, but the first team defensive guys were not too thrilled at being embarrassed by this. I always hated to think that it was deliberate, but on the very next play, as I dropped back in the pocket and then threw a pass, two of the biggest defensive linemen came crashing down on my right ankle as I followed through. I writhed in pain as the coaches wanted to take me to the doctor and have it X-rayed.

I refused, making the worst decision I have ever made in my life. I had never been to a doctor before, being brought up as a Christian Scientist. At Dundee, when all the kids left the classroom to get vaccinations for polio or smallpox, I would have a "note" from my mother about being exempt from these shots due to our religious beliefs. But I always felt weird sitting there all by myself, and I knew the other kids talked about me. My maternal grandmother was even a faith healer. If it had been a year later, I would have definitely gone to the doctor, had it set in a cast, healed up, and rehabbed to be able to play basketball in two months. I limped home on one leg and Dad kind of set the bone in place, (he was from the "old school" mentality, as he used to just have his separated shoulder slammed back in place, and continue playing football.) This probably cost him a potential pro career as a pitcher in baseball, as he was on the same Syracuse baseball team and pitching staff as Jim Konstanty from 1937-1939. Konstanty made his mark in sports history as a relief pitcher, leading the Philadelphia Phillies of 1950, the team that was called the "Whiz Kids," to the National League pennant and won the National League's Most Valuable Player Award that year.

Dad taped my ankle up, and in his defense, told me to stay off of it for six weeks. But I *had* to play junior varsity football and begged Mom to let me do it. She gave in, much to my Dad's chagrin. This other quarterback on the team was more the running quarterback, and I was more the passing quarterback. When it was an obvious passing situation, I was sent in, even with my ankle heavily taped. There was not much creativity in the play calling in those days; no spread formations, bubble screens, or draw plays. The opposing team just blitzed and creamed me repeatedly. I was pretty ineffective the rest of the season. I did heal up enough to play junior varsity basketball, but my ankle would never be normal again.

I lived with this pain for over 41 years, with these floating bone chips always poking me, probably why I had a lot of irritable moments. I played varsity football, basketball, baseball, and track my last two years of high school at Pebble Hill, and won the Best All-Around Athlete award both years. I finally had surgery in late December, 2002 to remove these bone chips. My ankle will never be 100 percent, it still has a lump on it and "acts up" now and then, but it is a major improvement over what I had to live with and endure all those years. I played basketball on teams in leagues in Syracuse and Wisconsin, and pick-up games in gyms and parks all over the country; as well as softball teams in leagues in Syracuse and Wisconsin, and in tournaments all over the country; and in tournaments all over the country and on National and Canadian Championship teams in Senior Softball. I always wondered what might have been with a normal right ankle, but looking at people with serious disabilities, and crippled and lost limbs, I guess you have to be thankful *for what you do have*.

    Getting back to my front tooth situation, my next traumatic incident happened in late January of 1962, also in my sophomore year. Maybe because I had a new body, or maybe just really bad luck, but my sophomore year was the worst year for my two main nemeses, my right ankle and my left front tooth. I was in gym class and was attempting to do a triple flip on the trampoline, the same flip that I used to do in my freshman year. Well, I only managed to do two and a half flips before smashing my face on the galvanized steel frame on the outside of the trampoline. The guys that were supposed to be spotting me were too busy checking out the girls. It happened so fast that I don't think there was much they could have done to save me. My nose was bleeding, but I had blood pouring out of my mouth. My left front tooth was just hanging by a thread.

My dad just happened to be a substitute teacher that day. Usually I cringed when he came to sub, as it kind of crimped your style when you are 15 years old, if you know what I mean. But it was lucky that he was there that day. He heard about what had happened and immediately came to the gym and took me to the nurse's office. I remember that it was brutally cold that day, and when we were walking down the hallway, someone entered through a side door and the wind just whipped its bitter coldness throughout my mouth. The nurse cleaned me up and gave me some gauze to hold against my mouth. Dad drove me to the dentist, and per "Murphy's Law," my regular dentist was away on vacation. So, the substitute dentist decided to try a procedure that was unheard of at that time. He took the dangling tooth and shoved it up into my gum, first asking me if it looked straight. How was I supposed to know? I was dazed, in pain, there was blood everywhere; and don't forget, this tooth was the same one that had been chipped in second grade. He then went ahead with this new procedure, wiring the tooth into the gum, as if you had braces. Amazingly, it grew back, although it was now a chipped tooth and a little crooked. (It remained like this for over 12 years.) I could only have things like milkshakes, soups, mashed up bananas, and juice, for 6 months and I had to wear this protective mask when I played basketball, hearing the abuse of the opposing teams' fans.

In 1973, Mom told me of this new dental treatment where they take a plastic cap and fit it on a chipped tooth and then fill in the missing part with this composite material called Restodent. I went to her dentist and had it done. His first attempt didn't turn out so well, as it was slightly longer than my other front tooth, enough so that my unmerciful friends were calling me "chiclet" or "shovel tooth." And it also had a yellowing effect on my tooth as well. I had it redone and for the first time since the start of second grade, over 20 years ago, I didn't have a chipped left front tooth.

  A year later, I had just come back for a visit to Syracuse from Austin, Texas, and for some unknown reason was playing one on one basketball with my friend, "Moon," who was a great swimmer, but not much of a basketball player; when in normally guarding him on defense, he elbowed me in the mouth with his burly forearm and knocked the Restodent cap out. Back to the chipped tooth. I had the procedure redone, but two weeks later, eating a salad with nothing hard in it, the tooth fell out. After all these years of trauma, the root had finally dissolved. I had to go to my regular dentist and he did a procedure known as a Maryland Bridge, installing a permanent left front false tooth, which has remained intact to this day.

  We had decided to sell our house in May of 2004, when we returned from our Fort Myers vacation; to get away from all the students and transient people in our area and get out in the country, not as backwoods as Erieville, but out of the Syracuse University neighborhood. We sold it at the end of June, just as I started to go through all those dental problems that summer. I was up in our hot attic, sorting out all my National Geographic magazines; when I came across this article about the coquí frogs of Puerto Rico, which inspired me to write my children's book, "The Forest That Rains Frogs." It has also been translated into Spanish, "El Bosque Donde Llueven Ranas Coquí."

  Later in July, we went up to the Thousand Islands to hang out with Gary and Patty at their camp on Mink Island and on their boat, cruising the Saint Lawrence River. We stayed at the old camp.

Tom and Debbie invited us to go with them and Willie on a vacation to Kiawah Island, South Carolina, the first week and into the second week of August. This was the first of several vacations that we would take with them. It was somewhat of a "working vacation," as they paid our plane fares, and we could stay with them in the house that they had rented from a friend associated with Syracuse University; in turn we would watch Willie, so that they could have some personal time for themselves. I didn't mind hanging out with Willie, playing basketball in the pool, throwing a frisbee around on the beach, and boogie boarding for hours in the ocean. Debbie could read and relax on the beach, go get a massage, have a glass of wine with Sylvia later in the afternoon. Tom could read, wander around, and sometimes get some extra work done for his classes. Plus having friends to spend time with, go out to dinners, play miniature golf, ride bicycles together, and enjoy each other's company.

Kiawah Island is a barrier island, 25 miles southwest of Charleston. The house we were staying at was a really neat place, just a short walk on the wooded path to a big pool and then to the beach. They invited Ursula and Ben to come up to visit one day and we all went to the Kiawah Island Golf Club and had a nice lunch.

Willie and I played golf at the Kiawah Island Golf Resort, where they have had the 1991 Ryder Cup, World Cups, the 2007 Senior PGA, the 2012 PGA, and will host the 2021 PGA. We played on one of their five championship courses. It was a father and son event that was set up for the younger kids, the tees being moved up 100 to 150 yards on each hole, so the adults couldn't just blast long drives. You had to adjust your game for the shorter drives. I couldn't convince Tom to play with Willie, he insisted that I play instead, maybe he didn't want to look bad. I hardly ever played, just playing a lot of softball. Tom finally consented to play one hole at our urging, got a birdie, and rested on his laurels.

Another day, Willie and I played a round of golf on a different course. Syl and Debbie walked the course, as Tom and one of us alternated riding in the cart. On one of the holes, I hit my ball near the marsh where this big alligator was lurking. I checked it out from a distance and decided to just hit another ball. When we came to the final holes, it was so dark you could hardly see. We were putting on the final hole using the outdoor clubhouse lights to see. Syl and Debbie were getting eaten up by mosquitoes and were anxious to leave. It was definitely a privilege being able to play on a prestigious course like this.

Tom had arranged for a professional chef, who had been the head chef on a cruise ship, to come to the house and prepare a "low country" dinner for us. The chef had every course planned out, from the first glass of wine to the after-dinner liqueur. When Willie came in, he wondered what that awful smell was. It was the chef cooking with garlic. Willie now looks back on this and laughs, as he loves garlic. But he had just finished third grade, soon to begin fourth grade, and was by himself with four adults. We had all these courses: salad, she-crab soup, homemade bread, seafood dishes with rice and vegetables, and desserts. The only drawback was that Tom was feeling bad that Willie didn't want to join us, maybe just being overprotective, and kept going upstairs to check on him. The chef kept having to wait, throwing off his timing, while waiting for Tom and drinking more wine himself. In hindsight, Tom should have gotten Willie some burgers, fries, and a milkshake, put ESPN on the television, and Willie would have been fine. But even with this distraction, it was delicious and a unique experience.

Ursula and Ben came back up to spend a day at the pool and the beach. Tom and Debbie invited them to spend the night, but they felt awkward about it and decided to return home. They went back to the house to shower and change, but Ursula tripped on an uneven part of the driveway and fell; scraping her chin, nose, and knees. It was an unfortunate ending to an otherwise pleasant day for them.

Willie and I were boogie boarding one day and kept feeling the current getting stronger and stronger on our feet. This was the precursor of Hurricane Charley. We would start off even to where Tom, Debbie, and Syl were sitting, but after riding the waves for a while, the undertow had caused us to drift a mile down the beach. Syl would go down the beach after us, worried for our safety and motioning for us to come back. That's the kind of person she was, always concerned about the welfare of others. We had no idea how far we had gone away from our starting point, so we changed our starting point to a half mile in the other direction; but after riding the waves for a while, the undertow caused us to drift down the beach where we were before. Once again Syl came down to motion us back. This happened a few more times before she eventually, and exhaustingly, told us to come back to the beach.

Tom, Willie and I drove into Charleston one evening to catch a Minor League Baseball game. We were all big baseball fans: Tom, being from Cleveland, was a lifelong Indians fan; Debbie, brought up in New York City, was a lifelong Yankees fan; I've been a lifelong Yankees fan, watching them win the World Series so many times, since I was a little kid; Willie chose to split his allegiances between the Indians and Yankees; and Syl, because of me, rooted for the Yankees.

Syl and Debbie stayed in the resort area and walked over to have some wine and a nice dinner. Joseph P. Riley, Jr. Park, known as "The Joe," home of the Charleston RiverDogs, is situated on the banks of the Ashley River. The RiverDogs play in the Class Single-A, South Atlantic League, South Division. When we saw them, they were an affiliate of the Tampa Bay Devil Rays, (now just the Rays.) This turned out to be the last year of this affiliation. In 2005, they became an affiliate of the Yankees, and have been ever since, and want to remain so, well into the future. Even to this day, we all agree that this was one of the most memorable games that we have ever seen. It was between the RiverDogs and the Charleston, West Virginia Alley Cats, then an affiliate of the Toronto Blue Jays.

We started off with some unique food choices and then experienced an hour rain delay. The game featured outfielders, like Delmon Young, playing right field for the RiverDogs, and a future major leaguer, throwing out runners at home to send the game into extra innings, and into extending the game into more extra innings; rundowns between bases, sacrifice and suicide bunts to score runs, great defensive plays, using just about every player on both teams; promos between innings, like guys sumo wrestling in huge rubber suits; this game had it all and then some. We had to drive in the dark and didn't get back to the house until after midnight.

Syl and I drove into Charleston on one of the last days, strolled around, had lunch with Syl's Aunt Lori, her daughter Peggy and family, then took the 30-minute ride on a tour boat to Fort Sumter National Monument. Fort Sumter was where the Civil War began on April 12, 1861, when Confederate artillery opened fire on this Federal fort in Charleston Harbor. Fort Sumter surrendered 34 hours later. Union forces would try for nearly four years to take it back.

We returned home and had to begin the process of packing up all of our things, to move to our new house, on Broadfield Road, outside the Village of Manlius, which is actually located in the Town of Pompey. It is the second highest elevation, at 1,457 feet, in Central New York; only behind the 1,940 feet at Song Mountain in Tully. Actually, at Pompey Hill, where you can see seven counties, it is 1,728 feet. It can tend to be very windy here. Now we were only five or ten minutes from Mom's townhouse, the store, pharmacy, and library in the village of Manlius; and fifteen minutes from Tom and Debbie's house and our teaching jobs at MPH.

The movers came on Tuesday, August 17th. We were needed to stay at Tom and Debbie's house that night to watch Willie, as Tom had an early morning appointment. We didn't feel comfortable leaving Jeopardy alone in a strange new house and we didn't want to bring her to Tom and Debbie's, fearing this strange environment might cause her to run away. So, we left her alone that night at Jerome Street. Poor Jeppy. We felt really bad doing this, yet this seemed like the best solution. At least she had her food dish and water bowl and her small pet bed. But she must have wondered what was going on, with the house being totally empty, and her usual resting places no longer there. She must have felt abandoned. We picked her up in the morning and she was happy to see us, but gave us a look that said,

"What are you trying to do to me?"

We spent our first night on Broadfield Road on Wednesday, August 18th. There was a lot of work to be done the first couple of years: painting, peeling off old wallpaper, (which Syl did), power washing and staining the deck, cutting down and hauling away overgrown bushes, trees, and vines; so many projects to get the house in shape.

My brother in law, John, helped us and we paid him for painting ceilings. Chuck, a close friend I've known since high school, drywalled above the fireplace, and made small wooden frames around each end of the wood beam that extends the full length of the living room. He was nice enough to do these things as a housewarming gift. We also paid him to install a steel door, from the basement to the garage.

The woman that we bought the house from had held on to it for seven years, after her mother, who owned the house, had died unexpectedly at 70. She thought about taking over the house herself, but finally decided to sell it.

We were put into a limbo situation, as our lawyer wouldn't let us officially close on the house, until he tracked down one of the previous owners, who were married, but the husband died and the wife had never signed off on the house. Luckily, she was still alive and signed off on the house, otherwise legally she could have claimed the house, or if she had died, her heirs could have done this also. So, it was for our protection to have this done. But we couldn't proceed on any home improvement projects, so every day we would wait for the news, and had to keep the roofers and plumbers on hold. He had arranged it so that we were paying rent on a daily basis until this issue was resolved. We went ahead with our interior projects, wondering if it was a waste of our time and money. They finally found her, but not until the end of September and much stress, when we could go ahead and have a new roof installed, a new water purification system installed, new hot water heater and well pressure tank and other plumbing; the basement ceiling had to be repaired and painted, had the house insulated, had all the heat ducts cleaned out, and numerous other improvements.

The following spring, Tish and Mary came up from Florida, and we paid Tish to paint the exterior of the house, put in outdoor lights on the house, new top boards on the deck railings, and install new closets in the bedroom and hallway. We paid John to install shingles around the windows. I sealed all the basement and garage walls, painted the beams, pipes, and floors in the basement and garage, garage doors, and the drain tubs in the basement. I also repainted the exterior trim from brown to blue. There is always a lot of work to do on this 1.3 acre property: shoveling, raking, picking up fallen branches, cutting down and trimming broken tree limbs, sweeping the deck and driveway, cleaning up the trash that people throw in the ditches by the road, sealing and painting, maintaining the water purification system, cleaning windows, on an on.

2005

June: New York City

    Park Avenue

    Battery Park

    World Trade Center Memorial

    Central Park (Carriage Ride)

    St. Patrick's Cathedral

    Rockefeller Center

    Broadway

    Times Square

Yankee Stadium (Monument Park)

July: Erie Canal
Green Lakes
Cazenovia Lake
Chittenango Falls

Cape Cod
Truro (Cape View Motel)
Head of the Meadow Beach
Highland Light
Salt Pond Visitor Center

August: Myrtle Beach, South Carolina
Ripley's Aquarium
BB & T Coastal Field

Skaneateles (Ursula visit) & (Mom)
October: Highland Forest

December: New York City

Park Avenue

Fordham University

Saint Patrick's Cathedral

Syl and I drove to Parsippany, New Jersey with Debbie on Friday night, June 17th, the weekend in between the two weeks of our annual Playscape Program at MPH. This trip was a combined celebration of Debbie's birthday on the 9th, Sylvia's birthday on the 18th, and Father's Day for both Tom and Debbie's father, Seelig.

Seelig was a renowned surgeon in New York City, who during World War II, served as Chief Medical Officer on the Queen Mary, which had been converted into a troop transport ship, and crossed the Atlantic Ocean *forty-four times*. His grandson, Debbie's brother, John's son, had done a documentary about him.

It was pouring rain as I drove Debbie's SUV, with Debbie sleeping in the back seat, and Syl up front to navigate. Tom and Willie were supposed to go with us, but Willie was playing in a Little League baseball playoff game. We couldn't believe that the game was not canceled, but they played it in the rain. We arrived at a nice hotel in Parsippany around midnight. In the morning, we met Debbie for breakfast in the hotel. They had a really nice spread that I was still enjoying, when Debbie was anxious to get going, and had Syl go with her to deliver a model train set to Tom's Uncle Joe. He was a brother of Tom's mother from Cleveland, who lived with his wife, Joan, and their family in New Jersey. I finished my breakfast, got our things together, and waited for them outside on a hot and humid day. Debbie drove into the city and as we passed

Harlem Motors on our way to Seelig's apartment, I wondered why it said Harlem Motors. Debbie informed us that it was because we were in Harlem. A few blocks later, we were at the building where the apartment was on Park Avenue. I never realized how close these two completely different worlds were to each other.

This building was 1185 Park Avenue, between East 93rd Street & East 94th Street. It is in the Carnegie Hill neighborhood, one of the very few grand courtyard apartment buildings left in Manhattan, and the only one still standing on Park Avenue. Built in 1929, it has an impressive Gothic triple-arch entrance. There are 172 apartments with 16 total floors. You can walk to Central Park, Museum Mile, Guggenheim Museum, Fifth Avenue, and Madison Avenue. Anne Roiphe wrote her novel, "1185 Park Avenue," about her family life growing up here in the 1940's and 1950's, published in 1999.

We put the car in a parking garage and took a taxi down to Battery Park, where you have a great view of the Statue of Liberty. We then went to the World Trade Center Memorial, which was then still under construction, opened on September 11, 2011, and the museum opened on May 21, 2014. From there Debbie treated us to a carriage ride around Central Park and seeing The Dakota, where John Lennon and Yoko Ono lived, and where John was gunned down on December 8th, 1980. Debbie went to buy a Father's Day gift for Seelig, and Syl and I went to see Saint Patrick's Cathedral, and then to Rockefeller Center to have a couple of beers for Syl's birthday. I ordered two Coors Lights and they said it was $13. I thought that was expensive, until they said it was $13 *each*. I exchanged one, as it had a chip at the top of the bottle. I wasn't going to pay $13 for a Coors Light and have a chip in the bottle.

We returned to the hotel to shower and change for dinner. This was an older hotel, right off Times Square, to be near the Broadway play that we would be going to that night. Tom and Willie would be flying in and joining Debbie and Seelig to go see "Chitty Chitty Bang Bang," but Syl and I had decided to go see Glengarry Glen Ross, David Mamet's 1984 Pulitzer Prize-winning play. Debbie, Syl and I walked for many blocks to meet Seelig for dinner at Shelley's, a renowned seafood restaurant. I don't know why we didn't take a taxi, as it was very humid out, and a long walk, especially for them wearing high heels. But the timing was good, as Seelig was just getting out of his taxi. They brought this huge fountain, an actual fountain, of seafood. One level would be different types of shellfish: crab legs, lobster, shrimp, clams, mussels, oysters, scallops; another level would be: salmon, tuna, and swordfish; another level was sushi. It was so much, but it was so good.

We all got in a taxi and were headed back to Broadway, when Debbie told us that we needed to get out of the taxi and start walking. She was not kidding, saying we would never make our play on time, due to all the congested traffic, if we didn't start walking. So, we got out of the taxi and started walking, making it to the Jacobs Theatre on time. Glengarry Glen Ross was our first Broadway play and it was excellent, with fantastic performances by Alan Alda, Liev Schreiber, and the entire cast. The dinner and the play were really nice birthday presents for Syl. We walked around Times Square after the play, taking in all the sights and sounds, then headed back to our hotel.

Syl and I met them for breakfast the next morning and then on to Yankee Stadium to see the Yankees and the Cubs play an interleague game. Seelig was supposed to go with us, but he wasn't there. It turned out that after we got out of the taxi, Seelig, who was then 92 and 7 months old; had a mild heart attack, if there is such a thing as a mild heart attack. He had several similar attacks before, but this one was enough for Debbie to take him to the hospital. She met Tom and Willie for their Broadway play, but Seelig needed to stay at the hospital for a few days.

"Beatrice Story"

This was not one of the main stories, more of a backup story, when the lunch tables went longer than the normal three-week rotation, and the main fourteen of "Dusty's Lunchtime Stories" had been told; but nevertheless, still a good story to tell. Debbie had been brought up living in her parents' Park Avenue apartment. Her mother, Charmian, was a lifelong Yankee fan. She had some friends that moved to Columbus, Ohio and Charm used to put the radio, with the Yankee game on, up to the phone when they called, as there was no cable television back then. When George Steinbrenner bought the Yankees in 1973, these friends would arrange for Charm and Seelig to sit with them in the owners' box for some Yankee home games. Charm and Seelig became well known in Yankee stadium.

Seelig was expected to be with us in our original plans, but that was obviously not the case now. Even though we would have had to go slower with him being with us, as he was now basically just shuffling along, it still would have speeded things up in other areas; as the ticket takers would have recognized him, and also being the husband of Charm, who had passed away in 2002. And they would have issued the blue security passes needed to get around the stadium, as security was still very tight then after 9/11, as it remains today, but extremely tight back then.

We pulled in to the "players, owners, and special personnel only" parking lot; where they have these road spikes which make it impossible to back up after you've entered. People were lined up on the sides, trying to get a glimpse of their favorite players. They peered in our car and commented,

"I think it might be an assistant trainer." I felt like yelling out, "No, I still play third base for the Syracuse Cyclones."

We parked our car next to A-Rod, as he got out of his car, sunglasses on and nicely casually dressed. Then Mariano Rivera, on his cell phone, also with sunglasses and nicely casually dressed. Other players, like Bernie Williams and Jorge Posada, started to arrive and get out of their cars. Debbie went to get our tickets and had to explain that she was Charm's daughter at the V.I.P. window. She didn't know to ask, or they forgot to inform her, about getting the blue security passes. So, we all went in and headed down to the V.I.P. Room for breakfast. Debbie explained who we were as we entered past the security guys. There was a woman there at her desk that greeted us.

She said, "Hi, my name is Beatrice. If there is anything you need, just let me know."

We thanked her and entered the room and sat at a table. Amazingly, I had never been to a game at Yankee Stadium. Neither had Willie. We both really wanted to see Monument Park and decided to go. Surprisingly, Tom didn't want to go. Syl stayed with Tom and Debbie for breakfast. They said that we had better hurry if we were going to go to Monument Park, as it closes 45 minutes before the start of the game. In our haste, I had taken nothing with me: no wallet, money, or identification. Luckily, I had our ticket stubs in my pocket. I asked one of the ushers, a younger guy, how to get to Monument Park. He pointed at the long line of people waiting to get in and said,

"Monument Park is open to the public, but as the waiting line to get in is filled, because of Father's Day, it is closed for today."

Well, the forlorn look on Willie's face, wearing his Yankees hat, and mine as well, telling him we had just come down from Syracuse for the game; must have struck a chord with him, especially if he had kids, being Father's Day. Whatever his reasons, he motioned for us to follow him, as he led us down in the stadium's underground through alleys and mazes that only ushers and maintenance people would know, past dumpsters and right into Monument Park. I thanked him profusely and felt guilty that I didn't have any money with me to tip him. I'm sure he would have accepted it, but he didn't have his hand out or look angry. I think he felt good about doing something nice for a kid, and whom he assumed was his father, on Father's Day.

I felt like a little kid in there, taking pictures next to the monuments of Babe Ruth, Lou Gehrig, Joe DiMaggio, and Mickey Mantle. The Cubs were taking batting practice as Willie watched them bang balls off the plexiglass window. It was time to head back to the V.I.P. room, as reality was now setting in, as the eventual crowd of 53,000 fans were filling up the stands. We couldn't go back the way we had come and started walking up through the crowd. I kept my hand on Willie's shoulder as we navigated our way to the open area at the top of the stadium. I found an usher and asked him how we could get back to the V.I.P. room.

He said, "Do you have your blue security passes?"

"No, but Beatrice told us that if ....."

"Oh, Beatrice? C'mon, follow me."

It was like a magic word.

He led us to a private elevator and told us that this would take us up to the correct floor. We got on the elevator and arrived at the floor where we had first entered. We were met with a group of security guards.

"Excuse me, can we help you?"

"Yes, we are trying to get back to the V.I.P. room."

"The V.I.P. room is down the hall, but do you have your blue security passes?"

"No, but Beatrice told us that if ....."

"Oh, Beatrice? Okay, we can take you there."

Again, it was like a magic word, as they led us down the hall to the V.I.P. room, and there was Beatrice at her desk.

"Hi, Beatrice, we are so glad to see you! You are a famous person here at the stadium."

She smiled as we told her our story.

We joined Tom, Debbie, and Syl and told them what had happened with us. It was too late for us to have breakfast and we went to our seats and watched the Yankees beat the Cubs, 6-3, to sweep the three-game series.

A couple of weeks later, Syl and I took Willie up to the Syracuse University Bookstore to get his supplies for the upcoming school year, which we had been doing for several years. I didn't enter through the guardhouse we usually went to, instead going to the one down by South Crouse. We explained who we were to a young woman, that we had the Vice-Chancellor's son with us and were taking him to the bookstore. She said that she didn't have Debbie's name on her list. I told her to call her, but she couldn't reach her. I then gave her Tom's name, explaining that he was Debbie's husband and an Economics Professor. She said that she didn't have his name on her list either. She was really being a stickler and we just couldn't get through to her. We called Tom and he told us to just go back to our usual gate. The guard at this gate looked inside our car, after we explained who we were, and recognized Willie.

He said, "Hi Willie. My name is Willie also."

He let us in and Willie said to us,

"See, I was your Beatrice today."

In July, Karen and Andrew came up from Atlanta for another visit. We went for walks on the Erie Canal, Green Lakes, and Chittenango Falls; and went swimming at Green Lakes, Cazenovia Lake, and over at Tom and Debbie's pool.

This next story would be the 14th and final story, of the main stories, of "Dusty's Lunchtime Stories." This was determined by categorizing four other stories as backup stories: "My Front Tooth," "Space Mountain," "Sand Dollar Heaven," and the "Beatrice Story;" as well as stories about my horse, "Torch," my dog, "Scooter," and stories about our three cats.

"The Shaving Story"

Later in July, Syl and I once again went to Cape Cod, staying in Truro at the Cape View Motel. It was a beautiful morning, as we got up to have breakfast and then spend the day at our favorite beach, the Head of the Meadow Beach in Truro. For some reason, maybe I wasn't hydrated enough, I was having a migraine headache attack. I took two Excedrin Migraine tablets and then went in the bathroom to shave. I had been using an electric shaver since Syl had bought me one for a Christmas present in 2004. I had used a straight razor all my adult life, but I had now switched to the electric shaver, and was used to using it for the past almost seven months now, without any problems. I began to shave and felt a pull and saw that I had a nick in my neck that was bleeding. I checked the shaver and noticed that one of the shaving heads had a bent blade that had become jagged. I tore off a piece of a paper towel, folded it, and held it on the nick. This seemed to do the trick, as the bleeding had apparently stopped.

I didn't worry about it too much as I started to do my workout routine. I did some stretching exercises and sit-ups and then began to work my arms with a set of 30-pound barbells that I had brought with me. In hindsight, this turned out to not be a very wise move. I found out later, which I probably should have been aware of, that Excedrin, or any acetaminophen, or aspirin product, are serious blood thinners. Exercising, especially lifting weights, was the worst thing I could have done to keep the blood from flowing from the nick. The blood was coming out nonstop now, as I kept tearing off pieces of paper towels to try and control the bleeding. I usually have a styptic pencil in my toiletry kit, but there wasn't one in there. This stick's medication is aluminum sulfate and acts as a vasoconstrictor in order to restrict blood flow. You apply it to the bleeding site and it seals small cuts and nicks.

I must have nicked an artery or vein, as the bleeding would not stop, and I had already gone through an entire roll of paper towels. We decided to drive to Provincetown to go to a store and buy a styptic pencil. I was driving, one hand on the steering wheel, and the other hand holding folded pieces of paper towels, that would just saturate the towels and the blood would be running through my fingers. Syl kept handing me clean towels as she would take away the blood-soaked ones. I don't know why I didn't have Syl drive, just being macho or something. (I always drove: to work, store, trips, vacations, all the time. Syl did pick me up when I came out of anesthesia after all my medical and dental surgeries and was a good driver. But I was a more confident driver in heavy traffic and strange places and Syl was a much better navigator than I was.) We went into the store and I bought a styptic pencil. The plan was to drive to the beach, where I would apply the styptic pencil to my neck for a while, and then go swimming where the salt water would further help to seal the nick and everything would be fine.

This turned out to be wishful thinking. We arrived at the beach and I went into the bathroom, as Syl waited outside for me. I attempted to apply the styptic pencil, but it was totally useless, as the blood kept gushing out. I think this was when I finally realized that this was a really serious situation. Syl probably realized this from the start, always being wiser than me, but went along with my plan, up until this point.

Syl and I left the beach and decided to go to the Truro Fire and Rescue Station, to have this checked out and see what they could do. We had been there two years earlier, in July, 2003, when Syl had been stung by a bee and was afraid of having a serious allergic reaction. She was allergic to a certain kind of bee, the honey bee, and had been stung while sitting around the hotel pool. She was wearing a bathing suit with flowers on it, evidently attracting the bee's curiosity. Luckily, she had no allergic reaction, just some redness. They gave her some Benadryl and she was fine. Syl had a few incidents in her childhood and was told a sting from a honey bee could be potentially life threatening if allergic symptoms were not treated immediately. She had been stung years before in our backyard on Jerome Street and started to get hives, rashes, and swelling almost instantaneously. I rushed her to the doctor, where they gave her an antihistamine, and a few days later she was back to normal. We should have always carried an EpiPen with us, especially on trips and vacations, but we didn't. We went to the Rescue Center and they checked me out and tried using a thicker type of styptic stick, which left a black circle mark, to no avail. They suggested going to the Emergency Center in Wellfleet, one of only two on the Cape, the other in Hyannis. They called up the one in Wellfleet;

"Yeah, we've got a guy here that is coming down to see you, that cut his neck with an electric shaver."

The E.R. doctor probably didn't think that it was a big deal the way he said it.

We left and drove down to Wellfleet, the whole time applying the folded-up paper towels to the gushing blood from the nick. By now, I had gone through almost two rolls of paper towels and my face looked very pale with all the blood that I had lost. Syl was extremely worried now. We arrived in the parking lot of the Wellfleet Emergency Center, a very small building. Just as we were parking, another car pulled in and the people were urgently taking a young boy inside, who we found out was having a serious asthma attack. There were only two doctors there, and one was already treating someone, so I had to wait for them to treat the young boy. They asked me to fill out the paperwork, as I did while dripping blood from the saturated paper towels, onto the forms and the counter.

Finally, we got to see the doctor, who was a very nice woman. I told her about taking the Excedrin and then exercising. She said that the Excedrin can thin your blood out for a week. She checked me out and told me that I was very fortunate that I hadn't cut the jugular vein or the carotid artery, which could have had catastrophic results, as it brings the blood from your brain to your heart. She tried putting this "new skin" patch on the nick and that didn't work. She informed me that she was going to try again with a thicker "new skin" patch, and if that didn't work, they would have to airlift me to Hyannis by helicopter for more immediate drastic measures to stop the bleeding. She applied this thicker "new skin" patch and it worked. It eventually blended in and I haven't had any more issues since. She told me,

"You look like an athletic, always in motion, kind of guy. But you need to chill and not do anything strenuous for at least three days. That means no swimming, running, exercising, or lifting weights. And even after that, to just take it easy for a while."

Now I was feeling really weak from all the loss of blood and I had all these bruises on my neck, a black circle from the stuff the rescue guys had used, special bandages to keep the skin patch in place, and other bandages over them. We went back to the hotel pool, where Syl and other people were swimming, and I could only wade in up to my waist on a picture-perfect day on the first day of our vacation. I felt very self-conscious as we got ready to go out to dinner and wore a turtleneck on a warm summer evening. I bought a new shaver and was afraid to shave near that area for months. I was also afraid that the pressure of the water while taking a shower might cause the "new skin" patch to come off, so I held my hand over that area every time that I took a shower for months.

After three days of sitting by the pool, (wading for me), and driving through the towns, we hiked the trails at the Salt Pond Visitor Center at the National Seashore, walked up to Highland Light, and eventually went back to the beach, where I took it easy on the boogie boarding.

One day a baby seal washed up on the beach. He was trying to get back out to where his mother was, frantically calling for him to swim out and join her. She was about 100 feet out, swimming parallel to the shore. She couldn't risk getting any closer for fear of getting beached. The baby would try to swim out, but the waves would engulf him and he retreated back to shore. People started milling around and the lifeguards told them to not get too close, for fear the mother would leave. People can be such jerks sometimes. They were trying to touch the baby, making him more frightened, and taking closeup pictures of him. I have a couple of pictures of him, but taken from a distance. This scenario went on for over an hour as the mother kept calling for him. The baby did go down the beach and around the corner, out of sight, so hopefully they were reunited and it was a happy ending.

  Syl and I returned home and there was Jeppy waiting for us. Bruce had watched her and the house while we were gone. She gave us a growl and a look that said, "Where have you been?" Jeppy was getting frail now, she was our only cat left, after having cats for almost 22 years. Roxy had lived for almost 12 years and was the only one to live on Clyde Avenue, before we moved to Elm Street in North Syracuse. She was our only cat for eight months, until her solitude was disrupted when we got Mandu in July, 1984. Roxy and Mandu were together for about two and a half years, before we got Jeppy around Christmas, 1986. All the cats lived in North Syracuse, Erieville, Canastota, and the Syracuse University area. Roxy was only at Jerome Street for a little over eight months. Now it was Mandu and Jeopardy at Jerome Street, for six years and about two months together, before Mandu was put to sleep on March 6, 2001. I remember us taking him in at 3 o'clock in the morning because he was howling in pain. He was 17 years and 2 months old. It was only Jeppy with us from this point on, for 4 years and 4 and a half months. She was the only one to make it out to Broadfield Road in Pompey. So, this brings us back to returning from Cape Cod. Jeppy had been holding on, waiting for us so that she could say goodbye. We had to take her in later that night, actually early in the morning, and had her put to sleep on July 20, 2005. She wasn't her normal self for these 11 months that she lived out here on Broadfield Road, but she lived the longest of our cats, 18 years and 10 months.

Our three cats provided laughter, affection, and funny stories over almost 22 years. I already mentioned some about Roxy. One time she decided to climb up on the barn roof in Erieville and she refused to come down all day and half the night, for no apparent reason, at least not to us. Another time she escaped into the backwoods at Mom's townhouse, when we were staying there with the three cats, before we could move into our townhouse in Canastota. We had to search for her and finally got her, as she was almost down to the village in Manlius. I think her being in that crowded and chaotic apartment that she was in when we adopted her, always made her skittish, especially when she was confronted with a new environment.

Mandu was a classic character. He was a big cat, not unbelievably fat, I've seen worse; but he could have dropped a few pounds. He would get in between us in bed and there was no way you could lift the covers. There would have to be an emergency to get him to move, where Roxy was just the opposite, she would hightail it at the drop of a hat. We would call him "Comfy-do," or "Lazy-do," any name we would just add the "do" at the end of it. He would be outside all day in Erieville, having five acres of property to go to the bathroom any time that he wanted to; but he would prefer to wait until he was back in the house, and I had finished cleaning out the kitty litter, nice and neat, then he would hop in the litter box and go. Every time. Unbelievable.

One day a guy came over to check out the Buick Regal that we were selling, (which he did soon after), and had his dog, a big mean looking dog, a German Shepherd, with him and left him in his car with the window rolled only a third of the way down. The dog spotted Mandu, and I have no idea how he managed to get out of that window, but he did. He chased after Mandu and Mandu went up this huge pine tree in front of the house, at least 60 feet, with no exaggeration. After the guy took his dog and left, I called for Mandu to come down. He refused and it was starting to get dark. I went and got the metal extension ladder, extended it to its maximum height, and propped it against the tree. I climbed up over halfway and called for Mandu to come down. Again nothing. I climbed up to the top of the ladder and called him again. It was dark out now. Finally, he decided that the coast was clear and he just flew down. I mean this was not a gradual descent; he came crashing down, breaking branches and limbs, as I caught him in my arms and broke his fall. It didn't break my fall, as the ladder went tumbling backwards and hit the ground, as did my head. I was very fortunate not to break any limbs myself or suffer a serious head injury. Mandu just looked at me, like "thanks," stretched, and walked away to go into the house.

  Jeopardy had the most stories and the funniest. One day when we lived in Erieville, the neighbors who lived behind us, had a black border collie named Tasha, who decided to come over and start chasing Jeppy. They were going around and around the barn, a flurry of black chasing orange and white. It looked like something out of a cartoon. After a while, Jeppy put on her brakes as if to say, "What's wrong with this picture?" She then did a u turn and started chasing Tasha full speed, now orange and white chasing black, around and around the barn. If we could have captured this on video, I think we would have had a great chance at winning the funniest video on the $100,000 video television show. It was really funny watching these two.

  Jeppy used to sit on the foot rest part of the recliner chair when I watched television in my room on Jerome Street. When I would put the footrest down, to go to use the bathroom that was right around the corner, she would jump off and run into the bathroom. I would sit on the toilet, and she would be on the edge of the bathtub, which faced the toilet. The first time this happened, as I was sitting there, I started petting her. After this, Jeppy started *expecting* to be petted, and wouldn't leave until she was. I could be watching television and just move my legs for a better position, and she would jump off and run into the bathroom. *Every time.* She watched every move that you made. She would paw down the toilet paper roll. She would try to flush the toilet, using her head to push down the flush handle. She just wasn't strong enough to do it, but she knew *exactly* what to do. Then she would watch the water being flushed, all the way down, like it was the greatest thing in the world. She did this from the time she was a kitten, to the very end, when she was old and frail.

When Syl and I went to bed, she would wait until we were under the covers and then she would walk around the entire perimeter of the bed, walking across our heads on the pillows, *exactly three times*, before she got between us and settled down. If you had a leg twitch or moved your legs to a different position, she would get up and walk around the perimeter of the bed, walking across our heads on the pillows, *exactly three times,* before she would settle in between us. Sometimes in order to get some sleep, we would have to close the door on her. Then she would growl and scratch the door to let her in. We felt bad, but she would eventually go sleep somewhere else. She just couldn't help herself with her compulsions, but she certainly provided us with some comical moments.

As long as I am telling stories about our cats, I also want to tell you about my horse, "Torch," that I rode in my childhood. He was a Hackney horse, a breed that was developed in the United Kingdom, popular now for carriage driving. When in motion, it seems like it is floating. They are known to be intelligent, gentle, and loyal. "Torch" was black with a perfect red star on his forehead, red markings on his legs, and red streaks in his tail, thus his name. He was my horse, but I didn't actually own him. There was a man from Florida who owned several horses, to be ridden at the summer camp at Lakemont, and boarded them here. If you took care of them, hosed them down, brushed them, fed them, and cleaned out their stall, you were able to ride them. I took care of "Torch" and we had a strong bond between us.

I was 10 years old in 1956, when we had the annual horse show at the end of the summer camp. The judges would shout instructions: "Riders, walk. Now trot." You would have to demonstrate that you were posting, up and down, in rhythm. "Now canter. Now gallop." After this, you had to complete a series of jumps, jumping over wooden posts, some with two posts, some with three, and some with four. "Torch" was a great jumper; we had practiced all summer and he had cleared all the jumps with no problem. On the day of the show, he went over the two and three post jumps, but refused to jump the four post ones. He almost threw me off when he stopped abruptly. I was in tears, as I was disqualified for not completing the required jumps. I couldn't be mad at "Torch," I loved him too much.

The next summer, 1957, when I was 11, I was confident that "Torch" would come through, as we had practiced really hard all spring and summer. And he did! I won first place, and it was on my birthday, so a great present. I was so proud of him. I took him back to his stall, hosed him down, and placed the first-place blue ribbon on his bridle. People were congratulating me and when I came back to see him in his stall, he had eaten the ribbon! I couldn't get mad at him, I loved him too much.

Our family also had a dog when we lived in Lakemont. It had been given to my older sister, Linda, by a good friend of hers from high school. When she went away to college, he stayed with us and became the family dog. He was a mixed breed of half-dachshund and half-beagle. His name was "Scooter." This was a perfect name for him, as he would scoot across the athletic fields where my dad was coaching, with his short little legs barely off the ground, and his long beagle ears almost touching the ground; as fast as he could, to greet us as we got off the school bus from Dundee.

"Scooter" was affectionate and a great friend. It was a sad ending for him however, as he was hit by a car and died. (I didn't tell this part to the kids.) What actually happened to him, nobody knows, only the person who hit him and the person who put his dead body on our front porch. Mom confirmed this, when I asked her if my recollection of this was accurate, when she was in the nursing home. She didn't think that the person who put him on the porch was being mean, rather found him on the road and wanted us to know what had happened. The details are fuzzy whether that person was the same person that had hit him with the car. It still seems weird to me to place him on our porch. Dad buried him in a remote area of the back yard. Either way, a sad and strange way to end such a loyal and loving dog's life. All I remember is that it was a traumatic childhood experience.

Faraway Friends

Faraway friends

Lost in my desert of memories

Inside some stolen silhouette

Framed and left to hang

In August, we went on another vacation with Tom, Debbie, and Willie, to Myrtle Beach, South Carolina. Myrtle Beach is a city and vacation resort on South Carolina's Atlantic coast, the main attraction on the Grand Strand, a 60 mile stretch of beaches. We stayed at a hotel right on the ocean. They were nice enough to give Syl and I the front bedroom with an ocean view. We all went to Ripley's Aquarium, where they have 10,000 exotic sea creatures in exhibits like Rio Amazon, Dangerous Reef, and Ray Bay. We touched prehistoric horseshoe crabs and gentle stingrays.

We played a lot of miniature golf. Myrtle Beach is known as the golf capital of the world, but also as the self-proclaimed mini-golf capital of the world; as there are more mini-golf courses per square mile than in any other city in the United States. Plus, it is the home for the ProMiniGolf Association's "Masters" tournament, this year being played at "Hawaiian Rumble" in North Myrtle Beach. We played this course and many others.

Tom, Willie, and I went to a Minor League baseball game to see the Myrtle Beach Pelicans, at this time an affiliate of the Atlanta Braves, in the Carolina League,

Single A, at Coastal Federal Field. Jarrod Saltalamacchia, a future major leaguer, and also having the distinction of the longest, non-hyphenated last name in professional baseball; was the catcher for the Pelicans.

Willie and I did a lot of boogie boarding again. One day, we were way out there trying to catch the biggest waves, and as it turned out, it was a good thing that we were. There was a guy where we were with his two sons. He was showing his older son, around 9 or 10 years old I would guess, some boogie boarding tips; as his younger son, 6 or 7 years old I would guess, was maybe five yards away. (Willie was 10 years and 7 months old at this time.) All of a sudden, this big wave came crashing down and engulfed the younger boy, who had drifted farther away from his father and brother. He went under and started to struggle and then was not in sight anymore. Willie and I saw this as it was unfolding. There was no time for me to do anything but to dive under the waves. I grabbed the boy as he had swallowed water and was in dire straits. I got him to the surface and slapped him on the back and the water that he had swallowed came bursting out. By now, the father had realized that he had lost sight of his younger son and was panicking. He saw me carry the boy over to him and he was extremely grateful. He was feeling so guilty, and if I hadn't been there, in the right place at the exact right time, to save the boy's life, he would have never forgiven himself. That's all it takes, just a quick minute for a tragedy to occur. You read about these stories all the time, children being unattended swimming in the pool, or losing sight of them for an instant in a lake, ocean, or river. You have to be vigilant at all times. But it was a great feeling that you were able to make sure that it was a happy ending for that family.

Ursula came up for a visit later in August, enjoying Tom and Debbie's pool, checking out yard sales with Syl, and we took her and Mom out to Skaneateles, where we all went on the Skaneateles Lake Boat Tour. In October, Syl and I went on our fall foliage drives and took nice hikes through Highland Forest, Green Lakes and Pratt's Falls.

In December, over Christmas vacation, Syl and I drove down to New York City with Tom, Debbie, and Willie and stayed for a few days at the Park Avenue apartment. We went down to see the lights and decorations in "The Big Apple;" go to The Metropolitan Museum of Art, where they had an exhibition of Vincent van Gogh: The Drawings; and for Willie to attend this baseball clinic, that Derek Jeter was putting on, at Fordham University.

When I first heard about the clinic from Tom, I envisioned an indoor baseball field of Astro Turf, where the fathers and sons would be able to throw the ball around with Derek Jeter and other Yankee players. As Tom usually had me take his place in these situations, I packed an equipment bag of my cleats, glove, hat, and softball uniform. If there was even the slightest chance of playing catch with Derek Jeter, I definitely wanted to be prepared. As it turned out, there was no way that was going to happen. The clinic took place in the Fordham University gymnasium and it was for the kids only, parents had to stay behind these metal gates they had set up on the sidelines. While everyone was waiting for Derek and the players to arrive, Tom had gone into the bathroom, and as he started to take a pee, Derek Jeter comes in and is taking a pee in the urinal next to Tom's, and says hello. A future talking point.

There were three stations: one was a fielding station with Derek, where he would throw a grounder to the kids waiting in two single file lines, then they would throw the ball over to a college kid, simulating a throw to first base; then jog back in line, giving Derek a high five on the way back. Willie went through and was so focused that he ran right past Derek without giving him a "high five," while we were shouting at him to do so. Then all the kids in this station would take group pictures with Derek. This clinic was mainly a public relations forum for Jeter and a nice bonus from the clinic fees, probably some extra money for him to buy Christmas presents while in New York City, before returning home to Tampa, Florida. The second station was with Tino Martinez, a close friend and former Yankee teammate of Jeter's, who had just retired. The kids would take swings in the batting cages and get hitting instructions from Tino and then take group pictures with him. All these group pictures were part of the package in this clinic. The third station was with Jim Leyritz, former Yankee teammate and a big part of the Yankees 1996 World Series win over the Atlanta Braves. He had fallen on some hard times with some serious off the field issues, where I think Derek was trying to help him out. His was a pitching station, where the kids would pitch to a college kid and get throwing instructions from Leyritz, and then the group photo. It was still a cool experience seeing the players up close and personal and Willie had a lot of fun.

  Somehow, I wound up back at the apartment after the clinic, as they all went to do something else. Maybe to bring my equipment bag back, so I didn't have to carry it around. I was to meet Syl at Saint Patrick's Cathedral and Seelig's personal Korean driver would drive me there. He was going to let me out several blocks away, but I asked him if he would drop me off in front of the Cathedral, as I had no clue where I was. I kept waiting for Syl, ducking inside every now and then, because it was so bitterly cold out; but not for long, as I didn't want her to think that I wasn't there, and she would be outside freezing. I was so glad to finally see her. We walked around the cathedral and lit some prayer candles in there before venturing outside into the bitter cold once again.

We all met for dinner at this restaurant in Grand Central Station, and we took pictures of Tom and Willie standing in front of the Grand Central Station sign used in the Madagascar movie, which they loved.

So, just to summarize, in order, with dates, the fourteen main stories that I told during lunch:

"Dusty's Lunchtime Stories"

#1. August, 1951: "Quicksand"

#2. March, 1957: "Falling Through The Ice"

#3. 1953-1960: "Stories About My Brother"

("Flying On The Roof") & ("Hitting My Head With A Baseball Bat") & ("Pitching A Baseball In My Ear and The Twenty-Third Psalm")

#4. 1963 (& beyond): "Nightmares"

("Alien Dreams") & ("Stopping The Train")

#5. November, 1969: "Hercules Caves"

#6. May-July, 1970: "Frisbee Trilogy"

#7. February, 1971: "Desert Cactus"

#8. March, 1973: "Stepping On A Sea Porcupine"

#9. November, 1978: "The Almost South American Plane Crash"

#10. April, 1986: "Moon Jellyfish"

#11. April, 1986: "Dead Man's Curve"

#12. April, 1986: "Shorty's Glass Bottom Boat"

#13. February, 1989: "The Long Walk Leaving The Mayan Ruins"

#14. July, 2005: "The Shaving Story"

2006

May: Alexandria, Virginia

July: Thousand Islands
    Mink Island

September: New York City (Liam & Willie)
    Park Avenue
    Yankee Stadium
    Statue of Liberty
    Ellis Island

October: Penn Yan (Keuka Lake)

Dundee

Lakemont (Seneca Lake)

    In May, Syl and I drove, taking Mom with us, 386 miles south to Alexandria, Virginia; for the wedding of Emlyn, Tom and Julie's daughter, and Brian. For some reason, maybe she wasn't feeling well, Linda decided not to go. I'm sure John would have been glad to drive them there. Tom and Julie were nice enough to take care of our hotel rooms. Syl and I walked around down by the harbor in Alexandria and the next day we got dressed up and went on the boat, "Celebrity," for the wedding. This boat went down the Potomac River, all the way where you felt like you could touch the Washington Monument. The wedding ceremony was very nice and Mom read "An Apache Blessing." The boat felt like it was swaying when the music got going and everyone was dancing. Brian and Em are still happily married today, with three wonderful children: Brady, Lila, and Morgan.

    In July, Syl and I went up to the Thousand Islands, spending a few days on Mink Island with Gary and Patty at their camp. We again stayed at the old camp, having our breakfast in the morning, then walking down the long line of wooden steps, and swimming in the river in front of the camp. We had fun going out on the boat, cruising and swimming in the Saint Lawrence River, nice dinners, looking at the stars and listening to music at night. This would turn out to be the last year that we would stay at the camp. We didn't know it at this time, it didn't even enter our minds, but other issues and circumstances arose. For several years, we talked about going back up, even if it was just for the day, but it never happened.

I think that the trip to Virginia had taken its toll on Mom, but it didn't manifest itself until the third week in July. Actually, Mom had gotten a new car a month earlier. She always drove a Toyota Camry, but when her lease was up, she decided to get a smaller car. She had gone to a different car dealer than the one who knew her and wound up being talked into, by some young and indifferent salespeople, buying a purple Dodge Neon. This car was small, uncomfortable, and about the farthest thing in the world that my mom should be driving and relying on, to get her safely where she needed to go. I was furious and went down to the dealers to give them a piece of my mind, like,

"What were you people thinking, or were you even thinking about what's best for my mother?"

There was a grace period that was still in effect to return this car and get her down payment reimbursed. We took her to the dealer that knew her and she got a smaller Toyota, a Corolla. She drove over to show us during our Playscape Program in June and was so happy. She was like a teenager, driving a new car, and still being able to drive.

For several years, for a week during August, Mom had driven to Chautauqua, a town and lake resort community in western New York, about a four hour, 220 miles west, trip from Syracuse. There she would stay at the Christian Science house, and greet people and give those who were interested, information about the religion. Chautauqua is an Iroquois word meaning "a bag tied in the middle" or "two moccasins tied together," and describes the shape of Chautauqua Lake. Chautauqua was an adult education movement in the United States, highly popular in the late 19th and early 20th centuries. Today they have many lectures, concerts, and plays. Mom always wanted us to go with her and stay for a few days, swim in Chautauqua Lake, see a concert, and walk around the grounds. I always felt guilty about not going, at least driving her up there, as she had to drive up and back by herself. She was proud of herself for driving there, especially when she was older. It always seemed that there was a conflict for us at the time she would go; whether we were on vacation with Tom, Debbie, and Willie, or taking care of Willie, or a softball tournament. They were the main factors, but having to stay at the Christian Science house, (we couldn't afford to stay elsewhere), was never appealing to us.

Mom had planned another trip to Chautauqua in August, but things changed forever for her the last week in July. She had suffered an apparent stroke. We had been over at her townhouse the day before, helping her with some gardening. Every time that we would leave Mom, whether it was after going out to dinner, a walk, hanging out with her; I always felt close to her, but sad at the same time. She was all alone in her townhouse. We would give each other the universal sign language for "I Love You" every time we left.

Mom had been doing a lot of sorting, lifting boxes and moving other things around. I told her not to do that, just call us and we would lift anything that she wanted us to, especially now that we were just five minutes away. I came in the house the next day and things did not look right. There was food all over the floor in the room where she watched television, as soon as you entered from the garage. I went around the corner and there she was, not being able to move or speak, or make it to the bathroom. One positive thing was that she had not gone up her long stairs to her upstairs bedroom, and then had the stroke, and fallen down the stairs. That would have been catastrophic. She looked into my eyes, and as helpless as she was, was so glad that I had found her and was there to help her. At first, we thought she had been there for 48 hours, but through her emails, it showed that she had been there for 24 hours, still obviously way too long.

There had been warning signs before.

Several years earlier, we had come over to pick her up to go out to the Brewster Inn in Cazenovia for Easter brunch. She was all dressed up when we got there, but said that she wasn't feeling well and to go on without her. We didn't want to do that, but she insisted, and we went to brunch. We came back to check on her, but she said she just wanted to lie down. This was always the problem with the Christian Science faith, her "not feeling well" could actually be a heart attack or stroke, you never knew the severity. We had to go over to her townhouse every night after Extended Day for months after this, as she did not feel confident going up and down her stairs. Syl would prepare dinner for her, have a hot plate up there, and fruit, and other food; and I would empty out the bucket where she was going to the bathroom, as she didn't want to risk walking over to the actual bathroom. Amazingly, through her strong faith, she recovered from this, and was fine for a few years; even driving, as I mentioned earlier, before this major stroke. The only visible sign of that previous stroke was that it had affected her hip, which she now had a limp and had to kind of drag it when she got in the car. Many years before, she had a minor episode on a school function, where she had to ask Baxter to help her get a lifesaver out of her purse.

Instead of just calling 911, which was the realistic and humane thing to do, I had to call Julie in Virginia, so that she could call Mom's Christian Science practitioner, *to get permission* to call 911. I always thought that Mom, being an intelligent woman and a highly respected educator, would be the renaissance woman to bring the Christian Science religion into more progressive thinking; out of the 19th century and into the 21st century. Their philosophy of "mind over matter" is a convincing one, that the mind can control our getting sick by not letting worry, stress, or negativity rule our thought process. But they always rationalized, wrongly so, about going to the dentist, (even if they didn't take novocaine), but not to the doctor. A dentist is still a Doctor of Dentistry, no matter how they try to spin it. And if you break or fracture a bone, or have an infection, you go see a doctor, with his or hers medical education and expertise, and modern technology, to set the bone in a cast, or treat the infection with antibiotics; and then you can utilize your faith to help you heal better and faster. But you could never break through the wall of dogma that Christian Scientists put up, no matter how plausible your logic. They were still entrenched in the teachings of Mary Baker Eddy, who healed herself of life-threatening injuries sustained after a fall, by spiritual means alone; and founded Christian Science in 1866. She published the textbook of Christian Science: "Science and Health," later called "Science and Health with Key to the Scriptures," in 1875. In 1908, at the age of 87, she founded The Christian Science Monitor, a global newspaper that has won many Pulitzer Prizes. She passed away in 1910. Mom was born ten years later into this religion.

    The paramedics came and took Mom to the Emergency Room. I explained to the doctors about her religious beliefs. She was taken to Crouse Hospital where she stayed for a week, taking no medicine, except on the first day there they had given her something for her extremely high blood pressure. They had put compression stockings on her legs to aid in her blood circulation. I was of the mindset to give her this medication, where Linda and Julie were not, to honor her free will and religious beliefs. Marty originally sided with me, then changed his mind when listening to what they were saying. Now it was them feeling one way and only me the other way. So, no medication for Mom.

   After a week, we put Mom in the Iroquois Nursing Home in Jamesville. For a while, she had her own room, but then had to be with a roommate with a curtain in the middle. Mom's strength of conviction in her faith was truly extraordinary, as she lived for 2 years and over 3 months there, taking absolutely no medication. Mom had been on her own for 22 years and 2 months, since Dad passed away in the middle of May, 1986.

   Dad had gotten sick over that winter and was retaining fluids, my guess from either a kidney infection or worse, or a prostate issue. He could have seen a college roommate of his, one of the leading urologists in the country, to diagnose his problem. But he was trying to show Mom how much he loved her by trying to heal himself through Christian Science. I could see if the doctor told him he would have to be on a dialysis machine, or procedures that could cost thousands and thousands of dollars, which they didn't have; to not take this route.

   But what if antibiotics or radiation treatments would have cured him? We'll never know. And Dad, not drinking or smoking, could have gotten a good ten years or more; sixty-nine and almost five months was way too early for him. I found a letter after he had passed away, where he said, "I feel like the fat man in the circus." They had to cut his suit coat in the back to fit him in the casket.

Julie lived in Syracuse then and would feed him, clean him, and do nursing type things for him during the day while Mom was at work. I brought over a spare bed and set it up in the dining room, so he didn't have to climb the stairs up to their bedroom anymore. At least he passed away peacefully in his sleep. So, you can see, with my lifelong ordeal with my right ankle, and the way my Dad's life was cut short, without any attempt to change the outcome; why I get frustrated and irritated by the limitations of the Christian Science philosophy.

It was hard to see Mom, an educator for over 33 years, not being able to speak. Syl and I would come up to the nursing home almost every night after Extended Day, trying to balance it out on the nights where Linda and John came to visit her. This went on for nearly four months.

It was an unusually warm night, for Syracuse, in late November, as I wheeled Mom outside to get some fresh air. What I am about to tell you reminded me of a scene in the 1975 movie, "One Flew Over the Cuckoo's Nest," where R.P. McMurphy, (Jack Nicholson), offers Chief Bromden, (Will Sampson), a stick of gum and the Chief thanks him. McMurphy looks at him in astonishment, not sure if he actually said that, as the Chief has not said a word in the movie up to this point, pretending to be deaf and dumb. McMurphy hands him another stick of gum with the wrapper on and the Chief looks at it and acknowledges that it is Juicy Fruit.

I looked up at the clear night sky and said to Mom,

"Wow, it's a beautiful full moon tonight."

A couple of minutes went by with Mom not saying anything, as had been the case for four months.

Then, out of nowhere, in a higher pitched voice than her normal one, Mom said,

"When there is a ring around the full moon, that means it's going to rain tomorrow."

I looked at her in utter amazement and said,

"Whoa, Juicy Fruit!"

I think Mom was just as astonished as I was, that all these words came out at once, and clearly, after four months of silence. It was a wonderful feeling for both of us, a special connection between mother and son.

In September, over Labor Day weekend, Tom and Debbie had made arrangements for us to drive Willie and Liam, 250 miles to New York City to go to a Yankee game. Debbie had the Yankee tickets all set to pick up at the stadium, so we wouldn't have to tell another "Beatrice Story." And also, to stay at the Park Avenue apartment. Now almost all parents are overprotective of their children, but to say that Tom was overprotective of Willie at this time, would be an understatement. And Joe, then the Assistant Headmaster at MPH, said to us:

"I love you and there is nobody else that I would trust more than you guys in driving my kid to New York City; but if anything happens to him, I will have to hunt you down and kill you."

And knowing Joe as well as we did, I think maybe he was only half-kidding. There were weather reports of a hurricane coming up the east coast, due to come in over the weekend. Plus, I had never driven into New York City before, although I had a great navigator in Syl. *So, with all this in mind, off we went.*

When we pulled into the entrance of the Park Avenue apartment building, there was no one in sight. Then seemingly out of nowhere, six doormen appeared, who also handled security. We explained who we were, and then they recognized Willie in the back seat, and we were good. They gave us the keys to Seelig's apartment. One of the doormen said to us, in his Irish accent,

"Oh, Syracuse. I was there one night in December, 1994, to see the Rolling Stones in the Carrier Dome. Coldest night of my life!"

Sounds about right. We took the boys to the ESPN Zone, and Syl had to hold on to Liam's hand, as he was so fixated on the ESPN Zone sign, that he was oblivious to the traffic in the middle of Times Square. The next day we went to see the Yankees play the Detroit Tigers. We took the subway and then the West Side D train to 161st Street in the Bronx. We all went to Monument Park. Our seats were about ten rows in back of home plate, behind the screen. Liam looked disappointed, instead of having a free and prime seat at Yankee Stadium. It turned out this was because he wanted to be able to catch a foul ball and couldn't behind the screen. That was his most important priority at this age. In the sixth inning, I let the boys sit several rows over, away from the backstop, but where we could still keep our eyes on them, to see if they could catch a foul ball. They weren't successful, but at least they had the opportunity, and they appreciated that.

We took the boys to this Italian restaurant, Nick's, at 1814 Second Avenue, at 94th Street, that Tom had told us about. We were seated in the back room with a big Italian family with their children having a birthday dinner and party. This place felt just like Louis' Restaurant on White Plains Road in the Bronx, where in "The Godfather," Michael Corleone shoots Sollozzo and Captain McCluskey.

The following day we took the Statue Cruises ferry over to Liberty Island to see the Statue of Liberty. None of us had ever seen it up close. You can't really see how enormous it is: 305 feet from the ground to the tip of the flame, as tall as a 22-story building, until you see it up close and personal. In 1886, it was the tallest structure in New York City. It weighs 225 tons. The security was tight, and you couldn't go all the way inside to the top, as it was undergoing renovations. "Lady Liberty" is truly an amazing sight.

We took the ferry to Ellis Island, in Upper New York Bay, the gateway for over twelve million immigrants to the United States. It was the busiest immigration inspection station in the United States for 62 years, from 1892 until 1954. Actually, 98 percent of those examined at Ellis Island were allowed into the country. (Certainly, a far cry from our present immigration system.)
The Immigration Museum is impressive, depicting the incredible journeys these people took to reach freedom. The boys had a good time running around outside, looking up their great and great, great grandparents; trying to find their names on The American Immigrant Wall of Honor.

The next morning, we had a nice breakfast, and were trying to make the decision whether to head back home, as the weather reports indicated the hurricane was getting closer, or to stay an extra night at the apartment and leave the following day. The air was still, probably the calm before the storm, as we decided to get the car out of the parking garage and hit the road. We made it out of the city okay, but as soon as we were on the main highway, the winds started howling at over 70 miles per hour. I had to hold on to the steering wheel with both hands, with every ounce of strength that I had, to keep the car on the road. I pulled over a couple of times, but the danger there was that the car could flip over. We decided to keep going. We made it back in one piece, but it was a harrowing ride that we won't ever forget.

In October, Syl and I drove down to Keuka Lake, referred to as Crooked Lake, unusual because it is Y-shaped, in contrast to the long and narrow shape of the other Finger Lakes. We were going to Hilary and Jeremy's wedding, two students who watched Willie for several years. Tom, Debbie, and Willie were driving themselves there. It was a very nice ceremony, outside with a beautiful view of the lake. There was music and dancing at night and then we went back to our room. All of a sudden, a guy burst into our room, as we hadn't locked the door and settled down for the night yet. Fortunately, we weren't being intimate, as this guy was drunk and had gone to the wrong room. It reminded us of that similar incident when we were staying at the Royal Dane, in the Virgin Islands, in March, 1987.

The following day we drove around Keuka Lake, then over to Dundee, Lakemont, and Seneca Lake.

2007

August: Seaside, Florida

The Truman House

Pensacola, Florida

September: Cape Cod (Cyclones)

Dennis Port

December: Charleston, South Carolina (Syl)

In August, Syl and I went on another vacation with Tom, Debbie, and Willie to Seaside, Florida. Seaside is a small resort community on the Florida Panhandle, on the Emerald Coast on the Gulf of Mexico. It is very pristine, with narrow, brick-paved streets, with pastel-colored houses with porches and white picket fences. This is where they filmed the 1998 movie, "The Truman Show," starring Jim Carrey as Truman Burbank, and Ed Harris, as Christof. He doesn't know it, but everything in Truman's life is part of a massive television set. "The Truman Show" is a live broadcast of Truman's every move captured by hidden cameras, where Christof tries to control his mind. Truman is a naive insurance salesman whose every move, unbeknownst to him, is being telecast live around the globe, 24 hours a day.

If you've seen the movie, which we had, you can visualize the scenes in the shops around the town center. We visited The Truman House where Truman lived.

We stayed in a really nice rented house, just a short walk down a sandy path to the beautiful long sandy beach.

Willie and I went boogie boarding in the Gulf, and after we got back to the house, all of us would take turns in the outdoor shower; where it was private, but you could look over the wooden enclosure to see plants and trees. It is a great feeling taking an outdoor shower. After a nice dinner, Willie, Syl and I would walk down to the beach and walk up the wooden steps to the Pensacola Beach Pavilion, with a pelican weathervane on top, one of nine pavilions at the end of each street. We would sit up there, looking at the stars and listening to the waves. Sometimes Syl and I would go back again later by ourselves.

We all played miniature golf, driving around 40 miles to Panama City, to play there one evening. Tom, Willie and I drove 100 miles to Pensacola one night to watch a minor league baseball game. The Pensacola Blue Wahoos play in the Southern League, Double-A.

It would be seven years before we went on another vacation with them.

In September, over Labor Day weekend, Syl and I drove to Cape Cod for a softball tournament that I was playing in for the Syracuse 60's Cyclones. We stayed with the rest of the team and their wives at the Colony Beach Motel in Dennis Port, overlooking Nantucket Sound.

In October, I flew out to Phoenix, Arizona for the Senior Softball World Championships. We were a wild card entry, as the team that wins the Eastern Regionals in Raleigh, North Carolina, in early August, then goes on and meets the winner of the Western Regionals; in a single game during the World Championships, for the National Championship in your classification: Single A, Double A, Triple A, Major. We were 60's Double A at this time, and came in second in the Eastern Regionals; but the team that won it, from Oshkosh, Wisconsin, decided not to go to Phoenix. I don't think that they understood the significance of this at the time. We were the lucky benefactors of their decision and received invitations in the mail to play in the National Championship game, which we of course accepted, and beat a team from Reno, Nevada, "Last Call," to claim the National Championship. It was a major breakthrough for us, as we were hugging and jumping on each other after the final out was made. Marty, Marti, and Brad, Marti's brother, who I had played basketball and softball with for many years in Syracuse, before he moved to Phoenix; came out to watch me play and I went back to their house for a family get together, which was fun.

In November, I went down to Fort Myers for the Winter Nationals with the Cyclones over Veterans Day weekend. This was the second of seven consecutive years, from 2006 through 2012 that I would play in this tournament. In 2006, we played our games in a beautiful new complex in Naples, a 40-minute drive one way each morning. After that first year, we always played in Cape Coral. In that tournament in 2006, I got one of my teammates, Rocky, to drive and hang out with me in Sanibel Island, doing similar things for the day, that Syl and I had done on our vacation in April, 2004: The Ding-Darling Wildlife Preserve, Bowman Beach, sunset on Captiva. The same routine for this year, 2007, with another teammate, Zeke. This was because we didn't make it to the final day of the tournament, and had a day to explore instead, before flying back home the following day.

Syl went down by herself to visit her mother and Ben, her sisters, nieces, nephews, and cousins, for Christmas. She hadn't spent Christmas with her mother and her family since 1979. This was something that she had talked about, and thought about doing for a long time, and she decided to do it over the Christmas Break at MPH.

We were always together and worked at the same place, especially the same hours, doing Extended Day together. I had these softball tournaments when I would be gone for three or four days, usually getting a personal day or two, as I never took a sick day in 21 years of teaching at MPH. We would arrange for someone to take my place and Syl would have to carry on without me at Extended Day.

It was nice getting a little space, but that lasted only a few days, before I began to miss Syl terribly. I was stuck here to fend for myself, to drive on icy roads, and shovel snow; while Syl was going to the beach, having lunch or dinner at restaurants, and home-cooked meals, and enjoying time with her family and the sights and sounds of Charleston. Sometimes she would need a personal day from school before returning from these trips, and I'd have to do Extended Day without her.

2008

February: Winter Haven, Florida

Lake Wales, Florida (Bok Tower Garden)

July: Montréal, Canada

Dollard-des-Ormeaux

Saint-Lazare

Mount Royal

Old Montréal

Mont-Tremblant

Lac Paradis

August: Dundee, Lakemont, & Watkins Glen

September: Cape Cod (Cyclones)

Dennis Port

December: Charleston, South Carolina (Syl)

This year, 2008, would become a life-altering year for both of us in so many ways.

Syl and I flew to Orlando, and then rented a car and drove 50 miles south to our hotel in Winter Haven, Florida, in the middle of February. This was because the Cyclones were playing in the Tournament Of Champions, the most prestigious of all the tournaments. In order to qualify, a team must win a major tournament, designated by Senior Softball, during the year to be eligible to play in this tournament. These don't include local or regional tournaments. Teams come from all over the country for this tournament. Syl was able to come to this one, as it was over the Winter Break at MPH. We played well, but came up a little short, coming in fourth place; but still a good accomplishment. Syl and I stayed a few extra days to enjoy our vacation. We stayed at the same hotel, and it was nice being the only ones from the team still there.

One day we drove 16 miles, through expansive orange groves, to Lake Wales, and then to Bok Tower Gardens, a 250-acre garden and bird sanctuary. We started off in the visitor center, where there is a small museum showing the history and some of the famous people who have visited here. The founder, Edward W. Bok, immigrated to the United States from the Netherlands at a very young age. He became a Pulitzer Prize winning author and created this masterpiece with landscape architect Frederick Olmstead. Bok's desire was to create an outdoor sanctuary that would "touch the soul with its beauty and quiet." He was definitely successful.

His motto was: "Give to the world the best you have and the best will come back to you."

There are beautiful gardens with many colorful flowers, giant Victoria water lilies, a reflection pool, and the Japanese Stone Peace Lantern.

The most impressive sight is the Singing Tower Carillon, made of marble and native coquina, standing 205 feet high, with 60 carillon bells ranging in weight from 16 pounds to nearly 12 tons. They have concerts every half hour during the day. You can hear the majestic sound of the bells from anywhere on the grounds. Syl and I agreed that there is a feeling of absolute joy and peace walking around here.

Both of our lives, especially Syl's, changed forever with a phone call in March. It was from her birth father,

Gunter, who had received a phone message from Sylvia. We had just gotten home from work when we checked our phone messages and he had left a message on our machine:

"Is this Sylvie? Sylvie Heer? This is Gunter Angeli, your father, if I have the right number."

He pronounced it, "On-gel-ee." We had always thought that it was pronounced, "On-gay-lee."

When I first met Sylvia, she was still using her married name on her Virginia driver's license and on her work identification card at St. Joseph's Hospital. I told her that she should think about changing it, especially if her former husband remarried and his new wife had her last name become his. I could see Sylvia retaining this name if there were children involved or issues with finances or property. But they had no children, I was certainly glad of that, and there were no financial or property issues either. She had kept it for a while when she first came to Syracuse, until the divorce papers came and the divorce was finalized. After that, she just hadn't bothered to change it. She wanted nothing to do with him or anything else at the end. She just wanted to get as far away from everything as she could. And she did.

Sylvia had gone by her grandparents' name, Ciemala, when she was born and for a couple of years before Ursula met and married Art, her stepfather. She went by his last name, Pine, through her childhood and her school years, until she was married. He did help raise her and her sisters, but he was gone on his military tours, and Ursula did the bulk of raising the three girls. In fact, it turned out that he never officially adopted Sylvia, Ursula told us. I told Syl that he had his other daughters to carry on his name, which Karen still does; and his son, Erik, from his second wife, Chris, will always carry on his name.

      I suggested to Sylvia that she might consider changing her last name to her birth father's last name; if she felt that he did nothing wrong in trying to go to Canada to find work, when she was less than five months old, that he didn't abandon them. As I mentioned earlier, I wasn't ready at that point to ask Syl to marry me. I didn't want anything to affect our new relationship. She thought about it for a while and then changed her last name to Angeli, Gunter's last name. Actually, pretty appropriate for Sylvia, when you think about it. I always told everyone it was: "*Angel with an i.*"

      They sort of Americanized it at MPH, pronouncing it as "an-jel-ee." The kids would goof around and call her "Mrs. Peanut Butter & Jelly." When we got married in April, 1994, she was now Mrs. Heer. But since Mom was such a legend at MPH for 33 years, this being her final school year before retiring in June, 1995; nobody could get used to calling Sylvia: Mrs. Heer. At this time, there was only one Mrs. Heer. It took a few years for everyone to get used to calling Sylvia: Mrs. Heer. Because of this, Sylvia had her paychecks, health insurance, taxes, and other documents under the last name of Angeli-Heer; and it stayed this way. In all other ways, she was Sylvia Ursula Heer.

      Syl had tried to track her birth father down her whole life. It was more than just a curiosity; it was something she needed to feel complete. It always seemed to us that Ursula knew more than what she would tell us, that she really didn't know where he was. All we knew was that he was somewhere in Canada. When we were in Toronto in July, 1995, to see "The Phantom of the Opera," we looked through all the phone books there and found nothing. We checked out genealogy sites and came up empty. Years went by, until we got a lead about a Gunter Angeli living in Augsburg, Germany. Syl wrote a letter explaining who she was, along with a picture of herself. She had high hopes, until she received a letter back from him, (he never did send the picture back), saying, "He was sorry to disappoint her, but that he would have only been twelve years old when Syl was born; so he was not her father, and he wished her luck in her search." That was a setback and more years passed by.

Things started to come together, coincidentally or not, when Art passed away in July, 2007. Somehow, we never knew how, word finally reached a cousin in Augsburg; that Sylvia was trying to find her birth father's whereabouts, and he was given her phone number. It turned out that Gunter's mother, Sylvia's paternal grandmother, was still alive. She was in her mid-90's and still went swimming three or four times a week. Why nobody knew that she was still alive was a mystery to us. If we had known that, we could have gotten in touch with her and tracked him down many years before. But it wasn't meant to be. *Until now.*

Syl was understandably apprehensive about returning his call, but excited at the same time. He had just returned from a family vacation to Cuba, as Canadians are allowed to travel there. Ironically, he had been living in Montréal all these years, just four hours from Syracuse. I mentioned the significance of Montréal earlier in this book, and here it is. Gunter had gone from Augsburg by boat to Québec City, and then headed south by train, arriving in Montréal around the middle of November, 1953. Syl and I had taken our first trip together to Saratoga for the Men at Work concert on August 7th, 1983; and then spontaneously had driven to Montréal to spend the night. Little did we know then what fate lay ahead here.

Syl returned his call and they carried on a nice conversation in German. She could speak fluent German, as she always spoke to Ursula in German, when she called her on the phone almost every night. Syl had no lingering German accent when she spoke in English, which was most of the time. They made arrangements to have us come up for his 75th birthday on July 18th. His birthday was on the same day as Syl's, just a month later. So, when Syl was born, he was a month away from being 20 years old.

They spoke several times over this interim period of April, May, June, and the first half of July. We finished the school year, did our Playscape program for two weeks in June, relaxed at the pool, and went out to Lakeside Park on Cazenovia Lake over the next three weeks. Then we got directions and headed up to Montréal in the middle of July, to finally meet and reunite with her birth father after 55 years. And to meet her new extended family.

When Sylvia's sister, Debbie, heard that we had finally made contact and were going up to meet him, she wrote a letter for us to bring to him from her.

"My name is Debbie, Sylvia's sister. Sylvia has always been a good sister and person. She was always very popular, no matter where we went. To know Sylvia was to love her. In Würzburg, she was a 'Homecoming Princess.' We were also on the Marching Drill Team together. Sylvia never got into trouble, but I sure made up for it! I am so very happy she found you and your family. There has always been a void in her heart that only *you* could fill. It was as though it was God's plan that it worked out the way it has! I was in Montréal in 1976. We sure were close, so was Sylvia! I did have you up on the computer, on ZABASEARCH, but I just was not sure. I did not want to take the responsibility of my sister being hurt, maybe you didn't want to see her. These situations are very emotional. Dusty is Great! You will see this. I love my sister Sylvia, and I know you all will too. I hope all of you have the best time. I am very happy for all of you!"

'Love from Sylvia's sister-Debbie'

Gunter was sitting on his front stoop in a lawn chair, waiting for us. I'm sure many thoughts were swirling around in his head as well. We pulled in the driveway and he immediately got up and came over to Sylvia, as she got out of the car, and they embraced in an emotional hug. *Fifty-five years!* I walked over to him and we hugged. Then Erna, his wife of over 60 years, and mother of their three children, came out into the front yard. She hugged Sylvia, and then put a gold chain around her neck, and said, "Welcome to the family." Erna and I hugged and then we all went out to the backyard. It was lovely, with a small above ground pool, a shed for chairs and tools, flowers, and beans and other things growing on stakes. It had a European feel to it. We sat around a glass table, with a big umbrella, drinking wine and eating cheese and crackers; having conversations like we had known each other all these 55 years.

Their charming townhouse, where they still live, is in a suburb of Montréal called Dollard-des Ormeaux. The next day, their daughter, Caroline, and her husband, Jacques, and their two sons, Seann and Ryan, came over and we walked a few blocks to eat at a Thai restaurant. We all hit it off right away. Syl now had a third sister, and Caroline now had a sister, before only having two brothers. Caroline had come along later in life, as she was 15 years younger than Syl. Actually, this meal was paid for by Gunter's mother, who was still alive at this time. Syl got a chance to talk with her grandmother on the phone, which was nice. She passed away a short time later.

   This is a good time to tell you that Gunter has been going by "Tex," for most of his life. The name was bestowed upon him because he learned how to read and write English by reading Western books and watching Western movies. Erna has always called him "Texel," putting a German spin on it. He liked the fact that I was "Dusty." "Dusty" and "Tex," names right out of the Old West.

   I've been called "Dusty" since I was born, in fact my dad wanted to name me that as my real name; but my mom wanted Charles, Jr., after my dad, and she won out. But everyone calls me "Dusty," or "Dust," if you know me really well. Syl always called me "Dust." Charles is only for formal purposes and documents. The reason "Dusty" came into the naming process was that my middle name was Rhoades, the same as my dad's. (A play on words, get it? "Dusty Roads.")

   I always had to tell everyone how Rhoades was spelled, with an a, as the more well-known spelling is Rhodes. I even emphasized this for my senior picture in the high school yearbook, and of course, per "Murphy's Law," they got it wrong and spelled it Rhodes, much to my chagrin. People were more familiar with the Rhodes spelling; as in the Greek island and the Colossus of Rhodes, a statue of the Greek sun-god Helios was erected here in 280 BC. It stood by the harbor of the city of Rhodes, on a platform of marble, and was 110 feet high, one of the Seven Wonders of the Ancient World. It was unfortunately toppled by an earthquake in 228 BC.

Other familiar Rhodes were: Rhodes Scholarship, an international postgraduate award, for students to study at the University of Oxford, in England, established in 1902. And there was James Lamar "Dusty" Rhodes, who helped the New York Giants win the 1954 World Series with his pinch-hits, two of them home runs. I remember him well, as a kid watching the World Series.

So, it's easy to see, with all these examples, why Rhodes was the more familiar and popular spelling of the name. I never knew where the origin of Rhoades had come from. Maybe I was told long ago and forgot, I'm not sure. But somehow the question came up when my mom was in the nursing home, and luckily, she was able to tell me it was my dad's aunt's maiden name. So that's where it came from.

The following day, we went out to Jacques and Caroline's house in Saint-Lazare, also known as Saint-Lazare-de-Vaudreuil; an off-island suburb of Montréal. It is 16 miles southwest, about a 30-minute drive from Tex and Erna's. They have a beautiful house, with trees all around, in an upscale middle-class neighborhood. In the backyard they had horseshoe pits.

We were here to celebrate Tex's 75th birthday and for everyone to meet and get to know Sylvia. Erna, and their close friends, had always known about Sylvia; but their children, and obviously their grandchildren, had no idea that she even existed. Erna had always told Tex that one day she would come knocking on his door. *And now she had.*

Tex was proud to introduce Sylvia as his daughter. Their oldest son, Bob, and his wife, Beata, (they are like how Syl and I were for our first 10 years and 9 months, not officially married, but married in every sense of the word, even longer); live far away in Edmonton and did not make it in to visit this year. Their second son, Ron, and his wife Lorraine, and their two sons, Lucas and Olivier, live in Ottawa. They drove in, except Lucas, who had to work. We obviously had no idea of this family connection when we spent a few days, including Canada Day, in Ottawa, in July, 1998.

Ron, who has kind of a cynical sense of humor, said to Tex, "So *what else* haven't you told us about?" I was wondering how I would get along with Ron, as he was formerly in the Canadian Army, and then spent most of his life in the police force, risking his life on many undercover narcotics assignments. I was in total contrast, living the lifestyle of the 60's and 70's, going to Woodstock and all. Everybody immediately loved Sylvia. We started drinking beers and Ron and I became partners in horseshoe matches. We won a couple of times and Ron would slap me five and say, "Way to go partner," if I made a winning toss. So, we got along very well and talked a lot about sports. Ron still plays hockey in local leagues to this day. Lorraine is French Canadian, pretty and very nice, and works at a hospital. So, there were conversations in English, French, and German going on. Jacques is a parts manager at Nissan and Caroline works for the Royal Bank of Canada. Syl joined in playing horseshoes, teaming with Caroline, who is really good, winning many matches with her left-handed tosses; of course, this was her home turf.

The food was wonderful, with Jacques cooking salmon and all sorts of meat on the grill, and the women making fantastic salads and vegetables and desserts. Music was in the air, as Syl danced with Tex on the deck. I have some great pictures of them in our photo album.

They brought out Tex's cake as we sang to him. It was a memorable evening.

    The next day, Syl and I went with Tex and Erna to Mount Royal Park, consisting of 470 acres. On October 3, 1535, Jacques Cartier climbed up the mountain and named it Mount Royal. Different pronunciations evolved over time; and by 1705, the city that grew up around it and the surrounding island, became known as Montréal. Mount Royal is west of downtown Montréal, part of the Monteregian Hills. It was inaugurated in 1876, designed by Frederick Law Olmstead, who also designed Central Park in New York City. He also designed the gardens at Bok Tower Gardens in Lake Wales, Florida, that we went to five months earlier; so, this was an extraordinary connection.

    We walked through the park, with kids playing, and people running or walking, and families having picnics. We reached the top of one of Mount Royal's three peaks, the highest is 764 feet above sea level; where you can see some amazing skyline views of Montréal. We took pictures up there and Erna pointed out in the distance the location of a house when she first came to Montréal. It was working as a housekeeper for a doctor and his wife.

    Erna had come over from Germany four years before Tex, when she was 16. They would load around 600 girls into these huge cargo boats, headed to Canada, looking for work there. Usually you had to be 18 to go, but Erna had received special permission from her priest to go at 16, due to some domestic abuse issues that she faced at home. She landed in Halifax, Nova Scotia, and then took the train to Montréal. She arrived at the train station, wearing only a dress, light jacket, and speaking hardly any English. There was a girl that she had met that held her hand and stayed with her, as all these men were sitting in the train station. It turned really cold and started heavily snowing, as they waited inside the station for their new employers to pick them up. Erna was glad to have a friend with her, as she was afraid of all these men; especially being so young, in a strange country, and being even more wary because of incidents in her past. Her friend was finally picked up and now she was alone. The doctor picked her up hours later, apologizing and explaining that he was delayed by the snowstorm.

Nothing bad happened, but Erna had to endure this fear and harrowing experience for her. She had written an article in recent years that was published in the newspaper, telling about her experience and trying to find her long-lost friend, that she never saw again. I told her this would make a great movie and I even envisioned myself maybe writing a screenplay. But nothing has been done, and to my knowledge, the friend was never found. Erna worked for them for a while, enduring the wife's eccentric behavior, before moving on. She became a waitress, met Tex, got married, and started a family.

After Mount Royal, we went to Old Montréal, where we took Tex and Erna for lunch in a nice restaurant with a musical group playing and singing jazz. We strolled the narrow cobblestone streets with charming shops and cafes, a definite European feel to it. We visited the impressive Notre-Dame Basilica of Montréal. It was a really nice day.

The next morning, we loaded up Tex's car with supplies and went to the store to buy food and alcohol to bring with us. We were driving up to what they like to call "The Country," to Lac Paradis, or Paradise Lake, about an hour's drive north through The Laurentians. Our destination for the next four days was Tex and Erna's cottage, in a community of German and Austrian friends. They have been going up there, almost every week for three or four days, from May through September, since the house was built. Tex drove up there almost every weekend, starting when the boys were really young, for 25 years, taking them with him, carrying up whatever he could scavenge from jobs that he worked on; any extra wood, doors, windows, anything he could use. He basically built this place by himself, on top of huge boulders, just incredible.

You walk on carved out "steps" of boulders, down to the lake. It is a beautiful view of the lake from their deck; where we have our breakfasts, lunches, dinners, and get-togethers, unless it is raining. Erna has put a lot of blood, sweat, and tears into the cottage as well; tending to flowers, plants, preparing meals, all sorts of things. Jacques and Caroline go there quite a bit now, especially in the summer and on their vacations. They installed a handrail all the way from the cottage to the lake; which is really nice, but we never had a chance to use it, as it was installed after our last visit to the cottage in July, 2014. The grandchildren, grown up now, take their girlfriends up there on weekends, so they have to plan their time to go up. So Tex and Erna don't go there now as much as they used to.

The rest of their friends in this community always knew about Sylvia, so getting the chance to see and meet her, was definitely the biggest event to happen up here in a long time. It was a scenic drive, winding through small towns and stopping at a country stand where we bought some corn. We arrived at the sign that said, "Lac Paradis." If you didn't know where to look, you would never find this place, that's how well it is hidden. We opened the gate and drove on the small road of dirt and stones. I think they all chipped in a few years ago and finally had it paved, as it would have huge ruts in it in the spring, after a harsh winter.

    Tex was repeatedly honking his horn, signaling our arrival, as we drove past the other homes. They were bigger, most of them you could live up there year-round, but hardly anyone did. They looked like Swiss chalets or Austrian mountain homes in the Alps. In fact, Karl, a master carpenter, from Austria, had built his house almost entirely out of mahogany. He was in his early 80's when he passed away a few years ago. Syl would have been sad to hear this, she really liked him. We unloaded everything from the car and got our little room set up.

    Word spread quickly and before you knew it, people started coming over with all kinds of homemade cakes and strudels, and homemade schnapps. Karl had brought his special pear schnapps. Everyone was enchanted by Sylvia, and she was truly enjoying it. Everybody was talking in German. They would say something to me and I would just shrug, before they realized I didn't understand and then spoke to me in English. We would get to know each other on our summer visits over six years, and carry on great conversations; but this trip belonged to Sylvia.

    There was always a lot of eating and drinking when we went to Montréal, even more so in "The Country." Tex and Erna would set the table at night for breakfast. If you said that you wanted cereal, they would put a cereal bowl at your setting by your chair. If you said you didn't, they wouldn't put a bowl there. No matter how much he had to drink the day and night before, Tex was always up bright and early, and would yell, "Breakfast!"

    He would do some yard work after breakfast, and around noon he asked me,

"Are you ready?"

"Ready for what?"

"For a beer."

This was the routine. He'd have a couple of beers, later in the day a rum and coke, a glass of wine at dinner, maybe more beers at night, and a small glass of brandy before bed. Maybe that was his secret, as he still does his yard work, does handyman work for some elderly women in the neighborhood, shovels, bowls in a league in the winter, plays golf, and does more work in the cottage in "The Country."

Paradise Lake has beavers and the men have to undo their dams sometimes so the water flows properly. They have a dock to lie on and you can take a "noodle" with you, for safety's sake, and swim across the lake. The bottom has tannin and Tex installed a platform with an outdoor carpet on it so you could get out without slipping on all the dead leaves.

The four of us drove up to Mont-Tremblant for the day. It is a ski resort, set within the Laurentian Mountains, northwest of Montréal. We walked around the shopping village, had lunch, and later in the afternoon, coffee in an outdoor cafe.

We drove back to Tex and Erna's and spent a couple more days there before driving home. It was a wonderful reunion and Syl was so happy.

In August, I went down to Raleigh, North Carolina, for the Eastern Nationals. This time we won and were now qualified to play for the National Championship in Phoenix, Arizona during the World Championships there.

This time there was no wild card entry involved. This year, 2008, turned out to be our most successful year that we ever had. We came in fourth at the prestigious Tournament of Champions in Winter Haven, Florida in February. This is the tournament where Syl went with me and we went to the Bok Tower Gardens. We came in second in the "Early Bird Qualifier" in York, Pennsylvania, at the end of April; getting robbed on a really bad call from the umpire, when we thought we had won the tournament in the final game, with a catch in the outfield. We won the "New England Classic" in New Branford, Connecticut, in the middle of May. We came in second in the "Crabtown Classic" in Glen Burnie, Maryland, at the end of June. We won the Eastern Nationals in Raleigh in early August. We came in second in the "Cape Cod Classic" in September.

Then on to Phoenix in the middle of October, where we won our second straight National Championship, beating a team called "Scrap Iron," from Colorado. We also came in fourth at the overall World Championships in Phoenix. Marty came to watch some of our games and I went over to their house in Peoria for a family get-together. We played in the Winter Nationals in Fort Myers, Florida, in the middle of November, but didn't win. (Our success was extended to early January, 2009, when we "put the cherry on top," by winning the Tournament Of Champions in Winter Haven, Florida.)

In August, we watched Willie again for two weeks, and one day took a day trip to where I grew up. We had lunch at the Belhurst Castle in Geneva, and then drove the 26 miles through the vineyards and the scenic views of Seneca Lake, to Lakemont and then Dundee. We went to the Little League field at Dundee Central School. It still looked the same as when I played there. We took pictures of Willie reenacting the second part of the three part

"Stories About My Brother," from "Dusty's Lunchtime Stories;" with Marty clocking me in the head with a baseball bat. From there, we drove 13 miles to Watkins Glen, where we hiked the spectacular gorge trails with its 19 waterfalls.

In September, Syl and I drove back to Cape Cod, for a tournament with the 60's Cyclones. We stayed again at the Colony Beach Motel in Dennis Port, before returning at night at the end of Labor Day weekend, to start another school year.

The following Saturday, we went with Tom, Debbie, and Willie, up to the Syracuse University Quad, where the Coasters were playing and Dennis Quaid was letting people take pictures with him in the V.I.P. tent, before the SU football game. We took some of Sylvia with him. He was there for the premiere of "The Express," the Ernie Davis Story, an excellent book and movie. He starred as Ben Schwartzwalder, the legendary coach at Syracuse.

After the tournament in Phoenix in October, I was down in Fort Myers for the Winter Nationals over Veterans Day weekend. Mom's health had been gradually going downhill and I was worried about her when I left. Syl and I had been diligent about going to visit her at night after work and at least once on the weekends. She had now been at the Iroquois Nursing Home for two years and three and a half months. As I mentioned earlier, the first four months after the stroke in the last week in July, 2006, were very tough on everyone. At the end of November came the memorable "Juicy Fruit" story. In December, we had Mom transported, (she was confined to a wheelchair), to her townhouse for a family Christmas. Julie and Em had come up from Virginia to join Linda and John, Syl and me. She was confused as to why she couldn't stay in her townhouse, but she needed full time care, which Syl and I couldn't provide. We wish we could have.

Over the Fourth of July, 2007, we had Mom transported out to Linda and John's house in Cazenovia for a family barbecue. Marty had come to visit, and there was Tom and Julie up to visit, Linda and John, Syl and me. Syl always brought things to eat for Mom at the nursing home, especially on important occasions like birthdays, Thanksgiving, and Christmas; so, she had a welcome change from the nursing home food and the dining room atmosphere. Syl would bring a tablecloth, linen napkins, everything planned and prepared with caring and love. *This is what Syl always did.* Mom would be the envy of her floor during these times.

I spent Christmas with Mom in 2007 when Syl went to Charleston to be with her family. On the Fourth of July, 2008, we had Mom transported over to our house for the day. Syl had prepared the dining room table, beautifully as usual, and we all had on our patriotic tee shirts. We took some pictures and then started to eat. Mom couldn't hold down her food and felt embarrassed. We told her not to worry about it, that we were just glad she could be with us. But deep down inside, we were beginning to worry. Tom and Julie came up later in July and with Linda and John, Syl and me, we took Mom to the Scotch 'n Sirloin restaurant in Dewitt. Mom was really looking forward to hearing about Syl's reunion with Tex and his, (now also hers), family in Montréal. Mom was really happy for Syl and said that nobody deserved it more. She really loved Syl like a daughter and I was happy that Mom was still around to hear that this father and daughter reunion had finally happened after fifty-five years.

On the day I was to fly back home from Fort Myers, I got a call from Syl that Mom had passed away in the early morning hours. I was sad and numb, but it wasn't totally unexpected. I felt a sense of relief that Mom was now no longer in physical pain. Her faith was so strong, that she had lasted as long as she did, not taking any medication whatsoever, not even a baby aspirin. I wish she had at least done that years ago. But that was her choice.

So, at the end of Veterans Day weekend in Fort Myers, I had already eaten my breakfast, checked out of my room, and went to sit by the pool, around ten o'clock in the morning, when I got the call from Syl. The plan was to go out to the airport with four other guys on the team, in a cab around two o'clock in the afternoon, a couple of hours before our flights. I just wanted to sit in the sun by the pool for a couple of hours, swim, rinse off in the outdoor shower, change, and go to the airport.

I was still trying to compute in my head the fact that my mom: who had given me life, raised me, cared for me, taught me, advised me, *was no longer here on Earth.*

Then these guys came out and said they wanted to move the leaving time up to one o'clock. I didn't tell them about Mom. I just wasn't ready to do it. I figured I still had some time, an hour less now, but I said okay. They were hanging out in the lobby, looking out at me, then one guy came out and was literally hovering over me. I was starting to get an uncomfortable feeling, instead of being in a reflective mode. Then they were getting antsy, and told me that they wanted to leave right now, to see if they might be able to fly standby to catch an earlier flight back to Syracuse.

In hindsight, I should have told them to go ahead without me, that I would take a cab at two o'clock and keep my original flight. It was about $8 per man for the cab fare and tip, whereas it would be $40 for me; $32 more that I could use to buy Syl a tee shirt and have lunch at the airport. But I shouldn't have let that become a factor. I could have been alone with my thoughts, having my coffee, with them not bugging me and being gone. But I went with them to the airport. They were unsuccessful on their earlier flight idea. They were on a different airline and went to their gate, in the opposite direction than mine. I went to my gate and now had four hours to wait before boarding. I bought a tee shirt for Syl and had a nice lunch. Then I sat down and started to write. This was the only good thing that came out of going to the airport hours earlier than necessary.

I had been struggling to complete the second half of my children's book, "The Forest That Rains Frogs," for quite a while now. I started writing and the ideas all just came to me, probably divine inspiration from Mom. It took me over four years to fine-tune it, find an illustrator and coordinate my vision with her; and go through the editing and publishing processes. It was published on December 20, 2012. I wish I could have finished it when Mom was still here. She would have loved the book and been very proud of me.

We waited a month, so everyone could make it back to Syracuse; to have Mom's services on December 13th, her birthday, and Santa Lucia Day.

Syl went back down to Charleston to be with her mother and family for Christmas. I had been alone for Christmas the year before, but could at least go visit and be with Mom. This year I was totally alone. I hadn't really broken down when Mom passed, keeping it together to prepare and read at the services; and to do my job at school and be there for the kids. I was listening to Abbey Road by the Beatles, while standing over the sink in the kitchen, looking out the window at the falling snow on Christmas; when the song "Golden Slumbers," sung by Paul McCartney, started playing. It was then that it all hit me like a ton of bricks, and I started bawling like a baby, for a long time.

Ghost of a Thought

I've seen many mothers, weary and cryin'

I've seen tired old men, alone and dyin'

I've seen the faces of miners, dingy and black

I've seen soldiers who left but never came back.

Looked at lost lovers, deep in thought

Seeking out, and being sought

Searching for treasures, sealed in a trance

Yearning for a second chance.

Heard them mocking a man gone lame

Watched them cringe at the sound of a name

Tasted the salt in another's wound

Stood on the soil of my father's tomb.

I saw the thunder in the prisoners' eyes

I sensed the anguish of their sighs

Felt their lonely dreams at night

Been down the road of an endless flight.

Barefoot beggars, cast aside by the flood

Left to wallow in the mud

Chained together by a hollow stare

Wanting to leave, but not knowing where.

Wondered who the stars are really shining for

As the sun fades away from the distant shore

It all turned shapeless, without any form

As I witnessed the calm before the storm.

2009

July: Montréal, Canada

    Dollard-des Ormeaux

    Old Montréal (Notre-Dame Basilica)

Québec City, Canada

    Old Québec

    Citadelle of Québec

    Parliament Hill

    Château Frontenac

    Chute Montmorency

    Basilica of Sainte-Anne-de-Beaupre

Saint-Lazare

Lac Paradis

Geneva, New York

    Seneca Lake

    Belhurst Castle

September: Cape Cod (Cyclones)

    Dennis Port

November: Charleston, South Carolina (Syl)

As I mentioned earlier, we, the 60's Syracuse Cyclones; won the Tournament of Champions in Winter Haven, Florida in January. I also went to play in tournaments for the Cyclones: to Loudoun, Virginia, in May, for the Atlantic Coast Championships; and to New Branford, Connecticut in June.

We survived another winter, finished another school year, and did our two-week Playscape program in June. We had some days to enjoy the park at Cazenovia Lake and relaxing time over at Tom and Debbie's pool.

In the middle of July, we drove back up to Montréal, now being part of our new extended family. This time we were going to be able to meet Sylvia's other brother, Bob, and his wife, Beata, who was from Slovakia. They were flying in from Edmonton, where they live. Tex and Erna had told us that Bob wanted to take us up to Québec City, around a three-hour drive, 163 miles north, for a few days. Bob had taken Tex and Erna on several vacations over the years; including a cruise to Alaska, Brazil, Cuba, Las Vegas, and Tucson.

Maybe there was some miscommunication about this, as I did the driving, in our car, and we paid for our hotel rooms and meals. Before we went up to Québec City, we spent a couple of days going to Old Montréal, visiting the Notre-Dame Basilica and walking around, and hanging out at Tex and Erna's.

Québec City, sitting on the Saint Lawrence River, was founded by Samuel de Champlain in 1608. It is Canada's mostly French-speaking Québec province and its capital city. We checked into our hotel and took a bus into Old Québec. We had lunch together and took a few pictures together. On this trip, Bob acted kind of aloof toward us. Maybe it was the realization that he now had a new sister after all these years, and that she was older. He was reluctant to take his picture with Syl. She was less than three years older than him, so give me a break. Syl didn't say anything, but I knew that it hurt her feelings. After this trip, when they came to visit Montréal in subsequent years, Bob warmed up to Syl and me, and we became close friends and family. Beata was always close to us from the start.

Bob wanted to split up and meet up again around five o'clock for dinner. It was sort of weird, but Syl and I went our own way, walking the narrow cobblestone streets, checking out the stone buildings, quaint bistros and shops of Vieux-Québec. We walked up to the Citadelle of Québec, the Plains of Abraham, Parliament Hill, and Château Frontenac. We ran into them there and said hello, as they were basically exploring the same sights as we were. They said they would meet us later. So, they went their way and we went ours. (Like the Dylan song.) The Fairmont Le Château Frontenac is an impressive luxury hotel, standing high on a bluff overlooking the Saint Lawrence River. We then walked on the boardwalk in front of the hotel with majestic views of the river. On the way back down, we saw a restaurant that looked like it would be a nice place to eat. This was before we all had cell phones, so we couldn't just call them and tell them to come up the hill to meet us. Instead, we had to walk all the way down the hill to meet them and then walk all the way back up this steep hill to eat at this restaurant. It was a great dinner, so it was worth it.

The following day we drove to Chutes Montmorency, large waterfalls on the Montmorency River, about 8 miles outside of Québec City. They are amazing,

272 feet tall, 99 feet higher than Niagara Falls. We walked the 480 stairs, up the cliffside to the top of the waterfalls, and crossed over this bridge to take more pictures. From there we visited the famous Basilica of Sainte-Anne-de-Beaupré, set along the Saint Lawrence River. It is one of the five national shrines of Canada, the oldest French-speaking Catholic Shrine in America. It has been credited by the Catholic Church with many miracles of curing the sick and disabled. This is evident with the collection of crutches and braces that were left behind by the healed, as you enter the church. We drove through the town and had dinner at this 150-year-old ancestral home, the Côte-de-Beaupré, where you could also stay in the rooms there. We thought about it, but instead drove home late at night.

All of us went out to Jacques and Caroline's house in Saint-Lazare to celebrate Tex's birthday. Bob and Beata returned to Edmonton and Tex, Erna, Syl and I drove up to the country house on Paradise Lake. Now we were not only part of the Angeli family, but part of this community as well. Several days of eating, drinking, conversations, and laughs. We had days of relaxing, swimming, and playing cards with Tex and Erna, before driving back to Dollard-des Ormeaux. We had another family get-together at Jacques and Caroline's before returning back home to Syracuse.

Julie came up to visit in late July and had arranged and paid a marina to have a boat take us out on Seneca Lake to spread Mom's ashes. The guy who owned the marina had his daughter take us out on the lake. I think she had just graduated from high school. We introduced ourselves and she was telling us about this festival that they were having at night, with music and fireworks. When we were out in the middle of the lake, I said to her,

"Do you know why we are going out here on the lake today?"

She had kind of a terrified look on her face, as she had no idea what we were going to tell her.

Hesitatingly, she asked, "No, why?"

We told her about spreading Mom's ashes on the lake, being the closest that we could come to Lakemont, where Mom said that this was the happiest time of her life. You could tell that she was not only relieved, but sympathetic to our mission as well. Julie opened the red velvet bag that the ashes were wrapped up in and we both took handfuls and spread them out on the lake. It was satisfying in a strange sort of way, for Mom to be set free and hopefully be reunited with Dad. We drove back to the Belhurst Castle and had lunch and spread the remaining ashes there.

I went down to Raleigh, North Carolina, with the 60's Cyclones to play in the Eastern Nationals in early August. We spent a lot of time at Tom and Debbie's pool and watched Willie again for two weeks. It was a little different now, as he was about to enter high school. I took him to varsity soccer practice and picked him up. But we still had time to play miniature golf with him and Liam, pool "pig" basketball, Bocce, and pitch card games and "pass the pigs."

Syl went with me, for the third consecutive year, over Labor Day weekend, to Cape Cod to play for the Cyclones in a tournament there. Again, we stayed at the Colony Beach Motel in Dennis Port.

Soon after Labor Day weekend, we had a big reunion with a lot of our close friends, on "Eff" and Kathy's deck, where most of these get-togethers took place. Wardie and Christie were back in town from Lake Tahoe for a visit. A lot of these friends live near Syracuse, but we'd never get together anymore, unless it was for a reunion. "Audie" suggested that we get cardboard cutouts made of Wardie and Christie, call for a reunion on "Eff" and Kathy's deck, pretending that they were there. Syl and I began another school year, taking weekend walks around Green Lakes and Pratt's Falls, and driving to many areas to see the colorful foliage.

I played for the Cyclones in Phoenix in the World Championships. There was no National Championship game this year. Marty saw a few games and I went back to his and Marti's house one evening for a family get-together with them, their sons Kenn and Justin, and Kenn's son, Braeden.

Over Veteran's Day weekend, I played for the Cyclones in the Winter Nationals in Fort Myers, Florida. We did not achieve the same successes this year as we had in the two previous years; including winning the Tournament of Champions in Winter Haven, Florida, in early January, 2009. There were several reasons, including many injuries to key players; unwanted additions that were made to the team; and a change in the team chemistry, that had made the 2007 and 2008 teams such magical ones.

In November, Syl returned to Charleston, for the Thanksgiving vacation this time.

Reflections of a Crystal Vision

Sitting here watching the rain

Each drop an eternity

How long will the slumber last

How cold it seems

Not holding you close

Feeling your tender warmth.

I can see you gently sighing

I can hear you softly crying

I want to kiss your fears away

Bringing life to dying dreams

I want to soothe your wounds

Pierced by the arrows of fate.

Silent glow of burning embers

Waiting to rekindle the flame

To soar again

Aching for your touch

To move me

From this chill in the wilderness.

2010

June: Cape Cod

    Nauset Beach

    Truro (Head of the Meadow Beach)

    Highland Light & Chatham Light

July: Montréal, Canada

    Dollard-des Ormeaux

    Saint-Lazare

    Saint-Saveur & Saint-Césaire

    Lac Paradis

    Another school year was finished, the last "normal" one, as I'll explain later. Syl and I did our Playscape program for two weeks, after all the graduations, and then went up to Cape Cod for the last week in June. We were offered a small house, more like a cottage, by MPH parents Wayne and Suzanne. I had just written and read their daughter, Julia's Lower School graduation speech from fifth grade.

    It was a cute house with an outdoor shower near Nauset Beach. We bought a seasonal pass for Nauset Beach and went there most days, as it was close to the house. I boogie boarded in the ocean and we took long walks on the beach. We drove up the National Seashore, hiked the trails, and went to Highland Light in Truro. We also went to Chatham Light. This would turn out to be our last trip to Cape Cod, a place we loved so much and held so many memorable moments for us.

In the middle of July, Syl and I drove back up to Montréal for the third consecutive summer. We again stayed at Tex and Erna's townhouse in Dollard-des Ormeaux; eating wonderful home cooked meals, relaxing in the sun in the backyard, and cooling off in the small above ground pool. We went out to Jacques and Caroline's house in Saint-Lazare for a birthday get-together for Tex.

We took a day trip with Tex and Erna to Saint-Sauver, about an hour away in the Laurentides region, in the Laurentian Mountains; and to Saint-Césaire. We walked around, took pictures, and had lunch and coffee at an outdoor cafe.

Then it was back up to the country house on Paradise Lake for several days of eating, drinking, sitting in the sun, swimming, and interesting conversations, with lots of laughs. Syl always loved it up here, it made her feel like she was back in Germany. And I did too.

I played tournaments for the 60's Cyclones in Loudoun in May, Syracuse in July, Raleigh in early August, Phoenix in October, and Fort Myers in November. We played a team in Raleigh called the Georgia-Alabama Masters, a team that could recruit players from two states. I didn't think that was legal, but I guess they were right on the border or something.

The Cyclones had gone from only guys from the Central New York area, to adding four guys from the Hudson Valley area, three hours from Syracuse.

They were instrumental in our success, elevating our team to a national championship level. Several more Hudson Valley guys were added later.

We played the Georgia-Alabama Masters in Raleigh. Every guy on this team looked like they were 6 foot 3 and 220 pounds. In Senior Softball, you can only score a maximum of five runs per inning, until the seventh and final inning, (unless the game is tied and goes into extra innings); where it is unlimited, which means your team can score as many runs as possible.

This sets up all sorts of strategies if the fifth run is on base; which base, how many outs, so that you could intentionally walk batters to set up force outs to try and prevent the fifth run from scoring. But if your team is not scoring, and the other team is getting their maximum five runs per inning, you could conceivably be losing, 30 to zero. A more likely scenario is that you get your maximum for two innings, and get two or three runs for two innings, and don't score any runs for two innings; you could be losing 30 to 15.

That's about what the score was when we played them in Raleigh, until the top of the seventh, when they kept us out in the searing over 100-degree heat and humidity, for what seemed like an eternity, scoring at will. We couldn't muster up any energy in our final at bat and the game was over.

At the end of the game, the teams in Senior Softball line up and "give five" to each other in a nice display of sportsmanship. A couple of guys and myself went through the line and were almost to our dugout, when we saw some of their guys put their arms around some of our guys and ask,

"Why don't you join us in a prayer session?

I don't like to be coerced into these types of things, but if the request happened while you were still in the line, you probably just go along with it. If you say no or walk away, you look like a jerk. We were already through the line and by the dugout, so we didn't have to worry about looking foolish. We could have run back out and joined the prayer session, but we didn't feel obligated to do so. You see professional football players kneel and pray in a circle after the game, but it is *your personal choice* to join in or not. This is the preliminary story, to a follow up story with this team, that I will tell you about soon.

I went out to Phoenix in October for the World Championships in October. Marty came to several of our games. We didn't make it to the final days, so I went with three other guys on a day trip to Sedona. I told them about Montezuma's Castle, so we stopped there for a break and a walk on the way. We ate lunch outside in Sedona and walked around town, then hiked up to the Chapel of Holy Cross, a Roman Catholic Church built right into the red rocks. We drove back toward Phoenix and Marty met me and took me back to his house. He was now separated from Marti after 40 years of marriage. Justin was living with him at this time and we had a barbecue and he drove me back to the hotel.

Over Veterans Day weekend in November, I went to Fort Myers for the tournament there. We played one day and on the second day we had an early morning game. The fog was starting to burn off and the sun was starting to brightly shine through. I've tried everything in these situations: from a hat pulled as low as I can, from wearing sunglasses, to eye black, to eye black stickers, to no avail. Nothing ever seemed to work. Just had to shield my eyes with my forearm and basically hope for the best. It was always a dangerous situation, especially at third base, "the hot corner," where I always played. To make it even worse, the sun was reflecting off the metal roof of the dugout, directly into my eyes.

      As fate would have it, this guy on the other team, a short but muscular guy, hit a wicked line drive down the third base line. I held my glove up high to shield the sun, and nine out of ten times, I would backhand and catch the ball. With no sun, I would *expect* to catch it, although it would be considered by the fans to be a great catch. At the worst, if it was the one time out of ten that I didn't catch it, I would at least deflect the ball off the top of my glove. This line drive had a tailspin on it, starting off foul and then curving back in, at over 100 miles an hour. I reached up to catch it, and the reflecting sun off the metal dugout roof was in my vision, and I was struck in the temple and right eye with a direct hit. I went down, but surprisingly was not knocked out. The players and fans were deathly silent. They led me off the field with blood pouring from my face. The people that managed the tournament were not much help, unless we were to call 911 for an ambulance.

      Two young guys, who were volunteers at the field, offered to take me to an Immediate Care medical facility, in a shopping mall plaza about 20 minutes away. I told them to tell my teammates where I was, so that they could pick me up after the game was over. I had no car, just pitched in for gas and tolls for whomever had rented the car, so I was totally reliant on them for transportation. They cleaned the blood off my face and the doctor came in to check me out. He was Greek and spoke in broken English, which I had a hard time understanding, besides being obviously dazed and confused. He put some ointment on the cut above my right eye and put bandages there and wrapped gauze around my head, giving me a "Van Gogh" look. (I remember them even charging $50 on my bill for this unneeded gauze.) The guys came and picked me up and took me back to the hotel.

I was sitting in the lobby when some of the other Syracuse teams in different age groups came in and were asking me how I was, as they had heard about what had happened. Some of the other guys on the Cyclones 60's team came in and my friend Ted took a look at me and said,

"So, where's your fife and drum?"

No mercy. I was woozy and probably had a concussion at the least, and should have gone to the Emergency Room for a Cat Scan, as the doctor had suggested. I probably should have, but I didn't. I had no car, and definitely was in no condition to drive myself, and the team had another game to play in the early afternoon. I really didn't know what to do. I should have sat by the pool for a while and then gone up to my room, taken a shower, and then a nap. I really wasn't trying to be a hero. I guess that I was afraid to be alone at this point and decided to go with the team back out to the field for the next game. One of the guys hit grounders to me before the game, with my bandaged eye, hardly being able to see. The manager didn't feel comfortable playing me in the field. I actually was a designated hitter for this game, but I was pretty worthless in the condition that I was in; compounded by the sun coming from right field, making it almost impossible for a right handed batter to see.

The next day I went with the team for an elimination game in the tournament. A couple of guys had pulled hamstrings and were unable to play. I didn't want the guys to be at a disadvantage playing short-handed; so, I volunteered to play, really having no business doing so in my condition, and risking further injury and possible permanent damage. The manager was appreciative, but still felt uncomfortable accepting this responsibility, if something worse were to happen to me.

He said, "Are you sure? We are playing the Georgia-Alabama Masters."

Fate couldn't have scripted it any better. I was nervous, but sometimes you just "have to get back up on the horse," as soon as possible. We played the game and actually kept it close and got out of the seventh inning in decent shape, not like the marathon fiasco in Raleigh over three months earlier. I think we only lost by four or five runs and surprisingly, I had no balls hit to me, especially playing third base, "the hot corner." There were some base hits to left field that I had no play on and that was it. As we walked through the handshaking line, several of the Georgia-Alabama Masters' guys put their arms around us,

"Won't you join us in a prayer session?"

There was no escaping it this time.

Their captain started off this session,

"It is a beautiful blue sky day today. The sun is shining and we are thankful to be alive and still being able to play ball. We would also like to give a prayer to the fellow who got hit with the line drive the other day and pray for his speedy recovery."

I raised my hand, "That would be me."

They had no idea that the guy that they were praying for had just played the entire game at third base against them, with a black and blue and yellowing and bandaged right eye.

"Well that is certainly welcome news. The Lord works in mysterious ways. Does anyone want to add any words to the prayer session?"

I again raised my hand and said, "Yeah, thanks for not hitting any line drives at me."

Everyone laughed and he said,

"See, the Lord has a good sense of humor. Just look at the guy next to you."

Then he went on a ten-minute religious speech before we could get out of there.

The next day was a beautiful, blue sky, sunny day in the 80's. Since we were now eliminated from the tournament, we had a free day before flying home the following day. I had always wanted to check out the annual American Sand Sculpting Championships, held on Fort Myers Beach at this time of year; but either we were still playing in the tournament or nobody wanted to go. One of the Hudson Valley guys, Bert, was interested and he had a car. It is an impressive festival, with over 30 sand sculptures, amazing works of art. There are 50 vendors, music, all taking place right there by the Gulf of Mexico. After that, Bert and I drove over to Sanibel Island and I showed him where to go: driving and walking the Ding-Darling National Wildlife Refuge, then driving down to Bowman's Beach for a swim and long walk, and then driving over to Captiva Island to watch the sunset. We had dinner on Sanibel Island and then drove back to the hotel. It was a really good day, even with my eye all different colors and bandaged up.

I really didn't want to tell Syl what had happened to me until she saw me when she picked me up at the airport.

I didn't want her to worry, as Syl was a natural born "worry wart" to begin with. She puts undue stress upon herself, when most of the time things are beyond your control anyway, and worrying about it is just a waste of your time.

I hung a framed picture in our bedroom, that my maternal grandmother had embroidered: a birdhouse with trees and flying birds around it, a border all around of flowers, and the words, "Today is the tomorrow" above the birdhouse and "You worried about yesterday" below the birdhouse. I hung this on the wall so that it was directly in her vision from her side of our bed.

I always called Syl every night when I was away at these tournaments, but I held out telling her about me getting hit in the head and eye. That last night I told her and she was not too thrilled that it had happened, and I had waited to tell her, and now started worrying.

I flew back home and went back to school and had to answer all the questions from everybody, especially the kids. Another story. I never did get a Cat Scan, but I did go to Dr. Ralph, our chiropractor here in Jamesville, ten minutes from our house. He analyzed me and said I had a cranial bone compression. He had to reach inside my mouth, way in the back, and press against it and manipulate it weekly for six months, before it healed back to normal. He was convinced I had suffered a concussion as well. I went on to play for two more years, although there were times of blurred vision and migraine headaches.

It was nice to have Syl home for both Thanksgiving and Christmas, for the first time since 2006; her spending Christmas in 2007 and 2008, and Thanksgiving in 2009, in

Charleston with her mother, Ben, her sisters, Debbie and Karen, and the rest of her South Carolina family.

An Early Snow This Year

We were thoroughbreds then

A singular breed

Content to roam together

Free and easy

She was nature's picture

Tranquil radiance

Raindrops upon a deserted pond

Blue jays flying

Tall corn growing

Walking lazy, in smiling fields of wheat.

I stand in a barren land now

Warped by storms and time

The blue jays have flown away

And the corn has turned brown

Even the wheat hide their faces

As I hurry by

Still searching for the rainbow

She must have left behind

Can't seem to shake this awful feeling

Not having her hand to touch.

2011

September: (Tex visit)

    Green Lakes

    Cazenovia Lake

    Skaneateles Lake (Boat Tour)

      In the middle of February, Baxter, our Headmaster at MPH, suffered a heart attack and passed away in the early morning hours. It was a severe blow to the school and changed its course and charm from that point on. We would become directly affected as well; our lives, especially our school lives, would never be the same again. Tracy, the business manager, would be named by the Board of Trustees to be the interim Head of School, as she knew the financial inner workings of the school. They also named her the interim Head of School for the following school year of 2011-2012 in June, as they would conduct a nationwide search for a new Head of School.

Syl and I survived another winter and in June there was another big reunion of close friends on "Eff" and Kathy's deck when Wardie and Christie came to visit. Also, in June, my brother Marty and his son, Kenn, and Kenn's son, Bready, came into Syracuse from Arizona for a visit.

We worked our usual Playscape program for two weeks in June and in the last couple of days went over to see Tracy for our contract talks. Syl had always gone over first to see Baxter for the contract talks, and after she was done, I would go over and see him. We were always one of the last to see him for our contract talks, being in the group with staff and maintenance. All the other administrators and teachers had their contract talks with him in late March. This was always the same routine for us, since after my first year was completed in late June of 1995. (Syl had been employed at MPH earlier than me, so she had seen him in June in 1993 and 1994.)

In March of 2009, we received an email from Baxter that he wanted to see us for our contract talks in late March. We were surprised, as we had always gone the last week in June for all those years. We didn't know why our status had seemingly been elevated, but we went in late March. It didn't change our salary though. We had started out extremely low on the pay scale, and would receive a raise each year of $1,000, (except a couple of years where there were no raises); so at least it added up over the course of our careers. We saw Baxter in late March again in 2010 for our contract talks. He would always say,

"So Dusty, how's it going? How's Extended Day going?"

He would always have praise for our teaching, our relationships with the parents and other teachers, and our caring and dedication for the students. We always felt some anguish before the talks, I think that's normal for everyone; but after some conversations and a couple of laughs, we would sign the contracts and look forward to another school year, starting after Labor Day weekend. (But getting away and enjoying the summer first.) You left there feeling good about your job and yourself. Even though I worked hard and dedicated myself to my job and improving myself, and earned everything on my own; I'll always give Baxter credit for taking a chance on me and believing in me, when a lot of people didn't at the start. I think Baxter was proud of his decision about me, silencing the critics and doubters.

This would be the last time we would ever have our contract talks with Baxter. I wrote a poem about Baxter, "The King of Hearts," and read it at the MPH's services for him in the gymnasium. Baxter was an eloquent public speaker and even had a talk radio show. His main passion, beside his family, was MPH. He cared deeply about the school, the administrators, teachers, parents, and especially the students.

I went over to see Tracy about my contract for the upcoming school year of 2011-2012. The meeting wasn't even in Baxter's office; rather it was a makeshift setup in the kitchen with Lynne, the Director of Admissions, there with her. Baxter never had anyone else with him for the contract talks. Right away, Tracy informed me that they were only offering me my Extended Day Co-Director position, nothing else. No Lower School Assistant position, that I had done for the past 17 years. No teaching Geography. Not even any position in the Physical Education Department. I was stunned, not believing what I was hearing. I think Lynne was shocked also, even embarrassed for me as well. I asked why and she just said it was a financial decision.

I was speechless, and not wanting to "burn any bridges," got up and left and returned to the Playscape program. I told Syl and she could not believe it. I think some other teachers and parents who were there to pick up their kids, must have overheard my conversation, and word spread quickly. It has been eight years and eight months since this meeting, and my blood still boils when I think about it.

Syl had kept her full-time positions as Kindergarten Assistant, as well as Co-Director, with me, at Extended Day. So that was good. Tracy called me over the next day and told me to stop "the parking lot chatter." As if I had any control over the parents, who were in disbelief over what had happened to me. They wrote letters on my behalf, extolling my virtues, and had meetings with her, but to no avail. So that summer was spent agonizing over the fact that I now only had a part-time job.

Syl had to hear all my grievances, similar to when I experienced the Merchants softball team letting me go at the end of June, 2001. We decided to not go up to Montréal this summer, dealing with this situation and hoping to still figure out something that could be added to my job description. My many emails fell on deaf ears. We tried to enjoy Tom and Debbie's pool under the circumstances, but this was constantly on our minds and in our discussions. Syl was happy that she still had her full-time job, but was so angry over what they had done to me.

Tex decided to drive down to visit us over Labor Day weekend. He came down by himself, following our directions, and found our house. We took him for a walk around Green Lakes the first afternoon, then to Cazenovia Lake, and went out to dinner. The next day we all drove out to Skaneateles; walked out on the pier, took the Skaneateles

Lake Boat Tour, strolled around town, ate at Doug's Fish Fry, and stopped for an ice cream on the way home. The following day we went over to Tom and Debbie's pool to swim and Tex met Willie and played pool basketball with him.

  The day after Labor Day began the four days of meetings, seminars, workshops, and getting the classrooms ready. I was required to attend some of the mandatory meetings, much to my dismay, still being the Co-Director of Extended Day. And to get things organized for Extended Day and meetings regarding the program. I needed to keep this job so we could still pay our bills. When I wasn't required to be there, I went over to the pool, five minutes away, and went back to pick up Syl and take her home when she was done for the day.

  The first day of school arrived, and for the first time since 1994, I had no job to go to MPH for, until I needed to be there by 3 o'clock in the afternoon for Extended Day. We only had one car, so I needed to take Syl in for her job, starting at 9:30 in the morning. I stayed out of Syl's way while she was getting ready, not even bothering to have coffee or anything. We left at 9:00 and by the time that I drove her in and drove back home, it was 10 o'clock. I had my juice, honey, coffee, banana, and smoothie, and went out to do some yard work.

  Before I knew it, it was 2 o'clock in the afternoon and I had to shower and get ready to leave for my Extended Day job. I never felt so lost in my life. Well, maybe in my younger days, when I was wondering where I was going to stay and how I was going to find work to make some money in order to eat; maybe not as lost as that. But after being married for over 28 years, and having a full-time teaching job for 17 years, I was feeling very lost.

Some days I would go down to the store, so we wouldn't have to do that after Extended Day. Some days I would take a walk around Green Lakes or Pratt's Falls, if it was nice out. Or go over and sit by the pool, even after it was closed, if it was a really warm day; bringing my school clothes with me and shower there, and then drive down to school for Extended Day. This was my routine for the rest of September and the first half of October. One day, I decided to go down to the Employment Bureau in downtown Syracuse, to see if I could sign up for unemployment insurance; not making much headway when I called, always seemingly talking to a voice on the machine, and not a real person.

I drove downtown and parked the car on South Salina Street at a parking meter. I was a dime short of the maximum time allowance when I got out of the car and it started raining. I walked to the old Chimes Building, where I thought the Employment Bureau was. (I didn't have a cell phone at this time.) I hadn't done any research on their location, that's how much my mind was stuck in a fog at this time. As I went to open up my umbrella, the wind started picking up and whipped the umbrella inside out, with the spokes going the wrong way, making it useless. Why I kept holding on to it, is beyond me. Again, the foggy mind syndrome, I guess. I kept asking different people for directions. They would send me over near the Federal Building, which wasn't it. Then over to a couple of more locations, and they weren't it either. I don't think these people really had a clue where it was. I walked past the Dinosaur Bar-B-Que and someone finally told me that the Bureau was on Franklin Street, past the Franklin Street apartments.

I really had to take a pee by now and thought that I could make it to the Bureau. I realized that I couldn't and it was too far now to walk back to the Dinosaur. Nature was calling big time and I noticed an empty alley. There were two choices for me, relieve myself in the alley or pee my pants. I don't think anyone would choose the latter. I had to pull down my jeans in order to go, as they were tight and it would be uncomfortable and tough to go, just by unzipping the zipper. So here I was, still holding on to the useless umbrella with my left hand, like a fool; while using my right hand to pee, with my jeans down to my ankles. I almost felt like crying, it was such an embarrassing and low moment in my life. I stood there thinking to myself,

"What did I do to deserve this?"

I could see it now in the paper in the police report: teacher arrested for indecent exposure. Luckily, that didn't happen, and I walked further and finally found the Bureau. It was a small office and you could call about job opportunities that were posted if you were interested. At this point in time, I was not, still hoping something would eventually open up at MPH for me. I couldn't qualify for unemployment insurance as long as I had my Extended Day job, and I wasn't about to give that up, for half pay for six months. I took some brochures and walked back to the car. I was surprised that there wasn't a parking ticket waiting for me, just to rub more salt into my wounds, as the meter had expired a few minutes before I got there. I decided to sign up for my Social Security benefits, earlier than I had planned on. I had to make all the calls, fill out all the paperwork, and go through all the procedures.

Most of October followed the same weekday routine, except for going over to the pool. I did a lot of yard work and took some walks when the weather was nice. Syl and I had our weekends to take walks, go for colorful foliage drives, and stop somewhere for dinner. In late

October, I made an appointment to have our leased Honda Accord serviced at the dealer, Honda City, out in Liverpool. I dropped Syl off at school and headed out to the car appointment. I didn't realize it, but I found out later that Joline, Head of the Lower School, had run after me as I was leaving the parking lot, wanting to talk with me. When I met with her the following day, they wanted to offer me the opportunity to do two Physical Education classes, if I was interested.

As it turned out, they were trying to get by with only one PE teacher in Pre-K and also just one in second grade; when the college student teacher finished with her internship the last week in October. There must *always* be at least two teachers in *every* PE class; not only for teaching skills, but monitoring, and most importantly, safety. So, one day after the student teacher was gone, the PE teacher in Pre-K, Bari, was all by herself when one of the kids got hurt. She had to get a teacher to walk the child across the parking lot over to the nurse's office. If there were two PE teachers there, one of us would walk the child to the nurse, as we always did in the past.

I set up an appointment with Tracy and was offered a position as a PE Assistant in Pre-K and in second grade. I had been the assistant in second grade for fifteen years before. We negotiated my salary, and it obviously wasn't close to what it once was, but it was an improvement over just getting paid for Extended Day the past two months.

So now we would both get ready in the morning, as we had for all those previous years, and leave for MPH at 9 o'clock. I would do my PE classes and have lunch, now just eating with the maintenance guys, no longer with the kids and no longer telling my "Dusty's Lunchtime Stories." I now had a few hours before I'd have to go down to the dining room at 3 o'clock to maintain some semblance of order, and take the kids across the quad to the Extended Day building, after the buses had gone.

I started putting this time to constructive use, going down to the library and using their computers to start typing up my children's book, "The Forest That Rains Frogs." It had been three years since that time in the Fort Myers airport, after hearing of my mom's passing, and having extra hours to wait for my plane, that I had finished the story.

One of the guys on the Cyclones, Joe, ("Pearl"), and his wife, Pat, were from Fishkill, near Poughkeepsie, in the Hudson Valley. We were at a tournament in Loudoun, Virginia in May, and between games, I noticed Pat drawing some landscape pictures. I didn't realize that she was an accomplished artist and had her work in many galleries. I only knew her as "Pearl's" wife, scorekeeper for the team, and going out to dinner. She only knew me as a guy from Syracuse, third baseman on the team, and a teacher. She had no idea that I was a writer. We had a few conversations here and there, but that was about it.

I started telling Pat about my children's book and she showed me a children's book that she had illustrated for a friend of hers, that had a disability and lived in Raleigh. I really liked her illustrations, as she had a unique style. She was actually in the process of illustrating a second book for her friend. I sent her a copy of the text of my book after the tournament was over. They had even been to the El Yunque rain forest in Puerto Rico, where the coquí frogs live, and where my story originates from.

The next tournament was in July in Syracuse and Pat and I talked in between games. She had not made any commitment yet, but she had circled certain passages of text, with a vision of what she might have an illustration idea in her mind. You could tell that the story intrigued her. Pat started sending me some pencil drawings of possible illustrations in the fall, although at that time we hadn't reached any kind of business agreement. But it was exciting to see the potential process begin to unfold.

I played for the Cyclones 60's in early August in Raleigh and in Fort Myers over Veterans Day weekend, playing there a year after getting hit in the head with the line drive incident.

We took Ileana with us out to Cazenovia Lake on Labor Day for a nice sunny day of sun, eating the lunch that Syl had packed, swimming, and playing on the playground. Ileana is the daughter of Traian and Ioana, two doctors originally from Bucharest, Romania. They were brought up under the regime of the former President, actually Dictator, of Romania, Nicolae Ceausescu. He was the General Secretary of the Romanian Communist Party from 1965 to 1989, and the second and last Communist leader of Romania. He was executed by a firing squad on December 25, 1989. He was a ruthless tyrant, causing people to struggle to buy daily food, as the grocery stores were empty. This was the environment that Traian and Ioana had to endure in their childhoods and had to win a lottery in order to escape their homeland.

They went on to become doctors, Traian as a Cardiologist and Ioana as an Internist and Pulmonologist. They completed their internships in Chicago and Virginia, Ileana was born, and they relocated to Syracuse to set up their practices. They enrolled Ileana in MPH when she was in Kindergarten and Syl taught her there and we had her in our Extended Day program. We got to know them from picking up Ileana and started a close and long-term friendship. We started giving Ileana a ride home occasionally when they both had to work late at the hospital. Syl would go over to their house on a Friday or Saturday night, so that they could go out to dinner and a movie. Syl and Ileana became very close and Syl could earn some extra spending money for herself.

In September, Debbie became the first female president of Claremont Graduate University, a private, all-graduate research university located in Claremont, California. Claremont is a city 35 miles east of downtown Los Angeles, in the foothills of the San Gabriel Mountains, with a sunny, Mediterranean climate year-round. Claremont Graduate University was founded in 1925 and is a member of the Claremont Colleges, which includes five undergraduate and two graduate institutions of higher education. The undergraduate institutions are: Pomona College, Claremont McKenna College, Harvey Mudd College, Scripps College, and Pitzer College. The graduate institutions are: Claremont Graduate University and Keck Graduate Institute of Applied Life Sciences. They are within walking distance of one another. This design was based on that of Oxford University and Cambridge University. Claremont Graduate University is the oldest all-graduate institution in the United States.

Expecting the Unexpected

A weeping willow quivers and twists

Put to the test, it bends but resists

Habitually jostling to maintain its space

Can't seem to halt the quickening pace.

Let bygones be bygones

Plead the destitute vagabonds

And before judging them as deserters who quit

Take a walk in their shoes, to see how they fit.

Plans fall by the wayside, schemes come and go

There will always be another fork in the road

Lurking around the corners of another year

Knowing even your shadow is no longer near.

2012

August: Montréal & Dollard-des Ormeaux
  Saint-Lazare
  Lac Paradis

 Syl and I survived another Syracuse winter, working our jobs at MPH and taking care of our home on Broadfield Road. Pat made a commitment to do the illustrations for my children's book and we reached a business agreement and signed a contract. She would send up colored illustrations, a few at a time, and I would show them to Syl, other teachers, and two art teachers, Jeanne and Linda. They were all very impressed.

During this school year, Tracy served as the interim Head of School. They narrowed it down to two finalists; and I, and most everyone else, think that they made the wrong choice. They picked a guy, Scott, a former federal prosecutor for seven years, before he entered the educational field. He had left a school in Massachusetts in turmoil, regarding a football scandal. A lot of parents at this academy protested to get him fired.

Syl and I did our two-week Playscape program after all the graduations in June, taking the kids on our usual twice a week field trips to Green Lakes. We spent many days, the last week of June, and most of July and August, sitting in the sun and swimming in Tom and Debbie's pool.

I played in tournaments for the Cyclones 60's in Loudoun in May, Hopkins Road in Liverpool in July, and Raleigh in early August. We decided not to go up to Montréal in the middle of July, our usual time frame for Tex's birthday; instead going up there for the last week of July. We went to see the White Chapel, had a nice lunch down by the water, and drove through the lovely neighborhoods by McGill University. Also, a get-together at Jacques and Caroline's house in Saint-Lazare. A few days later, back up to Paradise Lake in the country for good times of eating, drinking, and conversations with the people up there.

One night in late August, we went to Vernon Downs with Kyle and Cheryl, MPH parents of Mariah and Natalie. We taught them in the classroom, PE, and they were always part of our Extended Day program. We were going there to have dinner and watch Kyle's trotter horse in the harness races.

Over the summer, the administrators at MPH had contacted me about adding two more PE classes, Kindergarten and first grade, to my schedule; which was some welcome news for once. I had done both of these PE classes for the previous 15 years, so adding these to my Pre-K and second grade classes gave me four classes, helping out in fifth grade PE as well. My salary was better than last year's, but still not where it once was. Syl maintained her full-time status. Another school year began the day after Labor Day, with the four days of teachers' meetings. At least this year I was not facing the disappointment and disillusionment of the previous year. So, this was a good thing and our spirits were high for this upcoming school year at MPH.

MPH always had a small college atmosphere and close-knit community feel to it. There was a special connection between administrators, teachers, younger and older students, and parents. This would begin to eventually change under the new Head of School.

Syl and I took Ileana out to Plumpton Farms in Jamesville, to pet the animals and look at all the pumpkins and Halloween decorations, on Columbus Day. We would continue to do this over the next couple of years.

I went to Fort Myers once more to play in the Winter Nationals for the Cyclones 60's. We had an extra day after our tournament ended and spent the day at Fort

Myers Beach. This would turn out to be my last tournament for the Cyclones. I haven't put on my cleats, worn my glove, caught or thrown a ball, or swung a bat, since then. It has been seven years on Veterans Day of 2019. Sometimes I miss the competition going against teams from all over the country, the camaraderie, going out to dinner, sightseeing. It was even better when Syl was able to go with me. The new manager started adding several more players that he knew from the Hudson Valley and I didn't feel like going through any more of these scenarios. So, I just sort of faded away into the sunset from the Senior Softball fields.

   Pat and I coordinated our text and illustrations over the fall and I began the editing and publishing process with Outskirts Press, located in Parker, Colorado. The book was finally published and came out in both hardcover and softcover formats on December 20, 2012.

      A lot of friends, including softball friends, MPH teachers and parents, who were friends; were very enthusiastic about the book and bought copies of both formats, but mainly the hardcover edition in the beginning. I was very happy with my book. It is a good story of courage, loyalty, and perseverance; and Pat's illustrations are fantastic.

      Now that my children's book had been published, I had a vision of having it translated into Spanish and getting it into Puerto Rico, Mexico, South America, Spain, and Spanish speaking communities in the United States.

2013

July: Montréal & Dollard-des Ormeaux

Saint-Lazare

Lac Paradis

August: Skaneateles (Caroline & Jacques)

I asked Silviana, the Spanish teacher at MPH, if she would be interested in translating my book into Spanish. She was reluctant at first, quoting the fees that a translator would normally charge per page. I didn't think that I could afford this and the project went on hold. One day over the winter, she told me that she had decided to do it because Sylvia and I had always been so nice to her son, Chris, throughout his Lower School years at MPH. I gave her some gift cards at the end for all her work.

She was from Mexico City and went back there every summer to be with her family. Her husband, Chris, who taught Spanish at a public school outside of Syracuse, collaborated with her. We would meet when I had a break between classes, usually on her lunch break between her Spanish classes, during the rest of the winter and all of the spring and go over everything. I had made some revisions to my original text, so she had to make the appropriate revisions in her translation. It was a long process, but we finally got it done.

I had to go through the editing and publishing process once again through Outskirts Press, and "El Bosque Donde Llueven Ranas Coquí" was published in July, 2013. My vision has never been realized. Maybe I'm not persistent enough. It's like my screenplay, you make several efforts and then get no responses, and the years slip on by.

"Eff" and Kathy had been going on vacations to Puerto Rico for several years. I asked them if they wouldn't mind, if the opportunity arose, to mention my book. Kathy had a long career as a public school teacher, and "Eff" was a former professor at Syracuse University, before creating his environmental firm, Upstate Freshwater Institute. They had both read my book and really liked it. They said that there was a display of books in the lobby of the hotel where they stayed and they would ask the manager if he would display my book there.

When they returned from their vacation, they said the manager would do it and gave me his address. I wrote him and he wrote me back, to send him two copies, both the English and Spanish versions; and if I would autograph them for his children. I had to order and pay for some books through the publisher, sign them, put them in mailing envelopes, and go to the Post office and pay to send them to him. I also sent some color copies of the cover to have him put in some local bookstores. I was excited at the potential prospect of getting my book being known and selling in this new market. Especially since Puerto Rico is the origin of the story about these coquí frogs. Well, once again, I never heard back from him; not only if he liked the book and the illustrations, but if he ever received them in the first place. I even wrote him back to see if he received the books. No reply, so I'll never know. Frustrating. But at least I did it and had it published. Maybe someday my vision will be realized.

Syl and I survived another Syracuse winter and a busy school year. But as I alluded to before, the atmosphere at MPH was different than what it had been when Baxter was the Head of School, starting in 1990. (For Sylvia, it was almost 19 years, and for me, almost 17 years.) For the past two years, things had changed, and not for the better. Since the start of this school year, 2012-2013, with Scott as the new Head of School, things had dramatically changed. He would sit in the front lobby sometimes and just observe everything, which was his right to do. But you, and I mean almost everyone, felt as if you were being scrutinized and judged by him. Maybe his former federal prosecutor instincts. It just evolved into an atmosphere of feeling like people were talking behind your back, like you had this paranoid sense of constantly looking over your shoulder. And I know I wasn't the only one who felt this way. It was definitely not the atmosphere that we were used to all those years before with Baxter, that we now refer to as "the golden years."

Silver Shadows

Shimmering stars upon a frozen lake

Silver shadows stretch and begin to awake

Icy fingers flickering in the spotlight

Nocturnal charades in the dead of night.

Deceptive, like some will-of-the-wisp

Visions appear vague, obscured and eclipsed

Riddles as illusory as vanishing youth

Sorting out the ruins, veiled glimpses of truth.

On June 1st, Linda and John celebrated their 50th wedding anniversary, when they had gotten married in college in 1963. It was held in a really nice house that the President of Cazenovia College used for special events, near the Equine Center. Linda had been the secretary to the president for the past nine years, since they moved to Cazenovia from Padanaram. Linda had been going through some serious health issues and was confined to a wheelchair for this momentous event. I felt really bad for her. John was always diligent and loyal in taking care of her. Linda and John's children were there: Susan and her husband, Mike, whom Syl and I had never met before, and their daughter, Elise; Stephanie; Matt and his future wife, Kara; Julie and her daughter, Em; Syl and me; and some of their friends from college. There was plenty of good food, conversations, and laughs; we just wished Linda wasn't having to deal with her health issues.

Syl and I finished up the school year, and after all the graduations, did our usual Playscape program in June. This was our 20th year of doing this two-week program, and as we would find out the next year, it would turn out to be our last. We went in for our contract talks with Scott, and were informed that we would both only be retained to do the Extended Day program. They were taking away all my PE classes, that I had finally retained, and added to, for the past two years. And for the first time in her MPH career, Syl was experiencing having her Kindergarten and other teaching duties taken away. So here we were again, trying to figure out why, and wondering how we would be able to take care of our financial obligations.

During this school year, Tom had been going out to Claremont Graduate University, while still keeping his Professor of Economics position at Syracuse University. He had completed his tenure as Chair of the Department. He would go out there monthly, for three or four days, as a visiting professor. He was taking care of Willie when he was in Syracuse, but we were asked to stay at their house while he was gone; to drive Willie to school in the morning, bring him back after Extended Day, to make his dinner, go to the store, and take care of the house. So, this extra income was very helpful to us. Debbie had been coming back here the previous school year in the fall, when she could, to watch some of Willie's soccer games; and then for a month over semester break, from mid-December to mid-January, she was back here. Also, the Spring Break for her in March and the summer.

Willie could have gone to school in Los Angeles, but they decided, with his input, that MPH was the right place for him to be. He was an integral part of the soccer team, becoming the captain in his senior season, and earning All-League and All-Central New York team honors. Plus, all his friends were here and they remain close to this day.

As it turned out, this had become a very busy school year, with my added PE classes, working on the Spanish version of my book, and us taking care of Willie and staying at their house frequently. And now at the end of it all, having to deal with a diminished job position for both of us.

Before we got this news, we attended Willie's Baccalaureate and Graduation ceremonies. Most of the awards were given at Baccalaureate and we were certain that Willie would receive, or at least share, the

Martha L. Heer Citizenship Award, named in honor of my mom's influence and over thirty-three years of service to the school. Willie had gone fourteen years at MPH, and had been a model citizen, as well as a top athlete and scholar. We waited through all the awards and then they gave the Citizenship Award to the daughter of a long-time teacher at MPH, who was deserving of it, but nothing for Willie. We were very disappointed, but the next day at Graduation, Willie received the highest award, the Headmaster's Award, for all those attributes I just mentioned. One goes to a girl and Willie got the boy's award. That was a deserving and welcome surprise. Tom and Debbie had a big graduation party on their deck.

Later in June, we went over to Mary and Sheila's house for a high school graduation party for their daughter, Haley. Haley had been in Willie's class at MPH, but had left in Lower School, and graduated from Fayetteville-Manlius. The same applied to their younger daughter, Taylor, who graduated the next year and we went to her party as well. It seemed like a long time ago, in fact over ten years before, that we were with them in Disney World in April, 2003. Haley went on to graduate from, ironically, William Smith, and Taylor from Geneseo.

In the middle of July, Syl and I went back up to Montréal, to celebrate Tex's 80th birthday, as well as Syl's 60th birthday a month before. We had a great party at Jacques and Caroline's house in Saint-Lazare, so much to eat and drink, and to talk and laugh and dance. Ron and Lorraine drove over from Ottawa, and Bob and Beata flew in from Edmonton. Bob had warmed up to Syl over the years and now felt close to her and really loved her. Beata had felt close to her and loved her since we met and went to Québec City in the summer of 2009. Bob owns The Comedy Factory in Edmonton; manages the club, takes care of all the business and bookings, is the MC, and sometimes does a stand-up routine as well. Once you get to know him, he is really funny. He is also an accomplished deep-sea diver, having completed thousands of dives around the world. I've seen videos of him swimming with sharks all around him in the deepest depths. The deepest that I ever dove was maybe 30 feet down, off Shorty's Glass Bottom Boat in Antigua.

Bob and Beata rode with Syl and me, Tex and Erna drove their car, and we went up to the country house on Paradise Lake for several days. The usual, and never boring, routine of lots of eating, drinking, sunning, swimming, conversations, and laughing; with us and all the people up there. One day, Ron and Lorraine's sons, Lucas and Olivier, came up to spend the day. This was the first time that we had met Lucas.

We enjoyed the rest of July and most of August hanging out with Willie and his friends at the pool. Tom was having a hard time dealing with the reality of Willie about to begin college, at Occidental College in Los Angeles, which was only 35 miles away from them; but it was the separation factor, after all these years of doing so many things together, that was weighing heavily on his mind. It took him a year to work things out in his mind in order to move on. Tom was now at Claremont as well.

I now became the caretaker of their house; doing yard work, bringing in the mail and sending important mail out to them, giving them airport rides when needed, checking and monitoring everything in the house, and shoveling the snow off the walks and in front of the garage. This kept me busy, as well as supplementing our income. And Syl would sometimes take care of Ileana.

At the end of August, Caroline and Jacques drove down to visit us for a few days. We showed them the sights and went out to dinner. One day we took them out to Skaneateles to look at the lake, walk around the town, and eat at Doug's Fish Fry.

Syl and I started the new school year the day after Labor Day, attending the mandatory meetings and getting our Extended Day things in order. After that, we didn't bother with the other days of meetings, as it no longer pertained to us, in our view. We did yard work at our house, went to the store, ran errands, sat by the pool at Tom and Debbie's some days; before driving into school by 3 o'clock in the afternoon for Extended Day. We would occasionally give Ileana a ride home and Syl was still taking care of her once in a while on a weekend night. We took some nice foliage drives and walks to Green Lakes, Pratt's Falls, and Highland Forest. Then the long winter came and I had to shovel in front of our garage after the plower came; our deck, and get some of the snow off the roof with the snow rake, after a really heavy snowfall. And drive over and shovel over at Tom and Debbie's and take care of their house.

Next Stop Unknown

I woke up this morning

Or was it afternoon

The clock is still yawning

And way out of tune.

Gazing out at the drizzling rain

As mermaids of fortune collect their tolls

Bad news is tapping against my window pane

Reminding me of those bottomless holes.

It's not just coincidence

A new destination is near

Journey into suspense

Elusive, yet clear.

The seeds were sown

A long time ago

Next stop unknown

Next story untold.

2014

May: Fall River, Massachusetts

July: Montréal, Canada

    Dollard-des Ormeaux

    Saint-Lazare

    Saint-Sauveur

    Lac Paradis

August: Hilton Head, South Carolina

    Windmill Harbour

    South Carolina Yacht Club

    Shipyard Golf Club

    Harbour Town

   Savannah, Georgia

    Dolphin Watch Boat Cruise

    Coligny Beach

August: Dundee & Lakemont

    Watkins Glen

    Geneva (Belhurst Castle)

November: New York City

    Courtyard by Marriott (Third Avenue)

    Rockefeller Center

    Times Square

Over Memorial Day weekend, Syl and I drove five hours, 323 miles east, to Fall River, Massachusetts, for Matt and Kara's wedding. John drove Linda up and gave a blessing at the wedding. Tom and Julie came up from Virginia. Julie performed the wedding ceremony, as she had gotten her license to do this, and has performed many wedding ceremonies before and since. Susan, her son Geoff; and Stephanie, her daughter, Sara, and son, Luke; all came in from Oregon. Geoff was an usher and part of Matt's wedding party. Linda was able to stand up from her wheelchair, with Matt's help, and have the first dance with him. It was just a shame that she had to endure this. There was a lot of great food and Syl and I joined in for hours of dancing.

We finished the school year and maintained our Extended Day positions, but were offered nothing else. We had informed them that we were interested in any positions that might become available, but none was forthcoming. And they now replaced us with someone else for the Playscape Program, a popular program that we had done for the past 20 years.

I did go over to the end of the year clambake, the Saturday before all the graduations the following week, to attend the 50th reunion of our 1964 graduating class from Pebble Hill. There were only six of us that attended out of the class of twenty-seven. We had some good conversations and laughs. Syl stayed at the pool while I went down there for a couple of hours. Despite how the school was treating us, I just thought that it was the right thing to do.

In July, Syl and I drove up to Montréal once again. Bob was visiting during this week, by himself this time. We had our usual get-together at Jacques and Caroline's house in Saint-Lazare. We took a day trip to Saint-Sauveur, walking around town, a nice lunch and later a coffee at an outdoor cafe. Back to the country house on Paradise Lake for several days before heading back home. Because of circumstances beyond our control, as I will explain later, this would turn out to be our last trip to Montréal in the summer. We had enjoyed six wonderful summer trips, from the original reunion in 2008, through this trip in 2014; only skipping 2011, but Tex came down to visit us that year over Labor Day weekend. We now had an extended family and our new Paradise Lake friends as well.

In August, Willie wanted to relive some of his childhood vacations with us and Tom and Debbie invited us to go with them to Hilton Head, South Carolina. Hilton Head is in the Low Country southern end of South Carolina, 20 miles north of Savannah, Georgia, and 95 miles south of Charleston. We stayed in a beautiful house that Debbie's friends had offered to her. It was in Windmill Harbour. As you pulled in, there was a sign:

"You can say what you want about the south, but you don't see anyone retiring up north."

Windmill Harbour is a 172- acre private community along the Intracoastal Waterway. The brightly colored homes here display their true southern architecture. They had bicycles for us to ride around the community, checking out these beautiful homes, and a quick ride over to the South Carolina Yacht Club. At the Yacht Club, there was a beautiful pool, and a huge marina with 260 boat slips; and a locked harbor system that serves as a direct link to the Intracoastal Waterway. We all spent many days reading, sunning, and swimming in the pool. Will, (not calling him Willie anymore, but it was hard not to still refer to him that way), and I had fun playing basketball in the pool.

We all took a day trip on the Dolphin Watch Cruises Boat Tour, cruising down beautiful Broad Creek; observing the bottlenose dolphins, osprey, egrets, pelicans, bald eagles, mink, otter, and other birds and mammals on this impressive tour. We drove to Coligny Beach, where Will and I went boogie boarding for hours in the ocean, reliving our past vacations. There were many shops and food places on the boardwalk to check out and long walks on the beach.

Will and I played golf one day at the Shipyard Golf Club, as Debbie came with us riding a cart. The course had views of tall pines, magnolias, and moss-draped oaks. We all played miniature golf one day.

One night we all drove to Savannah, Georgia, to watch a Minor League Baseball game at historic Grayson Stadium, built in 1926. The home team was the Savannah Sand Gnats, and after the 2015 season, they moved to Columbia, South Carolina, to become the Columbia Fireflies. Now, Savannah's team is the Savannah Bananas, in the Coastal Plain League. The other teams in their division are the Florence Red Wolves, Lexington County Blowfish, and Macon Bacon; and in the other division, the Asheboro Copperheads, (love these team names!) The Bananas have been featured on ESPN and other cable stations with their wild promotions, notably in 2018, when they were the first team ever to play an entire game wearing kilts. We didn't see that, but have seen plenty of crazy things between innings at these games. Tom, Will, and I really get a kick out of watching all these promotional stunts, that's what makes Minor League Baseball so much fun.

One night we drove to Harbour Town, where the iconic Harbour Town Lighthouse is. We walked along the marina, listened to a guy playing and singing Jimmy Buffett music, and had a nice dinner. Most nights, Will, Syl, and I would walk down the long pier around the corner from the house, seeing the dolphins swim by, and listening to their sounds. We would try and talk Will out of his angst, about his upcoming transfer from Occidental to Syracuse University, to enroll in the Falk School of Sports Management, a very prominent school. As it turned out, it was the best decision that he ever made.

On our last night, we made plans for dinner and listening to music at the Jazz Corner, located in The Village at Wexford. Syl and I could see the darkening skies late that afternoon and the impending storm that was predicted. We left the pool, and were about to turn into our driveway, when lightning struck this huge tree as we ran toward the door. It was a good thing that we did, as the tree came crashing down, just narrowly missing us. This could easily have been catastrophic; possible death, or at the least, serious injury. Another time where fate smiled on us. There were trees and branches down all over this community and no way to be able to drive anywhere. When the storm subsided, we were all able to walk around the debris and navigate our way over to the Yacht Club for a nice dinner. By the time we were through with dinner, and hanging out drinking some wine, the crews had come and cleared the major debris from the driveways and roads; so, we were able to drive to the Jazz Corner. We had dessert there and listened to these guys who looked like they came from the sixties, with really long hair and beards, and some were barefoot. They were excellent, especially playing this amazing version of Desmond Dekker's "Israelites." We were all so glad that we were able to get out and listen to their music. This would turn out to be the last vacation that we would ever go on with them.

At the end of August, we took a day trip with Will down to Dundee and Lakemont and on to Watkins Glen, where we hiked the gorge trails. We stopped at Belhurst Castle in Geneva for dinner.

Another school year began with us being the Extended Day Directors, that being our only positions, for the second straight school year. Syl had been experiencing some digestive issues with bloating and pain. Sometimes you'd wonder if she wasn't becoming a hypochondriac; when every time she had a complaint about something, and she would go and see the doctor, everything would come out fine. Her blood work was good, her blood pressure was normal, better than mine, which always seemed higher than normal. She had colonoscopies, which I never have had. She had endoscopies for acid reflux, which I never have had. She had been dealing with having hot flashes the past several years, causing her great discomfort. Her complaints about her pain seemed different than they had been before, more intense, and with more urgency.

Syl went to see the doctors to undergo more tests. She even endured another endoscopy. But she continued to get up every day and do her Extended Day job for September and October. We still went to the pool during most of September, took our walks around Green Lakes and Pratt's Falls, and went on foliage drives on the weekends. Everything changed forever on October 27, 2014.

Linda had been dealing with serious health issues for several years. She was very private about it, at least to us. She had some form of cancer, female in nature, I'm not sure exactly what. She had over half of one of her lungs cut out, not having smoked anything her entire life. She was undergoing treatments on her brain, I believe radiation. None of this stopped her from drinking her several glasses of wine every night. She had the security and solace of her caring, faithful, loyal, and loving husband, John, and the comfort and love of her dogs. Linda had made her 50th wedding anniversary the year before, and Matt and Kara's wedding at the end of May. We had gone over to their house for several visits over the holidays. Linda had gone to this local rehab place just a few days before, when on October 27th, we received a call that she had passed away early that morning. *My older sister.* Later that same day, in the late afternoon, at Extended Day, Syl received a call from the doctor's office about the results of her tests; telling her that they had discovered a tumor and that she had stage four pancreatic cancer. *This was not a good day.*

Haunting Traces

Strolling down lonely paths

By cold black streams

Throwing pebbles in the night

Never landing

Never needing to.

Can't seem to keep my head

On the ground anymore

Stepping softly through the ashes

I am a mirage

A faded cowboy hero.

Total darkness now

Armies of walruses

Rode wheelchairs there

To watch faceless pirates

Get swallowed by the storm.

    Syl and I now faced a new reality. Ioana and many others suggested that we go down to the Sloan-Kettering Clinic in New York City, for further evaluation and treatment analysis.

    Nancy, an MPH parent and good friend, who does consulting and fund-raising work, took it upon herself to get some donations from MPH parents and friends, to cover the costs of going to New York City. Syl got all her test results and paperwork in order and sent them down, as she was asked to do, by Federal Express. We went down over Veterans Day weekend, so we wouldn't miss any Extended Day time, being as dedicated to our jobs as we were.

On the way down there, Syl receives a call from the clinic, asking her if she had sent her required paperwork by Federal Express. It turns out someone had misplaced them, which they eventually found. Another case of "Murphy's Law." Very frustrating start. We arrived at the Courtyard by Marriott on Third Avenue and they took our car and put it in the parking garage down below. We got settled in our room and walked a few blocks to Pescatore's, an Italian restaurant on Second Avenue, for a nice dinner. The next morning, we got up and had breakfast and got ready for our appointment, scheduled for noon. This clinic was located right in the Marriott; we just had to walk through these doors, take the elevator, and there it was. It was a depressing place to be, to say the least. To see all these people going through what they were going through. Why didn't good health and fortune shine down on them?

Why did they deserve this fate?

Syl was understandably apprehensive, as was I, waiting for the doctor to see us and having to look at all these people. We were starting to wonder if we had made the right decision coming here and what the hell we were doing here. He kept us waiting for over an hour and a half. Finally, we were led into this small room and I could see him looking at the test results on his computer on the way by. He was just checking this out now, instead of days before, when they should have gotten the test results to him. We sat there for ten minutes or so, seemed like an eternity to us, before he came in. He confirmed the tumor, and said with at least four aggressive chemotherapy treatments, that there was a 40 percent chance of doing a surgical operation called the Whipple procedure; a complex operation to remove the head of the pancreas, the first part of the small intestine (duodenum), the gallbladder, and the bile duct. Then the surgeon reconnects the remaining organs, to allow you to digest food normally after surgery. If they have to remove the left side, (body and tail), of the pancreas, they may have to also remove your spleen. If they have to remove your entire pancreas, you can live relatively normally without a pancreas, but you will need lifelong insulin and enzyme replacement. This seemed to be the direction of his potential outcomes.

Syl had her gallbladder removed in 2009, and Tammy, the surgeon and MPH parent at the time, had said it was a good thing that she did, as her duodenum was just lying on her gallbladder. It was too bad that Syl didn't have the pancreatic tumor at this time, in the sense that if she had, they could have removed it in its early stages. But she obviously didn't have it then. From what I understood from her oncologist later on, with her tumor markers, she might have had the undetected tumor for a year. Many people are not considered eligible for the Whipple procedure or other pancreatic surgeries if their tumors involve nearby blood vessels. He was not offering much in the way of telling us all these things. I just explained all these possibilities here, from doing research to know what we were dealing with, and the best course of action to deal with it. That's why we came down to New York City. Syl just looked at him and said,

"I don't want to die."

I was asking all the questions. I must say that this guy, Doctor Jarnigan, one of the leading pancreatic surgeons in the world, didn't have the greatest bedside manners in the world. At least not to us, not on this day. I think we were in there with him for a grand total of eight minutes! He was going to call an oncologist, Dr. Seth, that he knew, that Ioana had recommended, in Syracuse, to concur on the suggested chemotherapy for Syl's initial four treatments.

It's ironic now, as I recently saw a commercial for Sloan-Kettering on television with this older guy, who had just been cured, at least for now, after Doctor Jarnigan had performed pancreatic surgery. The guy sends Jarnigan reminders of the Red Sox winning the World Series, as you see a smiling Jarnigan, a long time Yankees fan, talk about it and the guy being thankful. I mean great for the guy, but to see Jarnigan in this commercial, and how his demeanor was to us that day, still makes me angry and frustrated.

Syl and I needed to get out of there and went to check out the Veterans Day Parade, in the heart of Manhattan, the largest of its kind in the nation. Unfortunately, we only saw the high school bands at the end. But if the doctor didn't keep us waiting for an hour and a half, we could have seen the whole impressive parade. Just another frustrating thing. We walked down to Rockefeller Center, hanging out there for a while, watching the people skating and taking a few pictures. Then we walked to Times Square, which in hindsight, we should have skipped. There were people all over us, with high pressure sales pitches, something in our fragile states of mind that we didn't need. It wasn't the relaxed atmosphere that we had felt walking around there, nine years and five months before, in the middle of June, 2005, after the Broadway play, we had gone to. Then all these pushy costumed characters swarming us as we took a picture, then demanding money for each one of them. Enough already. We walked back and had another nice dinner at Pescatore's. The next morning, we had breakfast, had our car brought up, and left for home. We got lost at first, had to ask directions a couple of times, before finally escaping the city.

Syl was feeling dazed and confused, as I tried to keep her having positive thoughts, and to be strong for her, which wasn't easy. Syl wanted to have dinner at Olive Garden when we got back. No matter what her physical condition and her digestive issues, Syl *always* wanted to go out to dinner. She just loved the whole *idea* of dinner: the getting ready, the ordering, the tastes, the wine, the ambiance. She never tired of it, even when she couldn't fully enjoy it, like she had for all those previous years.

We returned to our Extended Day jobs the next day and everyone wanted to find out what had happened. Syl was a bit overwhelmed, but she continued to do her Extended Day job through most of November. She had an appointment to surgically have a port installed near her neck, above her shoulder blade, so she wouldn't have to continually be injected in her arms and elsewhere, for all the blood samples and chemo and other infusions.

A couple of days before Thanksgiving, I took her down to Upstate Hospital, got her settled, and left for Extended Day. It was dark when I returned after work, and I parked the car, checked in, and went through all the security procedures, which was the same routine every time I went there; then took the elevator up to the cancer ward. Syl was not there. She was down on the 4th floor they told me. Syl was just lying there by herself, still groggy after the port procedure, and as it turned out, they were having trouble stopping the bleeding. She had been taking a lot of Advil lately for the pain. It reminded me of the "The Shaving Story," from "Dusty's Lunchtime Stories," in Cape Cod in July, 2005.

I felt so bad for her. I am crying right now visualizing this scene. Syl had bruises all over her neck area, where they had attempted to stop the bleeding. I went and got some doctors and they were just hovering over her and one said,

"Let's see her chart."

Another one, "Where's her chart?"

Another one, "I thought you brought it down."

The first one, "We need her chart."

I'm thinking these guys need a good smack with one of their clipboards. Why her chart wasn't with her is beyond me. Trying to keep my composure, I said that somebody needs to go and get her chart. I stayed down there until they had her chart, stopped the bleeding, and had her transported back to the cancer ward. She needed her rest, as they would begin the procedures soon. I kissed her good night and headed home.

Why this was happening to a person as caring and gentle and sweet as Sylvia, made no sense to me, or anyone else for that matter.

Syl had to undergo these infusions each time she had these treatments. One was antibiotics, to prevent infection. Another was to help with the nausea. These were about half an hour each and then wait an hour between infusions. Then the chemotherapy infusion, which came through this huge plastic bag, for 48 hours. She was down there for three or four days for these infusions. The problem with chemotherapy is that it not only kills cancer cells, it destroys healthy cells as well. And usually the loss of hair. How traumatic this was at first for Syl! Now here was Syl, having this port installed in her body, becoming bald, and losing weight. But she always handled everything with courage and dignity. She would have a treatment session, then a week off, before another session.

I would have to leave her for five hours, to drive in for Extended Day, put everything away and lock up, after all the kids had been picked up, around six o'clock; then drive back, usually had to go to the pharmacy and the store, to pick up what Syl wanted and needed; and sometimes something for dinner. Syl wanted to go out to dinner, at least on Friday nights, to Kirby's in Fayetteville. Syl would rest and read most of the time. She was a voracious reader; she could easily have four or five books going at once. She also liked watching her favorite shows, "The Waltons" and "Little House on the Prairie." They made her feel like she was revisiting her childhood, comforting her soul, with the hope of better days ahead.

Isn't it incredibly ironic, that one of Syl's favorite actors and the star of "Little House on the Prairie," Michael Landon, (real name was Eugene Orowitz), died of pancreatic cancer? In February of 1991, he began to suffer severe abdominal pains while on a skiing vacation in Utah. In April, two months later, he was diagnosed with pancreatic cancer, which had metastasized to his liver and lymph nodes. The cancer was inoperable and terminal. He died two months later in July, at the age of 54.

Syl endured her second treatment session in the middle of December and then was there for her third session over Christmas. This is where we were for the Christmas of 2014. It was a good thing that we had managed to get Syl qualified and accepted for Medicaid. Otherwise, we would have gone broke. I can see how people become homeless in a "New York Minute," if they have to pay for medical expenses for themselves or their children. I was off for Christmas vacation from MPH now, so I could go out to the pharmacy, store, pick up a take-out dinner, or shovel and do my chores at Tom and Debbie's house, during the day; for two weeks now, and not come home in the dark at seven or eight o'clock, or even later, if I was visiting Syl in the hospital.

Ioana had paid for Syl's wig and Karen, Mary Jo, and Vicki had gone with her to the hair salon for support. This first wig didn't look right on Syl, it was too bushy or something, even when she took it back and had it trimmed. Ioana again paid for her second wig. This one looked really nice on her. It was basically her blond hair color and was short, but not too short. She wore it anytime that we went out to dinner and to her treatments in the hospital. We both got used to it, but it is obviously something that you don't want to have to get used to. Syl still always looked beautiful to me.

The hospital tried to reschedule her fourth treatment appointment because her oncologist was going to be gone on his Christmas vacation. I had to have them keep her original scheduled appointment, as our mission was still to complete these four treatments, to see if the tumor had shrunk sufficiently; in order to be approved for the Whipple procedure operation at Sloan-Kettering.

Blessing in Disguise

Day fades into night

Night melts into day

I see Danger on the high road

Hitchhiking with two companions

Life and Death

Who have changed their identities

Somewhere along the way

Definitely not the ones

That I used to know

Memories drip from the jagged edge

From where you once stood.

2015

September : Chittenango Falls

Skaneateles

October & November: Green Lakes & Pratt's Falls

December: Montréal & Dollard-des Ormeaux

Saint-Lazare & Old Montréal

Syl completed her fourth treatment and they determined that she was not ready for the Whipple procedure at this time. They ordered an *additional six treatments.* This was definitely not the news that we wanted to hear. You have to wonder sometimes about how big a factor money plays into the equation. Who knows? Back to the drawing board for us. I always tried to be strong and to keep Syl having positive thoughts, but I was crying inside for her.

Syl completed her 5th treatment and the following week we went down for her consultation. There was an intern, a young Indian man, (it appeared that most of the oncologists and interns here are from India), waiting to talk to us.

He said, "It looks like you are doing beautifully. Your tumor markers are down to 55."

This was the first positive statement that we had heard since this whole process started in October.

Syl said to him, "You should put your name on the door."

"Why do you say that?"

"Because you look us in the eye when you speak to us. You show us respect and compassion. And you carefully go over all the information and test results with us."

"Thank you. I appreciate that."

He looked a little embarrassed almost, but you could tell that it made him feel proud.

The tumor markers had to be way down for any potential operation, and since hers were in the thousands to begin with, maybe like 1,300 or something; these treatments seemed to be showing great progress and felt like they were worth doing, even considering all the side effects.

Syl completed her 6th treatment and we were hopeful that the new results would be even lower. The new markers were 114, not lower as hoped, but as they have a tendency to fluctuate, as what was explained to us; were still "in the neighborhood." Two weeks later, Syl went down for her 7th treatment. This time, things not did not go well. Her weight had been steadily decreasing, down to the 120 to 115 range. She tried to eat as much as she was able to. Her normal weight was 125 in the summer to maybe 130 over the winter. During this 7th treatment, Syl's weight dipped to *109*. She fell as she went into the bathroom one day, hurting her wrist, but luckily not breaking it or anything else. Upon seeing and hearing of these developments, the oncologist cancelled her final three treatments that he had originally scheduled.

This was in the last week of March. The autumn of 2014 and this winter of 2015 had been the worst seasons that we had endured since we met. Syl took some time off to recuperate and to get her weight back, at least to the 120 level. We went for dinner at Kirby's on Friday evenings when I got home from work.

The oncologists decided to give radiation treatments a try for Syl's tumor. I would have thought that this might have been their first option, but obviously it wasn't. We drove down in the middle of April to the Hills Building, located near Phoebe's restaurant and Syracuse Stage, close to downtown Syracuse. Almost all of the radiologists appeared to be Russian. They consulted with Syl and a week later we went back to position where Syl would sit in this swivel chair, and to "mark" the area on her body with permanent marker, where the radiation would be administered; so, there would not be any radiation except for in this designated area. These treatments would be done on a daily weekday basis for five weeks.

Now we had a new daily schedule for the next five weeks, starting the last week of April and finishing up the first week in June. Syl had set up her appointments for two o'clock in the afternoon, so I had to do my chores in the morning and get ready earlier than before. Syl would get ready, putting her wig on. Her head was basically still bald, but there were little stubbles on it now from not doing the chemo infusions. We would leave by 1:30, take her to the Hills Building, I'd wait in the car for her to get her radiation treatment, usually just fifteen minutes; then drive her all the way home and turn around and race back in to MPH, to be there by 3 o'clock, to supervise the kids in the dining room before walking them over to Extended Day.

We would take some walks around Green Lakes on the weekends when Syl felt up to it. We had Tom and Debbie's pool opened, first dealing with the pool cleaning company, about getting it having the proper clarity. Finally got that resolved. We went to see the oncologist, Dr. Seth, in the third week in June for a consultation about the results of the radiation treatments. He came in and bluntly stated that the radiation had done absolutely nothing to get rid of, or at least shrink, the tumor. No compassion, no empathy. We wished that the young intern would have been our oncologist.

There was a 1991 movie, "The Doctor," starring William Hurt and Elizabeth Perkins, based on the book, "A Taste of My Own Medicine," by Edward Rosenbaum; that I feel should be required reading and viewing for every medical student, intern, nurse, doctor, and surgeon in the medical profession. William Hurt plays a surgeon who is emotionally disconnected from his wife and son and the people that he operates on. After he develops a life-threatening tumor, he sees life from a patient's perspective. He meets a fatally ill woman and begins to realize the necessity of showing kindness in the medical profession. It would do Doctor Seth and many others a world of good to see this movie.

In the last week of June, I was called into the new Headmaster's office for my contract talks. Scott had been unceremoniously dismissed over the Winter Break in February, the reasons not known, unless you were an administrator or on the Board of Trustees. This new guy, Jim, was serving on an interim basis through June, before they wound up hiring him for the position. He retired at the end of June, 2019 and I just read that they have found a new Head of School. Jim had a four-month period where he could have introduced himself to me and observed the Extended Day Program. I'm sure he was aware of our family's history: serving the school for over 100 years; Julie co-writing the Alma Mater; and where the Extended Day Program's full name had its origin. But he never bothered. I drove in and left Syl off at the pool and went in to see him. His office was located on the upper level of The Farmhouse, a floor above where Baxter used to have his office. This is where Scott had set up his office, and Jim just took it over after Scott's dismissal.

I came in, shook hands, and sat in a chair in the middle of the room. He was seated in a chair in the open doorway, facing me. He just started off, with no preliminaries whatsoever, saying,

"We want to make Extended Day a more academic oriented program, and since you don't have a four-year degree, we aren't going to rehire you in the fall."

Boom! Just like that. No acknowledging our family's or Sylvia's or my years of service. No mention of the fact that we developed the Extended Day Program from

20 kids per day in the early years to averaging 70 kids per day for most of our years as Directors. And the extra income that generated for the school. No mention or kudos for that. It didn't seem to matter to Baxter or any teacher or parent that Sylvia or I didn't have four-year degrees. I didn't even bother to mention, or bring our certificates from the State University of New York Education Department, of being certified to be Assistant Teachers in New York State. I didn't think that I would need them, and after what transpired in this meeting, I don't believe showing them to him would have made any difference in his decision. I had been going through these situations for the past five years, every year a new uncertainty, and Sylvia for the past two years, and affected by what happened to me the other years.

He expected me to just accept his decision and walk out after this five-minute evaluation of my status. He didn't know me. I kept him there for over an hour, telling him some of our family's history, even though there was so much more to tell. I told him I couldn't believe that they had not rehired Michael, the Music teacher, who was talented and loved by the kids, and did so many extra things; like putting together an annual Christmas Program and performing at all the graduations. And all the other 35 teachers and staff they had let go, most of them having been there for 20 years or more. He said nothing in response and showed no emotion. This was such a crock. I would rather have him be brutally honest with me and say,

"Here's the situation. You will turn 69 in two months and we can hire someone cheaper and younger. So, we are not going to rehire you."

Even though that's very cruel, I can deal with that better than him handing me a bunch of baloney, basically lying to me. I have driven by often, and they have about 20 kids in Extended Day now, back to the numbers when I first started in 1994. And looking at the different people they have had running the program since we left, and talking with some teachers, I don't see any academic oriented program going on here.

I didn't bother to mention to him that Sylvia and I were always available to help the kids with their homework; that we played intellectual games like "Brain Quest," "Twenty Questions," and others; and counting games like "Connect Four" and the always popular "Pass the Pigs." Sylvia always did coloring and arts and crafts projects with the kids. We were outside whenever possible. I invented and engaged the kids in the "On The Roof" game, and Sylvia had a huge gathering for swinging the jump rope and singing in unison:

"Cinderella dressed in yella,

Went upstairs to kiss her fella,

By mistake she kissed a snake,

How many doctors will it take?"

"1,2,3,4,5,6,7,8,9," and you keep counting until the person jumping misses and then another one jumps in. There were at least two more verses of this and Syl and the kids knew them by heart.

Jim had no clue about any of this and I don't think it would have mattered if he had.

"Is this decision coming from you?"

"No."

"Then is it coming from the Board?"

"No."

We knew most of the Board members and had taken care of their kids for many years and had their gratitude and respect. We would be surprised if this decision came from them. But we've certainly had our share of surprises over the past five years, so I guess we should not be surprised by anything that happened to us anymore.

"Is this coming from her?"

I sort of leaned my head in the direction of Sue, then the Director of Community Programs. He didn't say anything, kind of a non-denial denial. I really had no problem with her. She loved Sylvia, but I think she felt somewhat challenged by me, with my long years of experience and my popularity with the kids. Maybe not. She had recently lost her husband, Bill, I think he was only 42. I had met him a few times and he seemed like a really nice guy. Now she was left to take care of their three children by herself. We felt really bad for her.

In the previous fall, Traian had come to me about a complaint he had; that one of Ileana's classmates had taken pictures of them and posted them, including Ileana's, on the Internet, without their permission. I asked the kids who had taken the pictures and they told me that it was Sue's son. I confronted him about it and he denied it, lying about it. Maybe I should have let Traian talk to Sue directly about this, but since it happened on our watch, I decided to talk to her about this, especially when a parent had brought this to my attention. I would have done this to anyone else the kids had said took and posted the pictures, even if it was one of the teacher's children, which there were several. Even if it had been Ileana herself, taking and posting the pictures.

The parents through the years were appreciative when I spoke to them about an incident or bad behavior involving their children. I brought this incident up to her, with her son standing next to her, when she picked her kids up from Extended Day one afternoon; and again, he denied it and lied about to her. She should have demanded the truth from him, (why would all the other kids that were there lie about it?); and then maybe ground him from using his phone for two weeks for lying, or whatever punishment that she felt was appropriate. I understood it was an extremely difficult time for her, but it would have been an opportunity for an important life lesson for her son. Soon after, Traian came to me and said there was another picture that was posted with the kids and a MPH sign in the background. When I mentioned this to her, her response was that CBA kids do this all the time as a prank. I told the kids not to post any more pictures of their classmates. No more pictures were posted after this and I thought this incident had reached its conclusion. I was wrong. I was called in to meet with her right before the end of the school year. Rebecca, then the Assistant to her, and now the Director of Community Programs; was there to witness this exchange. Sue started talking about Extended Day and then said,

"I'm trying to save you from Jim."

I wasn't sure why she was saying this to me, but it was a precursor of things to come. I then was trying to explain the whole incident involving her son and a parent's concern, how it might be handled differently and better in the future; when she said, angrily, and unprofessionally I might add,

"You're not going to win any brownie points from me, bad rapping my kid."

This is the kind of thinking I was now dealing with. It turned out that after the fall of the next school year, she left MPH for another job, in a different capacity, elsewhere. Not before she influenced my job position. I've known Rebecca for many years, she had been at MPH for more than thirty-five years at this time, and we are friends. I believe that if she was the Director then, we could have talked this out, honored the parent's concerns, and come up with a resolution that was agreeable to all. Unfortunately for me, that was not the case. I guess the reason that I'm going into so much detail about this, is because if this was the end of my career at MPH after over 21 years, which became a reality; I wanted the truth to be told and the record to be set straight.

So back to my meeting with Jim. After this exchange, he looks at me and asks,

"Do you remember when Willie Mays played for the Mets?"

"Yeah."

"Do you remember when Joe Namath played for the Rams?"

"Yeah," I now said warily. I had a feeling about where he was headed with these questions.

"Do you remember when Michael Jordan played for the Wizards?"

"Are you trying to tell me that I'm over the hill?"

"Oh no, I'm about to turn 66 and I'm just thinking about my retirement."

Yeah, right, I'm thinking to myself. I can't believe this guy, the Head of School, is thinking I'm that stupid or naive to fall for that line. He must have thought that I was smart enough, or a knowledgeable sports fan, to even understand these analogies in the first place. I mean, this entire meeting, with the bogus reasons for not rehiring me, not being truthful about what influenced his decision, and these ridiculous references to players hanging on past their prime; was just one big lie and an obvious lack of respect for me. This is how my career at MPH came to an end. To reinforce all that I have recounted, he even said to me when I was ready to leave,

"I don't know what your wife's health situation is like, but if she still wanted to work at Extended Day, she could."

This guy had no tact whatsoever. He could have asked me how Sylvia was doing. He didn't even use her name. Maybe he didn't even remember it. He failed to mention if that offer was to remain the Co-Director or even Director of Extended Day. What, Syl was going to be an assistant to a new and younger Director, taking a huge pay cut, while he or she would be making more; after working at MPH for 23 years? And not rehiring me, and still facing an uncertain health future, undergoing more chemo treatments, dealing with the side effects; and having to face the kids and parents and answer their questions every day? I don't think so. She would have been interested in hearing their proposal. Maybe. But after I told her all about this meeting, enough was enough. The ways in which we were treated the past five years, made it clear to us that it was time to move on.

Syl and I started to go over to the pool again. She had asked her oncologist if she could take a break from the chemo infusions, and they gave her permission. They did order these chemo pills that were delivered to our house. They wanted her to take these on a daily basis for a week, then a week off. She took them for a week at the end of July, but was experiencing neuropathy in her fingers and toes, and did not want to take them after that. Her hair started growing back, not having this poison in her body. It was really short and curly. Syl had long, straight hair and used her curling iron and curlers frequently to get some curl in it, to have that look. I remember when she got a perm a year or so after we met. I have a picture of her with this perm on Christmas in 1984. She looked cute, but I liked her natural look better. Her hair was now white, and with a tan and wearing her turquoise earrings, someone told her that she had "the Nordic Look" about her. So, she would tell everyone that this was "her Nordic Look."

So really, except for those chemo pills for a week at the end of July; she had no chemicals going into her body after the first week in June, when the radiation treatments ended, until the last week in September. Basically, a three-and-a-half-month period, where she was enjoying sitting in the sun, reading outside, swimming, getting her hair, (at least somewhat back), and regaining her muscle tone. Her appetite came back and her weight was now close to normal. It makes you wonder if you are making the right decisions or not, undergoing all these infusions and treatments, that were deteriorating her body. That's not even considering the mental or emotional stress inflicted upon her. And me.

Syl was trying to get herself looking and feeling as good as possible, for Ursula's upcoming visit for two weeks after Labor Day weekend. And she was doing a great job. She looked beautiful with her new "Nordic Look," feeling close to normal again and smiling like she used to.

In fairness, through all the adversity, Syl never stopped smiling. *That's who she was.*

I had to go back to MPH in July and clear out all our things: Legos, toys, games, balls, books, all types of things; from our Extended Day storage room, that we had accumulated for over 20 years. I went over there for four separate, eight-hour sessions; throwing out things, recycling all I could, and loading some bins and boxes to bring home, of things to be saved. I've gone through some things, but those bins and boxes still sit in the basement and garage, from over four years ago.

I met Alexus, who had worked with us the previous year, and gave her all sorts of things for her mother, Brandi, who ran a day care center for minority kids. A few days later, I met Brandi and gave her even more things. She was very appreciative and wanted to pay me. I said no, I was glad to give these things for the kids to enjoy. She stuffed some money in my pocket anyway. It was enough to take Syl out for a nice dinner.

Alexus graduated from MPH in 2014. This is what Syl wrote to her:

"Dear Alexus, I hope you have a great summer! I am so happy to have met you and work with you. You are a wise, caring friend. (Mature for your age I might add.) I enjoyed our conversations and learned from you as maybe you have from me. You make me happy to be around you and I am sure your friends are too! Please keep in touch. Much Love, Sylvia & Dusty"

We went to Alexus' graduation party, one of the best parties we've ever gone to. Everyone made us feel welcomed, like a part of their family. Alexus has now gone on to graduate from the Newhouse School at Syracuse University in May, 2018.

That previous summer, 2014, had been a busy one, going up to Montréal in July and Hilton Head in August. Little did we know then what Syl was feeling internally and would have to start dealing with this reality. This summer, 2015, was now becoming more calm, Syl looking and feeling more like herself. Even with the disappointing ending at MPH, and having to figure out our financial income, it felt more like relief now; a weight that was finally lifted off our backs.

Syl and I went out to the New York State Fair on Sunday, September 6th, the day before Labor Day, to see the Steve Miller Band. I need to give you some history on this band. Steve Miller was from Milwaukee and went to the University of Wisconsin in Madison, starting in 1961. When I was a freshman at Wisconsin in the fall of 1964, he was playing with bands he created, the Ardells and The Fabulous Night Train. I would go with friends and see them at local clubs in Madison on Friday and Saturday nights. One club I remember was Mother Tucker's. Fellow students Boz Scaggs, Gary Gerlach, and Ben Sidran were in those bands. Of course, Boz Scaggs went on to his own successful solo career after being in the Steve Miller Band for their first two albums. Miller and Scaggs first started playing together in junior high in Dallas, Texas in 1955, as The Marksmen.

Ben Sidran, the keyboardist, who called himself "Doctor Jazz," later hosted a television show in Madison called "The Weekend Starts Now." It would start at midnight on Thursday night. This was a big deal, as there was obviously no cable television then, and everything was over by midnight; Madison being in the Central Time Zone.

"The Tonight Show" with Johnny Carson would start at 10:30 and end at midnight. This "TWSN" show would feature old movies and horror movies. We would get a big group of people and have beer, pizza, and other snacks, and watch these movies. Some of us even served as extras for commercials for a local business, like Gargano's Pizza. Sidran would bring in local musicians as guests, like Miller and Scaggs, for interviews.

Syl and I went to the New York State Fair in Solvay, near Syracuse, almost every year. We would check out the lineup of who was playing at the Miller Court, then it became Cole Muffler Court, and eventually Chevy Court, venue; and plan on who we wanted to see. These were free concerts, included in your admission tickets. Also, which artists were playing at The Grandstand venue, where you had to pay for the concert.

Our first stop was always the Dairy Building, where we would view that year's butter sculpture; and then we would each get two small cups of fresh milk, chocolate or white, one of each or two of the same. This would coat our stomachs for the food at the fair that we were about to consume. We would stroll around, checking out the animals and "Birds of Prey" exhibit. We liked to see the horse shows, with teams of Clydesdales, Friesians, Percherons, and others; all decorated and competing, an amazing sight to behold. There was the Art & Home Center; the Center of Progress Building, to see that year's incredible sand sculpture; the Pan-African Village, to hear some excellent music; and many more buildings and exhibits to explore.

We had dinner at the food court in the International Building before going to our concert. After the concert, we would wander down The Midway, people watching and listening to all the hawkers and vendors; and seeing the expressions on people's faces and listening to their screams, as they rode the scary rides, like "Top Spin." We were glad it was not us up on those rides. Had to get a fried dough from "Pizza Fritte," before we left The Fair for another year.

The Steve Miller Band concert at Chevy Court had the biggest attendance, around 37,000 people, of all time. This topped the 35,000 that attended Bruno Mars' concert at Chevy Court in 2011. We went in the main seating area two hours earlier to claim our seats, as it's on a first come basis. People were packed all around in droves by the railings behind the main seating area. There is also a big jumbo screen on the right-hand side of the stage. The band got everyone dancing and singing along, rocking the hot and humid night for over 90 minutes.

Two days later, Ursula arrived from Charleston for her visit. We spent some time at the pool, but Ursula didn't swim because she didn't want to mess up her new hairdo. I let them take the car so they could drive around and do their own thing. Syl had to wait, as Ursula had her hair redone, as she wasn't happy with the first one. I just waited at the pool. We drove out to Chittenango Falls one day to look at the waterfalls. Ursula was having problems with her hip, so she couldn't walk very far. Another day, we drove out to Skaneateles and looked at the lake from the park. Again, Ursula couldn't walk too far, just checking out some shops near the park. We ate at Doug's Fish Fry and had an ice cream on the way out of town. Traian and Ioana took us to Bonefish for dinner with them, Ileana, and Traian's mother, who was visiting from Romania and staying with them for several months.

Sylvia was so happy to be able to spend time with her mother and to be looking and feeling good about herself again. Ursula was glad to be able to spend time with Sylvia. This would turn out to be the last time that they would ever be together again.

This was the first year since 1993 that neither of us would be starting the school year teaching at MPH. Kind of sad, really, but this was our new reality.

After Ursula left, Syl started doing chemo infusions again, around the last week of September. We wondered if this was the right thing to do, but the oncologist said it was, if the goal was to not have the tumor metastasize to other organs of Syl's body. The new schedule was to just have the infusion one day per week, for an afternoon, and then she would have the following week off. So basically, two weeks between infusions, except having to go back down for a consultation. This was a lot better than three or four days straight, as was the case in the winter. And the daily weekdays, for five weeks, radiation treatments. He was also trying a new combo of chemo drugs, less powerful than the ones that did her in after that 7th chemo infusion this past March. Syl lost her hair that had grown back, and a little weight, but nothing as drastic as before. She got used to wearing her wig again and we took walks around Green Lakes and Pratt's Falls, foliage drives, and dinners at Bonefish, Kirby's, Olive Garden, Red Lobster, and Red Robin.

After Traian's mother left, Ioana was looking for someone to pick up Ileana after school, take her to her lessons, and wait for them to come home from the hospital. I said that I would do it. I still was the caretaker for Tom and Debbie's house, but we could use this extra income taking care of Ileana, to help offset the loss of no longer being the Co-Directors of Extended Day. I would leave around two o'clock in the afternoon, sometimes earlier, to do my chores at Tom and Debbie's, then go and pick up Ileana. The only drawback was that I had to go to MPH to get her, sometimes running into people or kids, curious as to why I was no longer the Director of Extended Day; and ask how Sylvia was doing. I would pick up Ileana, turn on her favorite radio station, 93Q, and take her to her lessons. Monday night was her fencing lessons at Shoppingtown Mall in Dewitt, where I'd go down to the library until she was done. Her piano teacher would pick her up at MPH on Tuesdays, and bring her home for her lessons, and I could run an errand and meet them there. Friday night was ballroom dancing in a studio in Fayetteville. It was a nice experience to see the teachers, they were Russian, the women dressed up in their beautiful costumes; and the men as well. I just waited, listening to the music and watching them dance. And swimming lessons at the YMCA in Fayetteville, where I could do a workout. The swimming lessons stopped after a few months, which was too bad because I could get a workout in.

    I would drive Ileana back home, in all kinds of weather conditions. I would then take their dog, Alexis, a little Bichon Frise with black eyes and a white fluffy coat, for a walk around the neighborhood; waiting until she pooped, picking it up in a plastic bag, and bringing her back home. Even in the freezing cold and heavy snow of winter. I would then help Ileana with her homework questions, especially math, and wait until one of them came home; sometimes it could be late. Then on to the store if necessary. Their house was outside of the village of Fayetteville, about 15 minutes from ours. This was now my new reality. I didn't have to watch Ileana most weekends, just once in a while, so they could go out to dinner and a movie. Syl would come with me a few times when she felt up to it. I got paid on a weekly basis, and I would give Syl half of it. Then I would have Syl put some in for groceries, like we always had. I was just trying to keep things as normal for Syl as I could.

We decided to go to Montréal, since we didn't make it up there in the summer, to visit our extended family for Christmas. Syl and I drove up to Tex and Erna's townhouse in Dollard-des Ormeaux. Syl was nervous as to how they would look at her now, with her wig and being thinner. I told her not to worry, that she looked beautiful. Tex confessed to me later that everyone, including himself and Erna, had no idea what to expect as to Sylvia's appearance. They were all pleasantly surprised.

We spent an enjoyable Christmas Eve with them, having a nice dinner and wine and conversation, trying to avoid talking too much about the medical issues. We all went over to Jacques and Caroline's house in Saint-Lazare for Christmas dinner and drinks and meeting some of Jacques' family. Ron and Lorraine, and Lucas, with his girlfriend, and Olivier; came in from Ottawa. Seann and Ryan were there with their girlfriends.

When it came time to open presents, it was like a "free for all." People were talking in English, French, and German. There was not a big announcement of the gifts, who they were for or who they came from. In our family's Christmases from childhood, each gift was announced, then presented by the giver of the gift to the person getting the gift. Then everyone would wait while that person opened their gift, showed it all around, and everyone commented on it. Then we would move on to the next gift. I guess in Canada, at least in this family, they wanted to do this as quickly as possible. People were opening gifts, left and right, all at the same time. Syl and I had no clue what was going on half the time, but it was a pleasurable Christmas evening; and spending it with family made Syl very happy.

Tex, Erna, Syl and I drove down to Old Montréal one day. Actually, this was my idea, as no one seemed that enthused about going there when I suggested it, but they were glad they went. It was very cold out, but feasible for quick walks on the cobblestone streets, before ducking into a shop or building. There were guys playing their violins around these fire pits in the historical Place d'Armes public square. Everywhere you looked, it was decorated and lit up with brilliant lights. Notre-Dame Basilica looked spectacular. We had a late lunch and coffee at a restaurant there before heading back to Dollard-des Ormeaux.

Syl and I spent a few more days there, all of us taking a brisk walk in the nearby park one day. We stayed an extra day, after a snowstorm, so the roads would be cleared for safe travel for us to drive back home. This would turn out to be the last time that they would see each other.

Lost Time Is Never Found Again

Sometimes you wonder how it could move so slow

Other times you're asking, where did it go

Time doesn't sit around waiting for you

It has planes to catch and things to do.

On the spur of the moment, anticipating its cues

Like the white rabbit, with no time to lose

"No time to kill," it shouts with alarm

Decides "a few more minutes can't do any harm."

Time after time, it teases you again

Doesn't waste time explaining where it's been

"All in good time," it whispers to you

"In the long run, I promise to leave you a clue."

"I'm sorry I can't help, but my hands are tied"

When I heard this, I nearly died

In no time at all, I was back on the mend

For the time being, keeping ahead of the end.

2016

March and April: Green Lakes & Pratt's Falls

June 18th: Manlius, NY (Eric & Nancy's house)

August 4th-14th & August 24th-September 9th: Upstate Hospital, Syracuse, NY

September 9th: (Maurer's) Liverpool, NY

September 16th: (Maurer's) Moyers Corners, NY

Another winter was upon us. I was leaving around two o'clock in the afternoon each weekday, to do my chores at Tom and Debbie's; before picking up Ileana at MPH at 3:30, to take her to her lessons before driving her home. Then walking Alexis, helping Ileana with homework, and waiting until Traian or Ioana came home. Then driving back home in tough conditions, picking up dinner, the store, or something at the pharmacy. Syl would be home reading her books and watching her television shows and resting. She was content, relatively speaking, as content as you can be under the circumstances. But I was always worried about her falling or something when I was away doing my jobs. She had to wear this Neulasta patch on her stomach after her chemo treatments now, to help prevent infections, due to having her white blood cell count being abnormally low after the chemo. This would save on not having to make an additional trip to see the oncologist. After 24 hours, she would show it to me to see if the medicine, essentially a white blood cell booster, was empty; and then she could remove the patch. Another thing she (we) had to deal with.

It was actually a milder start to spring in late March, at least by Syracuse standards. This winter was definitely a whole lot better than the previous winter of 2015, with Syl having to endure all those long days of the chemo infusions and the side effects that came with it. We still remained hopeful that these treatments would eventually shrink this tumor and we could move on with our lives. The possibility of undergoing an operation seemed remote at this point. Syl was never too enthused with this idea in the first place, always scared that things could get worse for her.

We started taking walks again, around Green Lakes and Pratt's Falls. We were excited about the Syracuse University basketball team playing in the NCAA tournament. Syl loved watching the SU games, but it also was stressful for her with my overboard enthusiasm. The team made a surprising run and made it to the Final Four. We continued our routines in April and Syl even came with me when I picked up Ileana at MPH, after I had picked her up at Upstate after a treatment; then I would drop her off at home.

Syl and I went out to Honda City in Liverpool in early April to pick out our next car to lease, as our present lease on the car that we had leased in 2013, was about to end. We picked out a champagne color and did all the paperwork. This was going to be our 7th leased Honda Accord, the first one in October of 1997. That was black, and subsequent colors were: emerald green, (from a distance, it looked almost black), champagne, "cool blue," silver, champagne again, and we decided to just stay with champagne once more with this one. All these leases were for 36 months, with one exception, I think the "cool blue" car was for 42 months. We went back out there on April 22nd and picked it up. Syl never even drove this car.

Things changed at the end of April. Syl fell while getting up from her recliner in the living room. She said that she had one leg tucked underneath her and it must have fallen asleep, so when she attempted to get out of the chair, she fell. I helped her up and it was definitely a bad ankle sprain, just like the one you get when you jump up and land on another player's foot in basketball. A situation that I'm all too familiar with, having sprained my ankles, (especially my right one, having that football injury to it in my sophomore year); literally hundreds of times in my over fifty years of playing basketball. Now she had to start putting ice packs on the ankle and keep it elevated, then compression. I went to the pharmacy to get her some things for this process and we both went to a medical supply store for some ankle supports. The ankle was swollen and all black and blue. We now had to go and see an orthopedic doctor for x-rays and evaluations, on top of the chemo treatments and Neulasta patch. I'm sure it must be as exhausting for you to read and absorb all this, as it is for me to write all this; and for Syl to endure this.

Two weeks later, in the middle of May, when the right ankle had come back to almost normal; Syl fell again from her chair, this time it was the left ankle. We couldn't blame the fall on her foot falling asleep this time, but we tried to rationalize it, that her right ankle was still in a weakened state; and by favoring it, she fell on her other ankle. Now the process began for this ankle: ice packs, elevation, compression, back to the orthopedic doctor for x-rays and evaluations. This is the treatment we learned in our First Aid classes, the RICE treatment: Rest, Ice, Compression, Elevation. By the first week in June, Syl's ankles were back to normal. But we never took our walks again. I told her to never walk down our steep stairs to the basement alone, fearing she could fall and seriously injure herself. (These are the only stairs in the house.) I would keep a supply of bottled water upstairs, as Syl drank a copious amount of bottled water on a daily basis. And I told her that I would do all the laundry from now on, which I had been doing most of it anyway.

I was over at Traian and Ioana's house one afternoon, and noticed that there was an ad in the paper for a concert to benefit the Syracuse Stage, with a performance by Madeleine Peyroux. I happened to comment on it out loud, and Traian, who was there with me in the kitchen, was excited to hear this. Ioana and Ileana had gone over to Bucharest, Romania, to visit Ioana's parents and Ileana's grandparents, for two weeks right after the school year had ended. I was still going over to their house, to bring in the mail and walk Alexis, while they were gone and Traian was working. He said he would like to take us to the concert and he would buy the tickets. Syl and I had a couple of her CD's and really liked her. She was really looking forward to this.

On Friday night, June 10th, we drove over to their house and went with Traian for dinner. Then up to the Syracuse University area, where he parked his car in a parking garage, and we had a long walk to the Schine Student Center, where the concert was being held, in the Goldstein Auditorium. It was exhausting for Syl in her weakened condition and wearing her ankle supports, but I held on to her and she made it. Some friends of Traian's met us, and after a long wait to get in, we sat in these balcony seats overlooking tables where patrons of the Syracuse Stage, who had paid for dinner and drinks, were still eating and drinking. They were still clearing dishes when she started to play, which was annoying. But after that, she put on an excellent show. This would turn out to be the last concert that we would ever go to.

"Music is a moral law. It gives soul to the universe, wings to the mind, flight to the imagination, and charm and gaiety to life and to everything."   -Plato

I can remember the first song that I ever heard, "I Walk the Line," by Johnny Cash; when I was almost ten years old. It was playing on somebody's portable radio, on the bus riding home to Lakemont from Dundee Central School in May, 1956.

Syl and I loved music. We loved listening to it, dancing to it, and singing along together with it, while driving in the car. It was a key factor at the beginning of our relationship, going to the Men at Work concert in Saratoga, on August 7th, 1983.

We went to many concerts:

(8/7/'83) Men at Work: (SPAC)

(8/21/'83) Diana Ross: (SPAC)

(8/18/'85) Don Henley: (SPAC)

(8/27/'85) Crosby, Stills, & Nash: (S.F. Grandstand)

(9/1/'86) Jimmy Cliff and Stevie Winwood: (FLPAC)

(2/10/'87) Bruce Hornsby & The Range: (Landmark)

(8/31/'87) Crosby, Stills, & Nash: (S.F. Grandstand)

(2/16/'88) Sting: (War Memorial)

(8/25/'89) Ziggy Marley: (S.F. Grandstand)

(6/27/'92) Santana: (SPAC)

(8/30/'92) Crosby, Stills, & Nash: (S.F. Grandstand)

(11/20/'94) James Taylor: (War Memorial)

(8/22/'96) Jackson Browne: (S.F. Grandstand)

(8/31/'96) James Taylor: (S.F. Grandstand)

(11/2/'98) Joni Mitchell and Bob Dylan: (War Memorial)

(6/24/'00) Ray Charles and Diana Krall: (Jazz Fest: Clinton Square)

(1/25/'02) Joanne Shenandoah: with the Syracuse Symphony Orchestra: (Civic Center)

(8/26/'03) Crosby, Stills, & Nash: (S.F. Grandstand)

(12/11/'05) Irish Tenors: (Landmark)

(6/24/'12) Billy Vera and Jaimoe's Jasssz Band and Donovan: (Jazz Fest: Jamesville Beach)

(10/28/'12) Jersey Boys: (Landmark)

(7/11/'14) Big Bad Voodoo Daddy and Trombone Shorty: (Jazz Fest: Onondaga Community College)

(6/10/'16) Madeleine Peyroux: (Goldstein Auditorium, Schine Student Center: Syracuse University)

Syl and I never had the opportunity to see Sade, (Helen Folasade Adu), perform live in concert; to hear her sultry voice and sophisticated blend of soul, funk, jazz, and Afro-Cuban rhythms.

Syl and I went almost every year to the free concerts at the New York State Fair, (the nation's first State Fair, held over September 29th & 30th, in 1841; that about 15,000 people attended.) In the early years, it was known as Miller Court; then in 1995, it became known as Cole Muffler Court, for eight years through 2003; then in 2004, it became known as Chevy Court, which it still is. Up until 2009, the performers would perform twice in the same day, once in the afternoon and once in the evening. I can remember José Feliciano not feeling very well in his afternoon session, looking very pale, like he had the flu. He toughed it out and came back even stronger for his evening show. It was especially great being able to see America, our favorite band to see at this venue at The Fair, perform twice in the same day. We saw them four different years, so that's eight total performances. In the 1980's, we were going up to the Saratoga Performing Art Center, (SPAC), for concerts; and also, to the Grandstand for concerts, when we went to The Fair.

The first one that I can remember at Miller Court was Bo Diddley in 1990. This was at the time when he was getting some name recognition, when Bo Jackson was doing all his commercials: "Bo knows this and Bo knows that;" and then where he sees Bo trying to play the guitar and says, "Bo, you don't know Diddley." He was playing the blues, sounding pretty good, when he abruptly stopped the show and started berating this photographer about not following his explicit instructions about no recording or photographing his performance. He went on this long rant, which was received by a stunned and deathly silent crowd. It turned out this poor young guy who had incurred Bo's wrath, was a reporter from Channel Nine News, just doing his job.

In 1996, we saw the Billy Dean Band. Syl and I were not passionate country music fans, although we liked a lot of country artists, like Chris Isaak, and their music. My cousin, Stephen, who went by his stage name, "Doc Hollister," (this was our grandmother's maiden name), was playing in this band out of Nashville. Billy Dean had kind of a Kurt Russell look, and there were plenty of adoring female fans standing outside the band's huge air-conditioned bus, waiting for him to come out and give autographs after their great show. Because we were family members, they let us: Aunt Gloria, (Stephen's mother), his older brother Bobby, (an excellent musician himself), and his wife, Cathy, Mom, Syl, and me come inside the bus. All the hundreds of fans who had been waiting, watched in disbelief as we were let inside the bus. It was a scene like when I was with Nicky that one night out in Las Vegas in

September, 2001. Even took some pictures of Syl standing next to Billy Dean.

In 2009, it was pouring rain during the Grand Funk Railroad show. We stood there for over an hour with our raincoats, that had these visors on the hood, that dripped water constantly; waiting patiently for them to play their signature song, "We're an American Band." They had just played, "I'm Your Captain/Closer to Home," and then left the stage. Syl hardly ever swore, but she said,

"They better come back and play it. I didn't stand out here in this pouring rain for hours for them to just f'in leave and not play that song."

They came back out and sang that song.

(8/29/'90) Bo Diddley

(8/29/'91) Bowzer's Rock and Roll Party

(8/23/'93) America

(8/25/'94) Blood, Sweat, & Tears

(9/4/'95) America

(8/23/'96) Billy Dean Band

(8/23/'97) Spinners

(8/28'98) Don McClean

(9/1/'99) KC & The Sunshine Band

(8/30/'00) José Feliciano

(9/2/'01) Johnny Rivers

(9/1/'02) America

(8/29/'07) America

(8/28/'09) Grand Funk Railroad

(8/31/'10) Peter Noone & Herman's Hermits:

(afternoon) & "1964": (Beatles Tribute): (night)

(8/26/'11) Three Dog Night

(9/3/'12) Joanne Shenandoah: (afternoon)

(8/27/'13) Chubby Checker

(8/25/'14) Peter Noone: (afternoon)

        & Steppenwolf: (night)

(9/6/'15) Steve Miller Band

    These are all the free concerts that we went to since 1990, with the years of 1992, 2003, & 2006, that we paid and went to concerts at the State Fair Grandstand instead. The only other years that I can't account for are: 2004, 2005 & 2008. I've researched who played there those years and nothing rings a bell. Either we didn't go to The Fair those years or we were content to just see Ted's band, Timeline, play if we went to The Fair those years. They are excellent, doing a Blues Brothers (dressed up like them) set, with many covers and "oldies."

    Syl and I would pick out which CD's to take with us on vacations, taking more if we were driving; going to: Alexandria, VA; Baltimore, MD; Cape Cod, MA; Catskills, NY (Woodstock & Bethel); Charleston, SC;

Delaware; Fall River, MA; Gettysburg, PA; Jacksonville, FL; Lake Placid, NY; Lancaster, PA; Letchworth, NY; Mount Lebanon, PA; Nags Head, NC; New York City; Niagara Falls; Old Forge, NY; Orlando, FL; Padanarum, MA; Saint Augustine, FL; Thousand Islands, NY; Westfield, MA; Williamsburg, VA; Winchester, VA.

And in Canada: Dorchester, Gananoque, Hull, Kingston, London, Montréal, Ottawa, Québec City, Toronto.

All these places do not include our many day trips.

Syl's favorite musician, by far, was Joni Mitchell. She knew all her songs and they touched a deep chord within her. She turned me on to Joni's early albums and I loved her as well. Syl also loved Sade, Stevie Nicks, Tracy Chapman, Nena, Bonnie Raitt, Linda Ronstadt, Sarah McLaughlin, Madeleine Peyroux, Joan Armatrading, Annie Lennox, Toni Childs, Diana Krall. I loved them also.

We both loved the Beatles, Bob Dylan, the Eagles, Buddy Holly, Roy Orbison, Elvis, Donovan, Tom Petty, Santana, Eric Clapton, John Lennon, George Harrison, Paul McCartney, Amos Lee, Bruce Hornsby, Michael McDonald, America, Bee Gees, Chris Isaak, James Taylor, Crosby, Stills, & Nash, Van Morrison, Boz Scaggs, Bob Marley, Fleetwood Mac, Simon & Garfunkel, Paul Simon, Jimmy Buffett, Neil Young, José Feliciano, John Prine, Marvin Gaye, and all the Motown artists, some Blues, Rolling Stones, "British Invasion" bands, and Soft Jazz like Craig Chaquico, Peter White, Lee Rittenour, Fourplay, Rippingtons.

I also loved Jimi Hendrix, The Doors, Pink Floyd; as well as Led Zeppelin and the Steve Miller Band. Syl liked some songs by these bands, but not with the same passion as I did.

I went to many concerts before I met Syl in July of 1983. As I mentioned previously, I went to see the Ardells and The Fabulous Night Train, (Steve Miller, Boz Scaggs, and others), in Madison in my freshman year at the University of Wisconsin in 1964-1965. There were also local concerts by a friend of mine, Al Craven, a fellow student from White Plains, NY; who went by the name of "The White Raven," in their group, Doctor Bop and The Headliners.

I returned to Syracuse after my freshman year at the end of May in 1965. I had no idea what I was doing at this point in my life. I wish that I had applied myself more in my classes, but I was more interested in socializing than studying. I look back at some of the courses that I took that year: Anthropology, Geology, Meteorology, Oceanography, and Sociology; and wish that I would have fully immersed myself in the learning process of these courses, as they all held great interest for me. I also took English and History courses as well.

Our family had taken a trip out to Madison, Wisconsin in late June of 1964, after my graduation from Pebble Hill, to look for a place for me to live and to check out the campus. Linda was not with us, as she was past due in her pregnancy. There were ambulances waiting on both sides of the stage, when Linda came up to get her diploma, at graduation from William Smith, a few weeks before. Her water had broken that morning, but she managed to make her way across the stage. She wouldn't deliver Susan, her and John's oldest daughter, until July 26th.

We found an ad about a room to rent, in a house near the football stadium, where I planned to play quarterback for the football team at UW. It was owned by an elderly woman named Mrs. Mosby. When we met her, my dad asked her if by chance that she might have a daughter named Janet. Well, as it turned out, she did. My dad had dated her in college, at Syracuse University, before he met Mom. *Just my luck.* We rented the room and signed the papers. My room was right next door to hers, with a common bathroom, on the second floor. There was a grad student from Milwaukee who lived down the hallway, but he had a fire escape for his own private entrance and exit, and his own bathroom. It was like having his own private wing. Mrs. Mosby also had a vintage classic 1950's car that she never drove anymore after her husband had passed away. The grad student could use her car, he just had to get her groceries and supplies.

I had a couple of guys that I met come over on a few Sundays, to watch the pro football games with me, and Mrs. Mosby would make us a wonderful home cooked dinner. It made her feel good to do this. She was actually a very nice lady. But it was weird for me, to finally believe that I was going to start having my independence for the first time in my life; after riding in the car with my parents for my last two years of high school, having my dad as a coach and teacher, and wearing a blazer and tie for school. I remember bringing a girl up to my room at Mrs. Mosby's and just talking and maybe kissing, but nothing else. But now, with this new found connection that she had with my dad because of her daughter, she had his phone number in Syracuse to report on me; which she did about bringing a girl to my room. Dad confronted me about this and that was the last straw for me. I applied to get into a dorm and moved out of Mrs. Mosby's after the first week in October into the Sellery Hall dorm on campus.

My roommate was a very tall, taller than me, Jewish guy with a bad complexion, named Marv Levy. I really liked him and got along with him with no problems.

But on our floor were a group of blond-haired, blue-eyed young Nazis. One night as we went to our beds to go to sleep, Marv woke up screaming, as he had discovered a gigantic snake in his bed. It was a Black Rat Snake. I was terrified as well, having had an experience as a kid at camp in Lakemont, where this Copperhead had wrapped itself around me while I was swimming. I was screaming as the counselor took a forked stick and got it off me. So, I have not been a big fan of snakes ever since, sort of like Indiana Jones. Somehow, we managed to get it into a pillowcase and throw it out the window. These guys came by the room, wondering what all the commotion was about, when they knew damn well what it was. I think they thought that I was one of them, but they were dead wrong. I've never been prejudiced against any race or religion, even then. Maybe it was because of all the diversity of the students at Lakemont Academy when I was growing up. From that moment on, we both checked our beds before going to sleep and kept our distance from these guys. I don't know how they got into our room in the first place, as we always locked our door. Strange. I heard years later that Marv was elected as an Alderman on the City Council.

      I had to work nights that first college year, as a janitor and security, at the Breese Terrace Cafeteria, which was near Camp Randall Stadium, and where the football players ate. It wasn't bad when I was at Mrs. Mosby's, but now that I was living on campus, it was miles to walk to work; a lot of it uphill and battling snow and strong winds during the long winter. I had decided not to play football, not needing any huge defensive linemen landing on my right ankle, injuring it further; on a cold November Wisconsin afternoon. Or any other afternoon for that matter. I worked from seven at night until midnight, for $1.25 an hour. This didn't include walking up there and back, so 6:30 until 12:30. Then try to sleep, and classes during the day, play basketball, and study whenever I could. I sponged off the tables and counters, mopped the floors, took out the garbage. The good thing was that I could drink all the milk that I wanted and take a lot of fruit home with me.

I got a job working for the Department of Parks that summer of 1965, and continued working for them through the fall, when I didn't return for my sophomore year at Wisconsin. My parents were greatly disappointed and concerned about me, especially when I won the Best All-Around Athlete Award both of my years and was inducted into the National Honor Society at Pebble Hill.

There was a group of us that started hanging around this bar, Jimmy Benham's, between East Genesee and East Fayette Streets; on Columbus Avenue, next to Columbus Park, not far from Westcott Street. There was this guy that we got to know, a muscular guy with a really low and gruff-sounding voice named Oscar. His real name was Mike with a long Polish last name. He was the first guy that I knew, besides athletes, that religiously lifted weights. Even athletes didn't lift the way that they do now, not even close, and not year-round like they do today. You would ask him where he was going when he left the bar, and he would reply, "I'm going to lift."

He had a nickname for almost all the regulars at Benham's: I was "Spring," after the popular singer, Dusty Springfield; Steve was "Cool Jew;" Gerry was "The Weasel;" Frank was "The Smoocher," or just "Smooch;" Paul and Noreen were "The Spider and the Fly;" Al C. was "Dill Pickle;" there was "Checkbook Ginny;" Shirley the Sparerib;" "Vivacious Vivian the Vestal Virgin;" and his sidekick, Ed, whom he dubbed, "The Conscience."

He definitely had a knack for this. There were many others, but these were the ones that I remember. There were rumors about some kind of a barroom brawl, the following summer of 1966, in Lake George, that he was involved in.

When I saw him, I said to him,

"Hey Oscar, I heard that you were in a fight in a bar up in Lake George."

"Who did you hear that from?"

"I just heard it through the grapevine."

"Who is this guy? Who's "The Grapevine?"

Perfect. I ran into him at Oneida Shores over twenty years later when I was with Syl. I introduced her to him. I had told her about him and these nicknames. He looked and talked exactly the same, when he saw me and said, "Hey Spring!"

I was being influenced by the words and music of Bob Dylan. It still resonates with me today. I was dressing like he did on the "Freewheelin'" album: jeans, boots, jean shirt, suede jacket, black "Dutch Boy" cap. Sometimes I wore a light green fatigue jacket. I went to check out the folk music scene in Greenwich Village on some weekends that fall in 1965. I had a 1960 Dodge that I had bought from my Aunt Carol, the wife of Mom's older brother, Dave. It was white with a red top and big wide tail fins and a huge back seat, good enough to sleep in. I really had no clue about what was happening, but some force was pulling me there.

There were all these clubs in those days: "The Bitter End," "Café au Go Go," "Café Wha?," "The Gaslight Café," "Gerde's Folk City," and "Kettle of Fish." This is where the music was flowing: Weavers, (Pete Seeger and Woody Guthrie), Dylan, Joan Baez, Joni Mitchell, Judy Collins, John Denver, Phil Ochs, Neil Young, Paul Stookey, Peter Yarrow, Mary Travers, (Peter, Paul, & Mary), Fred Neil, Dave Van Ronk, Buffy Saint-Marie, Simon & Garfunkel, Odetta, Josh White, Linda Ronstadt, Van Morrison, Loudon Wainwright III; and blues artists like: Sonny Terry, Brownie McGhee, John Lee Hooker, James Cotton, and Muddy Waters.

I was totally involved with the evolution of the Beatles, from the early albums, to: "A Hard Day's Night": July, '64; "For Sale": December, '64; "Beatles VI": June, '65; "Help": August, '65; "Rubber Soul": December, '65; "Yesterday and Today": June, '66; "Revolver": August, '66; "Sgt. Pepper's Lonely Hearts Club Band": June, '67; "Magical Mystery Tour": November, '67; "White Album": November, '68; "Yellow Submarine": January, '69; "Abbey Road": September, '69; "Let It Be": May, '70. I liked a lot of the British groups: Rolling Stones, Zombies, Kinks, Searchers, and many more; but none could ever come close to the Beatles, as far as I was concerned.

I still loved all the soul music and the Motown artists. In fact, we had a group of friends that included: myself, Steve, Patti L., Terry & Kathy, "Wally," and many others; that faithfully followed an upstate New York R & B band, named Wilmer & The Dukes. I still have their one and only album. Their hit single was "Give Me One More Chance." They also had "I Do Love You" and "Get It." We used to go see Wilmer at the old Suburban Park in Manlius, (now apartment buildings with the same name), and Thunderbird Lanes in Baldwinsville. Wilmer played a mean sax as well as piano and was a great singer and entertainer. He was like a pied piper and people swarmed to see him. And The Dukes were a solid band. We were always excited to go and see them. For us, this was from the summer of 1965 through 1966, 1967, and 1968. We would go and all dance together, doing the latest dance crazes, like "The Skate." If you're our age now, you know what I'm talking about. This iconic Geneva band was later inducted into the Rochester Music Hall of Fame. We went to see other bands at Thunderbird Lanes, like: Bobby Hebb, Gary U.S. Bonds, The Shirelles, Chiffons, and others; but no one did it like Wilmer.

 On the evening of July 25, 1965, Bob Dylan went electric at the Newport Folk Festival; as some cheered him, but many of the folk purists booed him. He took the stage in black jeans, black boots, and a black leather jacket; carrying a Fender Stratocaster in place of his familiar acoustic guitar. He only played three songs before leaving the stage, finally reappearing with a borrowed acoustic guitar and bid Newport a stark farewell, singing: "It's All Over Now, Baby Blue."

 Wow! It still sends chills through me, even to this day. I was right on this wave length, I just didn't know the direction that it would lead me. But I knew there was something out there that called for me.

 I had taped pictures on the dashboard of my car, some even on the bottom part of the front windshield and driver's window. I had cut them out of magazines and they included: Dylan, Donovan, The Byrds, Simon & Garfunkel, the Mamas & the Papas, Buffalo Springfield, Lovin' Spoonful, Turtles, and The Leaves, (what did they play with, electric rakes?); among others.

 I saw the Rolling Stones on October 30th and Bob Dylan on November 21st, both concerts at the War Memorial in Syracuse in 1965.

I continued to work at the Department of Parks through the fall, into the coldness of November and December. After the college guys had gone back to school, just working the summer, I was left with all the guys who had worked there for many years, and would probably work there for the rest of their lives. Some days they would knock off early and pull the trucks behind Loomis Bar on Burnet Avenue, and drink beers and play cards for a couple of hours, before returning back to the home offices. They would take great pains to camouflage the trucks with the tree branches that we had cut down earlier that day. I couldn't envision myself working here for the rest of my life.

It was early January of 1966 when I found out that Steve, along with two of his friends, Brian G. and Louie, were planning to drive out to Los Angeles in Louie's 1965 Bonneville. I asked if I could go with them, they talked it over, and they said I could. I also asked if "Ringo" could come along as well. I hardly knew this guy. I had met him at Benham's and all I knew was that he was from the Adirondacks and looked exactly like Ringo of the Beatles, with his hair and long nose. (Probably an Oscar nickname.) To this day, I don't even remember his real name. I must have known it back then, but I can't recall it now. I was surprised they agreed to let him come, just figuring on more money to help with gas and expenses. Nobody had hardly any money, maybe $100 each, except Steve, who was the "rich one," having $500 from his bat mitzvah savings.

So, we headed out in the middle of January, 1966, driving into the infamous "The Blizzard of 1966," that was fast approaching across the United States, and started snowing in Syracuse on January 30th and ended on February 1st; after 42 inches had fallen. Wind gusts of 80 miles per hour were reported along Lake Ontario. I kept a journal of our trip, called "Five Against The West."

First, the right rear window wouldn't go back up and we had to tape a towel there. Then we faced fierce winds in Ohio and Louie's car broke down. It was something to do with the transmission, and we had to stay in a room above this garage for a few days before this part came in and they could fix it. After this, we stopped in Albuquerque, New Mexico, where Steve's sister lived, for a night. We got a flat tire in the desert in Arizona, trying to fix it, with a rattlesnake rattling not too far away. I remember Steve trying to take a lug nut off, after they had been loosened by the wrench, but not all the way off; and burning his fingers as it was scorching hot. We arrived in Los Angeles at a high school friend's apartment, Jim G., known as "Ginso." We pounded on his door, but he would not let us in. It was understandable at this hour, being 3 o'clock in the morning, that he wanted nothing to do with us. He had a job in a grocery store and was taking courses at Santa Monica Community College at night. He didn't want anybody or anything to interfere with his routine. You can't really blame him. We just wanted to stay with him for a few days until we found our own place. Finally, reluctantly, he let us in. But we knew we had to find a place right away.

We found an apartment in the Harbor View Apartments in Culver City. Louie got a job as a mechanic and one of the other mechanics needed a roommate, so Louie moved in with him. Steve got the solo bed as he had the most money. Ringo arranged for a rollaway cot and put it in the living room. I felt weird sleeping with Brian G. in the queen bed and slept on the couch. I can't remember what jobs that Brian and Ringo got. Steve and I got jobs at Thriftimart, bagging groceries, stocking shelves, and bringing in grocery carts. We had to wear these green vests and small black bow ties and take a bus there. One day, as Steve was bagging a woman's groceries, he inadvertently had put the deodorant in the insulated bag along with the ice cream. When the woman complained about his mistake, Steve calmly said to her, "It's Ice Blue Secret, isn't it?

After a couple of months, we left there and got jobs at Fedco, short for Federal Employees' Distributing Company. They filed for bankruptcy in 1999, at that point being the longest-operating membership-based store in the country. Most of these stores became Target. Steve was assigned to bathroom accessories and I was assigned to automotive supplies, where I knew absolutely nothing and had to learn on the fly. Steve would continue his one-liners, as he still does today; telling customers inquiring about toilet seats,

"Mention my name and I'll get you a good seat."

We cruised the Sunset Strip on weekends when we weren't working. We went to the Troubadour and the Whisky-A-Go-Go and saw the Doors, The Byrds, and other bands. It was a happening music scene.

We had to take the bus back and forth to work and at this time, due to the fact that I had dropped out of college, I was getting drafted. This was before they started the draft lottery process, six years later in 1972. They had sent me notices, but I never opened them, so as not to acknowledge that I had received them. My "no mercy" roommates had pinned them on the walls of our apartment. We came back to Syracuse in the middle of June, after almost six months on the west coast.

I did some house maintenance for my dad, as he was now working for Eagan Real Estate, after getting his realtor's license. This happened because the administrators at Pebble Hill were getting rid of two of the most beloved and longest tenured teachers, Mrs. Alden in English and Economics and Mr. Van Wagenen in Biology, Chemistry, and Earth Science; mainly due to age discrimination. Ironically, this was the same thing that happened to me fifty years later. I heard that Mr. Van Wagenen had made a substantial amount of money by inventing some board games during World War II, and didn't need his teacher's salary. He taught because he loved to teach. Dad stood up for them and announced, "If they go, I go." And that's exactly what happened.

Dad was the one who got us to Syracuse in the first place, when he accepted the job at Pebble Hill in February of 1962. This is where Mom became a teacher, administrator, and legend for thirty-three years. This is where Marty met all his friends when he went to Nottingham for high school and would meet his wife, Marti, and have their two sons, Kenn and Justin. This is where Julie would finish high school, first Pebble Hill and then the merger to become Manlius Pebble Hill School; and then meet her husband, Tom, and have their daughter, Emlyn, and their son, Jeff. This is where I would meet all my close friends, that still are my closest friends to this day; and where I would meet my wife, Sylvia, the one and only love of my life; and where both of us would teach: me for 21 years, and Sylvia for 23 years, at Manlius Pebble Hill School.

I could no longer avoid these draft notices and had to go down to the draft board, downtown in the Old Chimes Building, to appear for induction into the Army. I was on the verge of boarding the bus several times, heading to Fort Dix, New Jersey for basic training and then to Vietnam. I would always list my misshapen right ankle, due to the football injury, and have them take x-rays and evaluate it. It was a legitimate claim, but in those days, if you could pretty much walk, they were going to try to send you to Vietnam. Some guys were lucky enough to get out on a medical deferment, like Steve having a doctor's note for having been diagnosed with Osgood-Schlatter Disease, a painful, bony bump just below the knee. I mean, good for Steve, but my ankle was definitely a stronger deferment claim. Louie, "Audie," "Whale," and Chuck wound up going to Vietnam, and making it back miraculously in one piece, though emotionally scarred. "Audie" and Chuck are still with us today.

    We would be up at Camp, on Rainbow Shores, and I would be asking guys, after many beers, to break my arm that night; before I had to go back to Syracuse to the draft board the next morning. This is how desperate I was to not wanting to go to Vietnam and kill anyone. I'm glad nobody followed up on my request. In the meantime, I had applied to join the Naval Reserves and took their standard qualification test. I have no clue on how I passed it, but somehow, I did, and nine of us guys from Syracuse were accepted out of hundreds of applicants. This was in October of 1966.

    I was living on Rugby Road, near Eastwood, with my parents; the same house we had lived in since we moved to Syracuse at the beginning of September in 1962. That summer, I had to go with my dad to Syracuse from Webster to work on the house. This was right after my injury-plagued sophomore year at Webster Central. I was enjoying the summer, except for still doing my newspaper route every morning, that I had been doing for two years, and having to go house to house for collections on Saturdays. But after that, playing basketball and baseball and hanging out with my friends, just enjoying being a teenager.

I celebrated my 16th birthday and then Dad and I drove to Syracuse. We had to eat and sleep there, and do all this work, so the house would be ready for the family to move in; about two weeks later. An elderly couple had owned the house for many years and had recently passed away. The house had a funky smell and we had to peel off all the old wallpaper and do a lot of painting. Dad had this small portable radio, (that I still have), that we would listen to while we were working. I remember turning it on and "Surfin Bird" by The Trashmen came blaring out.

My dad came down from the ladder and switched that song off as fast as he could. He put on some country station, where I can remember the song, "Please Pass the Biscuits," by Jimmy Dean was playing. One night Dad wanted to reward me for all my hard work and decided to take me to see "West Side Story" at a drive-in movie theater. I was sitting in the front seat, thinking to myself, "What's wrong with this picture?" (and I don't mean the actual movie), as there were couples in the front and back seats of every car, with everyone making out; and I was with my dad, who was passed out, loudly snoring in the driver's seat. I didn't know one person in Syracuse, and after my childhood in Lakemont, and even my two years in Webster, Syracuse felt more like New York City to me; not that I knew what New York City felt like, until over three years later.

I was now living in the small back room of my former bedroom, where Marty had taken over after I left for Los Angeles. The back room was a back porch that Dad had converted into a bedroom for Marty, so we both didn't have to live in the main bedroom. This was across the hallway from my parents' bedroom, and next to Julie's bedroom. I started working at Lamson Corporation in Eastwood in September. They made centrifugal blowers and exhausters, as well as those pneumatic air tubes that they use to send your information to the teller at bank drive-in windows. I was an Expediter, coordinated orders for domestic and foreign exports. I took a bus to work, having sold my car. I wore a suit coat and tie and had a small office. This was not what my parents had in mind for me, but in their eyes, it was an improvement in my life, compared to the previous year. Oscar and some of his friends worked in the factory and gave me information on when they would be finished building some of the products, which was very helpful to me.

    I was still going to Benham's some nights, mainly on weekends; and going to see Wilmer & The Dukes when they were playing around here. I had to attend weekly, on Monday nights, Naval Reserve meetings, and take courses in Electronics, in a building out in Liverpool. This building was next to Heid's, famous for its hot dogs, a Central New York landmark since 1917. We would go over to Heid's on our break to get some hot dogs and chocolate milks, then go behind the building and get a view of the movie that was playing at the Salina Drive-In. We did this in the summer of 1967.

    This was the time period, from just before Thanksgiving, 1966 until the middle of April, 1967; where I had a relationship, that led to coming within hours, I mean literally within hours, of getting married, and having a totally different life in all probability. During this time period, I had to go out to freezing Great Lakes, Illinois, to complete eight weeks of basic training in January and February, 1967. I was allowed a leave of absence from Lamson's and came back to work there for March and into

April. I wasn't much for the pressures of a corporate job, having to reach different quotas to please your bosses; and wearing a suit and tie. I'd had enough. And this relationship wasn't meant to be, a fortunate twist of fate for me.

I got a job with the Buildings & Grounds Department of Syracuse University, at the end of April, as did "Audie" and Steve. The pay was minimal, but you were outside in the fresh air, helping the environment, and keeping in good physical shape. And you were working with two good friends and could check out all the sights and sounds of a college campus. I was also taking six credits through Syracuse University, English History and Shakespearean Plays, at night. I applied to the University of Wisconsin for reinstatement; citing my jobs, my courses, and my Naval Reserves, including basic training. I was accepted back to UW for my sophomore year.

Steve and I went to see James Brown at the Syracuse War Memorial on May 24, 1967. We were two of the few white people there. But we didn't have a problem with that and nobody had a problem with us. Everyone was out of their seats, dancing to "Papa's Got A Brand-New Bag" and "Please Please Please."

After another week at the Rainbow Shores Camp, I got a ride at the end of August with some guys who were returning to college at Notre Dame in South Bend, Indiana. This was a nine hour, 590 miles west drive. From there, I took the four hour, 245 miles northwest, bus ride to Madison. I had arranged to stay with some friends for a few days while I looked for a room for rent. I didn't want to live in the dorms anymore. I saw an ad in the campus newspaper that a fraternity, the Tau Kappa Epsilon house, was renting out rooms to non-fraternity students, as their membership was very low. Of course, they would try to recruit you into joining their fraternity; but none of us, about a dozen of us, ever did. We called ourselves "The Independents." I became good friends with several of these guys. One guy, "Fireball," turned me on to Jimi Hendrix's "Are You Experienced" album.

    The TKE house was located on Langdon Street, where most of the other fraternities were located, overlooking Lake Mendota. Mendota, a Sioux Indian name, means "the mouth of the river." The other lake that borders Madison is Monona, a Chippewa word that means "beautiful." I've also heard that Mendota meant "sunrise" and Monona meant "sunset." They may not be historically accurate, but I like these meanings as well.

    I started my sophomore year and enrolled in the Naval ROTC program. I had new x-rays and doctors' reports about the status of my right ankle, being in a degenerative state. I applied for a medical discharge from the Naval Reserves and eventually received one, a medical and honorable discharge. I didn't officially receive it until October 10, 1968. Who knows what would have happened to me if I had gotten on those buses heading to Fort Dix after being inducted? And of those eight other guys from Syracuse that I went to basic training in Great Lakes, Illinois with? I only saw one guy again, as he was a graduate of Pebble Hill School as well. The other seven, I don't know what happened to them. I heard that some of them had the misfortune of being stationed on a gun boat near Da Nang. I hope they made it. They were hoping to be stationed in Hawaii or San Diego, but these were uncertain and volatile times. I had the experience of completing eight weeks of basic training and two years of Reserve duty and not having to go to Vietnam.

I got a job at Everson's Groceries, a small neighborhood Mom & Pop's type grocery store in Madison, owned by Mr. and Mrs. Everson, an elderly couple that had run the store most of their lives. I stocked the shelves and bagged groceries. Dave, the manager of the store, had a deformity of his right hand, kind of a claw hand. He handled the cash register. Both Mr. and Mrs. Everson became ill and I felt bad that I was only available to work the late afternoons. I started to work more hours after they became sick, helping Dave, and instead of working three until six, I worked three until nine, when the store closed for the day. I worked there from the middle of September until the middle of May, except for the holidays and school breaks. This curtailed my social life. I still had time to have fun with my friends on my days off, but it became harder to find enough time to study. I went to all my classes and applied myself this year, as opposed to my freshman year, two years earlier. I made my grade point average requirements and removed myself from academic probation. Looking back on it now, it was amazing to me that I fought my way back and returned to college after being out for two years.

There was a club called The Factory, a converted warehouse, on West Gorham Street, off State Street, in Madison, that started to book some nationwide bands. At first, there were regional acts, like Twistin' Harvey & The Seven Sounds, from Milwaukee. Harvey Scales was known as "Milwaukee's Godfather of Soul." He co-wrote, with Johnny Taylor, "Disco Lady." Also, the J. Geils band covered his song, "Love-itis." As a teenager, he was in a group with Al Jarreau, called The Playboys; and part of the Esquires in the late 50's. He opened for Chubby Checker, Stevie Wonder, and the Commodores. He and his band were rumored to be the inspiration for Otis Day and The Knights, from the 1978 movie, "Animal House."

We had our tickets, (they were $3) to see Otis Redding with the Bar-Kays. They were scheduled to play two shows that night, one at 6:30 and followed by another one at 9. This was the same format for all the performers that played there. There were rumors on the local radio stations that Otis Redding's plane had crashed into Lake Monona, that fateful Sunday afternoon of December 10th, 1967. Residents had seen a twin-engine plane plunge from the sky into the icy waters of Lake Monona.

There was an eerie fog that engulfed Madison that day. Otis and the Bar-Kays had played in Nashville two nights before and then in Cleveland the night before. They were flying to Madison from Cleveland to play two shows that night at The Factory. The crash remains a mystery, but one theory was that the pilot was told to put the plane on autopilot, because of the low ceiling caused by the fog. The fact that it was on autopilot would have hidden the fact that the plane had ice buildup happening, until it was too late. There were some other unsavory theories about what might have happened, but nothing was ever conclusive. The music promoter thought that they were traveling to Madison in a tour bus, unaware that Otis had recently purchased a twin-engine Beechcraft to travel by air.

When the promoter received the calls from the police department, they suggested to not turn people away that were standing in line to see Otis, due to all the student unrest at the time, these being the anti-Vietnam War protests. The promoter made the announcement of the tragedy and started to refund the tickets. He opened the doors for a free concert with The Grim Reapers, ((later to become Cheap Trick), to open the show, as they were scheduled to do for Otis. He made some calls and was able to get Lee Brown and The Cheaters, an eight-piece rhythm & blues band, to come to Madison and perform that night.

James Alexander, the bassist of the Bar-Kays, had volunteered to return the band's rental car in Cleveland, and take a commercial flight from Cleveland to Milwaukee; dropped them off at the hangar. He was waiting at the Milwaukee airport to be picked up that day. Instead, the police came and took him down to Madison to identify the bodies. Ben Cauley, who played trumpet with the Bar-Kays, was the only one who survived the fatal crash that claimed the lives of eight people, including Otis and four members of the Bar-Kays, originally called the Imperials. The Bar-Kays signature hit was "Soul Finger." In the summer of 1967, they backed Otis in a ten night stand at the Apollo Theater in Harlem and toured the country. That fall, Otis took some time off from the road to have some polyps removed from his throat; and to write and record what would ultimately become his most popular and his swan song, ("Sittin' on the) Dock of the Bay." Otis always looked and seemed older to me at the time, like he was 40. He was only 26. They would go back on the road in early December.

Cauley remembers the cabin of the plane was extremely cold that morning. They asked an attendant to crank up the plane so the cabin could warm up, but the attendant said he couldn't because the battery was kind of low and he would rather have the pilot do it. They all looked at each other, "Like what's going on, the battery's low?" But they took off for Madison with no problems. Then around 3:30, just a few minutes outside of Madison, the plane started violently shaking. Cauley remembers unbuckling his seatbelt and getting up and looking out the window. The next thing he remembers is waking up and being in all this water. He had been separated from the plane and thrown out of an opening in the fuselage. He had never learned how to swim and was struggling in the frigid lake. He had somehow gotten hold of a seat cushion, but the waves took it away from him. But another cushion floated by and he grabbed it. He saw two of his bandmates surface for a few seconds and cry for help. The waves prevented him from reaching them in time. The rescue team arrived in 17 minutes, their speed in getting to the crash site was the thing that saved his life; as he was a couple of minutes away from hypothermia. He was taken to the hospital and then was informed that he was the only survivor. He was in a total state of shock, just lying there with his eyes wide open, when Alexander arrived in Madison and went to see him in the hospital.

Alexander and Cauley, after months of mourning, re-formed the band in 1968, even touring with groups like the Temptations. Cauley left in 1972, not wanting to be on the road all the time. Alexander continues to lead the Bar-Kays to this day. Cauley suffered a massive stroke in 1989 and was given three days to live. But after months of rehabilitation, he recovered and was able to play his trumpet, something the doctors said he would never be able to do again.

In December of 2007, on the 40th anniversary of the crash, he returned to Madison, something he vowed he would never do. He performed as part of a ceremony, honoring Otis Redding and the fallen Bar-Kays, at the Monona Terrace. He performed his final show with Alexander and the Bar-Kays, as they were inducted into the Memphis Music Hall of Fame on November 24, 2013. Cauley, who seemingly had nine lives, died on September 21, 2015 at the age of 67. I always thought of writing a screenplay about Ben Cauley's life; traveling to Memphis, finding him, and conducting interviews with him. But I never did. I still think that his story would make for an excellent and unique movie.

We showed up at The Factory that fateful evening, and if memory serves me correctly, just got our ticket refund back. We were in no mood to hear any other music that night. But I wish that I would have held onto my ticket.

The Factory continued to book major musical acts. On February 27, 1968, we had the amazing experience of seeing The Jimi Hendrix Experience, with Mitch Mitchell and Noel Redding, *for two shows on the same night.* The Factory had a capacity of 750 people and the Fire Department was trying to get everyone out after the 6:30 show, before letting the new crowd in for the 9 o'clock show. We somehow managed to slip our way back in for the second show. We weren't the only ones, there had to be a thousand people packed in there for the second show.

On March 11, 1968, The Grim Reapers, (later Cheap Trick), opened up for Wilson Pickett. I remember dancing in front of our front row seats when Wilson Pickett invited us to come up and dance on the stage with him. We danced right next to and with him, as the band played and he sang his cover hit, "Land of 1000 Dances," recorded in 1966.

The original hit was recorded in 1962 by Chris Kenner. In 1965, Cannibal & the Headhunters, a Mexican-American group from East Los Angeles, added the "Na, na na na na" hook and popularized the song. They were the opening act on the Beatles' second American tour, backed up by the King Curtis band.

On March 27, 1968, we saw The Paul Butterfield Blues Band at The Factory, the last concert that we saw there.

I went with some friends as we took the 150 miles southeast drive, from Madison to Chicago, to see the Doors at the Chicago Coliseum on May 10th, 1968, at the end of the school year. It was a great concert and afterwards we went down to Old Town, a neighborhood and historic district on the North Side of Chicago. We went in this bar and these rough kinds of guys kept staring at me, wearing my silk Nehru shirt, looking like they wanted to beat the crap out of me. This was 1968, a deeply divided time in our country, pitting one group of people against the other; much the same as it seems to be today. It reminded me of that deeply uneasy feeling, fearing for your personal safety, when Steve and I were on the open deck of that boat, crossing the North Sea; with the drunken Norwegian sailors pointing to our heads with fingernail clippers. We made a quick exit and got out of there, avoiding what looked like an inevitable confrontation.

Dr. Bop & The Headliners played at an end of the year party with my friend, Al Craven, "The White Raven," as the lead singer. He had a great voice and was really acrobatic. He had climbed up on this roof and was singing an encore song, with the setting sun in the background; when he suddenly disappeared, seemingly into thin air, as the song ended and the sun made its final descent. It was a spectacular sight to behold, one I'll never forget.

I stopped working at the grocery store in the middle of May and I think they were able to find another student to work there. I stayed in Madison for another month, finally being able to enjoy myself without having to work, study, or go to Naval Reserve meetings. Just swimming in Lake Mendota, playing softball, hanging out with my friends. I remember a group of us watching Bobby Kennedy's speech at this house on June 5th, 1968 and see him get shot on live television, as we looked on in disbelief and horror.

I returned to Syracuse in late June and managed to again get a job working for the Department of Parks. I worked for July and August and my parents thought I was returning to Wisconsin for my junior year, especially feeling in their minds that I had put my life back in the right direction. It was the logical thing to do, to get my college degree and then see what the future held for me after that.

But I could not escape what I was feeling deep within my soul, this wanderlust, this feeling that *there was more out there for me to see and experience.* I think that they were more disappointed than they were the first time. I felt bad and never wanted to hurt them, but this pull of seeing and experiencing different countries and cultures was too powerful a force for me to ignore.

I rented a house with my friend Ronnie, on West Colvin Street on the South Side of Syracuse; not far from where Sylvia and I lived on Clyde Avenue, when we first met and started living together, 15 years later. I went with some friends to see Simon & Garfunkel at the Saratoga Performing Arts Center on August 19th. I continued working for the Parks Department in the fall.

The year 1969 arrived, and what an eventful year it turned out to be! I spent the winter in Miami, visited Madison in the spring, and came back to Syracuse for the summer, working for a landscaping company. Mom and Dad went to Europe during July, being chaperones for a group of students, including Julie, for The International Cultural Exchange School Program. They got their expenses paid doing this and managed to get Julie's paid for as well.

Marty and I were left to take care of the house. On July 20th, we had all these friends come over to watch the Apollo 11 Moon Landing on a small television in the living room. People would come to the door at Rugby Road, and if they were wearing a sweatshirt or football jersey, carrying a six or twelve pack of beer, and a pizza; they were probably Marty's friends. Marty and his friends had just graduated from high school at Nottingham a month before. If someone was at the door wearing a peasant shirt, bell bottoms, and love beads, carrying a bottle of wine, incense sticks, and some record albums; they were probably my friends, and headed up to the attic.

When it was time for Apollo 11 to make its landing, all of us watched together in awe, as Michael Collins landed the lunar module on the surface of the moon. Neil Armstrong stepped on the moon and was followed by Buzz Aldrin. That was a truly amazing and historic night, one that all of us will never forget; witnessing this in real time as it was happening.

The first three days of August, I went to the Atlantic City Pop Festival; and eleven days later, I went to Woodstock. Then back out to Madison in the fall, before returning to Syracuse and heading to Europe: London, Dover, Calais, Paris, Amsterdam, Bordeaux, Madrid, Algeciras, and staying in Tangier, Morocco.

In 1970, another winter in Miami; before heading back over to Europe: Madrid, Algeciras, Ceuta, Malaga, Rome, Florence, Venice, Pisa, Milan, Copenhagen, Skagen, Oslo, Lillehammer, Hamburg, Amsterdam. Returned to Syracuse and went out to Los Angeles, Glendale, "the Ranch in the Valley," San Francisco, Tucson, Miami, Phoenix, Flagstaff, Grand Canyon, Hermosa Beach, Tucson, New York City, Madison, Syracuse, Miami.

In 1971: Tucson for the winter and spring; Madison; McKeever, (near Old Forge); Madison in September; and then back to Tucson.

I went with some friends to see Chuck Berry at the Too High club in Tucson. The first half of his show he was great; playing all his old hits: "Johnny B. Goode," "Roll Over Beethoven," "Rock And Roll Music," "Sweet Little Sixteen," "Maybellene," "No Particular Place to Go," "Memphis, Tennessee," "Brown Eyed Handsome Man," "Nadine," "Little Queenie," "Reelin' And Rockin." During the intermission, I think he went out and got stoned. In the second half of the show, he was playing "My Ding A Ling" and some other nonsensical songs that were embarrassing for him to play and for us to listen to, especially coming from a true pioneer of Rock n' Roll.

On October 2nd, some friends and I drove up to Phoenix to see the Moody Blues at the Arizona Coliseum. There was a long delay to start the concert, as it turned out that their van, carrying all their equipment, had been in an accident. They had to use equipment, instruments, speakers, from a local high school band, brought in for their show. You would have never known the difference, as they sounded fantastic.

In 1972: Tucson for the winter and spring. On March 2nd, I went with some friends to see Savoy Brown and Fleetwood Mac, at Salpointe High School in Tucson. Later in the spring, driving with Chuck: from Tucson, 2,250 miles, through El Paso, Austin, New Orleans, to Miami. Chuck had returned from his tour of duty in Vietnam and was taking a cross country trip, visiting some Army buddies, one in Oklahoma, and coming out to Tucson to visit me. He hung out with me and some friends that I had met out there, for a week, before taking me with him back to Miami.

These were the three years: 1970, 1971, through 1972, that I decided not to eat meat or fish, becoming a vegetarian. I could never be a vegan, as I loved milk, whether by itself, a milkshake, on cereal, or a smoothie. I loved cheese, eggs, and yogurt. I also decided during these years to not wear any leather, and I'm not sure of my reasoning, but to not drive anymore.

So, on the first European trip, I was not doing any of the driving, leaving it all to Tomás and "Catman." I did always ride in the front passenger seat, to read the maps and navigate, and change the cassette tapes; so, the other guy who wasn't driving, could stretch out in the back seat and sleep.

Chuck could not believe I wasn't driving anymore and would not be helping him drive on this cross-country trip. He still brings it up, even to this day, over 47 years later. He does have a strong case, but it was what it was. On the flip side, in my defense, he fell asleep behind the wheel as we were approaching the city of New Orleans at dawn. Luckily, for both of us, I would stay awake in the front passenger seat, navigate, and take care of the music. Chuck was speeding across five lanes on the main highway, right to left, at 80 miles an hour; when I grabbed the steering wheel, straightened it out, and frantically woke him up. If I was asleep when this was happening, we would have, in all probability, been involved in a catastrophic crash, with death or life-threatening injuries being the end result.

When I started driving again in 1974, it was a strange experience for me, and took a while to get used to. It was like when you had your learner's permit and were practicing out on the road, preparing to take your driver's test in order to get your driver's license.

I think some of these abstention ideas stemmed from my thinking after the Woodstock experience. I started eating seafood again, then fowl, like chicken and turkey, then meat. I was eating all these things for nine and a half years when I met Sylvia. I continued eating all these things for our first six and a half years. I enjoyed chicken, turkey, a nice ham for the holidays, boneless pork chops, bacon, sausage, an occasional hamburger and hot dog. I was never a big steak eater, a nice filet mignon once in a while. Then I saw something on television about cows and the hoof and mouth disease and it just turned me off from eating meat ever again. I know it's psychological and I don't judge anyone else, but that was it for me. Syl could still make meals for me with chicken, turkey and seafood. Then several years later, I saw another thing on television about the bird flu and I stopped eating chicken and turkey.

Syl would bring home a container of tuna fish from the lunches at MPH and that would be one of my dinners. My other dinners during the week would be: fried egg sandwiches, grilled cheese sandwiches, and peanut butter and jelly sandwiches. I would usually eat salmon when we went out to dinner; sometimes crab, flounder, haddock, shrimp, or swordfish. I haven't eaten any meat since the end of 1989. I hadn't eaten any chicken or turkey since then either, but in this past year, I've had some chicken, chicken salad for a sandwich, turkey slices for a sandwich, and chicken soup. Syl would be pleasantly surprised. I'll see how it goes.

After the trip from Tucson, in 1972: Coconut Grove; Syracuse; New York City; Syracuse; Augusta,

Maine, (China Lake); Buffalo; Chicago; Madison; Miami.

In 1973: Coconut Grove; Madison; Syracuse; New York City; Syracuse; Madison; Miami; Coconut Grove; Austin; Los Angeles; New York City.

In 1974; Miami; Coconut Grove; Austin; Syracuse; Austin; Syracuse.

Our Coconut Grove crew consisted of: "Bush," "Fast," "Fox," "Hindustani," Ronnie, Steve, and me. We played "Tabletop Hockey," "Match Basketball," "Match Football," and "Morra," an Italian Fingers Game. "Morra" is a hand game that dates back thousands of years to ancient Roman and Greek times. Each player simultaneously reveals their hand, extending any number of *fingers,* and calls out a number. Any player who successfully guesses the total number of *fingers* revealed by all players combined scores a point. We just played one on one.

One night I was playing the "Tabletop Hockey" game with "Fast," when he started uncontrollably laughing for minutes. I asked him,

"What? What is so funny?"

"I just thought of a great one."

We all made up names for our hockey players, and would say them as we played, each doing our own play by play announcing and commentary.

"What is it?"

"Melancholy baby."

I had a puzzled look on my face.

"Mel and Colly Baby, the Baby Brothers!"

"Good one!"

We both started laughing.

Some of his guys were: Mo Mentum, Mel Baby, Colly Baby, Lefty Wright, Puckminster Fuller, Hans Stickey, and Al Ouette.

He came up with Ouette from the French song, "Alouette;" which goes: "Alouette, gentille Alouette Alouette, je te plumerai."

That gave me the idea of a good name for one of my players: Jean DePlumeray.

He said, "DePlumeray should be one of my guys. You would have never gotten him without me having come up with Ouette."

"True, but names are just out there for the taking. All that matters is that you come up with them."

My guys were: DePlumeray, Baga Trix, the Bridge Brothers: Tap & Zee, Y.B. Fatte, Sudden Stop Simmons, A.T. Random, (my goalie), and others that I can't remember. Sometimes you hear someone say something and a potential hockey name pops into your head. In fact, just recently I thought of a good one: Sir Cumference. You could make him French Canadian: Sir Cumferénce. Another one: Luke Warm. And Banque Teller.

This is one of those scenarios *where you had to be there* to fully appreciate it. We had a lot of laughs making up these names, and fun playing the hockey game, although very competitive while playing it. These were the years, in the early 70's, when we were hanging out in Coconut Grove, Florida.

In Austin, in 1974, I saw concerts with Boz Scaggs; Willie Nelson; Dr. John; and the Eagles. Dr. John, "the Night Tripper," (real name: Malcolm Rebennack); played at this small club in Austin and a group of us were sitting in the front row. At the end of his show, he takes out these two big bags full of glitter and empties them out over everybody in the first few rows. No matter how hard I tried to shake it all out from my hair, clothes, and apartment; it was futile, as I kept discovering more glitter for several months. (He just recently passed away.) We met the Eagles after their concert in Austin, and I can remember Glenn Frey wearing a University of Texas football jersey. (Glenn passed away four years ago.)

These previous five and a half years, from the beginning of 1969, until the summer of 1974 were my "wandering years." (In addition, the six months living and working in Los Angeles, in the first half of 1966.) I traveled extensively, being able to hitch rides with friends, take buses, and stay with friends on a couch or a mattress on the floor; sometimes renting a small apartment. Things were a lot cheaper then, that's for sure. I did a lot of landscaping and painting jobs to pay for my food, rent, and travel expenses. I lived those years on a "bare bones" budget, but I don't regret all the places I traveled to, all the people that I met, and all the experiences that I had.

Dad had gotten a job working for The New York State Department of Labor as a job counselor, around the end of 1969 or beginning of 1970; where he worked for 10 years, before they talked him into taking early retirement. He got me a job in January, 1975 as a courier for Federal

Express, (they had just begun operations in April, 1973), when they were first starting here in Syracuse; having their offices at a hangar at the old Sair Aviation building in Mattydale. I was hired as a temporary worker, lasting four months, before I was a victim of their numbers game and let go. I worked for Ace Landscaping for a few months before landing a job with P.E.A.C.E., Inc. I drove the van for the "Summer Lunch Program" for kids; then drove the van for the "Senior Citizen's Program;" and worked in their warehouse.

On June 3, 1978, I went to see Bob Marley & The Wailers concert, the "Kaya" tour, at the Landmark Theater in Syracuse. It was one of the greatest concerts I have ever seen. The only disappointing thing about it was that there was a rumor that Bob and his band were going down to Scratch Daniel's bar, in downtown Syracuse, after their concert. I chose to go to this party, where there were people getting high, and a place I didn't want to be, and I didn't stay too long there.

I found out the next day that Bob and his band had indeed gone to Scratch Daniel's, and had a drink or coffee there, and hung around for an hour or so. I would have loved to meet them, maybe carry on a conversation with them, just to be in their presence. What a thrill that would have been! I always have regretted making the wrong decision about not going down there and see if they came there, if the rumor was in fact true. Bob was scheduled to appear again at the Landmark, on October 1, 1980, a concert that I had tickets for.

He had started his "Uprising" tour in Zurich, Switzerland on May 30, 1980. He performed 33 concerts in Europe and 5 in the United States, including the September 23rd concert at the Stanley Theater in Pittsburgh; which would turn out to be his last one. He had been jogging in Central Park on September 21st, being in New York City for concerts at Madison Square Garden; when he collapsed, likely due to complications from the malignant melanoma cancer he was diagnosed with in 1977. He had this when I saw him in 1978. All the more reason for regretting not to go down to see him, after the concert, at Scratch Daniel's. He still went to Pittsburgh, two days after his collapse, to perform. He had to cancel the rest of the tour, including the October 1st show at the Landmark. He died on May 11, 1981, in a Miami hospital, at the age of 36. Way, way too young for one of the all-time greats.

In the late fall of 1978, I was staying at Rugby Road with Mom and Dad, up in the attic, where they had converted the main part of it into living quarters, but you had to come down the stairs to use the bathroom. I was there from late November until the middle of December. I had never missed a Christmas with my family, no matter where my travels had taken me; I always managed to find my way back to Syracuse for Christmas. This year, 1978, was different, as I wanted to drive back to Austin and find an apartment to move into by January 1st. I could stay at this ranch for a couple of weeks with a bunch of guys, a few from Syracuse, but I didn't want to get stuck there any longer than the end of December. I always loved Austin, I had only come back to Syracuse to pursue this relationship that I told you about earlier in the book; one that was ill-fated and similar in that way, to the one Syl had before I met her. It had run its course a year or so before, the same time table as Syl's had before we met. I was ready to move on and get back to a warmer climate.

I packed up my 1971 Buick Skylark, that I had bought at a used car dealership in Tampa in 1977, for $800, with everything I owned at this time. I had filled the trunk with my clothes. In the back seat, I had a big footlocker containing my possessions and my stereo equipment and speakers. I had put all my record albums on the floor under the back seats. In the front seat was my television, leaning against the window, and a small stand with wicker legs on the floor. I had to reach under the stand to use the car radio. (I still have this stand today down in the basement.) My parents were in obvious disbelief at this arrangement.

Mom had made me some sandwiches, along with some fruit and nuts, to take with me for the trip. She had put them in a paper bag and written "Dusty" on the bag. I put the bag on the top of my car as I kissed them good-bye, and inadvertently had driven away with the bag still on the roof of the car. They hadn't noticed it either, as I drove out of the driveway. It was late afternoon and getting dark out, as I drove down the steep Teall Avenue hill. Out of nowhere, I heard a police siren, and could barely see the flashing lights in my diminished vision in my back window. I pulled over, and the policeman walked up to the car, as I rolled down my window.

"Is your name Dusty?"

"Yes, why?"

I'm thinking, how could he possibly know that? I didn't recognize him from any basketball or softball teams that I had played on or even against. I didn't recognize him from any landscaping or painting crews, or from any other places where I had worked. Or a friend of any of my friends.

He held the bag of food that my mom had packed in his hand.

"Is this yours?"

"Yes, thank you."

I had driven on Rugby Road to the corner of Teall Avenue, and somehow the bag had managed to stay on the roof of the car. He was parked there to catch speeders, and as I turned left onto Teall, he saw the bag fly off the roof. He picked it up and followed me down the hill. He gave the bag to me, as he looked inside the car and told me that I should rearrange some things, for better vision for my safety and for the safety of other drivers as well. I thanked him again for his thoughtfulness and went on my way, for my solo 1,700 miles southwest trip to Austin.

It started intensely snowing, as a blizzard was fast approaching. I decided that it was too dangerous to continue, and headed back up the hill, back to Rugby Road. On the way, I got a flat tire, so it was a wise decision. I rang the doorbell and they had already gone to bed. Dad helped me get the car, which I had left on Teall, a block away, back into their driveway.

I wound up staying for three more days until all the snow had been cleared. I rearranged some things in the car for better vision, got the tire fixed, said good-bye to my parents again, and headed back on the road once more. I just slept in rest areas along the way.

Tuesday Mornin' Drivin'

Tuesday mornin' drivin'

Through the fog 'n drizzle 'n rain

I'm almost a thousand miles away now

From my loved ones and some pain.

And it just goes to show

That when you think you know

You've still got such

A long, long way to go.

Movin' down Forty West

To Nashville, Tennessee

Then two hundred miles to Memphis

I'll be beat as I can be.

Little Rock and Texarkana

Cruisin' through Dallas too

Look out below in Austin

I'm headed straight for you.

Tuesday mornin' drivin'

Seventeen hundred miles away

On my own highway now

Captain for the day.

Dreaming of my destiny

Reflecting on the past

Following a forgotten clue

But following it at last.

And it just goes to show

That when you think you know

You've still got such

A long, long way to go.

    I wrote this along the way, when I stopped to take some breaks. I always thought that this would make a really good country song, adding in the chorus a few more times. I would love to hear Willie Nelson play and sing it.

    I spent two weeks at the ranch, found a small apartment near the main part of Austin, and moved in at the beginning of January. I found some temporary work, unloading huge oriental rugs off of delivery trucks, for this carpet store. It was always hot and humid when we unloaded, the loose fibers from the rugs uncomfortably sticking to your skin. I played basketball with a group of familiar guys down in Adams Park, sweating like crazy for hours, then heading over to refreshing Barton Springs to cool off. I couldn't seem to find any painting or landscaping work, and decided to go back to Syracuse in the middle of July, 1979.

I have been here ever since. It turned out to be the greatest decision that I ever made, meeting Sylvia 4 years later; and eventually having a teaching career for 21 years. I wish I could have met Syl earlier, in 1980, and we would have had 3 more years together. She didn't come to Syracuse until the fall of 1979, and needed a year to have her divorce finalized and decide where she was going. Luckily for me, and for her, and for us; she didn't go with her mother to Charleston and stayed in Syracuse. Maybe it wouldn't have worked out if we had met in the summer of 1980, we'll never know. But it did work out 3 years later, so I guess that this was the way it was meant to be.

I found a place to rent near the Manley Field House at the end of July. It was a small house in the backyard of a house owned by two women that they had used as a guest house. It would have been a great place to live in when you were in high school. The ceilings were low and I had to constantly duck to avoid whacking my head, which I did frequently. The narrow stairs led to a loft where my bedroom was. There were several squirrels that hung out on the roof, you could hear them rolling their nuts across it, that sounded like "squirrel bowling," so that was annoying. The women had two big female dogs that would bark at me and literally keep me from leaving the house. Eventually I started to feed them dog biscuits and they became my buddies. They would be waiting at my door in the morning, in begging positions with their tails wagging, anticipating their daily treats.

I left there after a year, and moved into the Valley Court Apartments, on the south side of Syracuse, near Meachem Field. This is where we played most of our City League softball games, on a team that I was now on. I signed a one-year lease and was there from the end of July, 1980 until the end of July, 1981. As I was driving back to my apartment, on Route 81 South, after a softball game at Hopkins Road in Liverpool, one summer night in 1981; I heard a loud sound, like I had hit something on the highway. Well, it turned out that I had. I pulled into my apartment complex, parked the car, and went inside. I was looking forward to having an English Muffin and watching Sports Center on ESPN, which I had recently been finally able to get. I was jealous of some of my other friends who were getting cable television, with ESPN, for over a year now. I had just sat down when I heard some loud knocks on my door. There were several policemen. I was wondering what I had done to have them knocking at my door.

"Do you own that 1971 Buick Skylark?"

"Yes, I do."

"Well, you are going to have to get it towed out of here."

"Why, what happened to it?"

It turned out that whatever I had hit on the highway had put a hole in the gas tank, and I had unfortunately just filled it up earlier that evening; and it had now totally emptied out all over the apartment complex. They had to get everybody out of their apartments while three trucks from the Fire Department came and hosed down the parking lot, including all the cars, sides of the buildings, everything. If someone had thrown a lit match or cigarette, there would have been a catastrophic fire. All the residents, especially the women in their curlers and robes, were all standing there and pointing at me. They were obviously not too thrilled and it was well after midnight by now. Although it was a freak accident, I still felt guilty and embarrassed. I had to have my car towed, get a ride to pick it up two days later, and pay for a new gas tank and labor.

After a year living here, I was informed about a second floor of a house for rent on Clyde Avenue by Nick, a good friend of mine on the softball team. He and his roommate, Pierre, had been renting and living on the first floor of this house for a year or longer. A woman in Marcellus owned the house and I contacted her, signed the lease, and moved in at the end of July, 1981.

I had been living here on Clyde Avenue for about two years when I first met Sylvia. After she moved in with me in the middle of August of 1983, we lived there for six and a half months, before buying and moving into Marty and Marti's house in North Syracuse, at the end of February, 1984.

So this chronicles all the places that I lived: from the south side of Syracuse, 302 Marguerite Avenue, when I was a baby, in 1946, into 1947; to the village of Liverpool for a year or so; then to Fairmount Avenue in Liverpool, until the start of fall in 1953; to Lakemont, until the end of summer in 1960; to Webster, until the end of summer in 1962; to Syracuse, until the end of summer in 1964; to college in Madison, Wisconsin, until the end of May in 1965; Syracuse, until the middle of January, 1966; Los Angeles, from January to June, 1966; Syracuse, until the end of December, 1966; Great Lakes, Illinois, (Basic Training, Naval Reserves), for January and February, 1967; Syracuse, until the end of summer, 1967; back to college in Madison in September, 1967; Syracuse, Madison, Nassau, Miami, Madison, until the end of June, 1968; Syracuse, until late December, 1968; Miami, winter of 1969; Syracuse, Madison, Europe and Tangier, Morocco, 1969; Miami, Europe, Los Angeles, 1970; Tucson, Madison, Syracuse (McKeever), Madison, Tucson, 1971; Tucson, Coconut Grove, New York City, Syracuse, Augusta, Maine, Madison, 1972; Miami, Madison, Syracuse, NYC,

Madison, Coconut Grove, Austin, 1973; Austin, Syracuse, 1974; Syracuse, 1975; Syracuse, 1976; Syracuse, Tampa, Syracuse, 1977; Syracuse, Austin, 1978; Austin, Syracuse, (end of July), 1979.

Here is a list of all the concerts that I went to by myself, with a friend, or with friends, before I met Sylvia; when we went to our first concert together on August 7th, 1983. This list begins in the fall of 1964 and continues through the winter of 1983:

(Fall,'64 & Winter,'65): The Ardells and The Fabulous Night Train; with Steve Miller and Boz Scaggs: (Mother Tucker's, Madison, Wisconsin)

(Fall,'65) Folk Artists: (Greenwich Village clubs)

(10/30/'65) Rolling Stones: (War Memorial, Syracuse, New York)

(11/21/'65) Bob Dylan: (War Memorial)

(January-June,'66) The Byrds and The Doors: (Whiskey a Go-Go and The Troubadour, Sunset Strip, Los Angeles, California)

('66 & '67) Wilmer And The Dukes: (Suburban Park, Manlius, NY & Thunderbird Lanes, Baldwinsville, NY)

(April,'67) Mitch Ryder & The Detroit Wheels: (Bristol Mountain, Canandaigua, NY)

(5/24/'67) James Brown: (War Memorial)

(Fall,'67) Twistin' Harvey And The Seven Sounds: (The Factory, Madison, Wisconsin)

(12/10/'67) *Otis Redding & The Bar-Kays* (*The concert that never happened*): (The Factory, Madison, Wisconsin)

(2/27/'68) Jimi Hendrix Experience: (The Factory, Madison, Wisconsin)

(3/11/'68) Wilson Pickett: (The Factory, Madison, Wisconsin)

(3/27/'68) Paul Butterfield Blues Band (The Factory, Madison, Wisconsin)

(5/10/'68) The Doors: (Chicago Coliseum)

(8/19/'68) Simon & Garfunkel: (SPAC)

(Summer & Fall,'68) Wilmer And The Dukes: (Suburban Park and Thunderbird Lanes)

(Summer & Fall,'68) Gary U.S. Bonds; Bobby Hebb; Chiffons; Shirelles: (Thunderbird Lanes)

(August 1-3,'69) Atlantic City Pop Festival: (Atlantic City, New Jersey): Iron Butterfly; Procol Harum; Crosby, Stills, & Nash; Booker T. & the M.G.'s; Joni Mitchell; Chicago Transit Authority; Santana; Johnny Winter; Jefferson Airplane; Creedence Clearwater Revival; Lighthouse; Crazy World of Arthur Brown; B.B. King; Paul Butterfield Blues Band; Tim Buckley; The Byrds; Hugh Masakela; American Dream; Janis Joplin & The Kozmic Blues Band; Canned Heat; Mothers of Invention; Sir Douglas Quintet; Three Dog Night; Dr. John; Joe Cocker; Buddy Rich Big Band; Little Richard; Moody Blues.

(August 15-18,'69) Woodstock Music & Art Fair: (Bethel, New York): Richie Havens; Sweetwater; Bert Sommer; Tim Hardin; Ravi Shankar; Melanie; Arlo Guthrie;

Joan Baez; Quill; Country Joe McDonald; Santana; John Sebastian; Keef Hartley Band; The Incredible String Band; Canned Heat; Mountain; Grateful Dead; Creedence Clearwater Revival; Janis Joplin & The Kozmic Blues Band; Sly & the Family Stone; The Who; Jefferson Airplane; Joe Cocker and The Grease Band; Country Joe and The Fish; Ten Years After; The Band; Johnny Winter; Blood, Sweat & Tears; Crosby, Stills, Nash & Young; Paul Butterfield Blues Band; Sha Na Na; Jimi Hendrix/ Gypsy Sun & Rainbows.

(Winter,'71) Chuck Berry: (Too High Club, Tucson, Arizona)

(10/2/'71) Moody Blues: (Arizona Coliseum, Phoenix)

(3/2/'72) Savoy Brown and Fleetwood Mac: (Salpointe High School, Tucson)

('72) Dr. Bop And The Headliners: Featuring Al Craven, "The White Raven;" (Mother Tucker's and The Nitty Gritty, Madison, Wisconsin)

('72) Willie Dixon: (Nitty Gritty, Madison,)

('72) Charlie Musselwhite: (Nitty Gritty, Madison)

(1/19/'74) Bob Dylan with The Band; "Planet Waves" Tour: (Hollywood Sportatorium, Hollywood, Florida)

(4/12/'74) Boz Scaggs: (Armadillo World Headquarters, Austin, Texas)

('74) Eagles: (Austin, Texas)

('74) Dr. John: (Austin, Texas)

('74) Willie Nelson: (Austin, Texas)

(7/18/'75) Eagles: (War Memorial, Syracuse)

(10/14/'75) Fleetwood Mac: (Loew's State Theatre, Syracuse)

(2/24/'76) Joni Mitchell with L.A. Express: (War Memorial, Syracuse)

(5/8/'77) Dizzy Gillespie: (Tampa Theater, Tampa, Florida)

(4/24/'78) David Bromberg and Maria Muldaur: (Landmark Theater)

(6/3/'78) Bob Marley & The Wailers; "Kaya" Tour: (Landmark Theater, Syracuse)

(11/'78) Albert King: (Austin, Texas)

(12/12/'79) Southside Johnny & The Asbury Jukes

(5/5/'80) Bob Dylan; "Slow Train Coming" Tour: (Landmark Theater)

(8/2/'80) José Feliciano: (Civic Center, Syracuse)

(11/17/'80) George Thorogood & The Destroyers: (Club #37, North Syracuse)

(4/25/'81) Santana: (Carrier Dome, Syracuse): (This was the first concert in the Dome)

(10/9/'81) Journey: (Carrier Dome)

(2/9/'82) Gil Scott Heron with Full Force: (Drumlins Country Club, Syracuse)

(8/9/'82) Santana: (SPAC)

(2/22/'83) Eric Clapton & His Band: (Brendan Byrne Arena, East Rutherford, New Jersey)

(2/24/'83) Neil Young; Solo "Trans" Tour: (Madison Square Garden, New York City

There were several trips to Saratoga in the summers for the Jazz Festivals; one was: The Newport Jazz Festival Series.

I have been as accurate as I could listing all these concerts; through ticket stubs, research, and memory. (I have a ticket stub for Beatlemania: Landmark Theater, for Friday, September 19th, 19--; ticket stub was torn.)

Syl and I loved to dance together: cool, fast, or slow. We danced down at Rocky's bar, the Bridge Street Tavern in Solvay, after our Western Ranch softball games; at weddings; at Chuck and Lynn's annual Halloween party, in their living room; at MPH's "Cabin Fever Relievers," with Big Tony's Band, at the Lafayette Country Club; other places with other bands at MPH auctions and functions: in the fall of 1993, the year before I started teaching at MPH, it was in the gym, with the Miss E Band; another year it was Ted's band, Timeline, at the Marriott; to Bruce, with Out of the Blue or solo; to Timeline; to bands in clubs in Charleston; to steel bands in the Caribbean; on our deck; on Gary and Patty's deck at their camp in the Thousand Islands; on Jacques and Caroline's deck in Saint-Lazare; and bopping around while listening to music in the car. I loved looking at Syl while we danced, how she looked at me, the clothes that she wore, and the sexy way that she moved her body to the music.

Now she couldn't even take long walks anymore. Life is not fair sometimes, and it definitely was not now for us, especially for Syl. But we still had hope. We were not giving up. Tish and Mary had invited us, with two other couples, to go on a European trip with them. This included going to Tuscany, where Syl had always wanted to go. She loved that movie, "Under the Tuscan Sun," with Diane Lane. I had always planned on taking her on a trip to Germany, to revisit her childhood city, Augsburg; and Munich, and the other cities, Würzburg and Zweibrücken; where she went to school. She could show me around and we could visit some relatives, who were possibly still alive.

      Tish and Mary had been on about twenty European trips together, including a few with their daughter, Laura. They had showed us slides of their trips to Europe, hiking up in the Swiss Alps, and their stay in Capranica, Italy, 36 miles north of Rome. The slides of them walking through the olive trees at "The Farm" looked like something right out of "The Godfather" movie. We always wanted to go with them, but they always went in September; when most of the tourists were gone, it wasn't quite as hot as the summer, and the prices weren't as high. But we had our jobs and couldn't just take a five week leave of absence and obviously keep our jobs.

      They had come over at the end of June in 2015 for a visit, leaving for a European trip the next day for ten weeks. The usual length of their trips was five weeks. I don't think we could have afforded the ten-week trip. If it had been the normal five-week trip in September and early October, there was a good chance that we could have gone. Syl had gone through the intense chemo treatments in November and December of 2014, and January, February, and March of 2015. And then the radiation treatments from late April through the first week in June. She now had her "Nordic look," with her very short, but curly, white hair and a tan; and wearing her turquoise earrings. She was getting her weight back, getting her muscle tone back, and swimming in the pool. She was getting herself ready for Ursula's two week visit after Labor Day weekend.

It's ironic that Tish and Mary decided that this was the year to go to Europe for ten weeks, instead of the usual five weeks. I don't think they will ever do that again. We were still watching Tom and Debbie's house, but we could have closed the pool three weeks early; they wouldn't have minded, saving them cleaning expenses. We could have still been here to monitor the house for the summer and to help Will move into a house with some friends the third week of August. This house was on the same street, Lancaster Avenue, near Syracuse University, as the house Sylvia was living in when I first met her. We could have had Ursula come up after the first week in August instead, for her two-week visit. I had been let go at MPH at the end of June, and had cleaned out all our Extended Day supplies during July, so I had no more obligations at MPH. I didn't start watching Ileana on a regular basis until the end of September, so I'm sure I could have made arrangements to start a week later. Syl was not doing any more treatments over the summer, (except for those chemo pills that she took the last week of July.) She could have extended her non-treatments for an additional two weeks. Who knows, maybe after five weeks in Europe, she might have stopped doing the treatments altogether when we got back. We'll never know. There was nothing preventing us from going to Europe, except for the reality of them leaving the last day of June, instead of the first days of September. The only thing we would have missed was the Steve Miller concert at the State Fair. As long as we were here, I'm glad that we went to it, but that certainly wouldn't have mattered if we had been able to go to Europe.

Now, fast forward to the end of May, 2016. Tish made the arrangements for us with the air fares, rooms, and van expenses. I paid him for everything and we now had this trip to look forward to. Syl had justifiable fears about her health, being in foreign countries if she should require medical treatment. I tried to keep her mentally strong and that this would be an exciting adventure, a once in a lifetime experience for us, one that we had wanted to do for years ever since we saw their slides from Capranica, Italy.

Syl was healing from her severe ankle sprains, her second fall since the end of April. In the middle of June, we started going over to the pool again. She was swimming and getting her legs moving, to help her circulation, to deal with the neuropathy. She was getting a tan, reading her books, and things appeared to be optimistic; as the previous summer of 2015 had been. We went over to Eric and Nancy's house on June 18th, where they had planned a wonderful birthday party for Syl. Their daughter, Sarah, and LeeAnne's son, Cole, had decorated the house and we had to break through the streamers they had put on the door leading from the garage into the house. LeeAnne, who had worked with us at Extended Day at MPH for a few years, was there with her husband, Glenn. There was wonderful food, drinks, and conversation. They had a special cake made for Sylvia.

When they brought out the cake and put it in front of her, Syl had her hands clasped together against her chest, a pose that signified that she was so happy, usually for someone else, that being the kind of person that she was. There is a picture of her when she was a little girl, with her freckles and her short bangs, looking like Heidi, in the exact same pose. And when they brought out the birthday cake for Tex's 80th birthday, she is in the picture with the exact same pose.

This cake was decorated with blue frosting and then white frosting all around it. On the top row: was a big smiling sun on the left side, and on the right side was a square that read, in three lines:

"Happy Birthday Sylvia!"

"You Are Our Sunshine!!!!"

("and friend, mentor, other mother...")

In the second row, on the left side: was a square with a small sun with sunglasses, blue sky and wispy clouds, palm trees, and waves. On the right side: was a square with blue sky and white clouds, ocean, and a young boy and girl holding hands on the beach. In the third and bottom row, on the left side: there was a sun, palm trees, and two sandals on the beach. On the right side: was a gigantic sun. Syl was overwhelmed by this and made her birthday a very special one.

I took Syl down to Upstate Hospital for her weekly chemo treatments. She had to wear the Neulasta patch for 24 hours to prevent infections and an unneeded extra trip back to the hospital. I would monitor it and make sure it had emptied before she could take it off. She would get a week off from treatments, barring any extra evaluations and consultations. We were going over to the pool until 3:30, when I had to go and pick up Ileana from her summer camps at MPH. I would drop Syl off at our house and then take Ileana home, walk Alexis, and wait until Traian or Ioana came home. Syl came with us a couple of times. We were still going out to dinner, usually at Kirby's, something that Syl always looked forward to. I had two weeks off when Ioana and Ileana went to Bucharest, Romania, to visit Ioana's parents, and Ileana's grandparents. I had started to play some golf again, I hadn't played since playing with

Tish in Maui in 2002; with Tish, Mary, and Steve. We would play nine holes at scenic Green Lakes Golf Course, walking this hilly course, putting our golf bag in a "puller," pulling them around. We would play, on average, twice a week.

So, this was our routine. Syl had lost her hair again, the previous fall when the treatments began again, and wore her wig when she went out. She still looked beautiful sitting around the pool in her bikini and swimming. I started watching Ileana again when they returned at the end of June. At the beginning of July, I noticed a change in Sylvia. She didn't feel like going to the pool. I understood it right after a treatment, but this was when she had her week off. I tried to convince her to go with me to the pool, even if she just wanted to sit in the shade under the umbrella and read. The fresh air would make her feel better and get her out of the house. Whatever sun she could handle, the Vitamin D would be beneficial for her. Swimming in the pool would be therapeutic, moving her muscles and helping her circulation. I told her that she could go inside and take a nap if that's all she felt like doing. I just wanted her with me and to know that she was safe. This was the best time of the year in Syracuse; sunny, hot and humid; after a long, cold, snowy winter and so many other days during the year of gray skies, rain, and limited sunshine.

I thought of all our vacations together: Tampa; Antigua; Virgin Islands; Mexico (2); Tucson; Cape Cod (11 & 3 softball tournaments); Charleston (5); Lake Placid (7); Old Forge (2); Nag's Head; Virginia (3); Thousand Islands (9); Letchworth cabin (4); Catskills; Toronto; Ottawa; Amelia Island; Delaware; Maui; St. Augustine; Orlando; Fort Myers; Kiawah Island; Myrtle Beach; New York City (3); Seaside; Winter Haven; Niagara Falls (2); Montréal (7). And all our day trips, and days at lakes, and walks in the woods, around Central New York. Wonderful days of boogie boarding, snorkeling, swimming, catching rays, eating lunch, reading, just the ultimate joy of being together.

    Syl did sit out on our deck with me, to watch the fireworks from the village of Manlius, at night on the Fourth of July. I knew things were not right with her when she didn't want to go out to dinner anymore. No matter what, even after, and especially after a chemo treatment; Syl *always* wanted to go out to dinner. Not now. I was beginning to worry about her, more so than I ever had. I would play golf a couple of mornings, or go over to the pool, just to keep exercising and to maintain my sanity. I had to take care of Tom and Debbie's house and pool anyway, as part of my job. I would shower and pick up Ileana at MPH, take her home, walk Alexis, wait until they came home; then the store and pharmacy. I kept in touch with Syl by cell phone, in case there was any emergency.

    In the middle of July, Syl had a really horrible week. On Tuesday, she had a chemo treatment and wore the Neulasta patch for 24 hours. On Thursday, they had noticed something and called her, and she had to go back to the hospital for a blood transfusion. On Friday, she fell again in the living room. This time we couldn't rationalize that her foot had fallen asleep, and it was a fluke, like the first time at the end of April. Or that she was favoring her right ankle, as it was weak due to her first fall, and fell and sprained her left ankle in the middle of May. It was now two months later, and she had rehabbed and healed, but it happened again. Another weekend of RICE: Rest, Ice, Compression, Elevation. They wanted Syl to come back on Monday for another chemo treatment, as the oncologist was going away on vacation. *It's always about what they need to do, not what the patient needs.* I realize that they have families and their own lives to live, I get it; but it always seemed that Sylvia's needs came after theirs were taken care of. I'm sure there are many other patients who feel this way. We should have taken that week off, but they said that she needed this treatment, so we were stuck between a rock and a hard place. We also had to go back to take x-rays at the orthopedist, to make sure nothing was broken, and luckily there wasn't.

    For the rest of July, Syl just stayed home resting and healing her ankle. She wasn't eating very much, just her Activia yogurt and maybe some toast. I made her a glass of my smoothie every morning. I would go play golf or go to the pool, shower, pick up Ileana, walk Alexis. I would give Syl half of what I earned each week, to make her feel that she was still earning a paycheck; trying to keep things as normal as possible. But they weren't.

    Syl was still reading as many books as she could and watching her favorite television shows: reruns of "Little House on the Prairie" and "The Waltons." They made her feel good, like reliving her childhood in some ways. She was glad to see me when I got home. She watched her shows at night and talked with Ursula every night on the phone for an hour or longer. Tex would call and they would talk frequently also.

    It was still wonderful to cuddle up with Syl in bed, although you had to explore your way through the many obstacles that Syl had in the bed: heating pad; hot water bottle; extra pillows, one that she put between her legs; four or five books, at least two of them hard covers; an extra comforter on top of the usual comforter, (that we both used in the winter), on her side; and another comforter on top of that, on her side, in the winter. She was so funny like that, with a cuteness about it also. You had a hard time being able to maneuver your legs sometimes.

On Monday, August 1st, the plan was for Syl to have a treatment and then another one on the 8th. She had seemingly recovered from that horrible week, again coincidentally, not doing any treatments for two weeks. She had gotten permission from the oncologist, after these upcoming two treatments in August, to take two months off from the treatments; to be able to go on this trip to Europe. I wanted this trip to happen for Syl so badly; she deserved to go back and see Europe after all that she had been through. And for both of us to have this experience together. Who knew what the future would hold when we got back? We knew we were facing some seemingly insurmountable odds, but if we could at least have the memories of this trip; that would give us more inspiration. So that was the plan. I wisely took out travel insurance through AAA; I really had no choice but to do so.

I took Syl down on the 1st and the nurse told her that she would only have to get this treatment today and not do the one on the 8th. This was good news. Just come back a week before leaving on the trip for some tests and a consultation. That good news, as usual, since the end of April, was short-lived. The oncologist had noticed something in her tumor marker and decided that he would no longer be able to give her any more chemo treatments. So now what? Tish obviously knew of Sylvia's situation and we had a deadline of August 15th to cancel our trip, so he could cancel our rooms and make different arrangements with the vans. I still was not giving up hope, but our chances of going to Europe were fading quickly.

They called Syl the next day for her to come back down on Thursday, August 4th. They wanted to see if they could place a metal stent, which would be inserted into the bile duct, to unblock this obstruction. Syl could never catch a break, it seemed never-ending. I took her back on the 4th. The gastroenterologists evaluated her and were ready to do the surgery the next day. But the anesthesiologist did not want to take on the responsibility, due to the fact that Syl's tumor was wrapped around blood vessels, and this would be a delicate procedure to put this stent in. They wanted her to stay for the weekend and they would figure out a different plan of action on Monday.

I went home that night and on Friday picked up Ileana from her last summer camp day at MPH, took her home, walked Alexis, and talked with Ioana and Traian about what had transpired with Sylvia. Ioana had her practice at Upstate and looked in on Syl frequently. She said she would visit her over the weekend and keep me posted. I always felt guilty not being with Syl every minute at her hospital stays, but sometimes they didn't want visitors there after hours; and Syl had to be monitored and didn't need my angst around sometimes. It was a fine line between love and support and not helping the situation by being "in the way."

On Monday, they found a new anesthesiologist who was willing to take on the responsibility. They made all the arrangements and preparations on Tuesday, and on Wednesday, 10th, proceeded with the operation. They had to do an endoscopy procedure, which Syl had done several times in the past, to place this stent. There were complications, as they couldn't get the stent where they wanted to, because of the enlarged tumor. They managed to get a temporary plastic stent in, but not as well a placement as they would have liked. This is what they told me when I went down there on Wednesday. Ioana was there talking with the doctors. They wanted Syl to come back in a week or two, so that they could position the plastic stent better, if they couldn't again attempt to insert the metal stent. I helped one of the hospital workers wheel her up to her room on one of those huge carts. She was groggy and her throat was understandably sore. They wanted to keep her a few more days for observation, and Syl felt safer being here under medical care, for a few more days. I had a television hooked up for her, always in all her hospital stays, so that she could watch her shows and also the Summer Olympics had started.

  I was picking up Ileana at the MOST camp in downtown Syracuse, at the Museum of Science and Technology this whole week, as the summer camps at MPH had ended. This would be the end of picking up and taking care of Ileana and walking Alexis, as she was going to the Lourdes Camp on Skaneateles Lake for two weeks; before they were all going to Cape Cod for a vacation, and then the start of her 7th grade year at MPH.

  I picked Syl up at the hospital on Sunday afternoon, August 14th, and brought her home. This had turned out to be an eleven-day ordeal for her. I had held out as long as I could, but I had to call Tish the next day on the deadline, to tell him that we were not going to be able to go on the European trip. I think he knew that this would be the case. Syl was not eating hardly anything, not reading her books, not even watching her television shows. She was just lying in bed, resting and recuperating. I think she was relieved that the European trip was cancelled, but obviously disappointed. One morning, she sat up in bed and exclaimed, "I just want my life back."

  I just found this note recently that Syl had written around this time:

"My soul is upset, trying to find new ways, my brain is in standby mode, daring to pose, people are all around but friends few, hanging here or there."

I found another note from her recently:

"The wisdom you possess is one of your many strengths, use it wisely and 'the beauty of you' will always shine through."

I felt so bad for her. Why Sylvia? One of the gentlest, kindest, nicest, sweetest people you will ever meet. A person who cared for others more than herself. A prime example of that was on the morning of Saturday, August 20th, when she told me that she felt bad that she hadn't gotten me a birthday card, especially being my 70th birthday. There is no doubt in my mind that she was probably thinking about this ever since she returned back home from the hospital. I told her not to worry about it, that she loved me and was home with me, and that was all that mattered to me. I looked at the birthday card that Syl had given me the year before, on August 20, 2015; when things were really improving for her.

'Dust,'

"Thank you for

all you do for

me. I don't think

there is a better

husband than you!"

"I love

you very

much!"

"I couldn't do this

without you!"

'Syl'

    I thought of all the birthday dinners that we had for both of our birthdays, for thirty-three years. Getting dressed up, Syl doing her long hair, wearing a pretty outfit, turning heads as we walked in the restaurant. Talking, ordering, laughing, enjoying a delicious dinner and glasses of wine. Taking a stroll after dinner, driving home, later holding each other close in bed and being intimate with each other; *and knowing that there was no other place in the world that we would rather be, than in each other's arms.*

    I always felt guilty and worried about leaving her for a few hours during the day. I still played golf a couple more times in the morning, wanting to say good-bye to Tish and Mary; as they were leaving to visit their daughter, Laura, in Philadelphia, for a week before going on the European trip. I still had to go over and clean the pool and do my chores at Tom and Debbie's the other mornings that week. And go to the store and the pharmacy on the way home. I would spend the rest of the afternoon and evening just lying there with Syl, holding her gently. I would let her rest in the evening and go in my room next to our bedroom and watch some of the Summer Olympics. It was still nice to be able to sleep in the same bed with my beautiful wife, the love of my life.

But I was getting more and more concerned and worried about her. She was taking a lot of pain pills and her eyes had a yellowing around them, probably jaundice from a malfunctioning liver. I don't think that the stent was really working effectively. Her breathing started to get heavier and more shallow. Ioana had frequently asked me what I would do when faced with this situation. They always knew what the inevitable outcome would be. I always responded that I didn't know, I guess not wanting to deal with this reality. I always hoped and prayed for a cure, that things would miraculously turn around for Syl; but in the back of my mind, I feared the worst. I did my best to keep her positive, to keep her hopes alive, to care for her, and always be there for her, and be strong for her; no matter what the odds that were stacked up against her.

We woke up on Wednesday morning, August 24th, and I looked over at Syl, whose breathing was labored overnight and I said to her,

"I'm sure if I help you get ready, then I can take you down to the Emergency Room. I know that you don't want to go there, but I think we should. If you don't think that you can make it, I'm going to call 911. Okay?"

Syl said, "Okay."

I helped her up, and being the lady that she was, she wanted to clean herself up. She hadn't been able to take a shower since she had been back home from the hospital. She sat on the side of the bathtub, while I held her shoulders, and took a washcloth and soap and cleaned her private areas the best that she could, and then I dried her off. She brushed her teeth and managed, with my help, to get dressed. She held onto me, as we went out the sliding glass door off the dining room onto the back deck.

There was no way I was going to attempt to take her down the 12 steep stairs from the dining room down into the basement and risk a fall. There are only 3 small steps off the deck onto the back lawn, which we navigated with no problem. If we fell from there, it would be on soft grass. But we didn't, and I got her in the car, which I had pulled out of the garage earlier. We left around 2 o'clock in the afternoon, the last time Syl would ever be home. I didn't know what was going to happen on the way to the Emergency Room. Neither did Syl. We made it somehow, and the ER people came out and put Syl on a stretcher and took her inside.

    They had to wrap Syl up in an insulated and windproof hypothermia bag, called a "bear wrap," as her body temperature was so low, bordering on hypothermia. They told me it was a good thing that I brought her down when I did. It didn't help that they had the air conditioning blowing at full blast. I had shorts on and I was freezing in there. I realized that it was a hot and humid day outside, but it felt like the North Pole in there. I kept asking the nurses until they eventually turned the blower down. It was still freezing. A nurse came by and asked if Syl wanted some jello and a turkey sandwich. A male nurse was attending to Syl, with the usual blood tests and monitoring her temperature and functions. He was being relieved at 6 o'clock and admonished whomever had given Syl the jello, as it was cold, the last thing that she needed. She had only taken a spoonful and never touched the sandwich. It was after 11 o'clock, after I had been sitting beside and talking with her, for over 8 hours, when they took her from there up to the Intensive Care Unit. They had stabilized her temperature and she was falling asleep. They told me that it was okay for me to go home, they had my number to call me if needed.

I drove home in a complete daze, now knowing that unless a miracle occurred for Syl, that she was never coming home to me again. I can't possibly tell you how sad and painful this is to write, to relive all this, three years and five months later. I just feel Syl's complete story must be told, her courage in facing all these challenges, must be memorialized. She deserves that much. I still held out a glimmer of hope, that maybe this stay in Intensive Care would make a difference in another attempt at placing the metal stent where it would be effective. But that was beyond wishful thinking on my part.

My only focus was now going down to the hospital. I went down the next day to bring what Syl had asked me to bring for her: her phone and charger, a bag of extra clothes, her white fleece hat for her head that she wore in bed, her soft red velvet blanket, and her soft white terrycloth robe. I stayed all afternoon and night, beside her, talking with her, until she fell asleep. Her eyes didn't look as yellowish and her body temperature was getting closer to normal.

I always had to park the car in the parking garage when I went down there, walk across the street to the hospital; then wait in line to check in, go through the check-in procedures, go through security, find the correct elevator to take me up to the correct floor, then find the correct room that they put her in. Late at night, I had to get my parking ticket stamped at the front desk, walk to the garage, find my car, stop at the exit gate and sometimes have to pay something; and then drive all the way home, with my mind in a dense fog, and staring into the glare of the oncoming car lights. Friends started leaving food in styrofoam or regular coolers on my back deck. I ate a few things here and there, but I didn't have much of an appetite.

I put the frozen items in the freezer, some things I later ate; but eventually I had to throw a lot of things out.

This was my routine now. Every day and every night. After three days in ICU, Syl was transferred to another unit on another floor, which I had to find when I arrived on August 28th, and she was no longer in her room. That scared me. She had her own room now. A young Indian doctor and his team came to talk with us. He came right out and asked if we wanted to give our permission to DNR, (Do Not Resuscitate), if it came to that decision. He said if they were going to resuscitate her, they would probably have to break her ribs in order to do so. I looked at Syl, and we both agreed we didn't want that happening.

So, he goes through all the protocols and informs us that Syl probably only had six months to live. How many hundreds of times have you heard a doctor say that a patient will never walk again, or never play a sport again, or talk again, or come out of a coma, or have only so many months left to live? And some of these patients beat the odds and prove the doctors wrong in their predictions. Even with this optimistic approach, I thought that his prediction was generous, considering the survival time of pancreatic cancer patients. Anyway, after all this, he says,

"So, you *don't* want the DNR?" (Geez, does this guy have wax in his ears or what?)

This is how they make mistakes in hospitals, with wrong surgeries, on wrong body parts; *because they are not really listening.*

"*Yes, we want the DNR.*" We signed the papers and got that resolved, (hopefully.)

A couple of more days in this unit and they transferred her again. Once more, the anxiety of not finding her in her room and having to find her in a different room in a different unit. This time she had a roommate, a very nice black woman, probably Syl's age, maybe a little older, with a curtain in between them. I had talked to a young Indian woman doctor before I went up to see Syl and she informed me that Syl had about two weeks to live. Wow! From six months to two weeks, in a couple of days, it was shocking to say the least.

Maybe the first doctor was way too overly optimistic. This was our new reality. Two more days in this unit and they transferred her to the "Comfort Care" unit; which basically means they are not giving you any more treatments, only intravenous fluids and pain medications, to keep you as comfortable as possible. In blunt terms, your days are numbered, it's just a matter of when. This was on September 1st, and I had to find her again; this unit was on another different floor and tucked in the back corner.

I reluctantly took a ride out to Maurer Funeral Home in Liverpool, to discuss arrangements and terms for the seemingly inevitable conclusion I never wanted to face. They had known our family forever, and had performed services for everyone. I had to discuss all the options and costs, something you never wanted to deal with. I met with the hospice people at the hospital. They were very nice and looked in on Syl for some spiritual care. But I didn't like the religious overtones of it and neither did Syl. I even arranged for a woman from the Francis House to come and see Sylvia, where they evaluate the situation and see if the patient can come stay there. You are not in the hospital, you are able to live out your final days with dignity, with people in similar circumstances; where they have home cooked meals, spiritual guidance, and you can sit on benches looking at the beautiful flowers and gardens. It sounded like a good idea, but it's a small house and a space has to become available.

I was there beside Syl for 8, 10, sometimes as much as 12 hours a day. I wouldn't get home until 2 o'clock in the morning, bring the food inside that was put in coolers on the back deck, and try in vain to go to sleep. How could I sleep when I knew what Syl was going through?

I went over to the pool for a few hours in the late morning over Labor Day weekend, September 3rd, 4th, and 5th; to clean and maintain the pool and check on their house. I sat in the sun for a while, listening to my iPod, trying to maintain some semblance of sanity. I took a couple of swims for exercise, knowing I couldn't be there to help Syl, if I allowed myself to get sick. I showered and changed and went to the hospital, following the usual routine when I got there and when I left.

They were giving Syl morphine, so her pain must have been really bad. They also gave her Ativan. I always talked with the nurses and doctors about what was going on. Now this doctor that I talked with only gave her a few days to live. Syl was kind of out of it sometimes with the morphine, but would just come up with some great lines in moments of clarity.

One time, she sat up and looked at me and said, "Want me to make the coffee?" That was Syl, always thinking about someone else before herself. She would grind the whole bean coffee every morning into freshly ground coffee. We used to do Taster's Choice for many years, before they stopped making their whole bean coffee. Then we went to Eight O'clock coffee from then on. I still drink this today. I like the Columbian Peaks, but I don't grind the beans, I just buy the ground version. Syl looked so cute when she asked me that. Tears are pouring down my face when I am recalling these things. But I feel that I must keep going, finishing our story, honoring Syl's legacy.

There was a small sink in the corner of her room, with a mirror over it that you could see from Syl's bed. She had told the nurses that she had seen rats over there. The nurses told me that seeing them was a common sight with patients on morphine, having hallucinations. Syl said to me, looking over by the sink,

"Why are all those people dancing over there?"

The next day, out of nowhere, Syl sat up and exclaimed,

"Well, time to rock 'n roll!"

We both got a big laugh out of this. This was the first time, in a very, very long time, that we had laughed out loud together. It felt really good. I thought of all the laughs and funny stories and silly scenes and jokes that we had shared with each other for over 33 years. When Syl said this, it was such a profound moment for us; it was like the "Juicy Fruit" moment with Mom at the Iroquois Nursing Home in November, 2006. (It was hard to believe that happened almost 10 years before. Now it has become over 13 years ago.)

I had to adjust Syl's fleece hat, as it would slide down over her forehead. She originally had these two small tubes in her nose for oxygen, but then some nurse replaced them with this mask with two straps. If the straps were pulled too tight, they would pinch her cheeks, making them all red and put creases in her face. If they were too loose, they would wind up down around her neck, serving no purpose. This was a constant challenge to get the straps just right.

Syl sat up, attempting to get up, saying that she had to go to the bathroom really badly. One of the doctors had ordered her catheter removed, for no apparent reason, at least not as far as Syl was concerned. She had this small plastic bedpan under her, that definitely looked uncomfortable and cut into the back of her legs and her behind, leaving deep creases. The nurses thought that she was being delusional, imagining that she had to pee, as there was only a small trickle in the bedpan. You could tell that Syl was in agony; that feeling that we all get when we have to pee and can no longer hold it in. She kept trying to sit up, with all these tubes hooked up to her, as I held her shoulders.

"You are such a good husband."

"Thanks honey, but I'm not a nurse."

I got one of the nurses to finally listen to her situation. She agreed with me that the plastic bedpan was not the most comfortable thing in the world. She had to call the doctor, who had given the orders to have the catheter removed, to fax over permission to put the catheter back in. Meanwhile, Syl is somehow holding it in, in total agony. The first nurse attempted to put the catheter back in, with no success. Then another nurse came to help her, again they couldn't get it in. Then a male nurse came to help those two, but the three of them couldn't get it in. I couldn't believe that Syl was being subjected to this, on top of everything else that she was going through. Finally, the head nurse, somehow, and it wasn't easy, got the catheter back in. They were all amazed when Syl filled up the entire bag within minutes. She knew, contrary to what everyone else thought, what she was feeling. She could relax now and that stupid bedpan wasn't cutting into her anymore.

When the doctor came in later, I told him that there was no reason to remove the catheter in the first place; unless there was a situation of an infection or something like that. I told him that what my wife had to endure did not fall under the definition of "comfort care." He agreed with me and was going to bring this situation to the attention of other doctors at their next meeting. I hope that he did, so that another patient, in a similar set of circumstances, would not have to go through what Syl had to go through.

The next day, Syl again tried to get up, saying that she had to pee really badly. Now the nurses were skeptical, thinking she was just imagining this, as she now had the catheter back in her. Well, it turned out that the lines from the catheter to the bag had gotten twisted and crimped, thus not allowing the catheter to function correctly. I discovered this, as I was trying to find out what was wrong. They untwisted the lines and Syl filled up the bag again in a matter of minutes. As usual, Syl was right and knew what she was talking about. The nurses didn't doubt her anymore after this. That is why it is vitally important for patients to have someone, other than the medical personnel, there with them to advocate for them. I know Syl was thankful that I was.

It was Labor Day and I looked at Syl, hooked up to all these tubes, lying in a hospital bed; thinking about all, thirty-four of them to be exact, the Labor Day weekends that we had spent together. The thirty-three before this one had found us somewhere by a pool, a lake, or an ocean. Starting in 1994, when both of us together, began teaching at MPH; this would be the last day of summer vacation before driving home to begin the week of teachers' meetings at school. Many Labor Day weekends were at Cape Cod; one in Lake Placid; one in the Thousand Islands region in Gananoque, Canada; one in New York City; and the others were at: Cazenovia Lake; Eaton Brook; Skaneateles Lake; Southwick Beach State Park; or by the pool.

    Now we are trapped in this hospital room, looking out its windows at the sun gleaming off the buildings outside. What happened? What did we do to deserve this? Obviously, and especially, Syl. Did the angels need to take her so soon? I am grateful for every second that I had with Syl; I wouldn't trade it for anything else in the world. But nothing seemed to make sense anymore.

    As I watched Syl just lying there in this hospital bed, I had a flashback of a teacher at MPH. Jim L. was the Chair of the World Language Department, and taught Latin, Greek, and French for 38 years; from 1968 until his retirement in 2006. Mom always had the highest respect for him. We really liked Jim and he was fond of us. A couple of years before his retirement, he had open heart surgery. They had to split open his chest. We went down to visit him in the hospital, right after the high school graduation ceremonies in the middle of June. We went up to his room and he was on a lot of medication. We were all dressed up: me in a suit coat & tie, yellow dress shirt, dress pants and shoes; Syl in a pretty dress and shoes, and necklace. We had good tans. We visited with Jim for a while, and could see he was very tired and told him that we were going to leave.

    "Jim, we are going to leave now."

He healed and recuperated over the summer, and when we saw him again, when school started after Labor Day, he came up to us and confided to us:

"I was convinced that both of you were angels and coming to take me to heaven. You both looked so beautiful. I honestly thought you were my guardian angels."

It was now Tuesday, September 6th. I kept staying until way after midnight, sometimes until 2 o'clock in the morning; just watching Syl sleep. Ioana had returned from her family vacation in Cape Cod, and would come and look in on Syl and visit with her. She got rid of that breathing mask, and put the original two tubes back in Syl's nose, which was much better and more practical. I told Ioana about that catheter incident and she couldn't believe or understand it. She said she would definitely make sure that they followed up on their review of this. Todd, a doctor and MPH parent, came in a few times to look in on her. LeeAnne and Nancy came down to see Syl, but she told the nurses that she wasn't up to it. I think she wanted to, but felt embarrassed. An MPH teacher, with his two daughters, came to see Syl, unannounced and without permission. I think he thought he was doing a nice thing, but Syl did not want people, other than me, Ioana, and medical personnel, to see her like this. Especially his two daughters.

I had to deal with all the phone calls; Tex wanted to come down to see her, and Syl told me to tell him an emphatic *no.* The first week of this 16 day stay, Syl could talk with her mom on the phone. After that, I had to hold the phone to her ear when they talked. Now she couldn't even do that. Ursula wanted to come up. I realized that there is no greater love than a mother's for her child, and her ache must have been excruciating; made even deeper, as she had lost her middle daughter and Sylvia's sister,

Debbie, on April 27th, 2012. She was three years younger than Sylvia, and didn't quite make it to her 56th birthday. And losing her partner, Ben, of over 33 years, on February 4th, 2014.

But I was trying to convince Ursula to have the beautiful memory of Syl, when she came to Syracuse for two weeks in September, 2015; and to not have the haunting memory that she would have if she saw her now. She was being defiant, and said she was coming anyway. I talked with Karen, Sylvia's sister, who had been living with Ursula in North Charleston since June; to explain to her that I was trying to do the right thing. Ursula thought it over for a day, called me and apologized. I understood, the sadness and frustration creates anger. Every night I would return back home, 2 o'clock in the morning, bring in the food; realizing that not only would Syl never be returning home, but that I was going to lose her forever, at least on a physical plane.

Wednesday, September 7th, another afternoon and evening awaited me at the hospital. I spoke to this different doctor, one with absolutely no bedside manners whatsoever. As I mentioned before, it should be required viewing for all medical personnel, especially doctors, to see the movie, "The Doctor," with William Hurt. He was unfamiliar with Syl and I had never seen him before. He looked over her chart and history and matter-of-factly told me that she could go tonight. I wished I could have done something to this guy, to teach him a lesson, but I didn't know what. I felt like asking him,

"What if that was your wife lying there?"

But I didn't.

I sat next to Syl on the bed, looked deep into her eyes with mine, trying to convey all the affection, devotion, love, and respect that I had for her, and said,

"*I love you.*"

She knew what I was trying to capture, a lifetime full of wonderful experiences and undying love; and she answered,

"*I love you back.*"

I followed that up by saying,

"*I love you back to back.*"

I don't know, it just came out in this moment of uninhibited and unrestricted love. Our eyes met, and we laughed at this and hugged each other, a poignant moment that we both realized encompassed our love toward each other; a moment that will be sealed within our hearts forever. *I will never forget this moment as long as I live.*

Thursday, September 8th, I had to drive out to Honda City in Liverpool, in the rain, to get my windshield wipers fixed, as they were not working correctly. Another long afternoon and night awaited me at the hospital. Around 6 o'clock, Mary, our doctor friend, and the one who had let us stay in her timeshare in the Disney World Resort in April, 2003, came in to visit Sylvia. She had just come back from visiting her daughters in Europe; the same little girls that used to ride on my back, as if I was a dolphin. She said a prayer for Sylvia and gave her a kiss on the forehead. She squeezed my hand and then left.

I had an uneasy feeling about today. I had been as strong as I could be for Syl, at least when I was with her, for the past two years. I looked at her, and I could not hold it in any longer.

I told her, "That if she felt like letting go, if she wanted to go to her secret garden, that it was okay."

I said this as I put my head on her lap and started crying. She held my head and told me it was alright to cry. She was always thinking about someone else rather than herself. *She told me that everything was going to be okay.* After that, she would kind of fade in and out with the morphine going in her. I thought about spending the night in the chair beside her bed, but she was sleeping soundly and seemed to be at peace. There was an infomercial about these CD's from the 60's & 70's, with parts of songs being performed by the original artists: The Mamas and the Papas, Crosby, Stills, & Nash, Simon & Garfunkel, and many more. I put the remote on the pillow next to her ear, gave her a kiss, and decided to leave for home. I got back at 2 o'clock in the morning, brought in the food in the coolers from the deck, and got ready for bed.

I was just lying there, staring at all the framed pictures we have on our bedroom walls from our travels, when the phone rang. This was the home phone that we had kept, even after getting cell phones at least three years earlier. I wanted to get rid of the home phone, but Syl wanted to keep it for medical calls and appointments, which she was right about having this backup insurance. The home phone rang at 4 o'clock in the morning, the call I was dreading, and didn't want to answer, but I did. It was a woman doctor with a thick Indian accent, and it was hard to understand her.

"Is this Charles Heer?"

"Yes, it is."

"I'm calling to tell you that your wife, Sylvia, has just passed away at 3:45 this morning."

Silence on my end. She seemed very business-like in informing me about Syl.

"So, she is donating her eyes, is that correct?"

Dumbfounded on my end.

"No, that is not correct. There is no record of that request from her. So, no, please do not do that."

"Okay."

Now I think that donating your organs is a noble thing, and has given a new lease on life for millions of people; but I never heard anything about this from Syl. There was nothing in her will about this, there was nothing on her driver's license about this, she had never told me anything about this request; and she had two years to let me know about it, and never mentioned anything about this. If she had, of course I would have honored her request. But since there was none, I just felt that Syl had gone through enough; that it was time to leave her alone and to let her rest in peace. Plus, I don't know about eyes, but I wouldn't think someone's organs could be used when they have been subjected to chemotherapy and radiation for almost two years. I hate to think this, but I think that this doctor was maybe trying to orchestrate this donation on her own. Maybe not, but it seemed strange.

I called the funeral home immediately after this call and they picked up Syl at the hospital and transported her back to the funeral home. It was a good move that I had gone out there the previous week to make all the arrangements, although I obviously didn't want to.

I also asked him to get Syl's white fleece hat and red velvet blanket from the front desk. I had taken most of Syl's things, including her phone, back home with me in the previous days.

    I went back to bed and just stared at the framed pictures of us on the bedroom wall. There are twenty-one of them: nine on one side of the mirror over my dresser, nine on the other side, one under the mirror, and two on other walls. On the left side, top row: Half Moon Bay, Antigua, & Cramer Park Beach, St. Croix, Virgin Islands; second row: Makena Beach, Maui, & Napili Beach, Maui; third row: Bowman's Beach, Sanibel Island, & Head of the Meadow Beach, Truro, Cape Cod; and fourth and bottom row: Myrtle Beach, South Carolina, & Kiawah Island Beach, South Carolina, & Seaside Beach, Seaside, Florida. On the right side of the mirror, top row: overlooking the Mayan Ruins, Tulum, Mexico, & Mayan Ruins, Uxmal, Mexico; second row: Grand Canyon; third row: top of Whiteface Mountain, Lake Placid, & Letchworth State Park; fourth row: "Deadman's Point," Green Lakes State Park, & Haleakalā National Park, Maui; fifth and bottom row: National Aquarium, Baltimore, & "The Needle," Iao Valley State Park, Maui. Directly below the mirror is a picture of us on our honeymoon at Nags Head Beach, Nags Head, North Carolina. On a small wall to the left, next to the bathroom, is a picture of us at Nauset Beach, Cape Cod. On the far-right wall, high above a bookshelf, is a picture of us at the Lake Placid Hilton in Lake Placid. I put these pictures up by 2008, with the side pictures a few years later. This is what Syl was looking at when she was just lying in bed for ten days from August 14th to the 24th, before I took her down to the Emergency Room. This is what I was looking at now, and have been ever since.

I called Karen and Ursula, giving them the sad news. They had a family picnic and set off some balloons in Sylvia's honor. I called Julie, and Marty, and Tex & Erna with the sad news.

I drove out to Liverpool to the funeral home around 1 o'clock in the afternoon. I had to go over all the business things and pay all the expenses, and pick out cards. I decided to have the services at their other funeral home in Baldwinsville, which was a good decision. The one in Liverpool, where all our family services had been held; was in an older house, built in 1927, and had a musty smell to it. This is where Mom's had been on December 13, 2008; and there were so many people that they had to set up folding chairs in a small room adjacent to the main room. Plus, they had a tiny parking lot in back, so most of the people had to park out on the street.

The one in Moyers Corners, Baldwinsville, was bigger and more modern. Although originally built in 1980, they had made many updates to it; and it had a huge parking lot in back. I brought a multi-colored Oriental vase, that Syl used to put a plant in, for her urn; as she chose to be cremated. I have chosen this as well, and when my time comes, I have instructed Julie to take both of our ashes and mix them together; spreading them at Green Lakes, by her bench at the end of Round Lake; and maybe some at Cazenovia Lake and Skaneateles Lake as well.

I spent all afternoon there. I then had to write an obituary for Syl, a shortened version that went in the Post-Standard newspaper on Monday, September 12, 2016. This took a couple of hours, while they processed all the documents, and did all the things that they had to do on their end. I did the best that I could, having had no sleep, and being in a numb and shocked state of mind.

(Actually, I forgot to include Letchworth and Maui, so I'm including them now. Also, a few revisions from the original, which I have corrected now.)

Sylvia Ursula Angeli Heer

Sylvia Ursula Angeli Heer passed away on Friday after a courageous battle with a long illness. Our angel was born on June 18th, 1953, in Augsburg, Germany. She was a beautiful woman, both inside and out. She was an unselfish person, always thinking of others first. She was a voracious reader and loved animals, nature, taking walks around Green Lakes, and traveling to many places with Dusty. Her favorites were: Cape Cod; the Caribbean; Charleston, SC; Letchworth; Lake Placid; Maui; Mexico; Montréal; and Watkins Glen. Sylvia had many jobs: bank teller, receptionist at supply companies, working in hospitals and veterinary offices; before finding her true calling, teaching. She taught Kindergarten at Manlius Pebble Hill School for twenty-three years, and along with her husband, Dusty, as Co-Directors of the Extended Day Program. She cared for and nurtured thousands of children. Sylvia was predeceased by her stepfather, Arthur Pine; her sister, Deborah Pine Hibbs; her other stepfather, Benjamin Culpepper; and her sister-in-law, Linda Luques.

Sylvia's memory is left to cherish by her husband of over thirty-three years, Charles "Dusty" Heer of Manlius; her father, Gunter "Tex" (Erna) Angeli of Montréal; her mother, Ursula Ruth Pine of Charleston, SC; two sisters: Karen Ann Pine of Charleston, SC; and Caroline (Jacques) Filkin of Montréal; three brothers: Erik (Heather) Pine of Beaver Dam, Kentucky; Robert (Beata) Angeli of

Edmonton; Ronald (Lorraine) Angeli of Ottawa; a brother-in-law, Martin James Heer of Phoenix, Arizona; a sister-in-law, Julia Ann (Thomas) Chamberlain of Williamsburg, VA; Linda's husband, John Luques of Newport Beach, OR; and many aunts, uncles, nieces, nephews, cousins, and in-laws from: Arizona, California, Canada, Georgia, Germany, Massachusetts, New York, Oregon, South Carolina, and Virginia.

Sylvia saw the beauty and perfection in all living things. Her spirit will live inside of us forever.

I finally completed this and they now wanted me to view her body, to take as much time as I needed, before they sent her out to the cremation place. There she was, my beautiful wife, the love of my life, the answer to my dreams; just lying there with her arms folded across her chest, *lifeless*. She had a very peaceful look on her face, a hint of a smile on her lips. I sat with her for a while, talked with her about how much I will miss being with her. I kissed her on her forehead, which was cold to the touch. Then I felt *this presence*. Maybe I was imagining it. Maybe I just wanted it so badly. But I swear I could feel her floating outside her body, which she had now escaped. Forever. It was such an eerie, *yet totally harmonious feeling;* a feeling that I have never felt before or since. I saw this vision of Syl, and it was almost as if she was speaking these words to me:

"Death is nothing at all. It does not count. I have only slipped away into the next room. Nothing has happened. Everything remains exactly as it was. I am I, and you are you, and the old life that we lived so fondly together is untouched, unchanged. Whatever we were to each other, that we are still. Call me by the old familiar name. Speak of me in the easy way which you always used.

Put no difference into your tone. Wear no forced air of solemnity or sorrow. Laugh as we always laughed at the little jokes that we enjoyed together. Play, smile, think of me, pray for me. Let my name be ever the household word that it always was. Let it be spoken without an effort, without the ghost of a shadow upon it. Life means all that it ever meant. It is the same as it ever was. There is absolute and unbroken continuity. What is this death but a negligible accident? Why should I be out of mind because I am out of sight? I am but waiting for you, for an interval, somewhere very near, just round the corner. All is well. Nothing is hurt; nothing is lost. One brief moment and all will be as it was before. How we shall laugh at the trouble of parting when we meet again!"

-Henry Scott-Holland (1847-1918): was a Priest at St. Paul's Cathedral of London and a Professor of Divinity at Oxford University.

I could hear the soft sound of Syl's voice speaking these words to me. I can only hope that one day, the day I will see her again; that I can shout to the high heavens: "Truer words were never spoken!"

I left there at 5 o'clock and sat in the car in their back parking lot for a while. The directors were leaving to go home, waiting for me to leave. I think I saw the vehicle from the crematorium pull up to the back door. I drove back to the house, a place I knew would never again be called *our home*.

People saw the obituary on Facebook and started posting what they were feeling. Marty posted:

"I want to express just how proud I am of my brother. He lost his wife Sylvia yesterday, after a battle against cancer. I feel it takes tremendous courage to fight against this disease. I hope that I am not confronted with this type of decision. I don't believe I would go through with the treatments. I have tremendous respect for people that do fight and never give up, like Sylvia. My brother was there every step of the way. It was only Dusty and Sylvia going through this daily battle. Two people as one. I know that on my wedding day, even though I was only 20 years old, that I took the vows we say before God, very seriously. My brother kept his promise to love and hold, in sickness and health, until death do us part. He lived that promise every day of his and Sylvia's marriage. There is a movie with Graham Greene and Jon Voight titled, 'The Last of His Kind.' Graham is the last surviving member of his Indian Tribe. Jon runs a school to westernize Native Americans. Graham is very despondent because in his religion when one dies a member of the family sings the spirit to the 'other side.' Since Graham was the last of his kind, he feared he would never be reunited with his loved ones in the spirit world. Jon Voight was mainly the heavy in this movie and eventually, and unexpectedly, becomes the one to sing Graham over. My brother was there to sing the love of his life over. He shouldered the burden of fighting this disease with Sylvia every inch of the way. Dust, I love you, and I so admire how you dealt with this entire awful ordeal. I pray that Sylvia finds her Tuscany above, and I am so sorry for your/our loss."

Ashley K. posted: "Sylvia Heer, I remember the first time I met you. It was my first year at MPH, and my first time at Extended Day. I was in second grade, and afraid to talk to people. It was you who pushed me and encouraged me to express myself and make friends. I knew that I always had a friend in you, and that I could always come to you for any reason. And I will always remember being so excited to come see you and Dusty at

Extended Day after school to play 'Pigs.' The world has truly lost an amazing person, rest in peace, Mrs. Heer."

Melina posted: "Dusty, our deepest condolences. What you and your beloved wife Sylvia did for our children is immeasurable. We are so saddened by her loss. We still have a tough time telling our son. Know this: she is in a place where she has no pain. I cannot say a better place because that would be with you. Hang strong buddy, luv you."

Beata posted: "Just a few short years ago, a phone call from Sylvia to Montréal changed our lives forever. In her 50's she met her dad & discovered that there were also two brothers and a sister that she never met, Bob, Ron, & Caroline. The first time we met Sylvia & you, it was like we knew each other all our lives! You were a perfect fit to complete our family. Bob & I so enjoyed our road trip from Montréal to Québec City, our times at the country house, & our relaxing times at Tex & Erna's. The conversation just flowed like we knew each other a lifetime. It is unexplainable why Sylvia was taken from us so soon, but I'm confident there is a different plan for her now, she is helping all the little children in God's garden like she did on earth. We cherish our short time together; may she continue her journey in heaven & may you find some comfort in the fact that she is no longer suffering. You were her rock & she was your soulmate. We will all meet again on the other side & build the biggest fire in the garden, where we will roast marshmallows & have a few beers."

'Love you Dusty'

Abby posted: "Heaven truly gained a beautiful angel. I am so blessed I got to work with Sylvia and Dusty, as in our time we grew close, we were a team. This news shatters my heart. Sylvia was a beautiful and soft soul, so gentle and kind. She didn't deserve what happened to her. At least your pain and suffering has come to an end. I'm so sorry, Dusty. God bless."

  Alexus posted: "So sad to hear about the passing of my dear friend Sylvia Heer. I found this card she gave me on our last day working together at Extended Day. The tone and wording truly capture what a kind and thoughtful person Mrs. Heer was. I only wish that our phone calls, texts, and visits had not been so few and far between in the past year or so. Still, I am so fortunate to have known her. See you in Paradise, Sylvia."

  Colin posted: "Rest in peace to one of the most kind-hearted and loving women ~ Mrs. Heer, you were so incredibly loved and will be missed dearly. Thank you for everything you did for me, and for my family throughout the years. We love you always!"

  Keith posted: "I remembered with Cheryl today how when Devra was in Pre-K and at Extended Day, she didn't talk much to a lot of people, but always wanted to just sit on Sylvia's lap at the end of the day."

  Erica, Sylvia's sister Debbie's youngest daughter, posted: "I will miss you Aunt Sylvia Heer. I'll miss our long talks, our laughs about things only we could understand about our family, our beers on the beach. I will miss our talks about books, and your long hugs. I will miss your sweet kind words and ALWAYS positive attitude telling me no matter what in life, everything was going to be ok. I know you aren't in pain any more, I just can't understand why it had to be you. I wish I got to see your beautiful face one more time down here. It was an honor to be your niece. I will miss you."

There were many more tributes. I could go on and on, but you get the essence of how much Sylvia meant to students, parents, family, and friends; and how deeply she influenced their lives with her kindness and gentle spirit.

I went over to Tom and Debbie's house a few days later to go over the details of a Go Fund Me site that Nancy had organized and was posting on Facebook. Nancy was there, along with Debbie, Caroline, and Cheryl. The contributions to honor Sylvia came from far and wide: MPH families, parents and teachers; guys from the softball teams; close friends. It was truly amazing. It paid for all the funeral expenses, which was an incredible blessing for me; and to be able to donate to some causes in Sylvia's name.

I had made arrangements for Syl's services to be held on Friday, September 16th. The calling hours would be between 3 and 5 o'clock; and the services between 5 and 7 o'clock. I had to make many phone calls now and send many emails. I had to go buy poster boards and put them together, taking pictures out of our photo albums, making sure all the different families were represented. Then figure out which framed pictures I would take, wrap and place them in a plastic bin. Get my suit coat, dress shirt, dress pants, dress socks & shoes, and a tie picked out.

Julie was flying in from Virginia and would start off the services and introduce me. Kathy, "Eff"'s wife, asked if she could speak after me. But the calling hours ran long and they had to leave, as "Eff" was getting tired. He was fighting his own battle with cancer over the same years as Sylvia. Tex was going to drive to Ron's house in Ottawa from Montréal, and leave his car there, as Ron would drive them to the services. They would return to Ottawa around midnight; Tex would spend the night at Ron's, then drive back to Montréal the following morning. Erna said she just couldn't handle it and was not coming. I'm sure Jacques and Caroline had to work, maybe they could have left early and driven Tex to Ron's and come to the services; but for whatever reasons, they didn't make it. Bob and Beata were too far away in Edmonton, as was Marty in Arizona, Tom and Debbie in California, and all the families in Oregon.

Ursula was originally going to come. She needed to pay for hers and Karen's plane tickets and the car rental. I had a free place for them to stay at Tom and Debbie's. And Karen would be able to drive, (Ursula never had a driver's license), and help her walk, as she was having problems with her hip. I don't know, I'm not going to judge anybody. Ursula was so adamant about coming up when Sylvia was in the hospital; when it was uncertain how long she would be there and to have a haunting image in her memory. When it was definite that they weren't coming, I asked them if they wanted to say something about Syl at the services. They did and texted me what they wanted to say and I read both of theirs at the services.

During that week, I was going over to the pool and thinking about what I wanted to write and what I wanted to read at the services. I went down to the Manlius Public Library several times and made many copies of all these poems, sayings, and songs that I planned on reading. I took a long walk around Green Lakes one day, such a strange and sad feeling without Syl walking by my side.

On Friday, the 16th, I had my juice, two spoonfuls of honey, coffee with Natural Bliss creamer, a banana, and smoothie; shaved, showered, and put my dress clothes on. Then I loaded the bin with the framed pictures, the poster boards, and all the things that I was going to read. I arrived at the funeral home at 2 o'clock, and Nancy had volunteered to meet me there and help arrange the framed pictures and poster boards, which she did. Luckily, it was a beautiful and sunny day, at least as far as the weather was concerned.

There were at least 500 people who showed up that day to honor Sylvia. They kept coming in waves, it was an overwhelming tribute to her. Julie was just hanging out, meeting and talking with Tex and Ron, and making sure everything was going as planned. I was by myself to greet and talk with everybody. People kept bringing me bottles of water, putting them on the little stand next to one of the big soft chairs in the front row, below the podium. I probably needed to drink some to avoid dehydration, but I abstained, as I didn't want to have the feeling of having to take a pee when it became my turn to speak.

I was always afraid of that when I gave my fifth-grade graduation speech at the end of the school year at MPH. On the flip side, by not drinking water, I faced the real possibility of having severe cramps in my hamstrings, which could easily happen to me by being dehydrated. The poster boards were placed up front to the right of the podium, and there were flower arrangements some people had brought, along with the Oriental Vase containing Sylvia's ashes.

Close friends were there: Steve & Donna, Chuck & Lynne, "Eff" & Kathy, Craig & Leslie. Ioana and Ileana were there. There were guys from softball with their wives. From the Merchants: Tony & Anne; from the Cyclones: Vern & Carolyn, John H. & Ro, Gels & Patty, and Mel, who had just driven in from a tournament in Cape Cod. There was Nick D., with his girlfriend and his two daughters, Meghan and Justine. Syl and I used to hang out with them at the Camillus Pool when they were little girls. They are all grown up now. Nick lived on the bottom floor at Clyde Avenue, and told me about the availability of the second floor of that house; where I was living when I first met Syl, and the first place that we lived together. We played together on softball teams: Snafu All-Stars, Schaack Fabricating, and Western Ranch; in many different leagues through the 1980's and into the 1990's. And Karl, who played and was the sponsor of the Schaack Fabricating teams, and was a close high school friend of Marty's at Nottingham. Nabil, a regular in our weekly pick-up basketball games at MPH, and on other basketball teams, was there. I hadn't seen him in at least 20 years. There were hundreds of parents, students, and teachers, from MPH; and many other friends and families. It was a truly amazing outpouring of love for Sylvia.

It was getting close, about 10 minutes before 5 o'clock, when the son of the director came up to me, and wanted me to speed up the conversations and begin to wrap it up. What was I supposed to do? Not greet and talk to all these people that wanted to express their feelings to me about Sylvia? He wanted to start the services and the people waiting in line could greet me after the services. *I don't think so.* What, did he want to get going, to go out on a Friday night?

It would not have been fair to all these people who had been waiting for hours in the line for calling hours. A lot of them weren't planning on staying for the actual services, they just came for the calling hours and had plans for their Friday night. Julie was trying to appease him, but he kept coming up to me, reminding me of the time the services were supposed to start. My friend, Craig, overheard this and we were getting annoyed at his, in our opinion, unreasonable request. We related to him Jim Valvano's speech at the March 4th, 1993 ESPY awards, when they started playing the "time to wrap it up" music. Jimmy V. basically says,

"Yeah, I've got tumors all over my body, and I'm worried about this guy trying to tell me to wrap it up. Va fongool!"

There were no religious overtones in the services: no priests, ministers, or rabbis; no organ music or hymns to be sung. The funeral home did have some piped in music in the background. The services were just Julie speaking and then me. After that, several people gave testimonials. The services didn't start until 6 o'clock, but instead of the allotted 2 hours, they only lasted 1 hour and 15 minutes; so they were over at 7:15, instead of 7:00. Big deal. All that aggravation for nothing.

I received a survey a few weeks later, and I gave the funeral home high grades and recommendations, in answering all their questions; but under comments, I told them about this situation about the time, and in future situations like this, they needed "to go with the flow." This is a one-time event, one that you hope you will never have to deal with; but if you must, it needs to be done the right way. *I know that we did it the right way.*

Julie went up to the podium and started off the services.

"Thank you all for joining us today as we celebrate the life of Sylvia Ursula Angeli Heer. I am Dusty's sister, Julie, and Sylvia's sister-in-law... As you know, Sylvia was such a gentle spirit... She was a lover of animals, nature, and children. Everything she did, she did with grace~ from planting a garden to decorating her home.

She was a ray of sunshine, always spreading light and love. She was simply lovely through and through... She and Dusty had a beautiful relationship and life together. Sylvia was devoted to her family and loved them dearly... She and Dusty taught at MPH for over twenty years, and touched the lives of so many children, their parents, and the staff. She was well loved and loved well. She will be deeply missed by all who knew her."

"I would like to share a couple of poems and the following story of the caterpillar and the butterfly, all of which reminded me of Syl."

Julie shared the story of the caterpillar that leaves her family and doesn't return, leaving the caterpillars wondering what has happened to her; and why she hasn't returned. The caterpillar has now turned into a beautiful butterfly and realizes that she can't return to the caterpillars down below, who are munching on milkweed.

"At least I tried, but I can't keep my promise to come back and tell them where I went and why. Even if I could go back, not one of the caterpillars would know me in my new body. I guess I'll just have to wait until they become butterflies too. Then they'll understand what has happened to me and where I went."

And the butterfly winged off happily into its new world of sun and air.

Julie also read the poems "After Glow" and "Remember Me." We hadn't planned it, but "After Glow," by Helen Lowrie Marshall, was the poem that I had picked out to put on the back of the laminated remembrance cards of Syl; with nature scenes on the front.

Then she read "Remember Me," by Anthony Dowson.

Julie finished with, "Dear God, please remember those who have left the meadow and those of us who remain... Dusty would now like to share some poems and thoughts with you, and then open it up to those of you who would also like to share a remembrance of our dear Sylvia..."

I then went up to the podium.

"Thanks Jul, that was beautiful."

"Ursula, Sylvia's mother, and Karen, her sister, couldn't make it here today from Charleston, South Carolina, and asked me to read for them what they texted me what they wanted to say."

From Ursula: "To my sweet darling daughter Sylvia: You were my first born and it's hard to accept that you are gone. Never in my lifetime, thought you will be taken from me so soon.

As I look at your pictures, every day my heart aches that I will no longer have our nightly phone calls. And your visits to Charleston. My two weeks that I had with you last summer will be cherished in my thoughts and heart, but most of all your presence.

Your smiles, your goodness, your caring for others, will be missed. For you are a wonderful daughter and friend to all. You were an angel on Earth. Know you rest in peace, my daughter. God picked a perfect angel. I will love you forever. Your Mom. Here you go......"

From Karen: "My sweet sister Sylvia. My words can't express how I feel right now. Knowing that

I have not lost one sister, but two, has just been overwhelming. It's all kickin' in.

We had great times when I lived in Manlius, and not so great times, but I will cherish them all. I will not forget our nights watching TV and you calling to see if I am watching the sci-fi station. Then spending time talking and getting scared together and then laughing at how silly we got.

Our last visit together will not be forgotten. Folly Beach and the Mexican restaurant. Had some good laughs and the margaritas helped. And visit me in my dreams, 'cause you said you will.

So, my sister Sylvia, rest, you deserve it. I love you and will miss you."

I tried my best to read them as they would have read them themselves. I could feel their pain as I read them. I'm crying now as I write them down.

"I would now like to read some poems, sayings, and songs that I have chosen. The first one is 'On Death,' by Kahlil Gibran."

I then read two passages from my Native American Wisdom book. The first one is from Rina Swentzell, Santa Clara Pueblo:

"What we are told as children is that people when they walk on the land leave their breath wherever they go. So, wherever we walk, that particular spot on the earth never forgets us, and when we go back to these places, we know that the people who have lived there are in some way still there, and that we can actually partake of their breath and their spirit."

The second passage is from Wovoka, Paiute, (His vision of the Ghost Dance revival, 1889):

"When I was in the other world with the Old Man, I saw all the people who have died. But they were not sad.... It was a pleasant land, level, without rocks or mountains, green all the time, and rich with an abundance of game and fish. Everyone was forever young.

After showing me all of heaven, God told me to go back to earth and tell his people you must be good and love one another, have no quarreling, and live in peace...."

I then read seven of my own poems, (that I have included in this book): A Silent Life Within; Reflections of a Crystal Vision; Born to Ride the Morning Star; Wherever Freedom Flies; Cloud Dancers; Blessing in Disguise; and Once in a Blue Moon.

I started to read the poem that I had written a few days before. I had held it together pretty well up until this point, not looking out at all the people very often. As soon as I announced the title, For Sylvia, and started to read the first line, I lost it for a few minutes. I told them that I knew that I was going to lose it when I started reading this poem. I gathered myself and continued on.

When I think of you

I remember the sweet taste

Of your lips kissing mine

Your kindness and selflessness

Engulfing all those who knew you

Your elegance and grace

Following you wherever you go

Your gentle spirit

Guiding me once again forever more

When I see you

I see your reflection

Shimmering in the deep blue ocean

Within the endless ebb and flow

Of the ever changing tides

Where all life began

As we walk hand in hand

Upon the cool wet sand

Feeling universal harmony washing over us

When I think of you

I think of the connection

Of all living things

The perfection in nature

Flowers and plants and trees

Mountains on high and valleys below

    Rivers silently flowing

    To their ultimate destination

    The secret garden that you now tend

I see you

    Waterfalls cascading behind you

    As you whisper in the wind

    You are now free

    Floating above me

    With your eternal light

    Brightly shining

    Showing me the way

    Back into your waiting arms again

    This is so painful to relive again. But somehow, someway, it makes me feel closer to Syl. I then read three quotes about death.

    From an Irish headstone: "Death leaves a heartache no one can heal, love leaves a memory no one can steal."

    "Whoever said that loss gets easier with time was a liar. Here's what really happens: The spaces between the times you miss them grow longer. Then, when you do remember to miss them again, it's still with a stabbing pain to the heart. And you have guilt. Guilt because it's been too long since you missed them last." -Kristin O'Donnell Tubb, (The 13th Sign)

"I am always saddened by the death of a good person. It is from this sadness that a feeling of gratitude emerges. I feel honored to have known them and blessed that their passing serves as a reminder to me that my time on this beautiful earth is limited and that I should seize the opportunity I have to forgive, share, explore, and love. I can think of no greater way to honor the deceased than to live this way."   -Steve Maraboli

(I wish I would have discovered the "Death Is Nothing At All" poem before; and I would have read it at the services. But I didn't, so it is what it is. At least I discovered it to include in this book.)

Then I read the words to two songs. The first one was "In My Life," from The Beatles' Rubber Soul album, written and sung by John Lennon:

It started to get to a point while reading this, that I was almost singing it. If I was playing an acoustic guitar and had a decent voice, I would have sung it. When I got to the verse at the end, I was getting close to singing it and getting choked up doing it. I believe if I would have asked the people to join in with me singing, that they would have. They were right on the verge of doing so anyway.

The second song that I read was "All Things Must Pass," written and sung by George Harrison, from his debut solo album of the same name:

I then took out my ocarina, a small flute in the shape of an orca whale, from my suit coat pocket and played it for a minute or two. I had also played it at the end of my speech at Mom's services. It gives a feeling of a

Native American Prayer Ceremony, honoring those who are leaving us to join The Great Spirit, at least that is what I was trying to convey.

When I was finished, everybody gave me an ovation, which was nice. That meant that I must have done a good job in honoring Sylvia, but I sure wished that there was no reason to do it.

I sat down in the big soft chair in the front and could finally drink some water. Nancy came over by me and said some beautiful words. Will went up to the podium and told all about how we were like second parents to him and all the things that we did together. Cheryl got up, put her hand on my shoulder, and said some beautiful words. I commented, "I guess I've become the podium now." Caroline got up and stood behind me and said some beautiful words. Abby went to the podium and spoke about how we had become a strong team at Extended Day. Joe stood up where he was seated and spoke about how we had cared for his sons, and that you couldn't talk about Sylvia without including Dusty, and vice versa. Don went and stood near me, explaining that he had just returned from an MPH varsity soccer game; Don being the coach for over 40 years now. He spoke about how he remembered when MPH won their first state soccer title, that Sylvia and I bought the first tee shirts that went on sale commemorating that achievement. Sarah, Eric and Nancy's daughter, stood up on the other side of the room and spoke about how we were second parents to her growing up. I think Suzette spoke also. I can't remember anyone else speaking. Maybe there was. If I forgot anyone who did, I apologize; because it's not easy to speak in front of so many people, especially when it is so emotional to do so.

I went back up to the podium and introduced Tex and Ron. Tex told me later that he regretted not going up to the podium and saying something about Syl. I think he felt shy about his German accent and not knowing hardly anyone there except Will, now Julie, and me. I told him that just making the effort to drive down from Canada was enough.

    My close friends came up to me in the front after the services. Steve told me there was a woman sobbing throughout. That was Ioana. She came up to me, as well as Ileana, who was very sad, and we all hugged. I had a bag full of things for Tex to bring back with him: a couple of Syl's watches for Erna; a framed wedding picture of us, (that he keeps on a nightstand by his bed); a small wooden keg to put a plant in, two wooden plaques that Ursula had found in yard sales and given to Syl; one said "Willkommen," (welcome in German), and another one with a German saying on it, to put in the country house at Paradise Lake. I said good-bye to them and told Tex to bring back for Erna the flowers he had brought. I told Donna to take a flower arrangement up to hers and Steve's camp in the Adirondacks. Nancy and LeeAnne took some and I told anyone who wanted an arrangement to take them, I didn't want to bother with them. Nancy helped me gather up all the pictures and poster boards. I put them in my car and then carefully put the Oriental Vase, with Syl's ashes, in the car. I talked with Julie and Deb, a close family friend, in the parking lot for a while, and then left for home. I wanted to get the vase and the pictures and the poster boards back home safe and sound.

    Nancy posted: "Hundreds of Sylvia's and Dusty's friends and their families were there this evening to give tribute to Sylvia's life of compassion and giving. She will live on through all she has touched. Most touching were tributes from the small children they cared for who are now young adults. We and I will miss you always Sylvia. The harvest moon shines for you."

Julie posted: "Today we put my sister-in-law, Sylvia, to rest... My brother, Dusty, did a beautiful job at her service... He shared several meaningful Native American poems, Kahlil Gibran writings, poems he had written and one in particular that he wrote to her during this past week... Heartfelt and heart wrenching... Amazing tributes were shared by parents, students, family and friends acknowledging the numerous contributions of both Sylvia and Dusty. We were all so blessed to have her in our lives and will miss her presence every day."

I entered our dark, and now lonely house, and carried the vase up the basement stairs, and placed it on a wooden stand, next to the television in the living room, where it has been ever since. I brought the poster boards up and then the framed pictures. I began to put the pictures back where they belonged; when I was by the shelf next to the fireplace, I got too close to the brick frame around the fireplace and whacked my big toe on my right foot. I knew I had done a number on it, figuring it was definitely going to be a major contusion, like when you seriously stub your toe. I went into the bathroom to check it out, and I had severely sliced it in the middle of the toe, very close to the bone. It took a while to stop the bleeding. I put some antibiotic ointment on it and wrapped it up. Just what I didn't need to happen to me at this time. I didn't think that I deserved this. It took weeks for it to heal. Still have a scar there. *But the scar upon my heart will never heal.*

I went out on the back deck to gaze up at all the stars in the clear night sky. There was a full moon, the Harvest Moon, as it illuminated the backyard. To the right of the deck, covering almost the entirety of the right side of the back lawn, was a white-winged horse, like Pegasus. I hadn't had anything to drink. This was not like when you look up and see cloud formations: seeing a dragon, an elephant, a lion, whatever; this was a perfectly formed and shaped white-winged horse. And not a result of the moon's shadows or anything like that. I was not imagining this. Yeah, I was exhausted and emotionally overwhelmed after this long day, *but this was real.* I swear by this and it is something I had never seen before and I have not seen since.

Julie came over the next day and we hung out together for the rest of Saturday afternoon. Then we went out and had dinner at Kirby's. She flew back to Virginia the next morning.

The autumnal equinox started, the *first* event of the many *firsts* that I was now about to encounter without Syl; after doing them with her for over 33 years. Then the *first* Columbus Day weekend without her; the *first* Halloween; the *first* Veterans Day weekend; the *first* Thanksgiving; the *first w*inter solstice; and the *first* Christmas; being alone without Syl to share them with me.

I took my walks around Green & Round Lakes, such a strange and empty feeling, seeing the colors starting to change, knowing that my life was also changing forever; not experiencing it and sharing it with Syl anymore.

Wardie and Christie were in town, visiting from California; and called me on Tuesday, October 4th, to offer their condolences. It was good that I had kept the home phone, as they did not know my cell phone number. They came over and we talked for a couple of hours, and then they said they needed to get going to meet "Eff" and Kathy for dinner. I asked if they didn't mind if I came, and they invited me along. We went to Pascales at Drumlins and had a nice dinner. I felt like the "fifth wheel," as I have ever since. It wasn't their fault, they made me feel wanted and welcomed, it's just the way it is. Two days later, on Thursday, October 6th, there was a big reunion get-together on "Eff" and Kathy's deck, where all these reunions over all these years took place. Everyone was there, with lots of great food, drinks, music, and conversations, as usual. Syl would have loved to have been there, which she was for all the previous ones. She always told me she could visualize "Eff" dancing around the deck, with the Bee Gees' "One " song playing, his head bobbing up and down to the music, with a wry grin on his face. She liked that.

      Tish and Mary pulled up in their truck, next to the side of the deck, as Tish leaned out the driver's window and said, "Is this the toll booth?" They had just returned from their five-week European trip on Tuesday night, the trip that Syl and I had planned to go on. They had sent pictures on Facebook when they heard about Syl, raising a glass in her honor and toasting her. I was really sad when I saw this. They had flown back into Philadelphia, which they always do on these trips; to stay at Laura's for a week, before driving back home to Orlando. They decided to take the four-hour drive, stay overnight at a hotel, in order to attend this reunion. It was a great decision, as it turned out this was the last time that they would see "Eff." Everybody came and hugged me, talking about and missing Syl. Sometimes it was awkward. I understand, I would probably react the same way. I took a walk around Green lakes on Columbus Day, the 10th; with Wardie, Christie, and Emily, Wardie's brother, Jim's wife.

'Dear Dusty,'

"It is so difficult to know what to say to you at this time. I knew the impossibly sad day would come when we would have to say goodbye to Sylvia. I hope she knew--and I want to be sure that *you* know--that she (and you) were so important to Graham, Emmy, and me. You both looked after them so well, with such kindness and creativity, that they truly enjoyed their after-school hours and I felt supported knowing my children were cared for in the best way possible.

I remember Sylvia telling me about her joy and wonder at finding her father, forging that relationship, and discovering a new family. I remember her visiting me in the Campus Shop. And I remember when you both moved into your sweet house. But mostly I remember her style, her grace, and her enduring love for the children and families of MPH; and for *you*.

Emmy, Graham and I are better for having known Sylvia. I am so deeply sorry that her beautiful life was cut short. We send you our love and our heartfelt condolences."

-'Catherine, Graham, Emmy'

'Dear Mrs. Heer,'

"We have had many fond memories of Lower School, and 90% are in Extended Day. What you must put up with every day, with the screaming children and frustrating parents. We're sad to leave, never again to play pool with Dusty or fall on the playground or pick dandelion bouquets, but of all the things we'll miss, we'll miss you the most."

'With all our love, Rebecca L.'

I spent the rest of October and most of November taking walks around Green & Round Lakes and Pratt's Falls; doing work and looking after Tom and Debbie's house; yard work at this house; sorting all sorts of things.

Trying to get some sleep, but I was almost afraid to go to bed, always knowing that Syl would not be there to hold me tight. I kept hoping that she would appear in my dreams, that she would somehow show me that she was at peace; that she would be waiting for me.

I wrote a poem to Sylvia, hoping she could hear what I was trying to convey to her.

Still Waiting For Your Signs

I'm still waiting for your signs

Was it the white-winged horse

On the lawn

The night of the harvest moon

The silence is deafening

The hole in my heart

Is widening

Everyone can see through it

How it has been ripped apart

There is no magic cure

To repair this neverending ache

No magic wand

That will bring you back

Into my arms once again

Still waiting for your signs

The depth of my love for you

Has gone even deeper

Than I could ever imagine

I miss you more than you'll ever know

More than I could have ever known

Can you see my loneliness

Can you feel my pain

Do you understand

My life will never be the same

Without you with me

In my life

Full of emptiness

I keep thinking

Maybe this is all a bad dream

We will wake up tomorrow

Everything will be the way it was

Not the way it is

Still waiting for your signs

Please help me

I'm having a hard time

Holding on

I'm not finding a purpose

To carry on

Not being able to experience

The joy in life

Unless I'm sharing it with you

It has all become a blur

A cavernous void

A freefall with no way

Back up this ladder

They took away the steps

Made them invisible

You taught me so well

You taught me kindness

How to open up my heart

Truly open up my heart

I need you to show me

The way back home to you

Still waiting for your signs

They say it happened

For a reason

I'm hard pressed

To find one

To find any

Struggling to rationalize

Why they stole you away

Like thieves in the night

From me

Way too soon

I feel I'm the luckiest man alive

To have met you

To have you say yes

To be my wife

To have you share

Over thirty-three years

Over half of your life

On this earth

With me by my side

You were my destiny

The greatest thing to ever happen

To me

You have been my partner

My best friend

My wife

My lover

The love of my life

For all eternity

Where can I go

When half of me

Can't be there with me

Still waiting for your signs

I wonder all the time

What's the point anymore

They say it's the journey

Not the destination

Sometimes I feel

I wish I could join you

My mortality

Comes sinking into view

But I know I must hang on

Stay for a while more on this earth

To honor your legacy

I think you would want me to

I can't help but wonder

If this had happened to me

Not you

I would trade places

In a minute

But then you would

Have to endure this pain

This loneliness and sadness

I would not wish

Upon you

Turns your world

Upside down

Binds you inside

Like a twisted knot

A twisted fate

Still waiting for your signs

They say you don't know

What you've got

Until it's gone

That's not true for me

I knew what I had

An earth angel

The gem of all gems

Beautiful inside and out

A shimmering diamond

On an ocean of blue

Life will never be as wonderful

As it was being with you

Those are the cold hard facts

Stark reality

Ultimate truth

You were always wiser than me

Now I am left

To figure it all out

Pick up the pieces

Of this timeless puzzle

Decipher the unknown code

Unlock the forbidden door

Still waiting for your signs

No one can ever steal

Our memories that we shared

No one can ever deny

Our undying love

For each other

No one can ever find

The secrets that only we know

About each other

Every day

Every night

I pray you will wait for me

I don't know what else to do

It all seems so meaningless

Here without you

Still waiting for your signs

Longing for your tender touch

Your soft kisses

Your sweet smile

Your playful laughter

Your elegance and grace

Your caring and gentle ways

You always looked out for me

Now it all eludes me

Our sand castle dreams

Shattered into endless pieces

Our chance to fly

Grounded with broken wings

My mirror shows no reflection

Escapes into the other side

Where a vacuum of nothingness

Awaits with no reply

No answers

Still waiting for your signs

Visit me in my restless sleep

I see your face

In the pretty flowers

Your bouquet engulfs me

I see you flying

Like a dove in the morning mist

Reach out your hand to me

Guide me through the abyss

I am not far behind you

I don't want you to fade away

Disappear beyond the horizon

I don't even want

To end this poem

But I will for now

I can always

Begin another one for you

When I want to

When I need to

Still waiting for your signs

I was constantly going down to the Manlius Library and making copies of my poems and other writings and documents. I sent this poem to Bob & Beata, John, Julie & Tom, Karen and Ursula, Marty, Eric & Nancy, Steve & Donna, Tex & Erna, Tish & Mary, Tom & Debbie.

I sorted through some photo albums that Sylvia's sister, Debbie, had sent up years before she passed away. They contained pictures of the three sisters when they were growing up in Germany, when Ursula was a young mother and hanging out with her friends. Debbie had secured the pictures with staples in these albums, I guess that's the way they did it in those days. It was a painstaking process, (and painful for my fingers), to remove these old and rusted staples from every single picture, but I did it. I kept a few childhood pictures of Sylvia by herself, and some other pictures of her, through the years before I met her. The rest I sent to Ursula, as she would appreciate them and know the people in Germany. And they would get passed down eventually to Karen. I sent Karen any pictures of Art, her father. I sent them packages containing these pictures and also framed pictures of the sisters, when they were very young with Ursula. I sent them jewelry that was Sylvia's: pearls for Ursula, and a pair of Syl's favorite abalone shell earrings for Karen; among many more necklaces, earrings, and rings. I found a ring that Ursula couldn't find, that she thought she might have left on one of her visits. It was from Ben and it meant a lot to her. She was happy when I tracked it down. I also sent her the white fleece hat that Syl wore to bed and in the hospital. She hung it on her bedpost. I also sent Karen some beach hats and tee shirts that were Syl's.

I was constantly going to the Manlius Post Office and paying for these packages and also packages that I sent up to Canada for Tex and Erna. Erna wanted me to send her a ring that her mother had given to her and that meant a lot to her. That's how much she loved and thought about Sylvia, that she had given her mother's ring to her. Actually, it was included in the rings that I had sent to Ursula, when I was trying to send her the ring she had left here, with her description. Once that was resolved, I had to describe Erna's ring and have them send that back to me. Erna was happy to get her mother's ring back. There was also a gold medal on a gold chain from the 1976 Montréal Olympics, that Ron had given to Tex at that time; and Erna had put it around Syl's neck, when we first met in the middle of July, 2008, and said to her, "Welcome to the family." I sent that along with the ring and Tex was happy to get it back.

Eric and Nancy invited me over to their house for Thanksgiving dinner. Syl and I had gone there for Thanksgiving the year before, in 2015. They had their family and Nancy's sister, and a professor and some foreign students from Syracuse University. There was wonderful food, drinks, and conversations; *but there was no Sylvia.*

Traian and Ioana had also invited me for Thanksgiving, but I had already committed to go to Eric and Nancy's awhile before they invited me. Instead they invited me for dinner at Bonefish restaurant the following evening. I got ready and went down to the Post Office to put some bills and letters in the outside mailbox. Usually I would pull up to the mailbox in the car, roll the window down, and put the mail in the slot of the mailbox. There was a newspaper coin box nearby, so I parked the car and told myself if there was a newspaper available, I would get it. If not, I wasn't going to worry about driving around looking for another newspaper coin box or a gas station that had a newspaper. I got out of the car, put the mail in the mailbox, and walked over to see if there was a newspaper.

There is a big tree close to that newspaper coin box, that I've seen plenty of times in the past, that has some big branches sticking out from it. You can easily see them during the day, but now it was totally dark out. I put the coins in the slot, got the newspaper, and as I turned to go the car, I walked directly into one of the branches that were sticking out, a severe poke into my right eye. I knew that I had really hurt myself. I got in the car and checked it out in the mirror. My eye was bloodshot and bleeding. I couldn't believe it. This was two months and a week after I had sliced my big toe the night after the services. I had to stop at the bank to take care of some business. I drove to the bank, a few blocks away, and I asked the manager how did my eye look, explaining to him what had happened. He said it did not look good.

I still drove over to Bonefish and went inside and waited for them. Everyone seemed to be staring at me. Traian, Ioana, and Ileana finally came and we sat at a booth. In the light, they now saw my eye. They were very concerned, not only as friends, but both being doctors as well. Ileana had a horrified look on her face when she looked at me. Somehow, I managed to eat my delicious dinner and drink some wine, but my eye was hurting and also getting black and blue under it. They said that I needed to go to the Urgent Care place. I really didn't want to have to go to the Emergency Room and hassle with that, unless it was absolutely necessary. I stopped back at their house, as it was on the way, to give them some jewelry and other things that were Syl's, that I had brought for them.

Then I drove, basically with one eye, to the Urgent Care place on the outskirts of Manlius. They were closed for Thanksgiving and the Friday after, which was today. It was past 11 o'clock now, so I figured I would just go home, try to sleep, and go to Urgent Care the first thing in the morning, when they were open again.

    I got up early and drove to the Urgent Care place by 9 o'clock Saturday morning when they opened. Everybody else must have had the same idea, as it was packed with people needing medical attention. It's a small place, but there were a lot of people ahead of me, and I had to wait three hours to be seen, missing the first half of the televised SU basketball game. The doctor checked me out, putting this dye in my eye to see if there was a hole in the cornea or the retina. Fortunately, there was not. He diagnosed the injury as an eye subconjunctival hemorrhage, when small, delicate blood vessels break beneath the tissue covering the white of the eye. He prescribed some antibiotic eye drops. The Urgent Care visit was $45 with my co-pay, and I had to go to the pharmacy and get the eye drops, $12 with my co-pay. So, $57 for a newspaper, that I now couldn't read anyway. My eye healed up three weeks later.

    Steve wrote me a letter. (I had to correct some of his spelling, and clean up some punctuation; which he will readily admit was necessary. But by doing so, this does not diminish, rather it enhances, his words of passion and wisdom.)

    "I read your poem sent the other day. I wanted to take some time before responding. I was saddened at the thought of you standing on the corner of Heartbreak and Despair. Looking into a pothole of unfulfilled dreams. Tumbling and cartwheeling into a deeper cavern. A trick box of trap door feelings, a quicksand of endless emotions where the skylight above seems light years away. When every lyric of a song rips at your heartstrings, swelling you up with an ocean of teardrops. Especially now when joyful and smiling faces at this celebratory time of year for most, seems at the moment such a distant shore. With the dwindling light of shortened winter days unable to guide you to a safe harbor. All this compounded by the uncertainty of World News and the political climate and national negativity leaves us in a puzzled disbelief. Even your refuge of escape into sports, where every buzzer beater on TV or TD dance blaring from the tube seems a meaningless blur. Well-meaning friends who search for words of comfort seem like mirages of voices spewing out tired clichés. Dusty, perhaps the measurement of one's pure love for another can only be measured by the depth of one's freefall into the unknown void you now experience. Know this my old friend and Brother, you will emerge from this time of Darkness and Uncertainty. You will bask in the sunlight again. Aglow in the memory of your Soulmate and 'lover of life.' Your sweet Sylvia would have it no other way. She would have insisted upon it. Then the sign you ask from Her will be revealed in everything that breathes and blossoms in life. Sylvia touched so many things and brought a gentle kindness into the World so starved for love and understanding. You must continue that Legacy."

'Your Concerned Loving friend, STEVE'

It's a good feeling when you know that you have friends who care about you.

I bought the new CD by Barry Gibb, "In the Now." This was his second solo album, the previous one was "Now Voyager," released in 1984. His two sons play on this with him. Thank you, Barry, for stayin' alive, and creating an album that touched me deeply. When I listen to song #6, "The Meaning of the Word," it resonates to the core of my soul. From the first time that I heard it, and anytime I play it, I can't stop my tears from flowing.

This song reminds me of Syl so much and gets to me every time I hear it.

2017

April 24th: Installed the Bench Plate for Sylvia's Bench at Green Lakes, (end of Round Lake), Fayetteville, New York

August 1st: Memorial Brick put in at the Fayetteville Memory Garden, Fayetteville, New York

September 1st - October 5th (European Trip)

    Italy

        Capranica

        Civita di Bagnoregio

        Arezzo

        Pienza

        Santa Severa

        Toscano

        Narni

        Rieti

        Rome

        Trevignano on Lake Bracciano

- Corfu
    - Glyfada Beach
    - Downtown Corfu and Port
    - Halikounas Beach
    - Paleokastritsa Beach
    - Agios Spyridon Beach
    - Paleokastritsa Caves Boat Tour
    - Kassiopi
    - Perithia
    - Agios Gordios Beach
- Albania
    - Sarandë
    - Himarë
    - Berat
    - Gjirokastra
    - The Blue Eye
    - National Park of Butrint
    - Ksamil
- Greece
    - Igoumenitsa
    - Syvota

Ornella Beach Resort

Dodoni

Ioannina

Aristi

Metsovo

Vergina

Kalambaka

Meteora

Delphi

Athens

October and November: Green & Round Lakes; Mill Run Park; Pratt's Falls

November 29th: Installed the Bench Plate for Sylvia's bench at Mill Run Park, Manlius, New York

It was now a new year. A new reality that Sylvia would not see this year, unless she was somehow viewing it from the spirit world. I went over to Tom and Debbie's house for their annual New Year's Eve party. It was not a big one as it used to be in the past. Just a few friends and families, all of them missing Sylvia. This was the *first* New Year's Eve without Syl, not being there to kiss and welcome in the new year with me. It was the first *New Year's Day* without Syl, as I watched the college football bowl games. Syl was never a football fan, she just couldn't see the attraction. Not like she could watch SU basketball, especially when we went to the Dome, and could enjoy going to the Ernie Davis or VIP rooms with Tom and Debbie's tickets; she looked forward to that.

This reminds me of a story about a teammate of Dad's on the Syracuse University football teams of 1936, 1937, and 1938: Wilmeth Sidat-Singh. Syl and I had gone up to the Carrier Dome on February 26, 2005 to see the Syracuse vs. Providence basketball game. They were going to retire Sidat-Singh's #19 basketball jersey at halftime of the game. We went to the Ernie Davis room with Tom, Debbie, and Willie before the game for food and drinks. There were a few of his teammates there, invited to be part of the ceremonies. They were all in their late 80's now. Dad would have been 88 and 2 months, being born on December 19, 1916. I went over to them and asked them if they remembered my dad, Charlie Heer. They said,

"Charlie Heer, of course we do. He was a helluva player."

I introduced myself and Sylvia, telling them that Dad had passed away on May 14th, 1986. They were sorry to hear this. About three-quarters of that 1938 team, including Sidat-Singh, had passed away in World War II. I told them that Dad had done his thesis on Sidat-Singh and they recalled what a gifted athlete he was. He was being honored as a basketball player; the 5th player, along with Dave Bing, Sherman Douglas, Vic Hanson, and Pearl Washington, at this time. But he was really more famous for his football abilities, a quarterback described as the Donovan McNabb of his era.

Wilmeth Sidat-Singh was the first star African-American athlete at Syracuse University. The basketball team compiled a record of 40-13 during his career. He was a quick and fast guard, on both offense and defense, and led the team in scoring in his senior season. He was born as William Webb, but his father died when he was a child. His mother, Pauline, married a West Indian doctor, Samuel Sidat-Singh; who adopted him and moved the family to Harlem. Wilmeth Sidat-Singh was an All-New York City basketball player at Dewitt Clinton High School in the Bronx, leading them to the Public School Championship in 1933-34. He came to Syracuse on a basketball scholarship. He was encouraged to join the football team after an assistant coach, Roy Simmons, spotted him playing in an intramural game. He started his football career as a sophomore.

The following is a story that my dad and his other teammates always regretted. Sidat-Singh was the victim of segregation on a number of occasions. When SU played at Maryland and at the U.S. Naval Academy, the host schools refused to play Syracuse unless Sidat-Singh did not play. Early on, SU tried to declare that he was a West Indian Hindu; until teams found out about his real father and blew the cover off this ploy.

Syracuse went down to play Maryland in 1937. They refused to play Syracuse unless Sidat-Singh sat out. Even the hotel or restaurants wouldn't let him in. One of Dad's teammates was Marty Glickman, a speedy halfback who had qualified for the 4x100 relay team at the 1936 Olympics in Berlin. Hitler refused to let him participate because he was Jewish, eliminating Glickman's Olympic dreams. Because of that discrimination, he should have stood up and been the leader and boycotted the game; basically, announcing that if Sidat-Singh isn't allowed to play, that we are not going to play either. My dad felt the same way, but he and the rest of the team played the game without their star, Sidat-Singh, and lost the game. But they were 18 to 22 years old and did what the coaches told them to do.

    Glickman went on to become a prominent sports announcer for almost 50 years, doing the play by play for the New York Knicks, New York Giants, and New York Jets, on the radio. He became a close lifetime friend of Dad's, and they had many conversations about this and always regretted not standing up for Sidat-Singh and boycotting this game. Maryland came to play Syracuse in Archbold Stadium in 1938, and SU, with Sidat-Singh at quarterback, proceeded to punish the Terrapins, 55-0; remembering their actions of the previous season. My dad always felt deeply about this and wrote his thesis about Sidat-Singh.

    After graduation, Sidat-Singh played professional basketball with two barnstorming teams, the Syracuse Reds and the Harlem Renaissance. In 1943, he joined the Tuskegee Airmen, and was on a training mission, when the engine of his P-40 plane failed over Lake Huron and he died on May 9th,1943, at the age of 25. He is buried at Arlington National Cemetery.

    On November 9th, 2013, Maryland honored Wilmeth Sadat-Singh at their football game with Syracuse; 76 years after they banned him from playing against them in their stadium. I only wish Dad, Marty Glickman, Duffy Daugherty, (later to become a prominent football coach at Michigan State, from 1954 to 1972, and winning two national championships in 1965 & 1966); and the rest of that team could have been there to witness this.

    I had to endure another long winter in Syracuse, the *first* winter without Sylvia. I still had to take care of Tom and Debbie's house, shoveling in front of their garage and the front and sidewalks, after the plower had come; empty the dehumidifiers in the basement and make sure everything was okay inside the house. Plus, rides to and from the airport and other errands. This was my money for gas, groceries, wine, and miscellaneous; so, it was worth it. They had been back from California for a month, with visits to New Jersey and New York City, during their semester break. Will was in his senior year at SU, living in an apartment in a house on East Genesee Street, around the corner from where Benham's bar used to be. (It had burned down a long time ago, some thought suspiciously.) He would come back to his house occasionally, to watch a game and eat pizza and drink beers with some friends; or to come by himself, as a sanctuary to study or just be alone. I had to shovel in front of my garage, after the guy who plows here had plowed; and sometimes the entrance to the driveway, after the big road plow came by after that.

I felt an urgency to label our photo albums. Julie said that she would take them after I'm gone and pass them on to her children and grandchildren. Who knows what will happen to them, maybe they will just be in bins, buried in an attic, basement, or garage somewhere. Maybe somebody will discover them many years from now and see our pictures when we were young and traveling all over and be impressed. I guess that's about the best you can hope for.

A lot of time and effort went into filling up 29 photo albums, each album containing 300 pictures, plus several smaller albums of miscellaneous pictures. We're talking about *9,000 pictures.* That's a lot of pictures, to say the least. I had been very diligent about putting the pictures, after they had been developed, into the designated plastic sleeves in the photo albums almost immediately; and also labeling the places and dates of the pictures on the inside cover. I was very meticulous about this. Most people regret not doing this, as their pictures wind up in drawers, all mixed up and all over the place. I had always done the labeling through album #18, then I had for some reason stopped after that. I felt a need to label the rest of the photo albums before something happened to me. At least the pictures were all in the albums.

This became my winter project. I learned how to take pictures with the camera on my phone, from these pictures in the photo albums, and post them on Facebook. I had to get the right lighting, rotate and crop the pictures, then post them on Facebook with the correct dates and places. Except for errands, going to the store, shoveling here and over at Tom and Debbie's, and occasional walks when the weather permitted; this is what I was doing. I was also making a lot of calls, taking care of all the business things related to Syl's passing.

There was always something that came up, something that I had to deal with, more unneeded and unwanted reminders. I had to inform and send a copy of Sylvia's death certificate to Social Security, Internal Revenue Service, Department of Motor Vehicles, our TIAA retirement pension plans, and Key Bank for the mortgage loan and our bank account and her debit card. I had to call and cancel her credit cards for J.C. Penney's, Kohl's and Macy's. Sometimes promos came in the mail and I had to call back again. Medicare keeps sending information to her about supplemental plans. It is never-ending.

Every month, holiday, and special occasion became a *first* time for me, without Syl; after 33, and in the first fall, 34 years. There were the *first* (last three weeks of September), October, November, December, of 2016; and now January of 2017. I received an email from Tish in the middle of January, inviting me to go with them on their European trip in September. He said there was one seat left and it had my name on it. I had to make an immediate decision or miss out and I decided to go. I was going to go on this trip for both of us. Tish booked my ticket, along with his and Mary's; and made the room and transportation arrangements. I had to call the airlines and send in all the paperwork, along with Syl's death certificate, to get reimbursed for the 2016 trip that we had to cancel. I got most of the money back, losing some to the flights within Europe.

It was now the *first* February and then the *first* Valentine's Day without Syl. I displayed all the cards that I had saved from each other from all the Thanksgivings and Christmases, and now all the Valentine's Day cards. Valentine's Day was never as big a deal for us as was our anniversary, birthdays, or Christmas. We exchanged cards, but we were always teaching at school, since Valentine's Day of 1995. We would take some chocolate and cookies home with us from the classroom parties during the day. We would try to keep the kids under control at Extended Day, when they were all sugared up from eating their treats. After work, we would go out and have a nice dinner.

I put up the Valentine decorations, like Syl always did. I put all our past Valentine's Day cards out this year, and as I was reading through them, it hit me like a ton of bricks and I couldn't stop sobbing. I know that these cards can be somewhat maudlin sometimes, but it was *what Syl wrote to me,* expressing her feelings and love for me, that really got to me. I sat down and wrote a poem for Syl.

The Last Valentine

How was I to know

When I gave you

This card last year

That it would be

My last valentine

To you

How were you to know

When you gave me

My card

That it would be

Your last valentine

To me

How were we to know

That it would be

Our last Valentine's Day

Together

The forecast

Was not bright for you

Yet it was always bright
When we were together
Through the rain
Through the cold and snow
Through the gloom
We kept our hopes alive
It was always
A sunny day
Always a moonlit night
When we were together
We had it all
The world was ours
We filled the universe
With our love

It was always paradise
When we were together
Whether we were home
Or traveling the world
Paradise didn't have
Far to travel

In any way

Shape or form

From Seventh Heaven

Over to Cloud Nine

To find us

Yesterday's memories

Are burned deep inside

My soul

Deep inside

My heart

From the very beginning

When I first saw you

Floating softly

On a summer breeze

I knew you

Were the one

You found me

Just when I was looking

For you

You touched my heart

In so many ways

We grew closer and closer

As the days

Flew by

Filled with laughter

Filled with wonder

Very few people

Ever find true love

Their one and only

Like we did

You had this kinder, deeper

Unexplainable

Part of your heart

That not many people

Ever find

I can only try

To give of myself

As you did

You always cared

For everyone else

Above and beyond

Anyone I've ever known

I put up the valentine decorations

In our house this year

But the only heart

That really matters

Is missing

I can't seem to stop

My tears

From overflowing

Overwhelming moments

Suspended in time

Always remembering

All our Valentine Days

Together

Even though now

My heart has been shattered

Broken in half

The doctors said

In the end

That your heart had failed

Even though

You weren't able

To be with me

For Valentine's Day

This year

Your heart never ever

Failed me

Or all those

Who had the good fortune

Of knowing you

Feeling the incredible power

Of compassion and kindness

In your heart

This world

That I now live in

Doesn't have you

To hold me tight

Doesn't have you

To kiss goodnight

This world

That I now live in

Is a lonely one

Without the only one

Who could ever

Fill my heart again

You will always

Be my valentine

Forever feeling you

Beating inside my heart

    It became the *first* March, then the *first* vernal equinox: (first day of spring), without Syl. In early March, a good friend of ours, J.R., passed away in his sleep. He was a softball teammate of mine in the early 80's, and knew Sylvia before I met her. He had attended her services just six months before. I probably should have gone to his services, I always attended everyone's services; I just couldn't get it together for this one.

    On the last day of March, I met Ioana and Ileana for dinner at Bonefish and had a few more things of Syl's to give to them. This time they did not have to look at me having a bleeding eye at dinner.

It became the *first* April without Syl. I did a lot of yard work and stained the deck and put the deck furniture back out. I was cutting off some dead branches on the pine trees in the backyard, when I felt an irritation in my right eye, the same eye that was injured in late November. I had to go back to Urgent Care to have it checked out. It was a blister, probably caused by pine sap. I should have been wearing goggles, or at least sunglasses, which I usually do, but I didn't this time. I had to put the antibiotic drops in again and it cost me another $57.

In the middle of April, one of my closest friends, "Eff," the second guy that I met, after Wardie, when I first moved to Syracuse when I was sixteen, and one of the original "Campers;" passed away after spending a week at the Francis House. "Eff" had been battling brain cancer for a couple of years, during the same period that Sylvia had been battling her pancreatic cancer. He handled it with courage and grace, just as she had.

We spent many a Friday afternoon, after our week at our summer jobs from college had ended, drinking beers at local bars, like the Anchor Room, in Eastwood. "Eff" came to visit me in Madison in the spring of 1968, when I returned for my sophomore year at the University of Wisconsin; riding his motorcycle from South Bend, Indiana, where he was about to graduate from Notre Dame. All the graduation parties for his children, Erika, Damian, and Adam; and all the reunions, especially when Wardie and Christie visited from California; were always held on "Eff" & Kathy's deck, the ultimate hosts. In the early years, he even made his own beer: "F's Home Brew." We would help him cap off the bottles. It was very powerful.

"Eff" was a renowned scientist, a Limnologist, that studies lakes and rivers. He published an incredible number of articles, books, and periodicals on the subject. He was the first scientist to do extensive research on Onondaga Lake, a formerly beautiful lake, but it became the second most polluted lake in the United States; because Solvay Process had been dumping, unchecked, toxic waste in the lake since the early 1900's. This became his passion, to clean up this lake. He had to battle all sorts of political red tape, but eventually they had to go through him, as he became the ultimate authority on the condition of the lake. They used to hold the International Rowing Regatta, with teams from all over the country, for many years, on Onondaga Lake, even though it was polluted. A group of us guys used to go every year.

I worked for and with "Eff" for two years, 1982 and 1983, and this is where I was working when I first met Sylvia. I was trying to do something other than landscaping and painting. This was before he started his own research corporation, Upstate Freshwater Institute. I remember going out in his small boat in the early days and the boat broke down and we had to get towed into shore.

We used to drive down to the field station of the Naval Sea Systems Command in Dresden, New York, 70 miles southwest of Syracuse. We went there weekly, usually on Fridays. It is the Seneca Lake Sonar Test Facility, two large test barges, halfway out in Seneca Lake. Seneca Lake is 3 miles wide, so this was located about a mile and a half out. They do all kinds of sophisticated sonar and acoustic testing. This is because of the depth of Seneca Lake, one of the few freshwater lakes where you can conduct oceanographic studies. The Navy estimates its depth at 600 feet; but there was a Hobart professor who had a theory, that if you pushed through a layer of silt at that depth, it would go down an additional 600 feet. In that case, it would be 1,200 feet deep, and you could put the Empire

State Building in Seneca Lake, and only its antenna would break the surface. That has yet to be proven, but I bet it is a possibility. It is the Navy's primary active instrumented calibration and test facility.

"Eff" had received permission for us to conduct studies from the facility. We put on our life vests and they took us out in a rubber lifeboat to the barges. We collected samples of zooplankton, and put the Secchi Disk in to test water transparency or turbidity, and did some other tests. Because of its depth, Seneca Lake's temperature remains a near constant 40 degrees Fahrenheit. They have discovered sunken boats, with everything perfectly preserved and intact; like dishes, and a broom in the corner of the kitchen. I knocked on a door to ask where the bathroom was one day, and all these guys looked alarmed, like they were performing a secret mission; which they probably were.

We also conducted tests and collected samples from Otisco Lake, and brought them into the Onondaga County Water Authority in Skaneateles for testing. "Eff" had his basement set up as a test facility. He had two refrigerators down there, one had a keg in it with a tap on the outside for beer. The other one was full of all sorts of algae, zooplankton, and other samples. He had an annual "Lake Day" party in February; where scientists and professors, some local and some from all over the country, came to Syracuse for this. Some were even former students of "Eff's," when he was a professor at Syracuse University. All of us close friends came also. It started out being at his house, but soon became too big, and it was then held at local bars, until finding a permanent home at Klub Polski on Teall Avenue. There was all kinds of food, music, conversation, and good friends; something to look forward to in the winter.

It was late January of 1983 when we had the "Lake Day;" but in the morning before the party, we were to meet at Clark Reservation State Park in Jamesville. It was the site of a large waterfall formed by melting glacial ice at the end of the last Ice Age. The plunge basin at the base of the old falls is now a small meromictic lake, in which the surface waters and the bottom waters do not mix. "Eff" wanted to conduct studies and take samples in this lake. We were scheduled to meet in the parking lot there at 7 o'clock in the morning.

I got up at 5 o'clock, organized my notebook and things, and got ready. I put Vicks Vapor Rub all over my chest and wore thermal underwear under my clothes. I left early and stopped and bought coffees and doughnuts for all the guys. I arrived before 7 and there wasn't a car in the parking lot. It became after 7:30, and I was wondering if I was in the right place. There were obviously no cell phones then. Finally, they all arrived. I offered them the coffees, and they said,

"Coffee? We don't want coffee."

They were pulling a wagon loaded with two cases of bottled beer. That shot me doing a nice thing, being the new guy, theory. They had me, being "the rookie," carry the battery, a wooden box with all these components inside, that weighed 100 pounds. So, I did. I carried the battery down the 212 steps, down to the bottom of the basin, where the lake was. I had on these work boots that weren't really broken in yet and they were pinching my toes. Plus, they were not insulated, not the greatest choice of footwear on my part. The lake was frozen, but it had just recently become so, after a thaw in the middle of January. They were all reluctant to go out on it, except "Eff." He had no hat on and was wearing a heavy wool shirt. He started walking out on the ice.

Being one of my closest friends, I threw caution to the wind, and followed him out onto the ice.

Visions of my nightmarish "Falling Through The Ice" story in childhood flashed before my eyes. But nothing catastrophic happened, and eventually the rest of the guys came out onto the ice. By now, my fingers and toes were numb, having poor circulation from frostbite, due to the "falling through the ice" incident. We cut some holes in the ice and collected samples. "Eff" said that he would carry the battery and he gave me these long metal rods to carry back up those steps. They were lighter, but they became attached to my now wet gloves. I was literally frozen stiff. I was so happy to take off these gloves and get in my car and turn the heater on full blast.

In the spring and summer, "Eff" would have me drive up to Fulton and then Minetto, north of Syracuse on the Oswego Canal, once a week. I would have to first go to Lock #3 in Fulton and unhook this lid, where there were 24 big test tubes filled with water samples that would rotate around, each one for an hour, until they were all filled. Then place them in this case and replace the filled-up test tubes with empty ones and secure the lid. Then follow the same procedure up in Minetto at Lock #5, 6 miles north of Lock #4. What he neglected to tell me, as he had arachnophobia, was that there were these giant mutant water spiders, that started crawling out as soon as you opened these lids to get to the test tube water samples. The first time, I was so startled that I nearly fell in the canal. I got used to it after that, bringing a small broom to brush them away; but it was still a scary sight.

On the 16th of April, it was the *first* anniversary without Syl, since we were officially married in 1994. (We had been "married together" for 10 years and 9 months before this day.) I put all our past anniversary cards out, looking through them and seeing what Syl had written to me, crying for a long time once again. I took pictures of the cards from my phone and posted them on Facebook, as well as pictures from the wedding ceremony at Mom's townhouse and the reception at the Brewster Inn.

A few days later, we had "Eff's" services. He had just turned 70 at the end of January. There were hundreds of people there from all over the country: scientists, professors, former students, all of us close friends, family, friends; guys I hadn't seen since high school or college. There was a wonderful reception at Drumlins that followed. It was great to reminisce with so many people, but it's always the wrong cause that seems to bring us together. I miss "Eff."

I wanted to have a bench with an engraved name plate on it at Green Lakes to honor Sylvia. This is where we took the kids on so many walks, on field trips and the Playscape Program, for twenty years. And where Syl and I had taken walks, in all the seasons, in all kinds of weather, for all of our years together. I had given it a lot of thought over the fall and winter, and scouted out possible locations on my many walks. They weren't doing any new benches anymore, and I noticed that the benches that had name plates on them, except for the more expensive raised ones you might find on a gravestone; were black plastic and a lot of them had chips or pieces broken off. Many of the older benches had graffiti on them.

I was going to go to a company downtown that does engraving, when Nancy told me that LeeAnne's mother had an engraving business in Oswego, and LeeAnne worked with her. I asked her about the engraving, willing to pay for it, but LeeAnne said she would just do it to honor Sylvia. I told her what I wanted on the plate:

Sylvia U. Heer

Beautiful Angel

Elegance & Grace

Kind & Gentle Soul

Inside our Hearts Forever

June 18, 1953-September 9, 2016

And she put two small hearts on both sides. It was gold plated and looked really nice.

After much searching, I found the perfect location, at the end of Round Lake, around the corner of the end of Green Lake. It is a serene spot, looking out at a usually shimmering Round Lake, with trees bordering the lake. In front of the bench, there are trees literally sticking out of the water and a big rock wall. A few yards away, to the left of the bench, is a huge sign that asks:

"What is a National Natural Landmark?"

Round Lake is a rare meromictic lake, one of only eleven such lakes reported in the United States. It is surrounded by a forest that includes about 20 acres of diverse, old-growth maple-basswood forest. Some of these trees are between 100 and 400 years old. There are tulip trees, bitternut hickory, sugar maple, hemlock, and basswood. These components led to Round Lake's designation as a National Natural Landmark in 1973, one of 28 such sites in New York State. A meromictic lake is a lake that does not have complete mixing of the surface and bottom waters. This is due to the lake being very deep without a large surface area. Round Lake is over 180 feet deep, with a length of 700 feet; and Green Lake is almost 200 feet deep, with a length of 3,700 feet. Green Lake and Round Lake were formed during the last Ice Age, nearly 15,000 years ago. They have a beautiful turquoise color to them. On the sign, it gives you this information with a couple of photographs. On the lower left-hand side is a quote from George Carlin:

"Life is not measured by the number of breaths we take, but by the moments that take our breath away."

On April 24th, I met Nancy and LeeAnne in the parking lot in the late afternoon, and we walked until I showed them where the bench that I had picked out was. LeeAnne had her tools with her and put the name plate in the center of the top row of the bench. The bench itself was weathered, but still in good shape, and the serenity of its location was the most important factor.

On April 25th, the first episode of the "Genius" series on National Geographic began. The first season tracks Albert Einstein's life, from humble origins as a young, rebellious thinker to finally being accepted by his peers, following the disclosure of his theory of relativity. This was brilliantly played by Johnny Flynn. It also delves into his personal life and into the antisemitism in 1930's Germany. Also brilliantly played by Geoffrey Rush. There were ten weekly episodes. Syl would have really gotten engrossed in this and we would have watched all these Tuesday night episodes together.

It became the *first* May without Syl. In the middle of May, I took a walk with Will at Green Lakes, to show him where Syl's bench was. When I had taken walks with Nancy, I had always mentioned to her seeing the native Pumpkinseed Sunfish at Green Lake, in an area down below in the water; visible as you walk up the hill where there is a railing. They were never there when we walked. They were *always* there when Syl and I walked. We used to point them out to the kids and stop and watch them for a while. On my solo walks, I hadn't seen them now in a couple of years. I wondered if they had become extinct, or moved away to a different lake.

It was like when Holden Caulfield, in "The Catcher in the Rye," by J.D. Salinger, wonders where the ducks in Central Park go in the winter. This was one of my favorite books, and I always related to Holden Caulfield. I told Will all about this as we walked the trails. When we got to Syl's bench, seemingly out of nowhere, a family of Pumpkinseed Sunfish appeared, swimming directly in front of Syl's bench! I guess that they knew where to go.

I sent copies of my last four poems that I had written after Syl passed away, to George and Paula Saunders, renowned authors, former MPH parents, and good friends. Their daughters, Caitlin and Alena, graduated from MPH. I remember George and I carrying much of the equipment and supplies to the end of the year picnics when Alena was in the third and fourth grades, in "The Blend." I remember George bringing his glove and playing second base in the softball games with parents, teachers, and the kids.

Paula and Alena came into the classroom when Alena was in fifth grade and transformed half of the classroom into feeling like you were in Nepal, where their family had traveled to. They were dressed in traditional costumes and had hung colorful pennants all around the classroom. They gave a wonderful presentation and then Alena went over and gave an impressive demonstration of "the singing bowl." George and Paula had organized a school trip to Nepal and had invited me to join them as chaperones. They were not going to be staying in any hotels, just sleeping in an ancient temple. I was so looking forward to it. But the proposed trip did not generate the interest that they had hoped for and was canceled. We were all really disappointed.

I had requested Alena, as my choice, to write and read a 10 to 12 line "bio" at her fifth grade graduation; as all the other teachers did, when they received the decision from the administrators on which student they would be writing and reading their "bio," a synopsis of the student's interests and accomplishments. When I was reading Alena's, I saw George and Paula in the audience, with George tapping his chest, knowing that it really touched them. That was a nice feeling for me as well.

They invited us over to their house on Scott Avenue, a neighborhood of older stately homes on the outskirts of Syracuse University, for Alena's graduation party. We met George's parents and hit it off with them. There was a gigantic, and I mean *gigantic,* flower display and I asked them who that was from. They said to read the card, and it said, "Love from the Stillers." This was Ben Stiller, the famous actor, whom they had become friends with when they met in New York City many years before.

I had told George about my screenplay, "White Woman of the Genesee," and gave him a copy to read. He was nice enough to take the time to not only read it, but to critique it, writing suggestions on fine-tuning and improving it. He definitely thought it had merit and potential, which gave me inspiration. He also liked my children's book, "The Forest That Rains Frogs," and I gave him a signed copy of it. He had given me a signed copy of his book, a collection of stories, "Pastoralia," in 2000. His first collection of short stories and a novella, "CivilWarLand in Bad Decline," was published in 1996. Ben Stiller bought the rights to it, but it still "sits on the shelf," just like my screenplay. Ben was too involved in making all his movies. George called him and asked if he should tweak something about it, but Ben said to leave it just the way it was. So, if you ever see it in the movie theaters or on Netflix, this is George's book. I asked George what was the secret to get published and he said you just have to know the right people and have the contacts. Certainly, having his writing talents doesn't hurt.

We saw him in the spring of 2014 at Barnes & Noble in Syracuse, when he gave a talk on his book tour for his best selling book, "Tenth of December," winner of the 2014 Story Prize and 2014 Folio Prize. That's when I gave him a copy of my children's book. He has written children's books as well: "The Very Persistent Gappers of Frip;" and his latest, "Fox 8," a fable. His first novel, "Lincoln in the Bardo," won the prestigious Man Booker Prize in 2017. He has won many awards for his writing, and also was honored with the Guggenheim Fellowship and MacArthur Genius Grant.

George has remained a down to earth guy and a devoted family man. He gave a commencement speech at Syracuse University, "Congratulations, By the Way:

Some Thoughts on Kindness;" which went viral. He still is a professor at Syracuse University, where he teaches Creative Writing, and also where he met his wife Paula. Paula just published her debut novel, "The Distance Home," released in August, 2018, and now a best seller. They have traveled all over the country and the world on their many book tours. So, I emailed them my four poems and on May 22nd, 2017, George emailed me back:

'Hi Dusty,'

"Just wanted you to know that I'm sitting here in Melbourne, Australia, with tears in my eyes, because of your beautiful poetic tribute to dear Sylvia. You are such a dear heart and the purity of your love for her shines through. Miss you, brother- hang in there. You are the receptacle in which her kindness resides and it's for you to continue passing her love out into the world. You sent some of it my way through those poems, and you (you and her) made my day more beautiful, and made me feel more loving toward the world."

'Much love,'

'George'

I emailed him back,

"Tears are flowing reading your kind and wise words. I need to carry on and spread her love and kindness to all those who need it and want it. I want to write so much more. I'm trying not to feel sorry for myself, although it's so easy to go down that path. I'm so happy for your success with your new book and respect your talent so much. Have fun down under and safe travels. Hugs to Paula and keep in touch."

'Miss you brother.'

'Love, Dusty'

(Paula's book wasn't out yet.) I sent them twenty of my poems that summer and Paula said that they enjoyed reading them. I guess I want to have the approval of famous authors as affirmation and validation of my writing. It's nice to know that they are good friends and are supportive of me.

But now, with this book, nothing matters to me, as far as book critics or best seller lists are concerned. Or fame or money. All that matters are that my life story, and Sylvia's life story, and our life story together, gets written and told. Hopefully at least close friends and family will read it. Maybe many others will read it as well.

Two weeks later, it was the *first* Memorial Day weekend without being with Syl. It became the *first* June without Syl. My cousin Bobby, Aunt Gloria's and Uncle Bob's oldest son, passed away unexpectedly in the first week in June; after a three month battle with (what else?) cancer. He tried a couple of treatments, according to his wife, Cathy; and then just didn't want to deal with them anymore. I went to his services at the Maurer Funeral Home in Liverpool. It was a small gathering.

I hadn't planned on speaking, but except for a couple of quick comments, no one got up to say anything. They had stood up and spoken where they were seated, but I got up and went to the middle of the room and spoke. I recalled how Bobby and I used to set up these metal G.I. soldiers, on the stair steps at his parents' house, where our families got together on Christmas Eve; and then we would hide behind corners, and try to knock them down, using wooden clothespins. Bobby had a set of drums in his room.

He became an excellent musician, mainly on keyboards, but he could play drums and other instruments. He had played for many years with his band, "Smokin'," all over Central New York.

One of his early bands was "The Strangers," and a bandmate was Tom S., who was one of the guys that I had hitchhiked with to the Atlantic City Pop Festival at the end of July in 1969. He was at Bobby's services and I hadn't seen him since that festival, almost 48 years ago, at this time in 2017. He had lived in Boulder, Colorado for many years, working as a cook; and then had moved to Asheville, North Carolina, where he had driven up from for the services. We had fun reminiscing, but again, always the wrong cause to get together.

Bobby and Cathy had bought the same childhood house and lived there until the end. Bobby had the most amazing music collection you could ever imagine: albums, CD's, cassettes, you name it; filling the shelves in their living room. I talked about how we had played golf together several times, but wish we would have played more. Bobby was always funny with his wry wit. We played sports together at Pebble Hill; he was two years younger, being a sophomore when I was a senior. He left to play for Liverpool High School for his junior and senior seasons. We had both attended all these funerals over the years: our grandparents; Uncle Dave's; his youngest brother, Peter's; my dad's; a few months later, his dad's; Aunt Carol's; cousin Dave's; my mom's; his mom's; Linda's, (out at John & Linda's house in Cazenovia); Sylvia's. Now, unfortunately, I was attending his.

I went through the photo albums after I had finished labeling them, and compiled a notebook, listing dates and places, year by year, that we had traveled to; from August,

1983 through August, 2016. I titled it, "All Their Travels." This notebook became an important reference source in writing this book. I took pictures from the photo albums with my phone and posted them on Facebook. I learned how to make albums with my Facebook pictures and compiled many albums from different years; some of us together, and then pictures of Syl by herself, that I titled, "Only Sylvia."

On June 18th, it was the *first time* that I couldn't celebrate Syl's birthday with her in 33 years, since 1984. Couldn't give her my card, couldn't take her out for a nice dinner, couldn't go to bed and hold her tight. I wrote this to her, and posted it on Facebook:

"Well, Syl, today would have been your sixty-fourth birthday. It should have been your sixty-fourth birthday, if you had been allowed to celebrate it. In a more just and perfect world, you would not only be with me today, but for many years to come. I've written several poems about and for you, but my words can't truly express how much I miss you and how lonely my life is not sharing it with you. I think of all the things we've done together; all our homes, all our travels, all our times of fun and laughter, all our years of working together, all our own secrets we knew about each other, our intimacy, our hearts and souls entwined for eternity. You were and always will be my one and only true love."

I started playing golf again, nine holes at Green Lakes, usually twice a week, with Tish & Mary and Steve. When Steve couldn't make it, the three of us played. We played until the last week of August. I went out to Lakeside Park at Cazenovia Lake a few days and sat in the sun, thinking about all the wonderful days that Syl and I had spent there. I got Tom and Debbie's pool opened up and started to go there on nice days when we didn't play golf. I just sat in the sun, read, listened to my iPod, and swam in the pool. All those years with Syl at the pool, even just a year ago in 2016. I met Traian, Ioana and Ileana, who had now finished 7th grade; at the Arad Evans Inn one night. They treated me to a delicious dinner and I had some things of Syl's to give to them.

It became the *first* July without Syl, as I sat out on our back deck at night on the Fourth of July; watching the fireworks from the village of Manlius. This was the *first* Fourth of July without Syl, she had watched the fireworks with me last year. After this, things began to go downhill for her.

I went out on Tish and Mary's boat, "Xcuses," along with Tommy and Carolyn, on Skaneateles Lake. Once again, feeling like "the fifth wheel." We had a nice day cruising around, swimming, and eating at Doug's Fish Fry. Syl and I had gone on several boat trips with Tish and Mary over the years. A few weeks later, I went on another boat trip with Tish and Mary; this time we drove up to the Adirondacks, and went out on Fourth Lake. We stopped in Inlet first to get some sandwiches and snacks. It was a warm and sunny day, as we cruised around for a while; then anchored, swam, and ate our lunches. We told some jokes and had some good laughs, and talked about the plans for the upcoming trip to Europe. As we silently sat in the sun after this, I so wished Syl was sitting next to me, enjoying this day; and getting excited to go to Europe.

It became the *first* August without Syl. On the 1st, Nancy came with me to see the newly installed brick for Sylvia in the Fayetteville Memory Garden. You can pay for a small brick paver or a larger one, with an inscription on it. I paid for the larger one, with the same words on it as the bench plate at Round Lake, except they couldn't fit in the word forever on the last line, due to space limitations on the brick. Nancy had told me about this garden, having had a brick installed for a loved one herself. The pathway of bricks is shaped in the form of a ribbon, symbolizing hope and courage. It is a peaceful setting; with benches, a landscape wall, flowers, trees, lighting, and pergolas.

Never Before

Never before

In my life

Have I felt like this

Reliving all our timeless moments

That's all that I have left

Missing you so much

First summer since we met

We weren't together

Watching fireworks from our deck

Fireflies flickering in the night

Traveling to the Cape

Lying on the beach

Reading a book by the dunes

Eating the lunch

You so carefully planned

Riding the waves

Feeling the cool

Ocean salt on our bodies

Eventually

Finding our way

Through echoing footsteps

Back to where we began

   Never before

Has the lost treasure

Been so hard to find

Some people

Draw lines in the sand

We drew hearts in the sand

Watching the waves

Wash over them

Never fading

From our memories

Which seem so far away

Then again

Seem like they are

Right around the bend

As I see you

In my cosmic dreams

Standing on the distant shore

Waving for me

To come over

When I'm ready

Or when the tides

Carry me across

Never before

Have I had to carry on

Without you

Still hoping

You will appear

Like a lighthouse beacon

Through my daily

Morning fog

Never goes away

Only disguises the truth

Wraps its inevitable invisible

Shield around me

Won't let me inside

To hold you again

A never-ending mirage

Ultimate illusion

As the final curtain

Comes down

On this one act play

One trick pony

One last shot in the dark

One last sliver of light

One last shred of evidence

One last glimmer of hope

One last leap of faith

The show must still go on

    Never before

Have I felt

This deep a sting

Unequaled

By a thousand angry hornets

I think I'm still

In denial

Definitely not

A river in Egypt

That's a stone-cold fact

I reach out for you

In the middle of the night

You are not there

To feel

To hold

I miss your fragrance

I miss hearing your voice

Soft and sweet

In the stillness

I miss you listening to me

Offering some semblance of sanity

Now I talk to myself

Or I talk to you

Hoping you might hear me

In some far-off paradise

    Never before

Have I aimlessly wandered

Through so many mindless days

Through so many sleepless nights

I feel the rain

Softly falling on my face

Failing to wash away my tears

Failing to wash away my fears

A full yellow moon

Stares eerily down on me

Knows my fate

Hides its eternal secrets

Shadows without substance

Ghosts of reality

Endlessly haunt me

Solitary wilderness

Woman of the forest

Burned into my consciousness

In the blink of an eye

Became the long goodbye

I wish there was some way

You could come back home to me

As you spread your wings

Silently sitting

On the end of your rainbow

    In August: it was golf, the pool, starting to organize my clothes, toiletries, books, notebooks, for the upcoming European trip. On the 20th, it was my *first* birthday without Syl. In 2016, she didn't even have the energy to get me a card on my 70th birthday; as she laid in bed sick, and had felt bad about it. *But she was still here* and gave me a kiss and wished me a happy birthday last year. And that was good enough for me. No card today to look at from her, no going to the pool together, no going out for a nice dinner, no going to bed and holding each other tight. On the 23rd, the year before; it was the last night that she would ever sleep in her own bed. On the 24th, at 2 o'clock in the afternoon, the year before; it was the last time that she would ever be at her house. *Our home.*

    I had the pool closed for the summer the last few days of August. Packed up my clothes in a carry on-sized suitcase, and put the rest of my things, including an empty backpack, in an orange SU gym bag. Having them hold my mail at the Post Office, paying my bills, (some in advance), house things; trying not to forget anything that I needed: passport, debit card, driver's license, traveling money; because if you forget or lose any of these things, you are dealing with some major hassles.

It was now September 1st, the *first* start of September without Syl. Patty B. picked me up and drove me to Hancock International, the Syracuse airport. I flew to Philadelphia, where we were flying out of, to Europe. I took the shuttle over to the International Terminal and waited for the rest of the group to arrive. There was Tish and Mary, then I met Allie and Joe, and Dick and Nina. Wardie and Christie had flown from Sacramento to Venice a few days earlier, and were going to spend almost a week in Venice, before taking a train from there to Capranica; where we would pick them up at the train station.

We boarded the plane and I was seated next to Mary in the middle, with Tish next to her in the window seat. This plane had rows of four seats, so someone might be sitting next to me in the aisle seat. If no one sat there, I could move to the aisle seat for more leg room. I wasn't that lucky. A woman in her forties started to look at her ticket to verify if the aisle seat was hers. I was wearing this jacket that Will had bought for me at a discount sports apparel store. It was gray with a NY on it. It was a little tight on me, being a Large, when I took an Extra Large, but it wasn't too bad, and I decided to wear it anyway. Big mistake. It shouldn't have been, but it turned out to be. This woman looks at my jacket, before she even sat down, and exclaims in a really loud voice;

"I can't believe that they have me sitting next to a 'F'n' Yankees fan."

Tish and Mary and I were looking at her in total astonishment. She didn't stop there. She continued, looking directly at me with disdain;

"And do you know why?"

Before I could answer, which I wasn't going to anyway, she lifted up her pants to show this weird tattoo on her leg. It looked like an infinity symbol.

"Because I'm a Baltimore Orioles fan, that's why!"

I guess that her tattoo was supposed to look like an O, for the Orioles. If I was that passionate a Baltimore Orioles fan, and was going to get a tattoo on my leg; I would have gotten the team symbol, which is the face of a cute and smiling bird, wearing a baseball hat, and in the team colors of orange and black. She dropped a few more "F bombs" before she finally sat down.

I now realized that this 4,372 miles, almost nine hours flight, was about to seem a lot longer than that. If Syl was with me, she would have been sitting in my seat next to Mary, and I would have been sitting in the aisle seat. Or with the actual reality of Syl no longer with me; if this had been a plane with rows of three seats instead of four, then this crazy woman would not be sitting next to me. She started making phone calls and writing emails to people, I'm assuming friends, on her laptop; saying,

"I can't believe I have to sit next to a 'F'n' Yankees fan all the way to Europe."

After a few hours and dinner, I started talking to her, telling her that I've been a Yankees fan since I was seven years old. I told her about Sylvia, not going into all the details, and I think that made her soften a bit. She just had a relationship end, she didn't get into any details, which was fine by me; and was going on a two week trip around Italy with a tour group. I also told her about my children's books and gave her the information. We shook hands when we landed at the airport in Rome and that was the end of a long and uncomfortable flight. Hopefully, for them, she didn't encounter any Yankees fans on her tour. What was ironic after this, was that the Orioles were in playoff contention in the American League that year, and from this point on, went completely downhill. And the Yankees surged, making the playoffs, and even winning their first round matchup. And the Orioles have had losing teams ever since, while the Yankees have been getting even stronger. Call it karma or whatever, but I think it was sweet poetic justice.

Saturday morning, September 2nd, we arrived at the Rome airport, got our suitcases, and went through passport control. We rented our van and drove to Capranica, 36 miles north of Rome. It took us about an hour and a half to get from the airport to "The Farm." This was the place that Tish and Mary had stayed for many years, and was what Syl and I saw when they showed us their slides years ago, that reminded us of scenes from "The Godfather," and piqued our interest in the first place. Capranica lies among Mounts Cimini and Sabatini Hills, overlooking Via Cassia. It is in the province of Viterbo in the Italian region of Lazio. "The Farm" has many brick units to rent, as well as some beautiful classical homes that people live in. There is a very nice pool, where you can look out and see the town, with its ancient churches, bell towers, and buildings.

We would stay here for a week, picking up Wardie and Christie at the train station to join us. Each apartment had a kitchenette, with a small stove and refrigerator, a living room with a couch, an extra bedroom, where I put my suitcase and gym bag, and a bedroom with an armoire type closet to hang your clothes. There was no shower, only a bathtub with one of those hand held sprayers. This is the way it is in most hotels in Europe. And no shower curtains, which I find very strange and definitely not practical.

Anyone tall, and that's me, has to crouch down and attempt to not spray water all over the place when you took your so-called shower. It never worked for me, no matter how hard I tried, and I had to mop up the water on the bathroom floor afterwards with towels.

As you walked through the rows of lemon, olive, and pear trees, you felt magically transformed to an Old World atmosphere. The reason we called it "The Farm," is that they also have numerous hazelnut trees, and in September, they harvest the hazelnuts and transport them to a place that uses them to make the Nutella spread. This was our home base and from here we would drive to many sights in the towns in this region.

The next day, Sunday, September 3rd, we drove 35 miles north through Bracciano with the beautiful view of the big lake there, Lake Bracciano. Then to Civita di Bagnoregio, a hilltop village in the province of Viterbo. The only access to it is by a steep pedestrian bridge from the Bagnoregio village. We didn't walk over on the bridge, as we had a special festival to drive to and witness that day. Some of the other couples had walked the bridge in previous years. The medieval village of Civita di Bagnoregio was founded in the 7th century by the Etruscans. Civita became known as "the dying town," due to the forces of nature: earthquakes, landslides, and floods, that have threatened its survival since the 17th century.

We drove 78 miles north from Bagnoregio to Arezzo, through charming towns in Tuscany. Cortona is the picturesque hilltop town made famous in the movie, "Under the Tuscan Sun," with Diane Lane. We arrived in Arezzo and walked to the Piazza Grande, the most beautiful public square in the heart of this medieval city, and one of the most beautiful piazzas in Tuscany. The buildings come from different periods in history: The Palazzo delle Logge dates back to the 16th century, and dominates the highest part of the Piazza Grande; and the main square features the Town Hall, which dates back to the 6th century. There is the Duomo, cathedrals, palaces, and many shops and restaurants.

We found a small shop to get sandwiches and snacks, and stayed in front of it, just feet from the main street. People started coming from everywhere.
This festival, "Giostra del Saracino," The Joust of the Saracen; takes place twice a year, on the third Saturday in June and on the first Sunday in September. The people of Arezzo just call it, "Il Saracino," and we were here for it.

There were all these young men and women in their early twenties, looking fashionable, and greeting one another. This festival was a big deal and definitely a social event for them. They all had their cell phones in their back pockets. Ah, to be 23 again! Looking back on it, I was 23 and a couple of months when I went over to Europe the first time; and stayed in Tangier, Morocco, with Tomás and "Catman." And they were the same age. When Steve and I went to Europe, I was 23 and almost 9 months, and Steve was just 22 and 6 months. But we didn't have any extra money and definitely no cell phones. It was fun watching them interact with each other,

"Buon giorno;" "Come sta;" "Sto bene, grazie;" "Ciao."

People were packed in like sardines as the parade started with all these groups representing their different districts, or *contrade*, dressed in their colors in medieval costumes and helmets; parading along the historical center of Arezzo and ending in the Piazza Grande. The procession consisted of 350 people and 27 horses. Each group has separate rows of men and women with family flags, trumpets, drums, spears, swords, crossbows, and in the back row, some riding horses.

These horses are so close to you and can get easily spooked with all the people and noise. There were all these kids, I'd say seven to twelve years old, sitting high up on the church steps, watching the parade go by and cheering for the different groups, at least for their favorites. They were clapping and yelling in Italian, "Let's go Green!" Like we would be yelling, "Let's go Orange," at a Syracuse University basketball game. They looked like they were having so much fun. The sights and sounds of this Paleo Parade were truly amazing, something we will hold in our memories and never forget. *I wish Sylvia could have been here to experience this.*

After the parade, we walked up the hill to the Fiera Antiquaria, the Antiques Fair. It is held on the first weekend of each month, but because of the festival, it was moved from the Piazza Grande to the park at the top of the town. They had everything you could possibly imagine for sale here, from coffee mugs to chandeliers to furniture.

We walked around Arezzo and then got in the van and started driving 38 miles south to Pienza. There was a major accident on the main road, so everyone was diverted to the back roads. Normally an hour's drive, it took us over two hours. But it was well worth it, seeing the green rolling hills and valleys, the Val d'Orcia of beautiful Tuscany. *Sylvia would have loved it.* We went to Pienza for the famous "Fiera del Cacio," a festival dedicated to cheese. The Pecorino of Pienza is a tasty cheese made from sheep's milk. We walked around this quaint town, with its cobblestone streets and 15th century buildings, and spectacular views. The central Piazza Pio II has the Pienza Cathedral and the Piccolomini Palace. To the west of the Piazza, is the Pieve di Corsignano, a Romanesque church with a circular bell tower. We had a late dinner, featuring delicious homemade spaghetti. We drove back in the dark and didn't get back to Capranica until after midnight.

On Monday, September 4th, we just had a nice relaxing day at the pool here at "The Farm;" sitting in the sun and swimming, looking at the buildings and churches in Capranica. Later that afternoon, we drove to Toscano, a walled town, walked around and had dinner. We witnessed this beautiful scene of the full moon framing this castle on a distant hill.

Tuesday, September 5th, we drove to the medieval fortress of the Santa Severa Castle, located right on the Mediterranean Sea. It was an Etruscan port, Pygri, until conquered by the Romans. The castle was built in the 14th century. The Romans would build right on top of the Etruscan ruins, which you can see walking around inside the castle. They have an extensive display of artifacts, some just recently discovered. We started to walk up the stairs, 66 feet, to the top of the tower.

There were numerous doorways on the way up, with wooden beams, that had signs that cautioned you about low beams that you could easily smack your head on. For some reason, because usually I was in the back, I was in the front of the group; and kept shouting out at each doorway, "low beam," and making sure I was heeding my own advice. When we got to the last doorway, you could now see this was the end; there were only five steps, whereas all the other doorways had at least double that. Somehow Mary had managed to get in front of me. I was watching her climb the final five steps. She didn't say anything and had no problem going through the doorway, not having to worry about ducking her head. I came to the last step, watching her, and when I went to exit the doorway, I seriously compressed the top of my head into the metal strip of the doorway. This was not a wooden beam like the rest of them were, and there were no warning signs for this one, where they should have had them there. I sliced the top of my head and probably had a concussion. Blood was coming out as the women put antiseptic wipes on the slice and gave me some gauze to hold on it.

What's with me? I'm not a klutz, but you'd never know it, with the sliced big toe; two eye injuries; and now this; all within the past year. Maybe a lack of focus on my part, or maybe just being in the wrong place at the wrong time. So now I was dealing with this. The view from the top of the tower, looking out at the Mediterranean Sea, was spectacular. We walked around the village on the grounds, going inside some small museums with numerous ancient artifacts, and ate lunch there.

Wednesday, September 6th, we drove 37 miles north to Narni. We could see Orete in the distance, but Tish said it was extremely difficult to maneuver a van around its narrow streets, so we didn't go there. We took a tour of the Narni Sotterranea, the underground site of The Inquisition. I could have skipped this, with its gruesome devices of torture. In the adjacent waiting room, the prisoners had scratched their names and cries for help with their fingernails on the walls. What poor souls! I hope that there was a special place in hell that these sadistic torturers wound up in.

We drove 32 miles southeast from Narni to Rieti, where Tish had arranged a tour with a woman named Rita Giovannelli. You really had to give Tish a lot of credit, along with help from Mary, for all the research, planning, and organizing this entire five week trip. In addition, making all the calls and arrangements for our hotel rooms; and all the transportation: planes, vans, cars, buses, and trains. Tish did almost all the driving, which was exhausting and harrowing, with Mary as his navigator. I could never have driven where he did. There were a couple of occasions where Allie and Wardie drove, and they did an excellent job, but Tish was our main driver. He called it "The Get Lost in Europe Tour," and it certainly lived up to this slogan.

Rieti is surrounded by 13th century walls and 12th century cathedrals and palaces. We met Rita and walked down via Roma, then below street level she took us on a tour, Rieti Sotterranea, of underground 2,300 year old canals and stone work. There were Roman vaults and noble residences. After the tour, she invited us back to her house, located in the center of town. She rents out rooms also. We went into the kitchen and had coffee and pastries. I had told her about my children's books and it turned out that she had written several children's books herself: "Panfilo;" "Pammacchio;" "Porfirio;" & "Papiria;" beautifully illustrated by Luca Vannozzi. We all bought some of her books; I bought "Panfilo, Cat archaeologist."

Thursday, September 7th, we had to get up early to drive over to the train station and take a train to Rome. We spent the day walking all over Rome, marveling at all it has to offer in beauty and history. We went to the Colosseum, but didn't bother to take any tours inside, as there were so many people waiting to get in.

I was flashing back to when Steve and I had our picture taken, throwing a frisbee to each other, in front of the Colosseum; 47 years and almost 4 months before, in late May, 1970. Doesn't seem possible. There were no people around us when this picture was taken, although I'm sure there were still plenty of tourists in the vicinity. There are so many more today, just the result of the fact there are so many more people in the world.

We went to see many incredible sights: Saint Peter's Basilica; Roman Forum; Ancient Roman ruins; Piazza del Campidoglio; Teatro di Marcello, oldest theatre in Rome; walking around and taking pictures.

Then we went into the church of Santa Maria sopra Minerva; where to the left of the main altar, is a marble sculpture by Michelangelo, finished in 1521. It is called "The Risen Christ," also known as "Christ the Redeemer," or "Christ Carrying the Cross." This is the only sculpture by Michelangelo in Rome that you can get up close to it, and even take a picture with you next to it, which we did.

After the church, we continued on to: The Pantheon; Trevi Fountain; Castel Sant'Angelo; and The Vatican. At some point in our sightseeing, we took a break and had a nice lunch. Then we had to hustle to catch the train back to Capricana. It was an interesting experience to see all the local people getting off the train at their towns or villages where they lived.

Friday, September 8th, we needed a rest after a long day in Rome. We sat by the pool at "The Farm," sunning and swimming. In the late afternoon, I was reflecting on that this was *the last day*, one year ago; *that I would ever spend with Sylvia.*

We showered and changed and drove down to Trevignano Romano, a small town located on Lake Bracciano. We had dinner at Ristorantino Rustico di Rosella Mamma; they seated us outside, at tables close to the lake, with spectacular views. There was a wedding party that walked by, with the women trying not to sprain their ankles, while walking on the cobblestones with their high heels. They were all dressed up and taking pictures by the lake, a beautiful scene. We walked around the town and had our usual Italian gelato, while gazing up at the full moon. We drove back to "The Farm" for our last night of staying there.

    I cried myself to sleep, reflecting that this would be *the last night that I would ever be able to spend with Sylvia, one year ago; when she was still alive.* Since the day we left for Europe, that day, September 1st, and these seven days in Italy; were still the *firsts* for me without her.

    Saturday, September 9th, we all woke up really early, packed up our things, took some group pictures, and loaded up the van. "The Farm" lived up to my expectations and then some. I just wish that Syl could have been with me and shared this experience. We drove to the Rome airport, dropped off the van, and boarded a plane to Corfu, an island off Greece's northwest coast, in the Ionian Sea. We got another van after going through security and passport control. There were *always* security and passport checkpoints to go through on this trip. We drove to Kompitsi, Agios Ioannis, to Melitta Villa; the place we would be staying at for the next week. We got settled in and drove down to a small store nearby to buy our food and supplies.

    This day, September 9th, would be the last event that would be classified as a *first* for me; the *first* time, after a year, that I received the news about Sylvia and saw her for the final time at the funeral home. I cried all night long in my room at the villa. From now on, starting on September 10th, 2017, everything would now become a *second time;* the *second year without Syl* for: all the months, holidays, seasons, birthdays, anniversaries. This was always an inescapable reality for me. And I believe it always will be.

Sunday, September 10th, we drove through all these back roads until we found Glyfada Beach. We spent the day there; sitting in the sun, walking in the golden sand, swimming in the Ionian Sea, looking at the incredible scenery, with gigantic boulders protruding from the sea. We had a nice dinner there at the Glyfada Mexas Restaurant.

Monday, September 11th, we drove to downtown Corfu and the Port of Corfu to buy our tickets in advance for our upcoming ferry over to Albania. We walked around Old Town of Corfu and Corfu Town.

Tuesday, September 12th, we strolled around downtown Corfu. This was the day that all the kids went back to school, and because of this, I guess everyone is taking a shower at the same time; we learned that it is an annual commonplace situation where all of Corfu runs out of water. We found this out when we had no water at the villa. We had to fill buckets up from the pool, lug them back to the house, and use the pool water to flush the toilets. Then use bottled water to wash up and to brush your teeth. So, "when in Rome," or in this case, Corfu. The water was back on the next day.

While we were walking around downtown Corfu, I noticed these magnets that you can put on your refrigerator and I bought one of Corfu. This became a passion of mine, to buy and collect a magnet at each different place that we went to. I only wish that I had thought of this earlier; I could have collected magnets from all those cities and towns in Italy. I was now known for this and everyone would say, "Look, Dusty, more magnets!" They are very colorful to look at on my refrigerator now and to remember when we were in these amazing places.

After lunch in downtown Corfu, we drove to Halikounas Beach, a long sandy beach with shallow water, where you could swim way out. It was a more rustic atmosphere. They had all these really cool small rocks of many shapes and designs. I collected quite a few and brought them back with me; along with, of course, my magnets. We had a great dinner at the Alonaki Taverna restaurant overlooking Alonaki Bay.

Wednesday, September 13th, we drove to Paleokastritsa, its name meaning "old fortress;" and on to Paleokastritsa Beach, a picturesque village and beach resort on Corfu's spectacular west coast. We spent hours sitting in the sun, on lounge chairs in a grassy area, near the snack bar, where we had some snacks and beers. You had to traverse over pebbles and rocks, on the beach and in the water, until you could swim out to where it was sandy. The beach was surrounded by olive tree forests and gigantic boulders jutting out of the water. Tish and I swam way out past the protruding boulders for some spectacular views.

All of us then went across the street, to the beach of Agios Spyridon, to go on the Paleokastritsa Boat Tour into the caves. The panoramic views here are just so incredible that mere words don't do them justice. The guide takes you out on this boat and then *actually takes the boat inside the caves.* Before he maneuvered the boat inside the first cave, Tish, an experienced boatsman himself, could not believe what he was seeing. Tish asked him, in disbelief,

"You're not *really* going to take this boat inside that cave, *are you?"*

"Yes, we do it all day long, every day."

And he slowly, but surely, maneuvered the boat inside the cave with ease. Amazing. We visited the historical caves of Nausika; the spectacular colors of the underwater rocks; the San Nicolas; and the unique Blue Eye Cave. In one of the caves, the boat guide threw some pieces of bread, and the fish that live in these caves came leaping out of the water in a feeding frenzy. We cruised around the panoramic bays of Paleokastritsa, marveling at all the caves, rock formations, and gazing into the beautiful colors of the turquoise water.

As we got off the boat, the workers put down this wooden platform so that people could walk on it as they exited from their boats and walked to the beach. Joe happened to be standing there as they were doing this and got his foot caught under the platform. We saw this and yelled at him to get his foot out of there before all the passengers got on the platform. Their weight would have crushed his foot, and he would have had a really serious injury; definitely affecting him on this trip, and perhaps for the rest of his life. He was very lucky; he only sustained a bone bruise on his foot. If that was me, the way my luck was going, I would not have been so fortunate, and would have suffered the catastrophic injury. And I was standing right next to Joe, so that's one injury that I avoided.

After the boat tour, we walked up the steep green hills above the beach, to reach the Monastery of Theotokos; a Byzantine monastery that dates back to 1228. The road to the monastery passes through a forest of olive trees and cypresses. It is dedicated to Panagia, (Virgin Mary), of

Paleokastritsa. On top of this remote hill was another panoramic view of the island and the sea.

Thursday, September 14th, we drove around mountainous roads, with more spectacular views of the island and the sea; through small villages with incredibly narrow roads, where the local people would stop and stare at us, as we drove through in our van to the pristine village of Kassiopi. The women had an opportunity to go shopping; as the guys sat in front of this deli-type store, with great sandwiches and a wonderful array of pastries and sweets. We ate our food and enjoyed people watching. Then we all strolled around before getting back in the van and heading to Perithia.

The village of Perithia was built in the 14th century, while the island was under Byzantine rule. It is located on the northern side of Mount Pantokrator, at about 1,300 feet above sea level. The surrounding land was ideal for sheep farming and the cultivation of olives, and Old Perithia soon became prosperous. But times became harder by the 20th century, as tourism brought wealth and jobs to Corfu's coastal areas. Perithia's 1,200 residents were forced to come down the mountain in search of work.

Today it is a protected heritage site, its 130 Venetian style houses are abandoned and some are decaying. There is a school that remained in use until the middle of the 20th century and 8 churches surrounding the village. Today, it has a bed and breakfast and several tavernas. We walked all through this fascinating glimpse of history and had a nice lunch and a beer at one of the tavernas. We drove back to Glyfada Beach and ate dinner, with beautiful views of the Ionian Sea, at the Glyfada Mexas restaurant, where we had been on Sunday.

Friday, September 15th, we drove to Agios Gordios Beach, on the west coast of Corfu. It is surrounded by green olive trees. The water was crystal clear and you could walk way out on the sandy bottom. I was able to do some body surfing here, riding the waves into shore. We had our last dinner here and drove back to the villa, our final night after a wonderful week in Corfu. *I was thinking about how much Sylvia would have enjoyed it here*: staying at the villa; sitting in the sun and swimming in the turquoise waters at the beaches; walking around the picturesque villages, having lunch and shopping; seeing the panoramic views of the island and the sea, while driving or having dinner; eating great food and drinking wine; the Paleokastritsa Boat Tour; the history of Perithia.

Saturday, September 16th, we had to get up really early to pack up all of our things and drive to the port of Corfu, to take the ferry to Albania. None of us knew what awaited us in Albania, nobody had ever been there before. The famous catch phrase by Tish, when any of us asked him a question about what the game plan was, upon arrival in a new place, and especially in a new country, was:

"How do I know? I just got here."

Tish and Mary had an itinerary in mind, knowing which UNESCO World Heritage sites that they had planned on seeing. Everyone else was anxious for detailed information, but Tish liked to keep all of us in suspense, until we arrived at these sites. He enjoyed just springing it on you. I guess he had earned that right, as he organized and planned this whole trip, and did all the driving.

Next came passport control, security, lugging the suitcases and backpacks around, and finding seats on the ferry. We left the shores of Corfu, traveling two hours across the Ionian Sea; seeing the rolling rocky hills as we arrived in Sarandë, known as the "City of the Forty Saints," due to its religious past. Again, lugging the suitcases and backpacks, passport control, security.

We stopped in a town to get some money out of the ATM there. Tish or Wardie had helped me withdraw funds at previous ATM's in Italy and Corfu. Wardie was guiding me here in Albania, where the currency is the lek. Actually, we could have just taken out euros as it turned out. There was a glaring sun at this ATM, as I was planning on taking out 5,000 leks, which would be about $45, just for some spending money. Instead, I inadvertently hit the wrong button, which was 50,000 leks. Now I was stuck with the equivalent of $454 in leks! I was ready to tear my hair out. I became the bank for everyone; they gave me dollars for leks and paid their rooms and other things with leks, as did I. In fact, I got rid of all the leks and there were people still wanting more, but I was finally done.

Our first destination in our five days, four nights Albanian adventure was Himarë, a town in Southern Albania along the Albanian Riviera. After driving for 33 miles, we arrived. There is a well populated Greek community here. We were staying at Alex's B & B, a family owned place with Alex and his wife and their three-year-old son, and another child on the way. It was on a hilltop overlooking the town, with a tall iron gate and a guard dog. After dinner, I took a shower, with the sprayer and no shower curtain, with some water getting on the floor. I mopped it up with some extra towels, wrung them out, and hung them outside to dry.

When everyone went to bed, I went outside to gaze at the lights down below, and reflect that it had been a year now since Sylvia's services; and when I had returned home at night to a lonely house and had sliced my toe on the corner brick of the fireplace. The dog was barking at me and Alex came out to see what was happening. The dog was friendly to me, with Alex there, and I petted him as he lay down next to my feet. Alex and I started talking and he asked me why I was traveling alone when the rest of the group were couples. I told him about Sylvia, not going into lengthy detail. He asked me,

"Would you like to drink some homemade wine with me?"

"Sure."

"It actually tastes more like gin. It is called raki."

Raki is a sweetened, often anise-flavored alcoholic drink that is popular in Albania, Turkey, Greek Islands, and in the Balkan countries as an apéritif. Its main ingredients are grapes, figs, and plums, with an alcohol content of 45 percent. It is very powerful, and I was the first to be exposed to it in our group, at least on this trip. In the hills and towns of Greece and Albania, we saw many homemade stills where raki was being processed. I had a couple of shots with Alex and stumbled back to my room and went to bed.

It was about 5 o'clock in the morning, when I had to take a pee and went into the bathroom. I slept with my socks on, as it was chilly in the room. I didn't even turn the light on as I entered the bathroom, and to my unexpected and unwanted surprise, stepped into an inch or more of water on the bathroom floor. Now I turned the light on. The floor was dry when I went to bed, so I don't know how or why this happened, but it did. It must have seeped up from the drain, I guess. My socks were drenched and I had to wring them out, as well as the towels needed to mop this water up, and hang them outside to dry. Couldn't really get back to sleep after this. We had a nice homemade breakfast and coffee from Alex and his wife, loaded up the van, said our goodbyes, and headed out to our second Albanian destination.

Sunday, September 17th, we started driving up these winding, curving roads in the mountains with no guard rails or shoulders on most of these roads. Coming around the bends, you wouldn't think there was any room in the opposite lane for any vehicle, except for maybe a small car or a motorcycle, which there were those. But then there would appear vans, trucks, and even huge tour buses! There were herders guiding their goats or sheep across the road, while you waited for them to cross. There were cows grazing right on the edge of the road. There were dogs just lying on the side of the road.

It reminded me of Syl and I driving on "Dead Man's Curve" in Antigua in April, 1986. There were other incredibly steep drives on past trips: Syl and I driving down from the top of Whiteface Mountain in Lake Placid in July, 1987; Syl and I driving the mountain roads from Tucson up to Mount Lemmon, and back down, in March, 1993; and with Tish and Mary, with Tish driving, up to the Haleakalā Volcano in Maui, and back down, in February, 2002. They were scary enough, especially if something were to go wrong, but these drives in Albania rivaled those.

We planned on stopping in a small town on the way to get some snacks and take a break. The van carried us nine passengers in three rows, three in each row. This van had a faulty lever on the far-right seat in the second row, next to the sliding door. You had to lift this lever, and hold it, so that the seat would go up and stay up, to allow the three passengers in the back row to get in. The problem was the lever didn't hold the seat up automatically, as it was supposed to do. Previously, it had come flying back unexpectedly and Christie, sitting directly behind it, had a near miss of a serious injury to her ankle. I think Dick was holding the seat up as I got in the back row, the farthest seat to the left.

The ironical thing about what I'm about to tell you, was that Dick was almost *always* sitting in the second row seat by the sliding door. He always was there with an outstretched hand to help you make the step down while getting out of the van. So, this was one of the very few days that Dick was not sitting in that second row seat by the sliding door. I had reached over, after I got in my far left back row seat, and was holding the seat with the bad lever up, with my really long reach; until the other two back row people were in, as well as the first two in the second row. I was still holding on to the seat when Allie, about to sit where Dick usually did, let go of the seat as she sat down; unaware of my hand still being there, and crushed the fourth finger of my right hand. This was one of my few remaining fingers that wasn't bent or deformed from sports' injuries and now severe arthritis. Not anymore. It has now joined the group. I screamed in pain and couldn't help but swear a blue streak. Allie apologized and felt really bad, and I told her that I forgave her, but it didn't help my finger or the pain.

We stopped at this store and went inside. We were always quite a spectacle, nine seniors of varying looks and shapes. The local people welcomed us and brought trays with different kinds of cheeses and raki made from walnuts. I was wandering around the store, getting a few things, and dealing with my pain; when Tish came by with a big glass, not just a shot glass, of raki. He said,

"Here, drink this."

Either he was trying to give me something to ease my pain, or trying to "bust my chops," or both; but I thought that it was water, and he failed to tell me that it was raki. I took a big swig and nearly choked to death. We got back in the van and I kept my fingers out of sight. I had to deal with this pain for the rest of the trip, and my finger has never looked normal since, or will it ever. After 97 miles of driving on these roads, we arrived in Berat.

Berat is a city on the Osum River in central Albania. We drove up this really steep, narrow cobblestoned side road, to reach our hotel, Hotel Rezidenca Desaret, located on a hilltop with beautiful views. Berat is nicknamed "The City of a Thousand Eyes," with its white Ottoman stone houses, where all the windows seem to be watching you. We strolled around the old town of Berat, along its cobblestone streets and medieval architecture. There was the Berat Castle, (Kala), where there has been a fortress since the year 300, but this castle has been there since 1200 AD. There are so many churches in this city, at least 28 of them, some dating back to the 13th century, and historic mosques.

Monday, September 18th, driving these roads again for 100 miles to Gjirokastër; a city in southern Albania, in a valley between the Gjerë mountains and the Drina River, about 1,000 feet above sea level. Its nickname is the "City of 1,000 Steps." We stayed at the Hotel Gjirokastra, in the Partizani District, right behind the Bazaar Mosque. We walked up the steep hill to the Gjirokastër Castle, which dominates the town and overlooks the river valley. It contains a military museum featuring captured artillery, tanks, and memorabilia of the Communist resistance against German occupation. There is a captured U.S. Air

Force spy plane, forced down in 1957. There is the Ali Pasha Castle, where the tyrant, Ali Pasha, used his hilltop fortifications as a communist prison during his 19th century reign, and resided there until 1820. We walked the sloping cobblestoned streets with unique stone houses, giving Gjirokastër another nickname, "The City of Stone;" in Old Town, with many shops and restaurants.

Tuesday, September 19th, we drove 43 miles from Gjirokastër to Ksamil; a village on the Riviera of Southern Albania, and part of Butrint National Park. We stopped near Muzinë, at the famous Blue Eye, a water spring where the beautiful clear light turquoise river has a mesmerizing effect. There is a 164 feet deep pool, although its actual depth is still unclear. Divers have attempted to descend into the Blue Eye to calculate its true depth, but it's still unknown how far this mysterious hole goes. There were two guys diving off from above into the Blue Eye down below. One was a young man in his 20's from Britain, and the other one was a man in his 40's, there with his wife and daughters. They dove many times, definitely not something that any of us would ever attempt, even if we were really young again.

From here we drove 24 miles to the National Park of Butrint. Butrint was an ancient port city, situated on the Straits of Corfu, dating back to the 8th century BC. In ancient times, it was known as Buthrotum, and dedicated to Asclepius, the Greek God of Medicine. Its heritage includes Hellenistic, Roman, Byzantine, Venetian, and Ottoman cultures and civilizations. The theatre was originally built in the 4th century BC by the Greeks, and then the Roman built stage. It has a capacity for over 1,500 spectators and it is still used for summer performances today.

There is the Temple of Asclepius; Roman built courtyard houses and bath; the well-preserved mosaic floor in the Byzantine Baptistery, built in the early 6th century BC; 6th century Basilica; and spectacular circular walls dating back from Greek, Roman, Byzantine, and medieval times. There is also a well-preserved fortress, constructed by the Venetians in the 15th century, known as the Venetian Triangular Castle, on the south side of the Vivari Channel. There is a small structure, attributed to Ali Pasha of Tepelena, located at the mouth of the Vivari Channel, known as the Vivari Channel Fortress. This ancient city of Butrint was truly an amazing site.

We continued on to Ksamil, and had to drive down this really steep driveway to Hotel Kristal, located in a small bay next to Albania's Ionian coast. We arrived late in the afternoon, so we didn't get any beach time. The dinner was not the greatest and it was kind of a funky place, but we made the best of it. We were staying here so that it wouldn't be too far to drive back to Sarandë in the early morning.

Wednesday, September 20th, we drove 9 miles to Sarandë to take the ferry back to Greece. We crossed the amazing beauty and crystal-clear waters of the Ionian Sea and arrived at the port of Igoumenitsa. We encountered a long wait here, as there had been a mix-up in the van reservations, and we had to rent two cars instead. Tish drove one and Allie the other, 16 miles from Igoumenitsa to our new destination, the Ornella Beach Resort in Syvota. It was nice to be back in Greece, although Albania is a beautiful country, at least the central and southern parts that we explored.

Thursday, September, 21st, we woke up to being in the Ornella Beach Resort. This was a great place with pools, rooms with balconies, a fantastic breakfast buffet with everything you could possibly want. They had a small private beach where we lounged in the sun and went swimming in the bay of St. Nicholas Island. It felt good to take a break from all the driving, packing and unpacking. The only negative was dealing with my finger, which I had no choice but to do so. I was just concentrating on not sustaining any more unneeded or unwanted injuries on this trip. We had a relaxing couple of days here before packing up and heading out again.

Friday, September 22nd, we drove 59 miles to Ioannina. On the way, we came upon the Dodoni archaeological site, one of the most ancient of Oracles in Greece, dedicated to Zeus. The sanctuary of Zeus was a major spiritual place in ancient Greece. Only the Delphi Oracle was more famous than Dodoni in ancient times. It was the oldest of the Greek Oracles and ancient people traveled great distances in order to consult the priests who foretold the future. Outside the Temple of Zeus, the priests gathered under the Sacred Oak tree, and listened to the rustling of the leaves and the flight of the doves that nested in its branches, and glimpsed at the future.

Dodoni remained a vital center from 2000 BC, well into Roman times. The Oracle is located at the foot of the majestic twin peaks of Mount Tomaros. There are ancient ruins all around this site, but the most impressive feature is the theatre, which was used for theatrical plays in ancient Greece. It was later modified by the Romans to hold their gladiatorial games. There was a dog, probably belonging to one of the workers there, that took a liking to us and followed us around as we explored the ruins.

After Dodoni, we continued on to Ioannina, and eventually up these steep and winding roads to our hotel,

Mir Boutique, on top of this hill with spectacular views, overlooking Lake Pamvotida and the city of Ioannina. The buildings are connected with stone walkways, Mediterranean gardens, and secluded terraces. The breakfasts here were fantastic. Tish had booked every hotel on this trip to have our breakfasts included, which was a nice feature. We walked up the hill to eat dinner at a restaurant there, which had many homemade items.

Saturday, September 23rd, we explored the Perama Cave, believed to be a million and a half years old. It was discovered by accident in 1940 during World War II, as the inhabitants of the village were trying to find shelter against bombardments. The cave has 19 types of stalactites and stalagmites, where in most other caves there are no more than 10. The colors of red, white, and alabaster created a unique atmosphere. They have found the fossilized bones of a cave bear, thousands of years old. You have to be careful walking in these caves, as there are slippery areas, and to constantly duck to avoid low hanging rock formations. I had to stay focused and not whack my head again, like I did at Santa Severa, although there were plenty of close calls.

We went to Bizani, to see the Pavlos Vrellis Greek History Museum, also known as Pavlos Vrellis Museum of Wax Effigies. The museum was done by the sculptor Pavlos Vrellis, started in 1983 and finished in 1994. It has 150 wax figures in 37 different themes, inspired by events in Greek history. These figures are so lifelike, it is truly mind-boggling.

Sunday, September 24th, we took the ferry at the port across Lake Pamvotida to the island where the house of Ali Pasha, the tyrannical ruler, is located. There is also a small museum, which has unique historical relics from this time period, 1788-1822; and ones from the Greek revolutionary period in the 19th century.

We walked through the city of Ioannina, the capital of Epirus, with all the shops, restaurants, and ancient buildings. Ioannina was always multicultural, with Christian, Islamic, and Jewish influences, evident in the historic city center. The city has the feel of a bygone era.

Monday, September 25th, back in the van again, driving 30 miles on the mountain roads to Aristi. We stopped and got out of the van, to walk across the Missios Bridge, a stone bridge built in 1748, in the Zagori region in the Pindus Mountains. We were now in the northwest part of Greece in Zagorohoria, a region of dozens of villages that have their houses in the deep mountainsides. Many of them are Slavs, the Slavic "za gora," means behind the mountain; and the Greek "horia," which means villages. We arrived at our hotel, the Gamila Rocks Hotel in Aristi, at an altitude of over 2,100 feet, making it a lot cooler up here. It is near the Voidomatis River and the views here were spectacular. "Aristi " in Greek means excellence.

Tuesday, September 26th, we went to the Vikos Gorge, also known as the Vikos Canyon, in the Pindus Mountains, in Vikos-Aoös National Park. It lies on the southern slopes of Mount Tymfi, and is listed by the Guinness Book of Records as the deepest gorge in the world, at almost 3,000 feet. We hiked the rock trails, past the abandoned cliff face monastery of Agia Paraskevi at the southern end. The views were stunning, as the sunlight created magical illusions on the rock formations. We took pictures from above and looking down into the gorge. You get that feeling in the pit of your stomach when you look down.

Another day we drove to Monodendri and hiked through the woods along the Voidomatis River and then hiked up the summit to the Stone Forest, Petrodasos. This is where we found the most impressive views of the Vikos Gorge, with its natural monuments of rock formations.

Wednesday, September 27th, we drove 56 miles from Aristi to Metsovo, in the Pindus Mountains, at an elevation of 3,800 feet. We stayed at the Adonis Hotel with picturesque views of the mountains. It was chilly and rainy that night as we went out to dinner. The only other time that it had rained on this trip was one morning at Ornella Beach, and then it became sunny for the afternoon.

Thursday, September 28th, we drove 98 miles from Metsovo to Vergina. Vergina, in the foothills of Mount Pieria, was the first capital of the ancient kingdom of Macedonia, called Aigai. The people of Macedonia were Greeks, speaking and writing in a dialect of Greek. The city of Aigai was discovered in the 19th century. It is located between the modern villages of Palatitsia and Vergina, in the region of Hemathia, in northern Greece. Aigai, "goat town," the home of the royal dynasty of the Temenids, the family of Philip II and his son, Alexander the Great, 2,500 years ago.

Here we visited one of the most unique museums in the world, discovered in 1977, a giant mound of earth with ancient tombs under it. One of the royal tombs is that of Philip II, who conquered all the Greek cities, paving the way for his son, Alexander the Great, and the expansion of the Hellenistic world. Another royal tomb is that of Alexander IV, Alexander the Great's teenage son. There are other tombs here at Aigai, and all of them were discovered unlooted and in pristine condition. There are amazing artifacts: weapons, body armor, jewelry, free standing columns, temple-like facades, intricately woven and ornamented burial shrouds, carved human figures; and finely crafted ceremonial objects in gold, silver, bronze, iron, and ivory. These are under glass and everything is identified. There is an enormous palace and an adjacent theatre. It was truly a mind-blowing experience to glimpse at this ancient world.

We sat outside in a small cafe on a street corner in Vergina for lunch and then drove 106 miles to Kalambaka, a town in the Trikala region. Kalambaka means "powerful fortress." Here we stayed at the Spanias Hotel, where you had spectacular views of Meteora, a natural sandstone rock formation in the Thessaly region. This view was from the front of the hotel, as our rooms were in the back, facing the woods.

Friday, September 29th, we drove to Meteora after breakfast. There was a huge parking area at the top, with busloads of tour groups and many other tourists. Greek monks, out of fear, built the Meteora monasteries in Kalambaka on top of huge cliffs. Monks got in and out by sitting in a basket hanging on a rope; or by using wooden ladders, which could be drawn up in case of danger. The Meteora monasteries were built between the mid-14th century and the mid-16th century. There were 23 of them, today only 6 remain. There are 60 monks and nuns still living in the monasteries today. We climbed all the way up the steep steps, an exhausting climb to the top of Agia Triada Monastery, (The Holy Trinity.) It is a breathtaking view of the majestic rock formations, the monasteries, the Koziakas and Antichasion Mountains, and the valley below. Some of the scenes in the 1981 James Bond movie, "For Your Eyes Only," with Roger Moore, were shot here.

Saturday, September 30th, we drove 97 miles from Kalambaka to Delphi, formerly also called Pytho; lying on the slopes of Mount Parnassus, high above the Gulf of Corinth. It is the ancient town and seat of the most important Temple and Oracle of Apollo, now a major archaeological site with well-preserved ruins. Delphi was considered by the ancient Greeks to be the center of the world. Between the 6th and 4th centuries BC, the Oracle of Delphi was delivered by the Pythia, the priestess, and interpreted by the priests of Apollo.

Sunday, October 1st, we went into the Archaeological Museum of Delphi, adjacent to the site. It has artifacts that cover over 1,000 years, from the Mycenaean Era to Greco-Roman times.

We started our climb going through The Sacred Way, the main route through the Sanctuary of Apollo, leading from the gateway uphill to the Temple of Apollo. All that remains of the Temple of Apollo are the foundations. There is The Treasury of the Athenians, built around 510 BC and re-erected in 1903-1906, in the form of a Doric temple. It was built by the Athenians, using marble from the island of Paros, to house their offerings to Apollo. This is a copy; the original is in the Delphi Museum. Then up a flight of steps to the theatre, which dates back to the 4th century BC, and could accommodate 5,000 spectators, on 35 rows of stone benches. It was built to host musical contests at the Pythian Games, at Delphi, starting in 590 BC.

Continuing on to the highest part of the site, lies the Stadion, 164 feet above the theatre. It was built in the 5th century BC, but its present appearance was finished under the Romans in the 2nd century AD. Its tiered stone seating could accommodate 500 spectators, and like the theatre, was built to host the Pythian Games. Athletic contests were held here. The games occurred every four years, with each Pythiad marking the halfway point to the Olympics. Initially, the contests were musical, but athletic and equestrian events were added to the program after 586 BC, and were very similar to those held at Olympia. This stadium at Delphi is the best preserved in Greece.

I stepped over the low chain at the end of the stadium to take some full-length pictures. The track has a line of 2nd century Roman arches and you can clearly see the entire racing area, with the starting and finishing lines, and even the grooves of the runners. Below are the Gymnasium and Palaestra, situated close to the Temple of Athena Pronaia, used by athletes in training. There are two terraces: on the upper terrace were two practice running tracks. On the lower terrace was the Palaestra, which was used for wrestling, changing areas for the athletes, dressing rooms, and a large round pool for bathing. The remains date back to the 4th century BC.

We stayed at the Amalia Hotel, located on a slope of Mount Parnassus, at the exit of the town of Delphi. It had a really nice pool, gardens, and a panoramic view of the green valley and olive trees all the way to the Mediterranean Sea; and the towns of Itea and Galaxidi. We strolled all around the town of Delphi with its many shops and restaurants. One night we drove to Galaxidi, to have dinner down by the port, at Zygos Tavern.

Monday, October 2nd, we drove 127 miles from Delphi to Athens. You could tell that you were about to enter a large city with all the traffic. We returned the van and Tish was happy that he didn't have to drive anymore. From now on, it would be buses and walking, mainly on foot. We took a bus to the Arethusa Hotel, where we would be staying for our final three days. The hotel was located next to Syntagma, (Constitution) Square, and Plaka, (Old Town of Athens), on Mitropoleos Street, where the Cathedral of Athens is. There was a constant frenzy of vehicles: buses, cars, motorcycles, motor scooters, (so many motor scooters), taxis, trucks, and vans; all endlessly zipping around everywhere.

We went to the National Archaeological Museum, Greece's largest museum, where you will find artifacts, masterpieces of sculpture, treasures from the Royal Tombs of Mycenae, jewelry, and pottery; an incredible overview of ancient Greek civilization.

We strolled around the streets with all the shops and restaurants, people watching, and taking in all the sights and sounds of this ancient city. On one of the streets you could look up and see the Acropolis site. The sacred rock of the Acropolis was for many centuries a place of worship of Athena, the city's patron Goddess. In the 5th century BC, influenced by Pericles, the site was adorned with the monumental Propylaia, the Erechtheion, and the Parthenon, the eternal symbol of Greek and European civilization.

The Acropolis site has been inhabited since prehistoric times. Over the centuries, it has been a home to kings; a citadel; a mythical home of the Gods; a religious center; and a tourist attraction. It has withstood bombardment, massive earthquakes, and vandalism, yet still stands as a reminder of the rich history of Greece.

The next day, Tuesday, October 3rd, I asked Wardie and Christie if they wouldn't mind if I tagged along with them, to go see the Acropolis site and Parthenon. They said they didn't and we walked to the site to get our tickets. They wanted to get something to eat first. Christie waited in the ticket line as Wardie and I walked a couple of blocks to get the food. He got a gyro and I got a falafel. We walked back and Christie had the tickets. I thought we would just sit in the little park there, take ten minutes to eat our food, and then proceed to the site. Wardie had eaten over half of the gyro on the way back, and Christie ate the rest as we went on our way. I guess I could have just eaten my falafel on the way, but I wanted to sit down to enjoy it.

They seemed like they were in a hurry, as they quickly observed some ruins and were getting way ahead of me. I was starting to feel like "the third wheel," as I wanted to soak in and savor all the history that I was seeing. We stopped and took pictures of the Odeon of Herodes Atticus. This ancient theatre was built in 161 AD, designed with an auditorium fitted into a natural hollow. Semicircular rows of seating could accommodate 5,000 people. Live performances, like the Athens & Epidaurus Festival, presenting classical Greek operas, as well as musical and dance performances, are still held in this theatre in the summer. That must be an amazing experience.

We entered the Acropolis site through the Beulé Gate, a Roman-Era doorway, dating back to 280 BC; named after the 19th century French archaeologist, Ernest Beulé, who uncovered it in 1852. The Beulé Gate is below the west side of the Propylaia, the majestic entrance to the Acropolis. On the way up to the Propylaia is the Monument of Agrippa, built in the 2nd century BC. The Propylaia was built in 437-432 BC. A flight of marble stairs leads up to an entrance containing five gateways, which increase in width and height from the sides to the center. The porticos are supported by Doric and Ionic columns.

A woman worker at the gate informed me, observing the bag with the falafel in it that I was still holding, that there was no food allowed at the site. I told her that I promised not to eat anything up there and she trusted me. Why I was still foolishly holding on to this bag with the falafel in it, I can't really offer any logical explanation. So, I continued to constantly carry the bag around one of the most impressive and important sites in history, having to set it down each time that I took a picture on my phone.

By now, Wardie and Christie were nowhere in sight, having already gone through all the landmarks I was now experiencing. I saw them as I marveled at the elegant Temple of Athena Nike, an ancient sanctuary dedicated to the Goddess Athena as the bringer of Victory, (Nike.) I never knew that one, about how they got the name Nike. The temple was built between 432 BC to 421 BC, after the completion of the Parthenon and the Propylaia.

I think Christie was having problems with her hip, suffering nerve damage from contracting Lyme disease many years ago. She had sat down to rest, as Wardie returned from taking a few pictures on the other side of the Parthenon. I told them I wanted to take a few pictures of the Parthenon, and on the other side of it, just to give me ten minutes and I would walk back to the hotel with them. I only took ten minutes zipping around to take my pictures, at least that's what I thought, but when I returned to where they were before, they were long gone. It kind of annoyed me that they couldn't have waited for me, at least to tell me that they needed to get going. In their defense, Christie obviously was having a lot of discomfort and needed to get back.

It was a blessing in disguise for me, as I could now take some more pictures and take my good old sweet time in doing so. I mean, when are you going to be standing on the Acropolis site, next to the Parthenon, the Temple of Athena, and all the other temples, again; realistically? In all probability, never. I asked a young woman who was there if she would take a couple of pictures of me in front of the Parthenon. (I had to set my bag with the falafel in it by her, out of sight.) She was nice enough to do it, and took some good pictures.

The Parthenon was the most magnificent and sacred temple of the ancient world. It stands majestically on the highest point of the Acropolis hilltop, featuring 136 fluted Doric columns, in repeated rows of 8 times 17; creating a feeling of harmony and order. Seeing this awe-inspiring sight directly in front of me made me well up with tears, glad that I was privileged enough to be here to see it, *and sad that Sylvia was not here standing next to me, experiencing this together, and for herself.*

After serving as a temple for 900 years, the Parthenon suffered considerable damage in the 5th century. It was transformed into a Christian church, dedicated to the Virgin Mary, and remained in use for 950 years. After that, it became a Turkish mosque in 1456. Unfortunately, the temple, which had stood for more than 2,100 years, was destroyed by a bomb during fighting between the Turks and the Venetians in the 17th century. Another example of how senseless that war is. At least the ruins remain today as testimony to its former glory.

I continued to walk around the Acropolis site, taking more pictures and seeing more magnificent structures. There was: The Porch of the Caryatids at the Erechtheion; Old Temple of Athena Polias; and The Legendary Olive Tree of the Pandroseion. I reluctantly started to walk back down from the site, taking some pictures of things I barely had enough time to appreciate on the hurried walk up. So, I was glad for that. I started the long walk back to the hotel, having no clue where I was. Fortunately, I had the business card of the hotel in my wallet. I asked a guy waiting for a bus for directions and headed that way, still holding on to the bag with the falafel in it. I could have tossed it in the trash if it smelled bad. I checked it out and it didn't. I had carried it around all day and was determined to eat it. I probably should have sat on a bench and eaten it, but I wanted to get back to the hotel and see what the group plans were. So, I kept walking, crossing busy streets with all the crazy traffic, when everyone else did when the lights changed. I asked directions again when I knew the hotel was in the vicinity. Finally, I reached the hotel, went up to my room, and ate my soggy falafel. It wasn't as good as it would have been when freshly made, but it was still okay; and yet another story to tell.

  Wednesday, October 4th, we walked to the Ancient Agora of Athens, an archaeological site beneath the northwest slope of the Acropolis. These ruins, located in the heart of modern Athens, were once the site of the Agora, or gathering place. The term means marketplace in modern Greek. In the ancient world, it was a political, cultural, and economic center. Pericles and Socrates once walked here. Two magnificent buildings still stand among the ruins as testaments to its past glory. The Temple of Hephaestus, the best preserved ancient Greek temple from the Classical Era, and the Stoa of Attalos from the Hellenistic period. In the Stoa of Attalos is a small, but impressive museum, The Archaeological Museum of the Athenian Agora. It has art dating back to the Stone Age and artifacts from the Classical period.

  That night, we walked from the hotel, up steep stairs to a place where you get the cable car that takes you up to Mount Lycabettus, almost 1,000 feet above sea level. We met Lynn here. Lynn is a childhood friend of Laura, Tish and Mary's daughter. They became friends when they lived in Los Gatos, California, where Lynn is from. Lynn studied at the University of California, Santa Barbara, before deciding that she had always wanted to go to Greece and live. She moved to Athens and has been here ever since. She always maintained her friendship with Laura, and Tish and Mary had contacted her about getting together while we were in Athens. She was happy to see them and meet us. Lynn has a Marisa Tomei look about her. She became our guide for the evening.

We took the cable car to the top of Lycabettus Hill. There is a 19th century church here, the Chapel of Saint George, and also a restaurant and a theatre. Hundreds and hundreds of people were up here to watch the sunset, as it is a very well-known and popular place. They were all eating, drinking, talking, and taking pictures. It was a beautiful sight to witness the sunset, with a bonus of a rising yellow full moon, knowing you were a part of ancient, as well as modern, history. It became dark when the sun went down, and to see Athens transform into a city of lights, with the Parthenon lit up in the distance; was truly memorable. And the full moon shining brightly added a final touch to this portrait.

We took the cable car back down and Lynn helped us get taxis. There was some kind of protest going on back in the city and some of the taxi drivers had been caught up in that and wanted to go off duty for the rest of the night. Lynn finally got a couple of them to drive us into the city, so we could go have dinner at this restaurant next to her apartment. This taxi driver was zigging and zagging around the traffic and avoiding the congestion where these protests were taking place.

This restaurant was an upscale one with many Greek families eating there. You could look out the large window from your table to see the Acropolis site and the Parthenon all lit up at night, an amazing scene to look at while eating dinner! After dinner, we walked to Lynn's apartment, a block away. Surprisingly, it was sparsely decorated. We walked up the stairs out to an immense flat roof where you had an amazing view of the Acropolis site and the Parthenon all lit up.

Lynn is a yoga instructor and holds some of her classes up here. Tish and Mary had originally planned for all of us to participate in a yoga session with her, but it didn't work out. It had a dizzying effect on you when you looked down to the street below. I wouldn't want to be up here for a party, drinking a lot of wine, and wandering around up here. There were no barriers, and if you didn't focus on where you were, the fall would not have a happy ending. It would have been nice to spend some more days with her, as she could have taken us to places only she would know, living in Athens for around twenty-five years. But this night was it, at least we all had the chance to meet her, and hang out with her for the evening.

Thursday, October 5th, we got up early, packed all our things, had breakfast, and checked out. Tish and Mary and I walked several blocks with all our suitcases and backpacks to the bus stop. We had purchased our tickets the day before. We took the bus, with all its stops, out to the airport. The rest of them had taken taxis. Wardie and Christie were flying back to California on an earlier flight. The rest of us flew back to the Philadelphia airport, got our suitcases, said our good-byes, and went through customs. Joe and Allie were going to their house, Tish and Mary were spending a week with Laura before driving back home to Orlando, Dick and Nina were flying back home to

Orlando, and I was flying back home to Syracuse. I had arranged for Nancy to pick me up at the Syracuse airport, which she was nice enough to do, and gave me a ride home.

I got back to the house before dark and entered what used to be *our home*, now just a lonely house, as reality sank in once more. I'm glad that I went, I did the trip for both of us; seeing some amazing things, taking a journey back in time.

I drove over to Tom and Debbie's the next day to see what was going on. Will was now living at the house for the first semester of his senior year. This was actually his fifth year of college, needing the extra year to complete two majors, one in Economics and the other in Sports Management. He had gone to Occidental College, outside of Los Angeles, for his freshman year, and now four years at Syracuse University, spending the second semester of his junior year in London. The second semester of his senior year, he would be living in New York City, and doing an internship at production companies, Roadhouse and Jigsaw, where they did some of the "30 for 30" series for ESPN.

Tom and Debbie had allowed Will to have a roommate, Giuseppe, a good friend and a Mechanical Engineering student at SU, also in his senior year. He was originally from Brooklyn, but his parents now lived in New Jersey. There was another guy, I won't mention his name, that was also a good friend of Will's and Giuseppe knew him as well. He had already graduated from SU in May and was home living with his parents in New Jersey. When he heard that Will had the house with just him and Giuseppe living there, he decided to impose on Will's good nature and vulnerability, and ask to live there also. It was a rent-free place, out of his parents' house, and an opportunity to start up a computer business with his Syracuse connections and friends. Perfect for him. Not so perfect for everyone else. Will should have received permission from Tom and Debbie to allow him to live here, even for one semester. He knew that Will was too nice a guy to say no. Giuseppe would be staying for the entire school year, the second semester by himself. I'm sure the other guy would have tried to worm his way to stay for the second semester, if he could, when Will went to New York City.

    I tried my remote to open the garage door, but it wasn't working. Maybe it needed a new battery. I got out of the car and put in the number code on the side of the garage door to open the garage. This did not open the door either, so maybe this also needed a new battery. Didn't seem likely, but it was a possibility. I could hear a loud blowing sound coming from inside the garage, a sound I had never heard before. I went to the front door and rang the doorbell, and the other guy opened the door. He was friendly, I had met him once before, as we said hello and shook hands. I told him I couldn't get the garage door to open and was hearing a loud, strange blowing noise.

    "Didn't you hear what happened?"

    "No, I was away on a trip."

    "Oh, there was a fire in the garage and they are blowing the smoke smell out."

    "That's horrible. Is everyone okay?"

    "Yeah."

    As it turned out, admitting no guilt, and showing very little remorse, he was the one who caused the fire. In the middle of September, Will was on campus for classes, and this guy was leaving for wherever he was leaving for in his car. He had just finished smoking a cigarette, didn't bother to extinguish it properly, and just flicked it near the garage on an extremely hot day. It set fire to the garage, one entire side and most of the roof. Giuseppe happened to be taking a nap, in his basement apartment in the house, between classes, and smelled the smoke. It was extremely lucky that he was there, or otherwise the whole house would have burned down, along with all their possessions. Giuseppe's car was luckily out of the garage, safely out in the driveway. And Will had driven his car up to the campus. If those cars had been in the garage, they would have been burned up as well, and the distinct possibility of explosions. He raced upstairs and looked in the garage and called the Fire Department. They came and put the fire out.

    Because of this guy's careless actions, five people were directly impacted; Tom, Debbie, Will, Giuseppe, and me. So now this became a frustrating reality for the next six months. The house inside looked like it had been hit by a hurricane. There were dirty dishes, including greasy iron skillets, piled up in the sink. There were boots and shoes everywhere. The kitchen table was unusable, with all his computer things and papers on it. You would think that he would be doing everything in his power to make the place neat, but it was totally the opposite. He had left the window open in the room that he was staying in upstairs, with no screen in it, letting all these stink bugs in. He had spilled red wine on the couch. This guy was the roommate from hell. Will has a hard time being neat, but with my monitoring and Giuseppe's help, could have kept the house in decent shape. Giuseppe was neat and had his own space in the basement, away from all this chaos.

    It became worse when everything in the garage, including on the shelves, had to be taken out of there, so that the garage could be rebuilt and painted. This also included the mud room, which you entered from the garage, and it led to a door to the back deck and also a door to enter the kitchen and the rest of the house. There were many winter and other jackets in the mud room closet that had to be sent out to be dry cleaned. This guy and Will brought in everything from the garage and basically just threw it in the dining room and the space from the kitchen to the dining room. Balls, all kinds of balls: soccer balls, basketballs, footballs, buckets of baseballs and tennis balls; paint cans, automotive stuff, foldable chairs, recyclable bins, and on and on. This was all now in the dining room and spilled over into the kitchen. Sylvia would have been flipping out. I was now the only one with any maturity to deal with this. Eventually, just before Debbie came back for several days over Thanksgiving, I had Will help me carry all this stuff, (that I didn't throw away, that smelled like smoke, or recycle); down into the alcove area, and in the pool table room, of the basement, where it wouldn't impact Giuseppe's living quarters.

      This situation dominated a lot of my time for the next two months. I did yard work here and over there, and started taking my walks again, to Green & Round Lakes, Pratt's Falls, and Mill Run Park in Manlius, five minutes away. I had gone there, when I taught in Pre-K my first two years at MPH, to take the kids on their end of the year picnic there. Syl and I had also taken the kids a few times on field trips there in our earlier years. We also took Liam and Will there, for batting practice at a field up at the top, when they were in their Little League years. But Syl and I never went there after that, we just always went to Green Lakes, Pratt's Falls, and an occasional hike in Highland Forest or Beaver Lake, in the fall.

I rediscovered walking in Mill Run Park now, and noticed there were five wooden benches in the park, three of them that had bench plates dedicated to a loved one, and the fourth dedicated to a family dog. These benches were different than all the wooden benches in the main picnic areas. After walking past the pavilion, veering to the right, was a path with two benches with name plates, on the left-hand side of the path. The second bench was dedicated to Eric's (Nancy's husband) first wife, Joan, who passed away at the age of 50 in 2001, from cancer. I saw that bench, and then happened to notice another bench, further down on the right-hand side of the path, closer to Limestone Creek. It is partially hidden until you get close to it. It is wider than the other benches, with metal legs. This bench was pretty beaten up and weathered, with some bad words carved into it.

I got the idea to make this a bench for Sylvia. I inquired at the village offices and I don't think they even knew it was there. The other benches had their plates put on over 16 years ago. I was willing to pay for it, but after I explained about Sylvia, and what I planned to have engraved on the nameplate, they thought that was beautiful and to just go ahead and do it. They said they want to eventually add some new benches in there, but who knows when that will happen. I went back to the bench a few days later, and took a sharp stone and scratched the bad words out; and brought a hammer and thin nails, to secure some splintered pieces of wood on the seat of the bench.

LeeAnne engraved another bench plate for me, exactly the same and with the same exact inscription, as the one she had done for the bench at Round Lake. On November 29th, on a cold and windy day, I met Nancy and we walked in the snow to the bench. She had the screws and screwdriver and put the plate in. So now I have another bench to go to and hang out at, in all seasons, and talk to Sylvia.

Karen, Sylvia's sister, had posted on Facebook that Ursula had gone into the hospital just before Thanksgiving. She had been dealing with some health issues the past couple of years, and now had gotten sick. She was there for Thanksgiving and over Christmas as well, just like Sylvia was when she had her port installed, and her first three chemo infusions, in 2014.

Tom and Debbie came back to their house for a month, from the middle of December until the middle of January, during their semester break. Giuseppe went home over this time and the other guy finally knew that it was time for him to leave. Will was always stressed out all fall, as this guy was not making any effort to help out or clean up after himself, plus Will felt guilty about the fire.

But now he was gone, and Will could have some of his MPH friends over to spend time with over the holidays. Most of them were college graduates and now going to graduate school. I went over for a few dinners with them and hung out with the guys, telling them some of my stories from the European trip. Tom and Debbie had their annual New Year's Eve Party. As it turned out, this would be the last one in this house.

2018

August 31st-October 4th: (Second European trip)

Switzerland

Zurich

    Interlaken

    Sundlauenen

    Wengen

    Männlichen

Italy

    Stresa

    Lake Maggiore

    Isola Bella

    Portico di Romagna

    Brescia

    Lake Garda

    Varone

    Limone sul Garda

    Sirmione

    Milan

Romania

    Bucharest

    Sinaia

    Bran

    Râsnov

    Prejmer

    Targu Neamt
    Transylvania
    Probota
    Sighisoara
    Saschiz
    Biertan
    Vintu de Jos
    Alba Iulia
    Hunedoara
Bulgaria
    Sboryanovo
    Burgas
    Nessebar
    Plovdiv
    Kazanlak
    Shipka
    Kmetovtsi
    Gabrovo
    Brestnitsa
    Dryanovo
    Arbanasi

Veliko Tarnovo

Spain

Madrid

Yuncos

Toledo

Another year was upon me. Another year that Sylvia would never get the chance to see and experience. Another long winter in Syracuse in a lonely house without her.

On January 2nd, Will and I went to the Destiny Mall in Syracuse to see "The Magical History Tour": A Beatles Memorabilia Exhibition at "The Muzium" there. Will was fascinated by these exhibits, and so was I. There was an amazing collection of rare Beatle artifacts, photographs, and historical items, including the original stage from the Cavern Club. He loved to hear my stories about being a part of the Beatles era in real time.
We walked around, taking pictures, soaking it all in. After this, we went and had dinner in the mall. Syl would have enjoyed this day so much. Will left a couple of days later for his internship in New York City.

I went over to Tom and Debbie's several times to do my chores, have dinner, and visit with them until the middle of January. I gave them separate rides to the airport, as they had different departure dates, due to their teaching schedules.

I received an email from Tish about a second European trip. He only gives you a few days to think about it, either you are in or you are not. The intrigue of the Swiss Alps, northern Italy, *Romania, Bulgaria,* and Spain enticed me to make my commitment. This was something in the back of my mind to think about.

    I spent the rest of January and February shoveling snow in front of the garage here and over at Tom and Debbie's. I tried to pick the days where the roads were not icy to go over there and to the store. I had to go over there to meet with painters, contractors, and inspectors about them rebuilding the garage and painting it and the mudroom. I obviously couldn't put Will's SUV, a 2009 Ford Explorer, that Tom and Debbie had bought for him to use in Syracuse, back in the garage until the garage was finished, new roof and all. It was left around the bend in the circular part of the driveway, where the plower had to plow around it. When they finished the garage in early February, I had to shovel four feet of ice and snow around the SUV, like a solid brick wall. Then get the same amount of ice and snow off the SUV itself, finally get it started, and put it in the garage. It was my responsibility to start the SUV and take it for a spin frequently to keep it running properly. This became an additional chore to do.

    Giuseppe was living there by himself now and in his final semester at Syracuse University. I hung out with him when I was over there and told him some of my stories on our vacations, which he enjoyed hearing. I was planning on hand writing my book, just like I had done for my screenplay and children's books. He suggested getting a tablet and it was great advice. He ordered a Samsung Galaxy E, with a nice case, with a Fintie keyboard for me through Amazon. I reimbursed him and he gave me many technological tips. This is the device that I have been using to write this book.

I began to write this book, basically writing down notes and thoughts that were forming in my brain. This was the beginning of an over two-year process of writing my book.

The Winter Olympics, from Pyeongchang, South Korea, started on February 9th and ended on February 25th. I enjoyed watching them and I know that Syl would have also, especially the figure skating. I always think of watching the Winter Olympics in Salt Lake City, Utah, in 2002, with Syl, Tish and Mary, in their condo in Lahaina, when we were in Maui. It was such an extreme contrast, but we all were immersed in watching them, especially the figure skating.

In March, Earl, a good friend and softball teammate on the Cyclones; suddenly, and unexpectedly, passed away. I happened to see this sad news on a Facebook post. He was 70, way too young. I drove out to Baldwinsville, 12 miles northwest of Syracuse, where Earl had lived and taught History in their school system, for the services. Most of the guys on the Merchants' and Cyclones' teams were in a tournament in Florida. I saw Stevie J. as he was going through the line, talked for a few minutes, then he had to leave. "Stump," Angie, and I were the only ones from the softball teams there.

There were a lot of people there and many of them spoke. I had worn my Cyclones warmup jacket, as had "Stump," and I felt obligated to speak, honoring Earl and representing the Cyclones. So, I did. Earl always had a smile on his face, liked to "bust your chops," and keep things loose, on and off the field. Former students and teachers gave rave reviews about his teaching. When I went through the line, Pam, his wife whom he had just married in recent years, asked me how I was dealing with my loss and what to expect. I told her that everyone was different, but it is not an easy thing to deal with. This is true. Angie put a song on through the sound system that was very touching. I talked with them outside after the services, but it was cold and windy, and we all headed for home.

Made it through another winter, taking walks at Green and Round Lakes and Mill Run Park and watching college basketball on television. This was the year of all the *"seconds." The second New Year's Day; Winter: January, February, & most of March; Spring: rest of March, April, our anniversary on the 16th, May, & most of June; the second year of these things without Syl.*

Then the next round of sad news came from Karen in a Facebook post that Ursula had passed away on April 18th. Ironically, the 18th is Sylvia's birth date, (in June.) Syl would have been so sad if she had still been here. She would have been distraught starting in November of 2017 when Ursula became sick. She would have wanted to go down to Charleston to be with her. Karen was taking care of Ursula and being with her in the hospital. Syl could have helped her and stayed in Ursula's house on the foldable couch. But when Ursula came home from the hospital for a few months, Syl would have had to sleep on an air mattress in all probability, as Karen's son Andrew was now staying there as well.

When Syl would have returned home at some point over the winter, she would have had to go back down in the middle of April for the funeral arrangements and Ursula's services. It was good that Syl didn't have to go through this sadness. Yet to still be alive, and live for many more years and have her own life experiences, and our many more years of life experiences together; I think she would have chosen to endure this sadness. Ursula lived to be 82 and almost 4 months, 19 years more than what Syl got. Two months later, on June 20th, Ursula's sister and Karen and Sylvia's Aunt, Lori, passed away. Syl would have been very sad about this as well.

I found this recently among some of Syl's notes and writings:

"My mother is a woman like no other. She gave me life, nurtured me, taught me, dressed me, fought for me, held me, shouted at me, kissed me, but most importantly she loved me unconditionally. There are not enough words to describe just how important my mother is to me. What a powerful influence she continues to be. I love you."

At the end of April, I started to bring, with Giuseppe's help, all those things from the garage that had been stored in the basement, back into the garage. Tom and Debbie returned home after the first week in May for Will's graduation. Will had completed his internship in New York City and Giuseppe drove down there and brought him back to Syracuse. Debbie's brother, John, and his wife, Linda, came in from northern California; and Tom's Uncle, Joe, and his wife, Joan, and their family came in from New Jersey.

I had written a four-page summary of all of our years together, of Syl and I doing things with Willie, and all the vacations with them, and gave a copy to Will. He sent me a picture from his phone of these four pages being put in a frame by Tom, and hung on the wall in their house in Claremont. It had been 18 years and almost 4 months since we first met Willie in Pre-K at MPH in September, 1999.

We all went to his graduation at The Carmelo K. Anthony Basketball Center, where the Syracuse men's and women's basketball teams have their practice facilities, near The Manley Field House. It opened on September 24, 2009. These graduations were for the David B. Falk College of Sport and Human Dynamics. The different fields were: Food Studies; Human Development and Family Science; Marriage and Family Therapy; Nutrition; Nutrition Science and Dietetics; Public Health; Social Work; Sport Management. They had to read the names of almost 600 graduates from all these fields. Will received the Academic Excellence Award in Sport Management, the highest award that you can receive. He also was to get his degree in his other major, Economics, the following day in the graduation ceremonies in the Carrier Dome. Everyone was proud of Will.

    There was a big reception party at Tom and Debbie's house after the Falk College graduation. Giuseppe's parents and family came up from New Jersey, to see him graduate in Mechanical Engineering, and I met them. It was a great party, catered, and so many family and friends who had been there to support Will on his successful path. I only wish that Syl had been here for the graduation and the reception, she would have loved it. She was an integral part of Willie's, (Will's), development and growth.

    Will flew out to Phoenix immediately after the graduation at the Carrier Dome the following day. He was going on a ten day, hiking and whitewater rafting expedition, with a group, in the Grand Canyon. He had an exhilarating experience.

    I had figured out that through May 31st of this year, 2018, it had been *646 nights,* that I had been sleeping alone in our bed, without Syl being there. The last night that she had slept there was the night of August 23rd, 2016.

The next day, the 24th, I took her down to the hospital, never to return home. This fact only covers this time period; it does not include a week in March, 1986, when I went to a golf reunion with some old friends in Dallas Texas. Or the 11 years of 3 days and 2 nights that I was gone, being a chaperone for the fifth-grade field trips at Silver Bay in Lake George, New York. Or in 2004, 3 weeks after we had moved into this house; when I was also gone for 3 days and 2 nights, as a chaperone for the sixth-grade field trip at Frost Valley, New York, in the Catskills. I did both field trips that year. Or all the softball tournaments over the years; 2, 3, or 4 nights that I was gone, the ones that Syl was unable to go with me on. Or the 3 years that Syl went on vacation, two Christmases and one Thanksgiving, where she was gone visiting her family in Charleston for a couple of weeks.

On June 1st, Traian and Ioana invited me over to their house for a wonderful dinner. Ioana always made great meals. Ileana was finishing up her 8th grade year and graduating from Middle School at MPH. If Sylvia was here, we would have gone to her graduation ceremonies. We started talking about my upcoming trip to Romania.

I had been invited to attend Mariah's, Kyle and Cheryl's daughter, graduation, (from MPH), party at the Lakeshore Yacht and Country Club in Cicero, on Oneida Lake, on Friday night, June 15th. I assumed, being held at a Country Club, that it was a dress-up affair. I was dressed in my dress pants and shoes, dress shirt and tie, and even brought along my suit jacket, in case you were required to wear one to get in. Boy was I wrong! Everyone was happy to see me and Kyle and Cheryl were so glad that I came. I was saying that I was way overdressed, as everyone else was dressed in casual shorts and golf shirts, and the women in shorts or a casual dress.

They said I looked great and that I stood out in a positive way. The MPH kids that were there came running over to me like I was a rock star, so that was a nice feeling. It was a beautiful setting with a spectacular view of the lake on a warm night. There was great food, drink, and conversation. I gave Mariah one of Syl's necklaces as a gift. Syl would have loved to have been here and would have looked beautiful in whatever she had chosen to wear.

The following day, Saturday the 16th, Nancy and LeeAnne were having a graduation, (from MPH), party at Green Lakes for Sarah and Cole. It was a cookout, more informal than the night before. There were many parents, teachers and kids from MPH. I gave Sarah one of Syl's necklaces as a gift; and a pair of Syl's earrings to Bianca, Andre and Suzette's daughter, and another MPH graduate.

It was now June 18th, *the second year of not being able to celebrate Syl's birthday with her.* I wrote to her and posted it on Facebook:

"Well, Syl, today would have been your sixty-fifth birthday. I miss you more with each passing day, each lonely night. I love you more than ever. I will never stop missing you. I will never stop loving you."

I started playing golf again at Green Lakes with Tish, Mary, and Steve a couple of times a week for the summer. I was also watching the World Cup Soccer games being played in Russia, from the middle of June until the middle of July; and watching the Yankees games.

Tom and Debbie had the pool opened again, mainly to see if the filter pump and other equipment was still working, being next to the garage and the fire. The pool company they had for all these years was kind of inept and there were always issues with them. I agreed to do the weekly cleaning, which I did most of the time anyway, so Tom and Debbie wouldn't have to pay the company to do it. It was opened the third week in June and took a while to get functional. I could swim in it the first two weeks in July, but it still didn't have that shimmering look, like it normally should.

It became a nightmare for me after this, and I wish it had never been opened in the first place. It was a very hot and humid summer and the water kept turning green, like a pond. They came over and put chemicals in it, and it looked like it was starting to clear up; then I'd come back a few days later, and it would be green again. They said even newer pools were turning green with the humidity this summer. I backwashed it, kept everything functional, but I don't think the chlorinator was ever working correctly. I was constantly calling them, meeting them to check the chlorinator, and they would put more chemicals in, but it would turn green again. This was a very frustrating situation and it was a daily hassle for me. I had them close it and put the cover on it, in the middle of August, so I didn't have to deal with it anymore.

This was the summer, except for two okay weeks at the beginning of July, where there was really no pool. I remember all the years of fun with the kids, and swimming, and it being a sanctuary for us sometimes. This was the end of the pool days. Syl would have been very frustrated. *This was now the second summer: the rest of June, July, August, and into September, through the 8th, without Syl.*

I went up to Steve and Donna's camp on Kayuta Lake, in the foothills of the Adirondacks, near Remsen. They had invested so much time, effort, blood, sweat, and tears into making it what it is now. They have the main house, a guest house, a boat house, a dock, kayaks, a pontoon boat. They have put in wooden stairs from the parking area down the hill to the camp. They have all these unique metal sculptures all over.

They had invited us up for years, and now being here, I know how much Syl would have loved it, something Donna always told me. I told Donna to take one of the flower displays after Sylvia's services, and she finally did, putting it on the kitchen table at camp. She had sent me a picture of it from her phone, and said that she was glad she had taken the flowers, as it felt like Sylvia's spirit was there at the camp.

There was always a tight window of possible times to go up there for most of those years. We weren't done with school, graduations, and the Playscape program until the last week in June. After that, there were softball tournaments, taking care of Mom, visits from Ursula, going up to Montréal, vacations with Tom, Debbie, and Willie, our vacations to Cape Cod, and watching Willie for the last two weeks in August. Then back for a week of teachers' meetings and the start of another school year.

Then they started to rent out their guest house, sometimes for weeks, even for the month of July. In later years, we tried to arrange to come up there, but the guest house had been rented out.

I followed their directions and drove up there, 53 miles northeast from Manlius to Remsen, in July. I sat down by the dock and then Steve and I went out in the pontoon boat with their dog, Charly. We cruised around the lake, checking out all the camps. Donna made a nice salad and dinner, and we took a walk up on the railroad tracks. I wasn't sure if I was going to stay overnight. I had some extra clothes in my trunk. It was starting to get dark and I didn't want to have to drive at night on strange roads if I didn't have to. They invited me to stay and I accepted. Steve and I sat by the outdoor fire, drinking wine, and flashing back on some old memories.

I spent a pleasant night sleeping in the guest house, waking up to a beautiful view of the lake. We spent the day down by the water, swimming and sitting in the sun on a little strip of sand. They were doing some yard work here and there, and I helped out as well. Donna made some lunch and we went out on the pontoon boat for another cruise on the lake. They were picking up some friends to take for a ride and they dropped me off back at the camp.

I thanked them, gathered up my things, and headed for home. I took a different route back to Syracuse, not the back roads one I had come up on. There was a confusing exit sign and I went past it and wound up close to downtown Utica. I had to ask for directions and turn around and get back on the main highway. At least it wasn't dark out yet.

On August 15th, Traian and Ioana invited me over to their house for dinner. This was the last chance to see them before my trip, as they would be going on their vacation to Cape Cod a couple of days later. I showed them our itinerary and we talked about these places that we were about to see in Romania. They wrote some information down for me and gave me the phone number of Andreia, Ioana's sister, who lived with their parents in Bucharest. We exchanged emails and I was hoping to see her and have dinner on our last night in Romania, but it didn't work out. She was a veterinarian and would be out of town for that night.

It was now August 20th, my 72nd birthday, and the second one without Syl. In normal years, the last one being in 2015, (even though Syl had endured 10 months of tests, chemo infusions, and radiation treatments; but was now taking a break and she was looking better, with her hair growing back, and feeling better, getting her weight back to normal); we would spend the day at the lake or the pool, eat our lunch, sit in the sun, swim, read, talk, and hang out together. Then we would shower, put on casual dress clothes, and go out to the Brewster Inn or Bonefish for a nice dinner.

Well, this was not my scenario today. It was a sunny day and I decided to go over and sit by the pool at Tom and Debbie's house, even though the pool was closed and had the cover on it. I could get away from all the commotion happening near my backyard; and just sit in the sun, listen to my iPod, and spray myself with water from a plastic squirt bottle when I needed to. It sounded like a decent plan, at least at the beginning.

I had been there for several hours when I noticed this tall weed several steps from where I was now sitting. Who knows why I do some of the things that I do, as alluded to with my past injuries in this book. Fortunately, I had put on my old sneakers, even though I didn't tie them, and the left one had a huge rip in it. I got up from the lounge chair, walked a few steps, and pulled out this weed.

I know I tend to exhibit traits of OCD, Obsessive Compulsive Disorder, maybe this is why I can't help doing some of the things that I do. I don't know. Anyway, I threw the weed over the fence, behind the lounge chair, and as I turned around, I tripped over the strap holding down the pool cover. If the pool had been okay, I would have waited another week before closing it. Having those sneakers on, even though ripped and untied, was a good thing, or it probably would have been a serious foot and toe injury; worse than slicing my big toe that night after Syl's services.

I could feel gravity taking over and hurtling me forward. There was no time to lean back and nothing to hold on to or break my fall. Break being a word I didn't want to think about as this was happening. I crash-landed, doing a faceplant onto the patio bricks surrounding the pool. I tried to brace my fall with my hands, but to no avail. I didn't break my wrists anyway. But I had seriously smashed my chin, with a direct full force hit, as well as both knees and my chest. I knew that I was in a lot of pain and didn't know what the extent of my injuries entailed. Blood was pouring out of my chin and my knees were all bloody. All I could think of was that I had knocked out my front tooth, the same one that I had suffered traumatic injuries to, ever since "Skippy" Evans pushed me off the monkey bars in second grade at Dundee, in 1953, 65 years ago. I went into the house, shocked and stunned, hoping that I hadn't cracked or knocked any teeth out. If so, that would mean having emergency dental surgery, cost me lots of money, pain, discomfort; and face the possibility of not being able to enjoy food, as you normally would, on this upcoming European trip, leaving in ten days. I checked myself out in the mirror, not knowing what I would be seeing, and it didn't appear that there was any damage to my teeth. I cleaned the blood up from my chin and knees and started to put ice on them. If Syl could have seen me now! She would not have believed it. But if she was here, this probably wouldn't have happened in the first place, because my mind now was always in the clouds thinking about her. I managed to take a shower, bandage myself up, and drive back home.

Forgotten Dreams

The wheel of fortune has turned cruel

Your pride and heart, ready to duel

Shocked and bewildered, drawing a blank

Maybe fate is playing a fickle prank.

A startling bolt out of the blue

Has split your paradise in two

Castles crumble into oblivion

Utopia is now merely a delusion.

Songs are better left unsung

Words get stuck at the tip of your tongue

Flowers without a chance to bloom

Only memories remain in this lonely room.

Once again you are alone

Your emotions have been stripped to the bone

A shivering chill gripped the air

Ominous omens of dread and despair.

From your branchless tree

Hanging on now desperately

Another night of silent screams

Bleeding inside the forgotten dreams.

    I emailed Tish about this incident, and was hoping that they were going out boating and not playing golf the next day. But of course, per "Murphy's Law," they were. I've always had a warrior's mentality in playing sports with injuries and pain; like playing in the game the next day against the Georgia-Alabama Masters, after getting hit in the temple with the line drive, in Fort Myers in November, 2010. With my swollen and black and blue chin, and bandaged knees, I somehow played golf and walked the course at Green Lakes the next day. Maybe foolishly so, but I did.

    So there were several stressful incidents that I had to endure this year: dealing with the aftermath of the garage fire, with all the extra work involved; Earl passing away; Ursula passing away; Syl not being there for Will's college graduation and reception; Syl not being there for the MPH students' graduation parties; Lori passing away; my neighbors digging out a pond below my backyard, with bulldozers and excavators starting before 8 in the morning, going on from June through August, with all the noise and lost privacy; the pool not functioning properly and just becoming a daily hassle; the scare and ensuing pain of my fall onto the brick patio by the pool on my birthday.

When I wasn't dealing with all these things, I was writing this book. I completed 50 pages and took the tablet with me on the trip, with the idea that I would write some more, but I think I only wrote a few more pages: always packing, unpacking, driving, traveling, walking, hiking, exploring, then dinner and wine; too exhausted to do much writing.

My brother Marty came to visit from Arizona for almost two weeks and stayed here at my house. But I only would be seeing him for a couple of days, as I would be leaving for Europe on August 31st. Julie and Tom were visiting from Virginia for a week at this time and staying in a hotel. They came over and I had some things to give to Julie.

On August 29th, I drove them to Green Lakes to walk and show them Syl's bench. It was a very hot and humid day as I took them on the trails, taking the long route by Round Lake. Tom was having some issues with a balky knee and was wondering how much farther it was until we got to the bench. The catch phrase was that I kept telling . them, "it is just around the next bend." They were getting more and more impatient with me, when we finally reached Sylvia's bench.

We rested there, looking at the shimmering lake, and took some group pictures. We walked back to the car and then drove up the hill to the restaurant by the golf course, Brian's Landing, and had a nice lunch there.

I packed up my things on the 30th and Marty drove me to the airport in the morning on Friday, the 31st. He had come back here to see some old friends and to scout out the possibilities of moving back here. But he could never get past the thought of enduring the long, cold Syracuse winters with all the snow.

I flew to Philadelphia and met Tish and Mary, Laura, Tish and Mary's daughter, and her partner, Marcy, Joe and Allie, and Dick and Nina, in the airport. We were flying out of there to Zurich, Switzerland. I sat next to a college girl who went to a university in Zurich and had been visiting some friends here in the United States.

She was very pleasant and we talked for a while, until she got on her smartphone, and didn't talk too much after that. But this was a major upgrade from that crazy woman Baltimore Orioles fan, from last year's flight over to Europe. Wardie and Christie were going to Ireland for about a week and then flying into Bucharest and meeting us there. Laura and Marcy were going to Switzerland and Italy with us.

Saturday, September 1st, we arrived in Zurich, rented our van, and drove 60 miles to Interlaken. Tish, Mary and I left the rest of the group at the Victoria Jungfrau Grand Hotel for a few hours, while we drove to Beatenberg to explore the Saint Beatus Caves. We parked the car and had to walk up these steep wooden stairs in the rain to reach the caves. Tish and Mary had to take a break while walking up these stairs. I was relieved that they were feeling it too, because I definitely needed to take a few breaks on the way up. We finally made it to the top.

These limestone caves lie high above Lake Thun and are millions of years old. Legend has it that these caves served as a refuge for Saint Beatus, an Irish monk, who was believed to have driven away a dragon, who lived there in the 6th century. It was impressive with its gorges and waterfalls. We walked back down the stairs and drove back to Interlaken, leaving the van here, as our next destination did not allow any vehicles there.

We took the train to Wengen, where we would be spending the next few days, high in the Swiss Alps. Wengen is a Swiss Alpine village in the Bernese Oberland region, over 1,300 feet above the Lauterbrunnen Valley. Our hotel, Hotel Bernerhof, was right in the center of town, and I could look out the window in my room and see the Swiss Alps.

The next day, Sunday, September 2nd, we took a cable car up to the slopes of Männlichen and walked the trails. You could hear the tinkling of the cow bells in the mist. When you looked up at the spectacular white Alps, it made you feel like singing, which we did, like Julie Andrews did in the 1965 movie "The Sound of Music."

There was a thick fog that day, but then it would lift, and the majestic mountains would appear. It was as if God spread a curtain over the mountains, then pulled it back so you could witness this magnificent display of nature, and take some pictures, then cover them up again for a while and constantly repeat this process. Syl would have been thrilled to be here, it would have made her feel like Heidi in her childhood days in Augsburg. We hiked for hours on the trails, stopping for lunch and coffee at a quaint restaurant up there; then took the train back into Wengen, and spent the rest of the day walking around this charming resort village.

Monday, September 3rd, we took the train back to Interlaken and to our van. We drove 120 miles south from Interlaken to Stresa, in northern Italy. Stresa is a resort town on Lake Maggiore, looking out at the Borromean

Islands. We stayed at the Hotel Belvedere on Isola Pescatori, with beautiful views of the islands.

Tuesday, September 4th, we took a boat across the lake to Isola Bella, "beautiful island," a tiny island with a palace and gardens, where we went to the Palazzo Borromeo. This place is like something right out of a fairy tale. In 1670, Count Vitaliano Borromeo decided to turn this huge rock in the middle of the lake into a "place of delights." And he certainly did. It took four centuries to complete this magnificent Palace and scenic gardens. The tour of the house was fascinating, with all the gold-framed paintings and other works of art, and so many rooms, it boggles your mind. There are six grottoes on a lower floor, covered with stucco and marble, for cool relief from the summer heat. The baroque garden, with the Teatro Massimo at its center, is world famous. It consists of ten terraces in the shape of a cropped pyramid. Obelisks, statues, and two towers, remind you of being at Delphi or the Acropolis site. There are camphor and citrus trees, as well as camellias, roses, and rhododendrons, all around the gardens. There are white peacocks freely roaming around. This place is an unforgettable experience to see.

We took the boat back to Stresa and then drove 97 miles east to Paratico. We stayed in a nice hotel, Hotel Ulivi, with a beautiful view of Iseo Lake, and decided to stay an extra day here, foregoing Tish's original plans of going to Lake Como.

Wednesday, September 5th, we spent all day, a beautiful sunny, blue sky day, just relaxing by the pool. This pool was the cleanest pool that I have ever seen in my life, really big and the water was filled right to the brim. Syl would have really enjoyed sitting in the sun and swimming in this pool. I know I did.

Thursday September 6th, we drove 22 miles to Brescia, a city in the region of Lombardy. Here we visited the former monastery of Santa Giulia and the Santa Giulia Museum, with Roman bronzes and medieval frescoes. We walked to the Piazza del Foro, in the historic old center. This square is surrounded by ancient buildings and Roman ruins, like the Capitolino Temple.

We drove another hour to our hotel, Hotel Capo Reamol, right on Lake Garda. It had a distinctive pink facade and was set amongst cypress and olive trees. It is a haven for windsurfing and kitesurfing, and they even have a school for lessons for both sports here. You could look out your balcony from your room, the first thing in the morning, and see all the windsurfers and kitesurfers out there in the lake in a colorful display. On the other side of the lake was the Monte Baldo mountain range, part of the Italian Alps. There was a large terrace outside my room where I could sit and look at this magnificent scenery, and at night sit out there and look at the stars. *But there was always something missing, an unfulfilled feeling, without Syl being here with me.*

Friday, September 7th, after a great breakfast looking out at Lake Garda and Monte Baldo; we drove to the town of Tenno in Trentino, to see the Cascata del Varone, Varone Falls. The falls are 328 feet high. We hiked all through beautiful gardens and then the caves, where you can see the waterfalls. It never stops amazing you what the forces of nature can create.

We sat by the pool for several hours in the afternoon, and then took taxis to Limone sul Garda, 15 minutes away. It is a historic town in the province of Brescia, in Lombardy, on the shore of Lake Garda. Limone is the Italian word for lemon and this shore was once renowned for growing lemons and other citrus fruits. Most everyone bought a bottle of Limoncello, an Italian lemon liqueur, to take back with them. We strolled all around this pleasant town, with some of the houses built right into the Garda Mountains surrounding the town. Every house, shop, and restaurant has beautiful flower boxes, creating a harmonious atmosphere. The rest of the group ate at different restaurants and were going to take taxis back to the hotel. Tish, Mary, and I found this restaurant right on the lake and had a nice dinner, watching the big paddle steamers, steamships powered by a steam engine that drives paddle wheels to propel the ships through the water; pull into shore, leaving off its passengers. We walked over three miles, through scenic views in the hills, looking down on the lake, until we reached our hotel.

Saturday, September 8th, we drove 45 miles to Sirmione, a resort town on a peninsula, on the southern bank of Lake Garda. There was so much traffic there, that we drove around and around to find a place to park the van. All the big parking lots were filled. Finally, one of the lots had an opening and we parked the van. We walked into town to the Scaliger Castle, a fortress that was first being built in 1277. You have to climb up 150 steep stairs, to the top of this well-preserved medieval castle, where there are spectacular views of the moats and the lake. We strolled all around the narrow streets and alleys, having a nice dinner and a gelato.

We drove around picturesque Lake Garda, 107 miles to Milan, and out to the Malpensa airport to drop off the van. We took taxis into the city and our hotel, Hotel Metro, located in the Fiera Milano City area of Milan.

Sunday, September 9th, we walked around the city and went to the Piazza della Scala, at the entrance of

Galleria Vittorio Emanuele II; where we went into the Leonardo Da Vinci Museum. We saw the amazing exhibit of: "Leonardo3-The World of Leonardo Exhibition;" the artist and inventor, with working models of his machines and digitalized restorations of his paintings, including "The Last Supper." His library was impressive. This exhibit is a worldwide first and started on March 1, 2013 and runs through December 31, 2019. We were lucky enough to see it. The "Submarine," the "Time Machine," the "Mechanical Dragonfly," the "Rapid-Fire Crossbow," the "Mechanical Eagle," and the reconstruction of musical instruments, are just a few of the exhibits. An incredible experience.

We walked to the Duomo of Milan. Allie had read in her tour book that they don't allow shorts in the Duomo. It was hot out and Tish and I wore shorts, but Joe wore jeans to be on the safe side. I brought along my Yankee pajama pants, blue pin-striped with the interlocking white NY on the front left pocket, rolled up and stuffed into my fanny pack. Milan is known as the fashion capital of the world, and I would agree with that, as women dress the way they choose to, regardless of age or body type. When we neared the Duomo, I slipped my Yankee pajama pants over my shorts. I was walking the streets like this, and nobody thought a thing about it. The guy who took our tickets noticed the NY on my pajama pants and said he liked them and was a Yankees fan. I wonder what the crazy woman Orioles' fan, from the flight to Rome from Philadelphia the year before, would have thought of these pajama pants. I think I could offer a guess.

The Duomo of Milan tells a story of faith and art spanning over six centuries. It is dedicated to the Nativity of Saint Mary, Santa Maria Nascente. It is the largest Christian church in Italy, (as the larger Saint Peter's Basilica is in the State of Vatican City); the third largest in

Europe and the fourth largest in the world. It covers an entire city block. The Duomo is 354 feet high. Construction on the Duomo began in 1386 and was not completed until 1965. They decided to use Candoglia marble instead of the traditional Lombard brick, and to have a Gothic look.

Architects, engineers, and skilled workers came from all over the continent. Its imposing stained-glass windows, the Great Spire on top, the statue of the Madonna, (1774), pillars, columns, altars, monuments, sculptures; you name it, the Duomo has it. There are more statues on this cathedral than any other in the world. There are 3,400 statues, 135 gargoyles, and 700 figures. We climbed to the top to see fantastic views of the city of Milan. The Duomo is truly a mind-blowing experience.

Everywhere you turn is another church or cathedral in this city, another photo opportunity. We walked all around and had dinners at night.

On Monday, September 10th, we flew from Milan to the Henri Coandă International Airport in Bucharest, Romania. Laura and Marcy left from the Milan airport to fly to Paris for a few days, before flying from there to Philadelphia. So now there were just seven of us for almost all of the Romanian part of the trip. There was an over two-hour delay for Tish to arrange for a van to travel into Bulgaria, after our upcoming ten-day excursion into Romania. We found out that the rental agencies don't want to rent vans going to Bulgaria, as there is a strong possibility that they will be stolen. We would have to rent two cars for our trip to Bulgaria after the Romanian trip was over. We finally got our van for Romania, loaded our luggage, and headed for Sinaia, 87 miles away.

It was dark and rainy as we arrived at our hotel. We unloaded our luggage in the pouring rain as Mary went up to the hotel. The guy looked dumbfounded, having no idea who we were. It turned out to be the wrong hotel. We put the luggage back in the van and drove further up the hill and found our hotel, Pension Casa Tom, the right one this time. Gabriella met us and was very nice. She did everything there: the front desk duties, cleaned the rooms, and made us our breakfasts. It was past midnight now as we dragged our luggage up the stairs to our rooms and got ready for bed. There was a small balcony outside the room where you could sit and look out at the stars. The only problem with this serenity was the constant sound of all these barking dogs, seemingly trying to outdo each other with their echoing volume.

Sinaia is a town and mountain resort in central Romania's Bucegi Mountains. It is situated in the historical region of Muntenia. The town was named after the Sinaia Monastery of 1695, around which it was built. The monastery was named after the Biblical Mount Sinai. In the morning, you could see these mountains shining in the sun from your balcony. There was construction going on, starting in the early morning, across the street from the hotel. But other than this distraction and the barking dogs at night, it was a good hotel with beautiful views of the mountains.

Tuesday, September 11th, we went down the hill in the town to go to the ATM and get some supplies at the store. In the main square in front of the store, everybody was feeding the pigeons. This is what the townspeople apparently liked to do. Pigeons were flying everywhere, even over our heads as we sat there, battling each other for the food. We got in the van and drove to a gas station, to check on why the oil light was on. A mechanic checked it out and said it needed this additive, called "blue," which he put in half of the gallon plastic container and the light went off. We carried the half full container with us while we were in Romania. While we were at the gas station, a guy was there that owned a restaurant up the hill from our hotel and invited us to come for dinner. We walked there that night and ate dinner. He came in to greet us and they brought out shots of raki for us and some desserts. We went back there the second night, but the experience didn't measure up to the first night.

We went to the Sinaia Monastery, named after the great Saint Catherine's Monastery on Mount Sinai in Egypt.

We then drove to the Peles Castle, a Neo-Renaissance castle in the Carpathian Mountains, outside of Sinaia. It was built between 1873 and 1914, for King Carol I. We parked the car and walked up the long and steep cobblestones to the castle. It looked like something out of a Grimm's Fairy Tale from the outside. Inside there are three levels of intricate woodwork and alabaster sculptures. The main hall has a retractable stained-glass ceiling and a wood spiral staircase. There are elaborately decorated Moorish and Turkish rooms. The library had a secret door among the books you could push to escape your enemies. This castle was a memorable experience.

We stopped at an outdoor cafe on the grounds and had a beer and dessert. We had the Romanian Savarina, a cake made with a sweet yeast dough, which is soaked in a rum syrup overnight after baking. It was not only delicious, but I think we got a buzz from it.

Tish and Mary had researched all the World UNESCO sites on our trip. We went to just about every cave, church, citadel, fort, fortress, monastery, museum; that there was to go to.

Wednesday, September 12th, we drove an hour to cover 30 miles to Brasov. The main highway in Romania is a decent road, but only two lanes. You pass vehicles at your own risk. *At your own peril.* Tish was amazing driving on this highway. Even he couldn't believe it, when a car in front of us, would all of a sudden decide to pass five cars in front of him, around hidden curves, going over 100 miles an hour. There would be trucks, tour buses, and cars coming at him in the other lane driving in the opposite direction. Somehow, he would make it or duck back in.

I've never seen as many trucks on the road, all of them transporting something, as I did in Romania. There were dogs just lying on the side of the road. There were long wooden horse-drawn carts, carrying many people and their goods or supplies. They were just slowly going along on either side of the road, creating an Old World atmosphere, contrasting with the frenzied pace of the present day. Tish started getting into the flow of the traffic, passing several cars at once, before oncoming trucks and buses blocked his way. There were some hair-on-end moments and I know Sylvia would have been freaking out.

We went to the Bran Castle, a castle built in 1382 to defend Transylvania's border. This was the castle that Bram Stoker, an Irish writer, envisioned as the castle of Van Helsing, better known as Count Dracula, in his novel, "Dracula," published in England in 1897. It is said he based his character on Vlad Tepes, "Vlad the Impaler," ruler of Wallachia, from 1456-1462 & 1476.

From there we drove to Râsnov, where we went to Râsnov Citadel, Cetatea Râsnov. It is located on a rocky hilltop in the Carpathian Mountains, 650 feet above the town. It was built in 1331 by the Teutonic Knights as protection against invading Tartars. It became a refuge for the local Saxons, with 30 houses, a school, a chapel, and other buildings, creating a village inside the walls.

Thursday, September 13th, we left Sinaia and drove 23 miles through Brasov to Prejmer. Here we explored the Prejmer Fortified Church, with its Romanesque architecture, dating back to 1240. It was founded by the German Teutonic Knights, before being taken over by the Transylvanian Saxons. Today it is a Lutheran church. After this, we drove 155 miles to Targu Neamt, where our next hotel, Hotel Aristocratis, was located.

Friday, September 14th, we went to the Agapia Monastery, dating back to 1641. It is famous for its interior frescoes, painted in 1858 by Nicolae Grigorescu, one of the founders of modern Romanian painting. After this, we drove to the Monastery of Probota in Probota, Suceava, built in 1530 and known as the Church of Saint Nicholas. It is regarded as the most representative of the Moldavian painted churches.

Saturday, September 15th, we drove to Cetatea Neamtului, the Neamt Fortress, named after the nearby Neamt River, built in the 14th century. It is one of the most important medieval monuments in Romania, and the symbol of a glorious period of the territory of Moldavia, under the rule of Stephen the Great, 1457-1504.

We drove through the Cheile Bicazului, the Bicaz Gorge, in Bicaz National Park through the spectacular Carpathian Mountains. This road serves as a passageway between the Romanian provinces of Moldova and Transylvania.

Driving through a small village, we came upon a wedding party with young people, probably in their early twenties, dressed in traditional costumes, dancing right in the middle of the road. They looked like they were having a great time. We stopped and said hello and they didn't mind us taking some pictures of them. A burly farmer sitting in his horse-drawn cart, came over to the van and gave us a big jug of homemade wine. I never drank any of it, I'm not sure if anyone else did, but it was a nice gesture.

We drove 130 miles to Sighisoara in the Transylvania region. We drove all over Romania, miles and miles of vast green farmlands. Endless fields of cabbage, corn, potatoes, and sunflowers. Rows and rows of sunflowers brilliantly glistening in the sunlight. Ioana told me they process the sunflowers to make sunflower oil. The houses in these villages are so close to the road. Each one has a wrought-iron gate in front of their house. We observed that each gate was different: in size, style, and painted in a different color, making each one unique. There were numerous fruit and vegetable stands in these villages, with sacks of potatoes hanging everywhere. People were walking home with their sack of potatoes and cars would stop to buy a sack of potatoes to take home.

We arrived in Sighisoara in the late afternoon, and Tish and I dropped everyone else off up top in the historic center, and drove back down where you had to park your vehicle. We walked back up the steep cobblestoned driveway to our hotel, Casa cu Cerb, located next door to the house where Vlad Tepes, Count Dracula, was born. Casa cu Cerb was built in the 17th century and is the best-preserved house in Sighisoara. It is called "The Stag House" because of the stag head fixed on the corner of the building.

Sunday, September 16th, after breakfast, I wandered around the historic center. Sighisoara is Europe's last inhabited medieval citadel. With its majestic guild towers, ancient churches, cobbled streets, colorful buildings, and walled town center, it is an impressive place. I met the group and we walked up to the main centerpiece atop Citadel Hill, The Clock Tower, with its multi-colored tiled roof. It has also been called The Council Tower and The Gate Tower. The lower part was built in the 14th century, with higher floors built in the 16th century.

The clock was built in Switzerland and installed in 1648. There is a History Museum inside. You can also see the seven figurines, made from linden wood, each representing a day of the week. Every day the clock's mechanism rotates one of the figurines on the outside. The Clock Tower stands 210 feet high and forms the main gateway to the central walled city. When you reach the top, you are rewarded with a panoramic view of the town.

After The Clock Tower, we walked the 176 steps known as the "Pupil's Stairway"; 1,400 feet, the highest point of School Hill, to "The Church on the Hill," Biserica din Deal. It is dedicated to Saint Nicholas and is one of Transylvania's greatest churches, the most important monument of religious architecture in Sighisoara.

Monday, September 17th, we drove to Saschiz, a village known for its carpentry and metallic-blue ceramics. The ceramics shop was closed, but we asked some women there about it, and they found the person to come and open it up for us. The women bought some "blue pottery" to take home and for gifts. We went to the nearby Saschiz Fortified Church, dedicated to Saint Stephen of Hungary, built between 1493 and 1525, by the German Transylvanian Saxons, when the area belonged to the Kingdom of

Hungary. Initially it was Roman Catholic, it became Lutheran after the Reformation. It has Gothic elements of architecture and an impressive clock tower. The interior decor is mostly baroque and has a 1786 organ.

Tuesday, September 18th, we drove 30 miles to Biertan, to see the 15th century Biertan Fortified Church in Biertan; the strongest fortified one, among 150, in Transylvania.

From Biertan, we drove 90 miles to Vintu de Jos, a commune composed of 18 villages in Alba County, on the Mures River. It is a prominent wine country region, since the 1st century AD, of Transylvania. We would be staying at the Hotel Cardinal, a very nice hotel in Vintu de Jos.

We went to go see Alba Iulia Citadel, considered one of Romania's top attractions. It did not disappoint; it has a Taj Mahal look and feel to it. Its history goes back 2,000 years, when the Roman Empire conquered the Dacian Kingdom. But this impressive citadel is most famous for the day of December 1, 1918, when Transylvania decided its union with Romania, celebrated today as the National Day of the country. The impressive baroque gates connect most of the landmarks from the citadel: The Orthodox Cathedral; the 12th century Roman Catholic Cathedral, one of the most important in Transylvania; the Princely Palace; the Museum of the Union; the Union Hall; and the Batthyaneum Library, that has some of the rarest books in Europe. Alba Iulia is definitely one of Romania's top cultural and historical attractions.

Wednesday, September 19th, we drove 40 miles to the Castle Corvinilor, also known as Corvin's Castle, Hunyad, or Hunedoara Castle, in Hunedoara. It is one of the largest castles in Europe and considered one of the Seven Wonders of Romania. Bran Castle and Peles Castle are also on this list. On another list was the Sighisoara Citadel, with its Clock Tower, and the Alba Iulia Citadel. We saw all of these.

Corvin Castle, a Gothic Renaissance castle, dates back to 1440, and is the largest medieval castle in Transylvania, surpassing Bran Castle and Peles Castle. It was designed as a defense fortress against the Ottoman Empire. Many believe that Vlad the Impaler was imprisoned here during his exile.

Thursday, September 20th, we drove 215 miles to Bucharest, the capital of Romania, where the drivers are totally insane. I told Traian and Ioana that when I returned from this trip, and they just laughed. It's like driving in Boston, Chicago, New York City, Los Angeles, San Francisco, or many other big cities in the United States or Europe; when you live and work there, you know the routine and get used to it. I'm not sure that I could ever get used to driving in Bucharest.

We checked into the Hotel Giuliano, probably at the bottom of our hotels on the trip. Adequate for a night. The same could be said for the Hotel Krystal in Albania on the trip the year before. Both just for logistical purposes. Wardie and Christie met us here in Bucharest, after their week in Ireland. There was a big storm in Ireland on the day of their departure, and we weren't sure if they were going to make it and we discussed alternative plans. They drove through some high winds to the airport, but they made it. Now we were nine again.

We returned the van and had to rent two cars now. They gave us Nissan Passats. I told Tish that I would be willing to drive one of the cars, until I realized that they were standard and not automatic. I hadn't driven a stick shift in fifty years. I'm sure I could have gotten the hang of it fairly soon, like riding a bicycle after many years, just driving around on country roads. But I didn't feel confident learning on the fly on these mountainous roads and crazy traffic, and putting other passengers in dangerous situations. Allie and Wardie alternated driving the other car and both did excellent jobs.

Friday, September 21st, we left Romania and headed for Bulgaria. When you think of these countries like Albania, Bulgaria, and Romania, you think of drab, bleak, Communist countries. That is not the case. There are friendly people, natural wonders, rich history, with magnificent castles and churches and fortresses. Bulgaria is actually south of Romania and borders Greece.

There was a delay at the border with all the cars waiting to get in. They have a separate lane for the trucks. An official told us that there are 60 trucks lined up all the time waiting to get into Bulgaria. We drove through these remote villages, having to avoid huge pothole craters on these roads, finally reaching our destination, the village of Sveshtari, in Razgrad province, in northeast Bulgaria. We were here to see the Thracian Royal Tomb of Sveshtari. We figured that there was not going to be anyone else here in this remote place. We were wrong. There were two huge tour buses full of German tourists. There are tourists from all over when you travel, especially Chinese and Japanese tourists, as well as many other ethnic groups; but none of these matches the volume of the Germans. They are everywhere. Sylvia would have loved talking with them. She always talked with them when we ran into them on our travels. She loved talking about her childhood in Augsburg and Munich. And high school in Würzburg and

Zweibrücken. It made her happy to speak German, like she did on the phone with Ursula every night. We had to wait for an hour until they had taken the tour, until a guide could take us on our tour.

The Thracian Royal Tomb of Sveshtari was discovered in 1982, during the excavation from the Eastern Mound Necropolis of Sboryanovo. It is a 3rd century BC Thracian, three-chamber burial tomb, made of large limestone blocks. Each chamber is covered with a separate vault. The tomb has a unique architectural decor, with half-woman, half-plant reliefs and painted murals. When the woman guide took us to the tomb and pressed a button to open the doors, Tish and I looked at each other with anticipation, at this mystery which was hidden inside, and was about to unfold. It felt like something right out of a Star Trek episode.

From here we drove 123 miles to Burgas, a city on the westernmost point of Bulgaria's Black Sea coast. The Port of Burgas is the largest port in Bulgaria. Burgas is the fourth largest city in Bulgaria; after Sofia, the capital, Plovdiv, and Varna. We would be staying at the Primoretz Grand Hotel & Spa, a five-star hotel where we would be able to relax for four days. Each of us had our own suites, and you had to go down a special hallway, and through a private door, to reach them.

From my living room window in the front of my suite, I could look out and see the Black Sea. Looking out my windows on the left-hand side of the suite was a park. There was a beautiful pool, with all these square concrete "islands," with trees growing in them, which I could also see from the front window of my suite. You did have to watch where you were going when swimming in the pool. Birds would hang out on these "islands" and dip their feet and beaks in the pool water. There were many German tourists here, probably the same ones from the two tour buses at the Thracian Tomb. They would all be out at the pool, putting their towels on their lounge chairs, early in the morning.

The rest of our group had taken a several mile walk through the park to where they had all these sand sculptures. I wasn't aware that they were going on this walk; I was content to sit by the pool, catching rays, listening to my iPod, and taking a few swims. I guess that I could have gone on this walk the following day, but I followed the same routine as the previous day. Tish and Mary had gone down by the beach at the Black Sea, a short walk from the pool, probably to get a little space for themselves. There were foam beds under canopies for the hotel guests. Tish and Mary had left, when I walked down there later in the afternoon that first full day, so I wasn't aware these beds were free for hotel guests. I assumed you had to pay to use them.

I just put my things in the sand and took a dip in the Black Sea. I saw this thing floating in the water, it looked like a gray glove that a train conductor would wear. I dove in and this "glove" floated right next to my face. It was a big jellyfish, and startled me, but for once I didn't get stung, like Sylvia and I had, on our first evening in Antigua in April, 1986; the "Moon Jellyfish" story, one of "Dusty's Lunchtime Stories." I read that there are Moon Jellyfish in the Black Sea, but this one was probably a Rhizostoma Pulmo; commonly found in the Black Sea, Mediterranean Sea, North Sea, and the Sea of Azov.

After the second full day by the pool, I walked down to the foam beds and canopies and joined Tish and Mary there. Joe and Allie joined us also. After they all left,

I went body surfing in the Black Sea, as the waves had picked up. When I walked back to the hotel, there was a wedding about to start, under the now beautifully decorated arches on the outside of the pool area. I didn't want to walk through the wedding, so I went around through the park, then down a few blocks until I reached the front of the hotel.

Monday, September 24th, we drove 23 miles to Nessebar, an ancient city in Burgas province on the Black Sea coast. Originally a Thracian settlement, it became a Greek colony at the beginning of the 6th century BC. Nessebar became one of the first places in the world to start making coins: bronze and silver in the 5th century BC, and gold in the 3rd century BC, to buy goods. Before this, trade was only goods for goods.

The cobbled streets of the old town are lined with ruins, such as Byzantine-era fortifications and baths. We walked all over, into shops that had no ceilings, just growing trees filling the empty space from above. We went inside the 11th century Church of Saint Stephen, with hundreds of mural paintings and a huge beautifully decorated altarpiece. We also explored the ruins of the 5th century Church of Saint Sofia, with its stone columns and large arched windows.

Tuesday, September 25th, we went down and had our breakfast. All the breakfasts on these trips were good, some great, but here at the Grand Hotel, it was exceptional. There was everything you could possibly imagine to eat and drink. We packed up and checked out, reluctantly, leaving this beautiful place. We drove 155 miles to Plovdiv, the second largest city in Bulgaria. Plovdiv is an ancient city built around seven hills, in southern Bulgaria. It is one of the oldest cities in Europe, dating back 6,000 years of the Thracians, Greeks, Romans, Byzantines, and Ottomans.

The people seemed very friendly here, mainly because of their "aylyak" philosophy. "Aylyak" means to be supremely relaxed, unfazed by external pressures, receptive to the pleasures of existence. I'm sure most of the people in the world would want to live their lives this way if they could. For Plovidians, "aylyak" isn't merely a passing mood, it's a way of life.

Wednesday, September 26th, we walked up to the Central Square to go on a free tour with many other people. Our guide was a young man, Alex, in his twenties, who was well spoken, funny, and really informative. He led us down the longest free pedestrian zone in Europe, almost two miles; surpassing the almost one-mile Strøget in Copenhagen, where Steve and I saw Liberace and his entourage in July, 1970. Alex showed us the smiling statues by the master sculptor, Danko Dankov, of real people and their stories. There was: Miljo, a gentle fool with big ears, who shared all the urban gossip with both acquaintances and strangers. He is on Main Street and you can touch him for good luck. You can tell your best joke to the musician, Sasho Sladura, known as Alexander the Sweetheart. You can sit for a while next to the artist, Tsanko Lavrenov.

We walked all around, to the Old Town, where artists have painted beautiful and colorful murals on some of the buildings. Then on to the ruined fortress of Nebet Tepe, above the old town. Nebet Tepe is one of the hills of Plovdiv where the ancient town was founded. The earliest settlements are dated back to 4000 BC, leading down to the Maritsa River. Alex took us to the Ancient Theatre of Philippopolis, one of the best-preserved ancient theatres in the world, located in the city center. This Roman-era theatre was built in the 1st century AD. It can hold as many as 7,000 spectators and is still in use today. Alex told us that Sting had performed a concert there a year before. That would have been a cool experience to have been there for that. We all gave him a $10 tip, and the rest of the people on this tour followed suit, giving him $5 or $10, so it was a good day for Alex. He does two tours a day, all week. After the tour, we went below the ancient theatre to see a 3D movie at the Emperor Hadrian-era Ancient Stadium, which recreates Plovdiv in the second century AD.

Thursday, September 27th, we checked out of our hotel, Hotel Ego, and drove 65 miles to Kazanlak, in the Stara Zagora Province, at the foot of the Balkan Mountains. Kazanlak is the center of the Valley of the Roses and the home of the Thracian kings. There is a Thracian tomb here. We were here to see the Rose Museum, the only museum in the world dedicated to the oil-yielding rose. The museum explores every aspect of the rose production industry, from rose oil to rose water production. It is a very unique place.

Eight miles from here, seemingly in the middle of nowhere, we found the Shipka Memorial Church in Shipka, a tiny mountain town in Stara Planina. This is The Memorial Temple of the Birth of Christ, opened in 1902. It is a Bulgarian Orthodox church, splendid with its 17th century Muscovite style and its gold domes. There is also the Shipka Monument here, dedicated to the soldiers that died for the liberation of Bulgaria in the Russo-Turkish War of 1877-1878. The church's bell tower reaches 174 feet and its bells, the heaviest weighs 12 tons, were cast from the cartridges that were collected after the battles.

From Shipka, we drove to our hotel, Hotel Fenerite, in the village of Kmetovtsi, at the foot of the Balkan Mountains. This hotel was located in a rustic setting, surrounded by woods in the back. We drove 6 miles to Gabrovo, in the valley of the Yantra River, to the Entho Village, Etar, an open-air museum on the northern edge of Bulgarka Nature Park. Here were Balkan buildings to learn about Bulgarian customs, culture, and craftsmanship. There were streams and water wheels.

Friday, September 28th, we drove 60 miles to Brestnitsa, and then to the Saeva Dupka Cave, called "The Underground Pearl of Bulgaria," considered the most beautiful cave in the Laveech region of Bulgaria. The cave got its name from two brothers who hid there during the Ottoman occupation. This cave is absolutely stunning, filled with massive stalagmites, stalactites, other cave formations, and five subterranean halls. It is impressive in its size, much more spacious than you would ever imagine, looking at it from the outside. You have to focus in any of the caves we visited, being aware to duck your head when needed, and to be careful walking in many slippery areas. Saeva Dupka is between one and three and a half million years old. Workers found Roman coins that were over 1,000 years old.

Saturday, September 29th, we drove to Dryanovo, in Gabrovo Province, along the two banks of the Dryanovo River, a tributary to the Yantra River. We visited the Dryanovo Monastery, "Saint Archangel Michael," a functioning Bulgarian Orthodox monastery situated in the Andaka River Valley, in Bulgarka Nature park. It was founded at the end of the 12th century; destroyed, rebuilt, destroyed again, then rebuilt at the end of the 17th century, in the place it is today. It was renovated in the 19th century, completed in 1845.

We went to the nearby Bacho Kiro Cave, opened in 1890, and the first visitors entered in 1938. Two years later, it was renamed in honor of Bulgarian National Revival leader, teacher, and revolutionary, Bacho Kiro. These caves were inhabited as far back as the Middle Paleolithic Age, 70,000 years ago. Some of the formations have been named: "Bacho Kiro's Throne;" "The Dwarfs;" "The Sleeping Princess;" "The Throne Hall;" "The Reception Hall;" "The Haidouti Meeting-Ground;" "The Fountain;" & "The Sacrificial Altar."

Sunday, September 30th, we drove 30 miles to our hotel, Sevastokrator, located in the historical village of Arbanasi; set on a high plateau between the larger towns of Veliko Tarnovo and Gorna Oryahovitsa, and located on the surrounding Yantra River. There was a wedding celebration going on right in front of our hotel, with people dressed up in traditional costumes, drums and music playing, and dancing in the street. We talked with a woman who had come here from Miami for the wedding. They had a very nice pool, but it was late in the afternoon, and we took taxis to Veliko Tarnovo. It is often referred to as the "City of the Tsars," known as the historical capital of the Second Bulgarian Kingdom. The old part of the city is situated on three hills: Tsarevets, Trapezitsa, and Sveta Gora. We walked all around, seeing a lot of street art in the Old Town, going in the shops, and walking up stairs to see the colorful houses on the hill. We had lunch in this small restaurant and bar with an unusual decor: framed pictures, musical instruments, and knick-knacks, hanging every which way and all over the walls, even in the bathrooms.

The hotel had all these extra people staying there because of this wedding, so dinners and breakfasts were more crowded than usual, and they were partying at night. But it was still nice. The views of the city from my room were spectacular, you could see the lights from the fortress on the Tsarevets hill at night. But it clouded up and the next day was a rainy one. We walked all around the Trapezitsa Fortress, a medieval stronghold where the Old Bulgarian capital, Tarnovo, was located, surrounded on three sides by the Yantra River. It was built in the 13th century and here were the main church buildings of the capital city, the Patriarchate and the Patriarch's residence. Walking along the walls of the ruins takes you back to a time long ago.

Monday, October 1st, we got up early, packed, ate a quick breakfast, and checked out. We were now heading for the airport in Bucharest, 120 miles away, to fly to Madrid, Spain. When Tish booked the trip, there was no direct flight from Bucharest to Philadelphia, so he chose this alternative. Tish and Allie were driving the cars in the crazy traffic and then we had a major delay at the border crossing, with cars backed up for miles. They had to check everyone's passports and this took a long time. Then dealing with the insane drivers in Bucharest and finding the place to return the rental cars, which was in a congested area a few miles from the airport. We found it and took a shuttle to the airport.

We presented our tickets and checked our suitcases after a long wait. We now faced the distinct possibility of missing our flight; which would entail staying at an airport hotel, without extra clothes, and additional costs for having to change our flights. Then we had to walk to another counter to present our passports, another unexpected delay. Why this couldn't be done at the same time as the tickets, seemed illogical to us. The airline people were very helpful in getting our boarding passes to us, as we made a mad dash, literally running, down to our gate. Miraculously we made it. I asked the woman from the airlines as I gave her my boarding pass, if she could give me a window seat, rather than the middle seat I was assigned, as my legs just can't handle sitting in the middle seat. She did, but this would turn out to be a mistake.

I was seated next to an old Romanian woman; small, frail, and in her nineties. She was wearing the clothes of a peasant woman, with her head covered with a scarf. She spoke no English and it appeared that she had never traveled anywhere before. You could tell that she had never flown on an airplane before. Sitting next to her in the aisle seat was her middle-aged son. I wasn't sure if he lived in Madrid or somewhere in Spain, as he wasn't really friendly. During the flight, he fell asleep and was sprawled out halfway across her seat, causing her to be halfway onto my seat. Later she got up and went to the bathroom and apparently had a bathroom issue. She must have peed herself, as the smell of urine was evident in the air. I felt bad for her, but the son was oblivious to this. She leaned against me for the 3 and a half hours, 1,537 miles trip, with this permeating urine smell invading my senses.

We arrived in Madrid, got our suitcases, went through security and passport control, and rented our van, driving 27 miles to Yuncos. We spent the night at our hotel, Hotel Carlos I.

Tuesday, October 2nd, after breakfast at the hotel, we drove 20 miles southwest to Toledo, our final destination on this European trip. We arrived at our hotel, San Juan De Los Reyes, a 19th century building located in the historic center of Toledo. This building used to be an old flour mill and is situated in the old Jewish Quarter of the city. The interior decor is in keeping with the original design and decoration of the property.

Toledo is an ancient city set on a hill above the plains of Castilla-La Mancha. It is the capital of the

Province of Toledo, and known for the medieval Arab, Jewish, and Christian monuments in its walled old city. The Moorish Bisagra Gate and the Mudéjar style Sol Gate open into the Old Quarter. After breakfast at the hotel, we walked down the Plaza de Zocodover; with all the shops and restaurants, and street musicians playing accordions, guitars, and violins. We walked all over Toledo's historic Old Town, marveling at the beautiful architecture. There seemed to be an endless array of photo opportunities around every street corner and down every alley. There were churches to be admired at every turn.

    We went on the tour of Santa Iglesia Cathedral, The Toledo Cathedral, one of the most majestic cathedrals in all of Europe. This gothic style cathedral is dedicated to the Virgin Mary in her Assumption to the heavens. Construction began in 1227, but during the 15th century, the gothic style was added to the cathedral by building the Chapel of Saint Peter and the Chapel of Saint James. The design of the cathedral was influenced by the Bourges Cathedral in France. There are 5 central parts within the cathedral, supported by 88 pillars, and there are also 72 vaults. You listen to the history and information, through headphones that they provide for you, as you wander around this beautiful cathedral. Santa Iglesia in Toledo and the Duomo in Milan are truly breathtaking visual experiences.

    Wednesday, October 3rd, after breakfast at the hotel, we walked all over this magnificent city. We went to the Santo Domingo Church, Convento De Santo Domingo El Antiguo; a Cisterian monastery founded in the 6th century, rebuilt in the late 11th century, and renovated in the second half of the 16th century. It contains one of El Greco's earliest Toledo works, "The Assumption of the Virgin Mary" in 1679, which fills a gold-fringed altarpiece.

Barely visible through an iron grating, is the crypt containing the wooden coffin of the painter. There are two other paintings by El Greco here, and interesting facts and documents relating to his life. Doménikos Theotokópoulos, known as El Greco, as El Greco means "The Greek;" was a Greek painter, sculptor, and architect of the Spanish Renaissance. He was born in Crete in 1541 and died in 1614 in Toledo at the age of 72. He moved to Venice in 1567, lived and worked in Rome from 1570-1576, before moving to Spain. It wasn't until he moved out to Toledo that he was recognized as a great artist.

 I walked around the city with Tish and Mary and we had lunch at an outdoor cafe. I then went on by myself for more exploring. At the end of Plaza de Zocodover, I walked down the stone steps and came upon the iconic Statue of Miguel de Cervantes. The statue is framed by El Arco de la Sangre, ("The Arch of the Blood"), the ancient Moorish arch that was the former gateway to the city. Cervantes was famous for his novel, then titled "The Ingenious Knight of La Mancha," better known as "Don Quixote." "Don Quixote" has been translated into over 140 languages and dialects; making it, after the Bible, the most translated book in the world. An interesting fact is that he died a day before, in the same year, that Shakespeare did; April 22, 1616. One of his quotes that I like:

 "Too much sanity may be madness and the maddest of all, to see life as it is and not as it should be."

 Thursday, October 4th, we ate breakfast, packed up, checked out, and drove to the Madrid airport. Wardie and Christie and Joe and Allie were keeping the van and spending an extra week in northern Spain. The rest of us were flying home. We checked our suitcases and went through security. Then later I was randomly selected to go through an additional special security check, as were many others. This happened to me twice on the previous trip, nobody else in our group had to go through this. I don't know why I tend to get singled out, maybe it's because I have the spirit of Woodstock running through my veins.

I had no incidents on the 9 hours, 3,680 miles flight to Philadelphia. We got our suitcases, said our good-byes, and went through customs. I had to wait in lines, with hundreds of other people that had connecting flights, to go through security. They had moved my flight up 30 minutes, which was ironic, as most of the time the flights to Syracuse always seem to be delayed. Once I finally got through security, I had to hustle to get the shuttle to a different terminal, then literally run down to the gate, which of course was at the far end. Somehow, I made it, just as they were about to close the door. I arrived in Syracuse, completing my second five-week European trip. Ioana was nice enough to pick me up at the airport and give me a ride home. It doesn't feel like home anymore, it hasn't since August 24, 2016. I entered my, (which used to be *our*, for over 12 years), dark and lonely house.

I spent the rest of October and most of November taking walks at Green and Round Lakes, Mill Run Park, and Pratt's Falls. I would sit on Syl's bench, eat an apple that I brought with me, appreciate the autumn colors and the shimmering water at Round Lake, and talk with Syl. I continued to monitor Tom and Debbie's house and do my chores and yard work over there. At least this fall there were no major disasters to contend with. There was plenty of yard work for me to do at this house as well. I watched the Yankees in the baseball playoffs. They won the Wild Card game, but then lost to the Boston Red Sox in the divisional playoffs. The dreaded Red Sox went on to win the World Series. I started watching college football games, especially Syracuse. They wound up having one of their most successful seasons in many years, and won the Camping World Bowl game. The snow came early, more than the average amount we usually get in November, and the shoveling began. SU basketball started again for another season.

On December 20th, Ioana invited me to join her and Ileana for dinner at Bonefish. This for me was my Christmas dinner. Ileana was now almost halfway through her freshman year at MPH. I went back to their house, where Traian was, to show them my pictures from my trip. Traian connected my phone to their large screen television and they really liked them, especially all the Romanian pictures, as they were familiar with these places.

Debbie came to Syracuse with Will for a five day visit the day after Christmas. Tom didn't come with them, staying in California. It was the first time in 20 years that he wasn't back in Syracuse for Christmas. I came over for a few dinners and to spend time with them. A bunch of Will's close friends from MPH, that I knew well, came over to hang out for several nights. Giuseppe drove up from New Jersey to spend a few nights, as he would be driving Will back to New York City. Will would be staying with him in a small apartment in the city. Will would be starting a job on January 2nd at Good Morning America, as a production assistant; but his hours, 9 at night until 5 in the morning, were not ideal. I played Trivial Pursuit with the guys one night until we just had to call it a night at 2 o'clock in the morning. Then I had to drive back home. Most of these guys were now college graduates, also had Master's degrees, and had started jobs, entering *the real world*. A couple of them were taking courses part-time and working a day job, still trying to find their way. I could definitely relate to that.

Another night, I was telling Will and Giuseppe all about my European trips, until 2 o'clock in the morning, before driving back home again. Giuseppe and Will left on December 30th, as did Debbie. She was going to the Rose Bowl game in Pasadena with Tom, to see Tom's favorite team, Ohio State, and some of the floats from the morning's parade, after the game, on New Year's Day.

Traian and Ioana invited me over to their house for their New Year's Eve party. I was casually dressed, but everyone else was all dressed up. This was the reverse of when I went to Mariah's graduation party at the Lakeshore Country Club in the middle of June. They had opened up their living room and had a couple of young guys being DJ's. *Syl would have loved this party.* She would have found out from Ioana what to wear and would have been dressed up and looking beautiful. She would have turned some heads as she walked in. Syl would have had so much fun dancing with me, dancing with Ioana and some other women in a big circle, and dancing with Ileana and her girlfriends. It seemed like yesterday that we gave her rides home in our car and she had to use a car seat in the back seat. She was way beyond those days.

Sylvia would have loved to talk with everyone, most of them she knew from previous parties at their house over the years. They were mostly Romanian friends, a lot of them in the medical profession. She could have told them all about our trip, telling them all the places and things we saw in Romania. The food was fantastic and plentiful, as Ioana always is a great cook and host.

Sylvia would have loved to eat all this wonderful food, drink wine, and dance. And just before midnight, there were glasses of champagne poured for everyone and several incredible desserts. Everyone kissed their loved ones and other close friends. I was just standing there, wishing I could be kissing Syl at this moment.

 The dancing started again soon after, and Traian and Ioana were dancing together, enjoying each other's company, as I silently slipped out the front door. I'm glad I went, but once again with these get-togethers, at the end I'm left with just memories and an empty feeling. I drove slowly back home, tears pouring down my face.

2019

Winter and Spring: Green & Round Lakes

Mill Run Park

Summer: Green Lakes (Beach)

September 5th-October 9th: (Third European Trip)

 Italy

  Rome (Airport)

  Capranica

  Florence

  San Gimignano

  Montalcino

  Capranica

- Trevignano Romano
- Bomarzo
- Viterbo
- Tolfa
- Sutri
- Paestum
- Agropoli
- Paraghelia
- Tropea
- San Giovanni
- Sicily
  - Messina
  - Sant'Ambrogio
  - Cefalù
  - Sperlinga
  - Enna
  - Piazza Armerina
  - Ragusa
  - Modica
  - Ragusa Ibla
  - Palazzo

 Santo Pietro
 Scicli
 Palazzo
Malta
 Valletta
 Floriana
 Birgu
 Msida
 Attard
 Mdina
 Rabat
 Mosta
 Mgarr
 Gozo Island
  Munxar
  San Lawrenz
  Victoria
 Mellieha Bay
 Sliema
Sicily
 Palazzo

    Avola

    Siracusa (Syracuse)

    Ortigia Island

    Marzamemi

    Porto di Capo Passero

    Noto

    Taormina

    Messina

Italy

    San Giovanni

    Lagonegro

    Ardea

    Rome (Airport)

October and November: Green & Round Lakes

Pratt's Falls and Mill Run Park

December (27th): Upstate Hospital

It was now a new year, 2019, *another year that Sylvia never got the chance to see.* Another year, starting with the last three and two-thirds months of 2016; all of 2017 & 2018; and now 2019; not having Syl by my side.

It hasn't gotten any easier for me, that's for sure. I've been writing this book for over two years now; planning, research, writing first drafts, revisions, editing, more writing, more revisions, and more editing. I'm getting close to wrapping it up now, I could just keep going on and on. I feel an urgency, like I did with labeling all our photo albums in the winter of 2017, to complete it before something happens to me.

I feel like I'm coming down the home stretch in my life. Tish asked me where I thought I was in my life, using a baseball analogy. I told him that I thought that I was sliding into third base. He was surprised and encouraged by this, as he was thinking that he had already rounded third and was halfway down the third base line, on the way to home plate. That was a couple of years ago. Today I feel more like he did then. I ran hard to first base in my younger days; then cruised into second base; then struggled, winded and exhausted, as I eventually made it to third base. Now I keep going, withstanding all that has gone on in my life, as I have rounded third, trying to reach home.

Nobody can predict their future, but I feel it would be an incredible feat for me if I made it to 80. Of course, when you reach 80, and are still going, you have a different perspective on your mortality then. I want no part of being dependent on others, whether it be in a hospital or a nursing home. I just want to move on at that point, optimistic of being with Sylvia again, for eternity, albeit in a spiritual form.

Nobody knows for sure what happens when we leave our earthly physical body. A lot of people feel that when you are buried or cremated, you just turn to dust or ashes and that's it, the infinite cycle of life. But *nobody* has ever come back from the dead and demonstrated eternal life. Billions of people would argue that's exactly what Jesus Christ did. Billions of people aren't true believers. But either way you believe, one fact rings true: we still don't know for certain what lies on the other side when we die. *Nobody knows.* I, like everybody else, will just have to wait for the day when your time here is up, "when your number is called."

Writing this book has provided great comfort for me. It has provided reliving all of our memories together: travels, danger, laughter, homes, teaching, affection, ultimate love. But it dredges up feelings of uncontrolled grief, guilt, frustration, and anger, of Syl being taken way too soon; emptiness and sadness. Looking through all the pictures puts me back in all those places and times, and once again Syl is with me.

Another Syracuse winter had come to endure. I had thoughts, if I could muster up the courage to do it, of driving by myself down to Florida and spending over a month, leaving the last few days of January; and spending February and the first week of March down there. But I was still taking care of Tom and Debbie's house and decided to stay here.

Where No Light Ever Shines

Wishing a new day would arrive

Leaving behind the gloom

Feeling trapped inside a heartless tomb

Null and void, and barely alive.

All the places are empty

All the people have disappeared

All the nightmares that I feared

Have now become reality.

And now the trial has begun

An endless winter alone

Turning my mind into stone

Sinking with the setting sun.

A constant longing, a timeless thirst

For all those dreams that you crave

It's only a one-way gamble to the grave

No escape from this wicked curse.

Surrounded by a quicksand of confusion

On the verge of becoming deceased

The outlook is grim, to say the least

It's all too late to be an illusion.

At midnight the phantom creeps

Whispering farewell in a voice so low

Making sure you're the first to know

The promise of darkness he always keeps.

As I read the sign, I gasp with horror

"Welcome all you dearly departed"

I'm not sure how this all got started

As I find myself knocking upon death's door.

As the curtain falls on this final act

I guess it wasn't that bad of a script

Except the part about the corpse and the crypt

A happier ending is all that it lacked.

Restless spirits rehearse their lines

With an eerie and piercing shrill

Waiting to meet me at the terminal

Where no light ever shines.

January, February, and March were spent writing this book as much as possible; all afternoon most days, and sometimes even into the early morning hours. The usual mundane chores: shoveling here and driving over to Tom and Debbie's, when the roads weren't icy, to shovel and check on their house; going to the store and errands; going to the liquor store in Dewitt, on the way to their house, to buy some bottles of red wine. I drank a glass or two almost every night during the long winter. When it was a decent weather day, I took walks at Green & Round Lakes and Mill Run Park, cleaning off and sitting on Sylvia's benches. I watched college basketball on television, especially the SU games.

Debbie and Will came back here in the middle of February for several days, taking a bus from New York City. Tom and Debbie had made the decision to sell their house. Now that Will had graduated from Syracuse University, and Tom and Debbie weren't coming for a month over Christmas, or the summer; it made no sense for them to keep paying taxes, homeowner's insurance, maintenance and repairs, for the pool, for plowing and mowing, and for me as the caretaker. Debbie started putting different color coded post-it notes on everything: what was to be moved, what was to be put in storage, what was junk to be hauled away, what was to be sold. I was there for a couple of dinners and to help with some things.

They asked me to sort out the clothes in their armoire and the piles of clothes that Debbie had sorted and put in two gigantic piles in front of their bedroom closets. I spent five, 8-hour days doing this; like I did sorting out over 20 years of our Extended Day things, in July of 2015, when we were unceremoniously let go at MPH. I got some of the huge plastic bags from the Bottle Return Center, and loaded *seventeen* of these bags full of clothes; in addition, blankets, stuffed animals, garbage bags of miscellaneous things, and drove them to the Rescue Mission in Dewitt.

    Tom and Debbie flew into New York City, on their Spring Break at Claremont, in the middle of March, for a week to spend time with Will. Debbie took a bus to Syracuse and Tom and Will took the train here the following day. They were all here as the movers came and packed up everything, taking hundreds of framed pictures down from the walls, and boxing it all up. Will was sad sorting out his things, as this house encompassed so many memories for him, ever since he was five and a half years old. They sorted out books, documents, DVD's & CD's.

    After they left, I spent many more days in March sorting through these items and packing them in boxes. I took 8 boxes of books, 4 boxes of DVD's, and 2 boxes of CD's; loaded them in my car, and drove them, in several trips, down to the Dewitt & Jamesville Library. Then I lugged them into the library to be donated. A lot of work doing all these things, and the clothes and trips to the Rescue Mission. I was glad when this was all done, to get back to writing this book, not wanting to drift too far away from it and slow my momentum.

    I posted this on Facebook, at 12:55 a.m., on March 31st:

    I haven't had a real vivid dream yet where I clearly saw and interacted with Sylvia. I still hope that it will happen. Anyway, Jeanne had emailed me on July 17, 2018: "Hi, Dusty. Just wanted to tell you I had a lovely dream about Sylvia. She was beautiful and very happy. She gave me a big hug and said, 'everyone handles death differently.' I'm not sure what that meant but it was a very uplifting dream."

Last Saturday night, actually Sunday morning, March 24, 2019; I had this dream where several of us teachers were at this conference. I was the only guy in the group. There was: Joline, Melissa, Barb R., Mir, Elizabeth, Sylvia, Karen, Vicki, Mary Jo, Ellen, Kathy, Barb D., and Kate. They all sat on two benches, upper and lower. I was taking pictures with everyone's smartphones, one phone at a time. We all had to wait as Sylvia got up and got this shiny silver case that she brought over to me. She opened the combination lock and opened the case. The camera inside seemed to be glowing. She sat back down and when I took the picture, it gave off a strange blue light. (Was this the camera from "the beyond?") After this, everyone went their separate ways, including Syl. Just sort of vanished. Then I woke up. I guess I'm not ready yet.

An old Indian legend says, "that if you have trouble going to sleep, it is because you are awake in someone else's dream."

At the end of March, I called Honda City in Liverpool, as the lease on my Honda Accord was about to expire on April 22nd. It is so strange to say *my*, instead of *our*, Honda Accord. It was *our* Honda Accord when we leased it on April 23rd, 2016. Syl was there with me then to pick out the color and sign all the paperwork, as she always was, throughout all the cars that we leased. She never even drove this car, not trusting herself to drive alone; with all the chemo treatments and then the falls and ankle sprains from her neuropathy, starting less than a week after we leased the car. This was the car I would drive her to the hospital and back in, out to dinner, and to pick up Ileana.

I was thinking of going with the champagne color we had on the past two leased cars, but they had no more of them in the 2019 models. They were out of the silver color ones also, but managed to find one at another Honda dealer and had it delivered. I picked it up on April 1st. It is a nice-looking car, streamlined, with a "dolphin fin" on the back roof, for the antenna, instead of the lines on the back window, as in the past. It has an array of technological advances, except for no CD player. They can't put in a small slit for CD's? Come on! I have hundreds of CD's and can't even listen to them. Syl and I would always listen to our CD's in the car and when we took trips. We would take CD's on all our vacations, for the car and the room. Even my iPods wouldn't sync up with Bluetooth in this car, I guess being too old. The only device that would sync up was the Pandora app from my smartphone. I use this, but unless you want to pay for ad-free, which I don't, ads come on. It is basically enhanced radio, although with more variety. So, this is the way it is for now.

  In early April, the For-Sale sign was put up in Tom and Debbie's front lawn. It was a strange sight to see this reality. They've had two purchase offers that fell through.

  In April, the baseball season began, so another year of watching the Yankees games. Watched the Masters golf tournament, with Tiger Woods winning his 15th Major title, an incredible comeback.

  On April 16th, it was now *three years* since Syl and I celebrated our anniversary together. I read over all the cards that we had exchanged over the years. This was now *all the "thirds":* the third winter, seasons, holidays, anniversary, birthdays; without Syl; through September 9th, 2019.

  Syl and I enjoyed watching Jeopardy together. There was a new star on the show, becoming famous enough to be nicknamed "Jeopardy James."

James Holzhauer is a 35-year-old professional sports gambler from Las Vegas, who went on an incredible 32 game winning streak from April until early June. He won: $2,464,216, falling just short of the record $2,522,700 of Ken Jennings. He had the biggest five-day total: $298,687; the biggest one game total: $131,127; largest "Daily Double" wager: $25,000; and largest "Final Jeopardy" wager: $60,013. It was exciting to see him keep going during this streak; usually just wiped out his competition, only a couple of close calls. He was even on the national news, when they started calling him "Jeopardy James." Syl would have loved to watch these shows with me and to see how long he could keep his streak going.

His streak ended when Emma Boettcher, a 27-year-old librarian from Chicago, upset him on June 3rd, 2019. She followed his strategy of going for the higher-value clues and finding the "Daily Doubles." She found both of them in the second round, preventing him from going way out in front, which he always did. Just last week, they were matched up again as two of the three finalists in the Jeopardy Tournament of Champions. On Friday, November 15th, 2019, James got his revenge and beat her, winning $250,000.

Starting on January 7th, 2020, there was the ultimate tournament called "Jeopardy! The Greatest of All Time." It was between the three highest earning Jeopardy contestants of all time: Ken Jennings, Brad Rutter, and James Holzhauer, competing in a best-of-seven primetime tournament; the winner getting $1 million and the other two guys getting $250,000.

Syl would be watching all these shows with great anticipation and we would be watching them together. Jennings wound up beating Holzhauer in extremely tense matches. (I didn't get the chance to watch them, as I'll explain later.) An ironic situation, and a depressing one, is that Alex Trebek was diagnosed with pancreatic cancer several months ago. Everyone is pulling for him.

May was the third rainiest one in Syracuse weather history, which is saying something. I was looking out the kitchen window one morning and saw a bluebird sitting in the gutter on the roof, dipping its feet and beak into the water collected there. This seemed like a good sign.

Henry David Thoreau said, "The bluebird carries the sky on his back."

The only good things about all this rain were that all the trees and everything else were really green, the rivers and lakes were nice and full, and I spent much of these days writing this book. I watched the wildlife in the backyard: the deer that survived the hunting season, the mother teaching her new fawns, they are following her, running and playing. They are all whisking the annoying flies away from them with their tails while they nibble the grass. There were bunnies coming out from the bushes, busy squirrels and chipmunks, an occasional woodchuck, raccoon, opossum, or skunk.

The birds are always here. Flying, swooping, landing gracefully in the trees, hunting and squabbling over worms and grubs. There are, including fowl, at least 33 species that I've seen and identified in the backyard: Baltimore Orioles, Blue Jays, Canada Geese, Cardinals, Cowbirds, Crows, Eastern Meadowlarks, Finches, (Red & Yellow), Grackles, Great Blue Heron, Grouses, Hummingbirds, Mourning Doves, Nuthatches, Orchard Orioles, Owls, Pheasants, Pied-billed Grebes, Quails, Ravens, Red-tailed Hawks, Red-winged Blackbirds,

Robins, Sparrows, Starlings, Terns, Thrushes, Tufted Titmouses, Turkeys, Vultures, Woodcocks, Woodpeckers, and Wrens.

When there were dry days, I took my walks, or if it was warm and sunny, I sat out in the back yard and listened to my iPod. On May 21st, it was now *one thousand nights* sleeping alone in our bed without Sylvia next to me.

At the end of May, I received an email from Tish that he was planning another five week "Get Lost in Europe" trip. I had to make an immediate decision, so I did and here I go again. At least on this trip we will only have the one van and that's it. No multiple vans, no cars, no trains. We will be taking a couple of ferries and buses.

After the first week in June, I stained the back deck and got the deck furniture out. I was taking care of my responsibilities over at Tom and Debbie's house, yard work here, sitting in the backyard, and taking walks. I decided to inquire about how much a seasonal pass would be for entry into Green Lakes, as they charge $8 per vehicle, from Memorial Day weekend through Labor Day weekend. The rest of the year is free, which makes it nice. I was asking about a Senior Citizen discount as well. The girl at their office told me that Seniors, 62 and older, get in free Monday through Friday. I never knew that, so now I can go there during the week and out to Cazenovia Lake on the weekends. Syl and I usually had the pool, or Caz Lake, or were on vacation. No more pool now, but that's okay, I'm glad I no longer have the responsibilities or the hassles that went with it.

On June 18th, it was Syl's birthday again. This was the *third one* that she never saw and that we were not together. The last one was that joyous day over at Eric and

Nancy's house in 2016. It was a pleasant day weather-wise, but I just spent it reflecting and writing. I posted this on Facebook:

"Well, Syl, today would have been your sixty-sixth birthday. Should have been your sixty-sixth birthday, in a just and perfect world. Sleep in, have our coffee sitting on our back deck. Give you your birthday card. We would be going out to Lakeside Park at Cazenovia Lake, eating our lunch, sitting in the sun, reading, talking, swimming in the lake. If the weather didn't cooperate, go for a ride and a walk in the woods. Then shower, put on some casual dress clothes, and I could take you to Bonefish for a nice dinner. Back home to cuddle and be together. I miss you more than words could ever convey. I will never stop loving you."

I wrote another poem for Sylvia:

In My Mind's Eye

You have gone

Become a newborn child

Welcomed by the angels

Tending your secret garden

I have a vision

Of you

Peacefully floating

Dancing endlessly

Across a cloudless sky

Without boundaries

Limitless

Gracefully gliding

Like a ballerina

On the tip of a crescent

Yellow moon

Beyond my comprehension

Beyond the beyond

Here is a list of the #27 poems that are interwoven throughout this book, in the order in which they appear:

#1: Born To Ride The Morning Star

#2: A Silent Life Within

#3: Cloud Dancers

#4: Once in a Blue Moon

#5: Whisper of the Wind

#6: Wherever Freedom Flies

#7: November Nights

#8: Lost at Last

#9: Where Hell Froze Over

#10: Faraway Friends

#11: Ghost of a Thought

#12: Reflections of a Crystal Vision

#13: An Early Snow This Year

#14: Expecting the Unexpected

#15: Silver Shadows

#16: Next Stop Unknown

#17: Haunting Traces

#18: Blessing in Disguise

#19: Lost Time is Never Found Again

#20: Tuesday Mornin' Drivin'

#21: For Sylvia

#22: Still Waiting For Your Signs

#23: The Last Valentine

#24: Never Before

#25: Forgotten Dreams

#26: Where No Light Ever Shines

#27: In My Mind's Eye

I actually have at least 75 poems that I have written in my collection, but chose these.

The rest of June and into July, I watched the Women's Soccer World Cup from France, where the United States Women's National Team won the World Cup for the fourth time, and back to back Cups, which is quite a feat; also winning it in 2015. There were a lot of exciting games.

Tish and Mary came back for the rest of the summer and we started, with Steve, playing golf again, walking nine holes at Green Lakes a couple of times a week, starting on July 10th.

The other days I was going to the beach at Green Lakes, sitting in the sun, reading, listening to my iPod, writing notes for the book, and swimming in the lake. I've never seen so many people, of all ages, with tattoos all over their bodies. Each to their own, and I know it is a more popular trend than ever, but sometimes I wonder what they were thinking. There are so many people with all these tattoos, obese, missing teeth, chain smoking, and they are still enjoying life. Maybe their quality of life isn't that great, but they are still alive. It makes me even more frustrated and wonder why Syl was taken way too soon. Doesn't make sense to me.

I finished reading Jonathan Livingston Seagull by Richard Bach, and Siddhartha by Herman Hesse. I'd read these books a dozen times over the years, but after all that has happened over these past five years, they were more enlightening to me than ever before.

I was thinking about driving down to Bethel Woods for the 50th anniversary of the Woodstock Festival, where I was all those years ago, staying overnight somewhere down there and seeing the Woodstock Museum, which opened in 2008. But I didn't make it. Maybe next year. Hard to believe all this time has passed. It has even been thirty years since Syl and I went down there in 1989.

I've been watching this solitary beautiful blue heron, hanging out at the pond below my backyard, while I sit on my back deck. It soars elegantly over the house when it decides it's time to move on. Sylvia would have been thrilled to see this.

This was my routine for the rest of the summer, through Labor Day weekend: golf at Green Lakes, Green Lakes Beach, Cazenovia Lake on weekends, monitoring and doing my chores at Tom and Debbie's house, until their house is sold; yard work, watching sports: the Yankees, golf and tennis.

Will came for a visit on Saturday, August 24th, taking a bus up and back from New York City. I picked him up in the University area, then took a scenic drive out to Skaneateles. We had lunch at Doug's Fish Fry, walked down the pier, sat in the park looking at the beautiful lake, and walked around town. Drove back to my house, had a beer on the back deck, and caught up on each other's news. Then driving to Denny's for an after-midnight breakfast, before taking him to the Greyhound bus station to get a 3 a.m. bus back to New York City.

It is now the beginning of September and I am starting to organize my clothes, toiletries, documents and papers; getting ready for my third five-week trip to Europe. It is the same group: Tish & Mary, Allie & Joe, Dick & Nina, and me; just the seven of us this trip. Wardie and Christie hadn't heard from Tish all winter and most of the spring, about any trip to Europe this year, so they made their own plans. They are meeting Jim, one of Wardie's younger brothers, and his wife, Emily, in Italy for two weeks, traveling along the Amalfi coast. Jim and Emily will return to Syracuse after this, while Wardie and Christie will continue on to Spain for another two weeks. We are going to meet them for the afternoon and lunch in Florence, so that should be fun.

I was thinking of the analogy of the lines in "Field of Dreams," which I just saw a few nights ago, for at least the tenth time, where Shoeless Joe Jackson, (Ray Liotta), asks Ray Kinsella, (Kevin Costner), if this was heaven, and Ray tells him that it is Iowa.

And at the end of the movie, when his father, John Kinsella, (Dwier Brown), asks his son if this was heaven, and Ray tells him that it is Iowa. John replies that he thought it was heaven and Ray says that maybe it is heaven.

When we all meet in Florence, in the afternoon on Saturday, September 7th, after driving from Capranica; and I see Wardie and Jim, and remember their house on Rugby Road, one house over from our house, where we moved to from Webster in September, 1962, where my family lived for 28 years; and from where Wardie's basketball hoop was on their family's garage, where I met Wardie, "Eff," Tish, Steve, and many other close friends and original "Campers." So, I say to them:

"Is this Rugby Road?"

"No, this is Italy."

"Oh, I thought it was Rugby Road."

"Maybe it is Rugby Road."

Thursday, September 5th, I woke up at 7, had my coffee and smoothie, got ready, finished packing my toiletries and my backpack; and Nancy picked me up at 10 and gave me a ride to the Syracuse airport. I checked my suitcase, got my tickets and boarding passes, went through security, then endured my usual mandatory full body scan and search. Must be the Woodstock spirit running through my veins. I flew to Philadelphia, took the shuttle to the International Terminal, and waited a couple of hours before meeting up with most of our group. Allie and Joe had left a day earlier. We boarded the plane, had over an hour delay for "bathroom maintenance," finally departing for our nine-hour flight to Rome around 7:45 in the evening.

This time I had a window seat directly behind Tish and Mary toward the rear of the plane. Our row only had two seats, with a woman sitting next to me. She wasn't crazy like that Baltimore Orioles woman fan from the 2017 flight to Rome, but she wasn't the friendliest person either. She never introduced herself, actually suggesting that there was a person willing to switch seats with me in 9C. That was pretty subtle, to get rid of me, and have her friend, I think they were in a tour group, sitting next to her. I politely said that I was fine where I was. Why would I want to move, having a window seat and being able to talk with Tish and Mary once in a while?

At one point during the flight, I leaned up to say something to Tish and Mary, my elbows resting on the seats in front of me; I guess my right elbow must have been slightly over her TV screen, and without saying anything to me, she actually physically moved my right arm over. A lot of nerve. I seem to attract some strange ones. She wasn't really intently watching her movie, dozing off, and fell asleep after this. So, this was the 2019 flight from Philadelphia to Rome.

Friday, September 6th, we arrived at the Rome airport at a little after 10 in the morning, close to our scheduled arrival time. We had a long wait to get our bags and then met Allie and Joe at Hertz where we would rent our van. They had spent the day in Rome and stayed at an airport hotel that night. We had some issues with the vans that they were trying to stick us with. I told them that they were unacceptable as one had balding tires. After over an hour of wrangling, checking out alternate vans, and finally Tish speaking with the manager, we secured a nine passenger Mercedes van with low mileage, automatic transmission, and almost brand-new tires. Tish, who did all the driving as usual, was so glad that we persevered because those other deficient vans would have been a nightmare for us. It took us two hours to get out of the airport, but it was well worth it.

We loaded up the van with our luggage and drove 36 miles north to Capranica, once again staying at: i Noccioli di Monte Casciano, "The Farm," for a week, from Friday, September 6th, to Friday, September 13th. I had the same brick unit (#12), that I did in 2017, across from Tish and Mary's. We will have a couple of relaxing days during the week, walking around here and sitting by the pool and swimming. Taking some day trips into Tuscan towns and having some nice dinners.

We stopped at the Todis store and got our supplies. This is a small store that has everything you could possibly imagine; you just have to search where things are located. The beer, liquor, and wine prices were ridiculously inexpensive. We unloaded everything, walked around the grounds, then drove back down to a local restaurant near the store for dinner. We all went to bed exhausted.

Saturday, September 7th, we left early in the morning for the aforementioned trip, driving 148 miles north to Florence for the day. We walked around for a while, then I stopped to take a picture and everyone had disappeared. It can happen just like that on these trips. I took a right and went down to the main square where I thought they would be. It turned out that they had taken a left into this market area at the corner where I took the picture. I waited for a while and then wandered back to that corner, where Tish finally came back to find me.

We then met the Kimples near this market. I related to Jim and Wardie my "Heaven/Iowa to Rugby Road/Italy" analogy, and they got a kick out of it. We all sat down inside a restaurant near this market for lunch. There were all sorts of conversations going on at once. I talked with Jim at lunch, and later with Emily, as we all walked around for a while. Never had much of a chance to talk with Wardie or Christie, but it was still great to see them in a foreign city. Wish we could have met them at another location in Italy, but it wasn't meant to be this time.

We walked around the streets of Florence, back to our van, and drove 36 miles southwest to San Gimignano, an Italian hill town in Tuscany. It is encircled by 13th century walls and a skyline of medieval towers, including the stone Torre Grossa and the 12th century Duomo di San Gimignano. We would be staying at La Locanda di Quercecchio, located in a medieval palace in the historic center of San Gimignano, around the corner from Piazza della Cisterna.

We had to park down below, quite a distance from the hotel, and walk up steep cobblestone walkways. We had only taken our backpacks for this overnight and the following day stay. Mine was still heavy on my back with several water bottles in it. We finally reached the top, looking at spectacular views of the Tuscan valley and vine-filled countryside. After checking in at the hotel, we ate dinner at a restaurant outside, across the street from the hotel. I walked around the streets, up to the main square, Piazza della Cisterna, people watching as I enjoyed my gelato. There were young people practicing playing their drums for the big festival that would take place on Sunday. I sat on these stone steps with no support for your back. I had a restless sleep that night in a not so comfortable bed and felt a few twinges in my back when I awoke in the morning.

Sunday, September 8th, we had originally planned to see the medieval festival in San Gimignano, "Rocca of Montestaffoli," with performances of drums, clarions, and flags of San Gimignano, and dance and archer groups. Probably similar to the festival in Arezzo that we went to two years before, which was spectacular.

It looked like a storm was brewing as we checked out and walked back down to the van. There were loads and loads of buses packed with tourists coming in for the festival. Tish decided that he wanted to get going for the long 182 miles drive back to Capranica. It started raining just as we reached the van. It did clear up later, so I hope that it didn't rain on their parade and that the festival went on after the weather delay.

On the way, 50 miles from San Gimignano, we stopped in Montalcino for the "Honey Festival," where we also would be able to sample some of their famous Brunello di Montalcino wine.

Montalcino is a hill town, elevation of 1,860 feet, and commune in the province of Siena, Tuscany. It is located in central Italy, west of Pienza, close to the Crete Senesi in Val d'Orcia. It is a 14th century medieval city, with narrow, steep streets. The Diocesan Museum of Sacred Art has collections of painting and wooden sculpture by the Sienese school. The late 13th century Town Hall, with its bell tower and a "Campanone," or big bell, still rings, marking the life of Montalcino to this day. There are many churches, including the 14th century Church of Sant'Agostino, the Sanctuary of the Madonna del Soccorso, and the Church of Sant'Egidio.

    We bought several jars of homemade honey, some sweets, and wandered around the streets of this beautiful town. Joe and I continued on from where the others stopped for lunch, trying to find a spectacular view while we had lunch, which we did. We each had a glass of the excellent Brunello wine. The others found us and joined us later. There were steep hills to climb up and back in here as well. We left Montalcino and drove the remaining 132 miles back to Capranica. I really liked the atmosphere in Montalcino, it had a harmonious feel to it.

    When I got back to my apartment at "The Farm," I started experiencing excruciating pain in my back. The last time that I could remember back pain this severe was in the winter of 1970, when Ronnie and I had an apartment in Miami, almost 50 years ago. I spent a couple of days just sitting with my back up against the wall then, not being able to stand up. I wasn't sure if I could have moved if the apartment caught on fire, that's how bad it was. I've had lower back pain over the years after extensive days of yard work, or playing all day long for three or four consecutive days in softball tournaments, or sleeping in an awkward position on a bad mattress. But I would not categorize myself as having chronic back pain. I probably threw it out carrying my backpack with the water bottles up all the steep hills to San Gimignano. Plus, all the packing, airplane flights, especially from Philadelphia to Rome; lugging the backpack, suitcase, and groceries, driving long distances, all within the first few days of the trip.

That night I strongly considered sleeping on the floor, but I tossed and turned all night in agony in the bed. I didn't even know if I could go to the bathroom and brush my teeth before bed, as I couldn't even stand up straight. Somehow, I managed to do it, all hunched over, and made it through the seemingly endless night.

Monday, September 9th, I was still in pain, but walked up to the pool for a few hours. The warmth of the sun and stretching out by swimming helped. I wore my Copper Fit back support as we drove to Trevignano Romano, a town on Lake Bracciano, where we had gone for dinner in 2017, for dinner. Mary gave me a salonpas patch to put on my back that night and that definitely helped immensely.

We were all dealing with a virus that Joe had been infected with before the trip and then infected all of us. We were calling him "Typhoid Joe." He had severe laryngitis for the first few days, which Tish got a touch of the following week. All of us were coughing and hacking and sneezing for the first two weeks or longer. Tish and Mary and I took our "Z-packs" that we had wisely brought with us, six pills over five days of azithromycin, used for bacterial infections rather than viral infections, but it did the trick for us.

It was now the beginning of all "the fourths." The fourth year of all the days, months, seasons, anniversaries, birthdays, holidays, without Sylvia being with me. And her not being here to be able to experience all these places and things, and vacations, and travels, and life itself.

    Tuesday, September 10th, we spent a few hours at the pool before driving to Bomarzo, in the province of Viterbo. We walked through the Sacred Bosco, the Sacred Forest. Bosco is similar to the Spanish word for forest, bosque. It is part of the title of the Spanish version of my children's book, "El Bosque Donde Llueven Ranas Coquí," from the English version, "The Forest That Rains Frogs."

    "The Park of the Monsters," or "Parco dei Mostri," in the Garden of Bomarzo, was not intended to be a pretty sight. Commissioned in 1552 by Prince Pier Francesco Orsini, it was an expression of grief designed to shock its viewers. The Prince, also known as Vicino, had just been through a brutal war, been held ransom for years, and come home only to have his beloved wife die. Racked with grief, the Prince wanted to create a shocking "Villa of Wonders" and hired widely respected architect Pirro Ligorio to help him do so. The park is filled with bizarre and fascinating sculptures. There is a war elephant, a monstrous fish head, a giant, (Hercules), tearing another giant in half, and a house built on a tilt to disorient the viewer. When you walk in there, you really do feel a weird motion and become disoriented. The most famous and frightening one is "The Mouth of Hell," an enormous head, mouth opened wide in a scream. The accompanying inscription reads "all reason departs." We stood inside the mouth to take pictures.

    This art was built during the Italian Renaissance, but was not like other Renaissance gardens, rather was in a rough "Mannerist" style, a sort of 16th century version of Surrealism. Salvador Dali visited the park and loved it, even shooting a short film there. The sculptures inspired his 1946 painting, "The Temptation of Saint Anthony."

It was definitely unique, not like anything you had ever seen before, yet really strange and weird. I coined the subsequent phrase, being "bomarzoed," if something happened that was strange and weird, or if someone said something that was strange and weird. This could now be included in the group of terms like: bamboozled, bewildered, discombobulated, and flummoxed. This term came up frequently during this trip. Tish really liked it and used it.

We drove to Viterbo, a medieval city an hour north of Rome in the province of Lazio, not that far from Capranica. We walked around the ancient streets and had dinner there.

Wednesday, September 11th, we drove 25 miles of back roads to Tolfa, a town in the province of Lazio. We walked all around this medieval town and the uphill street, Villa della Rocca, leading up to the top, where there are the remains of the Castle of the Fortress, built around 1000 AD, then restored by the Frangipane family, who took up residence in the Tolfa territory in the 14th century AD. We walked through the tiny streets of the old village of Tolfa, surrounded by gardens from the neighboring houses. It is amazing that people live up here. Next to the castle there is the small church, The Sanctuary of Madonna Della Rocca. The views from the top of the Castle, Rocca di Frangipane, were spectacular.

Thursday, September 12th, we had a relaxing day. I spent all afternoon at the pool, sitting in the sun, listening to my iPod on my headphones, and swimming. That night we drove to nearby Sutri, an ancient town believed to have been first inhabited by the Etruscans, even before the Romans. We had dinner there, eating outside under a partially enclosed canopy, looking up at a radiant full moon.

Friday, September 13th, we got up early, packed up our things, loaded the van, and left "The Farm." We drove 220 miles south to Paestum, pronounced "Pos-TOOM," like in "costume," in the province of Salerno.

Paestum was a major ancient Greek City on the coast of the Tyrrhenian Sea in southern Italy. The Archaeological Park of Paestum is in the Campania region, 25 miles south of Salerno. It contains three of the most well-preserved ancient Greek temples in the world, temples in the Doric order, dating back from 600 to 450 BC. There is the Temple of Hera, (the Basilica), the oldest of the temples; the Temple of Ceres, (or Athena); and the Temple of Neptune, (or Apollo or Hera II), the largest temple and the best preserved.

The city was colonized by the Romans in 273 BC, then added the Roman infrastructure of roads, forum, and theatres. Christians moved in around the 5th century AD. By the 9th century AD, the land had become swampy and the city and its great temples were abandoned. It was overtaken by forest until it was discovered in the 18th century during the building of a road.

There is also The National Archaeological Museum of Paestum to see, with many tomb paintings, including the famous "Tomb of the Diver." The later paintings date back to the 4th century BC, when the Lucanians occupied the site.

We stayed at the Paestum Inn Beach Resort, located a few miles from the ancient ruins, that overlooks a beach on the Tyrrhenian Sea. This resort had to rank close to the top in the places that we stayed on this trip. My room was close to the pool, where they played piped-in music until late at night. The rest of the group had their rooms in a section behind mine. They assigned me room #106, which coincidentally was our family's house number on Rugby Road. Every room had a little veranda with a table and chairs to look up at the full moon and night sky. There was a boardwalk for a five-minute walk to a beautiful sandy beach, surrounded by mountains. The water in the Tyrrhenian Sea had a sandy bottom, where I could walk way out and do some nice body surfing when the waves came in.

We arrived in the late afternoon on the 13th, checked in, unloaded our luggage, and got settled in our rooms. I wandered around the grounds, taking a bunch of pictures. There was lush foliage everywhere: flowers, plants, and trees, having a tropical feel to it. We drove over to Agropoli, a town located in the Cilento area of the province of Salerno, situated at the start of the Cilentan Coast, on the Tyrrhenian Sea, for dinner. We ate at a popular local pizzeria, with many families coming in there. Then our usual after dinner gelato.

Saturday, September 14th, after breakfast, we drove to the nearby Archaeological Park to see the Greek temples. We went into the National Archaeological Museum first, marveling at the vibrant colors of the still well-preserved tomb paintings. "The Tomb of the Diver" was special and I bought a magnet of it. We then walked across the street to see the temples, which were awe-inspiring. It is one of those things that words or pictures truly don't do them justice. It is one of those experiences that *you have to be there* to really appreciate what you are having the privilege to witness with your own eyes.

As we were leaving the impressive Temple of Neptune, a man looking like he was around the same age as us, wearing a black baseball hat with gold letters that read USS Oriskany, stopped and stared intently at me. The Oriskany was nicknamed "Mighty O," and sometimes referred to as the "O boat," was one of the few Essex-class aircraft carriers completed after World War II, over 900 feet in length, and was commissioned in September, 1950 for the United States Navy. The ship was named for the Battle of Oriskany, in August, 1777, during the Revolutionary War. Oriskany Falls is a town about 50 miles east of Syracuse. The USS Oriskany earned battle stars for service in the Korean and Vietnam wars to 1976. In May, 2006, it was deliberately sunk 22 miles off the coast of Pensacola, Florida, where it became the world's largest artificial reef.

This guy, who probably served in Vietnam, looked at me and did a double take, and then a triple take, and exclaimed,

"Tommy!"

I looked at him and said,

"Are you talking to me?"

"Tommy, is that really you?"

"Sorry, I'm not Tommy. I'm Dusty."

He looked at me in stunned silence. He thought that I might be pulling his leg or something. The expression on his face was in total disbelief that I was not his shipmate Tommy. I was in the Naval Reserves from October, 1966 to October, 1968, and went through Basic Training in Great

Lakes, Illinois in January and February of 1967; but was never on an aircraft carrier.

"Well, you have a twin somewhere. I'm still having a hard time believing that you are not Tommy. I would have bet anything that you were him."

"Sorry, but I'm not him."

He walked away, still shaking his head. Ask Tish how convinced he was that I was Tommy, and then so disappointed when he realized that I was not. They say we all have a twin somewhere in the world, not counting natural born twins. He mentioned Tommy's last name, but I don't remember it. I should have written it down right away, but I didn't, and now I can't recall what it was. It was definitely a strange encounter for both of us.

We ran into him again later that day and as he passed us, he gave me a wry grin and said,

"See you, Tommy."

To me, this was a prime example of: *the common thread, how we are all somehow connected to each other on this planet.*

We returned to the hotel later in the afternoon and went down to the beach. I walked way out on the sand bar and did some body surfing in the waves. The water in the Tyrrhenian Sea was clear and warm. We stayed on the beach to witness a gorgeous sunset.

We drove back to Agropoli and should have eaten at the same restaurant as the night before. Instead, we went to a different one down the street, claiming to have earned awards for their pizza. It turned out to be our worst dining experience on the trip. The place became really packed with large family groups and our waiter was having a hard time with trying to give us separate checks. In the last week of the trip, Tish discovered an app on his phone that you could speak into and translate what was being said in English and in Italian. That would have been very helpful during the trip, (although we managed our way pointing to the menu and hand signals), and especially this night. I think that the waiter forgot about Tish's and Dick's pizzas, after we all had our dinners. In their haste they brought Tish what he described as "the worst pizza he had ever gotten." The owner gave us unfriendly looks and eventually didn't charge Tish for the pizza, after bringing back a couple of reheated attempts. The waiter didn't do separate checks and it became a nightmare trying to figure it out, when some people drank and others didn't, and some drank more than others.

    We managed to get separate checks sometimes during the trip, but other times we had to write down and figure out who owed what. The service tip or comperto, per person, was always included in the check or checks. Everybody left, paying what they thought they owed, and Nina and I were left to figure out the discrepancy that was left to us, while the owner grew more impatient with us. There were people who had forgotten their second beer or extra glass of wine. We finally worked it out, but Tish's phone app would have saved a lot of confusion that night. We walked down the street and had a gelato and drove back to our resort.

    This incident reminded me of a funny skit in the early days of Saturday Night Live, when Father Guido Sarducci, a fictional character created by the American comedian Don Novello, does this routine about "The Last Brunch." Sarducci, a chain-smoking priest with tinted glasses, works in the United States as a gossip columnist and rock critic for the Vatican newspaper, "L'Osservatore Romano." When traveling in Mexico, Father Guido says he managed to obtain the actual check from "The Last Supper." But it turns out it was the check from "The Last Brunch." The check reveals that one guy only had a soft-boiled egg and tea, while everyone else stuffed themselves. But when the bill was paid, it was divided equally. The moral of the story, according to Father Guido: "in groups, always order the most expensive thing."

Sunday, September 15th, after breakfast, we spent a relaxing day at the beach. Our lounge chairs and umbrellas were complimentary here. I sat in the sun, people watched, listened to my iPod, wrote some notes for the book, and body surfed in the waves of the Tyrrhenian Sea.

That night we drove back to a restaurant across the street from the Greek temples, where people were coming in droves for an outdoor concert at the Temple of Neptune. It was an incredible sight, the temple all lit up, radiant against the night sky. You could faintly hear the music in the distance, I think classical or a symphony, but tough to hear with so many cars whizzing by. It would have been a thrill to be next to the temple for the concert, but we had a nice dinner, and the thought of witnessing an outdoor concert from across the street, with a 450 BC perfectly preserved temple all lit up at night in all its glory, was an experience never to be forgotten.

Monday, September 16th, we checked out of the Paestum Inn after breakfast. It turned out that I left my white tank top, with palm trees and Maui in blue letters, on the veranda, hanging on the rack to dry. I wasn't sure about it, although I had a premonition, until I repacked everything for the flight back to the United States. Syl and I had bought these tank tops when we visited Tish and Mary in

Maui in February, 2002, so I've worn mine in the summer, and to the beach on vacations and these trips to Europe, for 17 years and 7 months. It is only a piece of clothing, and was starting to fray, but it is the symbolism that it represented; if you can understand where I'm coming from. Syl's might possibly be around somewhere, I'll have to check.

We drove 226 miles south to Parghelia, a small town near Tropea. Tropea, pronounced "Tro-PAY-a," is a town on the east coast of Calabria, in southern Italy, the toe of Italy's boot. Tropea was built on a former Byzantine cemetery; the 12th century cathedral has marble coffins and a painting of the Madonna of Romania, the town's protector. Tropea is situated on a reef in the Gulf of Saint Euphemia. The town is perched above the Tyrrhenian Sea on the Coast of the Gods. One legend says that it was founded by Hercules, who is honored in the main square, Piazza Ercole. Tropea is known for its prized red onions.

We would be staying at the Borgo degli Dei-Affittacamere Poseidone Hotel in Parghelia, because the parking is incredibly difficult in Tropea. Borgo means village and Borgo degli Dei means "Village of the Gods." We finally found it after some U-turns and navigating some steep and narrow roads. We were really high up on the cliff overlooking the Tyrrhenian Sea down below. Our rooms were next to each other and all had a name for a Greek god, goddess, or mathematician next to our doors. Mine was Apollo, Allie and Joe's was Hera, Dick and Nina's was Archimedes, and Tish and Mary's was Hermes. You could walk around the corner of the hotel to see some incredible views. We could stare out at these incredible views while we were eating our breakfast. At night, we walked up back roads and under bridges to the local town, where we had dinner at a restaurant there and got a few supplies at the local store.

Tuesday, September 17th, we spent a few hours at the really nice pool, and then drove to Tropea. Tish navigated the traffic and somehow found a parking place. We then climbed up hundreds of steep and narrow steps, with fantastic views, until we reached the top. We gazed out at the Beach Castle, Santa Maria Dell'Isola, a small monastery located on the top of a hill on an island, on the beach. It is a holy place for pilgrims. It had the look and feel of a fairy tale castle, something right out of a Disney World setting. We walked down the long street of Corso Vittorio Emmanuale, a popular street of both locals and tourists, lined with small cafes where people are sitting at all times with coffees and drinks.

Wednesday, September 18th, we drove back to Tropea and went to the beach there. The beach for the hotels rented beach chairs and umbrellas, but they wanted $20, which was way too expensive in our view. Instead, we spent the day at the adjacent public beach, just lying on our towels, not the most comfortable thing. We built sand mounds to rest our heads on. It was still packed with people and families. It was a beach of tiny shells and pebbles, where you sink in like quicksand. The same was true in the water, and made it difficult to get out and back onto the shore. I still went swimming, looking up at the sensational rock cliffs and castles. After the beach, we walked all around the Old Town of Tropea, to the Piazza Ercole and the historic center. People were out walking in the evening with their families, a leisurely stroll that they call "passeggiata."

Thursday, September 19th, we packed up and checked out, leaving Parghelia and driving 60 miles to

San Giovanni, where the ferry terminal was. We would wait in a long line of cars, vans, and trucks, to load our van onto the ferry. It was a quick 20-minute ferry ride across the Strait of Messina to Sicily. Driving in Messina was crazy.

We got out of there and drove 100 miles west to Cefalù, pronounced "Chef-a-LOO," a coastal city in northeastern Sicily, in the province of Palermo. The name Cefalù, derived from the Greek "Kephaloidion," comes from the head-like shape of the rock, called Rocca di Cefalù, which towers above the town. The first inhabitants were Greeks, who had a small town on The Rock. Their life was concentrated around the Temple of Diana. The town was founded in the 4th century BC, and is known for its Norman Cathedral, a 12th century fortress with elaborate Byzantine mosaics and soaring twin towers. Cefalù's crystal clear blue waters and golden beaches give it the reputation as the "Pearl of the Mediterranean."

We would be staying at the Kefa Holiday-Case Saponara, a bed and breakfast about 4 miles outside of Cefalù. The name sounded nice, but this place was kind of funky and literally in the middle of nowhere. There is no way that Mary could have found this without the GPS. Tish was driving down endless narrow back roads through the woods and another vehicle would appear seemingly out of nowhere.

I named Tish: "The James T. Kirk of the Starship Enterprise in Star Trek," as he "drove where no man has gone before;" with his driving on steep narrow roads, over speed bumps and avoiding potholes, passing vehicles, cars tailgating inches from his bumper, that just are so impatient and *have to pass.* They can't stand to wait. When they have to wait, they start honking their horns. Not the loud and continuous barrage of horn blowing as you experience in New York City, but annoying enough. And parking in impossible, at least in improbable places; making U-turns, three-point turns, avoiding hitting people and animals. Nobody, at least in our group, could handle all this driving and maneuvering like Tish does.

Case Saponara is set in the Madonie Nature Preserve, and is a former farmhouse with gardens, beautiful plants and flowers, near Sant'Ambrogio. A young woman, Christina, was our host and met us as we got settled into our rooms. It wasn't a bad room, but my toilet seat lid was ripped in half and jagged and loose. I just removed it and told Christina about it.

Tish drove back down to the tiny town of Sant'Ambrogio, where many of its 250 inhabitants have lived here for a long time. These streets were so narrow, making it almost impossible for him to navigate. We found a parking place and had dinner at a local Sicilian restaurant. We walked around town after dinner and then had to find our way back at night to Case Saponara.

Friday, September 20th, we had our breakfast up on the terrace, looking out at the nature preserve and the Madonie Mountains. Christina bought the food for our breakfasts. There was a large male gray feral cat there, that I assume sired all the kittens roaming around, that had a large head and Mary nicknamed him "Pumpkinhead." So that's what we called him. Mary said, "That he will grow into his face." He hung around the kitchen and Christina had to grab him and bring him back inside when he snuck out on the terrace while we were eating our breakfast. The smell of cat urine was prevalent around the terrace and in the kitchen. Plus you had to walk up a couple of flights of narrow steep stairs to reach the terrace. But with all of that, the breakfasts were actually pretty good.

"Pumpkinhead" snuck out on the terrace and Tish was teasing him with a piece of cheese. I warned him about doing this and "Pumpkinhead" slashed Tish's index finger with razor sharp claws. Tish had a nasty gash with a lot of bleeding. It took over a week for his finger to heal up. "Pumpkinhead" also scratched Mary's leg. I have a picture of him, sitting in Tish's chair after they had gone, staring at Tish's plate, with an evil look on his face.

We drove into Cefalù after breakfast, seeing the spectacular Rocca di Cefalù towering above the town. We found a parking place near the beach and went to the Lido Angeli del Mare: "Angel Beach." The special significance of Angeli, the name that Sylvia took before she became Sylvia Heer; the last name of Tex and Erna and Sylvia's extended family in Canada. I took pictures of this sign in front of the stairs leading down to the beach.

The prices were more reasonable for the beach chairs and umbrellas, so we rented them and settled in on a beach packed with people. Cefalù deserves its title of "The Pearl of the Mediterranean." The beach was sandy and golden and the Mediterranean Sea was crystal clear and blue with a sandy bottom. I walked way out and body surfed in the waves. I floated on my back, looking up at the Rocca di Cefalù and the twin towers of the Norman Cathedral. They are impressive sights, especially while viewing them from the water. *Sylvia should have been here at this beach that was named after her.*

We witnessed a beautiful sunset, walked around town, had a nice dinner at a restaurant near the beach and our van, and Tish drove us through the woods on the back roads to Case Saponara.

Saturday, September 21st, we had asked Christina if she would buy two dozen eggs for us, when she bought the food for our final breakfast. Mary was going to make us omelettes or scrambled eggs, but Christina forgot to get the eggs when she bought the food for breakfast. She felt bad, and we were disappointed, but that's the way it goes sometimes.

We packed up and checked out and drove to Sperlinga, 47 miles south of Cefalú, a commune in the province of Enna, in central Sicily, with an elevation of 2,460 feet. The village winds upwards to the castle that sits at the top of a cliff. It dates back to Norman times, in the year 1,000, and is built into this rocky cliff. The name Sperlinga is derived from the Latin word spelunca, meaning cave, and the troglodyte caves of Sperlinga are amazing, spaces and rooms dug into the sandstone. The village carved in the wall has 50 caves, each one was used as a small house, with one or two rooms at most. We hiked all through these caves.

We then drove 25 miles south to Enna, known as Castrogiovanni until the 1920's. It is located on a mountaintop almost in the exact center of Sicily. It is Sicily's highest major city at an elevation of 3,055 feet. Enna is the only important city of ancient Sicily that was not founded by foreign invaders, inhabited as far back as early 1200 BC. Enna is also the capital of the only one of Sicily's nine provinces that has no coastline. We walked all around Enna, visiting many churches.

From Enna, we drove 45 miles south to Piazza Armerina, a province of Enna. We would be staying overnight at the Suite D'Autore Art Design Gallery, opposite the 17th century Piazza Armerina Cathedral, which is what we were looking at from our rooms. This hotel featured original artworks throughout the building, with an avant-garde art gallery on site, promoting young artists and designers. Each suite had different themes and artwork. It was definitely unique, to say the least. Tish and Mary's room had a huge pair of red lips for a couch, a round bed, and a gel-filled floor that appeared as if it was moving. Allie and Joe's room had a gigantic cork in the middle of the room.

    We walked down steep and slippery stairs on a rainy night, down narrow alleys and streets, with cars and motorcycles and motor scooters coming too close for comfort of running you over; until we found a restaurant to have dinner. Tish and Mary just stayed in their room and ate sandwiches. After dinner and the long walk back, I watched a group of teenagers, boys and girls, from my hotel window, just hanging out, kicking a soccer ball around, in front of and against the Cathedral. Later they formed a circle, then began using the soccer ball to play volleyball, laughing and having fun on a Saturday night.

    Sunday, September 22nd, church goers were coming to the Cathedral for services, where the teenagers had played the night before. We checked out after breakfast and drove to the Villa Romana del Casale, famous for having the most complex and largest collection of Roman mosaics in the world, as well as the most beautiful and best-preserved of their kind. This is why we came to Armerina, as well as the many tourists who were here also. The archaeologist Gino Vinicio Gentili discovered its ruins in 1950, after the reporting of the local people. This Imperial Villa was originally the property of a powerful Roman family and dates back to 320-350 AD. It most likely belonged to a member of Rome's senatorial class and gives a layout of a grand Roman house, how rich Romans actually lived.

These mosaics date back to a more advanced period of the mosaic art and were probably the work of artists from North Africa, considering both the quality and the scenes representing various themes: mythology, hunting, plants and wildlife, and domestic life. The most famous mosaic is called "the bikini girls," a group of young women wearing very modern bikinis, depicting scenes of Roman female athletes in the gymnasium. I bought a magnet of them. Tish even bought one also.

Piazza Armerina was built in the 4th century AD, covered by a mudslide in the 12th century, uncovered in the 1950's, and is still not complete. The 18th century Duomo sits majestically on top of a hill. Near the Duomo is the 13th century area around the Via Monte.

We left Piazza Armerina and drove 56 miles south near Ragusa, a hilltop city in southeast Sicily. In this area, there was an infamous 7.4 earthquake on January 11, 1693, called the "Sicily Earthquake;" that struck parts of southern Italy near Sicily, Calabria, and Malta. The earthquake was followed by tsunamis on the Ionian Sea and in the Straits of Messina, causing major destruction.

We arrived at Relais Cimillà Guest House, an 18th century fortified manor, located about two miles from the center of Ragusa. The couple that managed the property, Salvo and Eugenia, were very nice and made our breakfasts for us. Most of the cakes and pastries were homemade by her. There was an outdoor swimming pool and a garden, with beautiful views of the countryside. I sat by the pool and took a swim in the late afternoon. I also sat out there all three nights, gazing up at the clear night sky. There was the definitive aroma of a working farm, with cows and sheep. Some of the sheep were grazing down below the pool. There was a solitary donkey that we waved to and spoke to, as we entered and exited the property. The rooms were decent, except there were numerous millipedes crawling on the walls of my room. Nina said that she had them in her room also. The others didn't seem to have them, maybe one or two. I had to go around with toilet paper and grab them and flush them down the toilet. I had to sleep with one eye open, as I didn't want them crawling in my bed or on me. *Other than that,* it was a very unique place to stay.

    Monday, September 23rd, we drove to Modica, 10 miles south of Ragusa. Modica is a city in southeast Sicily, known for its baroque buildings. We finally found a parking place that Tish squeezed into, after driving around for quite a while looking for one. This was usually the situation in all the towns or cities that we went to. We walked all around and went into the impressive Cathedral of Saint George. We then went into Antica Dolceria Bonajuto, the oldest chocolate factory in Sicily. Since 1880, six generations of artisan confectioners of the Bonajuto family have been making chocolate. Their chocolate directly descends from Aztec Xocoàtl, brought to Europe by the Spanish in the 16th century. We sampled that and tried other samples of chocolate from around the world. We also bought some bread and rolls from well-known Panificio San Francesco. I started singing in front of the bakery,

    "I left my heart in San Franscesco."

    Sometimes you get a little looney on these trips....

We left Modica and drove to Ragusa, one of the principal filming locations for the Sicilian detective drama, "Il Commissario Montalbano." ("Inspector Montalbano.") Ragusa Ibla, the Old Town, is home to many baroque buildings like the Duomo di San Giorgio, with paintings and stained-glass windows. We went into the impressive Duomo and visited several other churches. There is the Giardino Ibleo, a public park with churches and fountains.

Tuesday, September 24th, we drove 23 miles south to Palazzo, where the ferry terminal was located, to get an idea of the driving time and the parking situation, as we would be leaving our van there and taking the ferry to Malta in the morning. We completed our scouting mission and afterwards drove through Santo Pietro, a small village of the Commune of Caltagirone, in the province of Palermo, with a population of 90 people. The sun was shining brightly on the Mediterranean, and it was tempting to go and spend the day at the beach there, but we weren't prepared to do that, and proceeded to drive 7 miles south of Modica to Scicli, pronounced "Sheek-ly." It is also a filming location for "Inspector Montalbano." We walked down Via Penna, the pedestrian street with baroque churches and palaces. The most striking are Palazzo Beneventano and San Bartolomeo. The elegant baroque buildings were built after the 1693 earthquake.

On Wednesday, September 25th, we got up at 6:30, packed and checked out. Salvo and Eugenia were nice enough to make breakfast for us an hour earlier than normal so we could drive to Palazzo, and make the 9:30 Vintu Ferry to Malta. We parked the van, paid for leaving it there, and left our suitcases in the van, as we would only be taking our backpacks for our five day stay in Malta. This we had to plan out the night before.

We took this two-hour ferry ride south, across the Mediterranean Sea, packed with people and vehicles, to Valletta, Malta, Europe's smallest capital city. Malta is an archipelago in the central Mediterranean between Sicily and the North African coast. It is a nation that has had a succession of rulers: Romans, Moors, Knights of Saint John, French, and British.

We got off the ferry and started walking to where we would be staying, the Hotel Osborne. Tish, Mary, and I put our backpacks on our backs and started walking. We climbed up this very steep incline until we reached the city. The others did also, but then decided to take a taxi from this point to the hotel. We continued on until we reached the Tritons' Fountain, located on the periphery of the city gates of Valletta, almost on the border of the town of Floriana. It was designed in 1952, then work began on the fountain in 1955, and it was completed in 1959. A restoration project to reinforce it was done in 1987.

It is a bronze fountain with three large figures of mythological tritons holding a dish from which water jets out. The tritons are located so that the face of each of them is visible from the side of the city gates. Triton was a merman in Greek mythology, messenger god of the sea, and son of Poseidon and Amphitrite.

We stopped for a break, took a few pictures, and made our entrance into Valletta. We decided to eat lunch at a fish and chips place. It sounded good to us, after eating plenty of pasta and pizza for almost three weeks. We then found our way to South Street and to our hotel, Hotel Osborne. After checking in and getting settled in the room, I went up to the rooftop, where they had six lounge chairs next to a small pool. And I mean *small*. Three or four strokes from end to end. There was one couple just standing in a corner of the pool reading their books. The views of the city from the rooftop were amazing and I took some pictures. It was hot as I sat in the late afternoon sun listening to my iPod. After a shower, I walked down South Street and around the corner to the mall where we had lunch, and had a falafel at a Lebanese place. There were restaurants everywhere in Valletta. I walked down to the Tritons' Fountain, all lit up and looking spectacular at night.

Thursday, September 26th, after breakfast, we all went on our own walking tour of Valletta. This walled city dates back to the 1500's, established by the Knights of Saint John, a Roman Catholic order. It is known for its museums, palaces, and grand churches, such as the Church of Saint Paul's Shipwreck. Baroque landmarks include Saint John's Co-Cathedral, whose opulent interior is home to the Caravaggio 1608 masterpiece, "The Beheading of Saint John," his largest canvas and his only signed masterpiece. We went inside this magnificent church, built between 1573 and 1577, and dedicated to Saint John the Baptist, the patron saint of the Order. They give you headphones for a free audio guide, but there is an admission charge and it was packed with tourists.

There are beautiful marble floors of tombstones for the Knights of Saint John, in the central part of the church. The more important knights were buried closer to the front of the church. These tombstones are richly decorated with in-laid marble, with the coats of arms of the knights, buried below. There are also images relevant to each knight, telling of his triumphs in battle and his virtues. This is an amazing visual display in the church. There are intricate carved stone walls and gold leaf paintings. The vaulted ceiling and side altars are painted with scenes from the life of Saint John the Baptist.

We then walked to the Grandmaster's Palace, built between the 16th and 18th centuries, as the palace of the Grand Master of the Order of Saint John, who ruled Malta. It eventually became the Governor's Palace and today houses the Office of the President of Malta. We went into the Palace Armoury, the main armoury of the Order of Saint John in the 17th and 18th centuries. It was the last arsenal established by a crusader military order. Only a part of the original armoury still exists, but it is still one of the world's largest collections of arms and armor still housed in its original building, open to the public as a museum since 1860. There are some fascinating styles of weapons and body armor, you can see the evolution of them through the years. Also, some really gruesome ways of maiming or killing your enemies.

We walked around the beautiful Upper Barrakka Gardens and then made our way down to the waterfront in Floriana. There was an elevator that you could take down, which if we had known about it, would have saved us that exhausting walk up the steep incline, when we first got off the ferry. We got on a small wooden boat, a traditional Maltese dghajsa, called a "tal-pas," dating back to Phoenician times. You get a feeling of being on a gondola in Venice. There are many of these, with skilled boatmen, ready to take you over and back across the Grand Harbour, to the "Three Cities." There is a mast and a small motor in the rear. They then maneuver the boat right up to where you get in or out of the boat. You know that they have been doing this for a long time.

"The Three Cities" are: Birgu, (also known as Vittoriosa), Bormla, (Cospicua), and Senglea, (Isla.) We were dropped off at Birgu, an old fortified medieval city on the south side of the Grand Harbour, which has existed since the Middle Ages, well before the Knights of

Saint John arrived. Birgu was the headquarters of the Knights and they built Fort Saint Angelo, over the ruins of a castle dating back to Norman times, at the tip of Birgu, for protection. Birgu also served as the capital city of Malta between 1530 and 1571, until Valletta was built. We walked around this city, feeling transported back in time, then went to the Inquisitor's Palace.

This Palace, also known as the Sacred Palace, was the seat of the Maltese Inquisition from 1574 to 1798, under the name Palazzo del Sant'Uffizio. The building is one of the few surviving palaces of its kind in the world, and the only one which is open to the public. But seeing where they held the prisoners and the untold tortures that went on there, it reminded me of Narni in Italy. I don't need to see any more of these types of places on our trips, I get the idea.

We took another "tal-pass" back across the Grand Harbour, returning to Valletta. After dinner, when the rest of the group would walk around and then go back to their rooms, I would buy a small bottle of liqueur, like mandorla, (almond), or anisette, (anise), and walk down to the Tritons' Fountain and hang out there for a while, sipping my liqueur and watching all the people. This was in the big square and was where the buses came in, one after another, to drop off people as they entered Valletta. A parade of people was coming and going at all times: families pushing a stroller or strollers, groups of girls or boys in their teens, or groups in their twenties, everyone taking selfies or having people take pictures of them on their cell phones in front of the fountain. Some kids would even have pictures taken of them while doing gymnastic poses on the concrete wall of the fountain. I went down there all four nights that we spent in Valletta, gazing at the people, the lit-up fountain, and the night sky.

Friday, September 27th, we had to get up early to walk up to the main square after breakfast, to go on our first guided tour, leaving at 8:45. A van picked us up and drove us down to Msida, where the buses would depart from. We had a long wait and it was hot, just trying to find some shade, which was limited. Malta stays hot right through October, residents told us, which stands to reason, being an island in the Mediterranean and near the coast of Africa. It must be unbearable during the summer and with twice as many tourists. Our bus finally came and we were paired up with other tourists and a large group of German tourists. The Germans are everywhere. The woman guide had to give all the information twice, in English and in German. *But Sylvia would have loved this and talking with all the German people.*

First, we went to San Anton Gardens in Attard, a town in the Central Region of Malta. Together with Balzan and Lija, it forms part of "The Three Villages," inhabited since the 5th century BC. The gardens have a large variety of flowers and plants, and 300-year-old trees from all over the world. They are surrounded by walls, giving it a private atmosphere. We strolled through the many walkways to discover fountains, sculptures, ponds of ducks, swans, and turtles. The gardens surround San Anton Palace, built by the Grand Master Antoine de Paule in the early 17th century, to enhance his country villa. Today it is the residence of the Maltese President. These gardens have been open to the public since 1882.

Then it was on to Mdina, also known as Città Vecchia or Città Notabile, a fortified city in the Northern Region of Malta, which served as its capital from antiquity to the medieval period. It was called "The Silent City," because it had a protected inland location surrounded by a wall, yet it was high enough to keep an eye on the seas.

Once the capital left Mdina, it became a virtual ghost town.

We entered the Vilhena Gate, the Main Gate leading into the city, built in the Baroque style in 1724. Mdina's walls have two other gates: the Mdina Gate and the Greeks Gate. Walking these ancient streets really takes you back to a distant time in the past. We visited Saint Paul's Cathedral. This golden stone Arabic walled city has a mysterious feel about it.

From Mdina, the entire tour group had lunch at a restaurant, set up with long tables for us. This was part of the tour package. They gave us both red and white wine for free, but ironically bottled water was an additional charge. I was enjoying my lunch, when I bit down on the hard crust of a piece of bread and felt something that I knew was not right. I looked at my bread, and sure enough, a piece of my tooth had broken off. *Just what I needed.* It was the tooth next to, and past my "eye tooth," on the right side of my mouth. This tooth had been looking darker to me over the course of the summer, not totally black or anything like that, but I could tell it was a different look when I smiled. I had gone to my dentist for a teeth cleaning on August 23rd and had mentioned it to him. He just said that it was because of the old and dark filling in there.

I went back on September 3rd, two days before I was leaving on this trip, to see if he could drill out the old filling and put a new white filling in there. He said that it wasn't necessary, instead saying it would be wise to replace two old fillings in the teeth next to and past this one. I had taken a full set of x-rays and a tooth on the bottom, below these teeth, showed some decay, along with having an old filling. He said it was a necessary "down the road" situation and it would be a good idea to take care of that one now and the other two upper ones as well. I went ahead and had all three teeth filled with new fillings, and although he gave me a discount on a package deal, it was still costly. And the tooth that I went to see him about, remained the same, and looked darker than normal. My assumption is that when I did that face plant on the concrete patio at Tom and Debbie's pool on my birthday, August 20th, 2018, that tooth must have had a hairline fracture in it as a result of this fall, and x-rays had failed to detect it. This stands to reason why it was becoming darker; it has had this old filling in it for many years and didn't look like this. I was disappointed when I left the dental office and this tooth had the same dark look to it. I think that it had this fracture in it, undetected for 13 months, and just finally broke apart when I bit into that hard crust. I saved the piece of broken off tooth and brought it back home. Now I had half a tooth there and exposed. I didn't feel any intense nerve sensations, fortunately, but I felt sensitivity there and had to be careful and favor that side of my mouth when I ate or brushed my teeth, for the last 13 days of the trip.

I had the sliced big toe and the branch in the eye in the autumn, (I don't want to say fall), of 2016; the blister in the eye in the spring of 2017; the sliced scalp and the broken finger on the trip in 2017; escaped with no major injuries on the trip in 2018, yet was dealing with the healing and soreness of the cut chin, elbows, and knees from the pre-trip faceplant, on my birthday in 2018; and the excruciating back pain and now this broken tooth on the 2019 trip. *What next?*

What does the 2020 trip have in store for me?

The bus tour continued for a stop to stretch your legs and take pictures at one of the highest points in Malta, the Dingli Cliffs, with spectacular views of the

Mediterranean Sea. Then we continued on the tour to the town of Rabat, its name derived from the Arabic word for "suburb," as it was a suburb south of the old capital, Mdina. We walked around its ancient narrow streets and wooden galerijas, (Maltese balconies), with many churches, like Saint Paul's Church and Catacombs, and Roman mosaics.

The final stop was in Mosta, the third most populous town in Malta, behind Saint Paul's Bay and Birkirkara. Mosta is famous for the Mosta Dome, with its massive rotunda, that is the third largest in the world. The Basilica of the Assumption of Our Lady, commonly known as the Rotunda of Mosta or the Mosta Dome, is a Roman Catholic parish church dedicated to the Assumption of Mary. It was built between 1833 and the 1860's, on the site of an earlier Renaissance church, which had been built around 1614. It has been called "The Miracle Church."

During World War II, Malta was heavily bombed, being a strategic outpost for the Allies. By the end of the war, Malta had become the most bombed nation of them all. On April 9th, 1942, two German bombs fell on this church. A Mass was going on at this time, with 250 parishioners in the church. Alarms rang out ahead of time, and while some people left the church, others stayed and prayed. The first bomb pierced the dome, ricocheted, and fell onto the floor of the church. The second bomb cleared the left side of the triangle of the church's facade. Neither bomb exploded and it was hailed as a miracle. It was thought that divine intervention prevented the church and the town from turning into rubble. The bombs were quickly defused by the military and dumped into the sea. Today the Mosta Dome is celebrated for its miracle. There is even a replica of the bomb that fell through the dome, in the back. We went inside this church to see this and read about its history and the dome itself is an amazing sight to see and experience.

Saturday, September 28th, we had to get up at 6:30, eat a quick breakfast, and walk up to the same square where we had met the van to take us to the tour bus for our guided tour the day before. The van driver was pretty much on time for our 8:00 departure. He drove us 22 miles down to Mgarr, where we would take the ferry over to Gozo Island, the second biggest island, after Malta, of the 21 islands that make up the Maltese archipelago. Gozo, an island in the Mediterranean Sea, called the "Isle of Calypso," as it has long been associated with Ogygia, the island home of the nymph Calypso, in Homer's Odyssey. It has been inhabited for thousands of years: ruled by the Phoenicians, Romans, Arabs, Sicilians, French, and British. Gozo is known locally as Ghawdex, and in antiquity as Gaulos. Its inhabitants are known as Gozitans.

We took the Gozo Ferry, a 45-minute ride across the Mediterranean Sea to Gozo, then on the bus tour. The first stop was Xaghra, a town on the island of Gozo, home of the Ggantija megalithic temples, which were inhabited dating back to 3,600 BC and the Xaghra Stone Circle.

This means these temples were inhabited 5,620 years ago! Think about that: The Megalithic Temples of Malta are, according to the Guinness Book of World Records, the oldest free-standing structures in the world; *older than Stonehenge, (5,020 years ago), the Egyptian Pyramids, (4,900 years ago), and the Mayan Pyramids, (3,000 years ago.) The oldest signs of human writing were created in Sumeria, in Mesopotamia, in 3,300 BC, (5,320 years ago), meaning these Ggantija temples are 300 years older than written language!*

The Gobekli Tepe in Turkey, uncovered in 1994, was built in 9,500 BC, which makes it 11,520 years old, the oldest temple in the world. The people that built Gobekli Tepe were what we would call cavemen, hunters and gatherers working with tools made out of stone. What they managed to build should have been impossible: pillars organized into great stone rings. The pillars are decorated with intricate sculptures, but they are also the foundations to a structure, holding blocks that some of which weigh more than 10 tons. How was that possible? Another mystery to ponder, along with all the other ancient mysteries that we don't have the answers to.

We went into the small museum on the site. It explained about all the artifacts found at the site. There are statues which have been found that are headless. It is said this represents death as well as fertility. The Temple People had an inner sanctuary for the Holy Priest. The Temple People vanished mysteriously, and were replaced by the early Bronze Age People, who used the site for cremating their people. The Temple People buried their dead.

We walked out to the edge of the Xaghra Plateau, where we witnessed the two temples with our own eyes. The temples were a ceremonial site in a fertility rite. According to local Gozitan folklore,

"A giantess who ate nothing but broad beans and honey bore a child from a man of the common people. With the child hanging from her shoulder, she built these temples and used them as places of worship."

The name Ggantija is derived from the word "ggant," Maltese for giant. Gozitans held the belief that a race of giants were responsible for building these temples. We walked around the site and into the two temples, transported back in time to an ancient culture. Some of these megaliths exceed 16 feet in length and weigh over 50 tons. We took many pictures, then headed back to the bus.

The bus took us to Munxar, where we ate lunch at Sea Shells Bistro there. It was a good lunch and free wine again, but I had to be careful what I ate now with the broken tooth. No more bread, at least not the crust. We stopped at a craft market near there after lunch.

Then the bus took us to the village of San Lawrenz. Its name is derived from Lawrence of Rome, the patron saint of the village. We walked down to The Inland Sea, known as Dwejra, a lagoon of seawater connected to the Mediterranean Sea, through an opening formed by a natural arch. Unfortunately, one of their famous natural wonders, "Wied il-Mielah Window," or the "Azure Window," no longer exists. This 92 feet, natural limestone arch, was one of the island's major tourist attractions, until it collapsed in stormy weather on March 8th, 2017. You can still see postcards of it around for sale.

We went on a fishing boat, known in Maltese as a luzzu, on a tour of the caves. Tish and Mary, for some reason, decided to skip this, but the rest of us went. It was well worth it. It reminded us of the boat tour into the caves in Paleokastritsa in Corfu in 2017. The boat guide takes you out through a narrow natural tunnel in the limestone archway, then for a tour of the nearby steep limestone cliffs, the "Fungus Rock," and the "Azure Window" ruins, where you can barely make out where it collapsed. They skillfully maneuver in and out of the caves. You can see many small fish swimming below the surface. There are people swimming and snorkeling in these caves. It was hot out, and if I had my bathing suit on, I would have been tempted to dive in also. The turquoise of the inland sea changes to azure blue as you pass through the cave and you can see multi-colored coral. It is a beautiful sight to behold.

After San Lawrenz, we continued on the bus tour to Victoria, Gozo's capital city, known among the Maltese as Rabat. We went to the Gozo Cittadella, also known as the Castello, the Citadel of Victoria. The area has been inhabited since the Bronze Age, and the site now occupied by the Cittadella is believed to have been the acropolis of the Punic-Roman city of Gaulos. For centuries the Citadel served as a sanctuary from attack by Barbary Pirates and Saracens, Arab Muslims. We walked to the top and the views of this capital city were spectacular. We also went inside to the Gozo Museum of Archaeology and The Gozo Citadel Cathedral, the Mother Church of all churches on Gozo since 1435.

We took the ferry back to Mellieha Bay, where the van picked us up and drove us 25 miles to Valletta. We got there in time to witness a gorgeous sunset and walked back to our hotel after a long, eventful, and historic day.

Sunday, September 29th, after breakfast, we packed up our backpacks, leaving them for the day in the hotel's luggage storage room, as we didn't need to be at the terminal until around 4:30, to catch the 5:30 ferry. We checked out and walked down steep steps to the "Sliema Ferry" pier on Boat Street, on the west coast of Valletta. We then took the twenty-minute water taxi ride across Marsamxett Harbour to Sliema, a resort town on the east coast of Malta. You could see Fort Manuel, built by the Knights of Saint John, on tiny Manoel Island, on the way over.

The women wanted to check out a big mall there, to buy some gifts to bring back home with them. We walked around the mall for a while and then left to explore the long promenade lining the coastline along the waterfront, known as the Sliema Front. Fort Tigné is to the north and Saint Julian's is a 17th century watchtower and battery to the south. The baroque-inspired Stella Maris Church dates back from the 1850's. It was then time to take the water taxi back to Valletta.

    We walked up the steep steps to the city and back to the hotel to get our backpacks from the luggage storage room. One last walk down the city streets of Malta, past the Upper Barrakka Gardens, and taking the elevator down to the Floriana waterfront. We still had to walk for miles along the waterfront, lugging our backpacks, before reaching the ferry terminal. We boarded the ferry and took the two-hour ride across the Mediterranean Sea, witnessing a fantastic crimson sunset, until we reached Sicily. Our van was safe, with our suitcases still inside, in the parking lot in Palazzo. We loaded our backpacks in the van and now Tish realized that he was going to be driving once again, after a reprieve of almost five days.

    The next destination was Avola, a tranquil seaside city in the province of Siracusa. We drove 30 miles northeast in the Sicilian countryside, through dark narrow back roads until we finally reached the Agroturism Val Di Noto, where we would be staying. We had to make a call, so the young guy who managed the place, could drive up to meet us and let us in the locked gate. He gave us the remote code to get in the gate after this. We parked the van and unloaded our luggage and walked past a pen of goats down stone walkways to our rooms.

    Monday, September 30th, in the morning, we walked up the stone steps to the open terrace for our breakfast buffet. There was a nice pool on the upper level.

Donkeys and horses roam around the hills and there are plenty of cats that live here on the grounds. Olive and carob trees are plentiful here in the Hyblaean hills, in the valley of the Cassibile River. Cava Grande Nature Preserve surrounds the spectacular canyon formed by the river, the reason why Avola is called "The Grand Canyon of Sicily."

We drove 17 miles northwest to Siracusa, a city on the Ioanian coast of Sicily. We found a parking place and walked around the streets. I was proud to have Siracusa as our "Sister City" of Syracuse, as were Tish and Mary. It is a beautiful city, very clean, and known for its ancient ruins. The central Archaeological Park Neapolis comprises the Roman Amphitheatre, the Teatro Greco, and the Orecchio di Dionisio, (Ear of Dionysius), a limestone cave shaped like a human ear.

Siracusa has a rich Greek history, dating back 2,700 years. The city was built on Ortigia Island, the site of an ancient Greek settlement founded by the Corinthians in 734 BC. Siracusa was home to Archimedes, the most famous mathematician and inventor of all time. The city has been ruled by the Romans, the Vandals, the Goths, the Arabs, the Normans, and the Byzantines. You can see the influence of all these cultures when looking at the city's ancient and medieval structures.

We stopped in a store selling hundreds of different kinds of spices. You could smell their fragrances from a block away. We came upon the remains of the Temple of Apollo in Ortigia, in Piazza Pancali, the oldest Doric Greek Temple, dating back from the 6th century BC.

We found an outdoor market selling everything that you could think of and Tish and I bought Siracusa tee shirts, black with white lettering. Had to have a Siracusa tee shirt. I wore my Syracuse tank top, blue with Syracuse in orange lettering, and later in the day I put on my blue tee shirt with 'Cuse in orange lettering. Siracusa is where we met up with Margot, one of Allie and Joe's daughters, who lives with her husband, Scott, in Los Angeles. She had flown to Rome for a few days, then flown to Catania, then took a train from there to meet us in Siracusa. Allie and Joe met her at the train station.

Margot brought an infusion of youthful energy to our group. She and I talked a lot and enjoyed each other's company. I told her about Sylvia, and my children's books, screenplay, and now this book. She would be traveling with us for the next six days, so now there were eight of us. We all had lunch at an outdoor cafe.

After lunch, we walked some more on Ortigia Island, and then went into the Cathedral della Nativité di Maria, in the Piazza Duomo, considered the most important church in Siracusa. It was built by the Byzantines in the 17th century, with a Baroque style outside and Greek Temple and Medieval inside. We marveled at the impressive Piazza Duomo while eating our gelatos. We walked down to the Piazza Archimede, where we found the Fountain of Arethusa, a natural fountain on the island in the historical center of Siracusa, one of the few places in Europe where papyrus grows.

According to Greek mythology,

"The fresh water fountain is the place where the nymph Arethusa, the patron saint of Siracusa, returned to earth's surface after escaping from her undersea home in Arcadia."

There were beautiful gardens all around as we walked down by the Ionian Sea. It was now time to leave this beautiful city, return to the van, find a place to have dinner, and drive back to Val di Noto.

Tuesday, October 1st, after breakfast, we drove 17 miles south of Avola to Marzamemi, a seaside village of fishermen, who mainly catch red tuna, located by the Ionian Sea coast. In 1959, a Byzantine merchant ship, dating back to the 6th century, was found near here. The beach was now closed for the season and the area looked kind of run down. We drove further south and came upon another beach that was closed. A woman who was leaving this beach told us about another beach further south that was open. This turned out to be valuable information and saved our day.

Porto di Capo Passero is the farthest point south in Sicily, and thus in Italy as well. We parked the van and walked down a boardwalk to El Caribe Beach, a beautiful sandy beach where we rented beach chairs and umbrellas. The water was clear and pleasant with a sandy bottom. El Caribe had to rank right at the top of our beach experiences, along with Paestum and Cefalù. It was a picture-perfect day, sitting in the sun, listening to my iPod, body surfing in the waves of the Mediterranean. There were great views of cliffs and rock formations, and a monument out in the distance served as the marker separating the Ionian Sea on one side and the Mediterranean Sea on the other. They were making preparations to close in a day or two, so we made a great find!

After getting supplies and sandwiches from a big store, then driving back to Val di Noto, and a shower, we sat outside our rooms in an open area, eating our sandwiches and whatever else we had for dinner. Margot started feeding the cats some cheese, and of course they started following her around. We called her "The Cat

Whisperer" from this point on. The only problem was that Allie had an allergy to cats and kept sneezing. Margot talked with the goats also, as did Mary.

Wednesday, October 2nd, after breakfast, we spent several hours at the nice pool there, sitting in the sun and swimming, and I listened to my iPod. We then drove 6 miles west of Avola to Noto, known for its baroque architecture. The 19th century Porta Reale, with its triumphal arch, marked the entrance to the city. We walked to the Palazzo Ducezio, with its Hall of Mirrors. This became an inside joke for us, much like the Royal Dane in the Virgin Islands, where Sylvia and I stayed in March, 1987. "Royal Dane" became a term Sylvia and I used after this, for the combination of high-priced dinners with small portions.

The Hall of Mirrors was modeled after the Hall of Mirrors in Versailles, France. Here in King Louis XIV's Palace of Versailles, there are 17 mirror-clad arches that reflect the 17 arcaded windows that overlook the gardens. Each arch contains 21 mirrors, with a total of 357 mirrors. We weren't expecting anything as grandiose as that, but something that was impressive enough to warrant the price of admission. It was in one room, with two large decorated mirrors on either side of the room. The furniture was styled after King Louis XV, not King Louis XIV. It took five minutes to see this room and we were definitely disappointed, expecting to see something more like Versailles. We felt like we were *bomarzoed*. The "Hall of Mirrors" became an inside joke term for us, for anything that had embellished advertising and didn't come close to our expectations.

We walked up to the top of the Palazzo Ducezio, where there were spectacular views of the city. We visited the reconstructed 18th century Noto Cathedral, a Roman Catholic cathedral dedicated to Saint Nicholas of Myra. As you enter, you see a painted wooden cross, made from pieces of driftwood by African immigrants. We walked the narrow, ancient streets, Via Corrado Nicolaci, coming upon the 18th century Nicolaci Palace and the Palazzo Battaglia, dating back to 1735. The 1757 Fontana d'Ercole, "Fountain of Hercules," is in the Piazza XVI Maggio, in front of Chiesa di San Domenico, built between 1703 and 1727. We people-watched as we had a gelato, walked back to the van, drove out of the narrow streets, and stopped for dinner.

There was a saying painted on the wall in the restaurant in Sicilian. I asked the waitress what it meant and she tried to explain it to me, something about the birth of Sicily; I took a picture of it and googled it:

"Diu talió la Sicilia cu stupuri

e tutu pria tu dissi a lu suli:

vasala, accarizzala,

tenila granni onuri,

chidda è 'na goccia lu me' suderi."

It is the fourth and final verse of a famous poem, "The Birth of Sicily;" it translates to:

"Our Lord looked with stupor at Sicily,

and, very pleased, said to the Sun:

Be nice to her, love her and kiss her,

Keep her in great honor,

She is a drop of my sweat."

On Thursday, October 3rd, after breakfast, we packed up, checked out, loaded up the van, leaving Val di Noto and driving 84 miles northwest of Avola, through the Sicilian countryside, to Taormina in the province of Messina. When I first saw the road signs for Taormina, I started singing the 1960 song, "Corrina, Corrina," by Ray Peterson, rhyming it with Taormina, Taormina. The rest of the group looked at me in amazement, after singing it and naming the artist, as I frequently did on these trips. Allie called me "The Jerry Seinfeld of Music," the analogy of me quoting all these lines and scenes from Seinfeld episodes, to knowing all these songs and lyrics and who the artists were.

Taormina, meaning "thanks" from the Latin word Tauromenium, is a hilltop town, sitting on the east coast of Sicily. It was founded in antiquity, and then by the Chalcidensians, as Sicily's first Greek colony in 735 BC. It sits near Mount Etna, an active volcano with trails leading to the summit. The town is known for the Teatro Antico di Taormino, an ancient Greco-Roman theatre that is still used today. Cliffs drop to the Ionian Sea, forming coves with sandy beaches. A narrow stretch of sand connects to Isola Bella, a tiny island and nature reserve. There are tranquil gardens in the Villa Comunale Di Taormina. We would be staying at the Hotel Mediterranée, close to the Palazzo Corvaia Palace, overlooking Villagonia Bay and near the beaches of Mazzaro.

Tish somehow navigated the incredibly narrow streets and up the driveway to our hotel. We unloaded our luggage after checking in, and got settled in our rooms. The rooms had an open veranda, with rows of flowers between the rooms, and a huge open balcony area past that with huge vases and beautiful flowers and plants all around. We were high up on the hill, overlooking Villagonia Bay down to the Ionian Sea. There was a huge cruise ship that was docked there for several days, and small boats that would

transport the passengers into Taormina and back to the ship.

We left the hotel, walking down the steep hill and many steep steps until we reached the town. We walked all over the town, packed with tourists, Taormina being a popular tourist destination. There were cars, motorcycles, motor scooters, and trucks coming out of nowhere, from alleys and side streets. You had to stay focused where you were walking. We walked past the many boutiques, restaurants, shops, historic churches and buildings on the Corso Umberto, the main street of Taormina, until we reached the Teatro Antico di Taormina.

This incredible horse-shaped theatre was founded by the Greeks in the 4th century BC. We found out that they had started building it in the 3rd century BC, having to move manually from the mountain over 100,000 cubic meters of rock. We walked up the steep stairs to witness a truly awe-inspiring sight. It has a spectacular view toward the Calabrian coast, the Giardini-Naxos Bay on the Ionian coast of Sicily, and the cone of Mount Etna.

The Greeks built this theatre to accommodate dramatic performances and musicals. It was transformed during the Roman times for games and gladiatorial battles. This theatre is the second largest theater in Sicily, after the one in Siracusa; but it is the world's best known and most admired. This 10,000-seat amphitheater is still being used for performances today: theatre, arts and film festivals, rock concerts, award ceremonies, symphonies, operas, and ballets. To see a performance there, all lit up at night, would be a thrill of a lifetime, as the acoustics there are said to be exceptional. It would be even more impressive than the one at the Acropolis site in Athens, and the one in Plovdiv, Bulgaria; and they were amazing.

In recent years, there have been performances by: Paul Simon, Simple Minds, Sting, Carlos Santana, Tony Bennett, Elton John, Duran Duran, Robert Plant, and Patti Smith. We walked all around the theatre, taking pictures and trying to grasp where we were, being transported back into ancient history.

We walked back and had dinner, then strolled the Corso Umberto, now all lit up at night. We had a gelato as we stopped and watched a Sicilian born operatic tenor, Antonio Nicolosi, perform in the main square, Piazza IX Aprile. We found out his name when he put out his CD next to his donation box. He had no microphone, just a small CD player playing opera music in the background. He wandered away from that and was belting out opera, so there was no lip synching going on here.

People that were strolling the streets stopped and listened and hung out. People gathered on the stone steps of the Church of San Giuseppe and sat there and marveled at what they were hearing. I had asked the girl at the gelato place behind us if she knew his name, and she wrote down Antonio on a piece of paper and gave it to me. She did not know his last name. When we found it out, I wrote down Nicolosi for her on a piece of paper. She was happy, now being able to tell people his full name when people asked her if she knew his name.

He has sung on Italian and German television. Now he is a freelance tenor, well known in Rome for his great tenor voice, singing outdoors for the tourists in the squares of Piazza della Rotonda, near the Pantheon, and Piazza

Navona; and now in Taormina, where we had the good fortune to see and hear him, his beautiful voice piercing the still night air. He also injects a little humor into his performances.

Friday, October 4th, after breakfast, we were picked up by a hotel van, which Tish had arranged for us for six euros each, to take us to and back, a private part of Spisone Beach, owned by the hotel. We got our beach chairs and umbrellas, but the guy who worked on the beach, wasn't the friendliest or most accommodating guy in the world. The views were spectacular, the cliffs and rock formations stretching around the Bay of Spisone, reminded me of Glyfada Beach in Corfu. But unlike Glyfada Beach, it had pebbly sinking sand, just like the beach in Tropea. I started to wade in, but noticed huge protruding rocks just below the surface and wisely decided against it. I didn't need another face plant, smashed head and teeth, facial cuts and bleeding episode. The van driver picked us up at 4 o'clock to return to our hotel. I went up to the pool for a late afternoon swim, gazing up at Mount Etna, then showered, and we all walked down the steep hill and steep steps to a nearby pizza place for dinner.

Saturday, October 5th, after breakfast outside, with the magnificent view of Villagonia Bay, I went up to the beautiful pool and spent the entire day there, sitting in the sun on a gorgeous day, listening to my iPod, writing down some notes for this book, and swimming. For the first couple of hours, it was just me and looking at Mount Etna at the pool, before eventually people came and filled up the lounge chairs. It was very peaceful while it lasted, but it was still good after that. The rest of the group had gone sightseeing and to the Comunale Gardens.

Margot came up to the pool to say goodbye to me, as Allie and Joe had arranged a taxi to take her to Catania. From there, taking an evening flight back to Rome, staying overnight, then flying back home to Los Angeles the following day. Tish and Mary came up to the pool later in the afternoon after their sightseeing.

We all, except for Tish and Mary, went back to the restaurant, Don Ciccio, where we had eaten on Thursday night, in the Palazzo Ciampoli. We had a nice dinner outside, and Tish and Mary joined us, after they had eaten at that same pizza place from the night before. Then we all strolled down the Corso Umberto on our final night in Taormina, having a gelato, people-watching, and once again watching and listening to an exhilarating performance by Antonio Nicolosi in the square. We had to once again climb up all the steep steps and the steep hill to get back to Hotel Mediterranée.

On Sunday, October 6th, after our final breakfast, eating outside, overlooking the beautiful view of Villagonia Bay; we packed up and checked out, leaving Taormina, our group now back to seven, and headed for Messina. We had thought about visiting Savoca, 17 miles away, and Forza d'Agro, 20 miles away, the towns they used for the town of Corleone in the 1972 movie, "The Godfather." But it started to rain and we had heard that the streets in these towns were impossibly narrow, and these towns are packed with tour buses, with people curious to see these film locations. Tish decided to just keep on going. It would have been cool to see these towns that they used for the scenes in Corleone, but at least we were "in the neighborhood," and we had been in many towns that they could easily have used for Corleone.

We drove 32 miles to Messina, where we would take the 20-minute ferry ride, with our van, across the Strait of Messina, leaving Sicily and going back to Italy.
We arrived in San Giovanni and started driving 190 miles north to Lagonegro, a town in the province of Potenzo, in the Southern Italian Region of Basilicata. It was founded in the 9th century by Byzantine monks. Lagonegro is a medieval town of narrow streets and steep stairways, on the western slope of a nature reserve, the Massif Sirino.

It was raining for most of the drive to Lagonegro, but we kept going, only making a pit stop for lunch and a few supplies. We arrived at the Hotel Caimo in the early evening and I was given room #106, the second coincidental time on this trip that I was given our old family house number on Rugby Road, the previous time was at the Paestum Resort and Inn. Tish was exhausted from driving and he and Mary were just going to make some sandwiches and not go anywhere for dinner. The woman at the front desk didn't speak much English, but we communicated to her that we wanted to go out for dinner. There were no restaurants within walking distance and nobody felt confident enough to drive the van. She was very helpful and called the owner of a restaurant in town, and he came in a van and picked us up at 8 o'clock, and drove us a few miles to his Italian restaurant, "La Stradella," which he told us meant "streetcar."

They had two trays of complimentary pizza, cut into small squares, for us and cute glasses of prosciutto wine. He toasted with us and we had a few squares of the homemade pizza, which he told us that all the ingredients were grown and made locally. The crust was soft and the sauce was ample and delicious. I thought it was the best pizza that I had on the entire trip. We were seated at a long table on the right-hand side of the dining room. A large

Italian family came and sat behind us. In the middle of the room was a big screen television with a Serie A soccer game being played. The teams were Inter Milan against Juventus F.C. from Turin, with superstar Cristiano Ronaldo.

All these local guys came in, sitting in front of the television in a big table in the middle. They were there to watch the game, like we would be watching a football or basketball game, cheering on their favorite team, Inter Milan. They were cheering and yelling, as the waiters kept bringing them baskets of bread, pasta dishes, pizza, and bottles of wine. Joe and I were watching the game and cheering along with them. Another man came in with his young son to watch the game. The game was 1-0 in favor of Juventus, then Inter Milan tied it up at 1-1. The guys were urging their team on and agonizing over nearly missed goals. But when Juventus scored in the 80th minute, to take a seemingly insurmountable lead, the guys all got up and abruptly left, going outside to smoke cigarettes and analyze the game. It was a fun experience to be involved with them watching the game.

The owner was nice enough to give us a ride back to our hotel. It would have been a very difficult journey for us, if we would have had to walk several miles up hills and winding roads, with no streetlights and raining; especially not knowing our way and after drinking beers and wine. We all chipped in two euros each, to give him a ten-euro tip, which he appreciated.

Monday, October 7th, after breakfast, we packed up our backpacks, as it was only an overnight stay, and headed out of Lagonegro. It was still raining as Tish drove the 257 miles north to Ardea, about 23 miles south of Rome. Ardea is an ancient town of the Rutuli people, founded during the

8th century BC, near the Mediterranean coast, in the region of Lazio. In ancient times it was an important center of the cult of Juno. There are 12th century churches and towers. The definition of Ardea: the type genus of Ardeidae, including a number of large strong-flying New and Old World Herons. We would be staying at Agriturismo Corte in Fiore, rustic rooms on a working farm, near Landriana Gardens. Corte Fiore means "Court Flower."

We drove all day, only making a pit stop and lunch. The rain finally stopped and it started to clear up. We arrived in the late afternoon, checked in, and hauled our luggage once again up some stairs to our rooms. We walked around the grounds, taking pictures. They had a nice pool, but it was closed for the season. There were beautiful flowers, plants and gardens everywhere, and you could see the Mediterranean Sea in the distance. On the brick archway, as you exited the grounds on the walkway to the parking area, was a saying in Italian in script writing:

"*Campagna che appaia come un sogno.
Cielo, terra, mare! L'occhio riposa e l'anima s'acquieta dolcemente.*"

I researched it and it translates to:

"*Campaign that looks like a dream.
Sky, earth, sea! The eye rests and the soul sits quietly.*"

We drove a few miles to see if there were any beaches that were still open and found one, Galapagos Beach, (great name), to go to the following day. We found a restaurant to have dinner and drove the back country roads in the dark to Corte Fiore.

Tuesday, October 8th, it was a beautiful sunny day, and after breakfast we drove into town for a while, and then back to Galapagos Beach. We rented lounge chairs and had a pleasant relaxing day. I called the Mediterranean Sea that day, *"Goldilocks water": not too hot, not too cold, but just right.* The beach was sandy and it was a sandy bottom in the sea, with no rocks. I waded way out and went body surfing in the waves. To be doing this on the 8th of October was pretty special! I sat in the sun, listened to my iPod, and gazed out at the clear blue Mediterranean, soaking up the atmosphere of the last full day of our trip.

I would rank Galapagos Beach right up there with Paestum, El Caribe, and Lido Angeli del Mare in Cefalù, as the best beach experiences on our trip. Reluctantly we left Galapagos Beach, seeing another gorgeous sunset while driving along the beach road, and finding a restaurant to have our last dinner on this trip. We managed to navigate our way back on dark country roads to Corte Fiore.

I imagine Syl being with me on all these trips. I visualize her on the beach, sitting in the sun in her bikini, reading a book, swimming in the seas, maybe later having a beer; walking around the narrow streets of these ancient cities, experiencing their beauty and history, people-watching, window shopping, staying at different hotels with some spectacular views, enjoying delicious dinners and drinking some wine.

Wednesday, October 9th, getting up early, packing up, breakfast, checking out, loading our luggage in the van at 8; driving 23 miles north through back roads and traffic to the Rome airport; leaving off the van, getting our tickets and boarding passes, checking our suitcases, going through security, and boarding the plane for the nine hour flight back to Philadelphia. Once again, I had a window seat on the left side, two-person row, toward the back. A friendly Hispanic woman, probably in her 30's, barely five feet tall, unique looking, sat next to me. She was returning after a week's tour of Italy with her woman friend, sitting across from her.

They were going to spend a few days in Philadelphia before going back to where they lived, in midtown Manhattan. She told me that she was a physician in palliative care and I told her about being a caregiver for Sylvia for two years. I told her about our trip and she was jealous that they couldn't stay longer. I wrote down some of the cities and towns that we went to, in case she ever returned to Italy or ever went to Sicily and Malta. I wrote down the titles of my children's books and this book. It was a very pleasant flight for once, with no complaints or incidents.

We arrived in Philadelphia around four in the afternoon local time. Then an incredibly long line for customs, then getting our suitcases, and going through passport control. I said goodbye to Tish and Mary, and Allie and Joe, until who knows when. I had said goodbye to Dick and Nina when we arrived at the Rome airport, as they were taking an earlier flight through Charlotte to Orlando, to avoid a five hour wait in Philadelphia.

I walked through the airport, now with both my suitcase and backpack, to take the shuttle over to the terminal for my flight to Syracuse, leaving around 8:30. I had to go through security again, one last time, then checked my suitcase to Syracuse. I walked down near my gate and had a burrito at Chipotle.

Ioana had told me, (at dinner, with her and Ileana at the Arad Evans Inn on August 21st), that she would pick me up at the airport and give me a ride home. I texted her when I arrived in Philadelphia and she was nice enough to come and pick me up. I told her a little about the trip as we drove to the house. She and Traian and Ileana were going to New York City on Friday afternoon for Columbus Day weekend and to celebrate Traian's 50th birthday and Ileana's 16th birthday. Hard to believe that she is 16, halfway through her sophomore year of high school. And now learning how to drive!

Once more I walked into my dark and lonely house. I had left the sliding glass door from the back deck into the dining room unlocked, with the drapes closed, in case Marty made it back for his 50th high school reunion from Nottingham. He had planned this a year before, but now it was an uncertainty, when he had a colonoscopy and the results showed that he had a tumor. It turned out to be cancerous and he underwent an operation to remove it. It was successful and he is now cancer free, so this was great news, especially for him. He had to avoid any strenuous lifting until the end of November. He did come back for his reunion on September 20th, and stayed here at my house for four days, and said he had a good time seeing some old friends.

Thursday, October 10th, I had to get up early on my first morning back, restless sleep, exhausted and jet lagged; for a 10:30 dental appointment with Paul, "Doctor Noz," Tish's college roommate at Brockport State, that Tish had texted from Europe and made an appointment for me. He had to drill and fill the broken tooth. The tooth was almost all filling now and will require a crown. Then on to getting some wine, errands, checking out Tom and Debbie's house, bank, post office, to get my held mail, store. The following day, pleasant in the high 60's, I did much needed yard work.

Sunday, October 13th, walked around Green and Round Lakes once again. Ran into Steve and Donna as I headed up toward Round Lake. We talked for a little bit, telling them briefly about the trip. I continued on, seeing the near peak colorful foliage, sitting on Sylvia's bench, eating a doughnut and an apple, looking out at the

shimmering water on the lake, reflecting and talking with Syl. I took another walk around these lakes on Monday, October 21st, the leaves a little past peak, but still plenty of brilliant colors. I ran into Paul, a good friend and teammate from my Senior Softball playing days with the Syracuse Cyclones. We talked for a while, catching up on the news about the team and the guys.

The Yankees won their division, (American League East), and swept the Twins in the Divisional Playoffs. They lost to the Houston Astros in the AL Championship, to go to the World Series. They almost forced a decisive Game #7, losing in extra innings. They let an earlier game slip away, and had plenty of near misses and lost opportunities. This became the first decade that the Yankees had not won at least one World Series in every decade since the 1920's. They have been in 40 World Series, winning 27 of them. The Washington Nationals became the team of destiny, winning an unprecedented four road games against the Astros to become World Champions, for the first time in their history; the only other Washington team to win a World Series was in 1924.

Sunday, October 27th, I brought the deck furniture down to the basement and garage to be stored for six months and put the cover on the air conditioner to protect it for the same amount of time. Also picking up a lot of fallen branches after storms.

It must have been a premonition when I was singing, "Corrina, Corrina," as we entered Taormina, Sicily, on Thursday, October 3rd. Today, Jeff, my nephew, Tom and Julie's son, and his wife Jess, had the great fortune of the birth of their first child, a daughter named Corrina Elise. This date was also the passing away of my older sister, Linda, in 2014. And the same day and year that Sylvia received the awful diagnosis that she had a pancreatic cancer tumor. *This illustrates the never-ending cycle of death and rebirth.*

Monday, October 28th, I took a drive to nearby Pratt's Falls. There was still a lot of colorful foliage, but it was definitely past peak for the leaves. I walked down the steep steps to the overlook, watching the mesmerizing patterns of the impressive waterfalls, and listening to its thunderous roar. There was a chipmunk, staring intently at me, flitting in and out of a hollowed-out tree trunk, next to me at the overlook; before deciding he had better things to do, busily preparing for the upcoming winter. I walked back up the steps and through the woods, *wishing that Syl was with me enjoying this day.* I thought of all the years that we took walks here in all the seasons.

Tuesday, October 29th, I took another long walk around Green and Round Lakes, smelling the pungent, earthy, wonderful aroma as I walked through the fallen leaves. I sat on Sylvia's bench, eating an apple, reflecting as I watched the shimmering rays of the sun upon Round Lake. It was a beautiful autumn day in Syracuse, as was the previous day at Pratt's Falls, mid-60's, sunny with a clear blue sky. All is right with the world when it is sunny and blue skies; *yet I guess it is not quite all right, that there is always something missing, and that something is not having Sylvia here with me.*

I just received a text from Ioana asking me if I would consider picking up Ileana from school at 3:30 every weekday, except on school vacation days and snow days when school is cancelled. This came out of the blue and I had to contemplate this from every angle before agreeing to it. This is very important to Ioana, and Ioana did so much for us, and has given me rides home from the airport, and taken me to dinner several times, and invited me to their house for dinner and parties.

But this is now a major commitment and responsibility for me, and to drive in the winter conditions, when I wouldn't normally have to. And to return to MPH, where I have not worked for 4 years and 4 months, since the end of July, 2015; when I finished cleaning out and packing up our Extended Day equipment and supplies, after we were let go. I haven't picked up Ileana from school and summer camps since the middle of August, 2016, when I did it for about a year during her 6th grade year and that summer.

So, this is a new chapter in this relationship. Ileana will now be able to sit in the front seat, instead of a car seat in the back seat when she was a little girl, and then in the back seat after that. Ioana doesn't want her to just hang around school, she wants her to be home doing her homework and studying; Wednesdays over to her piano lessons in Manlius. Ileana has always been a model student, and very conscientious about her courses, and Ioana wants to make sure it stays this way.

It is now November 1st, as I change the calendars, October has come and gone. I turned all the clocks back an hour on Sunday, the 3rd, the ominous first signal of another winter approaching, soon getting dark by 4 o'clock in the afternoon; until it slowly goes up by a few minutes each day, after the winter solstice on Saturday, December 21st, 2019.

In November, my routine is now finishing up the book, walks in the woods, yard work, possible snow shoveling, still taking care of Tom and Debbie's house, and now picking up Ileana in the middle of the afternoon. And watching sports: college football, golf tournaments, and college basketball, with SU beginning another season.

I watch these horrific wildfires in California on the news, with so many people losing their homes and all their possessions or worse, it is like Armageddon out there. The global warming crisis only seems to be intensifying. I hope that all my friends are okay and out of harm's way.

Tuesday, November 5th, back to the dentist for a 90-minute session with "Doctor Noz," to drill out the broken tooth and put in the temporary crown. I will have to return for a 60-minute session to put in the permanent crown in two weeks. I ran all my errands and then spent hours at Tom and Debbie's, picking up big branches and huge limbs from the lawn and driveway, after some storms with 40 to 50 mile per hour winds.

Wednesday, November 6th, I got my hair cut and then back over to Tom and Debbie's to turn their heat on and cover up the patio furniture by the pool. I came home and pounded in my stakes, close to my driveway, for the snow plower. And guess what? Today, Thursday, November 7th, into Friday, 8th, we've had six inches of heavy wet snow. I wasn't ready for this, you never are. But here it is again.

Monday, November 11th, (11/11), Veterans Day, as of today, I have now lived for 10 more years than Sylvia; being 6 years and 10 months, (minus two days), older than her, and then being 3 years and 2 months, (plus two days), since she passed away. *Ten years more on Earth than Syl got.* And every day, month, and year that I'm alive, adds on to these 10 years. This will never make any sense to me.

Ileana was off from school, but Ioana asked me to pick her up at home and drive her to Huntington Learning Center in Lyndon Corners, where she is being tutored in chemistry. We used to take Willie there when he was being tutored.

On Tuesday, the 12th, I drove into MPH to pick up Ileana by 3:30. Some of the kids that we used to watch, who are now in high school, spotted me and were really excited to see me.

Wednesday, the 13th, I picked up Ileana and drove her to her piano lesson at her teacher's house near Wellwood Middle School, on the outskirts of Manlius. I guess I won't have to pick her up on Fridays, as Ioana is going to pick her up. Now I've been informed that she has ski team practice on Tuesdays and Thursdays, so I will only be picking her up on Mondays and Wednesdays for the next two months, and we'll see about January after the Christmas vacation. I picked her up on Monday, the 18th. Today, the 19th, I had the permanent crown put in for that tooth from Dr. Noz. I picked Ileana up at MPH on Wednesday, the 20th, and took her to her piano lesson.

I remember taking piano lessons for a couple of years, starting when I was 8 years old. It was with Mrs. Colvin, the wife of the President of Lakemont Academy. They lived around the corner from our house in Lakemont, close to the school. The lessons were two days a week in the afternoons after school. I eventually begged out of them, wanting to play sports with my Dundee School friends. Now I wish I had continued, maybe I would be able to play the piano today.

After my first year of lessons, there was a recital for all her students. All the parents were there in the audience and were served tea and pastries. When it was my turn, I came up to the piano, wearing my dress clothes; I remember a white suit coat, black pants, white shirt with a black bow tie; and began to play "Dance of the Little Swans," Elementary Piano Sheet Music from Tchaikovsky's classical "Swan Lake."

I began to play, and after a few notes, I would make a mistake, go back to the beginning, and start again. Then play and go farther than the first attempt, make a mistake, and go back to the beginning, and start again. This was probably my OCD tendencies triggering this behavior, although I didn't realize it at the time. Mom and Dad must have had an inkling. I would begin again, go farther than the previous attempt, make a mistake, then go back to the beginning, and start again. Probably painful for everyone to watch. Mrs. Colvin was urging me, with her body language, to continue on after I made a mistake. But I kept doing the same routine. When each student was done with their piece, the parents would politely clap. When I *finally* finished, they gave me a rousing ovation, relieved for me, and I'm sure relieved that they didn't have to sit through this anymore. I probably wasn't even aware of the situation, just thinking that they really liked my performance.

This was similar to when Jeppy had to walk around the bed, across our heads on our pillows, *exactly three times,* before she settled down. And then if anything unsettled her, she would have to get up and walk around the bed, *exactly three times,* before she settled down again. I guess she had OCD as well.

I have completed writing about my experiences on the European trip, and recent additions right up to the present, adding 55 pages to my book. Now the final review and editing process, before submitting this book for publication and release. It has been an almost three years "Labor of Love."

Usually there are still some decent days left in November to walk in the woods. Nancy invited me over to her house, with family and friends, for Thanksgiving. There was plenty of excellent food and good conversations. Showed Nancy my pictures from the trip. Will came up for a five-day visit from NYC, arriving on the 29th and left on the 3rd. He is going to move back to California on December 10th. I showed him all my European pictures and told him all the stories.

In December: some walks in the woods when the weather permits, shoveling snow, cutting up and disposing of downed tree limbs, watching sports, reading, and there is so much sorting to be done, long overdue, in my "den," the room where I watch television.

I have no clue how most people get up every day and do the jobs that they do. I'm sure they could say the same about teachers: how they could put up with all the kids with their attitudes, issues, and learning abilities. But you learn how to do it and how to relate to the parents, when their child or children are the most important thing in the world to them. And you learn and improve and grow, until you excel in how and what you teach.

I could never be a prison guard, soldier, fireman, policeman, first responder, EMT, doctor, nurse, dentist, lawyer, judge, roofer, crane operator, window washer from skyscrapers, bridge worker, mechanic, plumber, bank teller, factory worker, car salesman, insurance agent, politician, mortician, snow plower, taxi driver, and on and on. Don't get me wrong, I respect everyone for doing what they do; working hard to make a living, providing for their family, and in some cases, saving lives. I just can't imagine myself doing what they do. Every day. I can do driving jobs, painting jobs, landscaping jobs; not so much anymore, but I could if I needed to. I can teach and I can write, that's what I can do now.

"What lies behind you and what lies in front of you, pales in comparison to what lies inside of you." -Ralph Waldo Emerson

I can get through December, with the newly fallen snow, walking in the wintry woods, and seeing all the houses decorated with their Christmas lights and displays. It is the grind of January, February, and March that wears you down, especially around here. Some people welcome it, because they love to ski or snowboard, or ride their snowmobiles. But that's not me. I'd rather be walking by the ocean, looking at palm trees and pelicans, feeling the warm sun upon my body.

It was another Thanksgiving and Christmas without Syl. Then New Year's Eve. *2020 will be another year without Syl, another year that she was not allowed to see and experience. It will continue with all "the fourths": the fourth Winter, Valentine's Day, Easter, Spring, Memorial Day, her birthday, Fourth of July, Summer, my birthday, Labor Day; this whole time period between New Year's Day into early September, without Syl being here with me.*

One interesting thing about 2020 is that anyone that has a birthday on the 20th day of their month will have three 20's for their birthday. For example, mine will be

August 20, 2020. My nephew, Jeff, Tom and Julie's son, has his in March; Mary, Tish's wife, has hers in April; Tom, my brother in law and Julie's husband, has his in July; mine in August; my nephew Justin, Marty and Marti's son, has his in October; and Wardie has his in December.

Hopefully I will be around to see this birthday. You never know what can happen these days, with physical issues, forces of nature, or some insane person or terrorist stabbing or shooting you, while you are having dinner and drinking wine at an outdoor cafe in Europe or anywhere. You just never know any more in this world that we live in today.

Truer words have never been spoken. December was going along as normal. Picking up Ileana on Mondays and Wednesdays, some yard work, shoveling, doing my chores and monitoring Tom and Debbie's house, store and errands, house things, reading, watching sports. I picked up Ileana on the 16th and drove her home. Ioana asked me to pick her up on the 18th, drive her home, walk Alexis, then drive Ileana to the Oncenter downtown, where she would be volunteering for the Salvation Army. It started snowing and snow squalls were in the forecast, as I'll admit that I was feeling a little anxious about this journey, but I was going to do it and do it safely. Then Ioana texted me that Ileana was feeling ill and she would pick her up from school. I was relieved and went about my business at home. This turned out to be the first day of changes that would alter my life in the present and into the future.

I thought that I was through writing any more in this book about the present, just summarizing and moving on from 2019, heading into 2020 and beyond. But I feel obligated to let you know what has now happened to me. My breathing felt labored and I was wheezing. Will was dealing with some kind of viral thing when he visited, so I thought maybe he passed on a viral infection to me or that I had bronchitis or something. I bought a bottle of cough syrup and chest congestion medicine and would take a capful late at night. I was getting fatigued easily and knew things weren't right when I would walk down the driveway to get my mail from the mailbox and back and be totally winded and out of breath. That had never happened to me before.

I was afraid to go to bed. I would lie on my side and the wheezing would now be accompanied by a whistle. I was afraid I would not wake up and nobody would find me for weeks. I got up and walked around the house, sat in the recliner, reading and watching television. I managed to get through the days, but my breathing was becoming shallower and more labored at night. I couldn't catch my breath and was gasping for air, like a fish out of water. I was having late night anxiety attacks and subsequent panic attacks. There were several nights that I strongly considered calling 911, but I held off. Every day my breathing was getting worse. I couldn't catch my breath, gasping for air, and the anxiety and panic attacks were getting worse and happening more frequently.

This was dredging up thoughts of similar panic attack situations, like "Quicksand" and "Falling Through The Ice," two childhood experiences buried deep into my subconscious, still the cause of my nightmares today. But this daily and nightly breathing, actually lack of breathing, was ongoing and continuing, and I knew I couldn't go on this way anymore. *What a horrible and scary feeling it is not being able to breathe!* I had now endured this feeling for nine days, hoping the cough medicine would help, but things were just getting worse. And to let people enjoy their Christmases. I couldn't sleep, I could hardly breathe.

I texted Ioana, giving her all the symptoms and scenarios, hoping I could come see her at her office, as she is a pulmonologist. Maybe I had COPD, emphysema, or lung cancer. I was thinking that maybe I would have to start doing chemotherapy treatments, enduring the side effects, thinking of all Sylvia had to go through for two years. Ioana said she thought this sounded more like a heart issue, and Traian, who is a cardiologist, agreed. She said that I should go down to the Upstate Hospital Emergency Room. I thought about it, gasping for air, and endured another long and sleepless night.

Friday, December 27th, I gathered up some extra clothes and toiletries in my backpack, and drove myself down to the Emergency Room. The room was packed, kids running around, everyone was coughing and wheezing. They took my vitals after an hour, then I waited *seven hours* before I got in to see a doctor. They listened to my story and my labored breathing, and thought that I may have pneumonia. But I had no fever, so they ruled that out. One doctor was noticing a heart murmur and the possibility of a leaky heart valve causing it. They did an EKG and put a nitroglycerin patch on my upper right arm. These transdermal patches are used to prevent episodes of angina, chest pain, in people who have coronary artery disease, narrowing of the blood vessels that supply blood to the heart. Nitroglycerin is in a class of medications called vasodilators. It works by relaxing the blood vessels so that the heart does not need to work as hard and therefore does not need as much oxygen. They wanted to do more tests and analyze me, and took me to the fifth floor around midnight, and checked me in.

There was a curtain between myself and this other guy, George, who had to be fed, cleaned up, the whole deal. I'm not sure what exactly was wrong with him, but he was spastic and couldn't really talk normally. I felt sorry for him, they just never let him alone, at any hour of the day or the night, constantly doing tests, in addition to all their other duties. I wasn't allowed to eat or drink after midnight, as early morning tests awaited me. I hadn't eaten anything since I had a banana and a smoothie in the morning at my house, before leaving at noon for the Emergency Room. The nurse brought me a slice of buttered white toast, a Lorna Doone cookie, and a chocolate pudding. Not your greatest dinner, but it was at least something, and hit the spot.

      Saturday, December 28th, they came in the middle of the night to take my blood, which they have done every six hours since I've been here. They also give me heparin shots in my stomach to prevent blood clots, constant blood pressure tests, taking all sorts of meds, several IV's hooked up in both arms, which I have to be very careful about not ripping them out when I get up to take a pee, which is all the time. I've learned how to unplug the IV pole from the wall, as I'm standing up and then maneuvering the pole into the bathroom. I also have to put this heavy monitor box, with all these wires that are connected to all these leads all over my chest, in my gown pocket, then tie up my gown, and then pee into a plastic urinal, without peeing on the gown or ripping the IV's from my arm, connected to bags of Lasix, nitroglycerin, flushes. (Sylvia had a similar situation with bags of chemo, anti-nauseam fluids, and flushes.) This routine was repeated dozens of times throughout the day and the night as well. The Lasix causes you to pee so frequently. It is a loop diuretic, a water pill, that prevents your body from absorbing too much salt. This allows the salt to instead be passed in your urine. Lasix is used to treat fluid retention, called edema, in people with congestive heart failure, liver disease, or a kidney disorder.

It also controls high blood pressure, which mine has always been, when I've had it checked.

They came the first thing in the morning and took me down to the first of many procedures to come. I'd had no sleep, hardly eaten, waited over seven hours in the Emergency Room before seeing a doctor, still having trouble catching my breath. I was sedated, but still conscious, as they ran this catheter, a wire they run through two arteries in your arm, (they can do it through your groin also), with a purple dye that they shoot into your heart to give them a better and bigger picture of your heart. It can actually be pretty risky. This was lots of laughs. Then back to the room for an all day and night of all the things they do to you that I mentioned previously. And all the activity and sounds coming from the other side of the curtain.

Sunday, December 29th, Traian told me that I would be "swallowing a camera" today. They took me down to have the back of my throat numbed with a swab, and then they passed this probe down my throat and esophagus, so they could take even more definitive pictures of the heart and its blood vessels. This is called a transesophageal echocardiogram, a TEE, that uses a long, thin tube called an endoscope, to guide the ultrasound transducer down the esophagus. This lets the doctor see pictures of the heart without the ribs or the lungs getting in the way. It provides a clearer image of the heart because the sound waves do not have to pass through skin, muscle, or bone tissue. This is about a thirty-minute procedure, more lots of laughs. More tests, blood work, peeing all the time, having to maneuver the IV pole and all the wires, every time; and all the commotion on the other side of the curtain.

Monday, December 30th, they took me down for an ultrasound on my abdomen and kidneys. They discovered that I had been living with Hepatitis C for all these years, probably a result of some lifestyle choices from the late sixties through the mid-eighties. They have better treatments these days, which I will have to undergo after the inevitable heart surgery. That's why I always avoided getting into the medical system. Once you are in the system, you are in it forever. This principle applies to the court, mental health, and prison systems as well. So, try to avoid getting in these systems in the first place.

Traian took me under his wing and had me transferred to the eighth floor late in the afternoon. This room was like the Hilton compared to the room that I was now leaving. It was a corner room at the end of the hallway, with a couch and a recliner. It was my own room and my own bathroom. This helped my mental state with all the things that were happening to me. The meals actually were pretty good. New nurses, who were all very nice, more tests and blood work, peeing all the time with the Lasix IV. Traian told me that they had removed the equivalent of a gallon of fluid from my lungs. They removed the nitro patch and added the nitro to my IV's. It was giving me headaches for a few days before they lowered the dosage, and then took it off the IV drips. Now they started an IV of milrinone, a vasodilator that works by relaxing the muscles in your blood vessels to help them dilate and widen. This lowers blood pressure and allows blood to flow more easily through your veins and arteries. It is used as a short-term treatment for life-threatening heart failure.

The nurses told me that I couldn't eat or drink anything after 10:30 p.m., as they would be coming to get me for an MRI at 3 a.m. I couldn't sleep with more tests and anxiety over getting my first MRI, magnetic resonance imaging, used in radiology to form pictures of the anatomy and physiological processes of the body. They didn't come until 6 a.m. on Tuesday, December 31st, the last day of the year 2019. They gave me a pill to relax, but I still felt anxious and claustrophobic about going in that imaging machine. It was a forty-five-minute ordeal with loud noises that sounded like a herd of moose in there, as well as machine guns. Somehow, I survived it. I still may have to take a Cat Scan.

    Traian had gotten Dr. Randy Green, one of the leading heart surgeons around, and Division Chief of Cardiac Surgery at Upstate, to come and talk with me. We hit it off as he explained what was going on with me and how we were to proceed. I have congestive heart failure and open-heart surgery is the only option if I want to stay alive. He said I could have died from heart failure, if I had fallen asleep, or any time during the nine days, before Ioana told me to come to the Emergency Room. He explained that I have three heart valves that are leaking. If there was only one, they could use other methods rather than open heart surgery. The heart has four valves: The mitral valve and tricuspid valve, which control blood flow from the atria to the ventricles. The aortic valve and pulmonary valve, which control blood flow out of the ventricles.

    My aortic and mitral valves are leaking, the mitral even more severely. He said the aortic and mitral valves could not be repaired, only replaced. They will use a cow's valve for the aortic and a pig's valve for the mitral. The tricuspid valve can be repaired. He will make two incisions in my chest and then split the ribs apart. My life will now be in his hands early next week. Traian told me that after surgery "you will feel like you have been hit by a truck." So at least two, maybe three weeks in the hospital to recover before going home. Can't use your arms to lift anything strenuous or drive for six weeks.

So here I was in the hospital, digesting all of this, not being able to go to Traian and Ioana's New Year's Eve party, "The Roaring 2020's," at their house, which I was invited to a couple of weeks before.

I texted Julie, Marty, Nancy, Tish and Mary to give them all this information. Nancy came by to visit and got my car out of the parking garage here and into my garage at home. She brought me this tablet and keyboard, so I could start writing again about this entire experience.

It was now Wednesday, January 1st, *2020*. This was now a new year, the last year of this decade to experience. It will test all the strength and willpower that I have over this winter, if everything comes out okay. I will also begin treatment for the Hepatitis C virus. It will be the end of April before I can resume normal activities.

Thursday, January 2nd, and Friday, January 3rd, were more days of blood work, tests, blood pressure, IV's and peeing all the time, maneuvering the dangling wires on the IV pole; another ultrasound, this one of the carotid arteries in the neck; and early Friday morning for a series of pulmonary breathing tests. It is all never-ending. They have now removed nine liters of fluid from my lungs. If I wasn't suffering so much for those nine days before I came to the Emergency Room, I might have opted to just go and reunite with Sylvia.

Over the weekend, Saturday, the 4th, and Sunday, the 5th, all the usual tests and routines and I watched the NFL playoffs and continued writing. I was watching the Syracuse basketball game late Saturday afternoon in the Carrier Dome, which I could look out and see from my hospital window.

Monday, January 6th, they will be coming very early in the morning, to take me down for more chest x-rays, this time from the side and back. They will be doing "preps" all day, cleaning me up, breathing exercises for the lungs, doctors coming to talk with me. Nancy is coming by with a few things where I can pay three bills: car insurance for six months, property taxes for a year, and the other half of my snow plowing service for this winter. Other bills will have to wait until after the surgery. I called Janine at the Hair Shed to cancel my haircut appointment on the 8th.

Tuesday, January 7th, today is the day that they will come get me and perform an all-day open-heart surgical procedure. I have been writing the past several nights trying to finally finish this book. There will be three weeks of recovery and physical therapy in the hospital and three months or so after that at home for more recovery and more physical therapy. Maybe I will make it to 80 after all, changing several things in my lifestyle.

I underwent open-heart surgery, doing to me what I had mentioned previously. When I woke up from the sedation, I experienced the worst sensation in my entire time in the hospital, and that's saying something. You wake up, still sort of out of it, to having this long, white plastic breathing tube shoved down your throat where you feel like someone is trying to choke you to death. Ioana and Nancy were with me. You have an uncontrollable urge to have a productive cough and they won't let you. They want you to demonstrate that you are able to breathe on your own. Some people have even had arm straps to restrain them. Ioana told me recently that some people have this breathing tube down their throats for a week! They sedate them at night. Nancy had to leave. They wanted to keep the breathing tube down me overnight, but Ioana convinced them I could get it taken out before that. It is like a medieval torture. *It is an indescribable horrible feeling.* Ioana kept holding my hands and telling me to "breathe, Dusty, just breathe." She got me through this helpless feeling. I then started coughing up all this mucus, (could have been worse, like vomit), until they finally took that tube out from deep in my throat. Ioana spoon-fed me some orange ice, which tasted and felt so good after this horrendous ordeal.

I was all stitched up with all these wires underneath and sent to a room in the ICU wing, still on the 8th floor. When the sedation wore off, I did feel like Traian had told me, "that I had been hit by a truck."

Six more days of blood work, IV's, peeing all the time and bowel movements, eating their meals: pretty good, but now with sodium restrictions, and also fluid limitations, when I felt like drinking large quantities of water. Constantly being woken up at 4 or 5 in the morning by the nurses to take all these medications, blood work, and taken in a wheelchair for x-rays and tests.

The good news was that the heart valves replacement and repair went very well. The bad news was that my heart, having a weak heart muscle, was not beating on its own. It needs to be operating at an efficiency of 60, not at 25 like mine was. Teams of doctors came to talk with me and the conclusion was reached that I required an operation to implant a pacemaker/defibrillator device, needed so my heart will beat properly and keep me alive. Boy, I was not prepared for this when I came to the Emergency Room on December 27th!

On Monday, January 13th, I had this device implanted below my neck, near my left shoulder, becoming a bionic man for the rest of my life. I was sedated, but not asleep. Jamal, Traian's "The Heart Group" partner, performed this intricate surgery. I could feel the wires for the leads kind of pinching me, a weird sensation. I am very grateful for being alive, having the finest care possible, almost all of these outrageous costs for these surgeries and everything in the hospital stay being covered by my health insurance, and people taking care of me. *Like in the second paragraph in this book, I do not take these things lightly or for granted.*

I am trying not to go into a deep depression. There are millions of people who have these devices. But I know my life will never be like it used to be. Doing the open-heart surgery was quite enough, thank you, and a long road of physical therapy and recovery. Did not expect that my life was now totally dependent on an electrical device. Usually a shelf life of 5 to 7 years, even 10. So, who knows, maybe I'll reach 80. I can't really imagine anything more. All things considered; I think that's okay.

I have to take medications and blood thinners every morning, Lasix at 4, then more meds in the evening. I just follow orders. Some of these meds I will have to take for the rest of my life. Traian and Ioana offered me their basement apartment for two weeks. Ioana took me and my stuff over here at 4 o'clock, four days after the pacemaker implant surgery; Thursday afternoon, January 16th. Traian said this was the fastest recovery by anyone he has ever seen, with what was done to me. Most people take at least three weeks to recover. I've been at their house for over two weeks now. Had to go to Traian's clinic several times for bloodwork and tests, monitoring the pacemaker. Getting spoiled with Ioana's fantastic and healthy dinners.

Wednesday, January 29th, Nancy picked me up at noon and took me to Dr. Green's office. She has been wonderful also, getting my mail, checking on my house, and bringing me extra clothes. They did some tests and said I was healing nicely. Then we went to Wegmans, got some supplies, and I decided it would be wise to get the flu and pneumonia vaccines while I was there. Ioana had come down with the flu late Monday night into Thursday, staying home from work. After getting the vaccines at their pharmacy, I caught what Ioana had late that night. My arms were so sore from the vaccines, I could barely move them. They were still sore a couple of days later. I had the chills, whitish facial look, hollow leg feeling, and slept all day Thursday. On Friday, after a night of night sweats, it started to break. Still rested most of the day. I was hoping to have Nancy take me back home today, January 31st, and move ahead with my recovery.

    Doesn't look like that's going to happen anytime soon. There has been oozing from the incision site of the pacemaker and Traian has been changing my bandages on a nightly basis. If I take Warfarin to aid in heart valve healing and blood clots, it causes the thinned blood to ooze out of the pacemaker. Rock and a hard place. So, it looks like I might have to go to Saint Joseph's Hospital on Monday, February 3rd, for another 30-minute surgery by Jamal, to fix this problem. Can't catch a break. I will stay here a little longer, to heal and not risk infection. Hopefully this will go smoothly and I can get back to my house by the time Julie comes to visit from February 11th-15th.

    Traian told me I didn't have to go to the OR on Monday, but he would monitor it and possibly have to go on Thursday, which is today, February 6th, around 4:30 in the afternoon, which is when I first arrived at their house three weeks ago. I have been stressing out for a week now, thinking about having to do another operation, with more pain and discomfort and healing. It is sore and uncomfortable enough the way it is right now. But last night Traian looked at it and said that I didn't need to go to the OR. I was so relieved to hear that, finally catching a break for once.

On Monday, February 3rd, I walked down their road until the end, where it meets Highbridge Road, 1.2 miles, 2.4 miles round trip. It was 45 degrees out; I wasn't even wearing a hat and gloves. Traian and Ioanna clapped happily when I told them I had done this. Yesterday, Wednesday, the 5th, it was only in the low 30's, so Ioana found a hat and gloves for me, (mine are still sitting in my car in my garage), and I repeated this walk, making it 4.8 miles; and walking around in the basement, so 5 miles total.

Took my first shower since Christmas, putting a protective patch over the pacemaker. Then removing the patch by myself. I have been using these antibacterial cloth wipes from the hospital, and shower caps with shampoo and conditioner, that you warm up and then massage into your hair and scalp. Trying to get more independent, as I will return to my house after six weeks and four days.

Nancy will take me home with all my stuff on Monday afternoon, February 10th. Then Julie will be here from the 11th, at night, until the 15th. We will have three days, the 12th, 13th, and 14th, to hang out together. She will come over on Wednesday, the 12th, and take me for a noon haircut appointment with Janine at the Hair Shed, five weeks overdue. Julie will help me convert my manuscript from Word into a PDF using Adobe Acrobat Distiller, required by Outskirts Press. We will have to go down to the Manlius Library, as I have no WIFI in my house. Then fine-tune a couple of things and hopefully have it printed, bound, and released. *Finally.*

Lots of physical therapy and recovery ahead. Could be playing golf by the summer if there are no major setbacks. I informed Tish and Mary about my surgeries. They are planning another "Get Lost in Europe" tour. Same time frame. Could be as many as 14 travelers, for two parts of the trip, some just going for Part One-Italy; and some just going on Part Two- to the Italian Alps and Europe. Obviously, we'll need two vans. Have to see how that all plays out. Asked him to once again book my airfares, take out travel insurance, and rooms. They can always cancel my rooms if I can't go, and I will get reimbursed for at least the domestic airfares. Still never got reimbursed from Ryan Air when Sylvia couldn't make it for the 2016 trip. Of course, per "Murphy's Law," this is the year he needed to know by the end of January, instead of by the end of May like last year. So, I signed up to go.

Might be my last trip, who knows? One thing I know for sure, is that I'm not going to wait until the trip is over, and write all about it for the rest of October. This book is long overdue to be finally published and released. I have written all about the 2019 European trip; the rest of 2019; now the surgeries and hospital experiences in 2020; some of the projected routines and experiences of 2020; and the upcoming, and my fourth, European trip in September and into October.

Leaving on September 7th from Philadelphia to Rome. I have to fly from Syracuse to Philadelphia and meet them there. Rome on the 8th, get the vans, drive to Capranica, get our supplies at the todis store, going to "The Farm" in Capranica again for almost a week. Some pool time and some day trips into Tuscan towns and dinners. Leaving here on September 13th and traveling to a hotel near the Venice airport. Part Two travelers will join us there.

Then on to the Italian Alps, to Selva di Val Gardena, in the province of South Tyrol, in northern Italy, on the 15th. After this, it will be Austria, Czechia, Poland, Hungary, Croatia, and Slovenia. Back to the hotel near the Venice airport on October 6th and flying back to the United States on October 7th. There could be changes and nobody can predict the unknown factors.

But we are witnessing these horrific wildfires burning up Australia. The military strikes against Iran. Now the global spread of the coronavirus from China. And on January 26th, the horrific helicopter crash that claimed the lives of nine people, including basketball legend Kobe Bryant and his 13-year-old daughter, Gianna. We live in a precarious world and who knows what the future will bring.

When you pass away, you no longer experience or feel any of the pleasures of the physical body. (At least that is what we assume.) Like the human touch. A back or foot massage. Walking with your arms wrapped around each other. The gentle stroking of your hair. A needed hug. Holding hands. A soft kiss. The intimacy of making love. Cuddling affectionately. Gazing into your loved one's eyes. *How I wish I could be doing these things with Syl right now!*

Relationships, I believe, are formed by three elements: Physical, (attraction, laughing, crying, dancing, hugging, intimacy); Friendship, (caring, trusting, sacrificing); and Intellectual, (communication, exploration, knowledge.) You have to have all three working together to form the perfect union, like tending a garden: you dig out the earth, plant the seeds, water it, eliminate the weeds from time to time, and constantly nurture.

Sylvia was many things: Heidi, little girl, woman, wife, lover, partner, lady, model, advisor, confidante, navigator, protector, daughter, sister, aunt, teacher, friend, companion, Gemini, dancer, chef, gardener, rebel, saint.

Sylvia knew how to listen to the dictates of her heart. Her clarity of mind was incredible. Her caring and kindness offered a glimpse into the window of her soul. Syl reminded me of Princess Diana and Linda Eastman McCartney, with some of their physical features and their moral attributes. *She was my soul mate, my kindred spirit, the angel who made my dreams come true.*

"Do not grow old, no matter how long you live. Never cease to stand like curious children before the Great Mystery into which we were born."   -Albert Einstein

I've always envisioned myself, when I watched and took care of the kids on the playground at Extended Day, or on field trips; to be like Holden Caulfield, watching thousands of little kids playing in a big field of rye, catching them before they go running over the edge of the cliff.

Sylvia was a Gemini, illustrated by The Twins symbol. It is an air sign, preferring to talk about thoughts and feelings, being likable and easy to approach, and having a joyful and positive energy. Syl definitely had all of these characteristics. They deal with unknown situations very well, are very flexible, and like almost every change. This would include Syl. Her moon sign was in Virgo. Her love compatibility was with the other three air signs, and the only other one was with Leo, a fire sign. That is my sign. I think Sylvia's air, (passion, wisdom), fanned the flames of my fire.

I am a Leo with my moon in Gemini, kind of a changeable and flexible Lion, which appealed to her. Leos are action-oriented, warm, attention-seeking, generous and kind; also known for having a short and hot temper, something Syl knew how to keep that in check and keep me balanced. My fire sign is the most passionate of all the elements. Leos tend to be highly nurturing, as well as helping others with their problems. They crave excitement and new adventures.

Whatever the astrological explanations, we knew how to make our love and relationship grow and thrive. Syl spent close to 75 percent of her adult life with me.

On the first day of spring, Thursday, March 19th, 2020, it will now be *one thousand, three hundred three nights of sleeping alone, in our bed, without hearing Syl's soft breathing next to me.* And every day, month, and year will unfortunately add to this total.

One thing to look forward to this summer is the Summer Olympics, from Tokyo, starting on Friday, July 24th, and ending on Sunday, August 9th. We always enjoyed watching the Olympics together; but in August, 2016, Syl was too sick to enjoy them. She watched a little at the beginning, but that was about it. Brings back painful memories.

There is also the "Field of Dreams" baseball game, to be played on Thursday, August 13th, 2020, at the newly constructed ballpark in Dyersville, Iowa, at the site of the beloved baseball movie; between the Yankees and the Chicago White Sox.

If I am still around, I will attend Natalie's, Kyle and Cheryl's youngest daughter's graduation (from MPH), party at the Lakeshore Country Club on Oneida Lake, in the middle of June, 2021; seeing a lot of the people I won't have seen since their oldest daughter, Mariah's, graduation party there in the middle of June, 2018, three years before.

The following year, in the middle of June, 2022, there will be a graduation party at Traian and Ioana's house, for Ileana graduating from MPH. That's an amazing reality! It is a crying shame that Sylvia won't be here for this; for all these graduations: Will, (from college), Mariah, Sarah, Cole, Bianca, Natalie, Ileana. Syl would have been nostalgic, of course, but happy; and would have had so much fun at these parties. And everyone would have been happy to see, talk, and hang out with her.

"Life's tragedy is that we get old too soon and wise too late."   -Ben Franklin

I don't have any regrets about being born in 1946 though. A long World War was finally over and atrocious evil had been defeated. My childhood was idyllic, kind of a "Leave it to Beaver," "Father Knows Best," "The Adventures of Ozzie and Harriet," "Wonder Years," childhood. In fact, I feel privileged to have lived through and experienced, in real time, the 50's, 60's, 70's, 80's, and 90's: the tragic and senseless assassinations of JFK, Martin Luther King, Jr., and Bobby Kennedy; the Beatles; Vietnam and the anti-war protests; the Apollo 11 Moon Landing; the Atlantic City and Woodstock Music Festivals; all the great music and groups in those years, that is still relevant today; the beginning of cable television; meeting and falling in love with Sylvia; witnessing Halley's Comet together; being married to, living with, teaching with, traveling with, being best friends with, and loving life with Sylvia.

I've always wondered, in the afterlife, is there a natural continuation of human consciousness after physical death? Do you look exactly as you are when you die and cross over "to the other side?" Are you the same gender and age? Is this the spiritual form that you retain for eternity? Do you get a chance to choose what your spiritual form will look like? Is it a "Benjamin Button," like in the movie, kind of scenario?

We won't know until we are there. Sylvia knows. I still remain optimistic that I will be reunited with Sylvia. *This time for eternity.*

Buddhists believe death is a natural part of the life cycle. They believe that death simply leads to rebirth. This belief in reincarnation, that a person's spirit remains close by and seeks out a new body and new life, is a comforting and important principle.

Jesus said to his disciples, in Matthew 18:3,

"I tell you the truth, unless you change and become like little children, you will never enter the kingdom of heaven."

I've always been in harmony with The Beatitudes, from Jesus' Sermon on the Mount, found in Matthew 5. He praises the virtues of those who hunger and thirst after righteousness, the merciful, the pure in heart, and the peacemakers.

I am not deeply religious by any means, and I don't go to church. I do believe in a higher power, one that is beyond our comprehension.

Jesus also said,

"But woe to you who are rich, for you have already received your comfort."

Some food for thought for all the rich and powerful who hoard their money, and disregard the suffering of the poor. This is the political climate of our country today. I hope they all get their just due when they leave this earthly plane.

I think I am most attuned to the "Great Spirit" of the Native Americans, where everything is connected: the earth, nature, animals, and humans; all intertwined and dependent on one another.

It has been three years and almost six months now since I lost Sylvia. I don't foresee me ever being with anyone ever again. I know, forever, that Sylvia was and is my one and only true love. Sometimes I wonder how it would have been if we would have had and raised children together. I know that they would have been beautiful and that Sylvia would have been a fantastic mother. She would hold babies with her maternal instincts and loving gazes. Without going into too much detail, I know there were physical complications preventing her from having children. And in our earlier years, we enjoyed having the freedom of traveling and going on long and many vacations. Then over 20 years of teaching and looking after and caring for thousands of kids at MPH, including watching Willie and Ileana.

Maybe we would have adopted a child in our later years. If it meant that much to Syl to do this, something she needed to do, I would have gladly done whatever she wanted me to do. Now it is a moot point. I guess it wasn't meant to happen for us. But I think about it.

I started driving again, taking care of the house, yard work, laundry, making my own meals. They definitely weren't like Ioana's. Debbie came back during the first week in March, as they finally sold their house after a year on the market. It is the end of an era, 20 years and over 7 months. No more work over there, no more extra income.

This evil pandemic has taken over the entire world. We will never be the same. It is like airport security after "9/11" and taking off your shoes before boarding a plane after the "shoe bomber" incIdent. We are required in New York State to wear facial masks when you are out in public, to help in stopping the spread of the Coronavirus. Those who don't are being selfish or stupid. I wear mine when I go to the grocery and liquor stores and for my weekly, for the past three months, of getting INR bloodwork done. This measures your blood clotting ability, as I take blood thinners along with my other daily medications. I am in the "most vulnerable" category to get the virus: over 65; pre-existing condition, with the heart failure and pacemaker; and a weakened immune system. "Social distancing" and "flattening the curve" have become part of our universal language. Over a quarter of a million people have died globally, and this number will keep rising until an effective vaccine is discovered. In the United States, over thirty-three million are unemployed, and people wait in their cars for hours to get food from food banks. We canceled our trip to Europe. Hopefully next year.

All sporting events were suspended. I was really looking forward, more so than ever before, after my surgeries and near-death and hospital experiences; to watching: the conference basketball tournaments, (Syracuse whomped North Carolina in the ACC tournament, then the rest of the tournament and the season was canceled), the NCAA tournament, the start of MLB and the Yankees, the

Masters and Players and U.S. Open golf tournaments, the NBA and NHL playoffs, Wimbledon. Some of these events are being rescheduled for the summer and the fall, albeit in different formats. The Summer Olympics have been rescheduled for the summer of 2021. ESPN has been airing a 10-episode series, "The Last Dance," about Michael Jordan and the Chicago Bulls winning their six NBA championships in the 1990's; which has been fascinating.

I have been taking walks around Green & Round Lakes, and Mill Run Park, sitting on Syl's benches. Bringing the deck furniture back out, after being stored in the basement and garage since November. Trying not to get too depressed, dealing with the reality of being a bionic man for the rest of my life.

On May 25th, 2020, Memorial Day, it will now be one thousand, three hundred seventy nights, since Sylvia slept next to me in our bed; since August 24th, 2016. I miss Syl more and more, as my empty life without her keeps passing by, three years and almost nine months now.

I carry on, trying to live life for both of us, keeping Sylvia's spirit alive. That's why I wanted to and needed to write this book, so that I could share our stories with everyone. *So, nobody would ever forget Sylvia, that her legacy would live on forever.* I owe that to her after all that she has done for me in my life.

Life is Eternal

"I am standing upon the seashore. A ship, at my side,

spreads her white sails to the moving breeze and starts for

the blue ocean. She is an object of beauty and strength.

I stand and watch her until, at length, she hangs like a speck

of white cloud just where the sea and sky come to mingle with each other.

Then, someone at my side says, 'There, she is gone.'

'Gone where?'

Gone from my sight. That is all. She is just as large in mast,

hull and spar as she was when she left my side.

And, she is just as able to bear her load of living freight to her destined port.

Her diminished size is in me - not in her.

And, just at the moment when someone says,

'There, she is gone,'

there are other eyes watching her coming, and other voices

ready to take up the glad shout, "Here she comes!"
-Henry Van Dyke

Sylvia awakened feelings in me that I didn't even know existed. My heart will never feel as full and joyous as it was with her. *She made my world, our world, a much more beautiful place.*

"I am in the night. There is a being who has gone away and carried the heavens with her. Oh! to be laid side by side in the same tomb, hand clasped in hand, and from time to time, in the darkness, to caress a finger gently, that would suffice for my eternity."   -Victor Hugo

This is how I feel.

I looked at the last written birthday card that Sylvia gave me on August 20th, 2015. (She gave me a "verbal birthday card" on my 70th, on August 20th, 2016.)

The card says:

"But now I know

without a doubt

the luckiest day of my life

was the day that I met you."

And Syl wrote to me:

'Dust,'

"You are the

only one I have & will

love forever."

'Syl'

This is all I needed to know.

This is all I will ever need to know.

Dusty is passionate about animal rights, the belief that animals have a right to be free of human use and exploitation; saving endangered species; preserving the beauty of nature and the natural wonders of the world; traveling and writing. A journey to a different country offers us the unique experience of seeing the ancient history, culture and people in all its splendid diversity. He believes that books can magically transport us to places that we have always and yet maybe never dreamed of.

Also by Dusty Rhoades Heer

> "White Woman of the Genesee"
The Mary Jemison Story (Screenplay)

> "From The Horse's Mouth"
The True Story of Zippy Chippy

> "The Forest That Rains Frogs

> "El Bosque Donde Llueven Ranas Coqu

> Readers can Google Search: Dusty Rhoades Heer and find information on my Children's Books.

> Readers can also access my Facebook Page, Dusty Rhoades Heer and see pictures and albums of us, by scrolling down all the way through.

Lakeside Park, Cazenovia, NY August 1986

St. Croix, Virgin Islands March 1987

Lake Placid Hilton, Lake Placid, NY July 1987

Whiteface Mountain, Lake Placid, NY July 1987

Mayan Ruins, Uxmal, Mexico February 1988

Mayan Ruins, Tulum, Mexico February 1988

Merida, Mexico February 1989

New York State Fair, Syracuse, NY (Early 90's)

Wedding Reception, Brewster Inn, Cazenovia, NY

April 16, 1994

Toronto, Canada July 1995

"Phantom of the Opera," Toronto, Canada July 1995

North Charleston, South Carolina April 1998

Grand Canyon, Arizona February 2001

Brewster Inn, Cazenovia Lake, Cazenovia, NY

June 18, 2001

Brewster Inn, Cazenovia, NY August 20, 2001

Pratts Falls, Manlius, NY August 2003

"The Needle," Iao Valley State Park Maui, Hawaii

February 2002

Times Square, New York City, NY June 2005

Cazenovia, New York July 4, 2007

Dust and Syl

CPSIA information can be obtained
at www.ICGtesting.com
Printed in the USA
BVHW032146030620
580887BV00001B/1